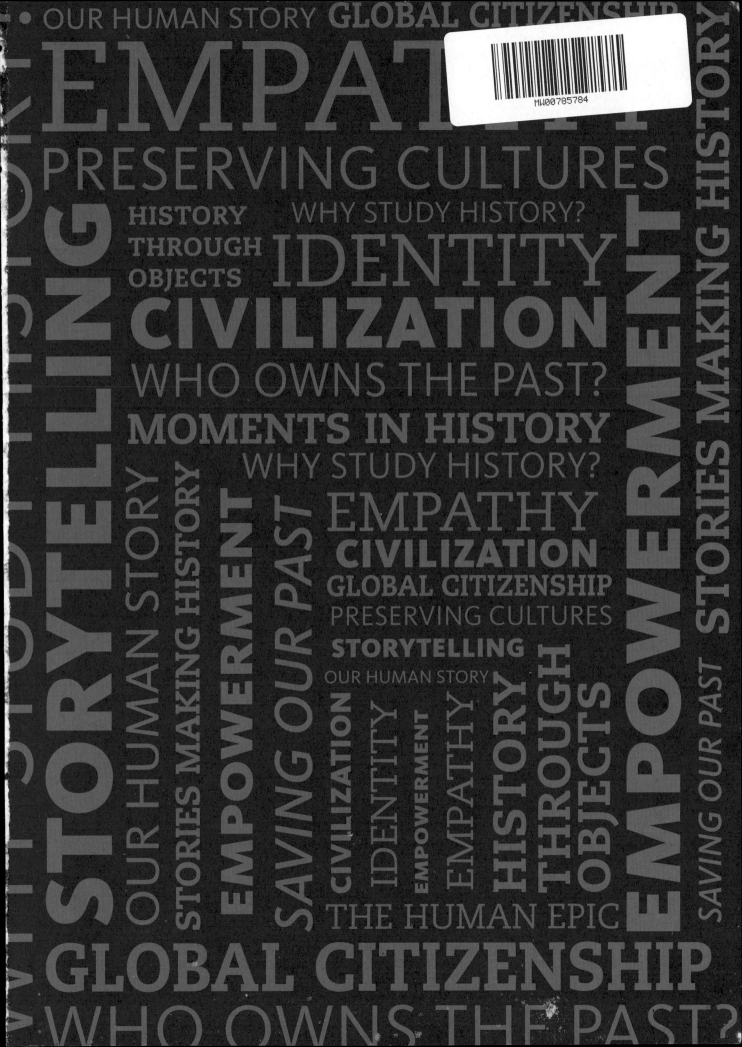

THE HUMAN EPIC GLOBAL CITIZENSHIP

STORYTELLING

WHY STUDY HISTORY? EMPATHY

IDENTITY **CIVILIZATION**

STORIES MAKING HISTORY

EMPOWERMENT

SAVING OUR PAST

EMPATHY

EMPOWERMENT

PRESERVING CULTURES

SAVING OUR PAST

WHY STUDY HISTORY?

GLOBAL CITIZENSHIP

IDENTITY

THE HUMAN EPIC

STORYTELLING

OUR HUMAN STORY

HISTORY

THROUGH

OBJECTS

EMPOWERMENT

CIVILIZATION

PRESERVING CULTURES

GLOBAL CITIZENSHIP

PRESERVING CULTURES

EMPATHY

OUR HUMAN STORY

CIVILIZATION THE HUMAN EPIC

WHO OWNS THE PAST

STORIES MAKING HISTORY

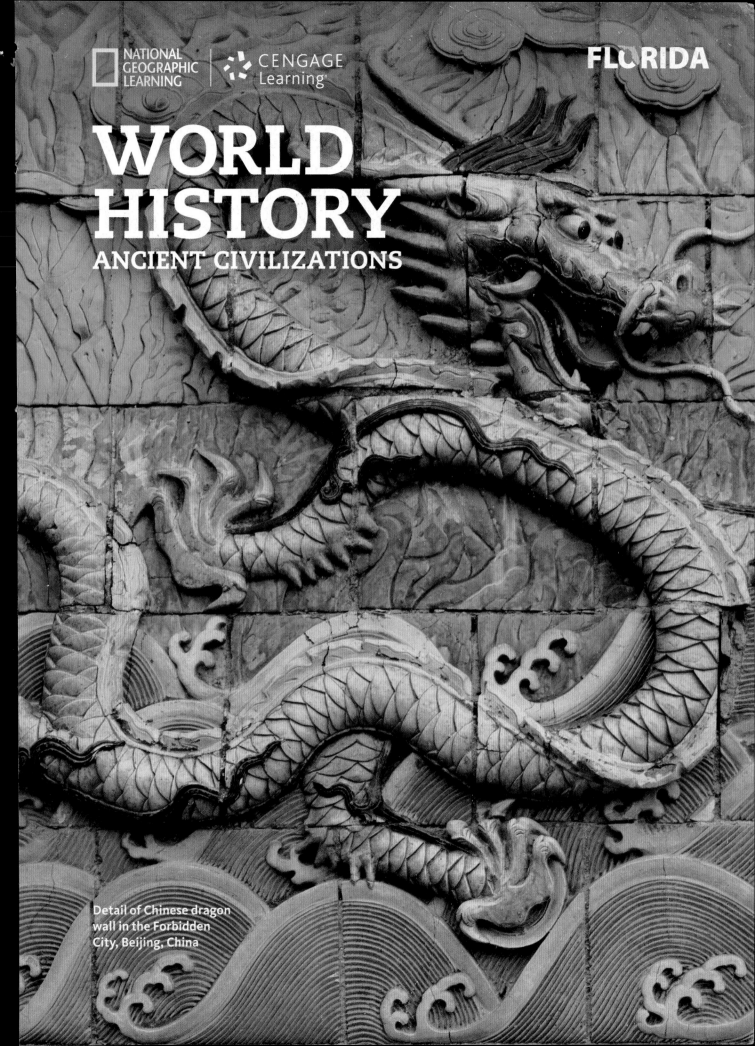

NATIONAL
GEOGRAPHIC
LEARNING

CENGAGE
Learning

FLORIDA

WORLD
HISTORY
ANCIENT CIVILIZATIONS

Detail of Chinese dragon
wall in the Forbidden
City, Beijing, China

NATIONAL
GEOGRAPHIC

FLORIDA

Acknowledgments

Grateful acknowledgment is given to the authors, artists, photographers, museums, publishers, and agents for permission to reprint copyrighted material. Every effort has been made to secure the appropriate permission. If any omissions have been made or if corrections are required, please contact the Publisher.

Photographic Credits

Front Cover: ©Neale Clark/Robert Harding World Imagery/ Alamy

Acknowledgments and credits continue on page R25.

"National Geographic," "National Geographic Society" and the Yellow Border Design are registered trademarks of the National Geographic Society ® Marcas Registradas

For product information and technology assistance, contact us at Customer & Sales Support, 888-915-3276

For permission to use material from this text or product, submit all requests online at **www.cengage.com/permissions**

Further permissions questions can be emailed to **permissionrequest@cengage.com**

National Geographic Learning | Cengage Learning
1 N. State Street, Suite 900
Chicago, IL 60602

Cengage Learning is a leading provider of customized learning solutions with office locations around the globe, including Singapore, the United Kingdom, Australia, Mexico, Brazil, and Japan. Locate your local office at **www.cengage.com/global.**

Visit National Geographic Learning online at **NGL.Cengage.com**

Visit our corporate website at **www.cengage.com**

ISBN: 978-13059-66871

Printed in the United States of America

Print Number: 03
Print Year: 2017

PROGRAM CONSULTANTS

Fredrik Hiebert

Dr. Fred Hiebert is a National Geographic Explorer and Archaeology Fellow. He has led archaeological expeditions at ancient Silk Roads sites across Asia and underwater in the Black Sea. Hiebert rediscovered the lost Bactrian gold in Afghanistan in 2004 and was curator of National Geographic's exhibition *Afghanistan: Hidden Treasures from the National Museum, Kabul*, which toured museums throughout the world. Hiebert curated National Geographic's exhibition *Peruvian Gold: Ancient Treasures Unearthed* and, most recently, the exhibition *The Greeks: Agamemnon to Alexander the Great*.

Christopher P. Thornton

Dr. Chris Thornton is the Lead Program Officer of Research, Conservation, and Exploration at the National Geographic Society, and Director of the UNESCO World Heritage Site of Bat in the Sultanate of Oman. Thornton works closely with NGS media to promote grantees and other scientists, overseeing research grants in anthropology, archaeology, astronomy, geography, geology, and paleontology. He also manages the Society's relationship with academic conferences around the world.

Jeremy McInerney

Dr. Jeremy McInerney is chairman of the Department of Classical Studies at the University of Pennsylvania. McInerney recently spent a year as Whitehead Professor in the American School of Classical Studies in Athens, Greece. He has excavated at Corinth, on Crete, and in Israel. Author of *The Cattle of the Sun: Cows and Culture in the World of the Ancient Greeks* (2010), McInerney has received top teaching awards, including the Lindback Award for Distinguished Teaching.

PROGRAM CONSULTANTS

Michael W. Smith

Dr. Michael Smith is the Associate Dean for Faculty Development and Academic Affairs in the College of Education at Temple University. He became a college teacher after 11 years of teaching high school English. His research focuses on how experienced readers read and talk about texts, as well as what motivates adolescents' reading and writing. Smith has written many books and monographs, including the award-winning *"Reading Don't Fix No Chevys": Literacy in the Lives of Young Men.*

Peggy Altoff

Peggy Altoff's long career includes teaching middle school and high school students, supervising teachers, and serving as adjunct university faculty. Peggy served as a state social studies specialist in Maryland and as a K–12 coordinator in Colorado Springs. She was president of the National Council for the Social Studies (NCSS) in 2006–2007 and was on the task force for the 2012 NCSS National Curriculum Standards.

David W. Moore

Dr. David Moore is a Professor Emeritus of Education at Arizona State University. He taught high school social studies and reading before entering college teaching. His noteworthy co-authored publications include the *Handbook of Reading Research* chapter on secondary school reading, the first International Reading Association position statement on adolescent literacy, and *Developing Readers and Writers in the Content Areas (6e).*

PROGRAM WRITER

Special thanks to Jon Heggie for his extensive contributions to *National Geographic World History: Ancient Civilizations*. Heggie became fascinated with history as a small child, a passion nurtured by his parents and educators. He studied history at Oxford University and received his Post Graduate Certificate in Education from Bristol University. Heggie has taught English and History at a number of schools in the UK and has written for *National Geographic* magazine for the past ten years. He is currently working on a number of history projects and serving as the editor of the recently launched National Geographic *History* magazine.

REVIEWERS OF RELIGIOUS CONTENT

The following individuals reviewed the treatment of religious content in selected pages of the text.

Murali Balaji
Hindu American Foundation
Washington, D.C.

Dr. Charles C. Haynes
Director, Religious Freedom
Center of the Newseum Institute
Washington, D.C.

NATIONAL GEOGRAPHIC SOCIETY

The National Geographic Society contributed significantly to *National Geographic World History: Great Civilizations*. Our collaboration with each of the following has been a pleasure and a privilege: National Geographic Maps, National Geographic Education and Children's Media, National Geographic Missions programs, and National Geographic Studios. We thank the Society for its guidance and support.

We BELIEVE in the power of science, exploration, and storytelling to change the world.

UNIT EXPLORERS

Each unit in this book opens and closes with a National Geographic Explorer discussing the content presented in the unit and explaining his or her own related work in the field. Within the Student eEdition, you can watch video footage of each Unit Explorer "on location" to expand and enhance your world history learning experience.

Steven Ellis
Archaeologist
National Geographic
Grantee

Francisco Estrada-Belli
Archaeologist
National Geographic
Grantee

Fredrik Hiebert
Archaeologist
National Geographic
Fellow

Louise Leakey
Paleontologist
National Geographic
Explorer-in-Residence

William Parkinson
Archaeologist
National Geographic
Grantee

Christopher Thornton
Archaeologist
National Geographic
Lead Program Officer of Research,
Conservation, and Exploration

CHAPTER EXPLORERS

In the chapters of this book, National Geographic Explorers tell the story of their work as it relates to the time in history you're learning about. Archaeologists, photographers, and writers explain their historical and cultural findings and the process involved in making the important discoveries that help us understand more about the past—and the future.

Beverly Goodman
Geo-Archaeologist
National Geographic
Emerging Explorer

Fredrik Hiebert
Archaeologist
National Geographic
Fellow

Patrick Hunt
Archaeologist
National Geographic
Grantee

Christine Lee
Bio-Archaeologist
National Geographic
Emerging Explorer

Sarah Parcak
Archaeologist
National Geographic
Fellow

Jeffrey Rose
Archaeologist
National Geographic
Emerging Explorer

William Saturno
Archaeologist
National Geographic
Grantee

NATIONAL GEOGRAPHIC

FEATURED EXPLORERS

Throughout the Student eEdition, National Geographic Featured Explorers take part in informal "video chat" style interviews to explain and discuss their fieldwork and explore high-interest topics covered in the book. Other Featured Explorers tell the story of important and ongoing world events in the Stories Making History section.

Salam Al Kuntar
Archaeologist
National Geographic
Emerging Explorer

Steve Boyes
Conservation Biologist
National Geographic
Emerging Explorer

Michael Cosmopoulos
Archaeologist, National
Geographic Grantee

Sarah Parcak
Archaeologist
National Geographic
Fellow

Thomas Parker
Archaeologist
National Geographic
Grantee

Matt Piscitelli
Archaeologist
National Geographic
Grantee

Shah Selbe
Conservation Technologist
National Geographic
Emerging Explorer

Soultana Maria Valamoti
Archaeologist, National
Geographic Grantee

Xiaobai Angela Yao
Geographer
National Geographic
Grantee

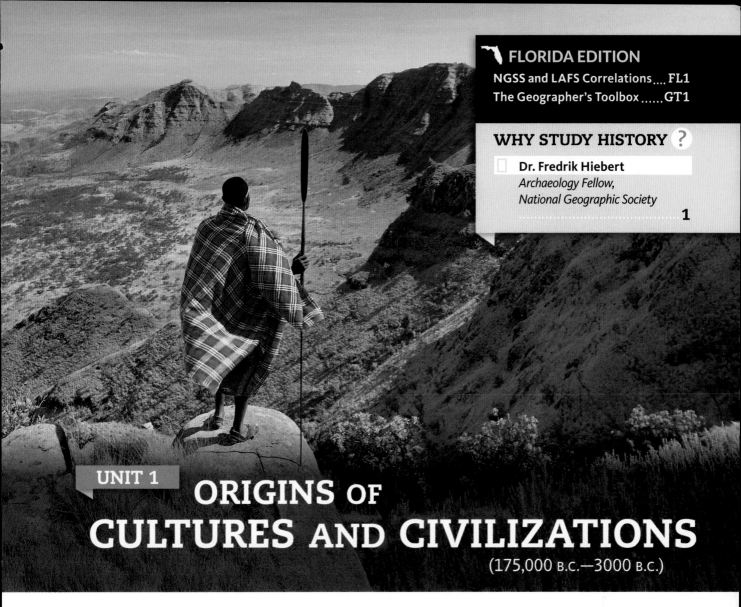

WHY STUDY HISTORY ?

☐ **Dr. Fredrik Hiebert**
*Archaeology Fellow,
National Geographic Society*

1

UNIT 1

ORIGINS OF CULTURES AND CIVILIZATIONS

(175,000 B.C.—3000 B.C.)

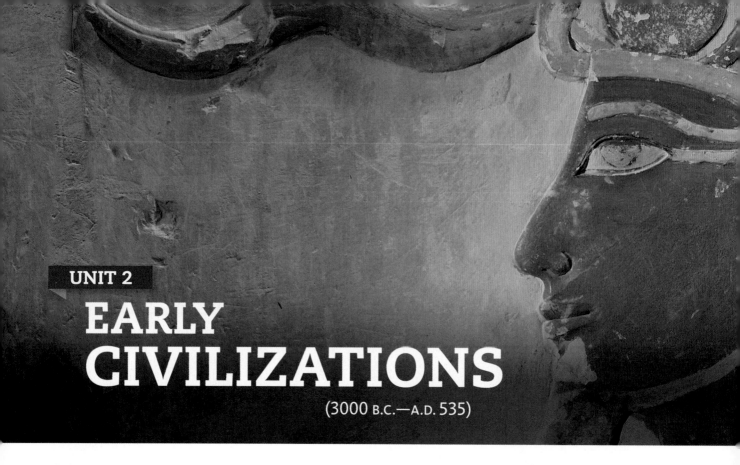

UNIT 2
EARLY CIVILIZATIONS
(3000 B.C.—A.D. 535)

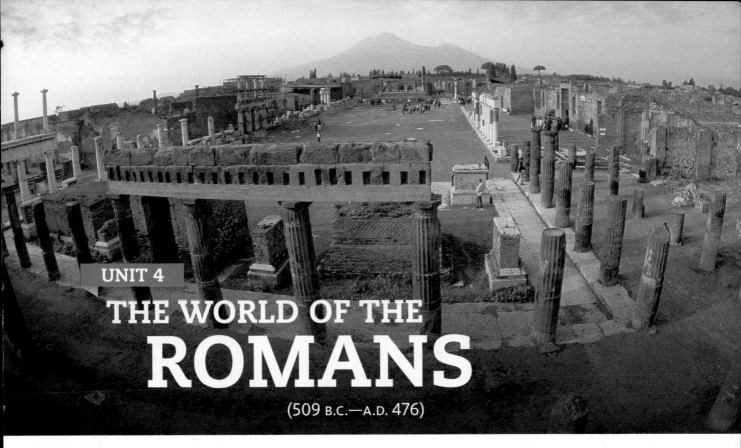

UNIT 4
THE WORLD OF THE
ROMANS
(509 B.C.—A.D. 476)

UNIT 5
AMERICAN & ASIAN
CIVILIZATIONS
(1200 B.C.—A.D. 1600)

The world changes on a daily basis, and National Geographic is there. Join five National Geographic voices as they tell the stories of five current global events. Learn about these newsworthy topics, discuss what might come next, and think about how these events impact you, the place you live, and the people you know—your global citizenship.

SPECIAL FEATURES

MAPS

DOCUMENT-BASED QUESTIONS

TIME LINES, CHARTS, MODELS, GRAPHS, INFOGRAPHICS

MOMENTS IN HISTORY

FLORIDA

WORLD HISTORY
ANCIENT CIVILIZATIONS

Next Generation
Sunshine State Standards and
Language Arts Florida Standards
Social Studies, Grade 6

NGSS Correlations

LAFS Correlations

Correlations to *World History: Ancient Civilizations*

NGSS Correlations

CIVICS AND GOVERNMENT

BENCHMARK	STUDENT EDITION
Standard 1: Demonstrate an understanding of the origins and purposes of government, law, and the American political system.	
SS.6.C.1.1 Identify democratic concepts developed in ancient Greece that served as a foundation for the American constitution.	221, 230, 254–255, 257, 261
SS.6.C.1.2 Identify how the government of the Roman Republic contributed to the development of democratic principles (separation of powers, rule of law, representative government, civic duty).	274–275, 303, 335
Standard 2: Evaluate the roles, rights, and responsibilities of United States citizens, and determine methods of active participation in society, government, and the political system.	
SS.6.C.2.1 Identify principles (civic participation, role of government) from ancient Greek and Roman civilizations which are reflected in the American political process today, and discuss their effect on the American political process.	230, 254–255, 274–275, 335

ECONOMICS

BENCHMARK	STUDENT EDITION
Standard 1: Understand the fundamental concepts relevant to the development of a market economy.	
SS.6.E.1.1 Identify the factors (new resources, increased productivity, education, technology, slave economy, territorial expansion) that increase economic growth.	66, 69, 81, 82, 104, 107, 108–109, 216–217, 270, 280, 293, 308–309, 406–407
SS.6.E.1.2 Describe and identify traditional and command economies as they appear in different civilizations.	36, 382
SS.6.E.1.3 Describe the following economic concepts as they relate to early civilization: scarcity, opportunity cost, supply and demand, barter, trade, productive resources (land, labor, capital, entrepreneurship).	24, 48, 107, 186–187
Standard 2: Understand the fundamental concepts relevant to the institutions, structure, and functions of a national economy.	
SS.6.E.2.1 Evaluate how civilizations through clans, leaders, and family groups make economic decisions for that civilization providing a framework for future city-state or nation development.	68, 94, 112, 126–127, 180, 214, 382, 397
Standard 3: Understand the fundamental concepts and interrelationships of the United States economy in the international marketplace.	
SS.6.E.3.1 Identify examples of mediums of exchange (currencies) used for trade (barter) for each civilization, and explain why international trade requires a system for a medium of exchange between trading both inside and among various regions.	186, 309, 407
SS.6.E.3.2 Categorize products that were traded among civilizations, and give examples of barriers to trade of those products.	107, 186–187, 188–189, 308–309, 414
SS.6.E.3.3 Describe traditional economies (Egypt, Greece, Rome, Kush) and elements of those economies that led to the rise of a merchant class and trading partners.	107, 112, 216, 308–309
SS.6.E.3.4 Describe the relationship among civilizations that engage in trade, including the benefits and drawbacks of voluntary trade.	107, 184–185, 186, 188–189, 216–217, 414

GEOGRAPHY

BENCHMARK	STUDENT EDITION
Standard 1: Understand how to use maps and other geographic representations, tools and technology to report information.	
SS.6.G.1.1 Use latitude and longitude coordinates to understand the relationship between people and places on the Earth.	GT6–GT7
SS.6.G.1.2 Analyze the purposes of map projections (political, physical, special purpose) and explain the applications of various types of maps.	GT10–GT11, GT12–GT13, GT14–GT15
SS.6.G.1.3 Identify natural wonders of the ancient world.	GT16–GT17, 12–13, 16–17, 45, 90, 145
SS.6.G.1.4 Utilize tools geographers use to study the world.	GT1, GT6–GT7, GT8, GT10–GT11, GT12–GT13, GT14–GT15, GT26–GT27, 8–9, 19, 21, 28–29, 33, 37, 53, 62–63, 67, 75, 80, 93, 97, 113, 125, 137, 139, 144, 149, 157, 158, 167, 181, 184–185, 193, 204–205, 211, 217, 227, 237, 245, 257, 266–267, 271, 291, 292–293, 309, 320–321, 328–329, 339, 348–349, 353, 359, 369, 379, 383, 403, 411, 418–419
SS.6.G.1.5 Use scale, cardinal, and intermediate directions, and estimation of distances between places on current and ancient maps of the world.	GT8–GT9, 53, 137, 158–159, 217, 245, 320–321, 339, 369, 383, 411
SS.6.G.1.6 Use a map to identify major bodies of water of the world, and explain ways they have impacted the development of civilizations.	28–29, 33, 37, 53, 67, 80, 93, 113, 125, 144, 167, 217, 266–267, 271, 353
SS.6.G.1.7 Use maps to identify characteristics and boundaries of ancient civilizations that have shaped the world today.	37, 53, 62–63, 67, 75, 80, 93, 113, 125, 157, 158, 167, 181, 204–205, 211, 217, 245, 257, 266–267, 271, 292–293, 328–329, 348–349, 353, 359, 369, 383, 403, 411
Standard 2: Understand physical and cultural characteristics of places.	
SS.6.G.2.1 Explain how major physical characteristics, natural resources, climate, and absolute and relative locations have influenced settlement, interactions, and the economies of ancient civilizations of the world.	16–17, 18–19, 24–25, 26–27, 28–29, 32–33, 36–37, 40–41, 42–43, 44–45, 66–67, 68–69, 80–81, 90–91, 92–93, 112–113, 120–121, 124–125, 144–145, 166–167, 204–205, 210–211, 214–215, 216–217, 244–245, 270–271, 352–353, 354–355, 356–357, 368–369, 378–379, 382–383, 388–389, 390–391, 392–393, 394–395, 396–397
SS.6.G.2.2 Differentiate between continents, regions, countries, and cities in order to understand the complexities of regions created by civilizations.	GT4–GT5, 40, 45, 48, 68, 74, 80, 82, 84, 126–127, 146, 174, 214, 216, 259, 292, 343, 397, 411
SS.6.G.2.3 Analyze the relationship of physical geography to the development of ancient river valley civilizations.	28, 36, 40, 45, 52, 62–63, 66–67, 68, 86, 88, 90–91, 92, 112, 120, 144–145, 166–167, 197, 352–353
SS.6.G.2.4 Explain how the geographical location of ancient civilizations contributed to the culture and politics of those societies.	36–37, 40, 42, 45, 57, 66–67, 68–69, 70–71, 80–81, 86, 92–93, 112–113, 124–125, 126–127, 144–145, 146–147, 148–149, 166–167, 208–209, 210–211, 214–215, 216–217, 270–271, 368–369, 378–379, 388–389
SS.6.G.2.5 Interpret how geographic boundaries invite or limit interaction with other regions and cultures.	81, 90–91, 166, 184–185, 204–205, 214, 216–217, 232, 247, 270–271, 291
SS.6.G.2.6 Explain the concept of cultural diffusion, and identify the influences of different ancient cultures on one another.	45, 52, 81, 84, 86, 112, 119, 136, 148–149, 186–187, 216–217, 247, 272–273, 282, 354
SS.6.G.2.7 Interpret choropleths or dot-density maps to explain the distribution of population in the ancient world.	GT12–GT13

Standard 3: Understand the relationships between the Earth's ecosystems and the populations that dwell within them.

SS.6.G.3.1 Explain how the physical landscape has affected the development of agriculture and industry in the ancient world.	36–37, 38–39, 40–41, 42–43, 44–45, 66–67, 68–69, 90–91, 92–93, 144–145, 146–147, 166–167, 352–353
SS.6.G.3.2 Analyze the impact of human populations on the ancient world's ecosystems.	GT26–GT27, 32, 36, 38, 40, 42–43, 45, 148, 352–353, 392, 396

Standard 4: Understand the characteristics, distribution, and migration of human populations.

SS.6.G.4.1 Explain how family and ethnic relationships influenced ancient cultures.	24, 32, 40, 94, 100, 128, 170, 218–219, 221, 278–279, 388
SS.6.G.4.2 Use maps to trace significant migrations, and analyze their results.	GT28–GT29, 19, 21, 137, 149
SS.6.G.4.3 Locate sites in Africa and Asia where archaeologists have found evidence of early human societies, and trace their migration patterns to other parts of the world.	16, 18, 20–21
SS.6.G.4.4 Map and analyze the impact of the spread of various belief systems in the ancient world.	136–137, 156, 163, 186, 193, 320–321, 404

Standard 5: Understand how human actions can impact the environment.

SS.6.G.5.1 Identify the methods used to compensate for the scarcity of resources in the ancient world.	66–67, 92–93, 148, 216, 308, 352–353, 378, 382–383, 392, 396
SS.6.G.5.2 Use geographic terms and tools to explain why ancient civilizations developed networks of highways, waterways, and other transportation linkages.	81, 82, 92, 156, 175, 184–185, 216–217, 308–309, 310–311, 382–383, 384–385
SS.6.G.5.3 Use geographic tools and terms to analyze how famine, drought, and natural disasters plagued many ancient civilizations.	16–17, 32, 66–67, 124, 138–139, 209, 316–317

Standard 6: Understand how to apply geography to interpret the past and present and plan for the future.

SS.6.G.6.1 Describe the Six Essential Elements of Geography (The World in Spatial Terms, Places and Regions, Physical Systems, Human Systems, Environment, The Uses of Geography) as the organizing framework for understanding the world and its people.	GT2–GT3
SS.6.G.6.2 Compare maps of the world in ancient times with current political maps.	167, 403

WORLD HISTORY

BENCHMARK	STUDENT EDITION

Standard 1: Utilize historical inquiry skills and analytical processes.

SS.6.W.1.1 Use timelines to identify chronological order of historical events.	6–7, 60–61, 141, 202–203, 264–265, 346–347, 376, 421
SS.6.W.1.2 Identify terms (decade, century, epoch, era, millennium, BC/BCE, AD/CE) and designations of time periods.	12, 28
SS.6.W.1.3 Interpret primary and secondary sources.	30–31, 33, 53, 72–73, 77, 87, 102–103, 121, 130–131, 141, 152–153, 163, 172–173, 193, 227, 240–241, 257, 298–299, 303, 322–323, 339, 366–367, 375, 399, 414–415, 425
SS.6.W.1.4 Describe the methods of historical inquiry and how history relates to the other social sciences.	5, 12–13, 15, 20–21, 30–31, 32, 54–55, 59, 96–97, 138–139, 190–191, 194–195, 201, 290–291, 340–341, 345, 362–363, 372–373, 422–423, 426–427

SS.6.W.1.5 Describe the roles of historians and recognize varying historical interpretations (historiography).	20–21, 30, 190–191, 362–363, 422–423
SS.6.W.1.6 Describe how history transmits culture and heritage and provides models of human character.	1, 15, 22–23, 198, 430, 433, 444

Standard 2: Describe the emergence of early civilizations (Nile, Tigris-Euphrates, Indus, and Yellow Rivers, Meso and South American).

SS.6.W.2.1 Compare the lifestyles of hunter-gatherers with those of settlers of early agricultural communities.	10, 24–25, 26–27, 32
SS.6.W.2.2 Describe how the developments of agriculture and metallurgy related to settlement, population growth, and the emergence of civilization.	28–29, 38–39, 64, 66–67, 68–69, 86, 168, 183
SS.6.W.2.3 Identify the characteristics of civilization.	46–47, 48–49, 50–51, 52
SS.6.W.2.4 Compare the economic, political, social, and religious institutions of ancient river civilizations.	100–101, 112–113, 120, 162
SS.6.W.2.5 Summarize important achievements of Egyptian civilization.	98–99, 100, 102–103, 114–115, 116–117, 118–119, 120
SS.6.W.2.6 Determine the contributions of key figures from ancient Egypt.	94, 98, 104, 106–107, 108–109, 110–111, 120–121
SS.6.W.2.7 Summarize the important achievements of Mesopotamian civilizations.	66–67, 68, 70–71, 72–73, 76–77, 84–85, 86–87
SS.6.W.2.8 Determine the impact of key figures from ancient Mesopotamian civilizations.	74–75, 76–77, 78, 82–83, 86, 124–125
SS.6.W.2.9 Identify key figures and basic beliefs of the Israelites and determine how these beliefs compared with those of others in the geographic area.	122, 124–125, 126–127, 128–129, 130–131, 132–133, 135, 136
SS.6.W.2.10 Compare the emergence of advanced civilizations in Meso and South America with the four early river valley civilizations.	352, 354, 374, 378, 398

Standard 3: Recognize significant events, figures, and contributions of classical civilizations (Phoenicia, Greece, Rome, Axum).

SS.6.W.3.1 Analyze the cultural impact the ancient Phoenicians had on the Mediterranean world with regard to colonization (Carthage), exploration, maritime commerce (purple dye, tin) and written communication (alphabet).	80–81, 84–85, 217
SS.6.W.3.2 Explain the democratic concepts (polis, civic participation and voting rights, legislative bodies, written constitutions, rule of law) developed in ancient Greece.	214–215, 221, 226–227, 230–231, 254–255, 257
SS.6.W.3.3 Compare life in Athens and Sparta (government and the status of citizens, women and children, foreigners, helots).	206, 218–219, 220–221, 226, 236–237, 238–239, 256
SS.6.W.3.4 Explain the causes and effects of the Persian and Peloponnesian Wars.	222–223, 224–225, 226–227, 233, 236–237, 238–239, 240–241, 256
SS.6.W.3.5 Summarize the important achievements and contributions of ancient Greek civilization.	208, 212–213, 230–231, 232–233, 234–235, 248–249, 250–251, 252–253, 254–255, 256
SS.6.W.3.6 Determine the impact of key figures from ancient Greece.	212, 230–231, 233, 240–241, 248–249, 250, 256
SS.6.W.3.7 Summarize the key achievements, contributions, and figures associated with the Hellenistic Period.	242–243, 244–245, 246–247
SS.6.W.3.8 Determine the impact of significant figures associated with ancient Rome.	272, 274–275, 284–285, 288–289, 290–291, 292–293, 294–295, 296–297, 298–299, 300–301, 302–303, 304, 306–307, 328–329, 330–331, 332, 338

SS.6.W.3.9 Explain the impact of the Punic Wars on the development of the Roman Empire.	288–289, 292–293
SS.6.W.3.10 Describe the government of the Roman Republic and its contribution to the development of democratic principles (separation of powers, rule of law, representative government, civic duty).	274–275, 277, 334–335
SS.6.W.3.11 Explain the transition from Roman Republic to empire and Imperial Rome, and compare Roman life and culture under each one.	294–295, 296–297, 306–307
SS.6.W.3.12 Explain the causes for the growth and longevity of the Roman Empire.	282–283, 284–285, 286–287, 308–309, 338–339
SS.6.W.3.13 Identify key figures and the basic beliefs of early Christianity and how these beliefs impacted the Roman Empire.	318–319, 320–321, 322–323, 324–325, 338–339
SS.6.W.3.14 Describe the key achievements and contributions of Roman civilization.	284–285, 310–311, 312–313, 314–315, 332–333, 334–335, 336–337
SS.6.W.3.15 Explain the reasons for the gradual decline of the Western Roman Empire after the Pax Romana.	326–327, 328–329, 330–331, 338–339
SS.6.W.3.16 Compare life in the Roman Republic for patricians, plebeians, women, children, and slaves.	268, 274–275, 278–279, 280–281, 302
SS.6.W.3.17 Explain the spread and influence of the Latin language on Western Civilization.	332–333, 335
SS.6.W.3.18 Describe the rise and fall of the ancient east African kingdoms of Kush and Axum and Christianity's development in Ethiopia.	112, 320–321
Standard 4: Recognize significant events, figures, and contributions of classical Asian civilizations (China, India).	
SS.6.W.4.1 Discuss the significance of Aryan and other tribal migrations on Indian civilization.	142, 148–149, 162
SS.6.W.4.2 Explain the major beliefs and practices associated with Hinduism and the social structure of the caste system in ancient India.	148–149, 150–151, 152–153, 158–159, 160–161, 162–163
SS.6.W.4.3 Recognize the political and cultural achievements of the Mauryan and Gupta empires.	156–157, 158–159, 160–161, 162
SS.6.W.4.4 Explain the teachings of Buddha, the importance of Asoka, and how Buddhism spread in India, Ceylon, and other parts of Asia.	154–155, 156–157, 160–161, 162–163, 186–187, 404–405
SS.6.W.4.5 Summarize the important achievements and contributions of ancient Indian civilization.	146–147, 156–157, 158–159, 160–161, 162–163
SS.6.W.4.6 Describe the concept of the Mandate of Heaven and its connection to the Zhou and later dynasties.	168–169, 192, 402–403
SS.6.W.4.7 Explain the basic teachings of Laozi, Confucius, and Han Fei Zi.	164, 170–171, 172–173, 192–193
SS.6.W.4.8 Describe the contributions of classical and post classical China.	168–169, 170–171, 174–175, 176–177, 178–179, 180–181, 182–183, 184–185, 402–403, 406–407, 408–409, 424, 429
SS.6.W.4.9 Identify key figures from classical and post classical China.	170–171, 172–173, 174–175, 176–177, 178–179, 180–181, 192, 402–403, 406–407, 410–411, 412–413, 414–415, 416–417, 418–419
SS.6.W.4.10 Explain the significance of the silk roads and maritime routes across the Indian Ocean to the movement of goods and ideas among Asia, East Africa, and the Mediterranean Basin.	184–185, 186–187, 188–189, 190–191, 192, 412–413, 414–415, 418–419

SS.6.W.4.11 Explain the rise and expansion of the Mongol empire and its effects on peoples of Asia and Europe including the achievements of Genghis and Kublai Khan.	410–411, 412–413, 414–415, 424
SS.6.W.4.12 Identify the causes and effects of Chinese isolation and the decision to limit foreign trade in the 15th century.	420–421, 424–425

LAFS Correlations

READING STANDARDS FOR LITERACY IN HISTORY/SOCIAL STUDIES	
BENCHMARK	**STUDENT EDITION**
Cluster 1: Key Ideas and Details	
LAFS.68.RH.1.1 Cite specific textual evidence to support analysis of primary and secondary sources.	33, 53, 73, 87, 103, 121, 131, 141, 153, 163, 173, 193, 227, 241, 257, 299, 303, 323, 339, 367, 375, 399, 415, 425
LAFS.68.RH.1.2 Determine the central ideas or information of a primary or secondary source; provide an accurate summary of the source distinct from prior knowledge or opinions.	15, 34, 39, 43, 45, 47, 52, 77, 86, 115, 122, 127, 139, 140, 191, 192, 213, 219, 243, 247, 251, 271, 273, 277, 283, 285, 295, 297, 302, 307, 311, 350, 365, 374, 379, 423
LAFS.68.RH.1.3 Identify key steps in a text's description of a process related to history/social studies (e.g., how a bill becomes law, how interest rates are raised or lowered).	20–21, 96–97, 138–139, 190–191, 290–291, 362–363, 422–423
Cluster 2: Craft and Structure	
LAFS.68.RH.2.4 Determine the meaning of words and phrases as they are used in a text, including vocabulary specific to domains related to history/social studies.	13, 17, 32, 41, 52, 71, 86, 119, 120, 140, 149, 151, 162, 177, 192, 215, 226, 228, 239, 256, 279, 302, 338, 357, 363, 374, 398, 424
LAFS.68.RH.2.5 Describe how a text presents information (e.g., sequentially, comparatively, causally).	10, 23, 25, 27, 31, 32, 41, 49, 69, 83, 91, 97, 101, 105, 109, 125, 142, 157, 161, 162, 171, 181, 183, 206, 209, 211, 215, 217, 219, 221, 223, 226, 231, 233, 237, 239, 243, 245, 249, 251, 255, 268, 275, 279, 289, 297, 302, 304, 309, 317, 319, 327, 331, 333, 335, 338, 353, 359, 365, 369, 371, 376, 379, 383, 391, 393, 397, 398, 405, 407, 409, 411, 413, 417, 421, 423
LAFS.68.RH.2.6 Identify aspects of a text that reveal an author's point of view or purpose (e.g., loaded language, inclusion or avoidance of particular facts).	31, 79, 164, 171, 191, 192, 363
Cluster 3: Integration of Knowledge and Ideas	
LAFS.68.RH.3.7 Integrate visual information (e.g., in charts, graphs, photographs, videos, or maps) with other information in print and digital texts.	5, 14, 17, 19, 21, 23, 25, 27, 29, 37, 39, 43, 47, 50–51, 67, 69, 71, 75, 79, 81, 85, 91, 93, 95, 101, 105, 109, 110–111, 113, 115, 117, 125, 127, 137, 145, 147, 149, 157, 159, 167, 169, 171, 177, 181, 185, 187, 188–189, 211, 213, 215, 217, 219, 221, 223, 233, 237, 239, 240, 243, 245, 251, 255, 263, 271, 273, 275, 279, 281, 283, 286–287, 291, 293, 295, 298, 309, 311, 321, 329, 330, 345, 353, 355, 356, 359, 361, 369, 371, 379, 380–381, 383, 385, 386–387, 389, 391, 393, 395, 403, 405, 407, 411, 417, 419, 421

BENCHMARK	STUDENT EDITION
LAFS.68.RH.3.8 Distinguish among fact, opinion, and reasoned judgment in a text.	19, 27, 30, 52, 85, 107, 159, 175, 183, 213, 295, 338, 374
LAFS.68.RH.3.9 .Analyze the relationship between a primary and secondary source on the same topic.	30, 298–299, 414–415

Cluster 4: Reading and Level of Text Complexity

LAFS.68.RH.3.10 By the end of grade 8, read and comprehend history/social studies texts in the grades 6-8 complexity band independently and proficiently.	The Lexile measure for the Student Edition falls within the stretch band for the Florida Standards.

WRITING STANDARDS FOR LITERACY IN HISTORY/SOCIAL STUDIES, SCIENCE, AND TECHNICAL SUBJECTS

BENCHMARK	STUDENT EDITION

Cluster 1: Text Types and Purposes

BENCHMARK	STUDENT EDITION

LAFS.68.WHST.1.1 Write arguments focused on discipline-specific content. Introduce claim(s) about a topic or issue, acknowledge and distinguish the claim(s) from alternate or opposing claims, an d organize the reasons and evidence logically.
    a. Support claim(s) with logical reasoning and relevant, accurate data and evidence that demonstrate an understanding of the topic or text, using credible sources.
    b. Use words, phrases, and clauses to create cohesion and clarify the relationships among claim(s), counterclaims, reasons, and evidence.
    c. Establish and maintain a formal style.
    d. Provide a concluding statement or section that follows from and supports the argument provided.
	87, 141, 193, 241, 303

LAFS.68.WHST.1.2 Write informative/explanatory texts, including the narration of historical events, scientific procedures/experiments, or technical processes.
    e. Introduce a topic clearly, previewing what is to follow; organize ideas, concepts, and information into broader categories as appropriate to achieving purpose; include formatting (e.g., headings), graphics (e.g., charts, tables), and multimedia when useful to aiding comprehension.
    f. Develop the topic with relevant, well-chosen facts, definitions, concrete details, quotations, or other information and examples.
    g. Use appropriate and varied transitions to create cohesion and clarify the relationships among ideas and concepts.
    h. Use precise language and domain-specific vocabulary to inform about or explain the topic.
    i. Establish and maintain a formal style and objective tone.
    j. Provide a concluding statement or section that follows from and supports the information or explanation presented.
	33, 53, 73, 103, 121, 131, 153, 163, 173, 227, 257, 299, 323, 339, 367, 375, 399, 415, 425

Cluster 2: Production and Distribution of Writing

BENCHMARK	STUDENT EDITION
LAFS.68.WHST.2.4 Produce clear and coherent writing in which the development, organization, and style are appropriate to task, purpose, and audience.	33, 53, 87, 121, 141, 163, 193, 227, 257, 303, 339, 375, 399, 425
LAFS.68.WHST.2.5 With some guidance and support from peers and adults, develop and strengthen writing as needed by planning, revising, editing, rewriting, or trying a new approach, focusing on how well purpose and audience have been addressed.	33, 53, 87, 121, 141, 163, 193, 227, 257, 303, 339, 375, 399, 425
LAFS.68.WHST.2.6 Use technology, including the Internet, to produce and publish writing and present the relationships between information and ideas clearly and efficiently.	197, 261, 343, 429, 444

Cluster 3: Research to Build and Present Knowledge	
LAFS.68.WHST.3.7 Conduct short research projects to answer a question (including a self-generated question), drawing on several sources and generating additional related, focused questions that allow for multiple avenues of exploration.	197, 261, 343, 429, 444
LAFS.68.WHST.3.8 Gather relevant information from multiple print and digital sources, using search terms effectively; assess the credibility and accuracy of each source; and quote or paraphrase the data and conclusions of others while avoiding plagiarism and following a standard format for citation.	197, 261, 343, 429, 444
LAFS.68.WHST.3.9 Draw evidence from informational texts to support analysis, reflection, and research.	33, 53, 57, 72–73, 87, 102–103, 121, 130–131, 141, 152–153, 163, 172–173, 193, 197, 227, 240–241, 257, 261, 298–299, 303, 322–323, 339, 343, 366–367, 375, 399, 414–415, 425, 429, 444
Cluster 4: Range of Writing	
LAFS.68.WHST.4.10 Write routinely over extended time frames (time for reflection and revision) and shorter time frames (a single sitting or a day or two) for a range of discipline-specific tasks, purposes, and audiences.	Writing opportunities throughout the SE fulfill this standard.

Correlations to *World History: Ancient Civilizations*

THE GEOGRAPHER'S TOOLBOX		
BENCHMARKS		
SS.6.G.1.1; SS.6.G.1.2; SS.6.G.1.3; SS.6.G.1.4; SS.6.G.1.5; SS.6.G.2.2; SS.6.G.2.7; SS.6.G.3.2; SS.6.G.4.2; SS.6.G.6.1		
Unit 1: ORIGINS OF CULTURES AND CIVILIZATIONS		
LESSON	**BENCHMARKS**	
Chapter 1 The Development of Human Societies		
1.1	SS.6.G.1.3; SS.6.W.1.2; SS.6.W.1.4; LAFS.68.RH.2.4	
1.2	SS.6.W.1.4; SS.6.W.1.6; LAFS.68.RH.1.2; LAFS.68.RH.3.7	
1.3	SS.6.G.1.3; SS.6.G.2.1; SS.6.G.4.3; SS.6.G.5.3; LAFS.68.RH.2.4; LAFS.68.RH.3.7	
1.4	SS.6.G.1.4; SS.6.G.2.1; SS.6.G.4.2; SS.6.G.4.3; LAFS.68.RH.3.7; LAFS.68.RH.3.8	
1.5	SS.6.G.1.4; SS.6.G.4.2; SS.6.G.4.3; SS.6.W.1.4; SS.6.W.1.5; LAFS.68.RH.1.3; LAFS.68.RH.3.7	
1.6	SS.6.W.1.6; LAFS.68.RH.2.5; LAFS.68.RH.3.7	
2.1	SS.6.E.1.3; SS.6.G.2.1; SS.6.G.4.1; SS.6.W.2.1; LAFS.68.RH.2.5; LAFS.68.RH.3.7	
2.2	SS.6.G.2.1; SS.6.W.2.1; LAFS.68.RH.2.5; LAFS.68.RH.3.7; LAFS.68.RH.3.8	

2.3	SS.6.G.1.4; SS.6.G.1.6; SS.6.G.2.1; SS.6.G.2.3; SS.6.W.1.2; SS.6.W.2.2; LAFS.68.RH.3.7
2.4	SS.6.W.1.3; SS.6.W.1.4; SS.6.W.1.5; LAFS.68.RH.2.5; LAFS.68.RH.2.6; LAFS.68.RH.3.8; LAFS.68.RH.3.9
Chapter 2 Origins of Civilization	
1.1	SS.6.E.1.2; SS.6.G.1.4; SS.6.G.1.6; SS.6.G.1.7; SS.6.G.2.1; SS.6.G.2.3; SS.6.G.2.4; SS.6.G.3.1; SS.6.G.3.2; LAFS.68.RH.3.7
1.2	SS.6.G.3.1; SS.6.G.3.2; SS.6.W.2.2; LAFS.68.RH.1.2; LAFS.68.RH.3.7
1.3	SS.6.G.2.1; SS.6.G.2.2; SS.6.G.2.3; SS.6.G.2.4; SS.6.G.3.1; SS.6.G.3.2; SS.6.G.4.1; LAFS.68.RH.2.4; LAFS.68.RH.2.5
1.4	SS.6.G.2.1; SS.6.G.2.4; SS.6.G.3.1; SS.6.G.3.2; LAFS.68.RH.1.2; LAFS.68.RH.3.7
1.5	SS.6.G.1.3; SS.6.G.2.1; SS.6.G.2.2; SS.6.G.2.3; SS.6.G.2.4; SS.6.G.2.5; SS.6.G.3.1; SS.6.G.3.2; LAFS.68.RH.1.2
2.1	SS.6.W.2.3; LAFS.68.RH.1.2; LAFS.68.RH.3.7
2.2	SS.6.E.1.3; SS.6.G.2.2; SS.6.W.2.3; LAFS.68.RH.2.5
2.3	SS.6.W.2.3; LAFS.68.RH.3.7

Unit 2: EARLY CIVILIZATIONS

LESSON	BENCHMARKS
Chapter 3 Ancient Mesopotamia	
1.1	SS.6.E.1.1; SS.6.G.1.4; SS.6.G.1.6; SS.6.G.1.7; SS.6.G.2.1; SS.6.G.2.3; SS.6.G.2.4; SS.6.G.3.1; SS.6.G.5.1; SS.6.G.5.3; SS.6.W.2.2; SS.6.W.2.7; LAFS.68.RH.3.7
1.2	SS.6.E.1.1; SS.6.E.2.1; SS.6.G.2.1; SS.6.G.2.2; SS.6.G.2.3; SS.6.G.2.4; SS.6.G.3.1; SS.6.W.2.2; SS.6.W.2.7; LAFS.68.RH.2.5; LAFS.68.RH.3.7
1.3	SS.6.G.2.4; SS.6.W.2.7; LAFS.68.RH.2.4; LAFS.68.RH.3.7
1.4	SS.6.W.1.3; SS.6.W.2.7; LAFS.68.WHST.1.2; LAFS.68.WHST.3.9
1.5	SS.6.G.1.4; SS.6.G.1.7; SS.6.G.2.2; SS.6.W.2.8; LAFS.68.RH.3.7
2.1	SS.6.W.1.3; SS.6.W.2.7; SS.6.W.2.8; LAFS.68.RH.1.2
2.2	SS.6.W.2.8; LAFS.68.RH.2.6; LAFS.68.RH.3.7
2.3	SS.6.E.1.1; SS.6.G.1.4; SS.6.G.1.6; SS.6.G.1.7; SS.6.G.2.1; SS.6.G.2.2; SS.6.G.2.4; SS.6.G.2.5; SS.6.G.2.6; SS.6.G.5.2; SS.6.W.3.1; LAFS.68.RH.3.7
2.4	SS.6.E.1.1; SS.6.G.2.2; SS.6.G.5.2; SS.6.W.2.8; LAFS.68.RH.2.5
2.5	SS.6.G.2.5; SS.6.W.2.7; SS.6.W.3.1; LAFS.68.RH.3.7; LAFS.68.RH.3.8

Chapter 4	Ancient Egypt
1.1	SS.6.G.1.3; SS.6.G.2.1; SS.6.G.2.3; SS.6.G.2.5; SS.6.G.3.1; LAFS.68.RH.2.5; LAFS.68.RH.3.7
1.2	SS.6.G.1.4; SS.6.G.1.6; SS.6.G.1.7; SS.6.G.2.1; SS.6.G.2.3; SS.6.G.2.4; SS.6.G.3.1; SS.6.G.5.1; SS.6.G.5.2; LAFS.68.RH.3.7
1.3	SS.6.E.2.1; SS.6.G.4.1; SS.6.W.2.6; LAFS.68.RH.3.7
1.4	SS.6.G.1.4; SS.6.W.1.4; LAFS.68.RH.1.3; LAFS.68.RH.2.5
2.1	SS.6.W.2.5; SS.6.W.2.6
2.2	SS.6.G.4.1; SS.6.W.2.4; SS.6.W.2.5; LAFS.68.RH.2; LAFS.68.RH.3.7
2.3	SS.6.W.1.3; SS.6.W.2.5; LAFS.68.RH.1.1; LAFS.68.WHST.1.2; LAFS.68.WHST.3.9
2.4	SS.6.E.1.1; SS.6.W.2.6; LAFS.68.RH.2.5; LAFS.68.RH.3.7
3.1	SS.6.E.1.1; SS.6.E.1.3; SS.6.E.3.2; SS.6.E.3.3; SS.6.E.3.4; SS.6.W.2.6; LAFS.68.RH.3.8
3.2	SS.6.E.1.1; SS.6.W.2.6; LAFS.68.RH.2.5; LAFS.68.RH.3.7
3.3	SS.6.W.2.6; LAFS.68.RH.3.7
3.4	SS.6.E.2.1; SS.6.E.3.3; SS.6.G.1.4; SS.6.G.1.6; SS.6.G.1.7; SS.6.G.2.1; SS.6.G.2.3; SS.6.G.2.4; SS.6.G.2.6; SS.6.W.2.4; SS.6.W.3.18; LAFS.68.RH.3.7
4.1	SS.6.W.2.5; LAFS.68.RH.1.2; LAFS.68.RH.3.7
4.2	SS.6.W.2.5; LAFS.68.RH.3.7
4.3	SS.6.G.2.5; SS.6.W.2.6; LAFS.68.RH.2.4
Chapter 5	Judaism and the Israelite Kingdoms
1.1	SS.6.G.1.4; SS.6.G.1.6; SS.6.G.1.7; SS.6.G.2.1; SS.6.G.2.4; SS.6.G.5.3; SS.6.W.2.8; SS.6.W.2.9; LAFS.68.RH.2.5; LAFS.68.RH.3.7
1.2	SS.6.E.2.1; SS.6.G.2.2; SS.6.G.2.4; SS.6.W.2.9; LAFS.68.RH.1.2; LAFS.68.RH.3.7
1.3	SS.6.G.4.1; SS.6.W.2.9
1.4	SS.6.W.1.3; SS.6.W.2.9; LAFS.68.RH.1.1; LAFS.68.WHST.1.2; LAFS.68.WHST.3.9
2.1	SS.6.W.2.9; LAFS.68.RH.2.5
2.2	SS.6.W.2.9
2.3	SS.6.G.1.4; SS.6.G.1.5; SS.6.G.2.6; SS.6.G.4.2; SS.6.G.4.4; SS.6.W.2.9; LAFS.68.RH.2.5; LAFS.68.RH.3.7
2.4	SS.6.G.1.4; SS.6.G.5.3; SS.6.W.1.4; LAFS.68.RH.1.2; LAFS.68.RH.1.3

Chapter 6 Ancient India	
1.1	SS.6.G.1.3; SS.6.G.1.4; SS.6.G.1.6; SS.6.G.2.1; SS.6.G.2.3; SS.6.G.3.1; LAFS.68.RH.3.7
1.2	SS.6.G.2.2; SS.6.G.3.1; SS.6.W.4.5; LAFS.68.RH.3.7
1.3	SS.6.G.1.4; SS.6.G.2.4; SS.6.G.2.6; SS.6.G.3.2; SS.6.G.4.2; SS.6.G.5.1; SS.6.W.4.1; SS.6.W.4.2; LAFS.68.RH.2.4
1.4	SS.6.W.4.2; LAFS.68.RH.2.4
1.5	SS.6.W.1.3; SS.6.W.4.2; LAFS.68.RH.1.1; LAFS.68.WHST.1.2; LAFS.68.WHST.3.9
1.6	SS.6.W.4.4
2.1	SS.6.G.1.4; SS.6.G.1.7; SS.6.G.4.4; SS.6.G.5.2; SS.6.W.4.3; SS.6.W.4.4; SS.6.W.4.5; LAFS.68.RH.3.7
2.2	SS.6.G.1.4; SS.6.G.1.5; SS.6.G.1.7; SS.6.W.4.2; SS.6.W.4.3; SS.6.W.4.5; LAFS.68.RH.3.7; LAFS.68.RH.3.8
2.3	SS.6.W.4.2; SS.6.W.4.3; SS.6.W.4.4; SS.6.W.4.5
Chapter 7 Ancient China	
1.1	SS.6.G.1.4; SS.6.G.1.6; SS.6.G.1.7; SS.6.G.2.1; SS.6.G.2.3; SS.6.G.2.4; SS.6.G.2.5; SS.6.G.3.1; SS.6.G.6.2; LAFS.68.RH.3.7
1.2	SS.6.W.2.2; SS.6.W.4.6; SS.6.W.4.8; LAFS.68.RH.3.7
1.3	SS.6.G.4.1; SS.6.G.4.2; SS.6.W.4.7; SS.6.W.4.8; SS.6.W.4.9; LAFS.68.RH.2.5; LAFS.68.RH.2.6; LAFS.68.RH.3.7
1.4	SS.6.W.1.3; SS.6.W.4.7; SS.6.W.4.9; LAFS.68.RH.1.1; LAFS.68.WHST.1.2; LAFS.68.WHST.3.9
2.1	SS.6.G.2.2; SS.6.G.5.2; SS.6.W.4.8; SS.6.W.4.9; LAFS.68.RH.3.8
2.2	SS.6.W.4.8; SS.6.W.4.9; LAFS.68.RH.2.4; LAFS.68.RH.3.7
2.3	SS.6.W.4.8; SS.6.W.4.9
2.4	SS.6.E.2.1; SS.6.G.1.4; SS.6.G.1.7; SS.6.W.4.8; SS.6.W.4.9; LAFS.68.RH.2.5; LAFS.68.RH.3.7
2.5	SS.6.W.2.2; SS.6.W.4.8; LAFS.68.RH.2.5; LAFS.68.RH.3.8
3.1	SS.6.E.3.4; SS.6.G.1.4; SS.6.G.2.5; SS.6.G.5.2; SS.6.W.4.8; SS.6.W.4.10; LAFS.68.RH.3.7
3.2	SS.6.E.1.3; SS.6.E.3.1; SS.6.E.3.2; SS.6.E.3.4; SS.6.G.2.6; SS.6.G.4.4; SS.6.W.4.4; SS.6.W.4.10; LAFS.68.RH.3.7
3.3	SS.6.E.3.2; SS.6.E.3.4; SS.6.W.4.10; LAFS.68.RH.3.7
3.4	SS.6.W.1.4; SS.6.W.1.5; SS.6.W.4.10; LAFS.68.RH.1.2; LAFS.68.RH.1.3; LAFS.68.RH.2.6

Unit 3: GREEK CIVILIZATION

LESSON	BENCHMARKS
Chapter 8 Ancient Greece	
1.1	SS.6.G.2.4; SS.6.G.5.3; SS.6.W.3.5; LAFS.68.RH.2.5
1.2	SS.6.G.1.4; SS.6.G.1.7; SS.6.G.2.1; SS.6.G.2.4; LAFS.68.RH.2.5; LAFS.68.RH.3.7
1.3	SS.6.W.3.5; SS.6.W.3.6; LAFS.68.RH.1.2; LAFS.68.RH.3.7; LAFS.68.RH.3.8
1.4	SS.6.E.2.1; SS.6.G.2.1; SS.6.G.2.2; SS.6.G.2.4; SS.6.G.2.5; SS.6.W.3.2; LAFS.68.RH.2.4; LAFS.68.RH.2.5; LAFS.68.RH.3.7
1.5	SS.6.E.1.1; SS.6.E.3.3; SS.6.E.3.4; SS.6.G.1.4; SS.6.G.1.5; SS.6.G.1.6; SS.6.G.1.7; SS.6.G.2.1; SS.6.G.2.2; SS.6.G.2.4; SS.6.G.2.5; SS.6.G.2.6; SS.6.G.5.1; SS.6.G.5.2; SS.6.W.3.1; LAFS.68.RH.2.5; LAFS.68.RH.3.7
2.1	SS.6.G.4.1; SS.6.W.3.3; LAFS.68.RH.1.2; LAFS.68.RH.2.5; LAFS.68.RH.3.7
2.2	SS.6.C.1.1; SS.6.G.4.1; SS.6.W.3.2; SS.6.W.3.3; LAFS.68.RH.2.5; LAFS.68.RH.3.7
2.3	SS.6.W.3.4; LAFS.68.RH.2.5; LAFS.68.RH.3.7
2.4	SS.6.W.3.4
Chapter 9 Classical Greece	
1.1	SS.6.C.1.1; SS.6.C.2.1; SS.6.W.3.2; SS.6.W.3.5; SS.6.W.3.6; LAFS.68.RH.2.5
1.2	SS.6.G.2.5; SS.6.W.3.4; SS.6.W.3.5; SS.6.W.3.6; LAFS.68.RH.2.5; LAFS.68.RH.3.7
1.3	SS.6.W.3.5
2.1	SS.6.G.1.4; SS.6.W.3.3; SS.6.W.3.4; LAFS.68.RH.2.5; LAFS.68.RH.3.7v
2.2	SS.6.W.3.3; SS.6.W.3.4; LAFS.68.RH.2.4; LAFS.68.RH.2.5; LAFS.68.RH.3.7
2.3	SS.6.W.1.3; SS.6.W.3.4; SS.6.W.3.6; LAFS.68.RH.1.1; LAFS.68.RH.3.7; LAFS.68.WHST.1.1; LAFS.68.WHST.3.9
3.1	SS.6.W.3.7; LAFS.68.RH.1.2; LAFS.68.RH.2.5; LAFS.68.RH.3.7
3.2	SS.6.G.1.4; SS.6.G.1.5; SS.6.G.1.7; SS.6.G.2.1; SS.6.W.3.7; LAFS.68.RH.2.5; LAFS.68.RH.3.7
3.3	SS.6.G.2.5; SS.6.G.2.6; SS.6.W.3.7; LAFS.68.RH.1.2
4.1	SS.6.W.3.5; SS.6.W.3.6; LAFS.68.RH.2.5
4.2	SS.6.W.3.5; SS.6.W.3.6; LAFS.68.RH.1.2; LAFS.68.RH.2.5; LAFS.68.RH.3.7
4.3	SS.6.W.3.5

4.4	SS.6.C.1.1; SS.6.C.2.1; SS.6.W.3.2; SS.6.W.3.5; LAFS.68.RH.2.5; LAFS.68.RH.3.7

Unit 4: THE WORLD OF THE ROMANS

LESSON	BENCHMARKS

Chapter 10 The Roman Republic

LESSON	BENCHMARKS
1.1	SS.6.E.1.1; SS.6.G.1.4; SS.6.G.1.6; SS.6.G.1.7; SS.6.G.2.1; SS.6.G.2.4; SS.6.G.2.5; LAFS.68.RH.1.2; LAFS.68.RH.3.7
1.2	SS.6.G.2.6; SS.6.W.3.8; LAFS.68.RH.1.2; LAFS.68.RH.3.7
1.3	SS.6.C.1.2; SS.6.C.2.1; SS.6.W.3.8; SS.6.W.3.10; SS.6.W.3.16; LAFS.68.RH.2.5; LAFS.68.RH.3.7
1.4	SS.6.W.3.10; LAFS.68.RH.1.2
2.1	SS.6.G.4.1; SS.6.W.3.16; LAFS.68.RH.2.4; LAFS.68.RH.2.5; LAFS.68.RH.3.7
2.2	SS.6.E.1.1; SS.6.W.3.16; LAFS.68.RH.3.7
2.3	SS.6.G.2.6; SS.6.W.3.12; LAFS.68.RH.1.2; LAFS.68.RH.3.7
3.1	SS.6.W.3.8; SS.6.W.3.12; SS.6.W.3.14
3.2	SS.6.W.3.12; LAFS.68.RH.3.7
3.3	SS.6.W.3.8; SS.6.W.3.9; LAFS.68.RH.2.5
3.4	SS.6.G.1.4; SS.6.G.2.5; SS.6.W.1.4; SS.6.W.3.8; LAFS.68.RH.1.3; LAFS.68.RH.3.7
3.5	SS.6.E.1.1; SS.6.G.1.4; SS.6.G.1.7; SS.6.G.2.2; SS.6.W.3.8; SS.6.W.3.9; LAFS.68.RH.3.7
4.1	SS.6.W.3.8; SS.6.W.3.11; LAFS.68.RH.1.2; LAFS.68.RH.3.7; LAFS.68.RH.3.8
4.2	SS.6.W.3.8; SS.6.W.3.11; LAFS.68.RH.1.2; LAFS.68.RH.2.5
4.3	SS.6.W.1.3; SS.6.W.3.8; LAFS.68.RH.1.1; LAFS.68.RH.3.7; LAFS.68.RH.3.9; LAFS.68.WHST.1.2; LAFS.68.WHST.3.9
4.4	SS.6.W.3.8

Chapter 11 The Roman Empire and Christianity

LESSON	BENCHMARKS
1.1	SS.6.W.3.8; SS.6.W.3.11; LAFS.68.RH.1.2
1.2	SS.6.E.1.1; SS.6.E.3.1; SS.6.E.3.2; SS.6.E.3.3; SS.6.G.1.4; SS.6.G.5.1; SS.6.G.5.2; SS.6.W.3.12; LAFS.68.RH.2.5; LAFS.68.RH.3.7
1.3	SS.6.G.5.2; SS.6.W.3.14; LAFS.68.RH.1.2; LAFS.68.RH.3.7
1.4	SS.6.W.3.14

1.5	SS.6.W.3.14
1.6	SS.6.G.5.3; LAFS.68.RH.2.5
2.1	SS.6.W.3.13; LAFS.68.RH.2.5
2.2	SS.6.G.1.4; SS.6.G.1.5; SS.6.G.4.4; SS.6.W.3.13; SS.6.W.3.18; LAFS.68.RH.3.7
2.3	SS.6.W.1.3; SS.6.W.3.13; LAFS.68.RH.1.1; LAFS.68.WHST.1.2; LAFS.68.WHST.3.9
2.4	SS.6.W.3.13
3.1	SS.6.W.3.15; LAFS.68.RH.2.5
3.2	SS.6.G.1.4; SS.6.G.1.7; SS.6.W.3.8; SS.6.W.3.15; LAFS.68.RH.3.7
3.3	SS.6.W.3.8; SS.6.W.3.15; LAFS.68.RH.2.5; LAFS.68.RH.3.7
4.1	SS.6.W.3.8; SS.6.W.3.14; SS.6.W.3.17; LAFS.68.RH.2.5
4.2	SS.6.C.1.2; SS.6.C.2.1; SS.6.W.3.10; SS.6.W.3.14; SS.6.W.3.17; LAFS.68.RH.2.5
4.3	SS.6.W.3.14

Unit 5: AMERICAN AND ASIAN CIVILIZATIONS

LESSON	BENCHMARKS
Chapter 12 Mesoamerica	
1.1	SS.6.G.1.4; SS.6.G.1.6; SS.6.G.1.7; SS.6.G.2.1; SS.6.G.2.3; SS.6.G.3.1; SS.6.G.3.2; SS.6.G.5.1; SS.6.W.2.10; LAFS.68.RH.2.5; LAFS.68.RH.3.7
1.2	SS.6.G.2.1; SS.6.G.2.6; SS.6.W.2.10; LAFS.68.RH.3.7
1.3	SS.6.G.2.1; LAFS.68.RH.2.4; LAFS.68.RH.3.7
2.1	SS.6.G.1.4; SS.6.G.1.7; SS.6.G.2.1; LAFS.68.RH.2.5; LAFS.68.RH.3.7
2.2	LAFS.68.RH.3.7
2.3	SS.6.W.1.4; SS.6.W.1.5; LAFS.68.RH.1.3; LAFS.68.RH.2.4; LAFS.68.RH.2.6
2.4	LAFS.68.RH.1.2; LAFS.68.RH.2.5
2.5	SS.6.W.1.3; LAFS.68.RH.1.1; LAFS.68.WHST.1.2; LAFS.68.WHST.3.9
3.1	SS.6.G.1.4; SS.6.G.1.5; SS.6.G.1.7; SS.6.G.2.4; LAFS.68.RH.2.5; LAFS.68.RH.3.7
3.2	LAFS.68.RH.2.5; LAFS.68.RH.3.7

3.3	SS.6.W.1.4

Chapter 13 South and North America	
1.1	SS.6.G.1.4; SS.6.G.2.1; SS.6.G.2.4; SS.6.G.5.1; SS.6.W.2.10; LAFS.68.RH.1.2; LAFS.68.RH.2.5; LAFS.68.RH.3.7
1.2	LAFS.68.RH.3.7
1.3	SS.6.E.1.2, SS.6.E.2.1; SS.6.G.1.4; SS.6.G.1.5; SS.6.G.1.7; SS.6.G.2.1; SS.6.G.5.1; SS.6.G.5.2; LAFS.68.RH.2.5; LAFS.68.RH.3.7
1.4	SS.6.G.5.2; LAFS.68.RH.3.7
1.5	LAFS.68.RH.3.7
2.1	SS.6.G.2.1; SS.6.G.2.4; SS.6.G.4.1; LAFS.68.RH.3.7
2.2	SS.6.G.2.1; LAFS.68.RH.2.5; LAFS.68.RH.3.7
2.3	SS.6.G.2.1; SS.6.G.3.2; SS.6.G.5.1; LAFS.68.RH.2.5; LAFS.68.RH.3.7
2.4	SS.6.G.2.1; LAFS.68.RH.3.7
2.5	SS.6.E.2.1; SS.6.G.2.1; SS.6.G.2.2; SS.6.G.3.2; SS.6.G.5.1; LAFS.68.RH.2.5

Chapter 14 Dynasties of China	
1.1	SS.6.G.1.4; SS.6.G.1.7; SS.6.G.6.2; SS.6.W.4.6; SS.6.W.4.8; SS.6.W.4.9; LAFS.68.RH.3.7
1.2	SS.6.G.4.4; SS.6.W.4.4; LAFS.68.RH.2.5; LAFS.68.RH.3.7
1.3	SS.6.E.1.1; SS.6.E.3.1; SS.6.W.4.8; SS.6.W.4.9; LAFS.68.RH.2.5; LAFS.68.RH.3.7
1.4	SS.6.W.4.8; LAFS.68.RH.2.5
2.1	SS.6.G.1.4; SS.6.G.1.5; SS.6.G.1.7; SS.6.G.2.2; SS.6.W.4.9; SS.6.W.4.11; LAFS.68.RH.2.5; LAFS.68.RH.3.7
2.2	SS.6.W.4.9; SS.6.W.4.10; SS.6.W.4.11; LAFS.68.RH.2.5
2.3	SS.6.E.3.2; SS.6.E.3.4; SS.6.W.1.3; SS.6.W.4.9; SS.6.W.4.10; SS.6.W.4.11; LAFS.68.RH.1.1; LAFS.68.RH.3.9; LAFS.68.WHST.1.2; LAFS.68.WHST.3.9
3.1	SS.6.W.4.9; LAFS.68.RH.2.5; LAFS.68.RH.3.7
3.2	SS.6.G.1.4; SS.6.W.4.9; SS.6.W.4.10; LAFS.68.RH.3.7
3.3	SS.6.W.1.1; SS.6.W.4.12; LAFS.68.RH.2.5; LAFS.68.RH.3.7
3.4	SS.6.W.1.4; SS.6.W.1.5; LAFS.68.RH.1.2; LAFS.68.RH.1.3; LAFS.68.RH.2.5

GEOGRAPHER'S TOOLBOX

THE GEOGRAPHER'S
TOOLBOX

Geographic Thinking

SPATIAL THINKING

Geography is about more than the names of places on a map. It involves spatial thinking, or thinking about the space on Earth's surface. Geographers use spatial thinking to ask questions, such as:

- Where is a place located?

- Why is this location significant, or important?

- How does this place influence the people who live there?

- How do the people influence the location?

By asking and answering these questions and many others, geographers can find patterns. Geographic patterns are similarities among places. The location of large cities near water is one example of a geographic pattern. Many geographers use computer-based Geographic Information Systems (GIS) to study patterns, such as those that affect population distribution, economic development, the spread of diseases, and water resources. They create maps and analyze their patterns using many layers of data.

The photo below shows the fertile land alongside the Nile River in Egypt. Thousands of years ago, many people settled along this river. They farmed along its shores and traveled and traded on its waters. In time, a great civilization grew in the Nile River Valley: the civilization of ancient Egypt.

Other ancient settlements and civilizations rose in river valleys in many parts of the world. Geographers note this pattern and others when they think spatially.

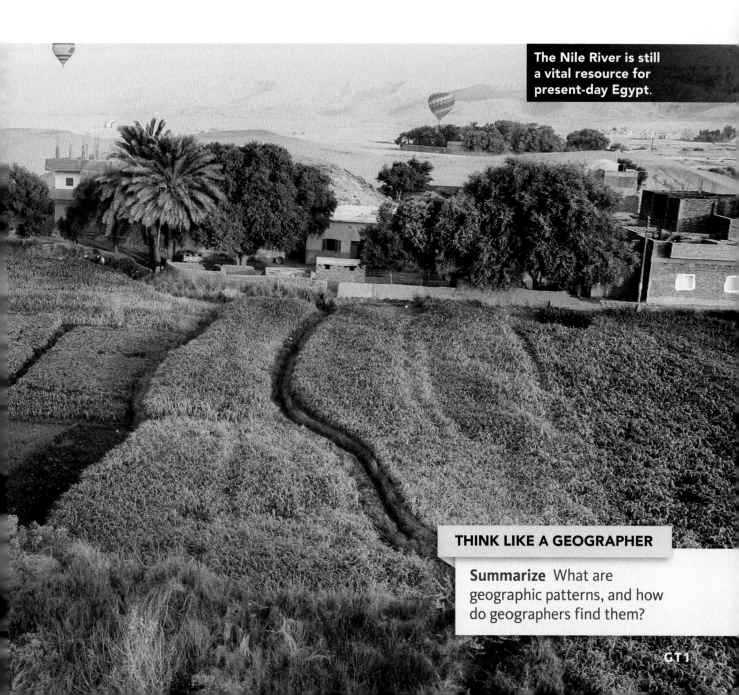

The Nile River is still a vital resource for present-day Egypt.

THINK LIKE A GEOGRAPHER

Summarize What are geographic patterns, and how do geographers find them?

Geographic Thinking THEMES AND ELEMENTS

Geographers ask questions about how people, places, and environments are arranged and connected on Earth's surface. The five themes and six elements will help you categorize, or group, information.

THE FIVE THEMES OF GEOGRAPHY

Geographers use five themes to categorize similar geographic information.

1. **Location** provides a way of locating places. Absolute location is the exact point where a place is located. Geographers use a satellite system called the Global Positioning System (GPS) to find absolute location. Relative location is where a place is in relation to other places. For example, the Great Wall of China is located near Beijing in northern China.

2. **Place** includes the characteristics of a location. A famous place in the western United States is the Grand Canyon. It has steep rock walls that were carved over centuries by the Colorado River.

3. **Human-Environment Interaction** explains how people affect the environment and how the environment affects people. For example, people throughout much of history have built dams to change the flow of rivers.

4. **Movement** explains how people, ideas, and animals move from one place to another. The spread of different religions around the world is an example of movement.

5. **Region** involves a group of places that have common characteristics. A region can be as big as a continent such as North America, which includes the United States, Canada, and Mexico. A region can also be as small as a neighborhood.

THE SIX ESSENTIAL ELEMENTS

In addition to the five themes, some geographers also identify essential elements, or key ideas, to study physical processes and human systems.

1. **The World in Spatial Terms** Geographers use tools such as maps to study places on Earth's surface.

2. **Places and Regions** Geographers study the characteristics of places and regions.

3. **Physical Systems** Geographers examine Earth's physical processes, such as earthquakes and volcanoes.

4. **Human Systems** Geographers study how humans live and what systems they create, such as economic systems.

5. **Environment and Society** Geographers explore how humans change the environment and use resources.

6. **The Uses of Geography** Geographers interpret the past, analyze the present, and plan for the future.

THINK LIKE A GEOGRAPHER

Make Inferences How do geographers use the themes and elements to better understand the world?

Critical Viewing Tourists climb the Great Wall of China. What physical land features can you see in the photo?

Critical Viewing The Great Wall runs through the Chinese countryside. Which themes and elements does this photo represent?

Geographic Thinking CONTINENTS

In 1413, a Chinese admiral and explorer, Zheng He, sailed from China to Arabia. When he arrived in Arabia, he saw people dressed in ways he had never seen. Yet, like him, these people wanted to trade.

Zheng He came to understand that regions of Earth have similarities and differences. The places within a region are linked by trade, culture, and other human activities. They also share similar physical processes and characteristics, such as climate.

As you've read, a region often contains an entire continent. A continent is a large landmass on Earth's surface. Geographers have identified seven continents: Africa, Asia, Australia, Europe, North America, South America, and Antarctica.

Geographers study the world's continents, but they also take a global perspective when they investigate Earth. They might, for instance, study ocean currents around the globe or how one region affects another. Both ways of looking at the world add to our understanding of it.

THINK LIKE A GEOGRAPHER

Draw Conclusions Why do geographers study the world by dividing it into continents?

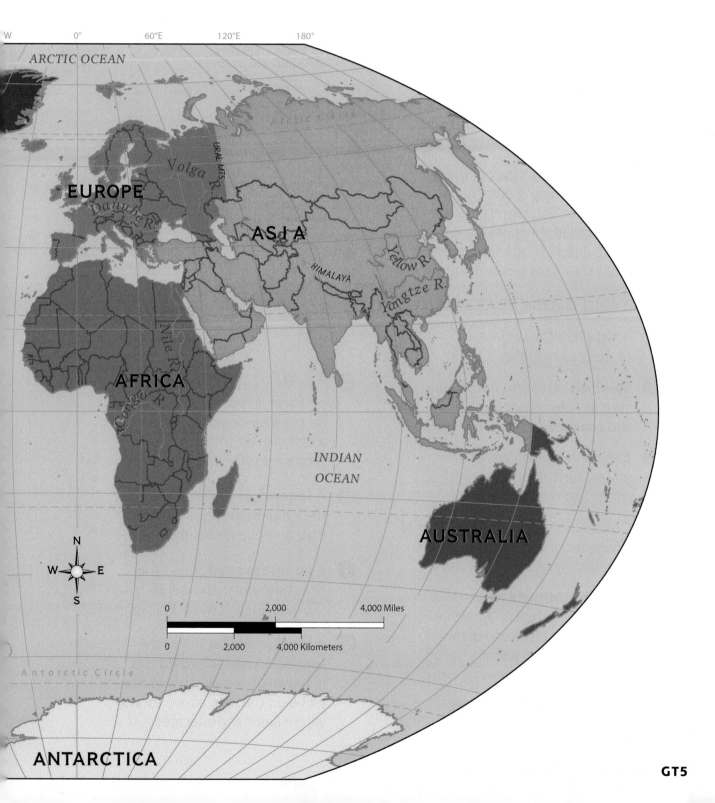

ARCTIC OCEAN

EUROPE

ASIA

AFRICA

INDIAN OCEAN

AUSTRALIA

ANTARCTICA

0 2,000 4,000 Miles

0 2,000 4,000 Kilometers

Maps ELEMENTS OF A MAP

Have you ever needed to figure out how to get to a friend's house? Maybe you usually use the GPS on your phone to navigate such distances, but imagine that the only resource you had was a globe. In order to see enough detail to find your friend's house, the globe would have to be enormous—much too big to carry around in your pocket!

GLOBES AND MAPS

A three-dimensional, or spherical, representation of Earth is called a globe. It is useful when you need to see Earth as a whole, but it is not helpful if you need to see a small section of Earth.

Now imagine taking a part of the globe and flattening it out. This two-dimensional, or flat, representation of Earth is called a map. Maps and globes are different representations of Earth, but they have similar features.

MAP AND GLOBE FEATURES

A A **title** tells the subject of the map or globe.

B **Symbols** represent information such as natural resources and economic activities.

C **Labels** are the names of places, such as cities, countries, rivers, and mountains.

D **Colors** represent different kinds of information. For example, the color blue usually represents water.

E **Lines of latitude** are imaginary horizontal lines that measure the distance north or south of the equator.

F **Lines of longitude** are imaginary vertical lines that measure the distance east or west of the prime meridian.

G A **scale** shows how much distance on Earth is represented by distance on the map or globe. For example, a half inch on the map above represents 100 miles on Earth.

H A **legend,** or key, explains what the symbols and colors on the map or globe represent.

I A **compass rose** shows the directions north (N), south (S), east (E), and west (W).

J A **locator globe** shows the specific area of the world that is shown on a map. The locator globe on the map above shows where Germany is located.

LATITUDE

Lines of latitude are imaginary lines that run east to west, parallel to the equator. The equator is the center line of latitude. Distances north and south of the equator are measured in degrees (°). There are 90 degrees north of the equator and 90 degrees south. The equator is 0°. The latitude of Berlin, Germany, is 52° N, meaning that it is 52 degrees north of the equator.

LONGITUDE

Lines of longitude are imaginary lines that run north to south from the North Pole to the South Pole. They measure distance east or west of the prime meridian. The prime meridian runs through Greenwich, England. It is 0°. There are 180 degrees east of the prime meridian and 180 degrees west. The longitude of Berlin, Germany, is 13° E, meaning that it is 13 degrees east of the prime meridian.

Remember that absolute location is the exact point where a place is located. This point includes a place's latitude and longitude. For example, the absolute location of Berlin, Germany, is 52° N, 13° E. You say this aloud as "fifty-two degrees North, thirteen degrees East."

HEMISPHERES

A hemisphere is half of Earth. The equator divides Earth into the Northern Hemisphere and the Southern Hemisphere. North America is entirely in the Northern Hemisphere. Most of South America is in the Southern Hemisphere.

The Western Hemisphere is west of the prime meridian. The Eastern Hemisphere is east of the prime meridian. South America is in the Western Hemisphere. Most of Africa is in the Eastern Hemisphere.

THINK LIKE A GEOGRAPHER

Monitor Comprehension How are maps and globes different? How is each one used?

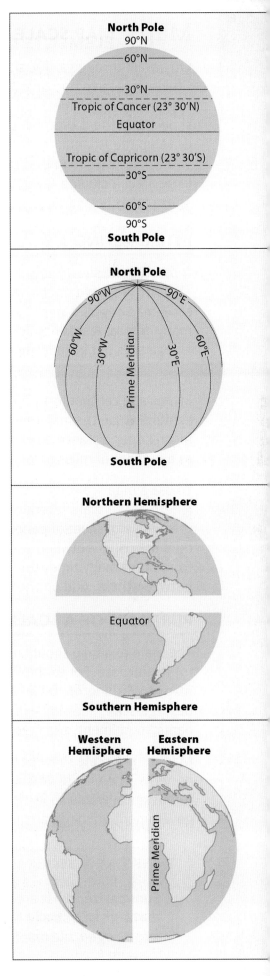

Maps MAP SCALE

On a walk through a city, such as Charlotte, North Carolina, you might use a highly detailed map that shows only the downtown area. To drive up the Atlantic coast, however, you would use a map that covers a large area, including several states. These maps have different scales.

INTERPRETING A SCALE

A map's scale shows how much distance on Earth is shown on the map. A large-scale map covers a small area but shows many details. A small-scale map covers a large area but includes few details.

A scale is usually shown in both inches and centimeters. One inch or centimeter on the map represents a much larger distance on Earth, such as a number of miles or kilometers.

To use a map scale, mark off the length of the scale several times on the edge of a sheet of paper. Then hold the paper between two points to see how many times the scale falls between them. Add up the distance.

PURPOSES OF A SCALE

The scale of a map should be appropriate for its purpose. For example, a tourist map of Washington, D.C., should be large-scale, showing every street name, monument, and museum.

Maps of any scale show geographic patterns. The map of Washington, D.C., for instance, would show that many government buildings are in one area.

THINK LIKE A GEOGRAPHER

Summarize What are the purposes of a small-scale map and a large-scale map?

LARGE-SCALE MAP

This detailed map shows only the city of Charlotte. On this map's scale, a half inch on the map represents a quarter mile on Earth.

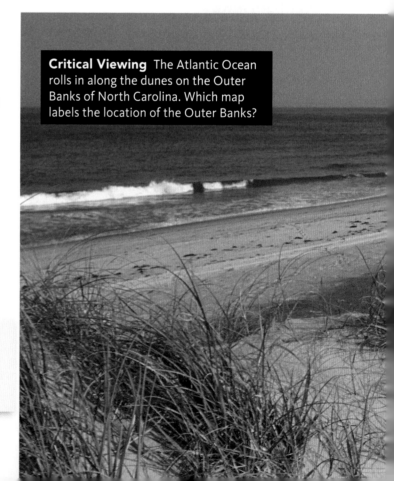

Critical Viewing The Atlantic Ocean rolls in along the dunes on the Outer Banks of North Carolina. Which map labels the location of the Outer Banks?

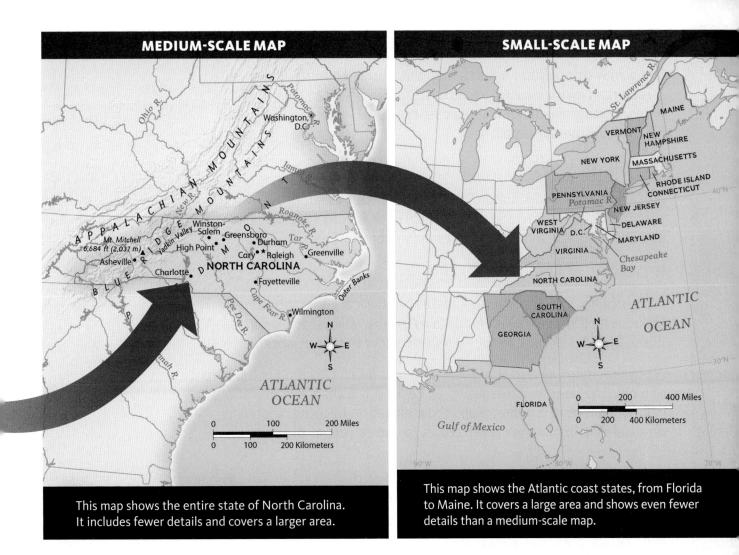

MEDIUM-SCALE MAP

This map shows the entire state of North Carolina. It includes fewer details and covers a larger area.

SMALL-SCALE MAP

This map shows the Atlantic coast states, from Florida to Maine. It covers a large area and shows even fewer details than a medium-scale map.

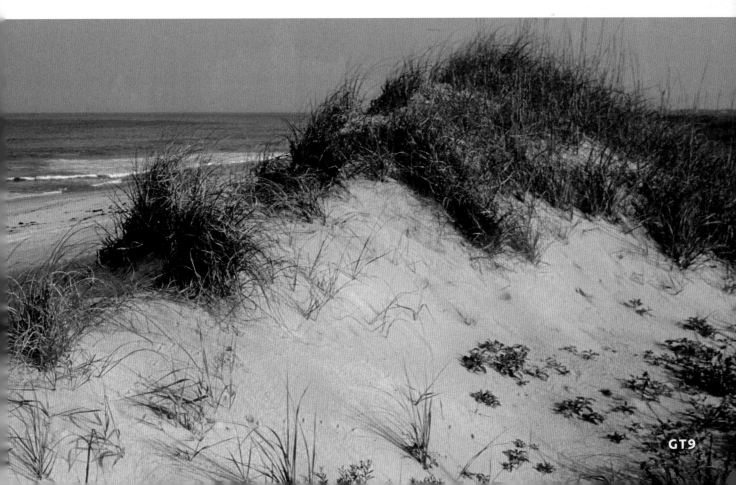

Maps POLITICAL AND PHYSICAL

The governor of a state needs a map that shows counties and cities. A mountain climber needs a map that shows cliffs, canyons, and ice fields. Cartographers, or mapmakers, create different kinds of maps for these different purposes.

POLITICAL MAPS

A political map shows features that humans have created, such as countries, states, provinces, and cities. These features are labeled, and lines show boundaries, such as those between countries.

PHYSICAL MAPS

A physical map shows natural features of physical geography. It includes landforms, such as mountains, plains, valleys, and deserts. It also includes oceans, lakes, rivers, and other bodies of water.

A physical map can also show elevation and relief. Elevation is the height of a physical feature above sea level. Relief is the change in elevation from one place to another. Maps show elevation by using color. The physical map below uses seven colors for seven ranges of elevation.

THINK LIKE A GEOGRAPHER

Monitor Comprehension How is a political map different from a physical map?

Critical Viewing The Sobaek Mountains cut diagonally across South Korea. Which map best indicates the location of these mountains?

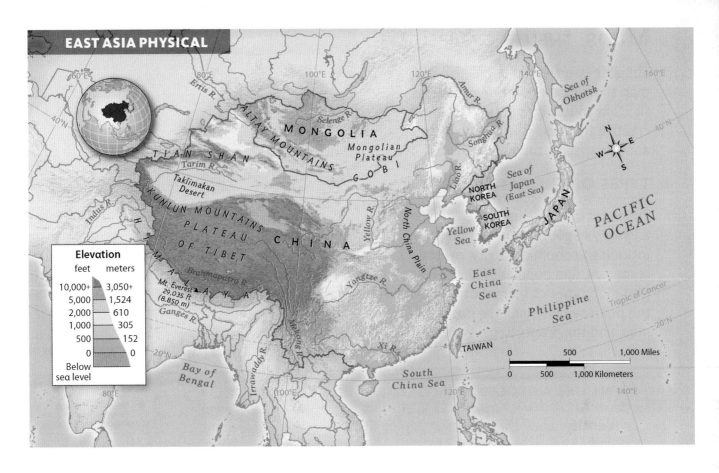

EAST ASIA PHYSICAL

Ertis R.
ALTAY MOUNTAINS
MONGOLIA
Selenge R.
Mongolian Plateau
TIAN SHAN
Tarim R.
G O B I
Taklimakan Desert
KUNLUN MOUNTAINS
PLATEAU OF TIBET
C H I N A
Amur R.
Songhua R.
Liao R.
NORTH KOREA
Sea of Okhotsk
Sea of Japan (East Sea)
SOUTH KOREA
JAPAN
Indus R.
H I M A L A Y A
Brahmaputra R.
Mt. Everest 29,035 ft (8,850 m)
Ganges R.
Mekong R.
Yangtze R.
North China Plain
Yellow R.
Yellow Sea
East China Sea
PACIFIC OCEAN
Xi R.
TAIWAN
Philippine Sea
Tropic of Cancer
Bay of Bengal
Irrawaddy R.
South China Sea

Elevation

feet	meters
10,000+	3,050+
5,000	1,524
2,000	610
1,000	305
500	152
0	0
Below sea level	

0 500 1,000 Miles
0 500 1,000 Kilometers

EAST ASIA POLITICAL

Ertis R.
Selenge R.
MONGOLIA
Ulaanbaatar
Tarim R.
Amur R.
Songhua R.
Liao R.
Beijing
NORTH KOREA
P'yongyang
Sea of Okhotsk
Sea of Japan (East Sea)
Seoul
SOUTH KOREA
JAPAN
Tokyo
PACIFIC OCEAN
C H I N A
Indus R.
Brahmaputra R.
Mt. Everest 29,035 ft (8,850 m)
Ganges R.
Chengdu
Chongqing
Yangtze R.
Yellow R.
Shanghai
Yellow Sea
East China Sea
Mekong R.
Kunming
Xi R.
Taipei
TAIWAN
Hong Kong
South China Sea
Philippine Sea
Tropic of Cancer
Bay of Bengal
Irrawaddy R.

0 500 1,000 Miles
0 500 1,000 Kilometers

Maps THEMATIC MAPS

Suppose you wanted to create a map showing the location of sports fields in your community. You would create a thematic map, which is a map about a specific theme, or topic.

TYPES OF THEMATIC MAPS

Thematic maps are useful for showing a variety of geographic information, including economic activity, natural resources, and population density. Common types of thematic maps are the point symbol map, the dot density map, and the proportional symbol map.

THINK LIKE A GEOGRAPHER

Identify Look through your world history textbook and identify an example of a thematic map. What geographic information does the map show?

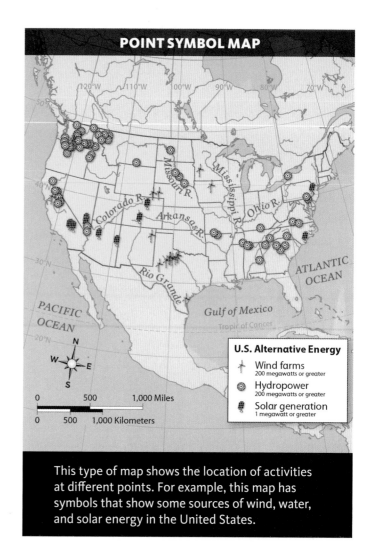

POINT SYMBOL MAP

U.S. Alternative Energy
- Wind farms
  200 megawatts or greater
- Hydropower
  200 megawatts or greater
- Solar generation
  1 megawatt or greater

This type of map shows the location of activities at different points. For example, this map has symbols that show some sources of wind, water, and solar energy in the United States.

DOT DENSITY MAP

Population Density

· One dot represents 50,000 people

This type of map uses dots to show how something is distributed in a country or region. Each dot represents an amount. For example, each dot on this map represents 50,000 people living in Thailand.

PROPORTIONAL SYMBOL MAP

Earthquake Magnitude

7.3–7.6
6.8–7.2
6.3–6.7
5.5–6.2

This type of map uses symbols of different sizes to show the size of an event. For example, the size of the circles on this map shows the severity of earthquakes in the Philippines.

Solar panels in the Nevada desert absorb light from the sun and turn it into energy.

Maps MAP PROJECTIONS

The world is a sphere, but maps are flat. As a result, maps distort, or change, shapes, areas, distances, and directions found in the real world. To reduce distortion, mapmakers use projections, or ways of showing Earth's curved surface on a flat map. Five common map projections are the azimuthal, Robinson, Mercator, Winkel Tripel, and homolosine. Each projection has strengths and weaknesses—each distorts in a different way.

When cartographers make maps, they need to choose a map projection. The type of projection depends on the map's purpose. Which elements are acceptable to distort? Which are not acceptable to distort? For example, if a cartographer is creating a navigation map, it is important that direction should not be distorted. It may not matter, however, if some areas or shapes are distorted.

THINK LIKE A GEOGRAPHER

Make Inferences How do cartographers decide which projection to use?

AZIMUTHAL PROJECTION

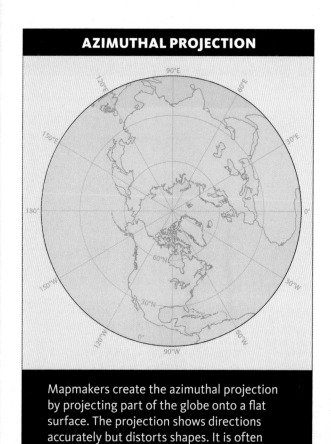

Mapmakers create the azimuthal projection by projecting part of the globe onto a flat surface. The projection shows directions accurately but distorts shapes. It is often used for the polar regions.

MERCATOR PROJECTION

The Mercator projection shows much of Earth accurately, but it distorts the shape and area of land near the North and South poles. This projection shows direction accurately, so it is good for navigation maps.

HOMOLOSINE PROJECTION

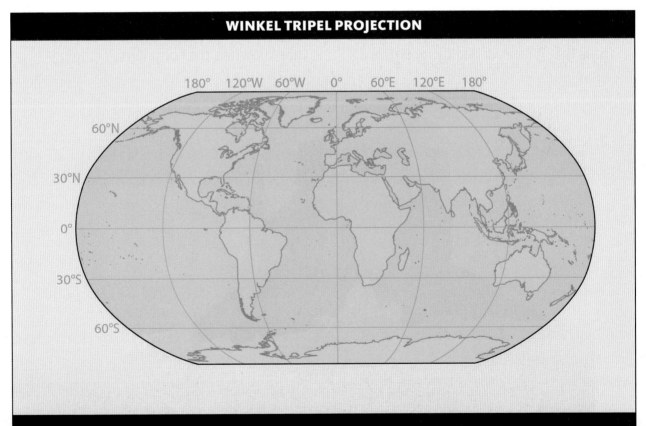

The homolosine projection resembles the flattened peel of an orange. It accurately shows the shape and area of landmasses by cutting up the oceans. However, it does not show distance accurately.

ROBINSON PROJECTION

The Robinson projection combines the strengths of other projections. It shows the shape and area of the continents and oceans with reasonable accuracy. However, the North and South poles are distorted.

WINKEL TRIPEL PROJECTION

The Winkel Tripel projection is a modified version of the Robinson projection. It has less distortion of area and shape. This projection has been the preferred projection of the National Geographic Society since 1998.

Physical Geography EARTH'S LANDFORMS

The Rocky Mountains rise more than 14,000 feet above sea level. The Grand Canyon is more than 5,000 feet deep. Both are landforms, or physical features on Earth's surface.

SURFACE LANDFORMS

Landforms such as the Rocky Mountains in western North America and the Grand Canyon in Arizona provide a variety of physical environments. These environments support millions of plants and animals.

Several landforms are commonly found on Earth's surface. A mountain is a high, steep elevation. A hill also slopes upward but is less steep and rugged. In contrast, a plain is a level area. The Great Plains, for example, are flat landforms stretching from the Mississippi River to the Rocky Mountains. A plateau is a plain that sits high above sea level and usually has a cliff on all sides. A valley is a low-lying area that is surrounded by mountains.

OCEAN LANDFORMS

Earth's oceans also have landforms that are underwater. Mountains and valleys rise and fall along the ocean floor. Volcanoes erupt with hot magma, which hardens as it cools to form new crust.

The edge of a continent often extends out under the water. This land is called the continental shelf. Most of Earth's marine life lives at this level of the ocean. Beyond the continental shelf, the land develops a steep slope. Beyond the slope, before the ocean floor, the land slopes slightly upward. This landform is called the continental rise. It is formed by rocks and sediment carried by ocean currents. Together, these landforms are known as the continental margin.

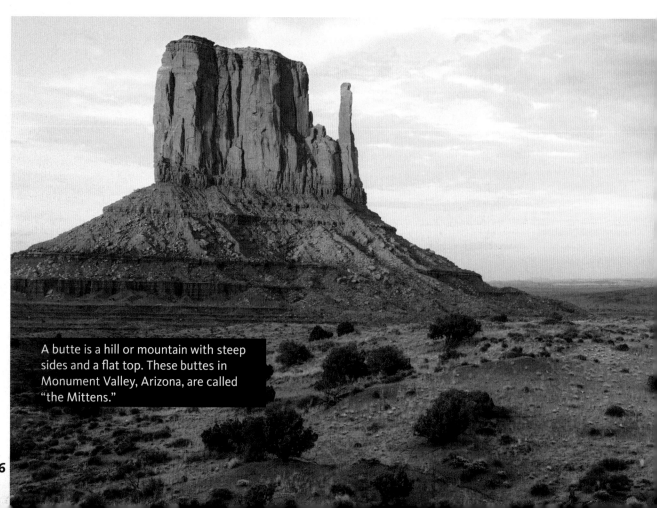

A butte is a hill or mountain with steep sides and a flat top. These buttes in Monument Valley, Arizona, are called "the Mittens."

The following natural wonders are landforms or events that have had an impact on world history.

1. Grand Canyon, North America
2. Iguazu Falls, South America
3. Great Rift Valley, Africa
4. Mount Kilimanjaro, Africa
5. Victoria Falls, Africa
6. Nile River, Africa
7. Sahara, Africa
8. Ngorongoro Crater, Africa
9. Okavango Delta, Africa
10. Red Sea Reef, Africa/Asia
11. Serengeti Migration, Africa
12. Matterhorn, Europe
13. Himalaya, Asia
14. Gobi, Asia
15. Uluru, Australia

THE CHANGING EARTH

Earth is always changing, and the changes affect plant and animal life. For example, a flood can cause severe erosion, which can ruin farmers' fields. Erosion is the process by which rocks and soil slowly break apart and are swept away.

THINK LIKE A GEOGRAPHER

Summarize How do physical processes reshape Earth's landforms?

GT17

Physical Geography NATURAL RESOURCES

What materials make up a pencil? Wood comes from trees. The material that you write with is a mineral called graphite. The pencil is made from natural resources, which are materials on Earth that people use to live and to meet their needs.

EARTH'S RESOURCES

There are two kinds of resources. Biological resources are living things, such as livestock, plants, and trees. These resources are important to humans because they provide us with food, shelter, and clothing.

Mineral resources are nonliving resources buried within Earth, such as oil and coal. Some mineral resources are raw materials, or materials used to make products. Iron ore, for example, is a raw material used in making steel. The steel, in turn, is used to make skyscrapers and automobiles.

CATEGORIES OF RESOURCES

Geographers classify resources in two categories. Nonrenewable resources are resources that are limited and cannot be replaced. For example, oil comes from wells that are drilled into Earth's crust. Once a well runs dry, the oil is gone. Coal and natural gas are other examples of nonrenewable resources.

Renewable resources never run out, or a new supply develops over time. Wind, water, and solar power are all renewable. So are trees because a new supply can grow to replace those that have been cut down.

SELECTED NATURAL RESOURCES OF THE WORLD

Energy Resources	Mineral Resources	
Coal	Gold	Iron
Oil	Silver	Diamonds
Natural gas	Copper	Aluminum
Uranium		

Natural resources are an important part of everyday life, yet countries with a large supply are not always wealthy. Nigeria, for example, is a major supplier of oil, but seven out of every ten Nigerians live in poverty. Japan is one of the wealthiest countries in the world—yet it must import oil from other countries.

Pumpjacks pump oil at a field in California.

THINK LIKE A GEOGRAPHER

Monitor Comprehension
Why are natural resources important?

Physical Geography CLIMATE AND WEATHER

People who live in Sacramento, California, have mild winters. When they go skiing in the nearby Sierra Nevada Mountains, they wear parkas to protect themselves from the colder temperatures. They have adapted to a different climate.

CLIMATE ELEMENTS

Climate is the average condition of the atmosphere over a long period of time. It includes average temperature, average precipitation, and the amount of change from one season to another. For example, Fairbanks, Alaska, has a cold climate. In the winter, the temperature can reach -8°F. Yet the temperature can rise to 90°F in the summer. The city goes through changes from one season to another.

Four factors that affect a region's climate are latitude, elevation, prevailing winds, and ocean currents. Places at high latitudes, such as Fairbanks, experience more change between winter and summer. Places close to the equator have nearly the same temperature throughout the year. Places at higher elevations have generally colder temperatures than places closer to sea level.

Prevailing winds are winds coming from one direction that blow most of the time. In Florida in the summer, the prevailing winds come from the south, making a warm climate even hotter.

Ocean currents also affect climate. The Gulf Stream is a current that carries warm water from the Caribbean Sea toward Europe. Air passing over the water becomes warm and helps create a mild winter climate in England and Ireland.

WEATHER CONDITIONS

Weather is the condition of the atmosphere at a particular time. It includes the temperature, precipitation, and humidity for a particular day or week. Humidity is the amount of water vapor in the air. If a weather forecaster says the humidity is at 95 percent, he or she means that the air is holding a large amount of water vapor.

Weather changes because of air masses. An air mass is a large area of air that has the same temperature and humidity. The boundary between two air masses is called a front. If a forecaster talks about a warm, humid front, he or she usually means that thunderstorms are headed toward the area.

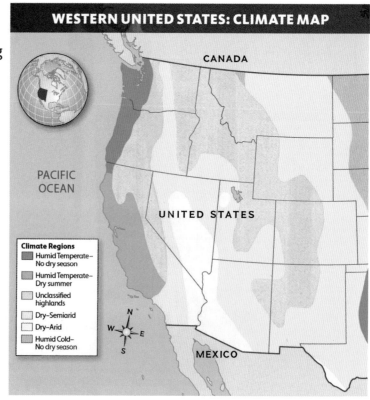

WESTERN UNITED STATES: CLIMATE MAP

CANADA

PACIFIC OCEAN

UNITED STATES

Climate Regions
- Humid Temperate– No dry season
- Humid Temperate– Dry summer
- Unclassified highlands
- Dry–Semiarid
- Dry–Arid
- Humid Cold– No dry season

N W E S

MEXICO

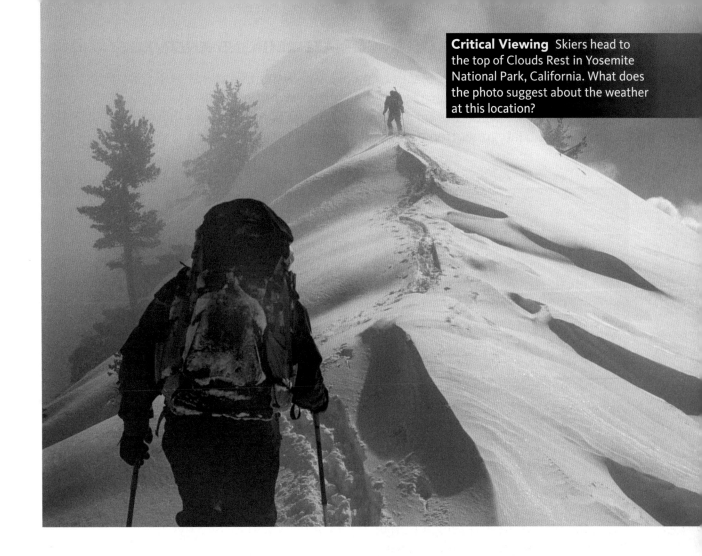

Critical Viewing Skiers head to the top of Clouds Rest in Yosemite National Park, California. What does the photo suggest about the weather at this location?

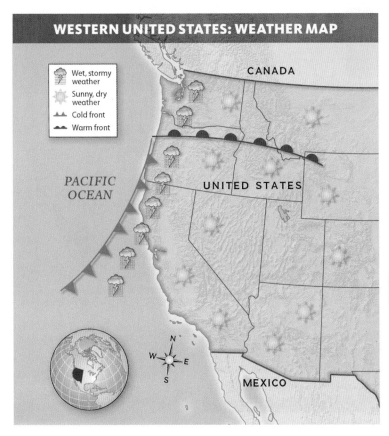

WESTERN UNITED STATES: WEATHER MAP

- Wet, stormy weather
- Sunny, dry weather
- Cold front
- Warm front

CANADA

PACIFIC OCEAN

UNITED STATES

MEXICO

N W E S

THINK LIKE A GEOGRAPHER

Make Inferences What is the difference between climate and weather?

Physical Geography CLIMATE REGIONS AND VEGETATION

A climate region is a group of places that have similar temperatures, precipitation levels, and changes in weather. Geographers have identified 5 climate regions that are broken down into 12 subcategories. Places that are located in the same subcategory often have similar vegetation, or plant life.

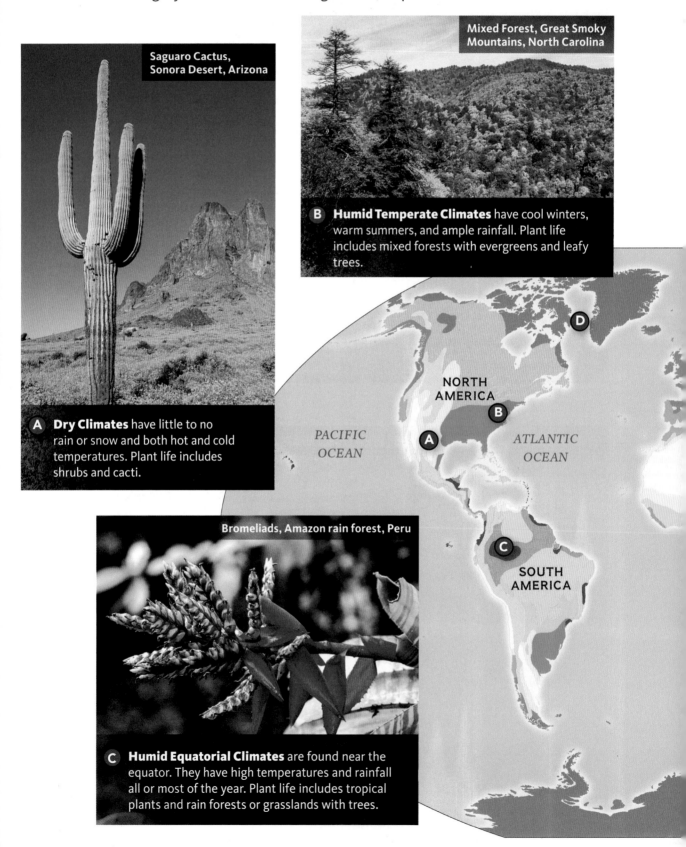

Saguaro Cactus, Sonora Desert, Arizona

Mixed Forest, Great Smoky Mountains, North Carolina

B Humid Temperate Climates have cool winters, warm summers, and ample rainfall. Plant life includes mixed forests with evergreens and leafy trees.

A Dry Climates have little to no rain or snow and both hot and cold temperatures. Plant life includes shrubs and cacti.

Bromeliads, Amazon rain forest, Peru

C Humid Equatorial Climates are found near the equator. They have high temperatures and rainfall all or most of the year. Plant life includes tropical plants and rain forests or grasslands with trees.

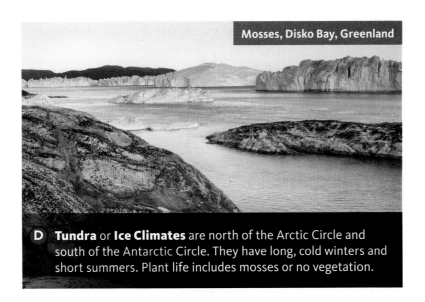

D **Tundra** or **Ice Climates** are north of the Arctic Circle and south of the Antarctic Circle. They have long, cold winters and short summers. Plant life includes mosses or no vegetation.

Mosses, Disko Bay, Greenland

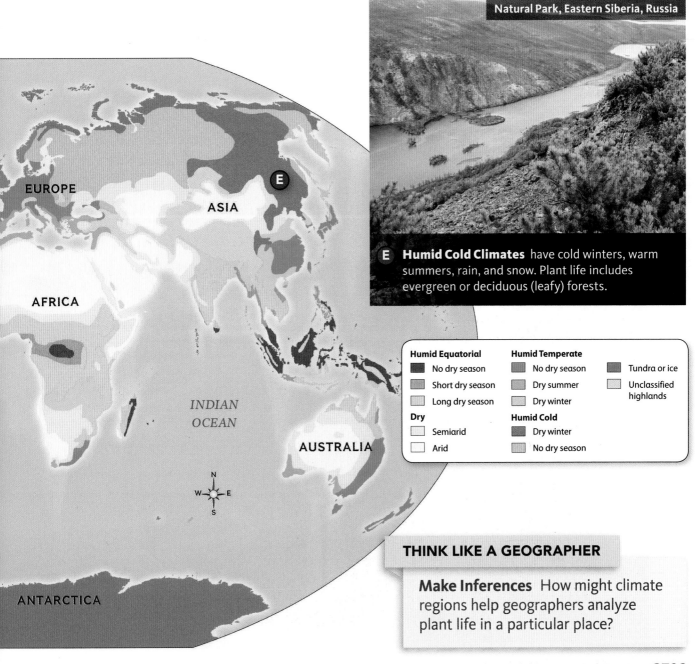

Natural Park, Eastern Siberia, Russia

E **Humid Cold Climates** have cold winters, warm summers, rain, and snow. Plant life includes evergreen or deciduous (leafy) forests.

EUROPE

ASIA

E

AFRICA

INDIAN OCEAN

AUSTRALIA

ANTARCTICA

Humid Equatorial
No dry season
Short dry season
Long dry season

Dry
Semiarid
Arid

Humid Temperate
No dry season
Dry summer
Dry winter

Humid Cold
Dry winter
No dry season

Tundra or ice
Unclassified highlands

THINK LIKE A GEOGRAPHER

Make Inferences How might climate regions help geographers analyze plant life in a particular place?

Human Geography ADAPTING TO THE ENVIRONMENT

Human geography explores the relationship between people and their surroundings. An important aspect of this relationship is the way in which people adapt to their environment.

Throughout history, people have had to adapt to their surroundings. Early humans did this simply to survive. They learned how to build a fire to warm themselves in cold weather and find plants and animals when food was scarce. In modern times, people have developed sophisticated technologies, including heating and cooling systems, to help them live in environments with challenging weather.

People have also learned to build structures to adapt to their environment. They build houses to protect them from the elements. They build dams to hold water back, bridges to span bodies of water, and tunnels to more easily travel over mountainous areas. In many cases, the materials people use to build these structures are obtained from the surrounding environment.

THINK LIKE A GEOGRAPHER

Make Connections What kinds of adaptations do you make in different types of weather?

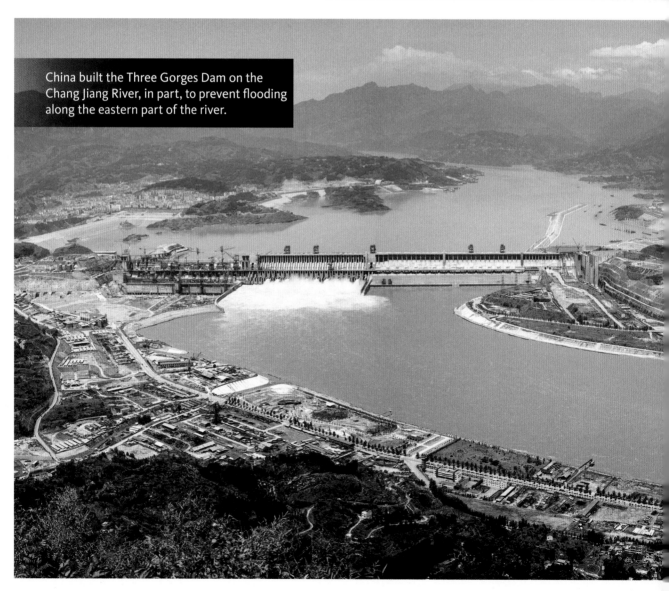

China built the Three Gorges Dam on the Chang Jiang River, in part, to prevent flooding along the eastern part of the river.

In the city of Noril'sk in the Russian region of Siberia, people deal with the snow and ice that covers the ground throughout much of the city's long winter.

Human Geography HUMAN IMPACT ON THE ENVIRONMENT

When people adapt to their surroundings, their actions sometimes have a lasting impact on the environment. Some adaptations have a positive impact on the environment, but some can be harmful.

NEGATIVE IMPACT

As people moved to cities over the last few centuries, they needed housing and ever-increasing supplies of energy to fuel their homes, businesses, and cars. As a result, entire forests were cut down, new mines were carved into the earth, and oil and natural gas were pumped from the ground and from underwater sources.

When forests and other natural environments are cleared, an entire ecosystem can be destroyed. An ecosystem is a community of plants and animals and their natural environment. The destruction of one ecosystem can affect another. For example, many scientists believe the destruction of rain forest habitats has led to global climate change.

The use of fossil fuels—including, coal, oil, and natural gas—has had a largely negative impact on the environment. Burning these energy sources has polluted the air and contributed to global warming. Even mining and transporting the sources has affected the environment. Oil spills from tankers and underwater oil rigs have damaged our waters, shorelines, and wildlife.

POSITIVE IMPACT

As understanding of human impact on the environment has grown, people around the world have taken steps to save ecosystems, preserve natural habitats, and protect our air and water. In 1973, for example, the United States passed the Endangered Species Act, which protects the habitats of endangered species. People have also restored, or brought back, habitats such as forests by planting trees. In addition, laws and regulations have been passed to limit the amounts of pollutants released into the air, land, and bodies of water by vehicles and industrial plants.

Scientists have worked to educate the public on pollution's impact on the environment. For example, some scientists have formed Mission Blue, a program that seeks to heal and protect Earth's oceans. One of the program's goals is to establish marine-protected areas in endangered hot spots, or "hope spots." These spots are ocean habitats that can recover and grow if human impact is limited.

Critical Viewing This satellite map of the world shows the location of 17 "hope spots," places that are important to the overall health of Earth's oceans. What patterns, if any, do you notice about the location of these spots?

EARTH'S "HOPE SPOTS"

In 2010, the Deepwater Horizon oil rig exploded in the Gulf of Mexico. The explosion killed 11 people and dumped more than 200 million gallons of oil in the Gulf. Thousands of birds, fish, and marine mammals were injured or killed in the disaster.

Elephants roam the Samburu National Reserve in Kenya.

THINK LIKE A GEOGRAPHER

Evaluate What can you do to have a positive impact on the environment?

Human Geography MOVEMENT AND SPREAD OF IDEAS

People have been on the move since early *Homo sapiens* first began moving within Africa about 100,000 years ago. The movement of people to a new location is called migration.

HUMAN MOVEMENT

Since our beginnings in Africa, we have migrated to new locations and populated the globe. Early humans moved because their survival depended on it. The climate changed, making food and water scarce. So people moved to find more hospitable homes and to follow the herds of animals they liked to hunt.

People have continued to migrate throughout history. The map on this page shows the Bantu migrations, which began about 2,000 years ago and continued for about 1,500 years. Historians say that this massive migration is the most important since our human ancestors first left Africa.

Historians don't really know why the Bantu people decided to leave their homes in West Africa and head south. Today, however, many immigrants are motivated to move by what are called push-pull factors. Push factors are those that drive people away from an area, such as war, political or religious persecution, and lack of job opportunities. Pull factors are those that attract people to a new place, such as higher wages, educational opportunities, and a more tolerant government. And of course, people are still drawn to a more favorable climate.

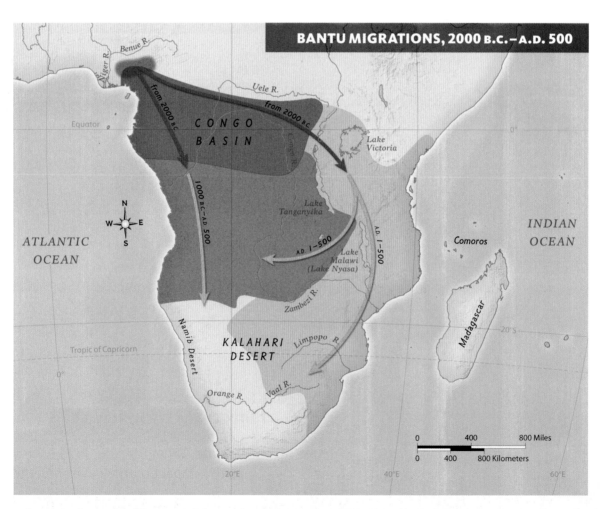

BANTU MIGRATIONS, 2000 B.C.–A.D. 500

SPREAD OF IDEAS

As people migrate, they bring their ideas, culture, skills, and language to their new homes. This spread of ideas results in great change. For example, the exchange of skills and ideas that occurred as a result of the Bantu migrations had an enormous impact on Africa's culture, economy, and government practices. You can see the impact of migration today in any large city. Restaurants, shops, and places of worship reflect the culture of the people who have moved to the city.

Trade has also spread ideas. The Silk Roads, a network of trade routes that began in China around 100 B.C., carried ideas as well as goods to Asia, Africa, and Europe. Over time, Chinese inventions and ideas reached Europe, and Indian traders brought Buddhism to China.

Movement isn't the only means by which ideas spread. Technological innovations can have the same impact. For instance, the invention of the printing press around 1450 resulted in an information explosion throughout Europe. The press produced books rapidly and cheaply and spread ideas quickly. Today, computers, the Internet, and social media carry ideas around the world at the touch of a button. These technologies—and those yet to come—are part of human geography and will continue to bring people together.

THINK LIKE A GEOGRAPHER

Evaluate What technologies and other means do you use to spread ideas?

The development of cell phones has connected people and their ideas in places where landline phone systems would be too expensive to install.

WHY STUDY HISTORY ?

Hi! I'm Fred Hiebert, National Geographic's Archaeology Fellow. We're about to embark on a journey all over the world and back through time—the history of the world as we know it today.

So why do we study past civilizations? The basis of civilization is identity—who we are and what we stand for. We express identity by creating unique ways to be housed and fed and to thrive. The basic building blocks of civilization are the same around the world: what kinds of plants and animals to tend and consume, how to find enough water, and how to survive the changes of the seasons. All core civilizations— from China, India, and Mesopotamia, to Europe and Mesoamerica— struggled with these issues.

Look at the sculptures shown below. These prehistoric "selfies" reveal a universal need to think about ourselves—in relation to the environment, the future, our religious beliefs—that dates from the earliest civilizations.

THE HUMAN EPIC

Historians, archaeologists, and anthropologists constantly update the story of human civilizations as new data surfaces from the latest dig site or the most recent scholarship. The Framework of World History at right is only one way to think about how human identity developed—there are many pathways from the past to the present.

I've lived and worked all over the world in lots of different cultures, and I know first-hand that you and others your age are more alike than you are different. You share the same need to understand yourself, your family, and your community and the same urge to hope and plan for your future. Your generation may be one of the first to truly be considered global citizens.

◀ **ARTEMIS**
This Greek marble sculpture dating back to the 4th century B.C. is known as *Artemis Hunting*.

◀ **NEFERTITI**
The bust of this famous Egyptian queen and wife of Pharaoh Akhenaten was sculpted more than 3,300 years ago.

FRAMEWORK OF WORLD HISTORY

The model below is one way to view the development of civilizations. For all cultures, it's not just the famous leaders who make history—it's all of us, through small actions that grow into world-changing events and ideas.

1 CORE CIVILIZATIONS

Humans begin to think about where they live, what they eat, and what they believe in—and plan for the future. Across the centuries and in all world cultures, humans use these building blocks to think about who they are and where they come from—the beginning of identity.

2 PRIMARY CIVILIZATIONS

Humans develop more effective responses to their environment, creating irrigation and other farming methods that make agriculture more predictable and more productive. People are able to form groups and move together, and eventually cities develop.

3 SECONDARY CIVILIZATIONS

Human understanding of identity comes into focus, and writing develops partly as an expression of identity. Codes of law and better rulers come to the forefront as cultures take on characteristics that embody those identities.

4 WORLD SYSTEMS

Civilizations reach out to each other, and trade develops along what would eventually be called the Silk Roads. The urge to move results in new road systems, new country borders with border guards, and new systems of taxation.

Fred Hiebert
▶ Watch the Why Study History video

The ancient cave painting in the background is located in Snake Cave in Australia. An Aboriginal artist created it by blowing pigment over his or her hand, leaving a blank hand shape.

◀ **TERRA COTTA BUDDHA**
This 5-foot tall statue was discovered at the site of Hadda in Afghanistan.

1

WHY STUDY HISTORY ?

TO BECOME A GLOBAL CITIZEN

As you study world history, you're going to meet some National Geographic Explorers along the way—men and women who are making incredible contributions to our lives through their work. Studying world history is part of what they do because they believe they can add to our understanding of the human story. Here are just a few.

MICHAEL COSMOPOULOS ▶
Cosmopoulos directs two major excavations exploring the origins of states and social complexity in Greece.

◀ WILLIAM SATURNO
Saturno supervises excavations in the jungles of Guatemala and determines the architectural history of a site by studying the little pieces that remain.

LOUISE LEAKEY ▲
Paleontologist Louise Leakey is responsible for some of the most important hominid fossils discovered in East Africa in the past two decades.

BECOME PART OF THE GLOBAL CONVERSATION!

Think About It

1. In what ways are you a global citizen?

2. Describe a situation or problem in which you think people should strive for global citizenship. What actions do you think should be taken to solve the problem?

3. Pick one action you named above and explain how you would go about accomplishing it. Develop a detailed action plan that could be put in place to make this happen.

STEVEN ELLIS ▶
Ellis directs the excavation of a working-class district in Pompeii, focusing on the use of public and private space and the role of ordinary people in the life of the ancient city.

◀ **SARAH PARCAK**
Parcak combines advanced technology such as satellite archaeology with good old-fashioned digging to reveal new Egyptian sites, including temples, pyramids, and tombs.

FUTURE EXPLORER ▶
WILL THIS BE YOU?

Write About It

SYNTHESIZE What does **identity** mean to you? Answer this question in two or three paragraphs in your notebook. Be sure to include your definition of identity, explain the various parts that make up your identity, and describe how you express your identity. Then designate a spot in your notebook where you can record how your understanding of identity changes as you read each chapter.

MAKE CONNECTIONS What different types of identities do you notice in your school and community? Create a chart that represents these identities and write your description of each.

ASK AND ANSWER QUESTIONS Imagine that you are at a panel discussion that includes the Explorers shown above. Write three questions you would like to ask the panel, including specific questions for individual Explorers.

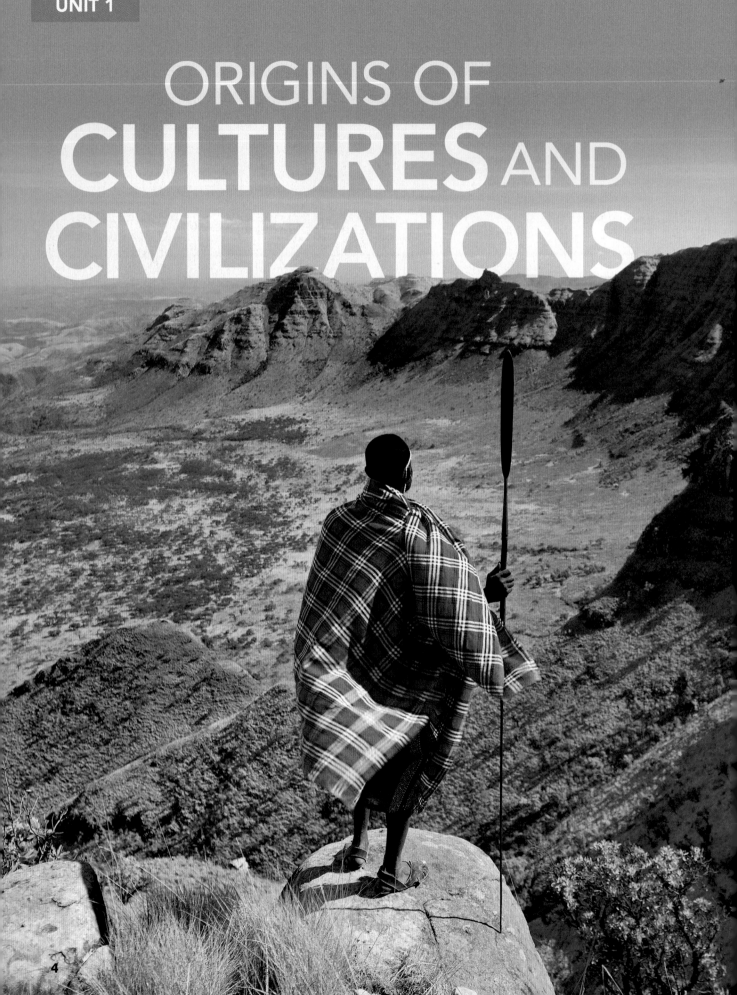

ORIGINS OF
CULTURES AND
CIVILIZATIONS

NATIONAL
GEOGRAPHIC

ON **LOCATION** WITH

Louise Leakey
Paleontologist

One of the first jobs of a paleontologist is finding a good place to dig. We look for places where fossilized bones, buried long ago by rivers and lakes, have been brought to the surface by tectonic activity and erosion. Lake Turkana in Kenya's Great Rift Valley is the world's best field laboratory for fossil discoveries going back several million years. My family has been working in this profession for three generations, uncovering the bones of human ancestors and other animals that lived in this region in the past. I'm Louise Leakey, and I help investigate and share the human story.

< CRITICAL VIEWING   A shepherd gazes out over East Africa's Great Rift Valley. How might the geography of the valley help archaeologists carry out their work?

The World

c. 10,000 B.C.
As the last Ice Age comes to an end, animals such as the woolly mammoth die out.

c. 15,000 B.C.
Lascaux Cave paintings are created.

c. 68,000 B.C.
Groups of modern humans begin to migrate out of Africa.

20,000 B.C.

175,000 B.C.

c. 9600 B.C.
Göbekli Tepe, the world's first temple, is built in present-day Turkey.
(Göbekli Tepe pillar)

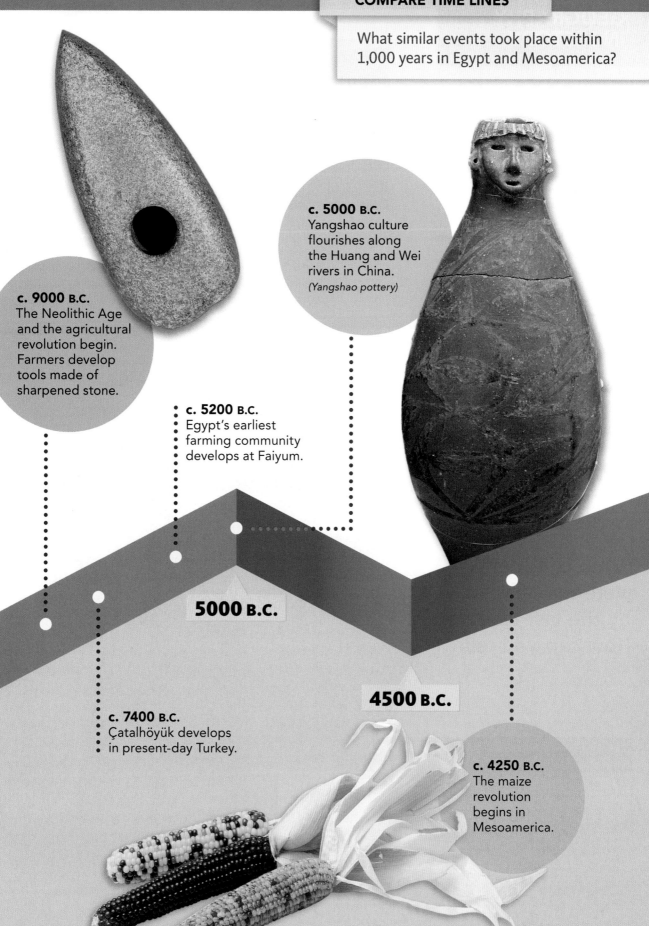

What similar events took place within 1,000 years in Egypt and Mesoamerica?

c. 5000 B.C.
Yangshao culture flourishes along the Huang and Wei rivers in China.
(Yangshao pottery)

c. 9000 B.C.
The Neolithic Age and the agricultural revolution begin. Farmers develop tools made of sharpened stone.

c. 5200 B.C.
Egypt's earliest farming community develops at Faiyum.

5000 B.C.

4500 B.C.

c. 7400 B.C.
Çatalhöyük develops in present-day Turkey.

c. 4250 B.C.
The maize revolution begins in Mesoamerica.

7

THE LAST ICE AGE

18,000 B.C.–10,000 B.C.

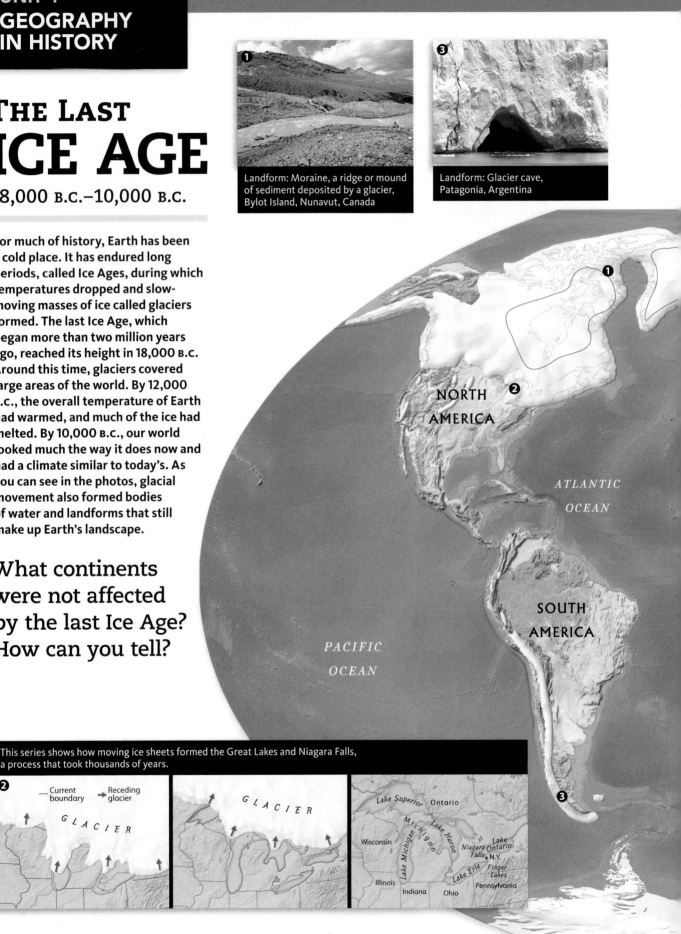

Landform: Moraine, a ridge or mound of sediment deposited by a glacier, Bylot Island, Nunavut, Canada

Landform: Glacier cave, Patagonia, Argentina

For much of history, Earth has been a cold place. It has endured long periods, called Ice Ages, during which temperatures dropped and slow-moving masses of ice called glaciers formed. The last Ice Age, which began more than two million years ago, reached its height in 18,000 B.C. Around this time, glaciers covered large areas of the world. By 12,000 B.C., the overall temperature of Earth had warmed, and much of the ice had melted. By 10,000 B.C., our world looked much the way it does now and had a climate similar to today's. As you can see in the photos, glacial movement also formed bodies of water and landforms that still make up Earth's landscape.

What continents were not affected by the last Ice Age? How can you tell?

NORTH AMERICA

SOUTH AMERICA

ATLANTIC OCEAN

PACIFIC OCEAN

This series shows how moving ice sheets formed the Great Lakes and Niagara Falls, a process that took thousands of years.

❷ — Current boundary → Receding glacier

GLACIER

GLACIER

Lake Superior Ontario
Wisconsin Michigan Lake Huron
Niagara Falls Lake Ontario N.Y.
Illinois Lake Erie Finger Lakes
Indiana Ohio Pennsylvania

Landform: Fjord, a deep glacial trough that filled with seawater, Norway

Landform: Glacial valley, Fagaras Mountains, Romania

Landform: Sediment-filled glacier, Karakoram, Himalaya

ARCTIC OCEAN

ASIA

PACIFIC OCEAN

AFRICA

INDIAN OCEAN

AUSTRALIA

Extent of ice coverage, c. 18,000 B.C.

Extent of ice coverage, c. 10,000 B.C.

Land area, c. 18,000 B.C.

Modern land area

0   1,000   2,000 kilometers

0   1,000   2,000 miles

Winkel Tripel projection

THE DEVELOPMENT OF HUMAN SOCIETIES

175,000 B.C. – 3000 B.C.

SECTION 1 THE PALEOLITHIC AGE

 SS.6.G.1.3; SS.6.G.1.4; SS.6.G.2.1; SS.6.G.4.2; SS.6.G.4.3; SS.6.G.5.3; SS.6.W.1.2; SS.6.W.1.4; SS.6.W.1.5; SS.6.W.1.6; LAFS.68.RH.1.2; LAFS.68.RH.1.3; LAFS.68.RH.2.4; LAFS.68.RH.2.5; LAFS.68.RH.3.7; LAFS.68.RH.3.8

KEY VOCABULARY

anthropologist
archaeologist
artifact
culture
drought
fossil
land bridge
megafauna
migration
oasis
technology

NAMES & PLACES

Beringia
Homo sapiens
Ice Age
Lascaux Cave
Paleolithic Age
Sahara

SECTION 2 THE NEOLITHIC AGE

 SS.6.E.1.3; SS.6.G.1.4; SS.6.G.1.6; SS.6.G.2.1; SS.6.G.2.3; SS.6.G.4.1; SS.6.W.1.2; SS.6.W.1.3; SS.6.W.1.4; SS.6.W.1.5; SS.6.W.2.1; SS.6.W.2.2; LAFS.68.RH.2.5; LAFS.68.RH.2.6; LAFS.68.RH.3.7; LAFS.68.RH.3.8; LAFS.68.RH.3.9

KEY VOCABULARY

agriculture
domestication
fertile
hunter-gatherer
nomad
oral history
primary source
secondary source

NAMES & PLACES

Fertile Crescent
Neolithic Age

READING STRATEGY

ORGANIZE IDEAS: COMPARE AND CONTRAST

When you compare and contrast two or more things, you note their similarities and differences. Use a Venn diagram like this one to help you compare and contrast Paleolithic and Neolithic people as you read the chapter.

Paleolithic People   Neolithic People

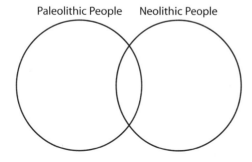

This rock art found in the North African country of Algeria dates back at least 8,000 years.

1.1 Discovering Prehistory

You probably think your parents are pretty old. Well, think again. They actually belong to the newest human species on the planet—*Homo sapiens*, or "wise man"—and so do you. We'll begin our story with this species.

MAIN IDEA

The evidence uncovered by scientists helps us learn about our early human history.

Time Travel

Throughout this text, you will see the abbreviations B.C. and A.D. A date followed by B.C. refers to the number of years the date occurred before the birth of Christ. A date preceded by A.D. refers to the number of years the date occurred after the birth of Christ. Many historians also use the abbreviations B.C.E. and C.E. for these time periods. However, B.C.E. stands for "Before the Common (or Christian) Era," and C.E. stands for "Common Era." Note that the year A.D. 1 took place immediately after 1 B.C.

GEOLOGIC AND ARCHAEOLOGICAL TIME

Earth is incredibly old: somewhere around 4.5 billion years old. Yet **Homo sapiens** (HOH-moh SAY-pee-uhnz) has existed for only about the last 200,000 years. Scientists know this because they have found fossils and artifacts that belonged to this species. **Fossils** are the remains, such as bones and teeth, of organisms that lived long ago. **Artifacts** are human-made objects, such as stone tools. These items provide some of the best clues to prehistory, or the time before written records existed.

Scientists called **archaeologists** search for, discover, and then interpret stones, bones, and artifacts left behind by *Homo sapiens*. Archaeologists are like the crime scene investigators of history. They piece together evidence that tells the story of what happened at a site hundreds, thousands, or even hundreds of thousands of years ago.

Archaeologists sometimes use geologic techniques to find out how old fossils and artifacts are. For example, they can figure out how old an artifact is based on how deeply it is buried in layers of dirt. In a site that hasn't been disturbed over time, dirt builds up in layers, with younger layers covering the older ones. Archaeologists know that fossils and artifacts lying in the deepest layers are the oldest.

ORIGINS IN AFRICA

Early *Homo sapiens* looked very much like humans do today. It is now widely accepted that the species first appeared in Africa. Earlier hominins, or human-like species, are believed to have lived in Africa for millions of years before *Homo sapiens*.

In 1967, a team of archaeologists led by Richard Leakey found the earliest fossils of modern humans. The team discovered two *Homo sapiens* skulls near the Omo River in the Great Rift Valley of East Africa. The skulls were originally thought to be 130,000 years old, but a more recent dating has determined them to be about 195,000 years old.

Homo sapiens lived during the **Paleolithic** (pay-lee-uh-LIHTH-ihk) **Age**, a period that began around 2.5 million B.C. and ended around 8000 B.C. The period is also called the Old Stone Age because the people living then made simple tools and weapons out of stone. It was a time of dramatic changes in geography and climate. It was also a time when modern human development— and human history—began.

12 CHAPTER 1

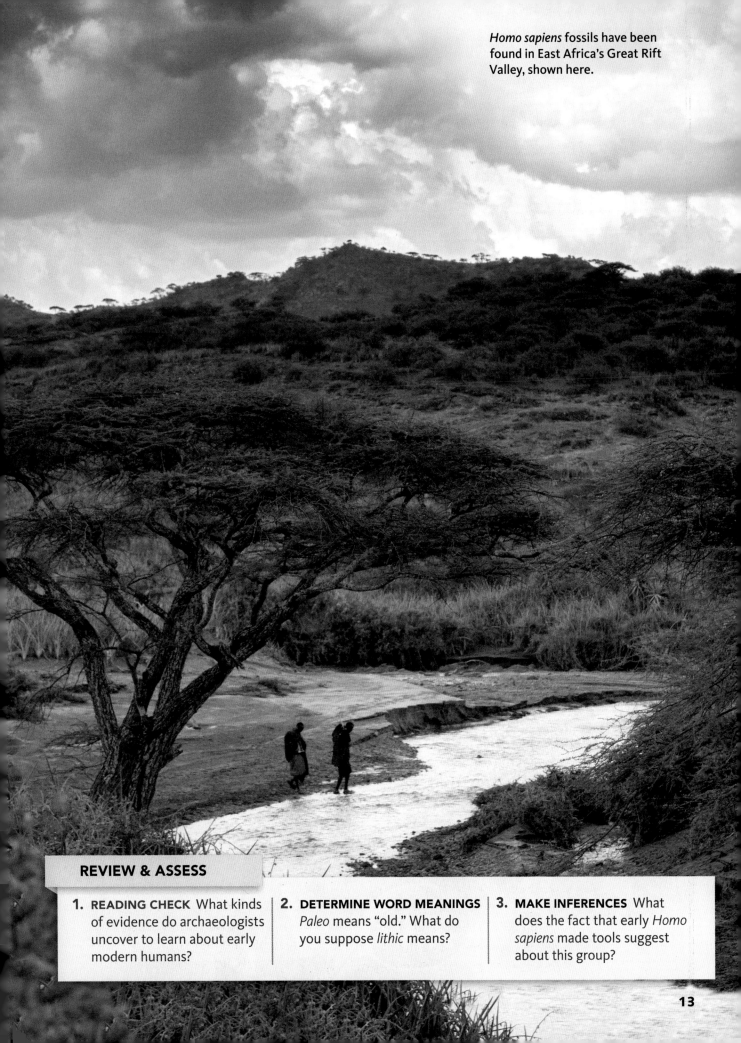

Homo sapiens fossils have been found in East Africa's Great Rift Valley, shown here.

REVIEW & ASSESS

1. **READING CHECK** What kinds of evidence do archaeologists uncover to learn about early modern humans?

2. **DETERMINE WORD MEANINGS** *Paleo* means "old." What do you suppose *lithic* means?

3. **MAKE INFERENCES** What does the fact that early *Homo sapiens* made tools suggest about this group?

Critical Viewing Friends and neighbors in a community in China sit down to a lavish banquet. What do details in the photo tell you about the community's cultural behaviors?

1.2 The Elements of Culture

Maybe you've heard the saying "You are what you eat," but did you know that you are also what you speak, what you wear, and what you believe? All of these behaviors—and many others—help identify you with your particular blend of cultures.

MAIN IDEA

Studying the culture of *Homo sapiens* in the Paleolithic Age helps reveal how people lived.

WHAT IS CULTURE?

Culture is a big part of human development. All the elements that contribute to the way of life of a particular group of people make up culture. These elements include language, clothing, music, art, law, religion, government, and family structure. Culture is passed down from parents to children and greatly affects our behaviors and beliefs. It influences people to do things in a particular way, such as eating or avoiding certain foods. It unifies a group and distinguishes that group from others.

Language, art, toolmaking, and religion are the elements that were most important in defining early cultures. Even early *Homo sapiens* communicated through speech, created cave paintings, made and used tools, and buried the dead. However, groups of people often did things slightly differently. These differences reflect each group's technical knowledge, artistic styles, and available natural resources.

WHY STUDY CULTURE?

As you've learned, cultural behaviors are passed down from generation to generation, but they can also change over time or—like the ability to make stone tools—be nearly lost altogether. In part, scientists study prehistoric cultures to learn how these cultures differ from modern cultures and discover what they all have in common. Information about modern cultures is often provided by archaeologists called **anthropologists**.

The artifacts archaeologists uncover help them piece together a picture of early humans' cultural behavior and daily life. For example, by studying tools uncovered at a prehistoric site, archaeologists learn how advanced the people who made them were and what jobs they needed to do. In addition, comparing artifacts from different sites can explain why one group was more successful than another.

Comparing artifacts from different time periods helps explain how people changed and developed. This knowledge helps us see thousands of years into the past so we can better understand the present and predict the future.

REVIEW & ASSESS

1. **READING CHECK** What do artifacts, such as stone tools, reveal about the culture of early *Homo sapiens*?

2. **SUMMARIZE** How do archaeologists and anthropologists work together?

3. **DRAW CONCLUSIONS** What might the discovery of tools used primarily as weapons suggest about a group of early humans?

1.3 Changing Environments

Today, climate change is forcing us all to make some adjustments—from switching off lights to turning off faucets. Still, we're not the first humans to be affected by shifting climate patterns. A big change in their environment drove Paleolithic people to take steps that would transform the world forever.

MAIN IDEA

A changing climate forced Paleolithic people to move to new places and develop new tools to survive.

COMPARING TOOLS

The stone tool on the left was made about 100,000 years ago. The fishhook made from bone on the right dates back about 42,000 years. You can see that early humans' technical skill had come a long way in about 60,000 years.

FINDING NEW HOMES

About 100,000 years ago, much of Africa had a very unstable climate. Some places became warmer and wetter, while others became hot and dry. These climate changes greatly altered the landscape in which Paleolithic people lived.

Archaeologists have discovered that East Africa suffered a terrible **drought** between 100,000 and 75,000 years ago. This long period of dry, hot weather had a huge impact on the landscape. Rivers and vast lakes shrank and left people struggling for survival. The plants they ate became scarce, and the animals they hunted disappeared. At the

same time, previously uninhabitable areas became livable and attractive. For example, the **Sahara**, which is one of the harshest deserts on Earth today, turned into an **oasis**, or a green area where plants can grow. These environmental changes may have encouraged some of the 10,000 Paleolithic people living in East Africa at the time to leave their homeland. They began their long **migration**, or movement, first to the Sahara in North Africa and then into the wider world.

ADAPTING TO NEW CONDITIONS

As people migrated, they responded to some of the challenges of their new environments by using technology. **Technology** is the application of knowledge, tools, and inventions to meet people's needs.

Critical Viewing Paleolithic people first lived on savannas like this one. Savannas are areas of flat grassland where animals roam. What might have made the savanna a welcoming environment?

The ability to capture and control fire was a particularly valuable technology. In addition to providing much-needed warmth and light, fire helped Paleolithic people scare away enemies and drive animals into traps. Cooking meat made it easier to digest and killed bacteria.

Paleolithic people also used technology to develop tools that helped them adapt to new environments and climates. Simple tools had been used for millions of years, but *Homo sapiens* refined them to create a really effective tool kit. A hard stone called flint was especially useful, as it could be split into hard, razor-sharp flakes. Early humans learned to design a tool to perform a particular task, such as chopping wood, carving meat, or skinning animals.

Over time, tools grew increasingly advanced. Humans crafted fishhooks out of bone and sewing needles out of ivory. These specialized tools helped our ancestors survive in an amazing range of new habitats and climates—from arctic areas to deserts.

REVIEW & ASSESS

1. **READING CHECK** What led some Paleolithic people to leave their home in East Africa thousands of years ago and migrate to new places?

2. **DETERMINE WORD MEANINGS** What context clues tell you that *uninhabitable* means "unlivable"?

3. **MAKE INFERENCES** Think about the adaptations Paleolithic people made to survive in new conditions. What can you infer about their intelligence?

1.4 Moving into New Environments

More than 60,000 years ago, the world witnessed movement on a scale never seen before as our restless ancestors began leaving Africa in waves. They set out on a worldwide migration that would permanently populate the entire planet.

MAIN IDEA

Between 70,000 and 10,000 B.C., Paleolithic people migrated from Africa and settled throughout the world.

SPREAD OF EARLY HUMANS

As you have learned, the changing climate made Paleolithic people search for homes outside of Africa. They first migrated into Southwest Asia around 70,000 years ago. The region was warm and tropical and provided lush vegetation and abundant wildlife.

In time, people spread across the rest of the world. From Asia they reached Australia around 50,000 years ago. By about 40,000 years ago, early humans had arrived in Europe. Around 30,000 years ago, *Homo sapiens* reached Siberia on the edge of eastern Asia.

The last continents to be populated were the Americas. This final migration may have been made possible by the **Ice Age**. At its height around 20,000 years ago, the Ice Age trapped so much water as ice that the sea level was nearly 400 feet lower than it is today. This trapped ice created **land bridges** that allowed humans to walk across continents. Many scientists have proposed the theory that hunters crossed the **Beringia** (beh-RIN-gee-uh) land bridge, which connected Siberia with North America, in a series of migrations between 20,000 and 15,000 years ago.

Scientists believe that during a period of glacial melting around 12,000 years ago, more travelers pushed southward through Central America and South America. However, new evidence has emerged that challenges this timing. The genes of some South American people suggest that their ancestors arrived from Australia 35,000 years ago, and *Homo sapiens* footprints in Central America have been dated to 40,000 years ago. These findings might support the theory that the earliest Americans arrived in boats, rather than by land bridge.

IN SEARCH OF FOOD

People migrated to many of these places, possibly in hot pursuit of the animals they liked to eat. Some of these creatures were **megafauna**, which means "large animals." Megafauna included the woolly mammoth, giant ground sloth, and saber-toothed cat, which are shown below.

Megafauna

Humans hunted herds of woolly mammoths in northern Asia and parts of Europe and North America. The giant ground sloth and saber-toothed cat lived primarily in North and South America.

Woolly Mammoth

Giant Ground Sloth

Saber-Toothed Cat

This map shows what Earth might have looked like many thousands of years ago. The purple shading indicates areas that were covered in ice from the Ice Age. The green shading shows land that once existed but has since eroded, or worn away.

The woolly mammoth, a relative of the modern elephant, was one of the largest megafauna. It stood between 9 and 11 feet tall and weighed as much as six tons. Its curved tusks grew up to 13 feet long.

At five tons, the giant ground sloth wasn't much smaller than the woolly mammoth. However, the sloth was fairly harmless. It mostly used its long claws to tear leaves and bark, not other animals.

There was more reason to fear the saber-toothed cat with its two huge, swordlike teeth. This creature was smaller than a modern lion but much heavier, weighing more than 400 pounds.

These megafauna became extinct, or died out, about 11,000 years ago. Many scientists believe they were overhunted or wiped out by climate change as the Ice Age began to come to a close.

REVIEW & ASSESS

1. **READING CHECK** What food did Paleolithic people eat when they migrated to Asia and other parts of the world?

2. **INTERPRET MAPS** What challenges do you think people encountered as they moved into the new environments shown on the map?

3. **FORM OPINIONS** Do you think the Americas became populated by land bridge, by boat, or by a combination of the two? Explain your position.

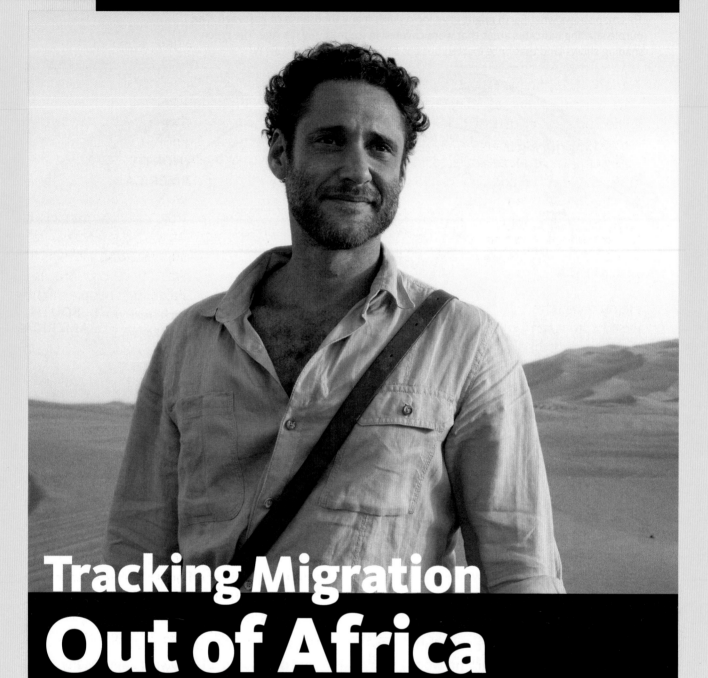

Tracking Migration
Out of Africa

Archaeologist Jeffrey Rose lives in a desert truck stop in the Southwest Asian country of Oman. He spends his days with his team of experts, sifting through rocks in 100-degree heat. Occasionally, he finds what he's looking for: small, sharp, egg-shaped stones. That may not sound like much, but his finds may dramatically rewrite our earliest history. Rose is looking for evidence to support his theory about who first migrated out of Africa and what route was taken. After years of exploration, he thinks he might have found the answer.

^ Jeffrey Rose has conducted work in many parts of Southwest Asia, including this desert outside of Dubai, United Arab Emirates.

Jeffrey Rose has found evidence to support a new theory about which Paleolithic people first left Africa and what route they took.

LOOKING FOR EVIDENCE

National Geographic Explorer Jeffrey Rose conducted his search in Oman. Geneticists—scientists who study DNA and heredity—have suggested that the first humans to leave Africa traveled through Ethiopia to Yemen and Oman, following the coast of the Arabian Peninsula. Rose went to Oman hoping to find archaeological evidence of this migration.

He recorded the earliest traces of humans: discarded flint tools. "Our geologist constantly reads the landscape to tell us where Paleolithic humans would have found water and flint. Find those and you find early people," Rose says. However, after years of surveying, he'd found no African-style artifacts and no evidence of Paleolithic humans on the Arabian Peninsula coast.

HITTING THE JACKPOT

Then in 2010, on the final day at the last site on his list, Rose hit the jackpot. He found a stone spear point with a design unique to people of the Nubian Complex, who had lived in the Nile Valley in North Africa. "We had never considered that the link to Africa would come from the Nile Valley and that their route would be through the middle of the Arabian Peninsula rather than along the coast," says Rose. Yet it made sense that people would migrate to Arabia from the Nile Valley. As Rose points out, "It's logical that people moved from an environment they knew to another that mirrored it." By the end of 2013, he had found more than 250 Nubian Complex sites in Oman.

When Rose dated the artifacts, he discovered they were roughly 106,000 years old, a point in time when people of the Nubian Complex flourished in Africa. The puzzle pieces fit. "Geneticists have shown that the modern human family tree began to branch out more than 60,000 years ago," says Rose. "I'm not questioning *when* it happened, but *where*. I suggest the great modern human expansion to the rest of the world was launched from Arabia rather than Africa." Rose's evidence suggests that perhaps it was a two-stage process. Paleolithic people might have left North Africa for Arabia more than 100,000 years ago. Then about 40,000 years later, they left Arabia and began to settle the rest of the world.

Now Rose wants to know why it was people of the Nubian Complex who spread from Africa. "What was it about their technology and culture that enabled them to expand so successfully," he wonders, "and what happened next?" As Rose says, "We've always looked to the beginning and wanted to understand how we got here. That's what it means to be human."

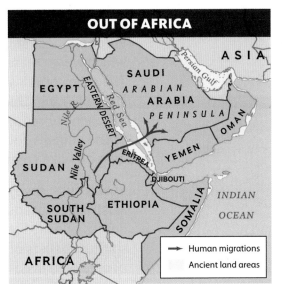

OUT OF AFRICA

→ Human migrations
▨ Ancient land areas

REVIEW & ASSESS

1. **READING CHECK** What theory has Jeffrey Rose proposed about the migration of Paleolithic people?

2. **INTERPRET MAPS** What body of water did the Nubians cross to get to the Arabian Peninsula?

3. **MAKE INFERENCES** Why would resources of water and flint have been important to early humans?

The Development of Human Societies **21**

Cave Art

It wasn't all about tools in the Paleolithic Age. Early humans had an artistic side as well. Prehistoric graffiti appears on cave walls all over the world. It turns out that the urge for artistic expression is almost as old as humankind itself.

MAIN IDEA

Cave paintings reveal much about Paleolithic people and their world.

ANCIENT ARTISTS

Art is an important part of culture. It shows a capacity for creativity, which separates humans from animals. Very early humans may have collected pretty rocks, carved wood, or painted pictures of themselves and their surroundings.

However, around 35,000 years ago, an artistic explosion occurred when humans began painting detailed images on cave walls. Examples have been found across the world, but it took archaeologists a long time to accept that the cave paintings had been created during the Paleolithic Age. They found it hard to believe that prehistoric people had the ability, time, or desire to produce such beautiful works of art.

The subjects of these cave paintings vary quite a bit, which is not surprising since they were created over a span of 25,000 years. The paintings often depict side-view images of animals, including woolly mammoths and horses. Some images feature everyday scenes, such as deer being hunted by men with spears. Other images consist of lines, circles, and geometric patterns.

One type of image that appears all over the world is considered by many to be one of the most moving: handprints. An artist often created this image by blowing paint through a reed over the hands—leaving behind the imprint of people who lived thousands of years ago.

GLIMPSE INTO AN EARLY WORLD

The **Lascaux Cave** in France has some of Europe's most amazing cave paintings, which were created about 17,000 years ago. The cave contains about 600 beautifully clear paintings, mostly of animals, many in shades of red, yellow, and brown. Some of the animals, including a nearly 17-foot-long bull-like creature, are now extinct.

Spectacular cave and rock paintings in Australia's Kakadu National Park show details of daily life and also reflect the spiritual beliefs of Aborigines, the earliest people who lived in Australia. These beliefs include a strong connection to the land and nature, which is still shared by the people who live in the region today.

The Sahara is also rich in rock art. The Tassili-n-Ajjer (tuh-sill-ee-nah-JAIR) mountain range in North Africa has spectacular paintings showing the once abundant wildlife and grasslands of this now barren desert. The Cave of the Hands in Argentina contains an incredible wall of handprints, as shown on the next page.

Despite many theories, it is unclear why Paleolithic people created such beautiful images in dark and hard-to-reach caves. Some researchers believe that most early art was actually created outdoors but has long since faded away. While we are unlikely to ever fully understand the meaning of Paleolithic art, it does provide insight into the lives and culture of our ancestors.

Researchers believe that this painting from the Cave of the Hands in Argentina shows the handprints of 13-year-old boys.

REVIEW & ASSESS

1. **READING CHECK** What do cave paintings reveal about Paleolithic people?

2. **INTEGRATE VISUALS** What different purposes might cave art have served in the Paleolithic world?

3. **COMPARE AND CONTRAST** What does the rock art in North Africa reveal about how that region has changed from the Paleolithic Age to today?

Nomadic Hunter-Gatherers

When you're hungry, you probably raid the fridge or head for the store. When Paleolithic people were hungry, they tracked down an animal, killed it with their handmade weapons, and then cooked it over a fire they had to carefully start and keep going. That's what it took to survive every day.

MAIN IDEA

Paleolithic people were constantly on the move to find food.

MOVING WITH THE SEASONS

The Paleolithic world had no farms or stores, but it did have a rich variety of foods. People just had to search them out. During the Paleolithic Age, humans lived as hunter-gatherers. A **hunter-gatherer** hunts animals and gathers wild plants to eat. These tasks were made easier and safer by the fact that early humans worked together and shared the jobs.

Most hunter-gatherer groups were small— around 30 people. The men hunted, often herding large animals into traps or over cliffs. Meanwhile, the women and young children gathered fruits and nuts. Scientists have learned a great deal about hunter-gatherers by studying the body and belongings of a later hunter known as the Iceman, seen at right.

Because the animal herds moved with the seasons, so did the groups hunting them. People who move from place to place like this are called **nomads**. Nomadic hunter-gatherers traveled light. They carried all their possessions with them, including stone tools and clothing.

As hunter-gatherers traveled in areas outside of Africa, they learned to adapt to their new environments—especially the cold. They made needles that enabled them to sew warm clothes out of animal skins. Caves offered the best protection from the worst winter weather. However, people also made shelters of wood, bone, and animal skins, which provided temporary camps.

FOLLOWING THE HERDS

Nomadic hunter-gatherers followed herds of megafauna as the animals moved from place to place. The herds migrated with the seasons and entered new environments created by the changeable Ice Age climate. For example, the Beringia land bridge allowed herds of woolly mammoths to cross into North America, with hunter-gatherers following close behind.

It wasn't easy to kill an animal as big as a woolly mammoth. It took intelligence, teamwork, and special tools. Paleolithic people developed deadly new weapons, including barbed harpoons, spear-throwers, and bows and arrows. These weapons allowed them to kill from a distance, which made the task safer and more efficient. The rewards were also great. A woolly mammoth could feed the group for months.

As humans spread around the world, various human groups competed for resources. Conflict would have been most common during cold periods when food and shelter were scarce. It's likely that in warmer periods of plentiful food, human groups interacted more happily, sharing their technology and culture. This interaction helped spread new ideas and paved the way for a remarkable new stage in human development.

THE ICEMAN

The Iceman lived around 3300 B.C. More than 5,000 years later, hikers found his frozen body in the Alps in Europe. His clothing, his tools, and even the contents of his stomach have helped scientists understand how prehistoric people lived. The graphic here offers some clues as to how he might have died.

1 The Iceman perches on a cliff. He tests the copper blade of his ax and the flint points of his dagger with satisfaction. They're razor sharp. He searches below for his prey. With any luck, he'll bring goat meat back to his community tonight.

2 Suddenly an arrow pierces the Iceman's shoulder. Another hunter has shot him from behind. The Iceman falls off the cliff into the snowbank below.

3 Desperately the Iceman rises and struggles to fight off his attacker, but he's too weak. He falls back down but manages to crawl into a cave in the ice. As the Iceman dies, snow begins to fall. Snow and ice will hide him from view for the next 5,000 years.

REVIEW & ASSESS

1. **READING CHECK** Why were Paleolithic people constantly moving from place to place?

2. **INTEGRATE VISUALS** What words would you use to describe hunter-gatherers such as the Iceman?

3. **ANALYZE CAUSE AND EFFECT** What impact did the changing climate have on hunter-gatherers?

2.2

The Beginnings of Domestication

A pet poodle might lick your hand and follow you everywhere, but dogs weren't always man's best friend. All dogs are descended from wolves. Humans transformed some of these wild animals into loyal helpers, which marked a major breakthrough in learning to control their environment.

MAIN IDEA

Early humans took control of their environment by raising useful plants and taming animals.

CHANGING CLIMATE

Around 14,000 years ago, Earth grew warmer, and the ice sheets melted. These changes raised sea levels, created freshwater lakes, and increased global rainfall. Large areas of land became covered with water. As a result, land bridges disappeared, and coastal waters formed that were full of fish. Animals moved, adapted, or died as their habitats, or environments, changed.

These environmental changes also began to transform the ways that hunter-gatherers lived in some areas. The warmer, wetter climate encouraged the development of forests and grasslands and resulted in longer growing seasons. These conditions proved to be perfect for the growth of grasses. In time, people learned to raise other plants and animals, making them useful to humans. This development, called **domestication**, led to the beginning of farming.

TAMING PLANTS AND ANIMALS

Hunter-gatherers had grown plants to increase their productivity long before the ice began to melt. Now the improved climate made growing plants even easier. After scattering seeds in wet ground, hunter-gatherers knew they could return and harvest the plants the following year. Some foods, especially grains from cereals such as wheat and barley, could be stored to feed people and animals year-round.

At about the same time, humans began to tame animals. The earliest domesticated animals were dogs. All around the world, wild wolf pups were caught and

Young nomadic girls corral sheep for milking in northeastern Afghanistan. What details in the photo tell you that the animals have been domesticated?

bred for hunting and protection. Other animals were domesticated for food: first sheep and goats, then pigs and cattle. As well as providing meat, milk, and wool, some domesticated animals could carry heavy loads and pull carts.

Although most humans remained nomadic, the warmer climate provided certain areas with such abundant resources that some hunter-gatherer groups decided to settle down. For example, areas around estuaries made perfect places to live. An estuary is formed where a river feeds into the ocean. The combination of fresh water, salt water, and land provided people with a year-round supply of food. Settling down to live permanently in such places would bring about a great change that allowed humans to make their next big leap forward.

REVIEW & ASSESS

1. **READING CHECK** How did humans use the plants and animals they domesticated?

2. **ANALYZE CAUSE AND EFFECT** How did the warmer climate and increased rainfall in some places affect people's ability to grow plants for food?

3. **FORM OPINIONS** What do you think were some of the advantages of the settled life over the nomadic one?

The Agricultural Revolution

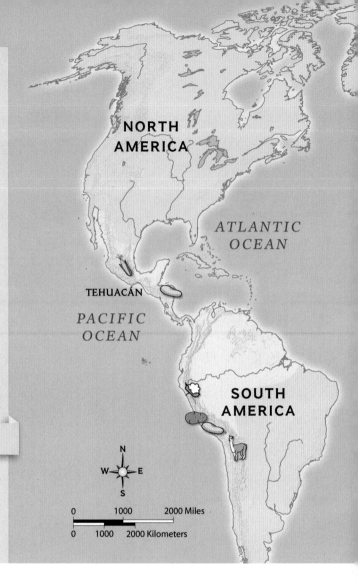

If you wanted to grow some crops, you'd probably look for a warm place with a reliable supply of water and soil full of nutrients. Thousands of years ago, a number of river valleys satisfied all of these conditions. They were at the heart of an important change in the way people lived.

MAIN IDEA

Humans settled down and farmed along river valleys and developed new farm tools and methods.

THE SICKLE

The sickle, which developed during the Neolithic Age, was crucial to harvesting certain grains. The tool was so important that in some places, people made sickles all the same size so that the tools could be repaired easily and quickly.

FERTILE RIVER VALLEYS

Imagine that a great change took place all over the world and transformed forever the way people lived. That is exactly what happened when farming largely replaced hunting and gathering. The slow shift to growing food began around 10,000 B.C. and ended around 8000 B.C. By then, many people had discovered that they could live year-round on what they farmed, rather than on what they found.

This shift in the way people lived is called the agricultural revolution. **Agriculture** is the practice of growing plants and rearing animals for food. The shift to agriculture also ushered in a new period known as the **Neolithic Age**, which began somewhere between 10,000 B.C. and 8000 B.C. In the early stages of this period, people began to build farming villages.

Many of the earliest farming villages were in an area called the **Fertile Crescent**. This region stretches from the Persian Gulf to the Mediterranean Sea. It includes the fertile, flat floodplains along the Tigris and Euphrates rivers in Southwest Asia. **Fertile** soil encourages the growth of crops and plants. The region provided a steady food supply. People were able to settle down and enjoy a much more comfortable lifestyle.

DOMESTICATION OF PLANTS AND ANIMALS, 5000–500 B.C.

EUROPE

ASIA

FERTILE
CRESCENT

INDUS

HUANG
HE

NILE

PACIFIC
OCEAN

AFRICA

ATLANTIC
OCEAN

INDIAN
OCEAN

AUSTRALIA

Agriculture established

By 5000 B.C.

By 3000 B.C.

By 500 B.C.

NILE Early agricultural center

Crops

Beans

Corn

Cotton

Other grains

Potato

Rice

Sorghum

Animals

Cattle

Llama

Pig

Sheep

NEW FARM TOOLS AND METHODS

Even so, farming was very hard work. To make it easier, Neolithic people developed specialized tools. They fashioned hoes for digging the soil and plows for preparing the land to plant seeds. They also made curved sickles that cut through the stalks of grain and millstones that ground the grain into flour.

Farmers used domesticated animals to make their new tools more efficient. For example, they tied cattle to the plows and led the animals up and down the rows. In addition to helping turn over the soil, the cattle left behind manure that fertilized the land.

Neolithic people also developed new technology for the home. They made clay pots and hardened them in kilns, or ovens. The kilns could also be used to heat and melt the metal from rocks—a process called smelting. The liquid metal was then cast in molds to create metal tools, which eventually began to replace stone tools. The Stone Age had come to a close.

REVIEW & ASSESS

1. **READING CHECK** What new farm tools did humans develop during the agricultural revolution?

2. **INTERPRET MAPS** Along what geographic feature had most agriculture developed by 5000 B.C.?

3. **DRAW CONCLUSIONS** In what ways was the agricultural revolution an important breakthrough in human history?

2.4 Studying the Past

Look around. Everything you can see tells a story. At a glance, the shape, size, age, and use of a particular object provide some clues to its history. However, with a team of scientists, you could learn a whole lot more.

MAIN IDEA

Archaeologists, historians, and other specialists gather and study evidence to tell the story of human history.

SCIENTIFIC DATA

As you have learned by reading this chapter, archaeologists piece together clues to tell the story of what happened in a particular place at a particular time. It is detective work, and like detectives, they rely on other specialists to help them find and analyze the evidence.

Some of these specialists include geologists, who can tell the story of a landscape by analyzing rocks and fossils. When geologists investigate rock layers, they sometimes uncover prehistoric plant and animal remains. These remains can reveal what the environment was like. The bones they find provide information about human health and diet. Geologists can also help archaeologists locate deeply buried artifacts.

Other specialists called radiologists study x-ray images to look beneath the surface of objects to show what the eye cannot see,

especially in bones and rusty metal. An advanced x-ray called a CT scan provides detailed images that can be manipulated on a computer and turned into three-dimensional representations.

As you may recall, geneticists are scientists who study genes, the biological blueprints for all living things. Genes are made up of DNA, which is encoded in every cell and transmitted from parent to child. *Encode* means "to put a message into a code," or set of symbols. By studying modern DNA patterns, geneticists can trace human ancestry back thousands of years to see how people spread around the world.

HISTORICAL SOURCES

Historians also work to understand the past. They take evidence from many different sources to explain what happened and when and why it did.

Some of the sources historians use include primary sources. A **primary source** is a document or other object that was created by someone who witnessed or lived through a historical event. These sources include letters, maps, paintings, and tools. Primary sources are very important, but they are not always completely reliable. The opinions of the author may distort, or misrepresent, the facts.

Historians also use **secondary sources**, documents or other objects created after an event by someone who did not see it or live during the time when it occurred. These are interpretations of events, often based on primary sources. History books and biographies are secondary sources. **Oral history** is an unwritten account of events that is often passed down through the generations as stories or songs.

Different historians can interpret the same evidence in very different ways. In addition, new evidence is continually being discovered. That means that history—especially the details—is always changing.

PRIMARY SOURCE: THE ROSETTA STONE

The Rosetta Stone, which stands nearly four feet high and weighs about 1,700 pounds, is a primary source from ancient Egypt. It is not from the Paleolithic Age. Instead, the three different types of writing carved onto it date back to 196 B.C. The stone was discovered in 1799, but no one could read the first two scripts until a scholar cracked the code in 1822.

HIEROGLYPHIC

Hieroglyphs are pictures that can represent people, objects, animals, plants, sounds, and ideas.

DEMOTIC

Demotic writing is an ancient Egyptian script that, like hieroglyphs, scholars could not read or write before 1822.

GREEK

The three scripts mostly contain the same text, so scholars used the Greek writing to read the other two.

REVIEW & ASSESS

1. READING CHECK How do archaeologists, historians, and other specialists work together to study historical evidence?

2. ANALYZE LANGUAGE USE How does the phrase "it is detective work" help explain the nature of an archaeologist's job?

3. COMPARE AND CONTRAST What is the difference between a primary source and a secondary source?

VOCABULARY

For each pair of vocabulary words, write one sentence that explains the connection between the two words.

1. **fossil; artifact**
   Both fossils, the remains of living organisms, and artifacts, human-made objects, provide helpful clues to understanding our history.

2. **archaeologist; anthropologist**

3. **culture; oral history**

4. **anthropologist; culture**

5. **hunter-gatherer; nomad**

6. **migration; land bridge**

7. **agriculture; fertile**

8. **primary source; secondary source**

READING STRATEGY

9. **ORGANIZE IDEAS: COMPARE AND CONTRAST** If you haven't already, complete your Venn diagram to compare and contrast the lives of Paleolithic and Neolithic people. Then answer the question.

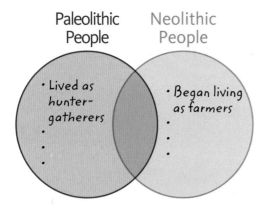

Paleolithic People   Neolithic People

- Lived as hunter-gatherers
- •
- •
- •

- Began living as farmers
- •
- •
- •

In what ways did the lives of Paleolithic and Neolithic people differ? In what ways were they the same?

MAIN IDEAS

Answer the following questions. Support your answers with evidence from the chapter.

10. What do archaeologists learn about early modern humans by studying their fossils and artifacts? **LESSON 1.1**

11. What effect did a catastrophic drought in East Africa have on *Homo sapiens* thousands of years ago? **LESSON 1.3**

12. Why were the Paleolithic people who left Africa probably attracted to the region of Southwest Asia? **LESSON 1.4**

13. How did groups of hunter-gatherers work together? **LESSON 2.1**

14. What were some of the first plants and animals domesticated by humans? **LESSON 2.2**

15. Why is the development of farming called the agricultural revolution? **LESSON 2.3**

16. What sources do historians use to study the past? **LESSON 2.4**

CRITICAL THINKING

Answer the following questions. Support your answers with evidence from the chapter.

17. **MAKE INFERENCES** What factors do you think were essential to the survival of humankind?

18. **COMPARE AND CONTRAST** How was the culture of prehistoric *Homo sapiens* similar to our own?

19. **DRAW CONCLUSIONS** What does the domestication of plants and animals suggest about the development of humans?

20. **YOU DECIDE** Some historians think that the agricultural revolution was the most important event in human history. Others claim that the ability to control fire was the most important. Which development do you think was more important? Support your opinion.

INTERPRET MAPS

Study the map of the Fertile Crescent. Then use the map to answer the questions that follow.

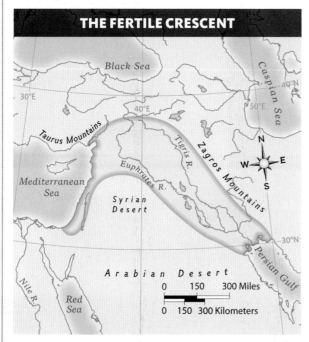

THE FERTILE CRESCENT

21. The Fertile Crescent is the area shown in green on the map. Why do you think the Fertile Crescent was so narrow?

22. What rivers were vital to the development of early farming in the Fertile Crescent?

23. What bodies of water bordering the region probably contributed to its fertility?

24. **MAP ACTIVITY** Sketch your own physical map of the Fertile Crescent. Be sure to label all bodies of water, deserts, and mountains. Use a different color for each type of physical feature. How does your map help you visualize the Fertile Crescent and its surrounding area?

ANALYZE SOURCES

Study this cave painting of two bison, or buffalo-like animals, from the Lascaux Cave in France. Then answer the question.

25. What details in the cave painting suggest that the Paleolithic artist who created it was highly skilled?

WRITE ABOUT HISTORY

26. **EXPLANATORY** Many new developments occurred during the Neolithic Age. Write a paragraph in which you describe one important development and explain how it changed the way people lived. Use the tips below to help you plan, organize, and revise your paragraph.

TIPS

- Take notes from the chapter on the development you chose.

- State your main idea clearly at the beginning of the paragraph.

- Support your main idea with relevant facts, definitions, specific details, and examples.

- Use vocabulary you learned from the chapter.

- Provide a concluding statement about the significance of the development you chose.

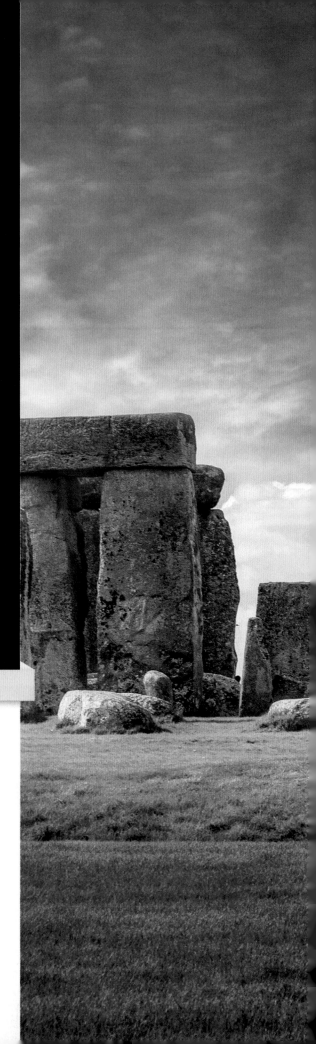

2 ORIGINS OF CIVILIZATION

10,000 B.C. – 3000 B.C.

SECTION 1 **EARLY VILLAGES**

 SS.6.E.1.2; SS.6.G.1.3; SS.6.G.1.4; SS.6.G.1.6; SS.6.G.1.7; SS.6.G.2.1; SS.6.G.2.2; SS.6.G.2.3; SS.6.G.2.4; SS.6.G.2.5; SS.6.G.2.6; SS.6.G.3.1; SS.6.G.3.2; SS.6.G.4.1; SS.6.W.2.2; LAFS.68.RH.1.2; LAFS.68.RH.2.4; LAFS.68.RH.2.5; LAFS.68.RH.3.7

KEY VOCABULARY

clan
cultural
 diffusion
cultural
 hearth
maize

matrilineal
metallurgy
staple
surplus

NAMES & PLACES

Banpo
Çatalhöyük
Faiyum
Mesoamerica
Nile River Valley
Oaxaca
Yangshao

SECTION 2 **THE SEEDS OF CIVILIZATION**

 SS.6.E.1.3; SS.6.G.2.2; SS.6.W.2.3; LAFS.68.RH.1.2; LAFS.68.RH.1.3; LAFS.68.RH.2.5; LAFS.68.RH.3.7

KEY VOCABULARY

city
civilization
government
record
 keeping
religion

scribe
specialized
 worker
temple
trade

NAMES & PLACES

Göbekli Tepe

READING STRATEGY

IDENTIFY MAIN IDEAS AND DETAILS When you identify a text's main idea and supporting details, you state the most important idea about a topic and determine which facts support that idea. As you read the chapter, use a diagram like this one to find a main idea and supporting details about cultural hearths.

Cultural Hearths

Main Idea:
Detail:
Detail:
Detail:

Stonehenge is an ancient stone circle that still stands on the Salisbury Plain in England. Archaeologists believe that work on this mysterious site began around 3000 B.C.

1.1 Centers of New Ideas

Where do new ideas come from, and how do they spread? Today's trends start with ideas that catch on all over the world. About 12,000 years ago, ideas began to spread in the same way. Groups of people living in different places invented new ways of doing things. These groups created the world's early cultural hearths.

MAIN IDEA

Cultural hearths promoted the spread of new ideas, practices, and technology in different parts of the world.

WHAT IS A CULTURAL HEARTH?

New ideas, practices, and technology began in places called **cultural hearths**. Remember that culture is a group's way of life, including the group's behaviors, beliefs, language, and customs. Ancient cultural hearths spread ideas and practices that influenced the way people did everyday things, from planting crops to burying their dead.

New practices emerged in several cultural hearths around the same time. Between 8000 and 5000 B.C., people living in different parts of the world began to develop new ways of community living. They began to practice new methods of domesticating animals and plants and living in settled communities. They developed traditional economies based on custom. Groups exchanged food and goods and made sure the needs of everyone in the group were met. As settled societies thrived, they began to form organized governments, build places of worship, and express themselves artistically.

Despite being separated by thousands of miles, ancient cultural hearths shared similar geographic features. These features included mild climates, fertile land, and access to rivers. Such favorable conditions allowed agriculture to flourish and attracted new people to the area. As populations grew and migrated to other places, they took the new cultural practices with them.

FOUR CULTURAL HEARTHS

Several cultural hearths developed during the Neolithic period. In this chapter, you will learn about four of them, specifically the cultural hearths that emerged in Southwest Asia, China, Mesoamerica, and North Africa.

As you can see on the map, these cultural hearths were located in widely scattered parts of the world. For example, Mesoamerica, in present-day Mexico and Central America, was thousands of miles away from Banpo, in China. Keep in mind that people living in these cultural hearths did not have the benefit of modern communication or transportation. Thousands of years ago, new ideas and practices emerged in and spread from very different places around the same time—without the benefit of the Internet or air travel.

Each of these cultural hearths made an important contribution to surrounding cultures and regions. Simultaneously, the people living in these cultural hearths accepted new ideas themselves. They learned new ways of doing things from people who traveled from other places, and they absorbed the new ideas into their own cultures. Later cultures would build upon the foundations established by these ancient cultural hearths.

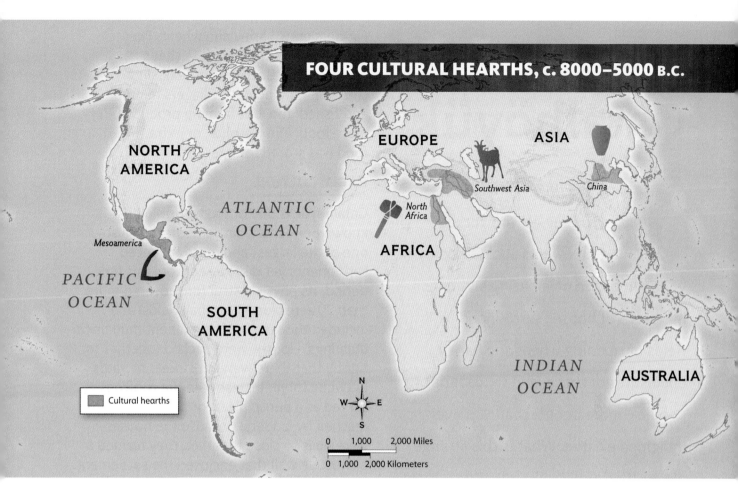

FOUR CULTURAL HEARTHS, c. 8000–5000 B.C.

NORTH AMERICA

ATLANTIC OCEAN

EUROPE

ASIA

Southwest Asia

China

Mesoamerica

North Africa

PACIFIC OCEAN

AFRICA

SOUTH AMERICA

INDIAN OCEAN

AUSTRALIA

Cultural hearths

N
W   E
S

0   1,000   2,000 Miles

0   1,000   2,000 Kilometers

Balsas R.

Oaxaca

Tehuacán Valley

Mesoamerica: Oaxaca
Farmers in Oaxaca introduced an important new crop: maize.

Faiyum

Nile R.

Nile River Valley

North Africa: Faiyum
Faiyum farmers adopted techniques from cultures across the Mediterranean.

Çatalhöyük

Göbekli Tepe

Tigris R.

Fertile Crescent

Euphrates R.

Southwest Asia: Çatalhöyük
Builders at Çatalhöyük demonstrated advanced construction techniques.

Wei Huang Valley

Huang He

Wei Huang

Banpo

Chang Jiang

China: Banpo
Yangshao potters at Banpo created functional, beautiful pottery.

REVIEW & ASSESS

1. READING CHECK What is a cultural hearth?

2. DESCRIBE What geographic features did ancient cultural hearths share?

3. INTERPRET MAPS Near what rivers did these four ancient cultural hearths emerge?

1.2 Southwest Asia: Çatalhöyük

Imagine you are a traveler crossing central Turkey 9,000 years ago. Suddenly, you stumble on an amazing sight: hundreds of houses surrounded by fields of ripening wheat and barley, enclosures of cattle, and thousands of people—more people than you ever imagined existed. What is this strange place? It's Çatalhöyük.

MAIN IDEA

Çatalhöyük was an advanced settlement and an early cultural hearth in Southwest Asia.

AN AGRICULTURAL VILLAGE

By modern standards, the Neolithic village of **Çatalhöyük** (chah-tuhl-HOO-yuk) was small and simple. To Neolithic people, though, it was incredibly advanced. Çatalhöyük developed in present-day Turkey beginning around 7400 B.C. This settlement was large, both in size and population. Çatalhöyük still fascinates people thousands of years later because of the rich cultural material left behind by those who lived there.

The people who built Çatalhöyük relied on farming for food. A stable food supply contributed to population growth and Çatalhöyük's agriculture eventually supported as many as 10,000 people.

Farmers grew barley and wheat. They also raised livestock such as sheep, goats, and cattle for meat, milk, and clothing. Çatalhöyük's villagers hunted and fished, too, but farming produced more food. The **surplus**, or extra, food was stored for later use.

EARLY CULTURE

Çatalhöyük is one of the world's oldest known permanent settlements. It is also one of the largest and most advanced settlements yet discovered from this time period. Its physical structure covered more than 30 acres (or 27 football fields) and included thousands of permanent mud brick buildings. Houses were packed together so tightly that there were no streets or yards between them. Instead, the flat rooftops served as a public plaza, or an open square, reached by ladders. Because the houses were built so close together, they formed a protective wall that enclosed the settlement.

People entered their homes through doors in the roofs. Most homes had a single main room where families cooked, ate, and slept. The main room had built-in benches and a fireplace. Plastered walls were covered with murals showing scenes of hunting, daily life, and important events.

At Çatalhöyük, archaeologists found evidence of religious practices and artistic expression. Horned bulls' heads mounted on walls and symbolic clay figures suggest that the villagers worshipped gods. Villagers also buried their dead, a fact revealed by human remains discovered beneath the floors of homes. The presence of pottery, cloth, cups, and bone utensils as well as tools and jewelry shows artistic expression. Archaeologists even found lead and copper, a sign of very early **metallurgy**, or metalworking. This was an important technological advance.

Discoveries at Çatalhöyük continue even today. Each new find sheds more light on the people who lived in this ancient settlement.

IMAGINING ÇATALHÖYÜK

Çatalhöyük was unknown to modern people until its discovery in the 1950s. Since then, archaeologists have carefully excavated the site. Their discoveries have revealed details of a unique settlement and culture. This illustration shows what archaeologists think Çatalhöyük might have been like. The cutaways let you peek inside the homes.

REVIEW & ASSESS

1. **READING CHECK** What archaeological evidence demonstrates that Çatalhöyük was an advanced culture?

2. **IDENTIFY MAIN IDEAS AND DETAILS** Why did the people of Çatalhöyük build their dwellings so close together?

3. **ANALYZE VISUALS** Based on the illustration, what might have been some advantages to living at Çatalhöyük?

China:
Banpo

About 1,000 years after the development at Çatalhöyük, a lightbulb went off on the other side of the world. Thousands of miles from Southwest Asia, another center of new ideas developed in China's rich river valleys.

MAIN IDEA

The Yangshao culture developed as a cultural hearth in northern China.

RIVER VALLEY AGRICULTURE

Around 5000 B.C., warmer, wetter weather prompted the development of cultural hearths in the fertile river valleys of China. As in Çatalhöyük, people here domesticated pigs, chickens, and dogs. They hunted and fished, too.

In southern China, which has a relatively warm climate, people began to settle in villages. Farmers grew rice, which they had domesticated from the wild rice that grew in the Chang Jiang (chahng jyahng) Basin.

Farming villages also developed farther north in the Huang He (hwahng huh) Basin. However, the colder, drier climate in the north was less favorable for growing rice. Farmers there domesticated wild millet instead. Millet is a tiny, yellow grain. It grows fast and is a low-maintenance, or easy-to-grow, crop. It was an important part of the diet of ancient people in northern China.

YANGSHAO CULTURE

The **Yangshao** (yahng-shou) culture was one of China's Neolithic cultural hearths. The Yangshao lived along the Huang and Wei (way) rivers from about 5000 to 3000 B.C. Archaeologists have discovered more than 1,000 Yangshao sites in northern China.

One of the best-known Yangshao sites is **Banpo**, a large farming village. This village contained many small houses that faced a community building in a central square. Archaeologists determined that Banpo houses were rebuilt many times. People may have abandoned the village when the fields were exhausted of nutrients and then later returned when the land recovered. Banpo villagers grew millet as their **staple**, or main crop. They also grew a fibrous plant called hemp and cultivated silk, which they crafted into textiles.

The Yangshao at Banpo left behind a unique style of pottery that demonstrates their artistry. Yangshao potters created bowls and vessels, or containers, that they formed by hand and baked in kilns, or ovens, just outside Banpo village. The Yangshao's painted pottery commonly features geometric designs. Other examples include shaped vessels used for food storage.

Archaeologists found many of these vessels and other useful items buried with the dead in neatly arranged graves. These "grave goods," as they are called, suggest that the Yangshao people believed in a link between the living and the dead, though their specific religious beliefs remain unknown. Because most graves contained similar grave goods, archaeologists believe that most people probably had equal status in society.

Early Yangshao graves also suggest that people were arranged into **clans**, or family groupings, when buried. These clans were **matrilineal**, which means they traced descendants through the mother rather than the father.

The Huang He in China provided fertile soil for ancient Yangshao farmers.

By about 3200 B.C. Yangshao culture had evolved into Longshan (lung-shan) culture. The Longshan crafted useful tools and beautiful objects from jade—a hard green or white stone. Longshan artists produced a distinctive black pottery using pottery wheels, and craftspeople made tools out of copper. The Longshan also established trade networks on which later Chinese cultures would build.

Yangshao Pottery

Formed in the shape of an owl, this tripod pottery vessel was used to serve food.

REVIEW & ASSESS

1. **READING CHECK** What is unique about the Yangshao culture?

2. **COMPARE AND CONTRAST** Why did farmers grow different types of crops in the southern and northern river basins of China?

3. **DETERMINE WORD MEANINGS** Based on its definition, what does the word part *matri-* mean?

Mesoamerica:
Oaxaca

Around the time the Yangshao were farming in China, another cultural hearth was forming across the Pacific in Mesoamerica. The people there were developing an important crop that you might recognize—corn.

MAIN IDEA

Maize domestication helped make Mesoamerica an important cultural hearth.

MESOAMERICAN NOMADS

Mesoamerica, which means "middle America," refers to the ancient geographic and cultural region that reached from central Mexico south through Central America. This region was another important Neolithic cultural hearth, similar in some ways to Çatalhöyük in Southwest Asia and Banpo in China.

For thousands of years, Mesoamericans traveled in small nomadic groups, moving from place to place with the seasons. They gathered wild plants but did little farming. For brief periods, these Mesoamericans may have tended small patches of land. However, they didn't settle in permanent sites, build permanent homes, or form villages. Eventually, though, Mesoamericans began to domesticate wild plants. In this way, they resembled people living in cultural hearths in other parts of the world.

CRADLE OF THE MAIZE REVOLUTION

One of the main plants Mesoamericans domesticated was **maize**, or what we know as corn. A cave is an unlikely place to find clues about an important development in farming, but that is where archaeologists found traces of an ancient plant. In fact, caves and rock shelters scattered across southern Mexico revealed the earliest signs of domestication in North America.

Archaeologists found prehistoric corncob fragments in the highland caves of **Oaxaca** (wah-HAH-kah) and the Tehuacán (tay-wah-KAHN) Valley. The pieces had been preserved for thousands of years by the region's hot, dry conditions. These fragments, which date to around 4250 B.C., came from an early variety of domesticated maize. Archaeologists also found stone tools for grinding the hard maize kernels into flour for baking. The first varieties of maize were probably neither juicy nor yellow, but they were easily harvested and stored, which made them a useful food source.

So where did maize come from? After decades of debate, scientists believe that maize was domesticated from a wild Mexican grass called teosinte (tay-uh-SIN-tay) that is native to the area around the Balsas River. Teosinte kernels are easily knocked off the plant, making it a difficult crop to harvest. However, hundreds of years of domestication solved this problem. Domestication also increased the number and size of kernels on the teosinte plant. Over time, it came to resemble modern corn.

As maize became a more productive crop, Mesoamericans relied on it for their annual food supply. By 2000 B.C., the maize revolution had taken place, and maize farming was widespread in Mesoamerica. Little did these farmers know they had invented a food that people would still enjoy thousands of years later.

DOMESTICATING CORN

Teosinte, the wild relative of modern corn, produced much smaller kernels. Note the size of the cobs of the teosinte plant as compared to a quarter. Now compare a quarter to the size of modern corn. In domesticating this plant, ancient farmers slowly began to encourage fewer branches on the plant. Less branching meant the plant could divert more energy into fewer cobs, which then grew larger. In addition, the hard kernel of the teosinte plant eventually gave way to the softer kernel we recognize as modern corn.

TEOSINTE

MODERN CORN

REVIEW & ASSESS

1. **READING CHECK** How did the domestication of maize help Mesoamerica become a cultural hearth?

2. **SUMMARIZE** How do archaeologists know that Mesoamericans domesticated maize?

3. **INTEGRATE VISUALS** Based on the illustration and text, what changes did domestication bring about to teosinte?

This photo of Faiyum today shows how access to a water source determines where crops can grow and people can live.

North Africa:
Faiyum

Long before building their extraordinary pyramids, the ancient Egyptians laid the building blocks of an advanced culture on the floodplains of the Nile River in North Africa. As in other cultural hearths, agriculture was at the root of cultural development in ancient Egypt, whose farmers adapted ideas from places far and wide.

MAIN IDEA

Early farmers established the Nile River Valley as an important cultural hearth.

MIGRANTS FROM THE SAHARA

As you may recall from the previous chapter, the Sahara was a tropical grassland 10,000 years ago. Then the climate changed drastically. Seasonal rains shifted south, and the grasslands dried into desert. This dramatic change forced people to migrate to more fertile lands with steadier water supplies.

The same climate shift that transformed the Sahara transformed the narrow **Nile River Valley**. Its swamps dried up, making the land usable and this fertile valley a perfect place for farming. The Nile floodplain was ideal for the agriculture that would later support a large population.

EGYPT'S EARLIEST FARMING VILLAGE

Faiyum (fy-YOOM) is an oasis about 50 miles south of present-day Cairo. Dating from around 5200 B.C., it is considered Egypt's earliest farming community. At Faiyum, archaeologists discovered storage pits for grain, postholes for building foundations, and the ruins of clay floors and fireplaces. They also stumbled upon a 7,000-year-old, Neolithic-era wood and flint sickle used for farming and left in a storage bin.

The agricultural practices used at Faiyum were not native to the Nile River Valley, though. According to archaeologists, people from neighboring cultures introduced new practices to Faiyum farmers. Grains of wheat and barley and bones of sheep and pigs found at Faiyum came from across the Mediterranean Sea or the Sinai Desert where domestication was already well established. People from these areas likely brought the domesticated grains and animals to the Nile River Valley.

The process by which cultures interact and spread from one area to another is called **cultural diffusion**. This process allowed Faiyum farmers to benefit from the skills of other cultures. It also helped establish the Nile River Valley as an important cultural hearth.

REVIEW & ASSESS

1. **READING CHECK** Why were early farmers attracted to the Nile River Valley?

2. **SUMMARIZE** How did a climate shift that took place 10,000 years ago change the Sahara and Nile River Valley?

3. **DRAW CONCLUSIONS** What impact did neighboring cultures have on the farmers at Faiyum?

Paths to Civilization:
Göbekli Tepe

An old riddle asks: Which came first, the chicken or the egg? Archaeologists have posed their own riddle: Which came first, organized agriculture or organized religion? Like most riddles, this one can't be easily answered.

MAIN IDEA

Throughout history, different cultures have traveled different paths to civilization.

THE WORLD'S FIRST TEMPLE

Over time, cultural hearths around the world transformed into civilizations. A **civilization** is an advanced and complex society. Two important markers of civilization are agriculture and organized **religion**, or the belief in and worship of gods and goddesses.

About 11,600 years ago in southeast Turkey on the edge of the Fertile Crescent, at least 500 people came together to create **Göbekli Tepe** (guh-bek-LEE TEH-peh), the world's first **temple**, or place of worship. Ancient builders formed massive limestone pillars into T shapes and arranged them into sets of circles.

The tallest pillars stood as high as 18 feet and weighed 16 tons. Keep in mind that Göbekli Tepe's builders did all this before the invention of the wheel. Stone workers carved ferocious animals onto the pillars after they were in place. Once completed, the immense pillars and the frightening images of deadly animals flickering in the firelight must have been an awesome sight.

Göbekli Tepe represents an important event in the development of organized religion. As one of the first known examples of monumental architecture, or large structures built for an identified purpose, it was specifically dedicated for religious use. Its commanding views over fertile plains, evidence of ceremonies, and high levels of artistic expression all suggest a religious purpose.

Göbekli Tepe is also remarkable because archaeologists believe that hunter-gatherers, not settled farmers, built it. The structures at Göbekli Tepe were constructed miles from any Neolithic settlement, water source, or agricultural land. The absence of harvest symbols found in later farming cultures reinforces the theory that hunter-gatherers—not a settled people—built Göbekli Tepe.

THE MEANING OF GÖBEKLI TEPE

Archaeologists argue over the meaning of Göbekli Tepe. Evidence found there has changed the way some think about the human transition from hunter-gatherer to farmer. For a long time, archaeologists thought that the need to ensure good harvests led to the belief in and worship of gods and goddesses. In other words, agriculture developed before religion. However, Göbekli Tepe turns that argument around, suggesting that here, at least, humans developed organized religion before farming. In this case, perhaps the need to feed religious gatherings led to the development of agriculture.

The fact is that in some places, agriculture came before religion; in others, religion came first. Göbekli Tepe teaches us that different cultures forged different paths to civilization. Either way, by 6000 B.C., both organized religion and agriculture—two of the fundamental building blocks of civilization—had been established in the Fertile Crescent.

Göbekli Tepe's builders constructed the site without the benefit of the wheel. They relied on human muscle—and lots of it—to move the 16-ton limestone pillars from as far as a quarter mile away.

PATHS TO CIVILIZATION

HUNTER-GATHERER

A warmer climate leads to more vegetation and wildlife, allowing for . . . ❯ Agriculture / Domestication of plants and animals / Permanent settlement   *which led to* ❯ Religion

Curiosity about the natural world encourages the beginnings of . . . ❯ Religion   *which led to* ❯ Agriculture / Domestication of plants and animals / Permanent settlement

FARMER

REVIEW & ASSESS

1. **READING CHECK** How does Göbekli Tepe show that organized religion sometimes developed before agriculture?

2. **IDENTIFY MAIN IDEAS AND DETAILS** What features made Göbekli Tepe such an important achievement?

3. **INTEGRATE VISUALS** Based on the diagram and description of the pillars in the text, what might the hunter-gatherers who visited Göbekli Tepe have worshipped?

2.2 Traits of Civilization

You might hear the word *civilization* a lot, but do you understand what it means? All civilizations, whether past or present, have certain things in common. So, what is a civilization?

MAIN IDEA

A civilization is a complex society that is defined by five key traits.

Cultural hearths prepared the way for the next development in human history: civilization. Ancient cultures around the world transformed into complex civilizations at about the same time, and they had five traits, or characteristics, in common: cities, complex institutions, specialized workers, record keeping, and improved technology.

CITIES

The first civilizations were born in **cities**. More than just large population centers, early cities were political, economic, and cultural centers for the surrounding areas. Cities often contained monumental architecture usually dedicated to religion or government. The city's heart was its trading center, where farmers and merchants met to conduct business. **Trade**, or the exchange of goods, allowed some civilizations to grow very rich. Some merchants traveled long distances to trade goods with other groups. Over time, they established trade routes, which helped spread ideas and practices.

COMPLEX INSTITUTIONS

As cities developed, complex institutions such as government and organized religion emerged as ways to manage resources and populations. **Government**, or an organization set up to make and enforce rules in a society, provided leadership and laws. Organized religion bound communities together through shared beliefs.

SPECIALIZED WORKERS

Food surpluses made possible by the agricultural revolution led to settled communities and to another key characteristic of civilizations: **specialized workers**. Specialized workers performed jobs other than farming. Some people specialized in pottery, metalworking, weaving, or toolmaking. Others became government officials, priests, teachers, soldiers, or merchants.

RECORD KEEPING

As societies developed, they had to manage information. **Record keeping**, or organizing and storing information, became an important job. Specialized workers called **scribes** recorded business transactions, important events, customs, traditions, and laws. The first writing systems used pictographs that looked like the things they represented, such as wavy lines for water. Eventually, complex writing systems helped people record important information and abstract ideas. As writing developed, so did calendar keeping.

IMPROVED TECHNOLOGY

The fifth key characteristic civilizations have in common is improved technology. As cultures became more complex, people developed new tools and techniques to solve problems and survive. Advances in technology included metalworking methods, inventions such as the wheel and the plow, and tools to create everyday items, such as the potter's wheel.

Giant's Tower, a temple in Malta, demonstrates evidence of complex institutions.

Specialized workers crafted this blue gemstone and gold necklace in ancient Iraq.

Pictographs carved on this clay tablet predated writing systems we recognize today.

Potters used the wheel long before it would be attached to vehicles around 3000 B.C.

FIVE TRAITS OF CIVILIZATION

COMPLEX INSTITUTIONS

SPECIALIZED WORKERS

RECORD KEEPING

CITIES

IMPROVED TECHNOLOGY

The great city of Ur was one of the busiest and most powerful trading centers of the ancient world.

REVIEW & ASSESS

1. **READING CHECK** What key traits, or characteristics, define civilizations around the world?

2. **DRAW CONCLUSIONS** In what ways were cities essential to the development of civilizations?

3. **ANALYZE CAUSE AND EFFECT** What is the connection between food surpluses and specialized workers?

2.3 NEW TECHNOLOGY

Ancient tools and technology reveal much about the cultures that used them. As early cultures advanced toward civilization, the design and manufacture of tools improved. Materials used to make tools also changed. For example, with the development of metallurgy, strong metals such as bronze allowed for the transition from stone to metal tools. Better and more complex tools developed by ancient people demonstrated the emergence of civilization around the world. Based on what you see here, what purpose did many early tools serve?

Harpoon
Reindeer antlers provided the bone for this hunting tool.

Flint Tool
Flint is a hard stone that can be shaped into a sharp point.

Copper Awl
This tool was used to pierce holes in leather and cloth.

Sickle
Hand-held tools called sickles were used to harvest grain.

Spearhead
Metals such as bronze improved a weapon's strength.

Arrowhead
Arrowheads of flint or other stone were tied to arrows and used for hunting.

Stone Hoe
This stone hoe, dated around 7000 B.C., is an example of an early agricultural tool.

Bone Needle
Needles made of bone were used for sewing and weaving.

Wheel
Early wheels were constructed simply: wooden disks with holes for axles.

Kitchen Utensil
This fork-shaped utensil made of bone was found at Çatalhöyük.

Flint Stone
When hit, flint stones helped spark fire.

Pottery
Pottery vessels of all shapes held liquids and food.

Flint Knife
The intricate handle on this knife was carved from a hippopotamus tooth.

Bronze Ax Head
Axes were used for chopping and hunting.

51

VOCABULARY

Use each of the following vocabulary words in a sentence that shows an understanding of the term's meaning.

1. **cultural hearth**
   A cultural hearth is a place from which new ideas and technology spread to surrounding areas.

2. **surplus**

3. **metallurgy**

4. **matrilineal**

5. **maize**

6. **temple**

7. **cultural diffusion**

8. **government**

9. **specialized worker**

10. **civilization**

READING STRATEGY

11. **IDENTIFY MAIN IDEAS AND DETAILS** If you haven't already, complete your diagram to determine a main idea and supporting details about cultural hearths. Then answer the question.

Cultural Hearths

Main Idea: *Cultural hearths promoted the spread of new ideas, practices, and technology around the world.*
Detail:
Detail:
Detail:

What is a cultural hearth? What impact did the four main cultural hearths have on the ancient world?

MAIN IDEAS

Answer the following questions. Support your answers with evidence from the chapter.

12. Why are cultural hearths referred to as centers of new ideas? **LESSON 1.1**

13. In what way was agriculture central to the people who built Çatalhöyük? **LESSON 1.2**

14. How did natural resources and climate influence the formation of cultural hearths in China? **LESSON 1.3**

15. In what ways did the Faiyum farmers demonstrate cultural diffusion? **LESSON 1.5**

16. What key characteristics do civilizations around the world share? **LESSON 2.2**

CRITICAL THINKING

Answer the following questions. Support your answers with evidence from the chapter.

17. **EVALUATE** What are some of the factors that contribute to the development of civilization?

18. **DRAW CONCLUSIONS** How did cultural hearths help lead to the emergence of civilization?

19. **MAKE INFERENCES** Why do you think government became necessary as cities developed?

20. **COMPARE AND CONTRAST** How did the lifestyles of hunter-gatherers compare with those of settlers of early agricultural communities?

21. **MAKE INFERENCES** Why is it significant that hunter-gatherers built Göbekli Tepe as a place of worship?

22. **FORM OPINIONS** Do you think agriculture or religion developed first? Support your opinion with evidence from the chapter.

23. **YOU DECIDE** Which of the five traits of civilization do you consider the most important? Support your opinion with evidence from the chapter.

INTERPRET MAPS

Study the map of the locations of the Yangshao and Longshan cultures that developed in China's cultural hearth. Then answer the questions that follow.

24. Which river was vital to the development of the Yangshao culture?

25. Why might the Longshan culture have expanded east from the Yangshao culture?

26. **MAP ACTIVITY** Create your own sketch maps of the other cultural hearths discussed in this chapter. Label the areas and bodies of water. Then study the maps and note the cultural hearths' physical similarities and differences.

CHINA'S CULTURAL HEARTH

Huang He

Yellow Sea

Banpo

Chang Jiang

0   250   500 Miles
0 250 500 Kilometers

N
W   E
S

Longshan
Yangshao

ANALYZE SOURCES

The dagger below is made of carved and chipped stone. Archaeologists who discovered it at Çatalhöyük believe it was made around 6000 B.C. Study the artifact. Then answer the question that follows.

27. What information might archaeologists learn about the skills of the Neolithic people who created the dagger? Use evidence from the chapter to support your answer.

WRITE ABOUT HISTORY

28. **EXPLANATORY** Choose two cultures discussed in this chapter. Write a 3-paragraph explanatory essay that compares and contrasts the cultures in terms of their agricultural and technological developments. Use the tips below to help you plan, organize, and revise your essay.

TIPS

- Take notes from the lessons about the two cultures you chose.

- State your main idea and supporting details in a clear, well-organized way.

- Use appropriate transitions to clarify the relationships among ideas.

- Use at least two vocabulary words from the chapter.

- Provide a concluding statement that wraps up the information about the two cultures.

- Use word-processing software to produce and publish your final essay.

ON **LOCATION** WITH Louise LEAKEY

NATIONAL GEOGRAPHIC EXPLORER-IN-RESIDENCE

▶ **Check out more on myNGconnect**

Meave Leakey (left) and Louise Leakey conserve a fossil found in Kenya. Their discoveries in the country's Turkana Basin have greatly contributed to our understanding of human origins.

ALL IN THE FAMILY

I've spent quite a bit of time on my hands and knees, carefully excavating the remains of our ancestors and other animals. I have been fortunate to have done this work alongside my mother, Meave Leakey. She is also a highly acclaimed paleontologist, so there's a lot to live up to! This is what happens when you're born into a family famous for finding prehuman fossils. My grandfather, Louis Leakey, made important discoveries in Tanzania, at Olduvai Gorge, that helped explain the human fossil record. I remember when my father, Richard Leakey, discovered a well-preserved 1.6-million-year-old skeleton of *Homo erectus*, one of our ancestors that left Africa for the first time 1.8 million years ago. I was twelve years old at the time, and they compared my teeth with the teeth of this skeleton, the Nariokotome Boy, to determine that it was about the same age as I was.

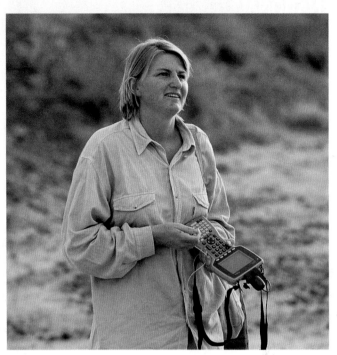

Louise Leakey uses GPS to locate fossils in Kenya. You can explore many of her family's fossil discoveries at www.africanfossils.org.

EARLY HUMAN FOSSILS

My mother and I continue with our field work, on the east side of Lake Turkana in Kenya's Rift Valley. We organize and coordinate the search for fossil remains in extensive fossil deposits in northern Kenya. During every expedition, we discover and collect exciting new fossils that help us answer important questions about the past. These fossils are kept at the Turkana Basin Institute or in the National Museums of Kenya. In 1999, we organized a National Geographic-sponsored expedition to the Turkana Basin. It was there that my mother and I uncovered a 3.3-million-year-old human skull and part of a jaw. The skull is very flat, and that makes it different from anything else ever found. In fact, it is so different that we believe it belongs to an entirely new branch of early human that we named *Kenyanthropus platyops*. To prove this beyond doubt, we still need to find more remains, ideally another intact skull! From this same site, the earliest stone tools known to the world have recently been announced, which strongly suggests that this species was also the earliest tool maker.

WHY STUDY HISTORY ❓

❝ When you look at the state of the world today, with its many conflicts and ethnic divisions, it's hard to believe that we are a single species with a common ancestor. We have to understand our past to contemplate our future. The fossils in east Africa are our *global heritage.* ❞ —Louise Leakey

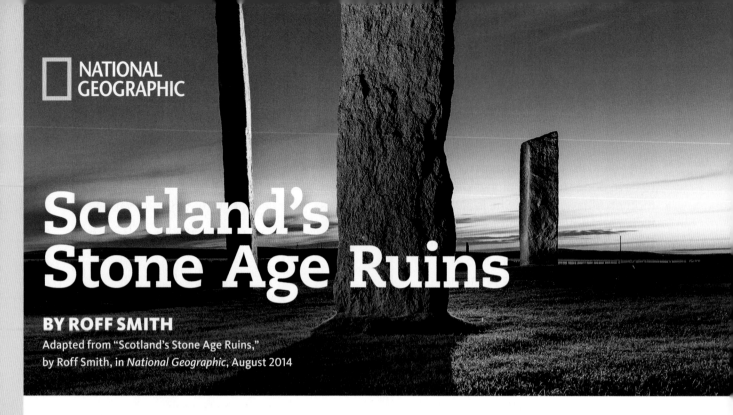

Scotland's Stone Age Ruins

BY ROFF SMITH

Adapted from "Scotland's Stone Age Ruins,"
by Roff Smith, in *National Geographic*, August 2014

Orkney is a fertile, green archipelago off the northern tip of Scotland. Five thousand years ago, people there built something unlike anything they had ever attempted before. They had Stone Age technology, but their vision was millennia ahead of their time.

The ancient people of Orkney quarried thousands of tons of sandstone and transported it several miles to a grassy hill. There they constructed a complex of buildings and surrounded them with imposing walls. The complex featured paved walkways, carved stonework, colored facades, and slate roofs. Many people gathered here for seasonal rituals, feasts, and trade.

Archaeologist Nick Card says the recent discovery of these stunning ruins is turning British prehistory on its head. "This is almost on the scale of some of the great classical sites in the Mediterranean, like the Acropolis in Greece, except these structures are 2,500 years older." Only a small part of the site has been excavated, but this sample has opened a window into the past. It has also yielded thousands of artifacts, including ceremonial mace heads, polished stone axes, flint knives, stone spatulas, and colored pottery. Archaeologists have also discovered more than 650 pieces of Neolithic art at the site.

"Nowhere else in all Britain or Ireland have such well-preserved stone houses from the Neolithic survived," says archaeologist Antonia Thomas. "To be able to link these structures with art, to see in such a direct and personal way how people embellished their surroundings, is really something."

Sometime around the year 2300 B.C., it all came to an end. Climate change may have played a role. Or perhaps it was the disruptive influence of a new toolmaking material: bronze.

Whatever the reason, the ancient temple was deliberately destroyed and buried under stone and trash. Card surmises, "It seems that they were attempting to erase the site and its importance from memory, perhaps to mark the introduction of new belief systems."

**For more from National Geographic
Check out "First Americans" on myNGconnect**

UNIT INQUIRY: CREATE A CULTURAL SYMBOL

In this unit, you learned about the origins of early human cultures and civilizations. Based on your understanding of the text, what elements of culture developed in early human societies? How did those elements help make each society unique?

ASSIGNMENT Create a symbol that represents the culture of an early human society you studied in this unit. The symbol should reflect one or more cultural characteristics that made that early society unique. Be prepared to present your cultural symbol and explain its significance to the class.

Plan As you create your symbol, think about specific characteristics that were unique to the society you have selected. For example, what elements of culture defined and unified early Stone Age humans? What customs, social structure, arts, tools, and major achievements distinguished them from other groups of early humans? You might want to use a graphic organizer to help organize your thoughts. Identify the early society and at least one specific detail about different characteristics of its culture. ▶

Produce Use your notes to produce detailed descriptions of the elements of culture that defined the early human society you

selected. You might want to draw or write descriptions of visual icons for each element.

Present Choose a creative way to present your cultural symbol to the class. Consider one of the following options:

- Write an introduction to the cultural symbol that describes the early human society it represents.

- Create a multimedia presentation showing different elements of the society's culture and what made it unique.

- Paint a flag of your symbol using colors that also express significance or meaning to the culture.

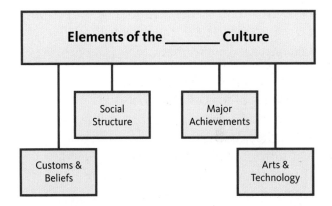

Elements of the _____ Culture

Social Structure

Major Achievements

Customs & Beliefs

Arts & Technology

1. Humans originated from a common ancestor who lived in Africa 60,000 years ago.

2. For thousands of years, humans lived in small, nomadic groups, hunted wild animals, and gathered edible plants.

3. Farming produced food surpluses that allowed rapid population growth and job specialization.

4. Agriculture encouraged people to group together in villages that grew into more complex cities.

5. Cultural hearths emerged around the world during the Neolithic period.

6-10. **NOW IT'S YOUR TURN** Complete the list with five more things to remember about the origins of cultures and civilizations.

EARLY
CIVILIZATIONS

NATIONAL
GEOGRAPHIC

ON **LOCATION** WITH

Christopher Thornton
Archaeologist
Lead Program Officer, Research,
Conservation, and Exploration,
National Geographic

The past is a window to the future. Early civilizations differ in many ways from those today, but there are also many similarities between then and now. Studying early civilizations is exciting because of what we can learn from the ancients, and also because what we know—or think we know— is always changing. I'm Christopher Thornton, and I time travel between the past and present. Join me on my journey!

< CRITICAL VIEWING This painted bas-relief shows ancient Egyptian king Thutmose III wearing the Atef crown, which was worn during religious rituals. What details in the artwork convey the king's strength and power?

Early Civilizations

Mesopotamia, Egypt, Israel, India, and China

c. 3500 B.C.
The world's first civilization arises in Sumer. *(stringed instrument from Ur)*

c. 1600 B.C.
The Shang dynasty emerges along the Huang He in China.

c. 1250 B.C.
Moses leads the Hebrews out of Egypt.
(Hebrew text scroll)

2334 B.C.
Sargon the Great conquers Sumer and creates the world's first empire.

1500 B.C.

c. 1790 B.C.
Hammurabi issues his Code of Laws at Babylon.

c. 2500 B.C.
Harappan civilization develops in the Indus Valley.

3500 B.C.

c. 1470 B.C.
Hatshepsut becomes Egypt's first female pharaoh.

c. 3100 B.C.
Upper and Lower Egypt are united under a single ruler.
(Horus, Egyptian sky god)

c. 1000 B.C.
Aryan civilization spreads through the northern Indian subcontinent.

What can you infer about the Qin dynasty in China based on this time line?

A.D. 320
Chandra Gupta I establishes the Gupta Empire, which oversees India's golden age.
(Gupta gold coin)

c. 269 B.C.
Asoka becomes ruler of the Maurya Empire and eventually rules by Buddhist principles.

A.D. 105
The Chinese invent paper.

200 B.C.

A.D. 100

563 B.C.
Siddhartha Gautama, the Buddha, is born.

202 B.C.
The Han dynasty comes to power.
(Han bronze dragon)

600 B.C.

c. 221 B.C.
The Qin dynasty begins with the reign of Shi Huangdi.

587 B.C.
Jerusalem falls to the Babylonians, beginning the Babylonian Exile.

61

FIRST CIVILIZATIONS

3500 B.C.–1800 B.C.

Most of the world's earliest civilizations, including Mesopotamia, Egypt, India, and China, developed in fertile river valleys. The good soil made the river valleys ideal for growing crops. By contrast, the Hebrews established their civilization along the Mediterranean. However, what really set them apart was their belief in one God. This belief would influence the rest of the world for centuries.

What landforms separated the civilizations?

ANCIENT MESOPOTAMIA

Water sources:	Tigris and Euphrates rivers, Mediterranean Sea
Civilizations and empires:	Sumer, Akkadia, Babylon, Assyria, Chaldea, Phoenicia, Persia
Significant leaders:	Sargon, Hammurabi, Nebuchadnezzar II, Cyrus
Legacy:	farming, writing, government, law, shipbuilding, math

ANCIENT EGYPT

Water sources:	Nile River
Civilizations and empires:	Egypt, Kush
Significant leaders:	Khufu, Ahmose, Hatshepsut, Ramses II, Piankhi
Legacy:	writing, math, science, medicine, art, architecture

JUDAISM & ISRAELITE KINGDOMS

Water sources:	Mediterranean Sea
Civilizations and empires:	Israel, Judah
Significant leaders:	Abraham, Moses, Saul, David, Solomon
Legacy:	education, religion, philosophy

0   250   500   750   1000 kilometers
0   250   500   750   1000 miles

ANCIENT CHINA

Water sources:	Huang He, Chang Jiang
Civilizations and empires:	Shang, Zhou, Qin, Han
Significant leaders:	Shi Huangdi, Liu Bang, Empress Lü, Emperor Wudi
Legacy:	philosophy, government, navigation, farming, writing, textiles, art

Aral Sea

A S I A

Huang (Yellow)

C h i n a

H i m a l a y a

Chiang Jiang (Yangtze)

Indus

I n d i a

Ganges

Arabian Sea

Bay of Bengal

South China Sea

I N D I A N   O C E A N

ANCIENT INDIA

Water sources:	Indus River, Ganges River, Indian Ocean
Civilizations and empires:	Harappa, Aryan, Maurya, Gupta
Significant leaders:	Chandragupta Maurya, Asoka, Chandra Gupta I
Legacy:	religion, art, medicine, math

3
ANCIENT MESOPOTAMIA

3000 B.C. – 500 B.C.

SECTION 1   **SUMER**

 SS.6.E.1.1; SS.6.E.2.1; SS.6.G.1.4; SS.6.G.1.6; SS.6.G.1.7; SS.6.G.2.1; SS.6.G.2.2;
SS.6.G.2.3; SS.6.G.2.4; SS.6.G.3.1; SS.6.G.5.1; SS.6.G.5.3; SS.6.W.1.3; SS.6.W.2.2;
SS.6.W.2.7; SS.6.W.2.8; LAFS.68.RH.1.1; LAFS.68.RH.1.2; LAFS.68.RH.2.4;
LAFS.68.RH.2.5; LAFS.68.RH.3.7; LAFS.68.WHST.1.2; LAFS.68.WHST.3.9

KEY VOCABULARY		NAMES & PLACES
artisan	polytheism	Euphrates River
city-state	ritual	Mesopotamia
cuneiform	silt	Sargon the Great
empire	social class	Sumer
famine	tribute	Tigris River
irrigation	ziggurat	

SECTION 2   **BABYLONIA AND LATER CIVILIZATIONS**

 SS.6.E.1.1; SS.6.G.1.4; SS.6.G.1.6; SS.6.G.1.7; SS.6.G.2.1; SS.6.G.2.2; SS.6.G.2.4; SS.6.G.2.5;
SS.6.G.2.6; SS.6.G.5.2; SS.6.W.1.3; SS.6.W.2.7; SS.6.W.2.8; SS.6.W.3.1; LAFS.68.RH.1.2;
LAFS.68.RH.2.5; LAFS.68.RH.2.6; LAFS.68.RH.3.7; LAFS.68.RH.3.8

KEY VOCABULARY		NAMES & PLACES
alliance	raw material	Cyrus the Great
colony	satrap	Darius I
legacy	tolerance	Hammurabi
province		Nebuchadnezzar II

READING STRATEGY

MAKE INFERENCES When you make inferences, you use what you already know to figure out the meaning of the text. As you read the chapter, use a chart like this one to make inferences about why civilization developed in Mesopotamia.

I notice...	I know...	And so...

Fierce lions decorated the walls of the street that passed through the Ishtar Gate. Standing 38 feet high and featuring hundreds of dragons and bulls, the Ishtar Gate was the entryway to the city of Babylon in Mesopotamia.

65

The Geography of Ancient Mesopotamia

Long after Çatalhöyük was settled, Southwest Asia was home to another group of people. They lived between two flowing rivers in a fertile land. Because of the advances in government, culture, and technology that took place there, the region is often called a "cradle of civilization."

MAIN IDEA

The geography of Mesopotamia helped create the conditions for civilization.

THE LAND BETWEEN THE RIVERS

As you have learned, the Fertile Crescent sweeps its way across Southwest Asia. In the west it bends down the coast of the Mediterranean. In the east it follows the course of the **Tigris** (TY-gruhs) **River** and the **Euphrates** (yu-FRAY-teez) **River** until they merge and empty into the warm waters of the Persian Gulf. Today this river valley lies mostly in the country of Iraq. Historians call this flat, fertile area **Mesopotamia** (meh-suh-puh-TAY-mee-uh), which means "land between the rivers." The people who once lived there are known as Mesopotamians.

The people of Mesopotamia called the Tigris "swift river" because it flowed fast. The Euphrates flowed more slowly. It frequently changed course, leaving riverside settlements without water. Both rivers flooded unpredictably. Mesopotamians never knew when or how much water would come. Too much, too little, or too late spelled disaster for crops.

On the plus side, the often-destructive floodwaters deposited **silt**, an especially fine and fertile soil, that was excellent for agriculture. In this way, the rivers brought life to the otherwise dry land of Mesopotamia and supported the early civilization that was developing there. As farming thrived in this river valley, populations grew and cities developed.

FARMING IN THE FERTILE CRESCENT

Farming began as early as 9800 B.C. in the Fertile Crescent. It eventually spread throughout Mesopotamia. However, Mesopotamia was far from perfect for agriculture. In addition to flooding, farmers had to deal with hot summers and unreliable rainfall. However, the region's fertile soils promised plentiful crops, such as wheat, barley, and figs—if the people could come up with a way to control the water supply.

Irrigation, or watering fields using human-made systems, was the answer. Farmers in Mesopotamian villages cooperated to dig and maintain irrigation canals that carried water from the rivers to the fields. Farmers also stored rainwater for later use and built walls from mounds of earth to hold back floodwaters. The people developed important new technology, such as the ox-driven plow, a tool that broke up the hard-baked summer soil and prepared large areas for planting. These creative methods enabled farmers to use the rich soil to their advantage.

The result was a reliable and abundant agricultural surplus. The ample food fed the area's growing population. Because food was plentiful, the people of Mesopotamia could afford to develop art, architecture, and technology. The agricultural surpluses allowed a great civilization to develop.

Black Sea

Caspian Sea

Caucasus Mountains

Rivers' Source
The Tigris and Euphrates rivers have their source in the mountains of Asia Minor (present-day Turkey).

Mountain Snow and Rain
Melting snow (from the mountains north of the Fertile Crescent) and rain flooded the Tigris and Euphrates rivers. This flooding deposited rich soil on riverbanks.

A S I A   M I N O R

Taurus Mountains

A S I A

M E S O P O T A M I A

• Nineveh

Ashur •

Tigris R.

Zagros Mountains

PERSIA

Mediterranean Sea

Byblos •
Sidon •
Tyre •
Mt. Lebanon Ra.

S y r i a n

D e s e r t

Euphrates R.

N
W   E
S

0   100   200 Miles
0   100   200 Kilometers

Babylon •

Umma •
Uruk • Lagash •
Ur •   SUMER

Susa •

Jerusalem •

Dead Sea

ile Delta

Nile R.

Giza •

Deserts
The Syrian and Arabian deserts created an open area, which made it easy for enemies to attack cities in the Fertile Crescent. As a result, people built walls around their cities for protection.

Persian Gulf

EGYPT

A R A B I A N   D E S E R T

Fertile Crescent
Mesopotamia
- - - Ancient coastline (about 5000 B.C.)

REVIEW & ASSESS

1. READING CHECK How did the Tigris and Euphrates rivers make the growth of civilization in Mesopotamia possible?

2. INTERPRET MAPS What forms the borders of Mesopotamia?

3. IDENTIFY MAIN IDEAS What new methods and technology did farmers in Mesopotamia use to take advantage of the fertile soil?

1.2 City-States Develop

The present-day location that was once Mesopotamia is made up of windswept deserts. It's hard to imagine that 5,500 years ago this dusty land was filled with people living their busy city lives. The city streets were not just filled with people—there were also buildings and temples so tall they seemed to rise up to the heavens.

MAIN IDEA

The city-states of Sumer formed Southwest Asia's first civilization.

Most residents lived in one-story mud houses that were crowded close together along the streets.

SUMER

Around 3500 B.C., Mesopotamia's first civilization arose in **Sumer** (SOO-mur), an area in the southern part of the region. (See the map in Lesson 1.1.) Sumer was not controlled by a single, unified government. Instead, the area was made up of a dozen advanced, self-governing city-states. A **city-state** included the city and its surrounding lands and settlements. These units developed when villages united to build major irrigation projects.

Most of Sumer's 12 city-states, including Ur, were built on the Tigris or Euphrates rivers. City-states also clustered close to the coast of the Persian Gulf, where the people developed fishing and trade. Frequent wars were fought between city-states to protect fertile land, limited natural resources, and profitable trade routes.

CENTERS OF CIVILIZATION

Surplus food gave Sumerians time to learn new skills and encouraged trade. Though Sumer had productive farmland, the area lacked important natural resources, such as tin and copper. These resources had to be acquired through trade. When combined, tin and copper produce bronze, a strong metal used by Sumerians to create tools and weapons. Because of the importance of bronze, the period around 3000 B.C. is called the Bronze Age.

THE CITY-STATE OF UR, c. 2000 B.C.

This large temple was built to honor Ur's moon god, Nanna. It was the highest point in Ur and could be seen for miles from outside the city.

Giant surrounding walls protected Ur from attack by other city-states and invaders from outside Mesopotamia.

Ur's residents accessed water from the nearby Euphrates River through a system of canals.

Surplus food also led to a growth in population. New government systems had to be established to meet the challenge of managing so many people. Kings arose to provide strong leadership, and administrators supervised taxes and kept order. Because of the wealth created by agricultural surpluses, Sumerians could afford to support these government administrators.

Sumerian society was organized by **social class**, an order based on power and wealth. Kings ruled at the top, with priests just beneath them. Next came administrators, scribes, merchants, and **artisans**, or people who are skilled at making things by hand. These groups in turn looked down on farmers and less-skilled workers. However, even people at the bottom of this system ranked higher than Sumerian slaves.

REVIEW & ASSESS

1. **READING CHECK** How did the organization of Sumerian society affect the way different roles were viewed by others?

2. **INTEGRATE VISUALS** In what ways did the rivers support agriculture and the city-states?

3. **ANALYZE CAUSE AND EFFECT** How did food surpluses encourage local and long-distance trade?

Religion in **Sumer**

In the blazing sun, Sumerian priests carry food offerings step by step to the top of the great temple. The purpose of this feast is to secure the gods' favor for another day. In the dangerous and unpredictable world of Sumer, it's important to keep the gods on your side.

MAIN IDEA

Sumerians took religion seriously and built monumental structures to please their gods.

VOTIVE STATUES

To demonstrate their devotion to the gods, Sumerians placed small statues called votives in temples. Sumerians believed that while they worked on earthly activities like farming or fishing, the statues would pray on their behalf.

LAND OF MANY GODS

Sumerian lives depended on natural forces they could not control, including rivers that flooded and changed course. The people worshipped hundreds of gods, who they believed could control these forces. A belief in many gods is called **polytheism**.

Sumerians believed that their gods ruled the earth and had created humans to serve them. They also believed that the gods possessed superhuman powers. Unfortunately, the gods could use these powers to cause droughts, floods, and disease. For example, Ishkur was a storm god who was believed to have the power to cause destructive rains and floods whenever he liked.

To keep the gods happy, Sumerian priests tried to please them. Everyone paid a temple tax, which was offered to the gods in elaborate public **rituals**, or formal series of acts always performed in the same way. By observing natural events, including the movement of the sun, moon, and stars, priests tried to predict what the gods were planning. These observations helped the Sumerians develop a calendar, astronomy, and mathematics.

OFFERINGS AT THE TEMPLES

City-states were important religious centers. The most important building within a city-state was a huge pyramid-shaped temple called a **ziggurat** (ZIH-guh-rat). *Ziggurat* means "mountaintop." Every city was dedicated to a major deity, a god or goddess, who was its guardian. Sumerians believed that the deity lived in a shrine, or sacred place, on top of the ziggurat. People reached the shrine by climbing long, external flights of stairs.

Priests were responsible for conducting religious practices at the ziggurat. These practices included various rituals, such as offering food to the city god or goddess. A statue representing the deity was placed in a space called the adytum (A-duh-tuhm), or holy place. A meal was set on a table before the statue. Sumerians believed that the god or goddess would eat the meal.

Priests also performed purification, or cleansing, rituals using holy water. This purification process was often used on kings before they entered shrines where the deities were believed to dwell.

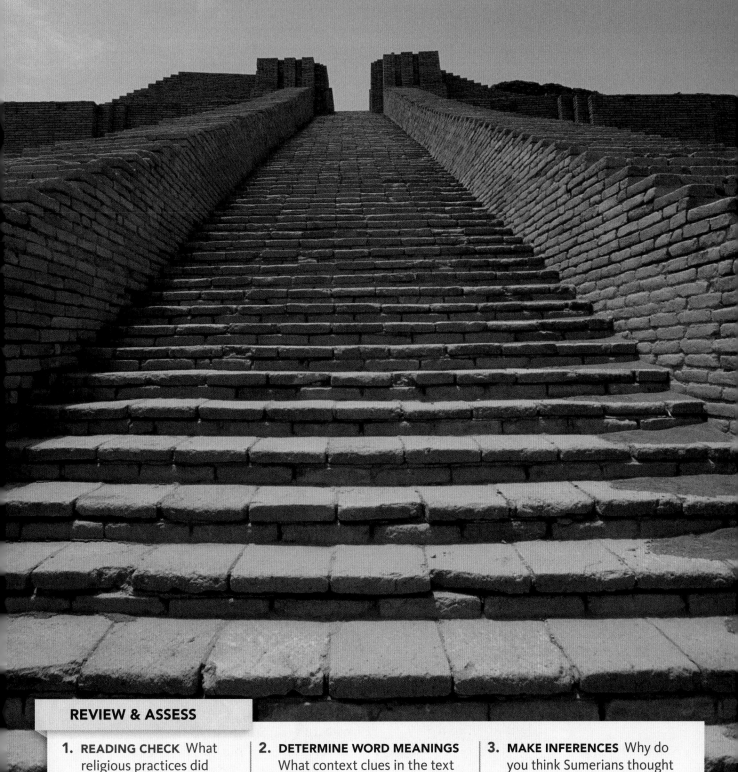

Critical Viewing Priests climbed 100 or more steep steps to the shrine at the top of a ziggurat to worship the city god. Why would the shrine have been positioned so high?

REVIEW & ASSESS

1. **READING CHECK** What religious practices did Sumerians observe to serve and please their gods?

2. **DETERMINE WORD MEANINGS** What context clues in the text tell you what *superhuman* means?

3. **MAKE INFERENCES** Why do you think Sumerians thought that cleansing was necessary before entering shrines?

Sumerians invented the earliest form of writing, known as pictographs, or images of objects. Detailed pictographs evolved into symbols called **cuneiform** (kyoo-NEE-uh-fawrm), which, over time, represented sounds rather than objects. Scribes began forming words and combining them into sentences in religious and scientific works and in stories. This change marked the beginning of written history and a major step forward in the development of civilization.

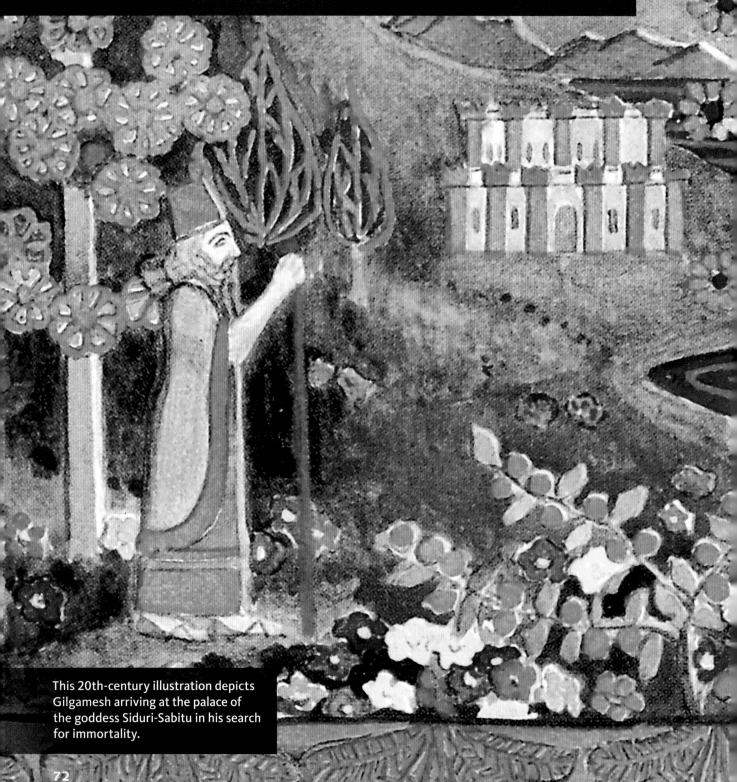

This 20th-century illustration depicts Gilgamesh arriving at the palace of the goddess Siduri-Sabitu in his search for immortality.

Cuneiform Tablet, Northern Iraq, c. 600s B.C.

Scribes used reeds, or sharpened blades of grass, to carve the wedge-shaped cuneiform symbols—600 in all—into wet clay tablets that were then dried. This tablet describes a flood scene from *The Epic of Gilgamesh*, explained in more detail below.

CONSTRUCTED RESPONSE Why did the Sumerians dry the clay cuneiform tablets?

from *Gilgamesh*, translated by Stephen Mitchell

The Epic of Gilgamesh is the world's oldest recorded story. The author is unknown. Gilgamesh was probably a real king of Uruk. In the story, he sets off on a fantastic adventure with his loyal friend Enkidu. This passage describes their encounter with a monster.

CONSTRUCTED RESPONSE Why would the Sumerians record a story about their king encountering a monster?

> They came within sight of the monster's den.
>
> He was waiting inside it. Their blood ran cold.
>
> He saw the two friends, he grimaced, he bared his teeth, he let out a deafening roar.
>
> He glared at Gilgamesh. "Young man," he said, "you will never go home. Prepare to die."

from *The Epic of Creation*, translated by Stephanie Dalley

This Babylonian creation story by an unknown author explains how the world was formed. In this passage, the chief god, Marduk, creates the stars and a 12-month calendar.

CONSTRUCTED RESPONSE Why might Babylonians want to tell and record their story of the creation of the world?

> He [Marduk] fashioned stands for the great gods.
>
> As for the stars, he set up constellations corresponding to them.
>
> He designated the year and marked out its divisions,
>
> Apportioned three stars each to the twelve months.

SYNTHESIZE & WRITE

1. **REVIEW** Review what you have learned about Sumerian writing and the world's oldest stories.

2. **RECALL** On your own paper, write down the main idea expressed in each document.

3. **CONSTRUCT** Construct a topic sentence that answers this question: What did the Sumerians' cuneiform writing system make possible?

4. **WRITE** Using evidence from the documents, write a paragraph that supports your topic sentence from Step 3.

1.5 Sargon Conquers Mesopotamia

Have you heard the expression, "Uneasy lies the head that wears a crown"? It applied well to Sargon the Great. He conquered many peoples, lands and cities, including Sumer. As ruler, Sargon was expected to keep his people safe, peaceful, happy, and fed. His role involved much responsibility. It was not easy being in charge of what was, at that time, the world's largest civilization.

MAIN IDEA

Sargon conquered Sumer and other lands in Mesopotamia to create the world's first empire.

AN OUTSIDER TAKES OVER

Sargon the Great was an ancient Mesopotamian ruler who has inspired stories for nearly 4,500 years. It is difficult to separate fact from fiction about his life. According to one story about his childhood, Sargon's mother was a royal priestess who abandoned him as a baby. A humble gardener from Kish raised him after finding him in a basket floating in a river.

Kish was a city-state in Akkad (AH-kahd), an area in central Mesopotamia. Akkadians and Sumerians shared a similar culture but had different ethnic origins and spoke different languages. Before becoming a ruler, Sargon was a servant to the king of Kish. After serving in the royal court, Sargon became a powerful official in Kish and eventually overthrew the king.

While Sargon gained power, Sumer was weakened by internal wars and invasions. In 2334 B.C., Sargon's armies swept through Sumer, conquering it completely. They also took control of northern Mesopotamia. These conquests created the world's first **empire**, a group of different lands and people governed by one ruler. Sargon's empire stretched from the Mediterranean Sea to the Persian Gulf. He ruled the Akkadian Empire from Akkad, his now long-lost capital city.

EMPIRE AND EXPANSION

The Akkadian Empire lasted 150 years, and Sargon ruled for 56 of them. He personally led the fight to expand the empire and claimed to have won 34 battles and taken 50 rulers prisoner. Sargon was an effective warrior and skilled at managing people and projects.

In the lands he conquered, Sargon allowed the people to keep their local rulers and customs. However, they had to obey him and pay a protection tax called a **tribute**. Sargon's policy helped keep peace and win the loyalty of people throughout his empire. He also introduced standard weights and measures and made Akkadian the official language of the government.

Sargon's powerful empire brought prosperity to his people and encouraged trade. Akkad's farmers managed agriculture so well that 100 years went by without **famine**, or widespread hunger. Sargon's wars were spread over large areas. As a result, Akkad traded with distant suppliers for timber, metal, and other raw materials Mesopotamia lacked. His wars concentrated

AKKADIAN EMPIRE, 2334–2200 B.C.

Reign of Sargon
(2334–2279 B.C.)

Sargon's Empire

- - - Ancient coastline
(about 5000 B.C.)

on controlling trade centers and protecting natural resources, such as cedar forests.

Despite Sargon's abilities, the empire became too big to control. After he died, his sons took over but were unable to maintain order. City-states rebelled, and a great deal of time and effort went into trying to keep the peace. Enemies from the northeast raided the empire's unprotected borders. Famine returned, spreading suffering and unrest among the people. By 2200 B.C., the Akkadian Empire had come to an end.

SARGON THE GREAT

To guarantee loyalty from the governors who ruled parts of his empire, Sargon gave trusted relatives powerful positions. To keep control of his army, he created a group of professional soldiers whose sole purpose was to fight for him.

< This sculptured head is believed to depict Sargon with his crown and long beard.

REVIEW & ASSESS

1. **READING CHECK** What measures did Sargon take to unite his empire?

2. **INTERPRET MAPS** Where were most of the cities of the empire located? Why do you think that was so?

3. **DRAW CONCLUSIONS** What conclusions can you draw about Sargon's abilities as a ruler?

Hammurabi's
Code of Laws

Would you know how to play a game if you didn't know its rules? Probably not. This is how people from Mesopotamia must have felt when it came to following laws enforced by rulers. Though they did exist, laws were not laid out in a clear fashion. This changed when a king decided it was time to literally spell out the laws for his people.

MAIN IDEA

Hammurabi changed civilization by organizing laws and displaying them.

NEW EMPIRE IN MESOPOTAMIA

After the fall of Sargon's Akkadian Empire, a tribe called the Amorites invaded western Mesopotamia around 2000 B.C. They established their capital at Babylon (BA-buh-lahn), a city-state overshadowed by powerful neighbors. (See the map in Lesson 1.5.) Then in 1792 B.C., **Hammurabi** (ha-muh-RAH-bee) became the sixth king of Babylon. Hammurabi was Babylon's most influential and powerful ruler. He expanded the kingdom and established his Babylonian Empire across Mesopotamia and other parts of the Fertile Crescent.

Hammurabi spent the first 29 years of his rule working on domestic improvements.

These included directing large projects, such as creating straight streets, strong city walls, magnificent temples, and efficient irrigation canals. Hammurabi also skillfully built up a network of **alliances**, or partnerships. This helped him conquer all of Mesopotamia in just eight years and claim the title "King of Sumer and Akkad."

HAMMURABI'S CODE

Hammurabi was a skillful ruler, but he is best remembered for his Code of Laws. His vast empire contained many different peoples who all followed different laws. To help unite his empire, Hammurabi took the best existing laws, added new rules, and then organized them into a clear, written system. The Code of Laws marked a major step forward for civilization. The code helped bring justice to everyday life. It also serves as an important primary source for historians because it offers insight into Babylonian society, including its structures, priorities, problems, and attitudes.

The Code of Laws was often applied based on a person's social class. For example, landowners could be fined more heavily than slaves. Hammurabi also laid down detailed laws about agriculture and the buying and selling of goods, highlighting the importance of these activities.

Three experienced judges heard cases. They listened to statements, examined evidence, and heard from witnesses. The judges even assumed the defendant's innocence. Guilt had to be proven. (Courts in the United States today also assume that people are innocent until proven guilty.) Hammurabi's Code of Laws influenced later legal systems, including those of ancient Greece and Rome.

After Hammurabi's death in 1750 B.C., the first Babylonian Empire declined rapidly and disappeared about 150 years later. However, Hammurabi's achievements ensured that Babylon remained a center of political, cultural, and religious importance for centuries to come.

Hammurabi's Code of Laws was carved into an eight-foot-high stone slab, called a stela (STEE-luh), for everyone to see and read. An introduction announced its purpose: "To prevent the strong from oppressing the weak and to see that justice is done to widows and orphans."

The code's 282 laws covered all aspects of life and dictated specific penalties for specific crimes. Punishments were often as brutal as the crime. For example, a son's hand would be cut off for striking his father, and those who robbed burning houses were burned alive. Additional examples of the numbered laws include the following:

 196 If a man put out the eye of another man, his eye shall be put out.

197 If he [a man] break another man's bone, his bone shall be broken.

∨ This top portion of the stela shows King Hammurabi receiving the Babylonian laws from Shamash, the god of justice.

REVIEW & ASSESS

1. **READING CHECK** How was Hammurabi's court system similar to the one we have today?

2. **IDENTIFY MAIN IDEAS AND DETAILS** What details illustrate the improvements Hammurabi made as Babylon's king?

3. **MAKE INFERENCES** Why was Hammurabi's Code of Laws displayed in public for everyone to see?

The
Assyrians
and the
Chaldeans

For 1,000 years after Hammurabi, Mesopotamia came under the rule of empire after empire. Then around 1000 B.C., the region shook with the sounds of an approaching army: marching feet, pounding hooves, frightening war cries. The Assyrian army had arrived.

MAIN IDEA

The Assyrians and then the Chaldeans conquered Mesopotamia.

THE ASSYRIAN EMPIRE

The Assyrians (uh-SIHR-ee-uhnz) were a people of northern Mesopotamia who developed a different culture. They were united by their worship of the god Ashur, for whom the Assyrian capital was named. (See the map in Lesson 1.5.) A strong agricultural economy and a large professional army helped the Assyrians conquer all of Mesopotamia, parts of Asia Minor, and even the rich state of Egypt by 650 B.C.

Destructive iron weapons gave Assyrian armies an advantage over their enemies, whose weapons were made of a weaker bronze. The armies also had horse-drawn chariots and soldiers who used bows and arrows while riding horses. Assyrian soldiers were experts at capturing cities.

It was not uncommon for soldiers to kill or enslave captured people and then burn their cities to the ground.

Villages, towns, and cities answered to the unforgiving Assyrian king, who held absolute power. Even the highest officials were closely watched. The government sometimes forced rebellious people to move to faraway lands. In time, however, the Assyrian Empire grew too big, and its subjects became tired of being treated so unfairly and violently. By about 626 B.C., the Assyrians were weakened by internal power struggles. This made it possible for a people known as the Chaldeans (kal-DEE-unz) to eventually defeat them.

CHALDEANS OVERTAKE THE ASSYRIANS

The Chaldeans were a seminomadic people who originally came from southern Babylonia. After overthrowing the Assyrians in 612 B.C., the Chaldeans became the ruling power of Babylon and extended their rule over all of Mesopotamia. **Nebuchadnezzar II** (ne-byuh-kuhd-NE-zuhr) was the most famous Chaldean king. Under his rule, which lasted for 43 years, the New Babylonian Empire included Mesopotamia and all of the Fertile Crescent.

Though he was often cruel, Nebuchadnezzar also made improvements to Babylon by rebuilding the city and adding incredible beauty to it. From miles away, the Tower of Babel, a soaring seven-story multicolored ziggurat, inspired awe. Visitors entered the inner city through the colorful Ishtar Gate with its gleaming blue-glazed bricks and images of dragons and bulls.

The king's most famous accomplishment was the Hanging Gardens of Babylon. Pumps operated by slaves irrigated a large, leveled terrace of trees and plants. The terrace formed a green mountain that seemed to float in the city. Although his empire outlasted him by fewer than 25 years, Nebuchadnezzar had built a monumental city fitting its name: Babylon, Gate of God.

Critical Viewing This painting shows what the Hanging Gardens of Babylon might have looked like. What reaction might the gardens have inspired in visitors?

REVIEW & ASSESS

1. **READING CHECK** In what ways were the rule of the Assyrians and the Chaldeans similar and different?

2. **MAKE INFERENCES** Why do you think the two empires did not last very long?

3. **ANALYZE LANGUAGE USE** What does "the terrace formed a green mountain that seemed to float in the city" mean?

from *Wonders of the Past*, J. A. Hammerton, ed., 1923

PHOENICIAN SHIP

The Phoenicians sailed their ships in the Mediterranean and beyond. Through trade, the Phoenicians also had contact with Mesopotamia. They established **colonies**, or outposts of people from one land who live in another land, in places as far away as Spain. Phoenicia's most famous colony was Carthage in North Africa.

Large Sail
The use of sail power and wind made it possible for ships to carry large cargoes without needing a lot of rowers.

Deck
The Phoenicians constructed space beneath the deck, where they could store cargo and supplies for the crew.

Figurehead
The ship's wooden figurehead was often carved into the shape of a horse's head. The eyes were meant to help the ship "see" where it was heading.

Ballast
Stones lining the bottom of the ship were used as ballast, or something that provides stability, for sailing in rough waters.

Goods
Slaves loaded such goods as wood, wine, and papyrus onto the ship.

Map legend:
■ Phoenician settlements
← Trade routes

EUROPE

Corsica ITALY
Sardinia
Black Sea
Tigris R.
Euphrates R.
MESOPOTAMIA
GREECE
Carthage
Sicily
Athens
PHOENICIA
Byblos
Sidon
Jerusalem
Tripolis
Mediterranean Sea
Tyre
Memphis
EGYPT
AFRICA
Nile R.
Red Sea

0   500 Miles
0   500 Kilometers

The Phoenicians

Do you have a well-traveled friend who always has interesting information about places you've never been? You can think of the Phoenicians as this worldly friend. While conducting trade throughout the Mediterranean and Mesopotamia, the Phoenicians spread cultural practices from one stop on their trade route to the next.

MAIN IDEA

Through their extensive trade network, the Phoenicians spread different cultures throughout the Mediterranean and beyond.

A TRADING PEOPLE

The narrow strip of coast along the eastern Mediterranean (present-day Lebanon) contained many natural resources and had good harbors. This combination was perfect for the development of industry and trade. About 1000 B.C., independent city-states emerged in the area. They shared cultural similarities, including language and a trading economy. The Greeks called the people from these city-states Phoenicians (fih-NEE-shuhnz), which means "purple dye people." The Phoenicians processed local shellfish into a purple dye used to color fabric. This dye was their most famous trade good. They exported wood from their highly desired cedar trees to Egypt and Mesopotamia. From other lands, they imported **raw materials**, or substances from which other things are made. Phoenician artisans crafted these materials into luxury goods for trade.

Phoenicia's most important export was its culture. To record trade transactions, the Phoenicians used their own 22-letter alphabet, which was adapted from Sumerian cuneiform. Each symbol from the Phoenician alphabet stood for a sound. First the ancient Greeks adopted the Phoenician alphabet, then the ancient Romans modified it to form the basis of our modern Western alphabet.

SHIPBUILDERS AND SEAFARERS

The Phoenicians were also skilled shipbuilders and sailors. They built strong, wide ships. Powered mainly by wind and a large, square sail, these ships carried huge cargoes thousands of miles. The Phoenicians became one of the first Mediterranean peoples to sail on the Atlantic Ocean. They sailed north to Britain, west to the Azores (nine volcanic islands located in the mid-Atlantic), and possibly even around Africa.

Despite their talents and enormous wealth, the Phoenicians were militarily weak and were eventually absorbed into the New Babylonian Empire. However, they performed a valuable service by spreading different cultures from one area to another. Their accomplishments show the importance of trade in building civilizations.

REVIEW & ASSESS

1. **READING CHECK** What goods and ideas did the Phoenicians spread through their sea trade network?

2. **ANALYZE VISUALS** Why might ballast have been important to the condition of goods transported by ship?

3. **MAKE INFERENCES** Why would the Phoenicians have established trading colonies in faraway places?

2.4 Persian Leaders

Palaces in the Persian Empire were built with diverse materials: bricks from Mesopotamia, timber from Phoenicia, ebony and silver from Egypt. This mix of materials was a deliberate celebration of the Persian Empire's rich ethnic diversity—a diversity that was encouraged by the wise leadership of two men.

MAIN IDEA

Under the rule of Cyrus and Darius I, the Persian Empire united different peoples and cultures.

CYRUS THE GREAT

The region of Persia was located in what is present-day southwestern Iran, just east of Mesopotamia. Around 700 B.C., the Persians were ruled by a people called the Medes (meedz). Then in 550 B.C., a Persian king known as **Cyrus the Great** led a successful uprising against the Medes. In 539 B.C., he captured the Babylonian Empire. Cyrus continued to add to his empire until it stretched from Afghanistan to the Aegean Sea, including Mesopotamia. Under Persian rule, these lands enjoyed 200 years of peace and economic well-being.

The secret of Cyrus's success was **tolerance**, or sympathy for the beliefs and practices of others. After winning a war, he showed mercy to conquered kings by allowing them to keep their thrones. Cyrus demanded only tribute that defeated people could afford, sparing them great hardships. He also honored local customs, religions, and institutions. His tolerance won him widespread respect and acceptance from conquered subjects.

DARIUS EXPANDS THE EMPIRE

After Cyrus's death around 529 B.C., his son Cambyses (kam-BY-seez) became king and added Egypt and Libya to the empire. The next king, **Darius I** (duh-RY-uhs), ruled Persia at its height. Darius expanded the empire until it grew to about 2,800 miles, stretching from India in the east to southeastern Europe in the west, with the Fertile Crescent in the middle.

Like Cyrus, Darius was a wise ruler. He avoided problems that had weakened other empires. For example, he divided his empire into 20 smaller **provinces**, or administrative districts, that were ruled by governors called **satraps** (SAY-traps). They helped him maintain control of his huge empire. Darius introduced regular taxation and fixed each province's tribute at only half of what the people could afford to pay. He also introduced a form of currency, which made it easier to pay taxes and buy goods.

Understanding that communications were essential to good government, Darius built the 1,500-mile-long Royal Road, running from Susa in Persia to Sardis in Anatolia (present-day Turkey). Other roads connected all 20 provinces so that messengers could carry his orders anywhere in under 15 days. The roads helped unify the blend of people and cultures that made up the Persian Empire.

Darius also built a new capital, called Persepolis, for his empire. Decorated with palaces and jeweled statues, Persepolis was meant to symbolize the magnificence of the Persian Empire—the largest, most stable, and most powerful empire of ancient Mesopotamia.

CYRUS THE GREAT

Job: Rebel and king of the Persian Empire

Education: Unknown; legend says a herdsman or a wild dog raised him

Home: Pasargadae, a city in ancient Persia

FRIENDS

Cyrus's friends included almost everyone he ruled.

TRIVIA

Cyrus remains a highly respected figure for modern Iranians, and his simple tomb is still visited by millions of people every year.

In this relief from ancient Persepolis, representatives from different regions of the Persian Empire carry gifts for the Persian king. The gifts are meant to symbolize their loyalty.

REVIEW & ASSESS

1. **READING CHECK** How did Cyrus and Darius each rule diverse groups of people peacefully?

2. **CONTRAST** In what ways did the governing policies of Cyrus and Darius differ from those of Assyrian rulers?

3. **SEQUENCE EVENTS** Identify four significant events, in order, that occurred while Cyrus and Darius ruled.

2.5
The **Legacy** of
Mesopotamia

 As you check your calendar, text a friend, or ride your bike, you probably aren't thinking about the people who walked the earth more than 3,000 years ago. But if it weren't for the people of ancient Mesopotamian civilizations, you might not be able to do any of these things.

MAIN IDEA

Mesopotamian civilizations were responsible for major cultural and technological developments.

CULTURAL DEVELOPMENTS

The advances developed in ancient Mesopotamia form the region's **legacy**—or the things, both cultural and technological, left to us from the past. Mesopotamia's cultural legacy touches our lives every day. For example, the written word took important leaps forward with Sumer's development of pictograph and cuneiform writing and then with the spread of the Phoenician alphabet.

Mesopotamia also left us a legacy in forms of government. The city-state unit that developed in Sumer, Babylon, and Phoenicia became an important governmental form in the ancient world. Equally important were the styles of government that emerged. Hammurabi highlighted the importance of law. His Code of Laws influenced later legal systems. Cyrus the Great demonstrated the power of tolerance to future leaders. Finally, the use of provinces, governors, and good communications are still essential to modern governments.

TECHNOLOGICAL ADVANCES

It is easy to take Mesopotamia's technological advances for granted because they seem so commonplace to us today. Yet at the time, Mesopotamian technology clearly furthered the development of human civilization. During the Bronze Age, tools and weapons became more effective than ever before. Strong axes, swords, and daggers were crafted from bronze.

Mesopotamian technology also had an impact on agriculture and on land and sea travel. The ox-drawn plow made it easier to cultivate large areas of land. Irrigation techniques pioneered by the Sumerians are still used around the world. The wheel revolutionized transportation and trade on land. Phoenician shipbuilding and navigation did the same at sea by spreading Phoenicia's Mesopotamian-influenced culture.

With advances like the abacus, people from Mesopotamia laid the foundations of mathematics and science. The abacus is a device that uses sliding beads for counting. The Mesopotamians were also among the first to perform complex calculations and develop a calendar. Additionally, they devised number systems based on 60, which is what we use today to keep track of time.

The application of mathematics made it possible for Mesopotamians to build larger and more complex buildings, including Mesopotamia's cultural and technological masterpiece, the ziggurat. So the next time you ride in a car, use a tool, or see a skyscraper, thank ancient Mesopotamia.

MATCH-UP: THEN AND NOW

These images show Mesopotamian inventions and their current forms—the ones we are familiar with today. Can you pair each Mesopotamian invention with its modern-day match?

MATCH-UP KEY
a. Phoenician merchant ship
e. Cargo ship
c. Abacus
g. Calculator
d. Message written in cuneiform on clay tablet
b. Text message on cell phone
h. Model of Sumerian plow
f. Tractor

REVIEW & ASSESS

1. READING CHECK
What are examples of Mesopotamia's cultural and technological legacy?

2. INTEGRATE VISUALS What other modern items would you add to the images above to illustrate Mesopotamia's legacy?

3. FORM OPINIONS Which cultural or technological advance from ancient Mesopotamia do you think is most important? Explain and support your choice.

VOCABULARY

Match each word in the first column with its definition in the second column.

WORD	DEFINITION
1. city-state	a. a pyramid-shaped temple with a shrine at the top
2. artisan	b. the governor of a district
3. polytheism	c. an order based on power and wealth
4. ziggurat	d. a person skilled at making things by hand
5. social class	e. an administrative district
6. province	f. a self-governing city that controlled the surrounding land
7. satrap	g. things left to us from the past
8. legacy	h. the belief in many gods

READING STRATEGY

9. **MAKE INFERENCES** If you haven't already, complete your chart to make inferences about why civilization developed in Mesopotamia. Then answer the question.

I notice ...	I know ...	And so ...
Two rivers flowed through Mesopotamia	Rivers provide water to sustain agriculture.	

Consider the traits of civilization that you learned about in Chapter 2. How did they develop in the region?

MAIN IDEAS

Answer the following questions. Support your answers with evidence from the chapter.

10. How did the geography of Mesopotamia contribute to the development of civilization? **LESSON 1.1**

11. What caused city-states to develop in Sumer and form the world's first civilization? **LESSON 1.2**

12. What purpose did the ziggurat serve in each Sumerian city-state? **LESSON 1.3**

13. What is important about the empire Sargon created in Mesopotamia? **LESSON 1.5**

14. What did Hammurabi establish to help unite his vast empire? **LESSON 2.1**

15. What factors helped the Assyrians of northern Mesopotamia conquer all of Mesopotamia? **LESSON 2.2**

16. How did Phoenician sea traders affect Mesopotamian culture? **LESSON 2.3**

17. In what ways were Cyrus and Darius wise rulers? **LESSON 2.4**

CRITICAL THINKING

Answer the following questions. Support your answers with evidence from the chapter.

18. **DRAW CONCLUSIONS** How might unpredictable natural forces, such as floods, have influenced the development of polytheism in Sumer?

19. **IDENTIFY MAIN IDEAS AND DETAILS** What are three details that support the idea that Sargon was a highly skilled administrator?

20. **ANALYZE CAUSE AND EFFECT** What led to Hammurabi's Code of Laws?

21. **SUMMARIZE** What were the important achievements of Mesopotamian civilizations?

22. **YOU DECIDE** Were the punishments in Hammurabi's Code of Laws appropriate? Support your opinion with evidence from the text.

Study the chart comparing letters in the Phoenician, early Greek, early Latin, and modern English alphabets. Then answer the questions that follow.

Phoenician	Early Greek	Early Latin	Modern English
⪤	⊲	⊼	**A**
𝕃	B	B	**B**
⌐	⌐	⟨	**C**
⌐	△	D	**D**
𝟛	⊟	⟨	**E**
𝖸	𝟤	⟨	**F**
⊞	⊟	H	**H**

23. Which letter is most similar in all four alphabets?

24. What conclusions can you draw about language in the ancient world?

ANALYZE SOURCES

Read the following translation of an Assyrian king's description of one of his raids. Then answer the question.

> I carried off his silver, gold, possessions, property, bronze, iron, tin, . . . captives of the guilty soldiers together with their property, his gods together with their property, precious stone of the mountain, his harnessed chariot, his teams of horses, the equipment of the horses, the equipment of the troops, garments with multi-colored trim, linen garments, fine oil, cedar, fine aromatic plants, cedar shavings, purple wool, red-purple wool, his wagons, his oxen, his sheep—his valuable tribute which, like the stars of heaven, had no number.

25. Based on this passage, what can you conclude about the nature of Assyrian attacks on city-states in Mesopotamia?

WRITE ABOUT HISTORY

26. ARGUMENT Of all the achievements of Mesopotamian civilizations, which one do you think has had the most significant and lasting impact on the modern world? Write a persuasive essay outlining your argument.

TIPS

- Take notes about the achievements of Mesopotamian civilizations discussed in the chapter.
- State your argument in a clear, persuasive way.
- Present strong evidence to support your argument.
- Use vocabulary words from the chapter as appropriate.
- Provide a concluding statement that wraps up the argument presented.
- Ask a teacher or a classmate to read your essay and make revisions based on their feedback.

CHAPTER

4 ANCIENT EGYPT

3000 B.C. – 500 B.C.

SECTION 1 **A SOCIETY ON THE NILE**

SS.6.E.2.1; SS.6.G.1.3; SS.6.G.1.4; SS.6.G.1.6; SS.6.G.1.7; SS.6.G.2.1; SS.6.G.2.3;
SS.6.G.2.4; SS.6.G.2.5; SS.6.G.3.1; SS.6.G.4.1; SS.6.G.5.1; SS.6.G.5.2; SS.6.W.1.4;
SS.6.W.2.6; LAFS.68.RH.1.3; LAFS.68.RH.2.5; LAFS.68.RH.3.7

KEY VOCABULARY		NAMES & PLACES	
cataract	pharaoh	Lower Egypt	Nile River
delta	vizier	Menes	Upper Egypt
dynasty			

SECTION 2 **THE OLD AND MIDDLE KINGDOMS**

SS.6.E.1.1; SS.6.G.4.1; SS.6.W.1.3; SS.6.W.2.4; SS.6.W.2.5; SS.6.W.2.6;
LAFS.68.RH.1.1; LAFS.68.RH.1.2; LAFS.68.RH.2.5; LAFS.68.RH.3.7;
LAFS.68.WHST.1.2; LAFS.68.WHST.3.9

KEY VOCABULARY		NAMES & PLACES	
hierarchy	pyramid	Ahmose	Old
mummy		Hyksos	Kingdom
		Khufu	Re
		Middle	
		Kingdom	

SECTION 3 **THE NEW KINGDOM**

SS.6.E.1.1; SS.6.E.1.3; SS.6.E.2.1; SS.6.E.3.2; SS.6.E.3.3; SS.6.E.3.4; SS.6.G.1.4; SS.6.G.1.6;
SS.6.G.1.7; SS.6.G.2.1; SS.6.G.2.3; SS.6.G.2.4; SS.6.G.2.6; SS.6.W.2.4; SS.6.W.2.6;
SS.6.W.3.18; LAFS.68.RH.2.5; LAFS.68.RH.3.7; LAFS.68.RH.3.8

KEY VOCABULARY	NAMES & PLACES	
barter	Hatshepsut	Nubia
	Kush	Ramses II
	New	
	Kingdom	

SECTION 4 **THE EGYPTIAN LEGACY**

SS.6.G.2.6; SS.6.W.2.3; SS.6.W.2.5; LAFS.68.RH.1.2; LAFS.68.RH.2.4; LAFS.68.RH.3.7

KEY VOCABULARY	
hieroglyph	scribe
papyrus	

READING STRATEGY

DRAW CONCLUSIONS
When you draw conclusions, you use the facts in a text to make educated guesses. As you read the chapter, use an organizer like this one to draw conclusions about the importance of ancient Egypt's geographic features.

```
        Conclusion
      /          \
  Evidence      Evidence
```

Egyptian ruler Ramses II built this massive temple at Abu Simbel to honor Egypt's gods—and himself. Each of the four 66-foot statues is an image of Ramses.

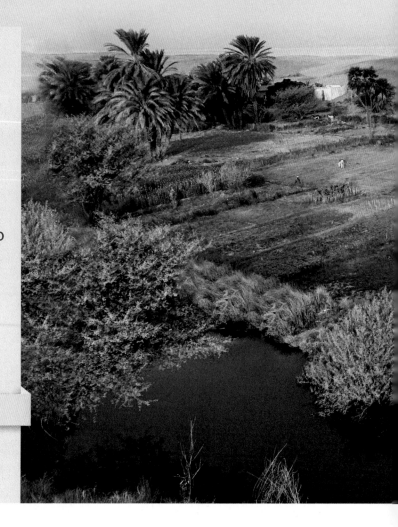

1.1 The Geography of Ancient Egypt

"Hail to thee, O Nile! Who manifests thyself over this land and comes to give life to Egypt!" These words written 4,000 years ago emphasize the importance of the Nile River to Egyptians: No Nile, no life, no Egypt. It was that simple.

MAIN IDEA

The Nile was the source of life in Egypt's dry, barren deserts.

THE GIFT OF THE NILE

The **Nile River** was central to the civilization that developed in Egypt. At around 4,132 miles in length, it is the world's longest river. It flows northward from sources deep in Africa to the Mediterranean Sea. Six **cataracts**, rock formations that create churning rapids, break the river's smooth course. The 550 miles from the most northerly cataract to the Mediterranean Sea formed ancient Egypt's heartland, which was divided into two distinct regions: the Upper (southern) Nile and the Lower (northern) Nile. The Lower Nile region included the Nile Delta, next to the Mediterranean. A **delta** is an area where a river fans out into various branches as it flows into a body of water.

The Nile was generally a peaceful river. Its current carried ships gently downstream, while the winds above it usually blew upstream, making it easy for ships to row downstream or sail upstream.

Water was the Nile's greatest gift. Without it there could be no agriculture in Egypt's desert. Every year faraway rains sent a surge of water downstream to Egypt, swelling the river with the annual flood.

Unlike the rivers of Mesopotamia, the Nile's flood was predictable, occurring every summer. The waters spilled over the riverbanks, depositing another great gift: silt, or very fine particles carried from upriver. The silt-enriched soil was fertile, or full of nutrients to support abundant crops. This soil made agriculture extremely productive—a key to the development of Egyptian civilization. With good management and a little luck, the soil delivered huge harvests.

THE BLACK LAND AND THE RED LAND

Egypt's climate was consistently dry, and sunshine was plentiful. Seven months of hot, sunny weather were followed by a

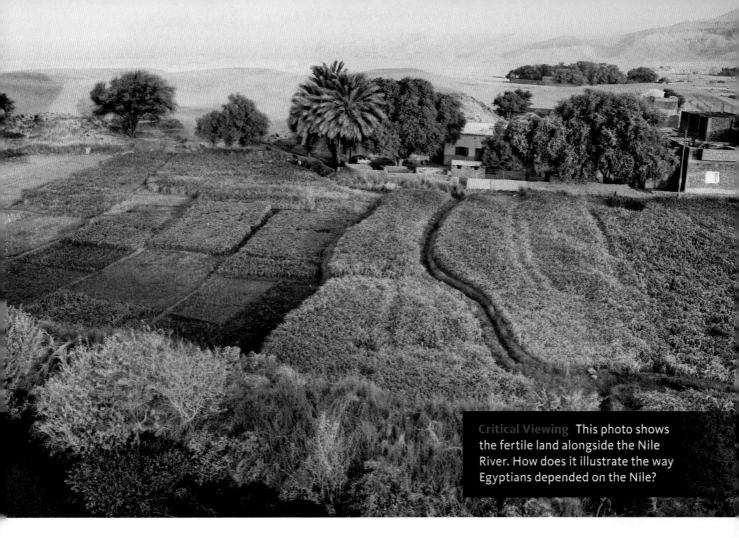

winter of mild, sunny weather. The lack of rainfall created a landscape of striking contrast, made up of regions called the "black land" and the "red land."

The black land was the narrow stretch that ran along both sides of the Nile. There, the river's waters and nourishing dark silt allowed plants to grow and people to live.

The red land was a vast, scorching desert that surrounded the Nile. This desert formed a powerful barrier against invasion and helped separate Egypt from the world beyond. The seemingly empty desert also held a treasure trove of raw materials, including stone for building and gold. The only major resource Egypt lacked was timber.

Egypt's geography, its climate, and—above all—the Nile River all played parts in the kind of civilization that Egypt would become. The land was rich in resources, produced a huge food surplus, and had well-protected borders. In addition, Egypt was a crossroads for trade, lying along important trade routes connecting Africa, the Mediterranean, the Red Sea, and the Middle East. The scene was set for Africa's most famous civilization of ancient times.

REVIEW & ASSESS

1. **READING CHECK** Why was the Nile River essential to life in ancient Egypt?

2. **ANALYZE CAUSE AND EFFECT** What effect did the annual flooding of the Nile River have on the development of agriculture in Egypt?

3. **COMPARE AND CONTRAST** What did the black and red lands have in common? How were they different?

1.2   Agriculture
Develops

It's August, and all that can be seen of the flooded fields is water lapping at the stones marking each farmer's boundary. In the dark of night, a farmer paddles nervously out and shifts the stones to steal a few feet from his neighbor. It's a profitable but serious crime—the penalty is death. Farmland in Egypt is so valuable that some are willing to risk it.

MAIN IDEA

Agriculture encouraged the development of communities and kingdoms in Egypt.

THE FERTILE NILE DELTA

Five thousand years ago, the lives of most Egyptians revolved around farming. Along with raising livestock, Egyptians grew a wide variety of crops such as wheat, barley, beans, lentils, peas, onions, and leeks. Fruits included grapes, dates, figs, and watermelons. Farmers grew flax to make cloth. Fish and birds were plentiful, and even poor Egyptians could eat well.

The cycles of the river dictated the farming year. From July to October, the fields were flooded, so farmers did other work. When the floods receded, farmers plowed the soft ground, scattered seeds, and used animals to trample the seeds into the soil. The growing crops were carefully watered through irrigation. Farmers captured floodwater in artificial lakes and channeled it to the fields. Later, the shaduf (shuh-DOOF) made irrigation easier. This tool was a long pole with a bucket on one end and a weight on the other. Farmers could use a shaduf to effortlessly lift water to their fields. The grain harvest started in mid-March. During the hot summer that followed, farmers prepared their fields before the next flood.

Irrigation and the Nile's fertile soil allowed for extremely productive farming. As in Mesopotamia, successful farming generated surpluses, which led to population growth, trade, and specialized jobs. Building and maintaining irrigation networks took a lot of labor, so farmers grouped together to create larger communities. Leadership was needed to coordinate and manage these increasingly complex societies. As villages grew into towns, village chiefs became kings.

TWO KINGDOMS ARISE

Some historians believe that by around 3200 B.C., two kings ruled over two separate kingdoms—**Upper Egypt** and **Lower Egypt**. Lower Egypt was the Nile Delta region with its wide expanse of fertile land and access to the Mediterranean Sea. Upper Egypt was the long, narrow stretch of the Nile south of modern Cairo and hemmed in by desert.

The Nile served as a superhighway, encouraging contact between Upper and Lower Egypt. Movement along the Nile was easy, and all the villages and towns were located near the great river. Goods and ideas were traded freely between the kingdoms, unifying Egyptians economically and culturally. Unlike Mesopotamia, Egypt would come to be a strong, unified state rather than a group of city-states.

However, Upper Egypt and Lower Egypt remained proudly distinct. Even after Egypt was united, it was represented by a double crown. Every time Egypt descended into disorder, the two kingdoms were usually on opposite sides of the power struggle.

Mediterranean Sea

Nile River Delta

Tanis

Pi-Ramses

LOWER EGYPT

UPPER EGYPT AND
LOWER EGYPT, c. 3200 B.C.

Giza
Saqqara   Memphis

Nile R.

Eastern

Desert

Western

Desert

UPPER
EGYPT

This map is a satellite photo with lines
and labels added to show the borders
of ancient Egypt and its important cities.

Desert lands

Fertile land near the Nile

Nile River

Nile R.

Red Sea

Luxor
Thebes

Hierakonpolis

S A H A R A

N
W   E
S

0   50   100 Miles

0   50   100 Kilometers

Aswan (Syene)

REVIEW & ASSESS

1. READING CHECK What role did the Nile play in Egypt's early development?

2. DESCRIBE What techniques did ancient Egyptian farmers use to make their farming more productive?

3. INTERPRET MAPS How does this map highlight the effect of the Nile River on agriculture?

Egypt Unites

Egypt's ancient civilization was unified for close to 3,000 years—twelve times as long as the United States has been a country. Of course, ancient Egypt witnessed its share of good rulers and good times and bad rulers and bad times. Still, ancient Egypt will be long remembered for its wealth and power.

MAIN IDEA

Strong kings united Egypt and ruled with the authority of gods.

DYNASTIES BEGIN

Egypt was governed by a long series of strong rulers. Exactly how Egypt united under a single ruler is uncertain. Tradition says that around 3100 B.C., the king of Upper Egypt conquered Lower Egypt and became ruler of all Egypt. Historians believe this king was called **Menes** (MEH-nehz). The complete unification of Egypt was probably a process that took place over the reigns of the kings who followed Menes. A double crown that combined the white crown of Upper Egypt with the red crown of Lower Egypt symbolized the newly unified country.

During this early period, the Egyptians built a magnificent new capital city at Memphis (MEHM-fihs). They also established the foundations of Egypt's political, economic, technological, artistic, and religious practices. The first kings founded a ruling **dynasty** (DY-nuh-stee)—a series of rulers from the same family. Egypt had 31 dynasties and was ruled by a total of more than 330 kings.

PHARAOHS RULE

Even though Egyptians did not call their kings **pharaoh** (FEHR-oh) until after 1000 B.C., the title is generally used for all Egyptian kings. The people used the term because they were afraid to speak the king's name. Why did the pharaoh inspire such fear in his subjects? He had complete authority over all religious, civil, and military matters. He exercised absolute power of life and death over everyone. A pharaoh was more than a man; he was worshipped as the son of Egypt's gods and a living god himself.

In Egypt, religion and government strongly overlapped. The pharaoh's main religious role was to keep harmony by maintaining communication between Egypt's people and their gods. He was high priest of every temple and led the most important ceremonies, especially the New Year rituals to ensure bountiful harvests. With this godly role came risk. Success reinforced the pharaoh's power. Defeat, disease, or famine threatened his authority.

On the government side, the pharaoh dictated all the important decisions. He also led his armies into battle as commander-in-chief. However, much of his day-to-day work was actually done by his **viziers** (vuh-ZEERZ), or chief officials. At first each pharaoh had one vizier. Later pharaohs had two viziers—one ran Upper Egypt and the other ran Lower Egypt. Thousands of lesser officials supported the viziers.

Most pharaohs were men and had many wives. Commonly, the eldest son of the pharaoh's principal wife inherited the throne. He often ruled alongside his father, learning on the job and ensuring a smooth succession (the passing of the throne to the next ruler) when the pharaoh died.

Critical Viewing This carving shows a pharaoh wearing the double crown of Egypt. Why was it important for the pharaohs to wear the double crown?

REVIEW & ASSESS

1. **READING CHECK** What made the pharaohs of ancient Egypt so strong and powerful?

2. **DRAW CONCLUSIONS** Why would disease or famine threaten the pharaoh's authority over the people?

3. **ANALYZE LANGUAGE USE** Why does the text refer to Egypt's rulers as *strong*?

Sensing Under the Surface

"Indiana Jones is so old school," laughs National Geographic Explorer Sarah Parcak. "I'm sorry, Indy, but things have moved on!" Parcak should know—she's a leading specialist in satellite archaeology. She is pioneering technology that archaeologists never would have dreamed of decades ago.

^ After identifying the likely location of an ancient city, Sarah Parcak and her team head for the site to begin the hands-on excavation. Together, technology and muscle power are revealing ancient Egypt.

MAIN IDEA

Sarah Parcak uses satellite imagery to guide her archaeological excavations in Egypt.

SATELLITE TECHNOLOGY

Sarah Parcak prepares for another tough day of searching beneath Egypt's desert for evidence of ancient Egyptian civilization and its people's daily lives. However, instead of digging, she boots up her laptop.

Parcak relies on remote sensing, using powerful infrared cameras mounted on satellites. These cameras use invisible rays of light to pinpoint even small objects buried beneath sand, soil, vegetation, or new buildings. "The Egyptians built with mud-bricks, which are denser than the surrounding soil," explains Parcak. "The infrared picks out this denser material. Computer programs refine the detail until we start to see recognizable shapes— houses, streets, temples, tombs, and pyramids. It's a real 'wow' moment."

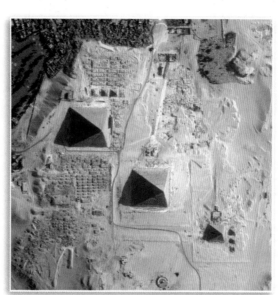

A satellite image of the Great Pyramid of Giza

Yet these revelations only happen after painstaking processing and analysis. "We don't just grab an image, flip it into the computer, and press a button. I've spent more than 10,000 hours of my life staring at satellite imagery to understand what I'm seeing," says Parcak. This effort pays off, saving enormous amounts of time and money. Before leading an expedition to Egypt, Parcak analyzed satellite imagery to figure out exactly where to dig. Within three weeks, she found about 70 sites. With traditional methods, this research would have taken around three and a half years.

MAPPING TANIS

Parcak's hard work has uncovered the main settlement area of Tanis, an important city in the eastern part of the Nile Delta. Over the centuries, Tanis was flooded and buried beneath Nile silt. Until recently only a tiny area had been excavated, but archaeologists, with the help of remote sensing, are changing that. Parcak turned the cameras onto Tanis with startling results. "We've created a map of this ancient city that's so clear it looks like something you'd use to navigate a town today," she says.

Excavations on the ground are proving the value of remote sensing. Scientists found an 80 percent match between the satellite image and the houses they unearthed. "This isn't just another 'gee whiz' toy," Parcak claims. "Less than one percent of ancient Egypt has been discovered and excavated, and, with the pressures of urbanization [the growth of cities], we're in a race against time. We need to use the most advanced tools to explore, map, and protect our past." Right now, satellites are just the tools for the job.

REVIEW & ASSESS

1. **READING CHECK** How does satellite imagery help guide Sarah Parcak's archaeological excavations in Egypt?

2. **COMPARE AND CONTRAST** What advantages does satellite archaeology have compared to more traditional methods of archaeology?

3. **MAKE INFERENCES** Why do you think urbanization creates a problem for the discovery and exploration of ancient Egyptian sites?

The Old Kingdom

It is taller than the Statue of Liberty, twice the area of the U.S. Capitol building, double the volume of the Rose Bowl Stadium, and 4,500 years older than all of them. For thousands of years, the Great Pyramid of Khufu was the largest structure on the planet.

MAIN IDEA

Old Kingdom pharaohs demonstrated their power by building monumental pyramids.

PYRAMIDS ALONG THE NILE

The **Old Kingdom** was Egypt's first great period of unity and prosperity, lasting from around 2700 B.C. to 2200 B.C. During these centuries, Egypt prospered under effective pharaohs, a strong central government, and an efficient administration. As Egyptian power grew, trade, technology, building, writing, and art also flourished. The pharaohs used their enormous wealth and power to build the **pyramids** (PEER-uh-mihdz), massive monumental tombs to house their dead bodies. The pyramids represented the Egyptian belief that life is a passageway to the afterlife, an existence believed to follow death. As a result, people made careful preparations for death.

Egyptian kings were originally buried beneath low mud-brick buildings. Around 2650 B.C., King Djoser (JOH-sur) took this idea to the next level—literally. Djoser's talented vizier, Imhotep (ihm-HOH-tehp), designed a 200-foot-high tomb made of giant steps. Beneath this step pyramid was a maze of chambers packed with items for the pharaoh's spirit to use in the afterlife. A huge complex of buildings and temples surrounded the step pyramid, creating a palace where the king's spirit could live in luxury for eternity.

THE GREAT PYRAMID

In Giza (GEE-zuh), near Cairo, the Great Pyramid of **Khufu** (KOO-foo) dominates the skyline. It is so extraordinarily huge that historians once assumed Khufu had been a cruel tyrant who used brutal methods to build it. In fact, he probably employed farmers unable to farm during the annual floods. Even so, Khufu must have commanded exceptional power and wealth to build his Great Pyramid.

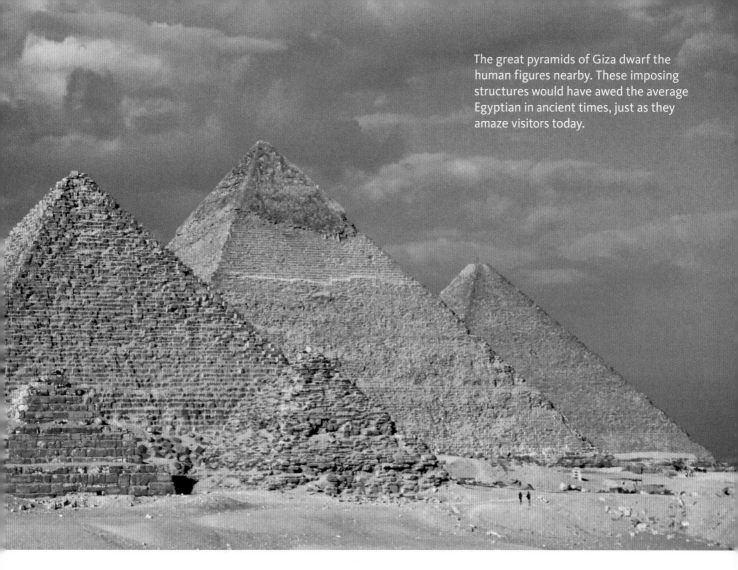

The great pyramids of Giza dwarf the human figures nearby. These imposing structures would have awed the average Egyptian in ancient times, just as they amaze visitors today.

The pyramids were an impressive achievement for a civilization with limited technology. Using copper tools, ropes, sleds, and ramps, some 18,000 workers quarried, cut, and precisely placed 2.3 million two-and-a-half-ton limestone and granite blocks. It took 20 years. The pyramid they built was symmetrical—all sides were the same. It covered 571,158 square feet and stood 481 feet high. Deep inside were Khufu's tomb and treasure. Two other large pyramids were built in Giza by Khufu's successors, Menkaure (mehn-KO-ray) and Khafre (KAH-fray). Khafre also built the Great Sphinx (sfihnks), a symbol of divine power with a lion's body and Khafre's head. The sphinx was carved out of a huge piece of limestone.

The Great Pyramid was a powerful symbol of the pharaoh's status as a living god and the unity of religion and government in Egypt. A proper burial within the great tomb would ensure the pharaoh's smooth passage to life after death. Until then, a vast city of pyramid builders surrounded Giza. Here, too, were palaces and government buildings that allowed the pharaoh to run the country while building his home for the afterlife.

REVIEW & ASSESS

1. **READING CHECK** Why did Old Kingdom pharaohs build pyramids?

2. **DESCRIBE** What was new and different about the design of King Djoser's burial building?

3. **DRAW CONCLUSIONS** What do the pyramids reveal about Egyptian society?

2.2 Daily Life and Religion

 There's a saying that "you can't take it with you" when you die. But Egyptians did! In fact, they were buried with everything they might need in the afterlife. The graves of wealthy Egyptians contained food, furniture, and jewelry. The Egyptians were ready for anything.

MAIN IDEA

The Egyptians had strong beliefs about religion and burial that affected all social classes.

Eight Gods of Ancient Egypt

Horus Sky god

Hathor Goddess of love, birth, and death

Re God of the sun (sometimes called Ra)

Nut Sky goddess

Anubis God of the dead

Osiris God of agriculture and judge of the dead

Isis Wife of Osiris and mother of Horus

Thoth God of writing, counting, and wisdom

EGYPTIAN SOCIETY

Ancient Egypt's society was a **hierarchy** (HY-rar-kee), meaning that people belonged to different social classes and each class had a rank in society. The social structure resembled Egypt's pyramids. At the top was the pharaoh, the all-powerful ruler and living god.

Beneath the pharaoh came the priests and nobles who ran the country and army. At the next step in the pyramid were all the officials and scribes who kept the government running smoothly by collecting taxes, organizing building projects, and keeping records. Beneath the officials and scribes were craftsmen and merchants. Farmers formed the next layer, and at the bottom came unskilled laborers and slaves who did all the hardest work.

Unlike in Mesopotamia, Egyptian women shared some rights with men. They could own property, conduct business, and take part in court cases. Poorer women often worked alongside their husbands, but they could do almost any job. Still, a woman's main role was to be a wife and raise children.

EGYPTIAN GODS

Like the people of Mesopotamia, the Egyptians believed in multiple gods. Modern scholars know 1,500 of them by name. The Egyptians believed that the gods controlled every aspect of life and death. The most important god was **Re** (RAY), the sun god, who created the world. The Egyptians also worshipped Osiris (oh-SY-rihs), the god of the underworld. The god Anubis (uh-NOO-bihs) weighed each dead person's heart against the weight of an ostrich feather. If the person was good, his or her heart would weigh the same as the feather, and the person would be admitted to the afterlife.

These beliefs encouraged Egyptians to lead good lives and take burial seriously. They believed a dead person's spirit needed food and a body to live in. The spirit would need to recognize the body after death. That is why the bodies of pharaohs and other powerful people were preserved as **mummies**. Specialized workers removed and preserved the internal organs (except for the heart, which Anubis had to weigh). Then the workers dried out the body and wrapped it in linen. Last, the body was placed in a coffin, and priests performed special rituals that were intended to give life to the mummy.

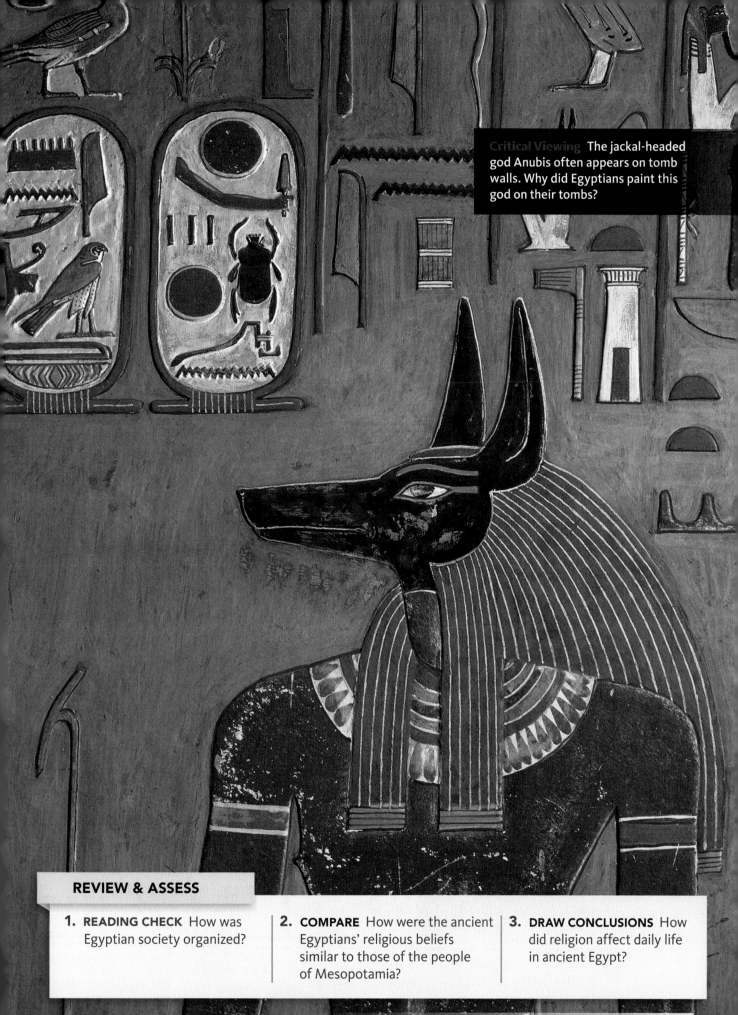

The jackal-headed god Anubis often appears on tomb walls. Why did Egyptians paint this god on their tombs?

REVIEW & ASSESS

1. **READING CHECK** How was Egyptian society organized?

2. **COMPARE** How were the ancient Egyptians' religious beliefs similar to those of the people of Mesopotamia?

3. **DRAW CONCLUSIONS** How did religion affect daily life in ancient Egypt?

DOCUMENT-BASED QUESTION

Life, Death, and Religion

The majority of ancient Egyptians could not read or write. Still, a vast amount of writing has survived in the form of official records, business transactions, religious texts, technical manuals, and stories. These documents tell us a lot about life in ancient Egypt.

The ancient Egyptian *Book of the Dead* helped archaeologists learn much about the civilization's religious beliefs. Here, a section of the book illustrates a vision of the afterlife that closely resembles the living world.

from *Hymn to the Nile*, c. 2100 B.C., translated by Paul Guieysse

Hymn to the Nile is a religious poem. It may have been read aloud at festivals celebrating the annual Nile flood. It has about 200 lines divided into 14 verses, although historians are not sure how the verses should be read. The hymn praises the Nile as the source of all life in Egypt. It expresses the people's joy when the flood brings water and silt and their misery when the flood fails. The author is unknown.

CONSTRUCTED RESPONSE Why might ancient Egyptians have wanted to praise the Nile River each year by reciting this religious poem?

> Hail to thee, O Nile!
> Who manifests [reveals] thyself over this land, and comes to give life to Egypt!
> Mysterious is thy issuing forth from the darkness, on this day whereon it is celebrated!
> Watering the orchards created by Re, to cause all the cattle to live, you give the earth to drink, inexhaustible one!

from the *Book of the Dead*, 1240 B.C., translated by E.A. Wallis Budge

The *Book of the Dead* was a series of texts that contained around 200 spells for helping the dead reach the afterlife. The texts were usually placed in the coffin or in the mummy's wrappings. This passage describes the sun god's journey as he rises and sets each day.

CONSTRUCTED RESPONSE What does this passage suggest about Re's role in ancient Egyptian beliefs?

> The gods are glad [when] they see Re in his rising; his beams flood the world with light. The majesty of the god, who is to be feared, sets forth and comes unto the land of Manu [a sacred place]; he makes bright the earth at his birth each day; he comes unto the place where he was yesterday.

Primary Source: Artifact

Sun God Re in Falcon Form, Ancient Egypt

This statue depicts Re, god of the sun and creator of Earth.

CONSTRUCTED RESPONSE What can you infer about Re's connection to nature from his representation in this statue?

SYNTHESIZE & WRITE

1. **REVIEW** Review what you have learned about ancient Egyptian religious beliefs from the text and these documents.

2. **RECALL** On your own paper, write down the main idea expressed in the artifact and in each document.

3. **CONSTRUCT** Construct a topic sentence that answers this question: What did the Egyptians believe about their gods' control of their world?

4. **WRITE** Using the evidence from the artifact and documents, write an informative paragraph that supports your topic sentence in Step 3.

2.4 The Middle Kingdom

First comes the thunder of hooves, then the whistling of arrows. Through the dust of battle bursts a line of horse-drawn chariots. From these wheeled wooden platforms, enemy archers rain arrows into your ranks before crashing through them, scattering your Egyptian army. These foreign war machines are effective; it's time to adopt, adapt, and fight back.

MAIN IDEA

The Middle Kingdom was strong and peaceful between periods of weakness and foreign rule.

CONFLICT AND STABILITY

The peace and prosperity of the Old Kingdom gave way to chaos and war between rival Egyptian groups around 2200 B.C. Building monumental tombs had drained the royal treasury. Water shortages and famines made the people doubt the pharaoh's power as a living god. The kingdom descended into a long period of conflict within its borders.

Then, around 2040 B.C., a king named Mentuhotep II (mehn-too-HOH-tehp) reunited the kingdom and launched a new era of peace and prosperity known as the **Middle Kingdom**. This period

lasted until about 1650 B.C. During the Middle Kingdom, the pharaohs restored the power of the centralized government. Farmers expanded agriculture into new regions, and the building of great monuments, including pyramids, resumed.

The pharaohs also pursued an active foreign policy to increase Egypt's wealth. Trade expanded greatly. Egypt's trade network reached to several nearby lands and possibly as far as East Africa. To support and expand the prosperity of the Middle Kingdom, the pharaohs increased Egypt's military power. In the northeast, they conquered lands along the eastern Mediterranean. They also extended Egypt's southern border further up the Nile by leading successful military campaigns against the kingdoms of Nubia (NOO-bee-uh).

INVADERS

Egypt's wealth made a tempting target. One group of foreigners, the **Hyksos** (HIHK-sohs), came to live in Egypt and rose to power in Lower Egypt. The Hyksos brought an end to the Middle Kingdom.

Hyksos means "rulers of foreign lands," and, from their capital Avaris (AH-var-ihs) in the Nile Delta, they controlled much of Egypt for more than 100 years. The Hyksos probably ruled pretty much as the pharaohs had, adopting native ways and practices. Even so, native Egyptians resented being under foreign rule. Finally, in Upper Egypt, King **Ahmose** (AH-mohz) rebelled. The Hyksos brought to the battlefield deadly new tools including horse-drawn chariots, powerful new bows, curved swords, and body armor. Ahmose adopted these deadly weapons and threw the invaders out of Egypt.

Although Ahmose reunited Egypt under native Egyptian rule, he faced new challenges. Egypt had been largely on its own for centuries, but now the pharaohs had to deal with the wider world. Armed with their new military might, the pharaohs set out to forge an empire.

Critical Viewing This pendant depicts the pharaoh Ahmose being purified by the gods Re and Amun. Why is the pharaoh shown with the gods?

REVIEW & ASSESS

1. **READING CHECK** Who were the Hyksos?

2. **ANALYZE CAUSE AND EFFECT** Why did the pharaohs lose control of the Old Kingdom?

3. **SEQUENCE EVENTS** What events marked Egypt's movements back and forth between disorder and order?

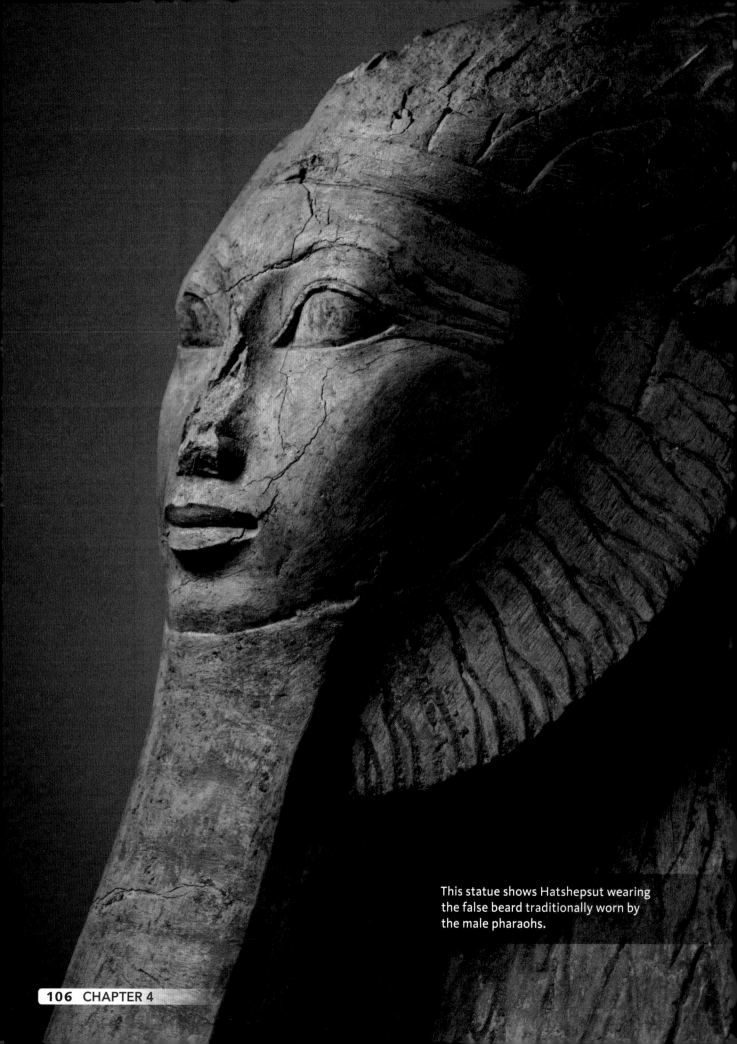

This statue shows Hatshepsut wearing the false beard traditionally worn by the male pharaohs.

Hatshepsut Expands Trade

At any grocery store, you can find exotic fruits from distant lands right alongside the crunchy apples from a nearby orchard. Like you, the ancient Egyptians had access to food and other goods from near and far.

MAIN IDEA

Under a great female pharaoh, Egypt grew wealthy through conquest and trade.

EGYPT'S GREAT FEMALE RULER

On the heels of the defeat of the Hyksos came the **New Kingdom**, which spanned nearly 500 years from 1550 B.C. to 1070 B.C. This period of prosperity saw Egypt grow more powerful than ever as it built a mighty empire. Its large professional army expanded the empire northeast into Palestine and south into Nubia. Plunder from war and taxes from conquered lands made Egypt rich, but so did trade. Under the rule of **Hatshepsut** (haht-SHEHP-soot), history's earliest well-known female ruler, trade flourished.

Hatshepsut came to power sometime around 1470 B.C. After her husband the pharaoh died, she ruled with her stepson, Thutmose III (thoot-MOH-suh), who was very young. Hatshepsut played a smart political game and won enough support to be crowned sole king. She performed all the religious, military, and political functions of the pharaoh, and she even dressed as a king.

TRADE AND EXPANSION

Like other pharaohs, Hatshepsut fought wars to expand the empire. But she also promoted trade in spite of the geographic barriers Egypt faced, such as deserts to the east and west and rapids on the Nile River and the Mediterranean Sea. Egypt had abundant resources to **barter**, or exchange, for things the land couldn't produce—especially timber and exotic luxuries. These goods traveled along routes over land and sea as far as East Africa. Egyptian merchants and traders bartered Egyptian beer, wine, food, and manufactured goods for myrrh trees, incense, ebony, ivory, leopard skins, and monkeys. The wealth generated through these expeditions stimulated Egypt's economy.

Back in Egypt, Hatshepsut moved the capital city to Thebes and ordered many great monuments constructed to celebrate her rule. After 15 years in power, she disappeared suspiciously, possibly murdered by her stepson. Thutmose III became a mighty pharaoh in his own right and tried to erase Hatshepsut's name from all monuments and records. Luckily, he did not entirely succeed, and historians have been able to reconstruct Hatshepsut's remarkable reign.

REVIEW & ASSESS

1. **READING CHECK** In what ways did Egypt prosper during the reign of Hatshepsut?

2. **DRAW CONCLUSIONS** Why did the pharaohs engage in trade with other countries?

3. **FORM AND SUPPORT OPINIONS** What details support the opinion that Hatshepsut was an ambitious leader?

RAMSES II

RULED
1279 B.C. – 1213 B.C.

The women and children wail, and the men look up to the sun god in desperation. After ruling for 66 years, the pharaoh is dead. Most Egyptians have known no other king, and the dead pharaoh wasn't just any ruler. He was **Ramses II**—also known as Ramses the Great, a man who earned his title. Egypt was never more powerful than during Ramses' long reign.

- 💼 **Job:** Pharaoh of Egypt
- 📝 **Education:** Ruled alongside his father, Seti I
- 🌐 **Home:** Pi-Ramses

FINEST HOUR

He led Egypt's army against the Hittites at the Battle of Kadesh around 1274 B.C.

WORST MOMENT

He saw 12 of his sons die before he did.

FRIENDS

The people loved him, affectionately calling him Sese (SEH-say), a nickname for "Ramses." He had about 200 wives and more than 100 children.

TRIVIA

His mummified nose was stuffed with peppercorns to keep its distinctive shape. When his mummy was exhibited in Paris, it received the Presidential Guard of Honor reserved for visiting royalty.

A LONG AND POWERFUL REIGN

Lasting 66 years, Ramses' (RAM-zeez) reign was one of the longest in Egyptian history. Ramses expanded Egypt's empire south into Nubia, west into Libya, and into the eastern Mediterranean. There he clashed with another ancient people, the Hittites (HIH-tyts).

The Hittites had a powerful empire centered around present-day Turkey, and they also sought to control the eastern Mediterranean. In his fifth year as pharaoh, Ramses fought a huge battle against the Hittites at Kadesh (kay-DEHSH). The battle stopped the Hittites' advance, but war with the Hittites dragged on for more than 15 years. At last, Ramses wrote letters to the Hittite king and negotiated a peace treaty. Peace with the Hittites and Egypt's territorial expansion helped Ramses create a strong economy.

Ramses went on to carve his legacy in stone and make himself unforgettable. First he built a new capital city, which he

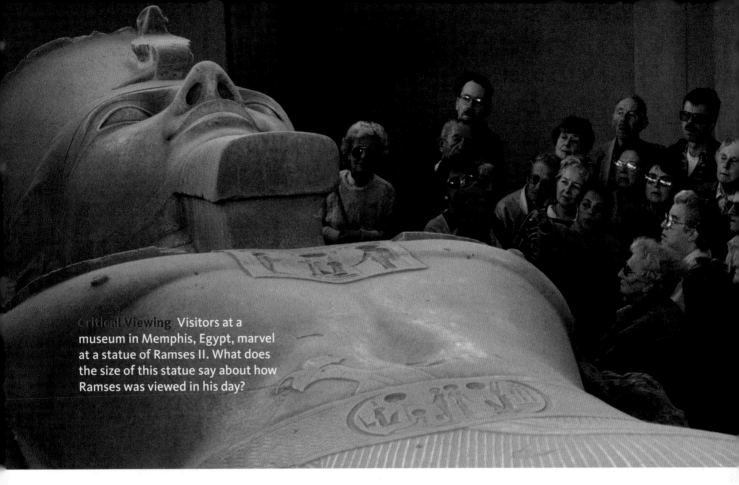

Critical Viewing Visitors at a museum in Memphis, Egypt, marvel at a statue of Ramses II. What does the size of this statue say about how Ramses was viewed in his day?

called Pi-Ramses (puh-RAM-zeez). Then he commissioned an awesome number of temples, monuments, and statues. At Abu Simbel (ah-boo SIHM-buhl) in Egyptian-controlled Nubia, Ramses had two cavernous temples carved out of the rock cliff face. His massive tomb at Thebes had a long wait for him—Ramses outlived 12 sons, dying in 1213 B.C. at more than 90 years of age.

THE NEW KINGDOM ENDS

Egypt's power was at its peak under Ramses the Great. After his death, several challenges emerged. Members of the ruling dynasty clashed with each other. In addition, Egypt was repeatedly invaded by a group known as the Sea Peoples.

Although they never conquered Egypt, the Sea Peoples waged a lengthy war that left Egypt's civilization weak and unstable.

In the years following the New Kingdom, Egypt was conquered and controlled by various foreign powers. First the Libyans and then the Nubians seized large areas of land. Later, another people from Southwest Asia, the Persians, conquered Egypt. After 332 B.C., Egypt came under the control of the Macedonians, a people from the Greek peninsula. The final pharaohs were all Macedonians, right down to the last one, the famous Cleopatra VII. When Rome conquered Egypt in 30 B.C., Cleopatra committed suicide. It was a suitably dramatic end to 3,000 years of pharaohs.

REVIEW & ASSESS

1. **READING CHECK** What weakened Egypt's power after the death of Ramses II?

2. **MAKE INFERENCES** Why did peace with the Hittites help strengthen Egypt's economy?

3. **COMPARE AND CONTRAST** Think about Ramses II and Hatshepsut. What did these two strong pharaohs have in common?

3.3

TUT'S TREASURES

Funerary Mask
The magnificent gold mask was placed over the mummy's head inside the coffin.

Ointment Jar
The alabaster jar held precious oil for the pharaoh's spirit to use in the afterlife.

In 1922, archaeologist Howard Carter broke through into tomb KV62 in the Valley of the Kings. There he discovered the first-ever intact royal tomb and treasures beyond the wildest imagination. The discovery turned an otherwise unremarkable pharaoh, Tutankhamen (too-tang-KAH-muhn), into a worldwide superstar. Sometime after 1330 B.C., Tutankhamen became pharaoh at the age of eight—he died just nine years later. The unique and priceless treasures of Tutankhamen's tomb have taught us a lot about the boy king, the pharaohs, and ancient Egypt. What do these treasures reveal about the ancient Egyptians' views of the afterlife?

Bed for a Pharaoh
The tomb contained a bed with gold hippopotamus heads for bedposts.

Bracelet
The lavish gold bracelet is adorned with a scarab beetle made of lapis lazuli, a precious stone.

Gold Dagger
The dagger was found in the mummy's wrappings.

Crook and Flail
Carried by the pharaoh in life, they were symbols of his power.

Gold Sandals
Tut's footwear for the afterlife was made of gold.

Pectoral
A pectoral was a jewel worn on the chest.

Necklace
Gold and semiprecious stones make up the falcon necklace.

Scarab Pendant
The jewel is inscribed with Tutankhamen's name.

Hawk Statue
The carving of a hawk is gilded, or covered in a thin layer of gold.

3.4 The **Rise** of **Kush**

How well do you know your neighbors? How do their lives affect yours? From annoyingly loud parties to borrowing tools or exchanging gifts, neighbors interact. Egypt couldn't ignore its closest neighbor, Nubia.

MAIN IDEA

The Nubian kingdom of Kush followed Egypt as a center of power, culture, and trade.

KUSH CONTROLS EGYPT

Just south of Egypt, across the first cataract of the Nile, lay the land of **Nubia**. Rich in gold, copper, and other important resources needed by Egypt, Nubia also provided a critical trade route for exotic goods from central Africa. This helps explain why the histories of Egypt and Nubia are so deeply connected. Early Nubia was a collection of chiefdoms dominated by Egypt. Later, when stronger Nubian kingdoms emerged, Egypt took more active control of its southern neighbor. It conquered and colonized large areas of Nubia, and Nubia's people adopted many Egyptian practices and customs during a thousand years of direct rule. Eventually, however, the tables were turned.

In the generations following the reign of Ramses II, the Nubian kingdom of **Kush** asserted its independence. It grew strong and ambitious. The Kushite king, Piankhi, invaded Egypt, sweeping north to take control of Thebes, Memphis, and Upper and Lower Egypt. In 728 B.C., Piankhi united the kingdoms of Egypt and Kush under a new line of Kushite kings.

Piankhi did not think of himself as a foreign conqueror but as a traditional pharaoh reviving Egyptian traditions. The Kushite kings styled themselves as pharaohs and continued classic Egyptian religious, social, and political practices. They built pyramids, mummified their dead, and worshipped Egyptian gods.

Eventually, the Kushite kings came into conflict with the iron-weapon wielding superpower of Assyria to the northeast of Egypt. In the course of the war, Kush lost control of Egypt to the Assyrians. Some of the fighting was fierce; the city of Thebes was destroyed before the Kushite kings abandoned Egypt.

TRADE IN IRON AND GOLD

After being pushed out of Egypt, Kush continued to flourish as an independent power. Its capital, Napata (nah-PAH-tuh), had a palace and a temple to the Egyptian god Amun (AH-muhn), one of the creator gods. The city's strategic location across two major trade routes ensured that Kush remained an important center of international trade. The Kushites had stores of gold, and they began to mine and produce iron as well.

Around 590 B.C., the Kushite capital moved south to another important trading city called Meroë (MAIR-oh-ee). Here the Egyptian influence continued with royal pyramids and temples to Amun and the goddess Isis. The Nubians expanded their kingdom and opened up many new trading routes, especially for iron.

Because of its resources, Meroë remained an important economic and political center for several centuries. However, around A.D. 350, the Ethiopian kingdom of Axum destroyed Meroë and conquered Kush. Axum adopted a form of Christianity and gained much wealth from trade. The kingdom began to decline as Arab powers rose in the region, and Axum fell around 1000.

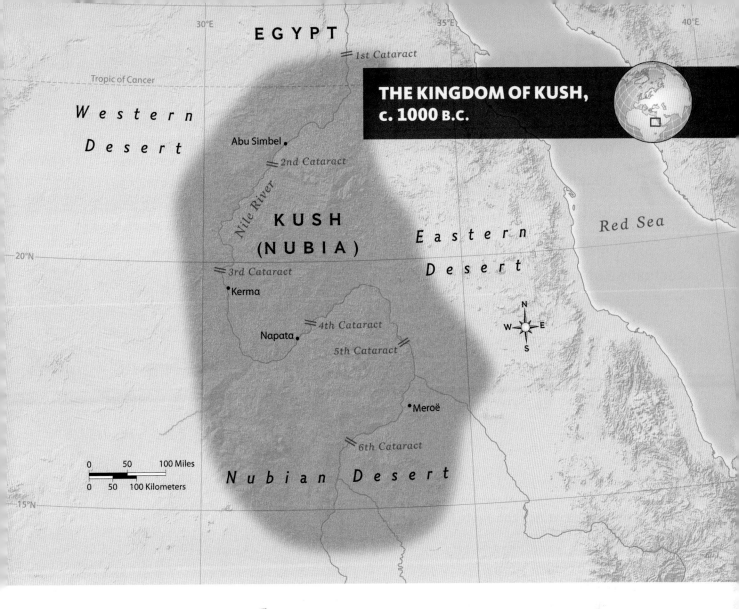

THE KINGDOM OF KUSH,
c. 1000 B.C.

EGYPT

Tropic of Cancer

Western
Desert

1st Cataract

Abu Simbel

2nd Cataract

Nile River

KUSH
(NUBIA)

Eastern
Desert

Red Sea

20°N

3rd Cataract

Kerma

Napata

4th Cataract

5th Cataract

Meroë

6th Cataract

Nubian Desert

0   50   100 Miles
0   50   100 Kilometers

15°N

GOLD

The importance of gold to Nubia is clear from its name. *Nub* was the Egyptian word for gold, and Nubia was rich with it. Skilled goldsmiths turned gold ore into intricate jewelry, such as this pendant of the goddess Isis.

REVIEW & ASSESS

1. **READING CHECK** In what ways did Kush follow Egypt as a center of power, culture, and trade in Africa?

2. **MAKE INFERENCES** Would life have changed a great deal for Egyptians living under the rule of the Kushite kings? Why or why not?

3. **INTERPRET MAPS** Why do you think Kushite kings established the kingdom's two capital cities—Napata and later Meroë—along the Nile River?

Hieroglyphs and Papyrus

You might be able to guess the meaning of some foreign words. But try reading a store bar code. The seemingly random arrangement of lines is actually a unique writing system telling you the product and price. To read it, you need to crack the code. Egyptian writing was just as baffling until archaeologists discovered the key—a slab of rock called the Rosetta Stone.

MAIN IDEA

The Egyptians valued writing and wrote for many purposes.

COMMON HIEROGLYPHS

Sun
(or day)

R
(a mouth symbol)

S
(a folded cloth symbol)

N
(water ripple)

WRITING AND WRITERS

Egyptian writing developed sometime before 3000 B.C., and it used **hieroglyphs** (HY-ruh-glihfs) instead of letters. A hieroglyph could be a picture representing an object, or it could represent a sound or an idea. By combining hieroglyphs, the Egyptians formed words and sentences.

The hieroglyphic writing system was very complex. There were nearly 800 hieroglyphs, no vowels, and very complicated rules. Few people mastered the skill of writing in hieroglyphs.

These special people were known as **scribes**, or professional writers, and they were among the most highly respected people in Egypt. It took five years of intense training to become a scribe, but the benefits made up for the hard work. Scribes were powerful, well paid, and had many privileges.

Reading and writing were just part of a scribe's job. Scribes were also skilled in art, mathematics, bookkeeping, law, engineering, and architecture. All scribes were important, but a really talented scribe could move up in Egypt's social hierarchy. One royal scribe eventually became the pharaoh Horemheb.

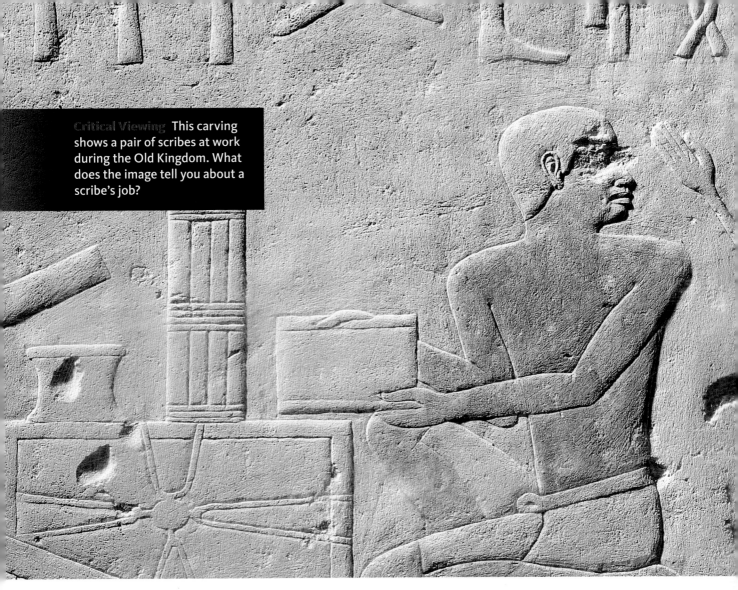

PAPER AND THE ROSETTA STONE

Hieroglyphs were painted and carved on tombs, temples, and monuments. For important documents, the Egyptians used sheets of a paperlike material called **papyrus** (puh-PY-ruhs), made from reeds that grew along the banks of the Nile. Sheets of papyrus could be glued together to make scrolls—some scrolls were several yards long. Papyrus was light and easy for a scribe to carry.

Eventually, the Egyptians abandoned the old forms of writing. For many years, scholars tried to crack the code of the hieroglyphs. Then, in A.D. 1799, a slab of rock was discovered near Rosetta, Egypt. On it was carved the same text in hieroglyphs, another form of writing, and Greek. Because scholars understood Greek, they were able to figure out what the hieroglyphs meant. Thanks to the Rosetta Stone, historians can read hieroglyphs and learn about the lives of the people who produced them.

REVIEW & ASSESS

1. **READING CHECK** How much time did it take to become a scribe in ancient Egypt?

2. **IDENTIFY MAIN IDEAS AND DETAILS** What details support the idea that scribes were among the most highly respected people in Egypt?

3. **MAKE INFERENCES** What does the complexity of the hieroglyphic writing system tell us about the role of scribes?

4.2 Medicine, Science, and Mathematics

The priest chants magic spells while the doctor applies a fragrant lotion to your wound. He carefully bandages it and gives you a foul-smelling medicine sweetened with honey. You gag on it, but the chances are you'll live. The ancient Egyptians were advanced medical practitioners for their time.

MAIN IDEA

Egyptians put their advanced knowledge of medicine, science, and mathematics to practical use.

CANOPIC JARS

Canopic (kuh-NOH-pihk) jars contained the internal organs of a mummified body. The head-shaped lids on the jars represent the sons of the god Horus.

MEDICINE

Egypt had the most advanced medical practices in the ancient world. Some ancient Egyptian science was so accurate that it formed the foundation of later medical practices in Europe. The Egyptians had developed a detailed understanding of anatomy through mummifying bodies. They identified the heart as the most important organ and the pulse as its "voice."

Doctors provided medicines made from plants and minerals, set broken bones, and even performed surgery. Researchers have found medical texts written on papyrus that give doctors instructions and advice for treating a variety of illnesses. Texts and carvings also show some of the surgical tools that doctors used to treat their patients. Magical spells to heal different illnesses were also considered part of medical treatment.

SCIENCE AND MATHEMATICS

Ancient Egyptians were gifted astronomers as well as talented doctors. Astronomy is the branch of science that studies the sun, moon, stars, planets, and space. By making observations of the moon, ancient Egyptian astronomers developed a 365-day calendar. It had 24-hour days, 10-day weeks, 3-week months, and 12-month years. The extra five days were added as birthdays for five gods and were considered unlucky.

The Egyptians were also excellent mathematicians. Like us, they used a decimal counting system that included fractions. However, they did not use zero. Egyptian mathematicians established several key principles of geometry, accurately calculating angles and areas. They could calculate the area of a circle and the volume of a pyramid or cylinder. These skills made it possible to design big buildings like the pyramids.

Less visible but equally impressive was their mastery of the mathematics needed to run an empire. Scribes accurately calculated how many workers would be needed for building projects and how much food they would eat. Similar assessments estimated trade profits, crop yields, and taxes. Along with trade and military might, math and science were foundations of ancient Egypt's civilization.

The mummy of Ramses II lies in the Cairo Museum. How did making mummies like this one advance medical knowledge?

REVIEW & ASSESS

1. **READING CHECK** How did ancient Egyptians put their advanced knowledge to practical use?

2. **MAKE CONNECTIONS** How was the calendar invented by the Egyptians similar to our modern calendar?

3. **SYNTHESIZE** How did science and mathematics help advance ancient Egyptian civilization?

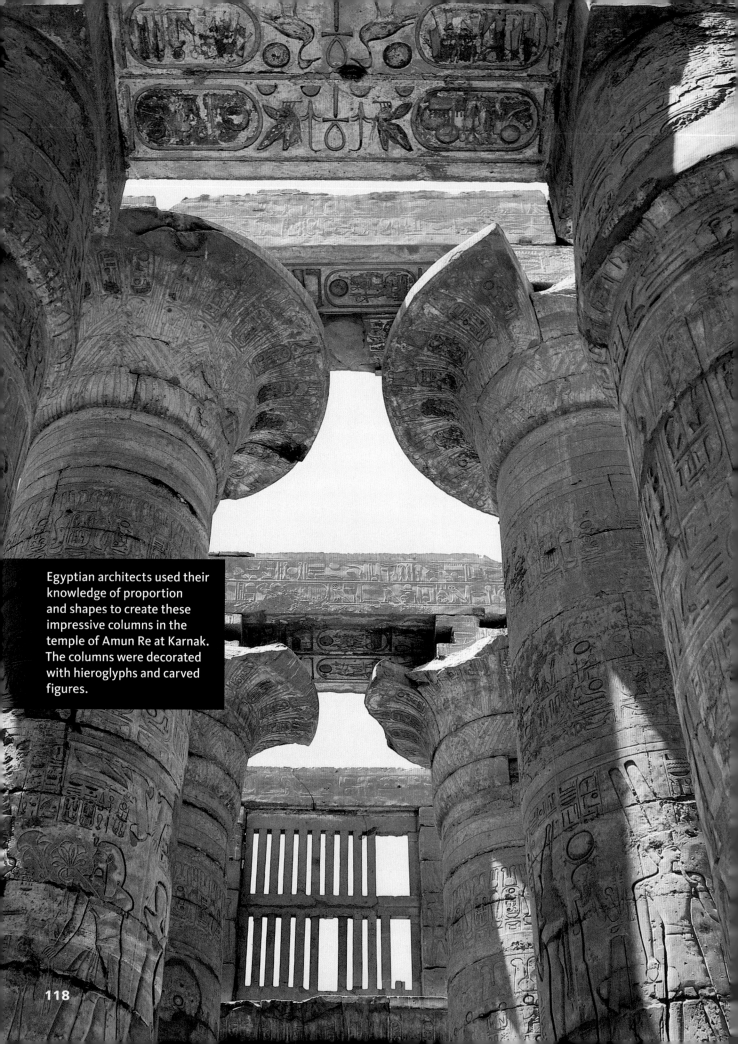

Egyptian architects used their knowledge of proportion and shapes to create these impressive columns in the temple of Amun Re at Karnak. The columns were decorated with hieroglyphs and carved figures.

4.3 Art and Architecture

The figures in ancient Egyptian paintings look awkward with their bodies facing the viewer, heads and feet facing right. Surely the artist didn't believe people really look like this!

MAIN IDEA

The ancient Egyptians created distinctive art and architecture.

A DISTINCTIVE ART STYLE

Ancient Egyptian art is easily recognizable. That is because artists used a distinctive style called frontalism. According to this style, the head and legs were drawn in profile, but the shoulders, chest, and arms were drawn as if they were facing front. The result looked pretty unnatural, but realism wasn't the goal. Most portraits were painted for religious purposes, which made it important to show as much of the body as possible. Frontalism achieved this goal.

Artists arranged each figure in a painting precisely to achieve balance and order. To get the sizes and proportions right, they followed a strict formula. Typically the human body was divided into three equal parts: from foot to knee, from knee to elbow, and from elbow to hairline. A figure's waist appeared exactly halfway up the body.

Most paintings showed scenes from everyday life. These included pharaohs performing religious rituals, fighting battles, or feasting, and ordinary people at work or play. Artists painted and carved figures and scenes like these in great temples, monuments, and tombs. This ancient art has revealed much about Egyptian life and beliefs.

ARCHITECTURE AND SACRED SHAPES

Egyptian architects also used clever techniques to make their soaring temples and other buildings look impressive. The architects used grid lines to create precise designs. They also applied mathematics to their designs using the "golden ratio." This mathematical formula helped architects achieve the most pleasing proportions— what looks good, in other words. The Greeks borrowed and developed the formula, and the golden ratio is still used today.

Certain geometric shapes, such as squares and triangles, were considered sacred, so architects included these in their designs. The most important shape, though, was the pyramid, which dominated Egyptian architecture throughout the civilization's 3,000-year history. In addition to the Great Pyramid of Khufu, architects built many other pyramids all over Egypt. Small pyramids even topped the tombs of the skilled craftspeople who built Egypt's great monuments.

REVIEW & ASSESS

1. **READING CHECK** What makes ancient Egyptian art and architecture stand out?

2. **DRAW CONCLUSIONS** What do Egyptian art and architecture reveal about the place of religion in ancient Egyptian society?

3. **DETERMINE WORD MEANINGS** How does the base word *front* clarify the meaning of the *frontalism* style of art?

VOCABULARY

Use each of the following vocabulary words in a sentence that shows an understanding of the word's meaning.

1. cataract
Cataracts make river travel difficult because boats must navigate around these rapids.

2. dynasty

3. pharaoh

4. hierarchy

5. mummy

6. hieroglyph

7. scribe

8. papyrus

READING SKILL

9. DRAW CONCLUSIONS If you haven't already, complete your organizer to draw conclusions about the importance of ancient Egypt's geographic features. Then answer the question.

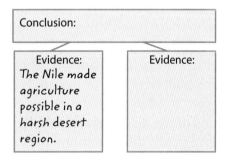

| Conclusion: |
| Evidence: The Nile made agriculture possible in a harsh desert region. | Evidence: |

How did the Nile River affect civilization in ancient Egypt? Explain.

MAIN IDEAS

Answer the following questions. Support your answers with evidence from the chapter.

10. Why was Egyptian agriculture dependent on the Nile? **LESSON 1.1**

11. What was the relationship between Upper Egypt and Lower Egypt? **LESSON 1.2**

12. What was the role of the pharaoh in Egyptian life? **LESSON 1.3**

13. How did the Great Pyramid of Khufu demonstrate the pharaoh's power? **LESSON 2.1**

14. How were the classes of Egyptian society organized? **LESSON 2.2**

15. What contributions did Hatshepsut make to Egypt during her reign? **LESSON 3.1**

16. In what ways were Kush and Egypt connected? **LESSON 3.4**

17. Why was it desirable to be a scribe in ancient Egypt? **LESSON 4.1**

CRITICAL THINKING

Answer the following questions. Support your answers with evidence from the chapter.

18. SYNTHESIZE How did the pharaohs use Egypt's resources to increase the country's wealth and power?

19. DRAW CONCLUSIONS What impact did the Nile have on Egypt's trade industry?

20. ANALYZE CAUSE AND EFFECT How did the absolute power of the pharaohs contribute to Egypt's cycles of order and disorder?

21. MAKE GENERALIZATIONS What position did women have in Egyptian society?

22. YOU DECIDE The Egyptians had many important achievements in math, science, art, and architecture. Which achievement do you think left the greatest legacy, and why?

Study the cross-section diagram of the interior of King Khufu's Great Pyramid at Giza. Then answer the questions that follow.

GREAT PYRAMID AT GIZA

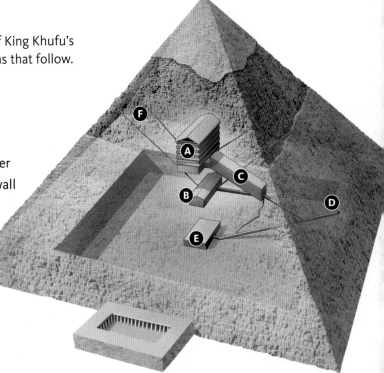

Ⓐ King's Chamber, where Khufu was buried

Ⓑ Queen's Chamber, which was found empty

Ⓒ Grand Gallery, leading to the King's Chamber

Ⓓ Entrance, which was sealed off by a heavy wall

Ⓔ Unfinished Chamber, built underground, beneath the pyramid

Ⓕ Air Vents

23. What features of the pyramid might help discourage tomb robbers?

24. What features of the pyramid were created to help the workers who built it?

Read the following translation of advice from an ancient Egyptian father to his son, who is training to be a scribe. Then answer the question.

> I have compared the people who are artisans and handicraftsmen [with the scribe], and indeed I am convinced that there is nothing superior to letters. Plunge into the study of Egyptian Learning, as you would plunge into the river, and you will find that this is so. . . . I wish I were able to make you see how beautiful Learning is. It is more important than any trade in the world.

25. What conclusions can you draw about the role of scribes in ancient Egyptian society?

26. **NARRATIVE** Ramses II was one of the key figures from ancient Egypt. Suppose you were a scribe who was alive then. Write an eyewitness account that tells about the greatest achievements of Ramses II.

TIPS

- Take notes from the chapter about the reign of Ramses II and his achievements.

- Make an outline of the achievements and events you will include.

- Be sure to include details and examples.

- Use at least two vocabulary words from the chapter.

- Provide a concluding statement that summarizes why Ramses II was an effective pharaoh.

- Use word-processing software or your class's online forum to publish your account.

5

JUDAISM AND THE ISRAELITE KINGDOMS

2000 B.C. – A.D. 70

 SECTION 1 **THE FOUNDING OF JUDAISM**

SS.6.E.2.1; SS.6.G.1.4; SS.6.G.1.6; SS.6.G.1.7; SS.6.G.2.1; SS.6.G.2.2; SS.6.G.2.4;
SS.6.G.4.1; SS.6.G.5.3; SS.6.W.1.3; SS.6.W.2.8; SS.6.W.2.9; LAFS.68.RH.1.1;
LAFS.68.RH.1.2; LAFS.68.RH.2.5; LAFS.68.RH.3.7; LAFS.68.WHST.1.2;
LAFS.68.WHST.3.9

KEY VOCABULARY

confederation
covenant
kosher
monotheism
rabbi
synagogue
tribe

NAMES & PLACES

Abraham
Deborah
Exodus
Hebrew Bible
Judaism
Moses
Talmud
Ten Commandments
Torah

 SECTION 2 **KINGDOMS AND EXILE**

SS.6.G.1.4; SS.6.G.1.5; SS.6.G.2.6; SS.6.G.4.2; SS.6.G.4.4; SS.6.G.5.3; SS.6.W.1.4;
SS.6.W.2.9; LAFS.68.RH.1.2; LAFS.68.RH.1.3; LAFS.68.RH.2.5; LAFS.68.RH.3.7

KEY VOCABULARY

exile

NAMES & PLACES

Cyrus the Great
David
Diaspora
Hanukkah
Israel
Judah
Solomon
Zealots

READING STRATEGY

IDENTIFY MAIN IDEAS AND DETAILS When you identify a text's main idea and details, you state the most important idea about a topic and list facts that support that idea. As you read the chapter, use a web like this one to identify beliefs and practices of Judaism.

Jerusalem is the religious center of Judaism. The Old City of Jerusalem is shown here.

Abraham and **Moses**

While mighty empires rose and fell, a group of shepherds grew into a small nation. These people never ruled a powerful empire. But they were bound together by a strong religious faith, and their influence has been greater than that of many empires. These people are known by various names, including Hebrews, Israelites, and Jews.

MAIN IDEA

Abraham and Moses were important leaders of **Judaism,** the first religion based on the worship of a single God.

THE PROMISED LAND

The Hebrews were a people who settled in Canaan (KAY-nuhn) around 1800 B.C. Canaan was on the eastern coast of the Mediterranean Sea. This region was later called Israel and also Palestine. The Hebrews differed from all other ancient people in an important way: they practiced **monotheism**, the worship of a single God. All other ancient people practiced polytheism, which you may recall is the worship of many gods. Monotheism was a significant development in religion and has had a great impact on cultures around the world.

Most of what we know about the Hebrews comes from the **Hebrew Bible**, a collection of ancient religious writings. According to these writings, God told **Abraham**, a Mesopotamian shepherd, to take his family and settle in Canaan. The region would be their Promised Land—a land that would belong to Abraham and his family forever. Abraham's descendants would have a special **covenant** (KUHV-uh-nuhnt), or religious agreement, with God. According to the covenant, God would protect the Hebrews if they accepted no other god and did what God asked.

The early Hebrews led a quiet, seminomadic life in Canaan. Seminomadic people move frequently with their flocks, but they often return to one place where they grow crops.

THE EXODUS

The land of Canaan sometimes became too dry for growing crops. According to the Hebrew Bible, a devastating drought, or dry period, caused such a severe shortage of food that the Hebrews left Canaan and settled in northern Egypt, perhaps around 1650 B.C. Here, the pharaoh enslaved them to work on his building projects. Around this time, the Hebrews became known as the Israelites.

The Hebrew Bible relates that the Israelites endured centuries of suffering before God chose a man named **Moses** to help them escape from Egypt. The Israelites returned to Canaan in a journey from slavery to freedom called the **Exodus**, possibly in the 1200s B.C. According to the Bible, the Israelites traveled through the desert for 40 years before finally returning to Canaan. Along the way Moses climbed Mount Sinai (SY-ny), where God gave him the **Ten Commandments** and other laws. This religious, moral, and civil code reaffirmed and expanded the Israelites' covenant with God. Today, the Ten Commandments form the basis of many modern laws, such as the law against stealing another person's property.

Black Sea

HITTITE EMPIRE

Haran

ASSYRIA

MESOPOTAMIA

Euphrates R.

Tigris R.

Mediterranean Sea

Damascus

CANAAN

Jericho

Dead Sea

Babylon

Pi-Ramses

Memphis

EGYPT

Ezion-geber

The location of the historical Mount Sinai is debated by scholars.

Mount Sinai

Nile R.

Red Sea

Ur

Persian Gulf

N W E S

| 0 | 100 | 200 Miles |
| 0 | 100 | 200 Kilometers |

→ Based on the Hebrew Bible, route of Abraham's journey to Canaan
→ Based on the Hebrew Bible, route of Israelites' journey out of Egypt and back to Canaan

ABRAHAM

The Jews regard Abraham, shown in this detail from a painting, as the father of the Jewish people. According to the Hebrew Bible, God changed his name from *Abram*, meaning "exalted father," to *Abraham*, meaning "father of many."

Detail from *Sacrifice of Isaac*, Michelangelo Merisi da Caravaggio, 1603–1604

REVIEW & ASSESS

1. **READING CHECK** Why are Abraham and Moses important in the history of Judaism?

2. **INTERPRET MAPS** What natural feature did Abraham follow on the first part of the long journey to Canaan?

3. **COMPARE AND CONTRAST** How did Judaism differ from the religions of other ancient peoples?

1.2 A Distinct Culture

You need a lot of nerve to go against a common belief. Abraham had this courage. But his strong belief ended up leading his people down a path filled with intolerance and harsh treatment, which continue in some places today. As you will see, acting out of strong belief became an important part of the distinct culture of the Israelites.

MAIN IDEA

As the Israelites fought to win control of their Promised Land, their religious beliefs and practices set them apart from the Canaanites.

DEBORAH

Deborah was the Israelites' only female judge. At the Battle of Mount Tabor around 1125 B.C., she led the Israelites to victory against a Canaanite king.

BELIEF IN ONE GOD

The belief in one God is central to Judaism. This idea may seem normal to many people today, but it was a radical idea in the ancient world. The Israelites were the first people to reject polytheism, making Judaism the world's oldest monotheistic religion.

Belief in one God helped unify the Israelites, but their beliefs and practices also set them apart from other ancient cultures. According to the Hebrew Bible, God gave Moses a code of religious practices that governed most aspects of life. The Israelites did not worship idols, or false gods. They ate only certain foods. They did not work on the Sabbath, a weekly day of rest. While they traded with other peoples, they tried to keep a distinct cultural identity. Most Israelites did not marry outside their faith, and they were careful not to adopt foreign customs. They generally avoided the cultural diffusion, or mixing, that was a major part of many other civilizations.

THE TWELVE TRIBES

According to the Hebrew Bible, when the Israelites returned to Canaan from Egypt, they consisted of 12 **tribes**, or extended family

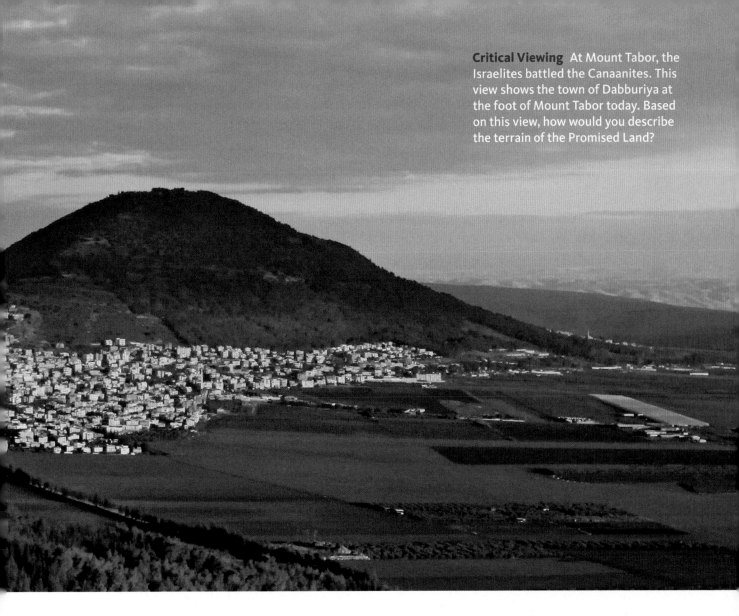

Critical Viewing At Mount Tabor, the Israelites battled the Canaanites. This view shows the town of Dabburiya at the foot of Mount Tabor today. Based on this view, how would you describe the terrain of the Promised Land?

units. Each tribe was descended from a son of Jacob, Abraham's grandson. Since Jacob was also called Israel, the tribes were called the Twelve Tribes of Israel, and Jacob's descendants were called Israelites. They referred to Canaan as the Promised Land.

Moses had died before the Israelites returned to Canaan. The Bible describes how a new leader named Joshua brought the Israelites into the Promised Land around 1250 B.C. Joshua went to war against local people known as the Canaanites, who practiced polytheism. After battling for about 200 years, the Israelites conquered most of Canaan. The tribes then divided up the conquered lands among themselves. They lived separately but acted together as a loose **confederation**, or group of allies. Powerful leaders called judges came to head the confederation of tribes. The judges directed battles, made decisions on policy, and helped keep the tribes united.

REVIEW & ASSESS

1. **READING CHECK** What was a major difference between the Israelites and the Canaanites?

2. **IDENTIFY MAIN IDEAS AND DETAILS** According to the text, how was Israelite society organized?

3. **MAKE INFERENCES** How did the Israelites maintain a distinct cultural identity?

1.3 Beliefs and Texts of Judaism

Your teachers probably have high expectations of you. At the very least, they'd like you to act responsibly and follow the class rules. Likewise, the Israelites believed that God had high expectations of them and wanted them to follow his rules. These rules were written down and covered almost every aspect of their lives.

MAIN IDEA

The Israelites followed religious teachings written down in their holy books.

JEWISH BELIEFS AND PRACTICES

The Hebrew Bible describes how Moses transmitted a religious code that governed the lives of the Israelites. It addressed all aspects of life, including how to worship God, how to treat all members of society well, and what to eat. For example, they could eat only **kosher** foods, foods that were specially prepared according to Jewish dietary laws. According to these laws, animals had to be killed humanely, dairy and meat could not be eaten together, and pork and shellfish were not allowed.

Judaism stressed the importance of treating others well. It promoted social justice, equality, and the holiness of human life. The Israelites also highly valued education, charity, and hospitality, or the kind treatment of guests. In addition, Israelite women were treated well for the time. Religious teachings told husbands to love and respect their wives, who were considered to be the heart of the family.

In time, Jews began gathering to worship in buildings called **synagogues** (SIHN-uh-gahgs), meaning "places of assembly." A spiritual leader called a **rabbi**, or "teacher," usually conducted services. Rabbis upheld Jewish customs and provided guidance for living a Jewish life.

An important practice of Judaism is the observance of a weekly day of rest known as the Sabbath. It begins at sunset on Friday and ends on Saturday night. On the Sabbath, the Jewish community gathers for prayer and to read from sacred texts. Families enjoy festive meals, and people leave behind weekday work and concerns.

SACRED TEXTS

The Hebrew Bible consists of 24 books in three sections: the **Torah**, Prophets, and Writings. The Torah consists of the five books of Moses. The name *Torah* means "the teachings." Jews believe that the Torah contains the word of God as revealed to Moses on Mount Sinai. The Torah includes religious and moral guidance covering most areas of life. In fact, it forms the basis of all Jewish law. Every synagogue has a Torah scroll, handwritten on parchment, which is treated with enormous respect and read from beginning to end over the course of a year. The Torah and other Jewish laws are discussed and explained in the **Talmud**, a collection of writings by early rabbis.

The books in the Hebrew Bible also make up the Old Testament of the Christian Bible, though the books are ordered, divided, and sometimes named differently. Many stories related in the Hebrew Bible and in the Christian Bible also appear in the Qur'an, the holy book of Islam. For example, stories about Abraham appear in all three texts.

This page from a Hebrew Bible dated A.D. 1299 is written in Hebrew script.

REVIEW & ASSESS

1. **READING CHECK** What are some important beliefs and texts of Judaism?

2. **MAKE GENERALIZATIONS** What were important values in Judaism, and why might they have stood out in the ancient world?

3. **DRAW CONCLUSIONS** Why do you think the Torah is treated with great respect by Jews?

DOCUMENT-BASED QUESTION
Writings from the
Hebrew Bible

Judaism was originally based on an oral tradition, in which stories are passed down by word of mouth. After the Israelites developed writing, they wrote down their religious texts. In 1947, a shepherd discovered a set of texts near the Dead Sea. Later known as the Dead Sea Scrolls, these texts included portions of the Hebrew Bible dating from around 150 B.C.

In this part of a painting by Italian artist Guido Reni, Moses is shown with one of the two tablets containing the Ten Commandments.

Moses with the Tablets of the Law, Guido Reni, 17th century

Primary Source: Sacred Text

from the Book of Genesis

Genesis is the first book of the Hebrew Bible. In this excerpt, God speaks to Abraham and tells him to bring his family to the land of Canaan.

CONSTRUCTED RESPONSE What does God promise Abraham?

> Go forth from your native land and from your father's house to the land that I will show you. I will make of you a great nation, and I will bless you.
>
> Genesis 12:1–2

DOCUMENT TWO

Primary Source: Sacred Text

from the Book of Exodus

Exodus is the second book of the Hebrew Bible. It describes the oppression of the Israelites in Egypt and their escape from slavery to freedom during the Exodus. It also depicts Moses' experience on Mount Sinai, where God gave Moses the Ten Commandments. According to the Bible, these laws were written on two stone tablets. This excerpt details the Ten Commandments.

CONSTRUCTED RESPONSE What do the first four commandments have in common? What do the last six have in common?

The Great Isaiah Scroll, one of the Dead Sea Scrolls

> **Ten Commandments**
>
> 1. I the Lord am your God. . . . You shall have no other gods besides Me.
> 2. You shall not make for yourself a sculptured image [idol].
> 3. You shall not swear falsely by the name of the Lord your God.
> 4. Remember the Sabbath day and keep it holy.
> 5. Honor your father and your mother.
> 6. You shall not murder.
> 7. You shall not commit adultery.
> 8. You shall not steal.
> 9. You shall not bear false witness against your neighbor.
> 10. You shall not covet [desire] . . . anything that is your neighbor's.
>
> Exodus 20:2–14

SYNTHESIZE & WRITE

1. **REVIEW** Review what you have learned about the covenant made between God and the Israelites.

2. **RECALL** On your own paper, write down the main idea expressed in each document above.

3. **CONSTRUCT** Construct a topic sentence that answers this question: What did God promise the Israelites?

4. **WRITE** Using evidence from the documents, write an explanatory paragraph that supports your topic sentence from Step 3.

2.1 Israel and Judah

Twelve friends decide to go to a movie, but everyone has different ideas about what to see. Finally, they agree to put one person in charge—a natural-born leader. His decision is quick and readily accepted. For a similar reason, the Israelites swapped decision-making by judges for rule by a single strong king.

MAIN IDEA

The Israelites united under a line of kings, but they later became divided and were defeated by external powers.

DAVID

David, a simple shepherd, attracted attention when he killed a gigantic warrior called Goliath using only his shepherd's sling and stones. David became one of the Israelites' greatest kings. His emblem, the six-pointed star called the Star of David or Shield of David, became a symbol of Judaism and modern Israel.

A LINE OF KINGS

The Israelites realized they needed greater unity and stronger leadership when they were attacked by another people called the Philistines (FIH-luh-steens), who lived in the area. The Israelites appointed a king named Saul to rule. In 1020 B.C., Saul defended Israel against the Philistines and other enemies.

When Saul died, **David** was crowned king. David united the tribes and continued the fight against the Philistines and other enemies. He captured Jerusalem and made it his capital, starting its transformation into one of history's most important cities.

David's son **Solomon** inherited a peaceful kingdom. He built a great stone temple in Jerusalem. Solomon's Temple became the focus of religious life. Solomon used trade and taxes to fund other huge building projects. However, most of the tax burden fell on the northern tribes, who came to resent Solomon's rule. Once again, trouble began.

Soon war broke out between the northern and southern tribes. Around 922 B.C., Israel was divided into two kingdoms: **Israel** in the north and **Judah** in the south. The northern kingdom consisted of ten of the original tribes, while the southern kingdom consisted of the remaining two. The kingdoms sometimes fought each other and sometimes formed alliances against common enemies. Eventually, Judaism and the Jewish people would be named after Judah.

INVADED AND CONQUERED

In 722 B.C., the Assyrian Empire conquered Israel. The ten tribes of Israel were scattered to other lands and disappeared from history. Judah, though, survived and was able to fight off Assyria.

However, Judah soon found itself the battleground between two warring groups: the Egyptians and the New Babylonians. Egypt conquered Judah first. Then the New Babylonian army, led by King Nebuchadnezzar, overran Judah.

Judah rebelled. In 597 B.C., the king responded by invading Jerusalem. He moved the elite members of society to Babylon, leaving the poor behind. In 586 B.C., Nebuchadnezzar's army destroyed Jerusalem, including Solomon's Temple. For the Jews, the age of kings was over.

SOLOMON'S TEMPLE

According to the Hebrew Bible, King Solomon built a magnificent temple in Jerusalem with walls and a floor of cedarwood overlaid in gold. The Bible indicates that Solomon's Temple housed the Ark of the Covenant, a container holding the stone tablets with the Ten Commandments. This reconstruction is based on descriptions of the Temple in the Hebrew Bible.

The walls, floor, and doors were overlaid in gold.

Two hollow bronze pillars flanked the entrance.

Offerings to God were burnt on an altar.

Religious leaders washed in a large basin of water.

REVIEW & ASSESS

1. **READING CHECK** What events mark the rise and fall of the Jews' age of kings?

2. **IDENTIFY PROBLEMS** What was one source of conflict between the northern and southern tribes of the Israelites?

3. **MAKE INFERENCES** What do you think the destruction of Solomon's Temple meant to the Israelites?

Jews come to pray at Jerusalem's
Western Wall, a remnant of the
Second Temple. Many visitors leave
written prayers in cracks in the wall.

2.2

Exile and Return

Psalm 137, from a book in the Hebrew Bible, captures the terrible upheaval the Jews suffered when they were forced to leave Judah and live in Babylon: "By the rivers of Babylon, there we sat, sat and wept, as we thought of Zion [Israel]. How can we sing of the Lord on alien [foreign] soil?" But the Jews found a way, and they grew stronger as a result of the experience.

MAIN IDEA

While in Babylon, the Jews maintained, developed, and strengthened their identity and religion.

BABYLONIAN CAPTIVITY

The removal of some of the Jewish people from their homeland to faraway Babylonia was a deeply distressing experience. Their captivity, called the Babylonian Exile, lasted about 50 years. **Exile** is the forced removal from one's native country. During the exile, Jews built their first synagogues.

Any remaining tribal divisions disappeared, to be replaced by a sense of religious and social unity among the Jewish people. Scribes started writing down the holy texts in a new script that is still used today. Most importantly, the Jews found that it actually was possible to "sing of the Lord on alien soil." Although they had lost control of the Promised Land, the Jews held on to their cultural identity and their religious faith.

CYRUS THE GREAT OF PERSIA

The Jews' efforts to maintain their faith were aided when **Cyrus the Great**, king of the Persian Empire, conquered Babylon in 539 B.C. As you may remember, Cyrus became known as "the Great" because of his impressive military conquests and wise rule. He adopted a policy of tolerance, allowing conquered people to keep their own customs and beliefs.

While Judah remained under Persian control, Cyrus freed the Jewish people in Babylon and encouraged them to return to their homeland and rebuild the Jewish state. Because of his policy of tolerance, Cyrus became a hero to the Jews.

Many of the Jewish people decided to stay in Babylonia. They formed a large Jewish community that thrived for centuries and remains in small numbers in present-day Iran and Iraq. However, in 538 B.C., about 42,000 Jews returned to Judah. There, they began rebuilding the temple in Jerusalem, called the Second Temple. Religious leaders began to refine Judaism into something like its modern form. In particular, they finalized the Hebrew Bible, which became the central document of the Jewish faith, and began public readings of the Torah.

REVIEW & ASSESS

1. **READING CHECK** Why did Cyrus the Great become a hero to the Jews?

2. **IDENTIFY DETAILS** While in exile, how did the Jews maintain their identity?

3. **MAKE INFERENCES** Why did a large number of Jews return to Judah in 538 B.C.?

The Diaspora

 If you moved to another country to live, you might adopt its language and customs to get along. But when Jews settled abroad, most tried hard to keep practicing their own religion and customs. The ability of the Jewish people to preserve their religion and heritage has been one of the most remarkable achievements in world history.

MAIN IDEA

The Syrians and then the Romans tried to destroy Judaism but ultimately failed.

YOHANNAN BEN ZAKAI

When the Romans destroyed the Second Temple, a Jewish teacher named Yohannan Ben Zakai asked permission to establish a school to teach Jewish scholars. The school was important in preserving Jewish traditions. Today, Jews regard Zakai as a great hero.

SYRIAN CONTROL

After the Persians, competing foreign powers controlled Judah. By about 300 B.C., Egypt took over the Jewish homeland. The Egyptian rulers tolerated Judaism and largely left Judah alone.

In 198 B.C., a Syrian empire, the Seleucids, conquered Judah. The Seleucids treated the Jews well until 168 B.C., when the Seleucid king tried to force the Jews to worship Greek gods. He dedicated the Second Temple to the Greek god Zeus. Outraged Jews rebelled, led by a family called the Maccabees. Their small army fought hard, defeated the Seleucids, and rededicated the Second Temple to Judaism.

ROMAN RULE

Judah's freedom from foreign rule did not last long. In 63 B.C., Rome seized control of the region. At first the Romans allowed the Jews to rule themselves. In time, however, Rome took direct control of Judah and insisted that Jews worship the Roman gods. Many Jews, including revolutionaries called **Zealots**, favored armed rebellion.

War finally broke out in A.D. 66. Unfortunately, Jewish resistance was no match for the powerful Roman army. Rome's soldiers destroyed much of Jerusalem, including the Second Temple. By A.D. 70, the war was almost over. The Zealots fought on from the mountaintop fortress of Masada, but the Roman army eventually crushed the revolt.

After the rebellion, many Jews were forced to leave Jerusalem and settle in new places. The migration of Jews to places around the world, which began with the Babylonian Exile, is called the **Diaspora** (dy-AS-puh-ruh). Yet even after leaving their homeland, Jews kept their religion alive and maintained a strong connection to the land of Israel. The rabbis transformed Judaism into a home- and synagogue-based religion that could be practiced anywhere. By holding on to their religion and customs, the dispersed Jews ensured Judaism would become a worldwide religion.

The legacy of the Jewish people is important in world history. Judaism was the first monotheistic religion. Its emphasis on justice and morality influenced later religions, including Christianity. Judaism also had a great influence on other aspects of Western civilization, such as law.

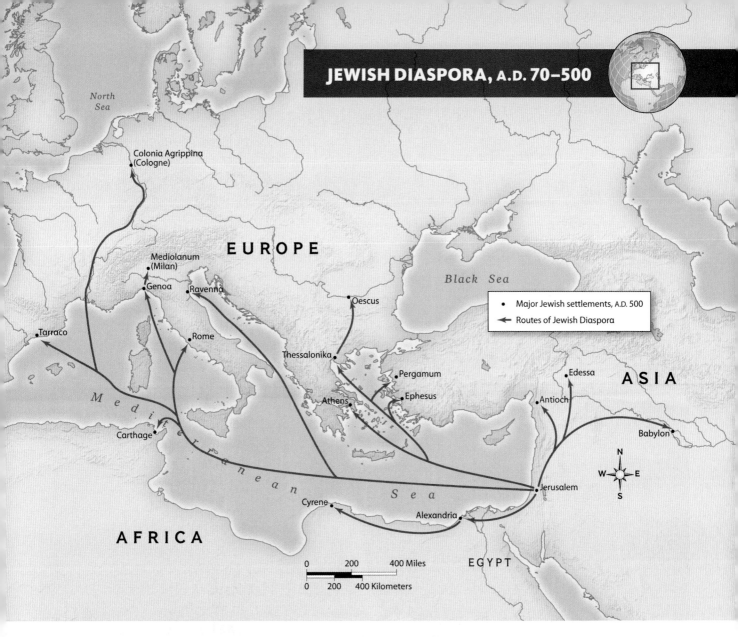

North
Sea

Colonia Agrippina
(Cologne)

EUROPE

Mediolanum
(Milan)

Black Sea

• Major Jewish settlements, A.D. 500
← Routes of Jewish Diaspora

Genoa
Ravenna

Oescus

Tarraco

Rome

Thessalonika

Pergamum

Edessa

ASIA

Athens

Ephesus

Antioch

Babylon

Mediterranean

Sea

Carthage

Jerusalem

N
W E
S

Cyrene

Alexandria

AFRICA

0   200   400 Miles
0 200 400 Kilometers

EGYPT

HANUKKAH

One of the holiday traditions Jews continued to celebrate after the Diaspora is **Hanukkah.** The holiday commemorates religious freedom and the rededication of the Second Temple to Judaism.

According to tradition, the Temple had only enough holy oil to burn for one day, but the oil lasted eight days. This event is symbolized by a special menorah used for Hanukkah. The Hanukkah menorah has eight main holders for candles, plus a ninth holder for the candle that is used to light the others.

REVIEW & ASSESS

1. **READING CHECK** How were Syrian rule and Roman rule of Judah similar?

2. **INTERPRET MAPS** In what direction did most Jews travel during the Diaspora?

3. **DRAW CONCLUSIONS** Why did Judaism become a worldwide religion?

Judaism and the Israelite Kingdoms   **137**

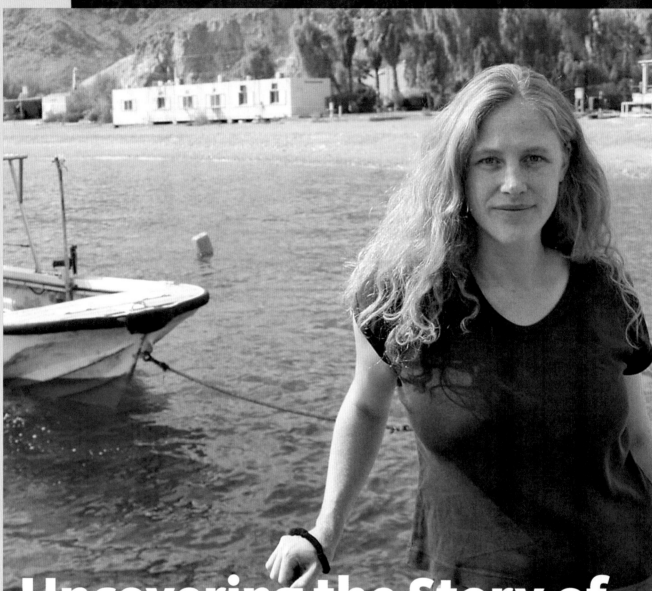

Uncovering the Story of Caesarea's Port

In the first century B.C., Judea was a province of Rome and was ruled by a Roman-appointed king named Herod. He founded the city of Caesarea on the coast of what is now Israel. Sometime in the A.D. 100s, the city's port was mysteriously destroyed. That's where National Geographic Explorer Beverly Goodman comes in. Goodman is a geo-archaeologist, a scientist who investigates ancient cultures by applying the tools of earth science. By studying broken seashells, she concluded that a natural disaster destroyed Caesarea's port.

> ^
> Beverly Goodman, shown above, studies archaeological sites along the Mediterranean coast.

MAIN IDEA

Geo-archaeologist Beverly Goodman has shown that a natural disaster likely destroyed the ancient port of Caesarea.

ISRAEL'S ANCIENT COASTLINE

Goodman's research focuses on the complex interaction between nature and humans along coastlines. "No place is more vulnerable than our coasts," she explains. Her findings from the port of Caesarea prove this thesis while ringing alarm bells that echo across 2,000 years.

At the end of the first century B.C., King Herod built a huge harbor at Caesarea to tap into the valuable trade between the East and ancient Rome. Caesarea had no geographic features useful for a harbor, so Herod relied on "modern" technology.

An aerial view of the ruins of Caesarea

Herod's builders used waterproof concrete to build huge breakwaters, or walls extending out from the coast. These breakwaters created a deepwater harbor where sailing ships could shelter from great storms. Nevertheless, the harbor could not escape the sea's deadliest force. That force came in the form of a tsunami (su-NAH-mee), a giant ocean wave caused by an underwater earthquake, a volcanic eruption, or a landslide. Tsunamis have threatened humans for as long as people have lived on the world's coastlines.

A 2,000-YEAR-OLD DISASTER

Before Goodman began her investigation, no researchers had ever found physical evidence of a major disaster. Scholars had always thought that the harbor had disappeared because of the builders' poor workmanship and inferior materials.

However, when Goodman began exploring the coastline, she uncovered an unusual concentration of shell fragments. "Instead of the normal half-inch layer, this band of shells was more than three feet deep!" she said.

To gather more evidence, she developed a new way of taking deep-sea core samples, sinking hollow tubes into the seabed and then pulling them out to show the layers of deposits. The layers can be read like tree rings. Analysis and dating suggested that a single, sudden, and violent event caused the shell concentrations. Goodman concluded that a major tsunami had destroyed Herod's great harbor.

Goodman is now putting her findings to the test. She's examining other archaeological sites around the Mediterranean region, looking for signs of tsunami damage. Goodman's research could help save lives in the future. "Analyzing the causes and effects of ancient environmental events like tsunamis can help tell us which types of coast are at greatest risk, and what kind of damage to expect in the future," Goodman explains. "I hope I'm collecting clues that will help us avoid catastrophic consequences down the line."

REVIEW & ASSESS

1. **READING CHECK** What natural disaster likely destroyed the ancient port of Caesarea?

2. **IDENTIFY MAIN IDEAS AND DETAILS** What findings support Goodman's conclusion about the cause of the port's destruction?

3. **MAKE CONNECTIONS** Why does Goodman's discovery have important implications for other sites on the Mediterranean?

VOCABULARY

Match each word in the first column with its definition in the second column.

WORD	DEFINITION
1. exile	a. a Jewish spiritual leader and teacher
2. tribe	b. the belief in only one God
3. monotheism	c. a place where Jews assemble to worship
4. covenant	d. an extended family unit
5. rabbi	e. a period of forced absence from one's homeland or native country
6. synagogue	f. a religious agreement with God

READING STRATEGY

7. **IDENTIFY MAIN IDEAS AND DETAILS** If you haven't already, complete your web to identify beliefs and practices of Judaism. Then answer the question.

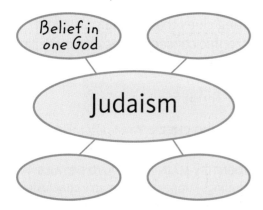

What are some of the beliefs and practices of Judaism? What is one way in which Judaism differs from other ancient religions?

MAIN IDEAS

Answer the following questions. Support your answers with evidence from the chapter.

8. What did the Israelites believe God wanted them to do in order to fulfill their special covenant? **LESSON 1.1**

9. What important religious belief set the Israelites apart from other ancient cultures? **LESSON 1.2**

10. Why is the Torah the most important holy book in Judaism? **LESSON 1.3**

11. What did Saul achieve as the first king of the Israelites? **LESSON 2.1**

12. Who was David, and what were his major accomplishments? **LESSON 2.1**

13. How did Cyrus the Great's policy of tolerance affect Jews during their exile in Babylon? **LESSON 2.2**

14. What was the Diaspora? **LESSON 2.3**

15. What natural disaster likely destroyed King Herod's harbor at Caesarea 2,000 years ago? **LESSON 2.4**

CRITICAL THINKING

Answer the following questions. Support your answers with evidence from the chapter.

16. **MAKE CONNECTIONS** How did the Jews develop and maintain their cultural identity?

17. **DRAW CONCLUSIONS** Why did the Israelites believe that the Ten Commandments reaffirmed their covenant with God?

18. **EVALUATE** Why was the Exodus such an important event in Jewish history?

19. **ANALYZE CAUSE AND EFFECT** What effect did the Diaspora have on the religion of Judaism?

20. **YOU DECIDE** Who do you think was the most important person in the history of the Jewish people? Why?

Study the time line of selected events in Jewish history. Then answer the questions that follow.

Jewish History

922 B.C.
Israel is divided into two separate kingdoms—Israel in the north and Judah in the south.

722 B.C.
The Assyrian Empire conquers the northern kingdom of Israel; the ten northern tribes are exiled.

538 B.C.
Cyrus the Great allows thousands of Jews to return to Judah.

1300 B.C.

1000

700

500 B.C.

c. 1250 B.C.
The Israelites finally reach Canaan.

c. 970 B.C.
King Solomon builds his temple in Jerusalem.

c. 1290 B.C.
The Exodus: Moses leads the Israelites in their escape from slavery in Egypt.

c. 1020 B.C.
King Saul defends Israel against the Philistines.

586 B.C.
King Nebuchadnezzar destroys Jerusalem and Solomon's Temple and exiles many Jews.

21. Who destroyed the First Temple and exiled the two tribes of Judah to Babylon?

22. Which empire destroyed the northern kingdom of Israel?

Read the following psalm, or sacred song, from the Hebrew Bible. Then answer the question.

The Lord is my shepherd; I lack nothing. He makes me lie down in green pastures; he leads me to water in places of repose [calm]; he renews my life; he guides me in right paths as befits his name. Though I walk through a valley of deepest darkness, I will fear no harm, for you are with me; your rod and your staff—they comfort me. You spread a table for me in full view of my enemies; you anoint [rub] my head with oil; my drink is abundant. Only goodness and steadfast love shall pursue me all the days of my life, and I shall dwell in the house of the Lord for many long years.

Psalms 23:1–6

23. What qualities does the author attribute to God in this psalm?

24. ARGUMENT Which one of the Ten Commandments do you think has had the greatest impact on society? Make a list of some of its important effects on society.

TIPS

- Reread the Ten Commandments in Lesson 1.4. Choose the one that you think has had the greatest impact on society.

- Write down the commandment. Under it, list at least three effects of this commandment on society.

- If you can think of more than three effects, add them to the list.

- Use vocabulary from the chapter as appropriate.

- If you have difficulty identifying three effects, you might draw evidence from informational texts. For example, you might look up the Ten Commandments in an encyclopedia or another reference book.

CHAPTER

6 ANCIENT INDIA

2500 B.C. – A.D. 535

SECTION 1 INDUS RIVER CIVILIZATIONS

 SS.6.G.1.3; SS.6.G.1.4; SS.6.G.1.6; SS.6.G.2.1; SS.6.G.2.2; SS.6.G.2.3; SS.6.G.2.4;
SS.6.G.2.6; SS.6.G.3.1; SS.6.G.3.2; SS.6.G.4.2; SS.6.G.5.1; SS.6.W.1.3; SS.6.W.2.4;
SS.6.W.4.1; SS.6.W.4.2; SS.6.W.4.4; SS.6.W.4.5; LAFS.68.RH.1.1; LAFS.68.RH.2.4;
LAFS.68.RH.3.7; LAFS.68.WHST.1.2; LAFS.68.WHST.3.9

KEY VOCABULARY

caste system   planned city
dharma   reincarnation
epic poem   subcontinent
karma   yoga
monsoon
nirvana

NAMES & PLACES

Aryans   Indus River
Brahmanism   Mohenjo-
Buddhism   Daro
Ganges   Sanskrit
  River   Siddhartha
Harappa   Gautama
Hinduism   Vedas

SECTION 2 INDIAN EMPIRES

 SS.6.G.1.4; SS.6.G.1.5; SS.6.G.1.7; SS.6.G.4.4; SS.6.G.5.2; SS.6.W.4.2; SS.6.W.4.3;
SS.6.W.4.4; SS.6.W.4.5; LAFS.68.RH.3.7; LAFS.68.RH.3.8

KEY VOCABULARY

golden age
inoculation

NAMES & PLACES

Asoka
Ayurveda
Chandragupta Maurya
Chandra Gupta I
Kalidasa
Mohandas Gandhi

READING STRATEGY

ORGANIZE IDEAS: ANALYZE CAUSE AND EFFECT When you analyze cause and effect, you note the consequences of an event, an action, or a condition. As you read the chapter, use a graphic organizer like this one to identify the effects of the Aryan migrations on Indian civilization.

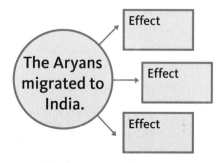

The Aryans migrated to India.

Effect

Effect

Effect

Schoolgirls offer a prayer before a performance of Indian classical dance in honor of Lord Shiva, one of the three major Hindu male deities.

Naryn R.

Toxkan R.

Yarkant R.

Syr Dar'ya

Zarafshon R.

Tejen R.

Panj R.

HINDU KUSH

Harirud R.

Indus R.

Helmand R.

H I M A L A Y A

Jhelum R.

Chenab R.

Ravi R.

Harappa

Sutlej R.

Saraswati R.

The Saraswati River has dried up and disappeared

Mohenjo-Daro

THAR DESERT

Mt. Everest
29,035 ft
(8,850 m)

Brahmaputra R.

Tongtian (Yangtze) R.

Lancang (Mekong) R.

Nu (Salween) R.

Chindwin R.

Tropic of Cancer

Chambal R.

Yamuna R.

Ganges R.

Ghaghara R.

I N D I A

Mahi R.

Narmada R.

Mahanadi R.

Mouths of the Ganges

Tapi R.

Wainganga R.

Irrawaddy R.

Arabian
Sea

Godavari R.

Bhima R.

DECCAN

Krishna R.

W E S T E R N   G H A T S

P L A T E A U

Tungabhadra R.

E A S T E R N   G H A T S

Bay of
Bengal

Cauvery R.

SRI
LANKA

Elevation

feet	meters
10,000+	3,050+
5,000	1,524
2,000	610
1,000	305
500	152
0	0

Below
sea level

Dry monsoon
winds

Wet monsoon
winds

I N D I A N   O C E A N

0	200	400 Miles
0	200	400 Kilometers

N
W   E
S

The Geography of Ancient India

Geographically, India has it all. If you were to travel around India, you could climb snowcapped mountains, cross wide grassy plains, hack through dense tropical forests, sail down mighty rivers, and skirt around sun-scorched deserts. You might travel under a bright blue sky or get soaked by seasonal rains.

MAIN IDEA

South Asia's physical geography affected the development of Indus Valley civilizations.

MOUNTAINS, RIVERS, AND MONSOONS

Present-day India, Bangladesh, Bhutan, Nepal, and Pakistan make up the large landmass, or **subcontinent**, of South Asia. This diamond-shaped landmass was originally an island. However, 40 million years ago, the large moving plates on which the continents lie drove the subcontinent into Asia. As the lands collided, they pushed Earth's crust upward to form the Himalaya, a 1,500-mile mountain range.

The Himalaya are the world's highest mountains. Many Himalayan peaks rise about 24,000 feet. Thirty peaks, including Mount Everest—Earth's highest point—are over 25,000 feet high.

On either side of the Himalaya lie lower mountain ranges, including the Hindu Kush, which separates what was once northwest India from present-day Afghanistan. These northern mountains form a natural barrier against invaders. The Arabian Sea, Indian Ocean, and Bay of Bengal have provided further protection. The Deccan Plateau, which contains smaller mountain systems, makes up much of southern India.

The two major rivers of northern India, the **Indus** and the **Ganges**, both start in the Himalaya. Like the Tigris and the Euphrates in Mesopotamia, these rivers provide water for irrigation and deposit fertile soil for farming.

Strong seasonal winds called **monsoons** have long been an important element of the subcontinent's climate. These winds bring a dry season in winter. In summer, they bring a wet season with heavy rainfall.

INDUS RIVER VALLEY

Physical characteristics of the Indus River Valley offered nearly ideal conditions for agriculture. The valley's fertile soil and plentiful water supply most likely encouraged nomadic herdsmen to settle there and farm. Villages emerged. Then, around 2500 B.C., some villages grew into cities—and a civilization developed.

REVIEW & ASSESS

1. **READING CHECK** How did physical geography affect the development of Indus Valley civilizations?

2. **INTERPRET MAPS** What physical feature separates India from the continent of Asia?

3. **MAKE INFERENCES** What positive and negative effects might the summer monsoons have had on farmers?

1.2 Harappan Civilization

Historians have studied ancient Egyptian civilization for many centuries. But evidence of ancient India's great civilization was not discovered until the early 20th century. Then, in 1921, archaeologists unearthed an Indian culture every bit as vast and sophisticated as that of ancient Egypt: the Harappan civilization.

MAIN IDEA

One of the world's earliest and most advanced civilizations emerged in ancient India's Indus River Valley.

WELL-PLANNED CITIES

Around 2500 B.C., civilization developed in the Indus Valley. Fertile soil and irrigation delivered food surpluses that generated wealth. As populations boomed, villages grew into large cities. **Mohenjo-Daro** (moh-HEHN-joh DAHR-oh), one of the civilization's major cities, covered over 250 acres. Another important city, **Harappa** (huh-RA-puh), gave the Harappan civilization its name. These cities were the largest of their time. Their influence spread across a 500,000-square-mile area, which was greater than that of either ancient Egypt or Mesopotamia.

Indus Valley cities were among the world's first **planned cities**. Many were built with the same layout and the same features. Such cities had an eastern housing and business area guarded by defensive walls. To the west were public buildings, as well as structures that may have been used to store grain. Main roads as straight as rulers intersected at right angles with streets exactly half their width. Wells were another common feature. People used bricks that were all the same size to build houses. Homes had indoor plumbing with a bathroom and a toilet that emptied into excellent underground sewers.

Archaeologists have found similarly styled pottery, jewelry, toys, and tools at more than 1,000 Harappan sites. These similar goods demonstrate strong cultural ties among people living hundreds of miles apart. The similarities also suggest that the Harappan civilization was a single state with a strong central government. However, historians have no idea how it was ruled.

AN ADVANCED CULTURE

In fact, there is a lot historians do not know about Harappan civilization because archaeologists have not figured out its writing system. It seems to be based, at least in part, on pictograms, like Sumerian cuneiform. The only writing found is on small items such as pottery, tools, and tiny square stone seals. Traders probably pressed these seals into soft clay to leave their mark on trading goods. Traders also used stone cubes as standard weights and measures.

The Harappans were long-distance traders, using boats and possibly the world's first wheeled vehicles. Their enormous trade network stretched over the mountains into what are now Afghanistan, Iran, and Iraq. There, archaeologists have found records of Harappan copper, gold, and ivory.

Historians know little about Harappan religion. In fact, much about the Harappans remains a mystery.

Critical Viewing This photo shows the ruins of Mohenjo-Daro. What detail indicates that the high mound had a specific purpose?

REVIEW & ASSESS

1. **READING CHECK** What is one characteristic of the advanced culture of Harappan civilization?

2. **INTEGRATE VISUALS** What details in the photo support the conclusion that Harappa was an advanced civilization?

3. **MAKE INFERENCES** Why do you think it is important to use standard weights and measures in trade?

1.3 Aryan Migrations

Historians believe the Indus Valley suffered a series of earthquakes from which the Harappan civilization never recovered. Other forces were also in play. Eventually, migrations of Aryan people from the north led to the establishment of another great Indian civilization.

MAIN IDEA

After the Harappan civilization declined, Aryan immigrants forged a new Indian civilization.

HARAPPAN SEAL

Found at Mohenjo-Daro, this soft stone seal was probably used to mark trade goods. The marks at the top are an example of the Harappan language, which archaeologists have not yet learned to read.

END OF HARAPPA

A combination of natural forces probably contributed to the Harappan civilization's downfall. First agriculture declined when rainfall diminished. Then earthquakes caused flooding and drastically changed the course of rivers. One river, the Sarasvati, no longer flowed near Harappan cities. With reduced access to river water for irrigation, agriculture became more difficult.

As food supplies declined, people abandoned the cities. By 1900 B.C., a simple village way of life had largely replaced the Harappans' advanced urban civilization.

According to many historians, around 1500 B.C., waves of new people began crossing the Hindu Kush into India. The migrants were a collection of tribes called **Aryans**, meaning "noble ones." They belonged to the Indo-European people who had populated central Asia. (Some scholars have begun to dispute this theory, however. They believe that the Aryans were descendants of earlier Indus civilizations and were not foreign invaders at all.)

The Aryans were seminomadic herders of horses and cattle and were also fierce warriors. They built only basic houses but rode horses and used wheeled chariots.

Around 1000 B.C., what became known as Vedic civilization expanded south and east. There the people adopted agriculture, cleared the forests to cultivate crops, and settled down in villages. The villages grouped together into chiefdoms and then into kingdoms. As they conquered and mixed with native people, the Aryans had a huge cultural impact on religion, class, and language.

IMPACT ON INDIAN SOCIETY

The Aryans worshipped many gods from nature. They also had gods for friendship and for moral authority. To keep their gods happy, Aryan priests, or Brahmans, performed complicated rituals in **Sanskrit**, the Aryan language. Their religion came to be called **Brahmanism** (BRAH-muh-nih-zuhm).

In time Brahmanism's rituals and hymns were recorded in sacred texts called the **Vedas**. The oldest text is the Rig Veda, which contains 1,028 melodic hymns.

VEDAS

The Vedas are four sacred texts that were probably composed between 1500 and 1200 B.C. For a thousand years, people passed the Vedas down orally.

After a written form of Sanskrit emerged, people were finally able to write down the Vedas. These texts tell historians what life might have been like in the Vedic period.

ARYAN MIGRATIONS, c. 1500 B.C.

Aryan migration

Brahmanism grew powerful because the priests established beneficial relationships with kings. The Brahmans preached that the gods granted the right to rule to the kings. In return the kings upheld the authority of the Brahmans.

Over time, a social class system developed that determined how people lived. Priests were at the top, followed by warriors and nobles. Freemen, farmers, and traders were third in importance. At the bottom were slaves, laborers, and artisans. Non-Aryans

made up most of the lowest class. Many centuries later, another group developed that was considered even lower.

The Aryan hierarchy developed into a rigid **caste system** that was hereditary and could never be changed. People's castes dictated the kind of work they did and whom they could marry. The caste system even dictated what people could eat. Such definitions applied to people's children as well.

REVIEW & ASSESS

1. **READING CHECK** Who were the Aryans?

2. **INTERPRET MAPS** What physical features did the Aryan migrations pass through?

3. **DETERMINE WORD MEANINGS** What does *waves* mean in the sentence, "Around 1500 B.C. waves of new people began crossing the Hindu Kush into India"?

Hindu Beliefs and Practices

If you are into computer games, you might have an online avatar, a character that represents you. The concept of avatars is nothing new. The Hindu god Vishnu had many avatars, including a godlike hero called Krishna. Unlike your avatar, Vishnu's avatars were versions of himself in various forms.

MAIN IDEA

Over 5,000 years, Hinduism absorbed and integrated many beliefs found throughout South Asia.

GODS AND SACRED TEXTS

The religion that grew out of Aryan beliefs and practices is **Hinduism**, the world's third largest religion. Hinduism developed over many centuries. Its many gods and goddesses, or deities, combine to form Brahman, a universal spirit. The three most important Hindu deities are Brahma, Vishnu, and Shiva.

Female deities include Saraswati, goddess of knowledge, science, and the arts, and Parvati, who is both a goddess and the beautiful wife of Shiva. She meditated for years in the Himalaya to attract his attention. Lakshmi, wife of Vishnu, is the goddess of wealth and prosperity. People who seek success worship Lakshmi.

The Vedas are Hinduism's holiest books, but two **epic poems**, or long narrative poems, are also important. One, called *Mahabharata* (mu-HAH-bahr-AH-tuh), teaches the importance of living and acting righteously. The other poem, the *Ramayana* (rah-mah-YAH-nuh), tells the story of Rama, the perfect king, who fought evil forces in the world.

Within the *Mahabharata* is a spiritual poem called Bhagavad Gita (BAH-gah-vuhd GEET-ah), or "Song of the Lord." In this poem Krishna praises duty. He also encourages action over inaction, knowledge over ignorance, belief over disbelief, and good over evil. This poem remains popular as a source of spiritual guidance and inspiration.

BELIEFS AND PRACTICES

Hindus occasionally worship in temples, but the home is the center of religious activity. Many homes have a temple room or corner where family members worship. Many Hindus still observe certain cultural practices related to the caste system, such as marrying within one's caste. They also believe the soul is eternal and is reborn in different bodies over different life cycles. This is known as **reincarnation**.

According to Hindu beliefs, people's actions and conduct create **karma**, which determines the kind of life into which they will be reborn. The karma of someone who leads a good and moral life leads to rebirth into a better life. A life filled with misdeeds creates bad karma, which leads to rebirth into a life of greater hardship and suffering. The ultimate goal of a Hindu is to end this cycle of rebirth by living selflessly and eliminating material desires.

There are many paths to the perfect life. One path involves the practice of **yoga**—a series of exercises intended to help a person achieve spiritual insight. An important idea underlying such practices is to seek and know the truth.

These women in northern India are throwing flowers in the air to celebrate the Hindu festival of Holi, which marks the coming of spring.

HINDU DEITIES

Brahma, *the Creator:* Brahma created the universe, the world, and the human race. His four heads represent the four Vedas.

Vishnu, *the Preserver:* Vishnu contains and balances good and evil. It is his job to maintain the divine order of the universe. If evil is winning, Vishnu comes to Earth in human form to restore the balance.

Shiva, *the Destroyer:* Shiva is responsible for all forms of change, from giving up bad habits to death. He is closely associated with yoga.

REVIEW & ASSESS

1. **READING CHECK** Who are the three most important gods in Hinduism, and what is the role of each?

2. **MAKE INFERENCES** How might the concept of karma guide a Hindu during his or her lifetime?

3. **ANALYZE LANGUAGE USE** How does knowing that *carne* refers to "flesh" help you understand the word *reincarnation*?

DOCUMENT-BASED QUESTION
Hindu Sacred Texts

The Bhagavad Gita and the *Ramayana* are two of Hinduism's most famous and popular sacred texts. They tell exciting stories about great warriors having heroic adventures, while also teaching important religious and moral lessons. People in ancient India originally memorized these epic poems and passed them down orally, as they did the Vedas.

This painting shows the Lord Krishna, an avatar of Vishnu, and Prince Arjuna as they head into battle.

DOCUMENT ONE

**from the Bhagavad Gita,
translated by Stephen Mitchell**
The Bhagavad Gita is a 700-verse poem describing a conversation between Vishnu's avatar Krishna and the hero Arjuna. In this excerpt, Krishna speaks to Arjuna before a great battle. Krishna tells the warrior about the soul—the "it" in the poem.

CONSTRUCTED RESPONSE According to Krishna, what is special about a soul?

> The sharpest sword will not pierce it;
> the hottest flame will not singe [burn] it;
> water will not make it moist;
> wind will not cause it to wither [die].
>
> It cannot be pierced or singed,
> moistened or withered; it is vast,
> perfect and all-pervading [everywhere],
> calm, immovable, timeless.

DOCUMENT TWO

**from the *Ramayana*,
a retelling by William Buck**
The *Ramayana* is a love story in which the good king Rama, an avatar of Vishnu, rescues his kidnapped wife Sita from Ravana, the evil ruler of an island off India's southeastern coast. In this passage, Rama speaks to his brother after they learn that their father has died.

CONSTRUCTED RESPONSE What comfort might his brother take from Rama's words?

> Life is passing as a river ever flowing away, never still, never returning. Life is changeable as the flashing lightning, a pattern of as little meaning, and impermanent. . . . Life is bright and colored for a passing moment like the sunset. Then it is gone and who can prevent it going?

DOCUMENT THREE

**from the Rig Veda,
translated by Wendy Doniger**
The Rig Veda is a series of 1,028 hymns grouped into 10 books. It is also the oldest of the Hindu sacred texts. This excerpt from a poem in Book 10 addresses a person who has just died.

CONSTRUCTED RESPONSE According to the passage, what happens to a person after death?

> May your eye go to the sun, your life's breath to the wind. Go to the sky or to earth, as is your nature; or go to the waters, if that is your fate. Take root in the plants with your limbs.

SYNTHESIZE & WRITE

1. **REVIEW** Review what you have learned about Hinduism, the Bhagavad Gita, the *Ramayana*, and the Rig Veda.

2. **RECALL** On your own paper, write down the main idea expressed in each document.

3. **CONSTRUCT** Construct a topic sentence that answers this question: What do the passages from the Bhagavad Gita, the *Ramayana*, and the Rig Veda suggest about Hinduism's attitude toward life and death?

4. **WRITE** Using evidence from the documents, write an explanatory paragraph that answers the question in Step 3.

Siddhartha and Buddhism

 Like many people, you might very much want to own the latest cell phone or tablet. But what if someone told you that your desire for such material possessions would only bring you suffering? That's exactly what a man who lived about 2,500 years ago said.

MAIN IDEA

Buddhism emerged in India around 500 B.C.

EIGHTFOLD PATH

Right View: See and understand things as they really are

Right Intention: Commit to ethical self-improvement

Right Speech: Tell the truth and speak gently

Right Action: Act kindly, honestly, and respectfully

Right Livelihood: Earn a living in a moral, legal, and peaceful way

Right Effort: Focus your will onto achieving good things

Right Mindfulness: Value a good mind

Right Concentration: Single-mindedness

THE LIFE OF BUDDHA

Earlier in this chapter, you learned about the development of Hinduism in India. Another major religion, called **Buddhism**, also began there. Buddhism is based on the teachings of **Siddhartha Gautama** (sih-DAR-tuh GOW-tuh-muh). According to tradition, Siddhartha was born in 563 B.C. He was a prince who lived a life of luxury in what is now Nepal.

Siddhartha enjoyed his life until, at the age of 29, he came across an old man, a sick man, a dead man, and a holy man who was poor but very happy. These men made Siddhartha think about suffering brought on by old age, disease, and death and wonder what had made the holy man so happy. Siddhartha gave up his wealth, his wife, and his child to search for the answer to this question. Then, after six years of wandering, he meditated beneath a tree and finally understood how to be free from suffering. Because of this revelation, or understanding of truth, Siddhartha came to be known as the Buddha, or "Enlightened One."

BUDDHIST BELIEFS

The Buddha spent the rest of his life teaching what he had learned. Much of what he taught is contained in a set of guidelines called the Four Noble Truths. The first truth teaches that all life is suffering. The second truth is that the cause of suffering is desire. The third truth teaches that the end of desire means the end of suffering; the fourth, that following the Eightfold Path can end suffering. The Eightfold Path is also called the Middle Way because it promotes a

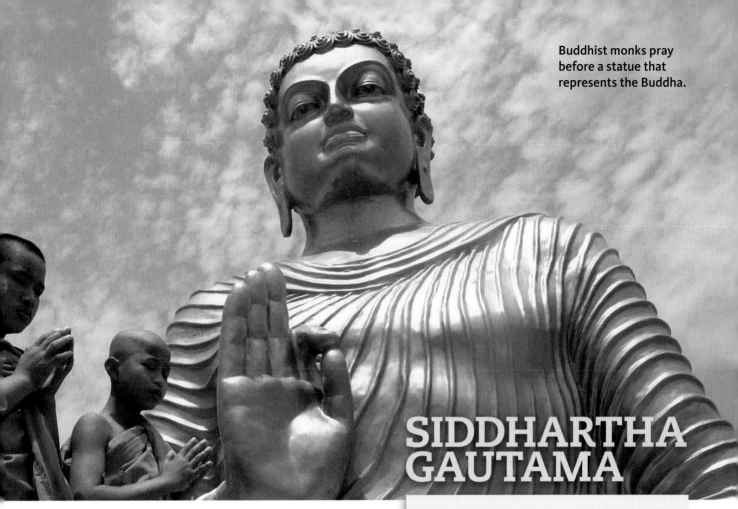

SIDDHARTHA GAUTAMA

life balanced between happiness and self-denial. Like Hindus, the Buddha believed in reincarnation. He taught that following the Eightfold Path would lead to **nirvana** (nihr-VAH-nuh), a state of bliss or the end of suffering caused by the cycle of rebirth.

The totality of the Buddha's teachings are known as the **dharma** (DUHR-muh), or divine law. The Buddha taught that a person of any caste could attain nirvana, and he also promoted nonviolence. Buddhism spread throughout Asia and beyond. After the Buddha died, his remains were buried under eight mound-like structures called stupas.

Job: Prince, poor man, Enlightened One, and founder of Buddhism

Education: Princely pursuits followed by soul searching

Home: Northeast India

FINEST HOUR

He finally achieved enlightenment after 49 days of intense meditation.

WORST MOMENT

He struggled to find the answers he sought, despite putting himself through much suffering and hardship.

MILESTONE

The Buddha is said to have received enlightenment at the age of 35.

REVIEW & ASSESS

1. **READING CHECK** Who is Siddhartha Gautama and what did he seek to learn?

2. **DRAW CONCLUSIONS** What is the purpose of the Four Noble Truths and the Eightfold Path?

3. **MAKE INFERENCES** Why do you think Buddhism became popular in ancient India?

The Maurya Empire

Bite into oven-hot food and you'll burn your tongue. But nibble away at the cooler edges and you can eventually eat the whole meal. That's the principle one king applied to defeat some weaker kingdoms until he was strong enough to conquer them all.

MAIN IDEA

The Maurya Empire united much of India under a single ruler.

A UNITED INDIA

Earlier in this chapter, you read about the Aryans who migrated to India. The Aryans established many kingdoms in the subcontinent. For hundreds of years, no major power arose. Then, around 550 B.C., a kingdom called Magadha in northeast India grew powerful.

Chandragupta Maurya (chuhn-druh-GUP-tuh MOWR-yuh) became king of Magadha around 325 B.C. Believed to have been a soldier, Chandragupta gained power with the help of Kautilya, a Brahmin who plotted Chandragupta's rise. Once Chandragupta became king, he conquered many of the other kingdoms and established an empire. His Maurya Empire united most of northern India and was the first great Indian empire.

Chandragupta established a strong central government. He used taxes to pay for a network of spies and a large army to crush troublemakers. Then, somewhat surprisingly, Chandragupta gave up the throne in 297 B.C. Instead of continuing to rule his empire, he chose to become a monk committed to nonviolence.

THE BUDDHIST KING

Around 269 B.C., **Asoka** (uh-SHOH-kuh), Chandragupta's grandson, became king. At first he earned a reputation for cruelty. His unprovoked attack on another Indian kingdom caused the deaths of hundreds of thousands of people. In the aftermath of so much violence, Asoka underwent a dramatic change. He converted to Buddhism and began to rule using Buddhist principles about peace.

Asoka made a pilgrimage to all the Buddhist holy places in northern India, preaching to his subjects as he traveled. He actively encouraged the spread of Buddhism by sending missionaries to preach abroad. This practice helped Buddhism reach other countries such as Sri Lanka and China, where it is still very popular today.

Asoka had his Buddhist policies inscribed on rocks and tall pillars across his empire. The inscriptions were written in the appropriate regional languages. These policies encouraged everyone to live good lives. State officials monitored moral conduct.

Asoka built more than 1,000 stupas in honor of the Buddha. He donated to charity and built hospitals for animals as well as for humans. To govern his vast empire effectively, Asoka built good roads with plenty of shade and water. These roads were useful for trade and allowed his instructions, inspectors, and armies to travel quickly.

Although Asoka may have been India's greatest king, his well-run empire did not last long. After his death, the Maurya Empire collapsed into many warring kingdoms.

THE MAURYA EMPIRE, c. 250 B.C.

60°E · 70°E · 80°E · 90°E
HINDU KUSH · HIMALAYA
30°N
Indus R.
Ganges R.
Pataliputra
MAGADHA
20°N
Arabian
Sea
Bay of
Bengal
Tropic of Cancer

☐ Maurya Empire

10°N

0   300   600 Miles
0   300   600 Kilometers

N
W   E
S

This pillar is one of many
that Asoka had erected
during his reign.

REVIEW & ASSESS

1. READING CHECK How did
Chandragupta Maurya unite much of
India into the first great Indian empire?

2. INTERPRET MAPS
Where was
Magadha located?

3. ANALYZE CAUSE AND EFFECT
What caused Asoka to renounce
violence? What was the effect?

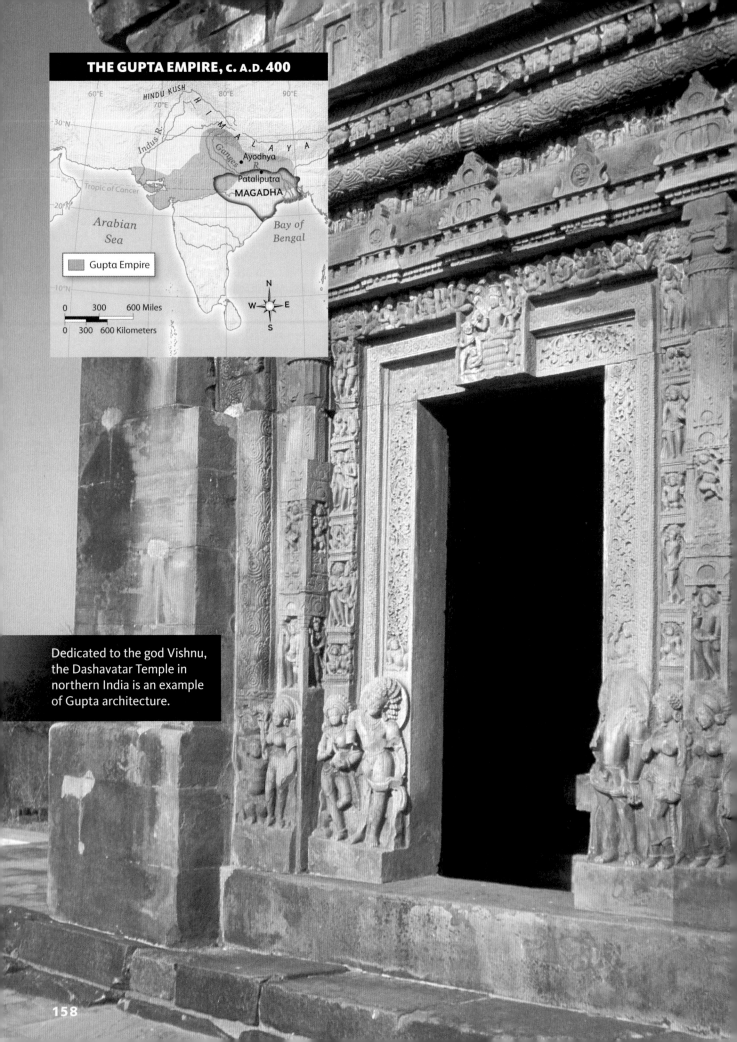

HINDU KUSH

H I M A L A Y A

Indus R.

Ganges

Ayodhya
R.

Pataliputra
MAGADHA

*Arabian
Sea*

*Bay of
Bengal*

Tropic of Cancer

60°E
70°E
80°E
90°E

30°N

20°N

10°N

Gupta Empire

N
W   E
S

0   300   600 Miles

0   300   600 Kilometers

Dedicated to the god Vishnu,
the Dashavatar Temple in
northern India is an example
of Gupta architecture.

The Gupta Empire

History has some weird coincidences. Two of India's greatest empires began in Magadha with a king called Chandragupta. But the kings weren't related. And both empires began around 320, although the Maurya Empire began in 320 B.C. and the Gupta in A.D. 320.

MAIN IDEA

The Gupta Empire brought 200 years of peace and prosperity to India.

A WISE RULER

The collapse of the Maurya Empire led to 500 years of fighting in India. Despite this disorder, the period brought continued economic, social, and cultural progress. Then around A.D. 320 a new unifying power arose. A leader in Magadha called **Chandra Gupta I** began gaining new land and established the Gupta Empire. A dynasty of strong Gupta kings continued to expand the empire until it covered most of northern India. Instead of establishing a strong central government like the Mauryas did, the Guptas allowed the defeated kings to continue to rule. In exchange the Guptas required obedience and tribute, or payment, from the defeated kings.

A series of strong, wise, and long-lived Gupta rulers brought India 200 years of political stability, peace, and prosperity. The expanding empire and its extensive trade routes spread Indian cultural influences around Asia and beyond. Hinduism was reestablished and eventually became India's main religion.

A GOLDEN AGE

Chandra Gupta II, grandson of Chandra Gupta I, ruled during India's **golden age**, a period of great cultural achievement. **Kalidasa** (kah-lih-DAH-suh), the greatest poet in Chandra Gupta II's court and one of India's greatest writers, composed poems and plays in Sanskrit. Scribes, or writers, finally wrote down the spoken stories, including the *Mahabharata* and the *Ramayana*.

Indian artists painted and sculpted statues of Hindu deities. Architects designed and built elegant new temples. Metalworking, improved dramatically. A 24-foot iron pillar weighing more than 6 tons still stands in Delhi some 1,500 years after being installed.

Medical understanding also increased. **Ayurveda** (y-uhr-VAY-duh), a traditional guide to medicine, diet, exercise, and disease, developed and remains an alternative form of healing. In medicine, as in many other areas, ancient Indian knowledge and culture reached far around the world.

REVIEW & ASSESS

1. **READING CHECK** How did the Gupta kings bring peace to their empire?

2. **INTERPRET MAPS** In which directions did the Gupta Empire spread out from Magadha?

3. **FORM AND SUPPORT OPINIONS** Which achievement during India's golden age do you think was most significant? Explain your answer.

The Legacy of Ancient India

Martin Luther King, Jr., championed nonviolent protest to win rights for African Americans. His methods were inspired by the nonviolent protests of Mohandas Gandhi, who helped India gain its independence in 1947. And Gandhi took his nonviolent principles from Hinduism and Buddhism. In that way alone, Indian thinking has had an immense impact on the modern world.

MAIN IDEA

The achievements of ancient India have influenced much of the world.

RELIGION

Two major religions had their origins in India: Hinduism and Buddhism. These religions remain important and influential in much of the modern world. Today four out of five Indians are Hindu, which greatly affects the country's culture. Although the caste system is now officially illegal, some people still observe certain cultural practices according to caste. The idea of reincarnation is especially widespread. Ancient Sanskrit texts continue to teach ethics through stories. Millions of people in many countries practice Hinduism, including more than two million people in the United States alone.

A number of great leaders, including **Mohandas Gandhi** (moh-HUHN-dahs GAHN-dih), have encouraged the Hindu and Buddhist principle of nonviolence. People throughout the world engage in nonviolence to protest injustice. Many vegetarians, people who do not eat meat, follow the Hindu and Buddhist principle of nonviolence toward animals. Today around one percent of India's population is Buddhist. However, Buddhism thrives in countries such as Sri Lanka, Thailand, Vietnam, Japan, Korea, and China. Buddhism also has a following in Europe and in the United States.

ARTS AND SCIENCE

You've learned that religion influenced Indian writing. The *Mahabharata* and the *Bhagavad Gita* are popular around the world. Religion also influenced Indian architecture, an influence that spread to other parts of the world. The temple of Angkor Wat in Cambodia, a country in Asia, is considered one of the world's greatest architectural achievements. The building's elaborate style evolved from ancient Indian architecture. Similar examples can be found in Myanmar (Burma), Vietnam, and Thailand.

Ancient India also contributed much to the fields of science and mathematics. Indians were among the first to practice **inoculation**, which stimulates mild forms of disease in people so that they do not develop more serious forms. Inoculation has greatly reduced the threat of smallpox.

Indian mathematicians created the decimal system and numerals (the number symbols we use today). They also developed the concept of zero, which is crucial to mathematics and computing. Indian astronomers, scientists who study the sun, moon, stars, and planets, accurately calculated the length of the solar year. They also asserted that Earth traveled around the sun and proved that the world was round 1,000 years before Columbus's voyage to America.

LEGACIES OF ANCIENT INDIA

Moral Conduct

Mohandas Gandhi's understanding of the Bhagavad Gita inspired his nonviolent protests in the mid-twentieth century against the British rule of India.

Science

Ancient astronomers determined that Earth is round. They also correctly calculated the length of the solar year.

Medicine

Inoculation protects people's health by increasing one's resistance to disease. It has virtually eliminated smallpox.

Mathematics

Mathematicians of ancient India devised both the decimal system and numerals. They were the first to use zero.

REVIEW & ASSESS

1. **READING CHECK** How did ancient India influence religion in other parts of the world?

2. **SEQUENCE EVENTS** How did mathematicians in ancient India contribute to the age of computers?

3. **MAKE CONNECTIONS** What is the legacy of India's ancient Sanskrit texts?

VOCABULARY

On your paper, write the vocabulary word that completes each of the following sentences.

1. Today, five countries make up the Indian _____, which is separated from the rest of Asia by the Himalaya.

2. Strong seasonal winds called _____ shape India's climate.

3. The *Ramayana* is an example of an _____.

4. Ancient Indians had a social hierarchy that developed into a rigid _____.

5. Hindus believe in _____, which means that when a person dies, his or her soul is reborn in another body.

6. According to Hindu teachings, _____ is the practice of breathing exercises as a path to spiritual insight.

7. The totality of the Buddha's teachings are known as the _____, or divine law.

8. Buddhists believe that the Eightfold Path leads to the end of suffering, or _____.

READING STRATEGY

9. **ORGANIZE IDEAS: CAUSE AND EFFECT**
If you haven't already, complete your organizer to identify the effects of the Aryan migrations on Indian civilization. Then answer the question.

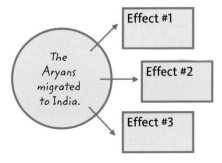

How did the Aryans change civilization in ancient India?

MAIN IDEAS

Answer the following questions. Support your answers with evidence from the chapter.

10. How did geographic features contribute to the development of the Harappan civilization? **LESSON 1.1**

11. In what way were the cities of Mohenjo-Daro and Harappa signs of an advanced civilization? **LESSON 1.2**

12. Who were the Aryans? **LESSON 1.3**

13. How did Hinduism develop in India? **LESSON 1.4**

14. What did Siddhartha Gautama achieve? **LESSON 1.6**

15. How did Asoka spread Buddhism? **LESSON 2.1**

16. In what ways was the reign of Chandra Gupta II a golden age? **LESSON 2.2**

17. What Hindu beliefs and values still deeply influence people's behavior in India today? **LESSON 2.3**

CRITICAL THINKING

Answer the following questions. Support your answers with evidence from the chapter.

18. **ANALYZE CAUSE AND EFFECT** How did the Guptas establish and maintain their empire?

19. **MAKE CONNECTIONS** What did early Indus Valley civilizations have in common with other ancient river valley civilizations?

20. **EVALUATE** How important were the contributions of ancient India to the fields of science and mathematics? Support your evaluation with evidence from the chapter.

21. **COMPARE AND CONTRAST** How are Hindu and Buddhist beliefs similar? How are they different?

22. **YOU DECIDE** What do you think were Asoka's two greatest leadership qualities? Support your opinion with evidence from the chapter.

INTERPRET CHARTS

Study the chart of the caste system that developed in ancient Indian society. Then answer the questions that follow.

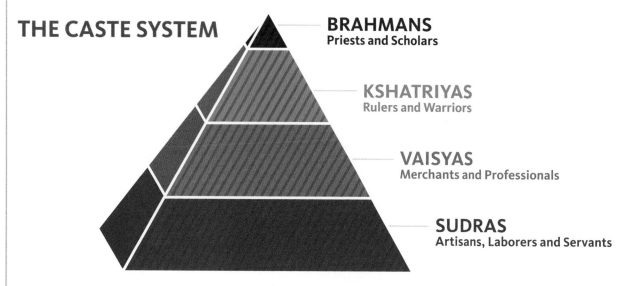

THE CASTE SYSTEM

BRAHMANS
Priests and Scholars

KSHATRIYAS
Rulers and Warriors

VAISYAS
Merchants and Professionals

SUDRAS
Artisans, Laborers and Servants

23. To which caste did most Indians belong?

24. Which caste was the smallest? Why do you think this was so?

ANALYZE SOURCES

Read the following words spoken by the Buddha. Then answer the question.

> Hold fast to the truth as a lamp. Hold fast as a refuge [place of safety] to the truth. Look not for refuge to any one besides yourselves. . . .
>
> And whosoever, . . . either now or after I am dead, shall be a lamp unto themselves, . . . shall look not for refuge to any one besides themselves—it is they . . . who shall reach the very topmost Height!—but they must be anxious to learn.
>
> from *The Last Days of Buddha*, trans. T.W. Rhys David

25. In the passage, the Buddha is telling his followers how to act. What is his message?

WRITE ABOUT HISTORY

26. INFORMATIVE Suppose you are writing a pamphlet for a museum exhibit about India. Write a short essay that explains the lasting influence of ancient India on religion.

TIPS

- Develop an outline that shows how ancient India's influence on religion continues to this day.
- Write the introductory paragraph of your essay using your outline as a guide.
- Develop the topic with relevant, well-chosen facts, concrete details, and examples.
- Use vocabulary from the chapter to explain your ideas.
- Provide a concluding statement that summarizes the information presented.
- Ask your teacher or a classmate to read your essay and make revisions based on their feedback.

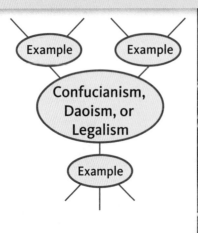

7 ANCIENT CHINA

2000 B.C. – A.D. 220

SECTION 1 RIVER DYNASTIES

SS.6.G.1.4; SS.6.G.1.6; SS.6.G.1.7; SS.6.G.2.1; SS.6.G.2.3; SS.6.G.2.4; SS.6.G.2.5; SS.6.G.3.1; SS.6.G.4.1; SS.6.G.6.2; SS.6.W.1.3; SS.6.W.2.2; SS.6.W.2.4; SS.6.W.4.6; SS.6.W.4.7; SS.6.W.4.8; SS.6.W.4.9; LAFS.68.RH.1.1; LAFS.68.RH.1.2; LAFS.68.RH.1.3; LAFS.68.RH.2.5; LAFS.68.RH.2.6; LAFS.68.RH.3.7; LAFS.68.WHST.1.2; LAFS.68.WHST.3.9

KEY VOCABULARY

dynastic cycle
dynasty
filial piety
isolate
oracle bone

NAMES & PLACES

Chang Jiang
Confucianism
Daoism
Huang He
Legalism
Mandate of Heaven
Shang
Warring States
Zhou

SECTION 2 CHINA'S EMPIRES

SS.6.E.2.1; SS.6.G.1.4; SS.6.G.1.7; SS.6.G.2.2; SS.6.G.5.2; SS.6.W.2.2; SS.6.W.4.8; SS.6.W.4.9; LAFS.68.RH.2.4; LAFS.68.RH.2.5; LAFS.68.RH.3.7; LAFS.68.RH.3.8

KEY VOCABULARY

bureaucracy
emperor
peasant
silk
terra cotta

NAMES & PLACES

Great Wall
Han
Qin
Shi Huangdi

SECTION 3 EAST MEETS WEST

SS.6.E.1.3; SS.6.E.3.1; SS.6.E.3.2; SS.6.E.3.4; SS.6.G.1.4; SS.6.G.2.5; SS.6.G.2.6; SS.6.G.4.4; SS.6.G.5.2; SS.6.W.1.4; SS.6.W.1.5; SS.6.W.4.4; SS.6.W.4.8; SS.6.W.4.10; LAFS.68.RH.1.2; LAFS.68.RH.1.3; LAFS.68.RH.2.6; LAFS.68.RH.3.7

KEY VOCABULARY

barter
caravan
cultural diffusion
maritime

NAMES & PLACES

Silk Roads

READING STRATEGY

ANALYZE LANGUAGE USE
When you analyze language use, you note how specific word choices indicate the author's point of view and purpose. As you read the chapter, use concept clusters like this one to analyze the language used to describe the philosophies of Confucianism, Daoism, and Legalism.

Example — Example
Confucianism, Daoism, or Legalism
Example

The lion's dance, a Chinese tradition for more than 1,000 years, is performed during a New Year's celebration in Beijing, China's capital.

1.1 The Geography of Ancient China

At about 240 years of age, the United States may seem like an old civilization, but it's young compared to China. The Chinese civilization has continued for more than 5,000 years. China's geography helped set the stage for the early development of its civilization.

MAIN IDEA

China's deserts, mountains, and rivers helped shape its civilization.

NATURAL BARRIERS

In the beginning of its growth, natural barriers somewhat **isolated**, or cut off, China's civilization from much of the rest of the world. As a result, ancient China developed differently from other early civilizations, with relatively little outside cultural influence. This early isolation helped unify Chinese culture and allowed China to establish a firm foundation for its civilization.

Some of China's natural barriers included vast deserts. The Gobi to the north and the Taklimakan (tah-kluh-muh-KAHN) to the west discouraged invaders and peaceful immigrants alike. The Himalaya, Tian Shan, and Pamir mountain ranges formed a significant obstacle in the west. The waters of the Pacific Ocean, Yellow Sea, and East China Sea on China's east coast separated the region from its nearest neighbors, Japan and Korea.

MAJOR RIVERS

Like the ancient civilizations of Mesopotamia, Egypt, and India, China's civilization arose along fertile river valleys. It developed on the land between China's two great rivers: the **Huang He** (hwahng huh) and the **Chang Jiang** (chahng jyahng).

The 3,395-mile-long Huang He lies in northern China. It is also called the Yellow River because of its high concentration of yellow silt, or fine, fertile soil. The river deposits this silt along its floodplains, creating good farmland. However, the Huang He is unpredictable. Its course, or the direction in which a river flows, has changed many times. Throughout China's history, heavy rains have also caused the river to flood—with deadly results.

At about 4,000 miles long, the Chang Jiang, or Yangtze, in central China is the third longest river in the world. Like the Huang He, the Chang Jiang carries fertile yellow silt. Unlike the Huang He, the Chang Jiang maintains a relatively predictable course. For thousands of years, the river helped unify China by serving as a useful transportation and trade network within its borders.

The area between the two rivers, called the North China Plain, is the birthplace of Chinese civilization. In Chapter 2, you read about the Yangshao culture, which developed along the Huang He. Another important culture in the area was the Longshan, which developed around 3200 B.C. Other advanced Chinese cultures arose in other river valleys. These cultures include the Liangzhu (lyahng-jew) and the Hongshan. Archaeologists have uncovered beautifully carved jade objects from these cultures in other parts of China. All of these ancient cultures contributed to the development of China's unique civilization and to the rise of its earliest rulers: the Shang and the Zhou.

Shang dynasty, 1300 B.C.
Zhou dynasty, 600 B.C.
Present-day China

TIAN SHAN

Taklimakan Desert

PAMIR

HIMALAYA

GOBI

HONGSHAN CULTURE

KOREA

Huang He (Yellow R.)

Wei He

NORTH CHINA PLAIN

LIANGZHU CULTURE

Yellow Sea

JAPAN

Chang Jiang (Yangtze R.)

East China Sea

Xi Jiang

PACIFIC OCEAN

Tropic of Cancer

South China Sea

0   200   400 Miles
0   200   400 Kilometers

REVIEW & ASSESS

1. READING CHECK How did China's natural barriers affect the early development of its civilization?

2. INTERPRET MAPS How do the borders of the Shang and Zhou dynasties compare with those of present-day China?

3. MAKE INFERENCES What might have been the advantages and disadvantages of China's early isolation from other civilizations?

1.2 Shang and Zhou Dynasties

According to Chinese tradition, a ruler named Yu learned to control the floodwaters of the Huang He and established China's first dynasty, the Xia (shee-AH). But no archaeological evidence of this dynasty has ever been found. The first dynasty for which evidence does exist is the Shang.

MAIN IDEA

The Shang and Zhou dynasties developed many cultural behaviors and beliefs that have become part of Chinese civilization.

CHINA'S FIRST DYNASTY

The **Shang** dynasty emerged along the banks of the Huang He around 1600 B.C. A **dynasty** is a line of rulers from the same family. The Shang developed many cultural behaviors and beliefs that rulers would continue throughout much of Chinese civilization. They established an ordered society with the king at the top, warlords coming next, and farmers at the bottom. The farmers helped advance agriculture in China and grew crops such as millet, wheat, and rice.

The Shang also developed a system of writing using about 3,000 characters. These characters became the basis for modern Chinese writing. They first appeared on **oracle bones**, which are animal bones used to consult the many gods the Shang people worshipped. Priests carved a question on a bone and then heated it. They believed that the pattern of cracks that resulted revealed the gods' answer.

In addition to their gods, the Shang people worshipped the spirits of their dead ancestors. The Shang believed these spirits influenced everything from the king's health to farmers' harvests. To keep the spirits happy, priests conducted special ceremonies, often using beautifully decorated bronze vessels. Shang craftspeople were among the most skilled metalworkers at that time. They also built elaborate tombs for the dead.

THE DYNASTIC CYCLE

In time, the Shang dynasty began to weaken. Around 1045 B.C., the **Zhou** (joh) overthrew the Shang and became China's longest ruling dynasty, lasting about 800 years. The rise of the Zhou also marked the beginning of China's classical period, a time of great social and cultural advances that lasted for about 2,000 years. The Zhou adopted many of the Shang's cultural practices, including ancestor worship and the use of oracle bones. However, the Zhou also developed a concept, known as the **Mandate of Heaven**, to be a guiding force for rulers. They believed that a king could rule only as long as the gods believed he was worthy. The mandate led to a pattern in the rise and fall of dynasties in China called the **dynastic cycle**.

During the first 200 years or so of their rule, the Zhou established a strong central government. However, during the last 500 years of the dynasty, the Zhou divided their lands among local lords. Eventually the ruling lords grew too powerful and independent. They fought among themselves and disobeyed the Zhou kings. By 475 B.C., China had descended into a time of constant war called the **Warring States** period. In 256 B.C., the last Zhou king was finally overthrown.

THE DYNASTIC CYCLE

1
The people believe that the gods approve of the new dynasty.

2
The dynasty weakens.

3
Disasters occur.

4
The people believe that the gods no longer approve of the dynasty.

5
The dynasty is overthrown.

6
A new dynasty re-establishes order.

REVIEW & ASSESS

1. **READING CHECK** What were some of the religious beliefs and practices of the Shang people?

2. **INTEGRATE VISUALS** Based on the diagram and what you've read in the lesson, what do you think happened after the Zhou dynasty fell?

3. **COMPARE AND CONTRAST** How does the development of ancient China under the Shang dynasty compare with that of ancient Egypt?

1.3 Chinese Philosophies

"What you do not wish for yourself, do not do to others." Sound familiar? You may have heard this saying before—or another version of it. It's a simple but powerful guide for moral behavior, and it was written 2,500 years ago by a man called Confucius.

MAIN IDEA

Chinese philosophers developed important ideas on how society should be organized.

CONFUCIANISM

As you've read, China began to fall into disorder during the Zhou dynasty. By the time Confucius was born in 551 B.C., China was already experiencing unrest. A teacher and government official, Confucius believed that Chinese society was breaking down as a result of the constant conflict. In an effort to restore order, he taught that people should respect authority and one another.

Confucius' teachings formed the basis of a belief system known as **Confucianism**. His teachings focused on the duties and responsibilities in the following five relationships: father and son, older brother and younger brother, husband and wife, friend and friend, and ruler and subject. Confucius also promoted education, family unity, and **filial piety**, or the respect children owe their parents and ancestors.

Confucius died believing he had failed to restore order to society. Yet after his death, his students collected his teachings in a book called the *Analects*, and Confucian ideas spread. In time Confucius' teachings became required reading for all government officials. Today Confucianism influences millions of people. The philosophy has been a unifying force in Chinese culture and civilization.

DAOISM AND LEGALISM

Another man called Laozi (low-dzuh) is believed to have lived around the same time as Confucius. He founded a belief system called **Daoism**, which emphasizes living in harmony with nature and the Dao. *Dao* means "the Way" and is believed to be the driving force behind everything that exists. Daoists seek order and balance in their lives by merging, or blending, with nature "like drops of water in a stream."

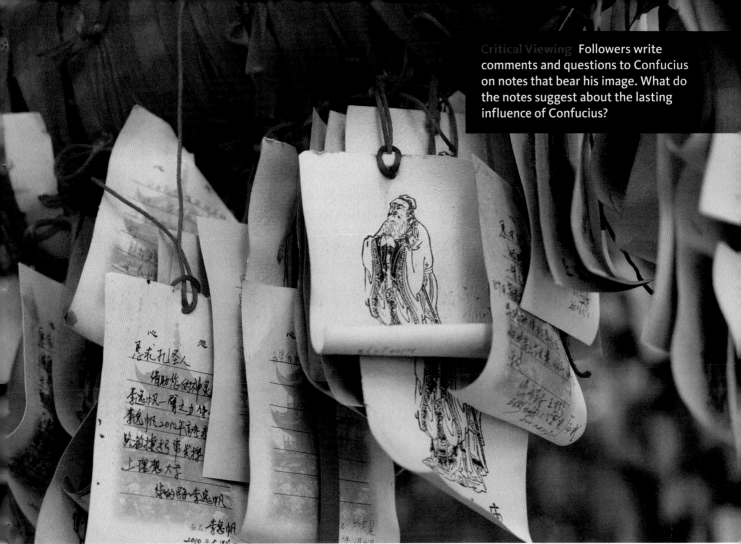

In contrast with both Confucianism and Daoism, **Legalism** emphasizes order through strong government and strictly enforced laws. Legalism developed after 400 B.C. This philosophy does not have a founder, but Han Feizi (fay-zee) set down its ideas around 260 B.C. He maintained that people were naturally bad and needed to be controlled through the threat of harsh punishment. As you will see, a Chinese dynasty would arise that would govern according to this philosophy.

YIN
dark
cold
soft
water

YANG
light
hot
hard
fire

DAOIST YIN-AND-YANG SYMBOL

This symbol is often used in Daoism to show how seemingly opposite forces form a whole. Daoists believe that everything contains aspects of both yin and yang. The symbol shows some of the aspects of each force.

REVIEW & ASSESS

1. **READING CHECK** What are the basic beliefs of Confucianism?

2. **ANALYZE LANGUAGE USE** What Daoist idea does the phrase "blending with nature like drops of water in a stream" help convey?

3. **COMPARE AND CONTRAST** How does Legalism's attitude toward people's nature differ from that of both Confucianism and Daoism?

Ancient China   **171**

DOCUMENT-BASED QUESTION

Contrasting
Belief Systems

You've seen that the suffering caused by weak government and conflict in China led many to think about the best ways to ensure an orderly and peaceful society. As a result, China produced some of the world's greatest philosophical thinkers and writers. Their ideas were so powerful that they not only shaped the future of China for 2,000 years but also continue to influence world thinking today.

Children dressed in traditional clothing perform in China during a celebration of Confucius' birthday.

Primary Source: Philosophical Teaching

from *Analects of Confucius*, translated by Simon Leys

The *Analects*, a collection of Confucius' ideas, sayings, and stories, was probably recorded by many people over many years. In this passage from the *Analects*, a lord asks Confucius (often referred to as "the Master") how to govern his people.

CONSTRUCTED RESPONSE What details in the passage support the idea that Confucius believed rulers had to set a good example for their people?

> Lord Ji Kang asked: "What should I do in order to make the people respectful, loyal, and zealous [enthusiastic]?" The Master said: "Approach them with dignity and they will be respectful. Be yourself a good son and a kind father, and they will be loyal. Raise the good and train the incompetent [those unable to do a good job], and they will be zealous."

DOCUMENT TWO

Primary Source: Philosophical Teaching

from *Dao de Jing*, translated by Stephen Mitchell

The *Dao de Jing* is a key text of Daoism. In general, it stresses inaction over action and silence over words. This passage explains the power of the Dao.

CONSTRUCTED RESPONSE According to the passage, how can powerful people live peaceful, happy lives?

> The Dao never does anything,
> yet through it all things are done.
> If powerful men and women
> could center themselves in it,
> the whole world would be transformed
> by itself, in its natural rhythms.
> People would be content
> with their simple, everyday lives,
> in harmony, and free of desire.

DOCUMENT THREE

Primary Source: Philosophical Teaching

from *Han Feizi: Basic Writings*, translated by Burton Watson

Han Feizi lived from 280 to 233 B.C. He did not believe Confucianism was the answer to the chaos brought about in China during the Warring States period. In this passage from a collection of his writings, Han Feizi describes the role of rulers.

CONSTRUCTED RESPONSE What does the passage suggest about the kind of ruler and government Legalism supported?

> Discard wisdom, forswear [reject] ability, so that your subordinates [those beneath you] cannot guess what you are about. Stick to your objectives and examine the results to see how they match; take hold of the handles of government carefully and grip them tightly. Destroy all hope, smash all intention of wresting [taking] them [the handles of government] from you; allow no man to covet [desire] them.

SYNTHESIZE & WRITE

1. **REVIEW** Review what you have learned about Confucianism, Daoism, and Legalism.

2. **RECALL** On your own paper, write down the main idea expressed in each document.

3. **CONSTRUCT** Write a topic sentence that answers this question: What ideas about leadership do each of the ancient Chinese philosophies convey?

4. **WRITE** Using evidence from the documents, write a paragraph to support your answer from Step 3.

Ancient China **173**

2.1

SHI
HUANGDI
259 B.C. – 210 B.C.

The flames rise higher as officials toss more books onto the fire. Their emperor, Shi Huangdi, has ordered them to burn any writing that contains ideas he doesn't like. High on the list is anything to do with Confucianism. Shi Huangdi is a cruel but skilled ruler—and he intends his dynasty to last for 10,000 generations.

Job: First emperor of China
Home: Kingdom of Qin

FINEST HOUR
After unifying and expanding China, he became its first emperor.

WORST MOMENT
He supposedly died after taking pills he thought would keep him alive forever.

HOBBIES
He built a huge tomb for himself filled with life-size statues of warriors and horses.

GREATEST FEAR
Convinced that his enemies wanted to kill him, he slept in a different apartment in his palace every night.

A RUTHLESS RULER

China's Warring States period finally ended when the leader of the **Qin** (chin) kingdom defeated all other kingdoms around 221 B.C. The leader's name was Ying Zheng, and he united the kingdoms to form an empire. He would come to call himself **Shi Huangdi** (shee hwahng-dee), meaning "first emperor." An **emperor** is the ruler of an empire.

Shi Huangdi established his government based on Legalist ideas. He set up his capital in Xianyang (shee-ahn-yang) and built magnificent palaces in the city to demonstrate his power. The emperor then forced thousands of China's most powerful families to relocate to the capital so he could keep an eye on them.

In addition, Shi Huangdi divided his empire into 36 areas governed by officials he himself had selected. He also followed Legalist ideas by punishing anyone who disagreed with or criticized him. Shi Huangdi is said to have put to death hundreds of Confucian scholars.

This digital re-creation shows how Shi Huangdi's army of terra cotta warriors might have been painted and posed around the emperor's tomb.

A UNIFIED EMPIRE

Although his methods were cruel, Shi Huangdi brought order to China. He made sure units used to weigh and measure items throughout the empire were standardized, or the same, to ensure that buyers were not being cheated. He also brought a single writing system and currency, or form of money, to China.

As Shi Huangdi conquered new lands and expanded his empire, he made further improvements that united his territory. He had thousands of miles of roads built to link different parts of the empire. These roads were all constructed at the same width. He also built canals and irrigation systems. Shi

Huangdi's most famous construction project was the **Great Wall** of China, which you will learn more about in the next lesson. Many historians believe these structures were built by forced labor and funded by high taxes.

Shi Huangdi's rule came to an end when he died in 210 B.C. Throughout his reign, the emperor had feared being murdered by assassins. It seems he believed evil spirits could also attack him in the afterlife. As a result, Shi Huangdi had an army of **terra cotta**, or baked clay, warriors buried beside his tomb to protect him. The burial site probably forms his greatest legacy—an odd twist of fate for a man who spent much of his life trying to cheat death.

REVIEW & ASSESS

1. **READING CHECK** How did Shi Huangdi link the new lands of his empire?

2. **DRAW CONCLUSIONS** What are the benefits of using a single currency within a country?

3. **FORM OPINIONS** What do you think was Shi Huangdi's greatest achievement? Why?

2.2 The Great Wall

Groaning under the weight of another brick, you set it in place on the wall. You didn't volunteer for this work, and you won't be paid very much for it either. It's possible you'll even die working on the wall. But under Shi Huangdi's rule, you do as you're told.

MAIN IDEA

Shi Huangdi began building the Great Wall to keep invaders out of China.

KEEPING OUT INVADERS

While mountains, deserts, and seas protected most of China, part of its northern border was vulnerable, or open to attack. Riding on horseback, nomadic tribes from Central Asia often swept over the border, destroying farms, villages, and towns. Small walls had been built along the border during the Warring States period, but Shi Huangdi decided to join them into one long wall that would stretch over 2,500 miles.

The emperor forced hundreds of thousands of **peasants**, or poor farmers, to build his wall. He also conscripted soldiers and prisoners to perform the backbreaking labor, often in extreme conditions. Many of the laborers died from exhaustion, hunger, and disease. After Shi Huangdi's death, the wall fell into disrepair. However, later rulers built and extended it. In fact, work on the wall continued into the 1600s.

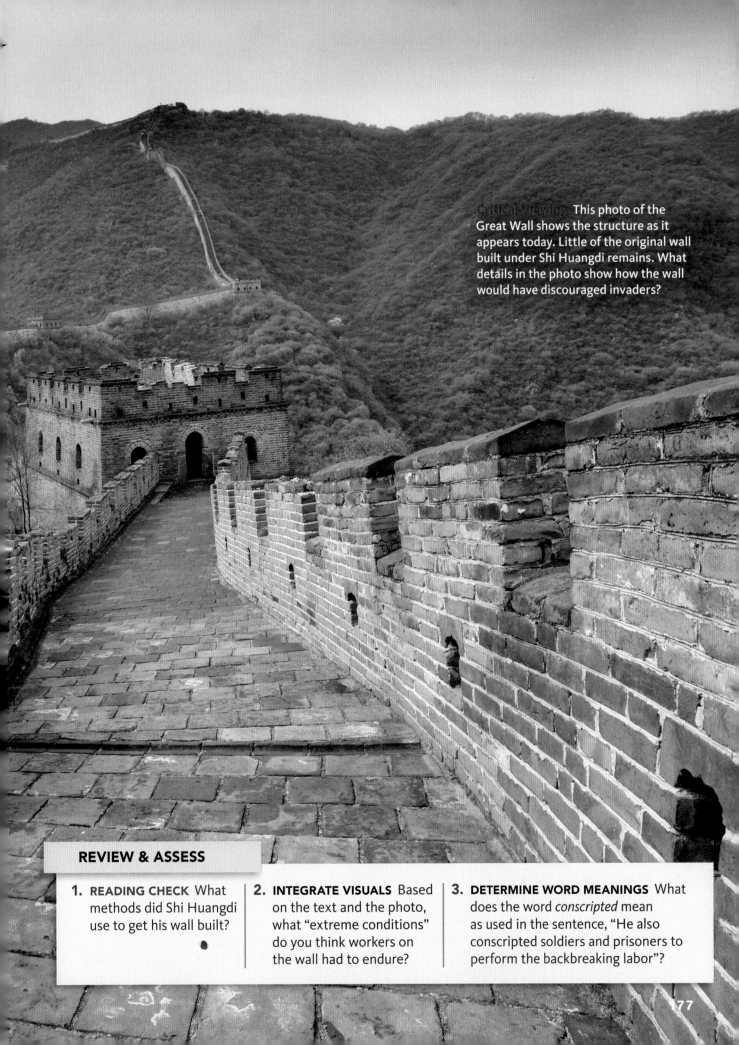

Critical Viewing This photo of the Great Wall shows the structure as it appears today. Little of the original wall built under Shi Huangdi remains. What details in the photo show how the wall would have discouraged invaders?

REVIEW & ASSESS

1. **READING CHECK** What methods did Shi Huangdi use to get his wall built?

2. **INTEGRATE VISUALS** Based on the text and the photo, what "extreme conditions" do you think workers on the wall had to endure?

3. **DETERMINE WORD MEANINGS** What does the word *conscripted* mean as used in the sentence, "He also conscripted soldiers and prisoners to perform the backbreaking labor"?

209 B.C.

On the morning of March 29, 1974, farmers digging a well in a village near Xi'an (shee-ahn), China, made an incredible discovery. They found a body—but one made of baked clay. It was one of an estimated 8,000 life-size terra cotta warriors that had been created to protect Shi Huangdi more than 2,000 years ago. The army of warriors—and their chariots and horses—stood in battle formation, ready to fight Shi Huangdi's battles in the afterlife. Historians estimate that more than 700,000 laborers worked for 38 years to complete the project around 209 B.C. As wonderful as the warriors are, archaeologists believe even greater treasures lie in the emperor's tomb itself, which remains unexplored. What details in the statues help make the warriors look lifelike?

2.4
The
Han Dynasty

Maybe you've gotten in trouble for coming to class late, but that predicament would be nothing next to this: In 209 B.C., some farmers arrived late to sign up for their required military service, and they were sentenced to death. The farmers got away and spurred thousands of others to rebel against the Qin dynasty.

MAIN IDEA

Han dynasty rulers reformed the government, expanded the empire, and brought prosperity to China.

GOVERNMENT

After Shi Huangdi died, his son became emperor but proved to be a weak ruler. The farmers who escaped their death sentence fueled a bloody rebellion that brought about the collapse of the Qin dynasty. Rebels struggled for power until Liu Bang (lee-oo bahng), a peasant from the Han kingdom, seized control and began the **Han** dynasty in 202 B.C.

Han emperors introduced practices that were less cruel than those of Shi Huangdi. They lowered taxes and put an end to laws that were especially harsh. They also required lighter punishments for crimes.

You may recall that Shi Huangdi had forced workers to labor for years on his building projects. The Han, on the other hand, had peasants work for only one month per year to build roads, canals, and irrigation systems.

The Han rulers also replaced Legalism with Confucianism and used Confucius' teachings as a guide. Furthermore, they valued the well-educated and obedient officials Confucianism produced. As a result, the officials they appointed had to pass an examination that tested their knowledge of Confucianism. The rulers established their government based on a **bureaucracy**, in which these appointed officials ran the bureaus, or offices.

Later Han rulers included Liu Bang's wife, who came to be known as Empress Lü. Women were not allowed to rule as emperor in ancient China, but Lü found a way around that restriction. After her husband died in 195 B.C., Lü placed their young son on the throne and ruled in his name. When she outlived her son, she held on to power by crowning a couple of infants emperor and ruling in their place. After Lü died in 180 B.C., all of her relatives were executed by a group of rival court officials. They made sure that no other member of her family could rule again.

Emperor Wudi (woo-dee), who ruled from 141 to 87 B.C., was another notable emperor. He used military conquests to expand the empire's boundaries—nearly to the size of present-day China. His reign lasted 54 years, which set a record that would not be broken for more than 1,800 years.

DAILY LIFE

China prospered under the Han dynasty. Many merchants, government workers, and craftspeople lived in large houses in the cities. Like modern cities, these were crowded places filled with restaurants, businesses, and places of entertainment. Some cities had populations of up to 500,000 people.

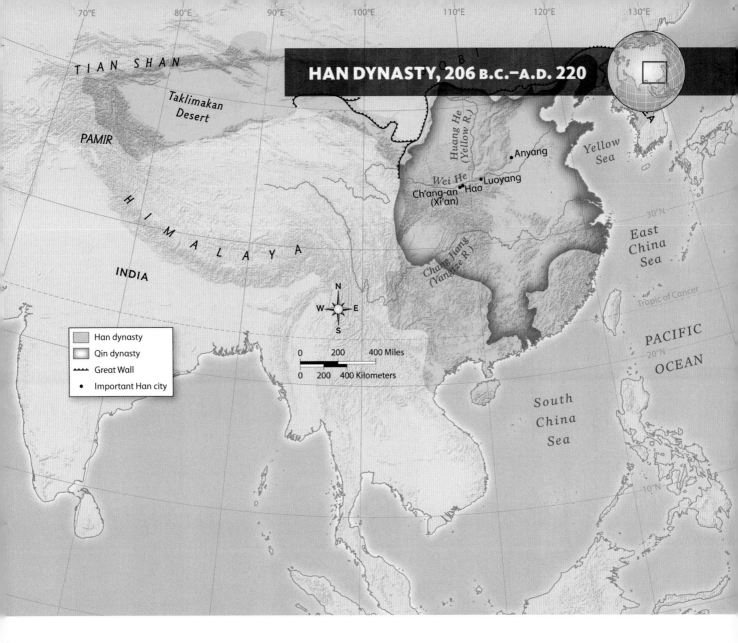

Most of the Chinese people, however, were peasants. They lived in small mud houses in villages close to their farms. Some peasants could not afford farm animals and so pulled their plows themselves. They had few possessions and barely produced enough to feed their own families. For the most part, peasants lived on the rice, wheat, and vegetables they grew on their farms.

Perhaps because the Han leaders ruled more wisely than Shi Huangdi had, their dynasty lasted about 400 years—until A.D. 220. Most Chinese people today are proud of their ancient civilization and of the contributions made during the Han dynasty in particular. As a result, many Chinese call themselves "people of the Han" in recognition of the dynasty's great achievements.

REVIEW & ASSESS

1. **READING CHECK** What government reforms did the Han rulers put in place?

2. **INTERPRET MAPS** How does the size of the Qin dynasty compare to that of the Han?

3. **COMPARE AND CONTRAST** How did the lives of poor peasants and rich merchants differ?

THE LEGACY OF CHINA'S EARLY COMPASS

Over the centuries, people have used the technology behind ancient Chinese inventions to develop their own inventions. For example, this Chinese compass from the Han dynasty paved the way for the development of the items shown below. The compass wasn't used for navigation, but it did show direction. The spoon is a special type of magnet that aligns with Earth's poles and can point in the eight main directions marked on the plate.

Sextant from the 1700s
Developed in the 1730s, the sextant measured the angle between a star and the horizon, enabling navigators to determine latitude.

World War II Radio Receiver
This navigational device was used on ships and planes during World War II. The device determines the direction of incoming radio signals.

Present-Day GPS Receiver
A global positioning system, or GPS, device uses satellite information to determine the location of almost any place on or near Earth.

2.5

The Legacy of
Ancient China

Ancient China's contributions to world civilization are so many and so varied that it's difficult to know where to begin. But consider that whenever you read a book, you're looking at one of China's most important inventions: paper.

MAIN IDEA

Early Chinese achievements, including inventions, cultural contributions, and ideas, left the world a lasting legacy.

INVENTIONS

Although historians believe the use of paper in China goes back even further, China is officially said to have invented paper in A.D. 105. The invention transformed writing. The ancient Chinese made paper from tree bark, plant fibers, and old rags. It was cheap to produce and easy to write on. The availability of paper allowed ideas to spread farther and faster than ever.

During the Han dynasty, the ancient Chinese also invented the first compass (shown opposite). The Chinese sometimes used the instrument to determine the best location for burials. However, this early compass would eventually lead to the development of the navigational compass, which made exploration of distant lands possible.

As you have learned, most Chinese worked as farmers. Many benefited from early agricultural inventions, such as an improved plow, a wheelbarrow, and a harness that fitted around a horse's neck.

CULTURE AND IDEAS

Not all of ancient China's contributions were strictly practical. One of its most valued inventions is the beautiful textile, or cloth, called **silk**. The Chinese developed the technique for making silk and kept it secret for thousands of years. (Hint: It had something to do with worms.) Demand for silk grew until it became China's most traded good. It is still a prized textile today.

Chinese craftspeople worked in metals as well. Remember reading about the advanced bronze sculptures developed during the Shang dynasty? Hundreds of years later, the Chinese would also teach the world to cast iron. This process involves heating iron until it becomes liquid and then pouring it into a mold to solidify into different shapes.

Finally, Chinese philosophies remain one of ancient China's greatest legacies. One of these philosophies—Confucianism—got a boost from the invention of paper. Confucian ideas were among the first spread by China's new writing material. Today, Confucianism continues to influence thinking, just as Chinese inventions make our lives easier.

REVIEW & ASSESS

1. **READING CHECK** What were a few of the inventions that ancient China contributed to world civilization?

2. **ANALYZE CAUSE AND EFFECT** What impact did agricultural advancements probably have on ancient China's food production and economy?

3. **FORM OPINIONS** Which ancient Chinese invention, cultural development, or idea do you think is the most significant? Explain your reasons.

3.1

The
Silk Roads

The desert sun beats down on your back as you trudge wearily across the sand. Peering ahead, all you see is a long line of camels, each loaded with bundles of silk. Still, you know that the profit you'll make from trading these goods will make your journey worthwhile.

MAIN IDEA

The Silk Roads were some of the world's most important international trade routes.

Traders had to deal with dangerous animals along the routes, including poisonous snakes.

CAMELS

Camels sometimes bite and spit, but they're terrific on a long journey—like one along the Silk Roads. They can store fat in their humps and survive without eating or drinking for days. When they get a chance to drink, however, they can take in as much as 25 gallons of water at one time.

ROUTES ACROSS ASIA

You have learned about ancient China's legacy of inventions, culture, and ideas. However, a series of international trade routes called the **Silk Roads** is also one of China's great legacies. The Silk Roads had been well established by 100 B.C., but the name for the routes was coined many centuries later. A German geographer came up with the name because silk was the main good China traded on the routes. The Silk Roads brought great wealth to China and its trading partners.

The Silk Roads began as a network of local overland routes. These eventually joined to form a huge network that connected China with the rest of Asia, Europe, and Africa. The main route stretched more than 4,000 miles and ran from China through Central Asia and Mesopotamia. Other land routes branched off the main road. Some of these routes brought traders to northern India.

The Silk Roads also included **maritime**, or sea, routes. Traders could sail along these routes to the Mediterranean Sea and to Europe. Other maritime routes led across the Indian Ocean to East Africa and across the Pacific Ocean to Korea, Japan, and Southeast Asia.

A DEMANDING JOURNEY

Chinese goods might have traveled thousands of miles, but Chinese traders did not. They traded their goods somewhere around Kashgar, near China's western border. They may have passed

SILK ROADS MAIN ROUTE, 150 B.C.–A.D. 500

While crossing the deserts, camels could close their nostrils against the blowing sand.

In time, market towns developed along the Silk Roads in places like Samarqand. Some of these, in turn, grew into great cities.

their goods along to Central Asian nomads. The nomads, in turn, may have gone on to trade the goods with other merchants from Asia, Africa, and Europe. The goods probably changed hands so many times that no one knew where they originated.

Actually, few traders made the entire journey from one end of the main Silk Roads route to the other. The trip over the rugged terrain would have taken at least six months. At best, traders followed rough paths or tracks. At worst, they scaled ice-covered mountain passes or encountered sandstorms as they crossed scorching-hot deserts.

These difficult conditions made camels the ideal pack animals because they were strong, sure-footed, and tough. They could carry huge loads—about 400 to 500 pounds of goods—for long distances in the driest, hottest weather.

The traders on the Silk Roads usually walked alongside the camels and traveled in groups called **caravans**. They found safety in numbers. The valuable caravans created a tempting target for the bandits and thieves who often lay in wait along the routes. After all, a single camel carried more wealth than most people could possibly imagine.

REVIEW & ASSESS

1. **READING CHECK** What continents were connected by the Silk Roads?

2. **INTERPRET MAPS** Why do you think the main route of the Silk Roads divided in two between the cities of Dunhuang and Kashgar?

3. **MAKE INFERENCES** What impact do you think the Silk Roads had on China's economy?

Trade on the Silk Roads

In the late 1930s, archaeologists discovered two sealed rooms in Begram, Afghanistan, an ancient city on the Silk Roads. Inside they found decorative bowls from China, ivory statues from India, and glassware from Europe. Stored away about 2,000 years ago, the objects illustrate the worldwide trade that flowed along the Silk Roads.

MAIN IDEA

Many different goods and ideas from three continents were traded on the Silk Roads.

GOODS

As you have learned, silk was China's chief trade good. Production of the fabric was not easy, though. Silk is made from the cocoons, or protective coverings, of silkworms, which live only on mulberry trees. Chinese workers had to remove strands of silk from the cocoons by hand and spin them into thread. Even so, the process was worth the trouble. Demand for the rare fabric allowed Chinese merchants to charge high prices for it. In fact, silk was so valuable that the Chinese government sometimes used it to pay its soldiers.

In addition to silk, China traded paper, highly polished decorative items called lacquerware, and objects made of iron or bronze. In return for these goods, Chinese merchants often sought gold, silver, and olive oil. One of the items the Chinese especially valued was Central Asian horses.

Market towns sprang up all along the Silk Roads. Major market towns in China included Chang'an, where the main route began, and Kashgar. A dazzling variety of items, including Central Asian rugs, Indian spices, and European wool, landed in the stalls in these towns. Traders from these and many other places used different currencies. Many had no money at all. As a result, the traders often **bartered**, or exchanged, items for other goods.

INVENTIONS AND IDEAS

Goods were not all that passed along the Silk Roads. With so many traders from so many parts of the world, the routes served as a network for the exchange of inventions and ideas as well. You have already learned that the process by which ideas spread from one culture to another is called **cultural diffusion**. By this process, Chinese ideas about papermaking, metalwork, and farming techniques began to spread beyond China's borders. In time, these ideas and inventions reached as far as Western Europe.

China also absorbed new ideas. Chief among these was Buddhism. You might remember that Buddhism began in India around 500 B.C. Indian merchants introduced Buddhist ideas to Chinese traders and even established Buddhist shrines along the Silk Roads.

Buddhism's ideas about ending suffering appealed to the Chinese, and eventually the religion became an important part of Chinese life. Many Chinese blended its practices with Confucianism. From China, Buddhism would spread throughout East Asia. Other ideas also reached China, including Greek and Indian styles in sculpture, painting, and temple building. All of these ideas enriched Chinese culture and civilization.

Critical Viewing It took artists more than 90 years to carve this Giant Buddha in southwest China, the largest carved stone Buddha in the world. What qualities does the Buddha's face convey?

REVIEW & ASSESS

1. **READING CHECK** What were some of the goods and ideas exchanged on the Silk Roads?

2. **DRAW CONCLUSIONS** Why do you think Buddhism's ideas about ending suffering might have appealed to the ancient Chinese?

3. **MAKE INFERENCES** Why were Chinese traders able to demand high prices for their silk?

3.3

GOODS FROM THE SILK ROADS

Imagine a market filled with delicate silk and gold and jewels that catch the sunlight. Rows of foods, including grapes, olive oil, spices, and honey, tempt you as you stroll along the stalls. Horses and camels stare back at you with bored expressions as they wait under a tent for potential buyers. Because of the long distances, difficulties, and dangers along the Silk Roads, only the finest and most expensive goods were traded. Very few of the actual goods traded have survived, but as you can see, the types of wares exchanged can still dazzle the eye. Who probably bought these goods in the markets?

Rugs and Blankets
Nomads from Central Asia used wool from their sheep and camels to weave the rugs and blankets they traded.

Grapes
European merchants traded grapes, which were used to make wine.

Ivory
Asian traders bartered ivory plaques, like this one, carved from elephant tusks.

The design on a rug traded on the Silk Roads often represented the nomadic tribe to which the weaver belonged.

Honey
Northern European merchants sold honey on the Silk Roads. This image shows honey in a honeycomb.

Spices
Spices were used to flavor food but were also believed to cure many diseases.

The spices shown here include cinnamon, coriander, and pepper. In ancient times before refrigeration, these and other spices were used to mask the flavor of food that had spoiled.

Pottery
Korean celadon, like this pottery jug, probably traveled to China over the maritime routes.

Silk
A pound of silk was as valuable as a pound of gold on the Silk Roads.

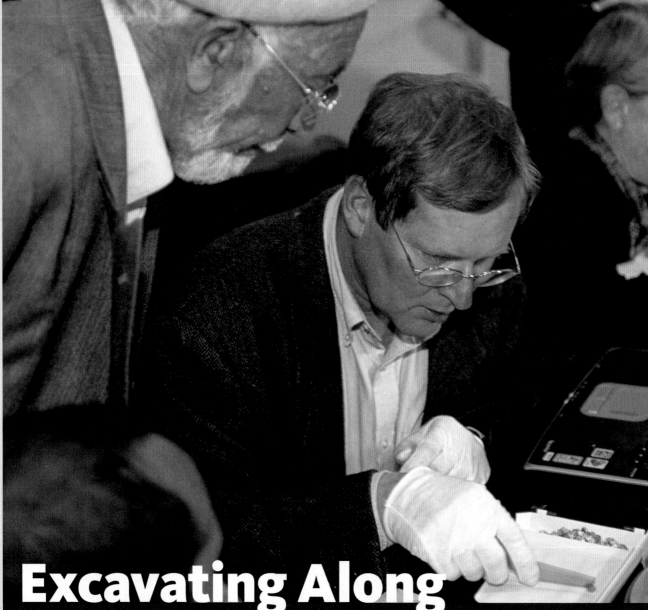

Excavating Along the Silk Roads

Fredrik Hiebert likes to challenge accepted ideas. "As an archaeologist," he says, "my main job is to try to make the textbooks go out of date. History is a living thing, and we're always rewriting it." Some of Hiebert's major excavations, or archaeological digs, have been in Turkmenistan, a country in Central Asia. Based on his discoveries there, Hiebert has concluded that traders began traveling along the Silk Roads about 4,000 or 5,000 years ago—much earlier than historians had once thought.

^
Fredrik Hiebert's study of the ancient trade routes led him to Afghanistan, where he uncovered a golden treasure. Here he examines some of the artifacts.

MAIN IDEA

Archaeologist Fredrik Hiebert's explorations have uncovered lost gold and challenged ideas about when trading began on the Silk Roads.

CONNECTED CULTURES

National Geographic Explorer Fredrik Hiebert has been conducting excavations at Silk Roads sites—like cities in Turkmenistan—for more than 20 years. "Historians thought the Silk Roads had emerged about 100 B.C.," says Hiebert. "But when we dug deeper into Silk Roads cities, we found they'd been built on much older Bronze Age settlements, which contained artifacts from as far away as India and Mesopotamia. This means that long-distance trade along the Silk Roads took place 2,000 years before we'd thought it had started."

Necklace from the Bactrian Hoard

The realization didn't surprise Hiebert. He believes that ancient cultures were always connected. "It's easy to argue that ancient cultures were isolated by geography and the lack of transport," he claims, "but that really didn't stop people from traveling and trading. They just did it more slowly."

LOST GOLD

Hiebert's explorations of the Silk Roads have also taken him to Afghanistan, which borders Turkmenistan in the south. In 1988, a Russian archaeologist told him about 21,000 pieces of ancient gold that he'd excavated ten years earlier near the Afghan region of Bactria. He later showed Hiebert photos of the collection, which came to be known as the Bactrian Hoard. The gold had belonged to nomads who herded and traded along the Silk Roads around the first century B.C. The collection was placed in a museum in Afghanistan. However, after war erupted in the country in 1978, the gold disappeared. The Russian archaeologist believed it was lost forever.

"Fast-forward to 2003 when I heard rumors of ancient gold hidden in the Afghan presidential palace," Hiebert continues the story. "I thought: Could it be the Bactrian Hoard?" Working with the National Geographic Society, Hiebert persuaded the Afghan authorities to let him open the safes where he thought the treasure might be found. Inside were all 21,000 pieces of gold, including a necklace, shown here, that Hiebert recognized from the photos he had seen of the hoard.

"Against all odds it had survived intact, thanks to a few dedicated museum workers who had kept it secret for so many years," Hiebert says. His study of the gold revealed more evidence of cultural connections. The items were imitations of Chinese, Greek, and Indian artifacts traded on the Silk Roads. The gold is beautiful and valuable beyond measure, but that's not what most interests Hiebert. As he says, "We don't actually search for treasure. We search for knowledge—that's our real gold."

REVIEW & ASSESS

1. **READING CHECK** When does Hiebert believe trade along the Silk Roads first took place?

2. **IDENTIFY MAIN IDEAS AND DETAILS** What evidence did Hiebert find to support his ideas about cultural connections on the Silk Roads?

3. **ANALYZE LANGUAGE USE** What does Hiebert suggest about knowledge when he compares it to gold?

VOCABULARY

Complete each of the following sentences using one of the vocabulary words from the chapter.

1. During China's early development, physical features such as mountains and deserts helped _isolate_ China.

2. The Han dynasty's government was based on a _____ run by appointed officials.

3. Rather than sell silk for money, Chinese merchants would _____ it for gold.

4. According to the _____, a dynasty is overthrown once it has lost the approval of the gods.

5. Many historians believe that hundreds of thousands of _____ were forced to build the Great Wall.

6. Confucius taught that children should show their parents _____.

7. Traders on the Silk Roads often traveled in groups called _____.

READING STRATEGY

8. **ANALYZE LANGUAGE USE** If you haven't already, complete your concept clusters to analyze language used to describe Confucianism, Daoism, and Legalism. Then answer the question.

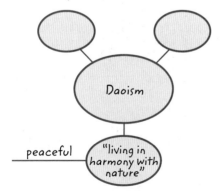

Based on the author's choice of words, how would you describe the overall theme of each philosophy?

MAIN IDEAS

Answer the following questions. Support your answers with evidence from the chapter.

9. Why did civilization in ancient China first develop with relatively little cultural influence from the outside world? **LESSON 1.1**

10. What was the Mandate of Heaven? **LESSON 1.2**

11. How did Shi Huangdi organize his empire? **LESSON 2.1**

12. Why did Shi Huangdi begin building the Great Wall? **LESSON 2.2**

13. How did Han rulers bring Confucianism into their government? **LESSON 2.4**

14. What were the benefits of traveling on the Silk Roads in camel caravans? **LESSON 3.1**

15. How did trade on the Silk Roads encourage the process of cultural diffusion? **LESSON 3.2**

CRITICAL THINKING

Answer the following questions. Support your answers with evidence from the chapter.

16. **SUMMARIZE** How did China establish one of the world's oldest continuous civilizations?

17. **DRAW CONCLUSIONS** How did the dynastic cycle help ensure the rise of new dynasties throughout China's early history?

18. **MAKE INFERENCES** Why do you think Shi Huangdi was drawn to Legalist ideas rather than Confucian ideas?

19. **COMPARE AND CONTRAST** What did the governments under the Qin and Han dynasties have in common? How did they differ?

20. **MAKE INFERENCES** What role do you think the Silk Roads played in the Han dynasty's prosperity?

21. **YOU DECIDE** Do you think Shi Huangdi was an effective emperor? Why or why not? Support your opinion with evidence from the chapter.

INTERPRET MAPS

Study the map showing the spread of Buddhism. Then answer the questions that follow.

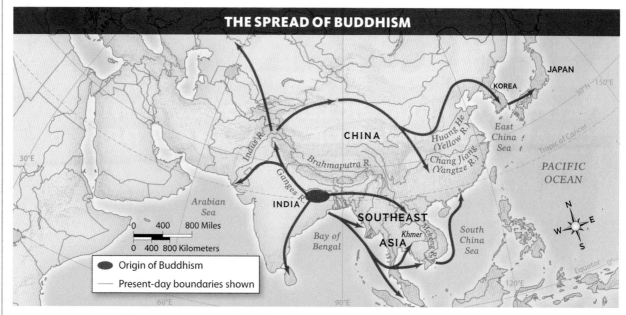

THE SPREAD OF BUDDHISM

JAPAN

KOREA

CHINA

Huang He (Yellow R.)

East China Sea

Chang Jiang (Yangtze R.)

PACIFIC OCEAN

Indus R.

Brahmaputra R.

Ganges R.

INDIA

Arabian Sea

SOUTHEAST ASIA

Khmer

Mekong R.

South China Sea

Bay of Bengal

Tropic of Cancer

Equator

Legend:
- Origin of Buddhism
- Present-day boundaries shown

0   400   800 Miles
0   400   800 Kilometers

22. Why do you think Buddhism spread to China before Korea and Japan?

23. What other region shown on the map was influenced by Buddhism?

ANALYZE SOURCES

Study this bronze statue of a flying horse, one of the finest examples of art from the Han dynasty. Then answer the question.

24. What details in the statue make it appear as if the horse is actually flying?

WRITE ABOUT HISTORY

25. ARGUMENT Which Chinese philosophy might be most effective as the basis for a governing policy? Choose one of the philosophies—Confucianism, Daoism, or Legalism—and create a bulleted list of arguments you might use in a debate on the subject.

TIPS

- Take notes from the lessons about each philosophy and its application in ancient Chinese government.

- Study the excerpt from each philosophy's teachings in Lesson 1.4.

- Consider what each philosophy offers governments and the people they rule.

- Use vocabulary terms from the chapter.

- Organize your ideas into a bulleted list of arguments. Include points that might counter, or answer, arguments proposed by the opposing side.

ON **LOCATION** WITH

Christopher
THORNTON

NATIONAL GEOGRAPHIC LEAD PROGRAM OFFICER, RESEARCH, CONSERVATION, AND EXPLORATION

▶ Check out more on myNGconnect

Christopher Thornton directs
excavations at the archaeological
site of Bat in Oman. He has
uncovered information that is
providing new insights into the
social history of the region.

EARLY PASSION

I'd always planned to major in chemistry in college, but in my freshman year, I took a seminar on archaeological chemistry and got hooked! From that moment on, archaeology became my passion and my career.

Today I specialize in late prehistory in Southwest Asia, from the beginning of agriculture to the rise of empires. I love working in this region because, while people's lives have been modernized, their cultures remain fairly traditional. You get a sense of "the old ways" while still enjoying hot showers!

Chris Thornton works near a 4,500-year-old Bronze Age monument in northwestern Oman at the site of Bat.

DIGGING FOR CLUES

Because this region had very limited literacy during the late prehistoric and early historic periods, it needs an archaeologist's eye to investigate and figure out what was going on then. One of the key questions I'm trying to answer is how and why people living in harsh regions like present-day Oman managed to create relatively large settlements 4,000 years ago but, 1,000 or so years later, were content to live in much smaller areas. A clue lies in copper.

Mesopotamian texts from the Bronze Age refer to modern Oman as "Magan," noting that it was then a major producer of copper for the entire region. Most archaeologists believed that the people of Magan were being exploited by traders from Mesopotamia and the Indus Valley. However, for nine years, my team and I have been excavating a site called Bat in northwestern Oman. In the course of our digs, we've discovered not only evidence of copper production, but also indications of the local use of copper in tools, weapons, and jewelry. This suggests that despite the harsh geography of the region, the people of Magan were a very important part of the Bronze Age economic trade networks that led to the rise of cities. This puts a whole new slant on the history of the region.

Now we hope to find clues that will help us understand how the adoption of farming led to early settled villages in Magan, and how these eventually grew into the large centers we find by 2200 B.C. These are the kind of answers we keep digging for.

WHY STUDY HISTORY ❓

❝ History helps us *to understand the similarities* between apparently different nations, peoples, and cultures. Studying history lets us look back on all that we have accomplished and to consider where we are going now! ❞ —Christopher Thornton

NATIONAL GEOGRAPHIC

China's Ancient Lifeline

BY IAN JOHNSON

Adapted from "China's Ancient Lifeline,"
by Ian Johnson, in *National Geographic*, May 2013

Barges sailing the Grand Canal have knit China together for 14 centuries. They carried grain, soldiers, and ideas between the economic heartland in the south and the political capitals in the north.

Old Zhu, as everyone calls him, is a modern barge captain. Barge captains live by tough calculations that determine whether they get rich or are ruined. One captain said, "The product owners set the price, the moneylenders set the interest, and the government officials set the fees. All we can do is nod and continue working."

On paper, the Grand Canal runs 1,100 miles between Beijing and the southern city of Hangzhou. But for nearly forty years, part of its course has been too dry for shipping. Today, the waterway's main commercial section is the 325 miles from Jining to the Yangtze.

Emperor Yang of the Sui dynasty built the original canal system. Ancient China's main rivers ran west to east, and he needed a way to move rice from south to north to feed his armies. The emperor forced one million workers to build the canal. It took six years to complete and many workers died, but goods began to flow. The Grand Canal also moved culture. Emperors inspecting the canal took some local customs back to the capital.

Along one section, Old Zhu pointed and said, "That's the old Grand Canal, or what's left of it," pointing to a channel about 15 feet wide curving between a small island and the bank. Today, local governments aim to boost tourism and development by beautifying the canal. But beautification can also destroy. In Yangzhou, the makeover required leveling nearly every canal-side building.

In 2005, a small group of citizens campaigned for the Grand Canal to become a UNESCO World Heritage site. "Every generation wants the next generation to look at its monuments," said Zhu Bingren, who co-wrote the proposal. "But if we wipe out the previous generations' work, what will following generations think of us?"

**For more from National Geographic
Check out "Faces of the Divine" on myNGconnect**

UNIT INQUIRY: WRITE A CREATION MYTH

In this unit, you learned about the development of early civilizations in Mesopotamia, Egypt, India, and China. Based on your understanding of the text, what crucial roles did geography and natural resources play in the development of early civilizations? What other factors were important to their growth and longevity?

ASSIGNMENT Write a creation myth for one of the civilizations you learned about in this unit. The narrator of your creation myth should be a geographic feature or a natural resource—such as a river—that was vital to the civilization's development. Be prepared to present your creation myth to the class and explain your choice of narrator.

Plan As you write your creation myth, think about the essential roles geography and natural resources played in that civilization's development. To describe the civilization, answer from the narrator's point of view the questions *Who? What? Where? When? Why?* and *How?* Try to incorporate these descriptions in your myth. You might want to use a graphic organizer to help organize your thoughts. ▶

Produce Use your notes to produce detailed descriptions of the factors that were important in the development of the civilization you selected. Begin your creation myth with an engaging introduction to capture your audience's attention.

Present Choose a creative way to present your myth to the class. Consider one of these options:

- Create a multimedia presentation using illustrations or photographs of the civilization's geography to produce a sense of place.

- Dress in costume and play the role of an ancient storyteller for an oral presentation of the myth.

- Illustrate cover art featuring the narrator of the creation myth.

Who?	_____
What?	_____
Where?	_____
When?	_____
Why?	_____
How?	_____

RAPID REVIEW
UNIT 2

EARLY CIVILIZATIONS

TOP TEN

1. Farming in the fertile lands of Mesopotamia led to the emergence of city-states such as Sumer and Ur.

2. The fertile farmland along the Nile River enabled the development of ancient Egyptian civilization.

3. Judaism was the first monotheistic religion.

4. Several important religions developed in India, including Hinduism and Buddhism.

5. Ancient China spread innovative forms of government, philosophy, technology, writing, and art via trade routes.

6-10. **NOW IT'S YOUR TURN** Complete the list with five more things to remember about early civilizations.

TO LEARN ABOUT THE BUILDING BLOCKS OF CIVILIZATION

In Units 1 and 2, you've learned about the origins of culture and how the building blocks of civilization allowed humans to move from individuals struggling to survive to groups creating a life together. All early civilizations faced the same challenges—and the urge to establish an identity was key to their survival.

The record of human occupation involves the study of stones, bones, and artifacts that go back hundreds of thousands of years. Archaeologists rely on that record to learn about the way we've lived on this earth. Artifacts represent people's identity. When an artifact is looted, or excavated illegally, we lose the context for that artifact—where it was found and who created it. It becomes lost to history. The human record is a non-renewable resource that can never be replaced.

Fred Hiebert
▶ Watch the Why Study History video

WHAT COMES NEXT? PREVIEW UNITS 3–5

3

ACROPOLIS

4

POMPEII

5

AZTEC SKULLS

GREEK CIVILIZATION
Learn how the Greeks left a legacy in government, art, and architecture that would have an impact on all civilizations.

THE WORLD OF THE ROMANS
See how the Roman developments in government, engineering, and religion continue to affect your life today.

AMERICAN AND ASIAN CIVILIZATIONS
Study the sophisticated cultures that developed in the Americas and in imperial China.

KEY TAKEAWAYS UNITS 1 AND 2

PATTERNS IN HISTORY: SIMILAR DEVELOPMENTS ACROSS LOCATIONS

All centers of civilization develop the same basic structures:

- the beginnings of social organization that lead to governments
- origins of religion as a way to make sense of the world
- the development of crafts that lead to technology
- basic economies that lead to today's economy

GOVERNMENT

Advancements include the rise of dynasties, such as those in Egypt and China; the creation of laws, including Hammurabi's Code; and the building of cities.

MOVEMENT OF PEOPLE AND IDEAS

People adapt to new places, environments, and climates, from the earliest exodus from Africa to migrations in India.

TRADE

Peoples and cultures gradually intermingle, a first step toward global citizenship.

ARTISTIC EXPRESSION

Cave art, including the handprints shown here, become early expressions of identity.

TECHNOLOGY & INNOVATION

Tools, settlements, and the development of agriculture increase chances of survival.

AS YOU READ ON

History is more than just one fact after another. Keep in mind the key takeaways from Units 1 and 2. Be sure to ask "how" and "why," and not just "what." Watch as the human story continues with the civilizations that may be most familiar to you: the Greek and Roman civilizations.

GREEK
CIVILIZATION

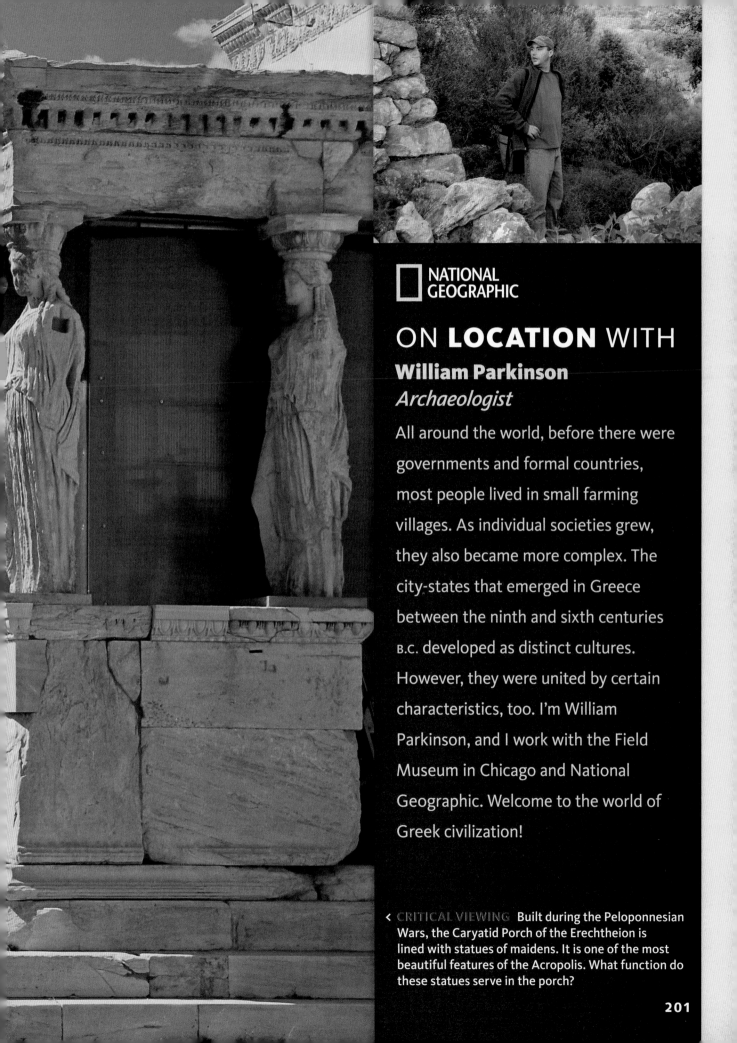

ON **LOCATION** WITH

William Parkinson
Archaeologist

All around the world, before there were governments and formal countries, most people lived in small farming villages. As individual societies grew, they also became more complex. The city-states that emerged in Greece between the ninth and sixth centuries B.C. developed as distinct cultures. However, they were united by certain characteristics, too. I'm William Parkinson, and I work with the Field Museum in Chicago and National Geographic. Welcome to the world of Greek civilization!

< CRITICAL VIEWING Built during the Peloponnesian Wars, the Caryatid Porch of the Erechtheion is lined with statues of maidens. It is one of the most beautiful features of the Acropolis. What function do these statues serve in the porch?

Greek Civilization

c. 1450 B.C.
Mycenaean civilization thrives on the Greek mainland and takes control of Crete, ending Minoan civilization.
(Lion Gate of Mycenae)

c. 2000 B.C.
Minoan civilization flourishes on the island of Crete.
(a lady of the Minoan court)

1500 B.C.

2000 B.C.

c. 2000 B.C.
EUROPE
Stonehenge is built in England.

1790 B.C.
ASIA
Hammurabi's Code is issued in the Babylonian Empire.

1300 B.C.
ASIA
The kingdom of Israel is established by the Hebrews.

1279 B.C.
AFRICA
Ramses II begins 66-year reign in Egypt.

The World

1200 B.C.
AMERICAS
Olmec culture rises in the Americas.
(Olmec stone head)

What happened in the world just before democracy was established in Athens?

334 B.C.
Alexander the Great enters Asia Minor in order to conquer Persia. He dies in 323 B.C., marking the end of the Classic Age. *(gold coin with Alexander's profile)*

431 B.C.
The Peloponnesian War between Athens and Sparta begins. *(Greek pot with scene from Peloponnesian War)*

800 B.C.
Greeks begin using an alphabet. Literature is written down, including the *Iliad* and *Odyssey*.

1000 B.C.

c. 750 B.C.
Phoenicia develops into wealthy city-states, including the colony of Carthage.

c. 500 B.C.
The first democracy is established in Athens.

1100s B.C.
ASIA
The Zhou dynasty rules China.
(Zhou vessel)

500 B.C.

509 B.C.
EUROPE
The Roman Republic is established.

551 B.C.
Confucius is born in China.

ANCIENT GREECE c. 500 B.C.

The area colored orange on the map may look like a small and fragmented collection of peninsulas and islands, but these areas of land formed one of the most sophisticated cultures and civilizations the world has ever known: the civilization of ancient Greece. Not even its geography stood in Greece's way. Greek traders used the waters of the Mediterranean to secure and control trade routes. Mountains made travel and communication difficult, but independent city-states formed around them. The city-states are labeled with dots on the map. In the city-state called Athens, a form of government developed that would change the world: democracy.

What empire might have challenged Greek power in the region?

Bosporus

Sea of Marmara

Dardanelles

Mount Olympus

G R E E C E

PERSIAN EMPIRE

Delphi

Thebes

Megara

Corinth

Mycenae

Argos

Athens

Olympia

Ephesus

Miletus

Sparta

Aegean Sea

Delos

Ionian Sea

Sea of Crete

Knossos

Crete

Mediterranean Sea

0   25   50   75   100 kilometers

0   25   50   75   100 miles

THE OLYMPICS

The first Olympic Games took place in 775 B.C. and lasted one day. Today's games include 28 different sports in summer and 7 in winter and last a couple of weeks. The early games had just a few events, not all of which are played today. You can read about the original events in the early Greek Olympics below. Emperor Theodosius banned the games in A.D. 393, calling them a "pagan cult." The first modern Olympics took place in 1896.

 Running   Contestants ran the 200-meter dash, 400-meter dash, and long distance events.

 Jumping   Athletes carried stone weights that they threw at the end of their jump to increase their distance.

 Discus   Athletes tossed a heavy disk made of stone, or later, of heavy metal.

 Boxing   Athletes fought one another using wrapped straps around their hands to strengthen their punches.

 Equestrian   Horse races and chariot-driven races took place in the Hippodrome, an ancient Greek stadium.

 Pentathlon   The pentathlon included five events: long jump, javelin throw, discus throw, foot race, and wrestling.

 Pankration   This event was a blend of wrestling and boxing and had few rules.

CHAPTER **8**

ANCIENT GREECE

2000 B.C. – 480 B.C.

SECTION 1   EARLY GREECE

 SS.6.E.1.1; SS.6.E.2.1; SS.6.E.3.3; SS.6.E.3.4; SS.6.G.1.4; SS.6.G.1.5; SS.6.G.1.6; SS.6.G.1.7; SS.6.G.2.1; SS.6.G.2.2; SS.6.G.2.4; SS.6.G.2.5; SS.6.G.2.6; SS.6.G.5.1; SS.6.G.5.2; SS.6.G.5.3; SS.6.W.3.1; SS.6.W.3.2; SS.6.W.3.5; SS.6.W.3.6; LAFS.68.RH.1.2; LAFS.68.RH.2.4; LAFS.68.RH.2.5; LAFS.68.RH.3.7; LAFS.68.RH.3.8

KEY VOCABULARY

acropolis	monarchy
agora	myth
aristocracy	oligarchy
epic poem	polis
hero	raw material
labyrinth	tyrant

NAMES & PLACES

Homer
Minoan
Mycenaean
Odysseus
Trojan War

SECTION 2   SPARTA AND ATHENS

 SS.6.C.1.1; SS.6.G.4.1; SS.6.W.3.2; SS.6.W.3.3; SS.6.W.3.4; SS.6.W.3.6; LAFS.68.RH.1.2; LAFS.68.RH.2.5; LAFS.68.RH.3.7

KEY VOCABULARY

alliance	helot
democracy	trireme

NAMES & PLACES

Athens
Darius I
Solon
Sparta
Thermopylae
Xerxes

READING STRATEGY

ORGANIZE IDEAS: COMPARE AND CONTRAST
When you compare and contrast information in a text, look for words such as *also*, *and*, or *too* to signal comparisons and *but*, *however*, or *unlike* to signal contrasts. As you read the chapter, use a graphic organizer like this one to compare and contrast life in Sparta and Athens.

Sparta   Athens   Both

The Temple of Aphaia, goddess of sailors and hunters, was built on the island of Aegina around 500 B.C.

Mysterious Minoans

You step forward and grasp the horns of the huge panting bull. Its head twitches; your muscles tighten in anticipation. Blocking out the cheers of the crowd, you spring over the bull's back and land behind the enormous animal. In ancient Crete such deadly games as bull-leaping are your way of worship.

MAIN IDEA

The Minoans established the earliest civilization in ancient Greece.

ANCIENT DISASTER

Around 1600 B.C., a volcano called Thira (THIH-ruh) erupted on an island 70 miles north of Crete. The eruption destroyed most of the island and caused death and destruction across the Mediterranean. Scholars disagree about whether this eruption caused the decline of Minoan civilization, but this is one possibility.

MINOAN CIVILIZATION

Historians trace the origins of Greek civilization to Crete, a mountainous island about 150 miles off the coast of mainland Greece. Neolithic farmers settled there around 7000 B.C. and agriculture flourished. By 2000 B.C., a sophisticated **Minoan** (mih-NOH-uhn) civilization had emerged, centered on cities governed from magnificent royal palaces.

Though the Minoans left behind written records, historians cannot read their language. Their knowledge of Minoan civilization is pieced together through archaeology and the writings of ancient Greek historians. There are also many myths about this civilization. **Myths** are very old stories told to explain events or to justify beliefs and actions. The word *Minoan* comes from a mythical Cretan king named Minos (MY-nuhs). According to the myth, Minos built a **labyrinth** (LAB-uh-rinth), or maze, beneath his palace. A monstrous Minotaur (MIHN-uh-tawr)—half man, half bull—lived in this labyrinth and was offered regular sacrifices of unlucky humans. Unlikely? Perhaps, but archaeological evidence confirms that a powerful Minoan king built a labyrinth-like palace, and Minoans did in fact worship bulls and perform sacrifices.

CITIES AND CULTURE

The Minoans grew wealthy through trade across the Mediterranean. One of the Minoans' strengths was that they were expert sailors. Their well-built ships carried olive oil, wine, cloth, pottery, and metalwork to Greece, Egypt, Cyprus, and Spain. The Minoans returned from trading voyages with important **raw materials**, or substances from which other products are made, such as tin, gold, pearls, and ivory. Minoans spread their culture throughout Greece and along the coasts of the Aegean (ee-JEE-uhn) Sea. Their strong navy controlled the seas, making the Minoans feel so safe they did not build city walls.

The great palace at Knossos (NAW-suhss) dominated Crete. The size and complexity of the palace may have encouraged some people to believe it was Minos's labyrinth. Home to almost 20,000 people, Knossos was more like a city than a palace. It was the center of Minoan culture, religion, and economy. The palace included a central courtyard for ceremonies, hundreds of rooms,

This painting from the palace of Knossos shows bull-leaping.

and even advanced plumbing. It also provided workshops for Minoan artisans and storerooms for surplus crops, such as grains. Minoans worked to support the palace and enjoyed a relatively prosperous life.

Minoan religion was polytheistic, which means that people believed in many gods and goddesses. Lifelike Minoan wall paintings suggest forms of worship involving bull-leaping, boxing, wrestling, and dancing as well as sacrifices to pacify the gods.

Mysteries surround the end of the Minoans. Around 1500 B.C., Minoan civilization declined sharply and its palaces fell into ruins. Possible causes for their collapse include natural disasters such as earthquakes, tidal waves, or volcanic eruptions. Some historians think all three factors—as well as an invasion by people from mainland Greece—contributed to the Minoans' decline. By 1450 B.C., a new civilization would overtake the Minoans.

REVIEW & ASSESS

1. **READING CHECK** What were some of the traits of the earliest civilization in ancient Greece?

2. **DRAW CONCLUSIONS** What does the great palace at Knossos reveal about the Minoan civilization?

3. **ANALYZE CAUSE AND EFFECT** How did trade help the Minoans develop wealth?

1.2 Mycenaean Civilization

The fascinating thing about history is often what we *don't* know. Though we know the Mycenaeans overtook the Minoans, we don't know for sure what caused their own violent end. Along with the Minoans, the Mycenaeans helped lay the foundation of Greek civilization.

MAIN IDEA

After copying Minoan culture, the Mycenaeans conquered the Minoan people.

CONQUERORS

Around 2000 B.C., a new group of people from farther east settled in mainland Greece. They became known as **Mycenaeans** (my-SEE-nee-uhnz) based on the name of their main city, Mycenae (my-SEE-nee). The early Mycenaeans established villages throughout Greece, picked up influences from Minoan culture which had spread there, and spoke an early version of the Greek language.

After invading Crete in 1500 B.C, the Mycenaeans adopted Minoan culture. The Mycenaeans copied Minoan art, architecture, religion, writing, trade, metalworking, and shipbuilding. Elements of Minoan and Mycenaean culture became part of the foundation of Greek civilization.

The Mycenaeans had an aggressive streak, though, and they eventually turned against the Minoans. The Mycenaeans seized and conquered lands across the eastern Mediterranean and Greece. Around 1450 B.C. they conquered the Minoans, taking their treasure, land, people, and palaces.

RICH KINGS

The city of Mycenae was the center of Mycenaean civilization. Built high on a hill, the city was surrounded by thick walls that protected houses, storerooms, and a grand palace. The Mycenaeans protected Mycenae and other cities with great stone walls—so huge that later Greeks believed they were built by mythical giants called Cyclopes (sy-KLOH-peez). A network of good roads connected Mycenae to other important cities.

While most Mycenaean farmers lived in simple mud-brick houses in the countryside, important officials, artisans, and traders lived in three-story stone houses in cities. Warriors had it even better. Mycenaean kings gave elite warriors fine houses and lands to rule. Everyone else worked to support the warriors.

Extensive trade and wars made Mycenaean kings rich. The fierce Mycenaean military, wearing metal armor and driving fast-moving chariots, raided and conquered surrounding people. Yet at the height of its power, around 1200 B.C., the Mycenaean civilization came to a violent end. Suddenly most Mycenaean cities and towns were mysteriously destroyed.

Historians have several theories about why Mycenaean civilization declined. One theory suggests that natural disasters caused shortages that turned cities against one another or led to peasant uprisings. Another theory suggests that Mycenaean cities were invaded by the mysterious Sea Peoples. The Sea Peoples were seaborne and land raiders who had also attacked the ancient Egyptians and fought the Hittites of Mesopotamia.

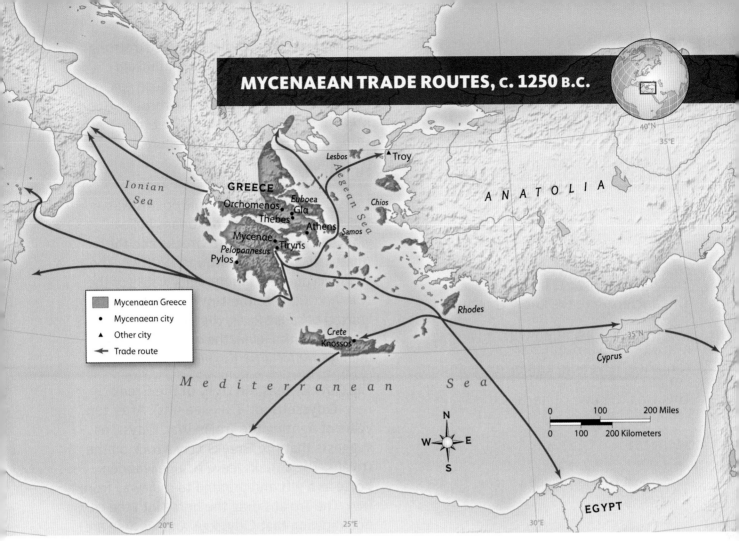

MYCENAEAN TRADE ROUTES, c. 1250 B.C.

Ionian Sea

GREECE
Orchomenos
Euboea
Gla
Thebes
Mycenae
Tiryns
Peloponnesus
Pylos
Athens
Aegean Sea
Lesbos
Chios
Samos
Troy

ANATOLIA

Rhodes

Cyprus

Crete
Knossos

Mediterranean Sea

EGYPT

Legend:
- Mycenaean Greece
- Mycenaean city
- Other city
- Trade route

Whatever the cause of the collapse, the end of Mycenaean civilization meant that ancient Greece entered a period of decline that lasted until about 950 B.C. The people abandoned cities, trade halted, and the economy floundered. During this time, the ancient Greeks also stopped keeping written records.

Without written records, historians know little about this 400-year period of Greek history. Luckily, though, the Greeks would learn to write again and record some of the greatest stories ever told.

MASK OF AGAMEMNON
This gold funeral mask discovered at Mycenae in 1876 is called the Mask of Agamemnon, named after the mythical Greek king. The mask most likely covered the face of a Mycenaean leader, though archaeologists are unsure which leader it was.

REVIEW & ASSESS

1. **READING CHECK** How did the Mycenaeans become so powerful?

2. **COMPARE AND CONTRAST** In what ways were the Mycenaeans similar to and different from the Minoans?

3. **INTERPRET MAPS** Describe the route Mycenaean traders used to reach Egypt from Tiryns.

The Age of Heroes

A good story needs an exciting plot, a little suspense, fascinating characters, and an exotic location. The ancient Greeks knew this and invented stories filled with adventure, romance, revenge, and intense action. This was the age of heroes.

MAIN IDEA

The ancient Greeks created a strong storytelling tradition.

HOMER'S EPIC POEMS

The ancient Greeks believed in many gods, goddesses, monsters, and heroes. Stories about these characters were told and retold. About 750 B.C., a man named **Homer** emerged. Historians do not know much about Homer, but tradition says he was a blind bard who lived in ancient Greece. A bard is a poet who tells stories as a rhythmic chant accompanied by music.

Homer composed two of the world's greatest stories, the *Iliad* and the *Odyssey*. Both are **epic poems**, or long poetic stories. Every epic poem has a **hero**, or a character who faces a challenge that demands courage, strength, and intelligence. Homer's epic poems dramatized how gods and goddesses influenced the lives of humans. They also helped establish the characteristics of Greek gods and goddesses.

The *Iliad* and the *Odyssey* followed a strong Greek storytelling tradition that mixed history, religion, and fantasy. These epic poems also united the Greeks through pride in their shared past and set the stage for future Western literature.

HEROIC DEEDS

The setting for Homer's epic poems was the **Trojan War**, which historians believe was fought between the Greeks and the Anatolian city of Troy around 1200 B.C. The *Iliad* tells of events in the final weeks of the war. According to the story, the Trojan War started because Paris, the prince of Troy, ran away with Helen, the wife of Menelaus (mehn-uh-LAY-uhs), the king of Sparta.

The *Odyssey* tells the story of the Greek hero **Odysseus** (oh-DIH-see-uhs). After ten years of fighting the Trojan War, Odysseus suggests that the Greeks play a trick on the Trojans. The Greeks leave a huge wooden horse as a gift and pretend to sail away from Troy. The Trojans drag the horse into the city, not knowing that Odysseus and his men are hiding inside. That night, Odysseus and his men sneak out of the horse. They open the city gates to Greek soldiers waiting outside. The Greeks take the city and recover Helen.

The *Odyssey* also tells the story of Odysseus's journey home after the war. He has many adventures involving creatures such as a one-eyed Cyclops and the Sirens—women whose singing lures sailors to crash their ships onto rocks.

FACT OR FICTION?

For thousands of years Troy and the Trojan War were considered nothing more than myths. However, Homer's stories inspired archaeologists to explore Greece. In the 1820s, they discovered the remains of a great city in Turkey. It matched Homer's description of Troy and had been violently destroyed about the same time, so Homer's war may have actually happened.

The Trojan Horse, Henri Paul Motte, 1874.

REVIEW & ASSESS

1. **READING CHECK** What is the setting for Homer's epic poems, the *Iliad* and the *Odyssey*?

2. **IDENTIFY MAIN IDEAS AND DETAILS** In Greek epic poems, why do heroes take action and what traits do they have?

3. **FORM AND SUPPORT OPINIONS** What details about the Trojan War do you think are fact and which are fiction?

213

1.4 City-States

Though ancient Greek cities seemed to lie quiet for 400 years, around 800 B.C. they began to thrive again. Eventually they would extend their influence across the Mediterranean.

MAIN IDEA

Ancient Greek city-states established different ways of governing as they gained power.

CITIES AND CITY-STATES

As population, trade, and wealth grew, the ancient Greeks began to build cities near coastlines for trade and on hilltops for defense. Greek cities were distinct from one another, each with its own personality. However, these ancient cities shared certain similarities, too.

The highest point in an ancient Greek city was the **acropolis** (uh-KRAHP-uh-lihs), or upper city. This stone-walled fortress was the city's last line of defense against invasion. From the acropolis one could see houses and narrow streets and easily spot the open space of the **agora**, the city's marketplace and social center for sports, festivals, and meetings.

A powerful city grew into an even more powerful city-state, also called a **polis** (POH-luhs). As you may recall, a city-state is an independent political unit in which a dominant city rules the surrounding area. A number of Greek city-states emerged after 750 B.C. Some city-states grew larger than others. Smaller towns and villages supplied food, trade goods, labor, and soldiers for the city-states.

Geographic isolation influenced how city-states developed in ancient Greece. High mountains surrounded plains and valleys, separating cities from one another. The mountains made it more challenging for some city-states to communicate and engage in trade with other city-states.

City-states developed at the same time all over ancient Greece, but they did so in different ways. Although they shared a common language, religion, heritage, and culture, city-states remained independent from one another. Each city-state had its own sets of customs and laws. Even more, citizens identified themselves as Athenians or Spartans—not as Greeks.

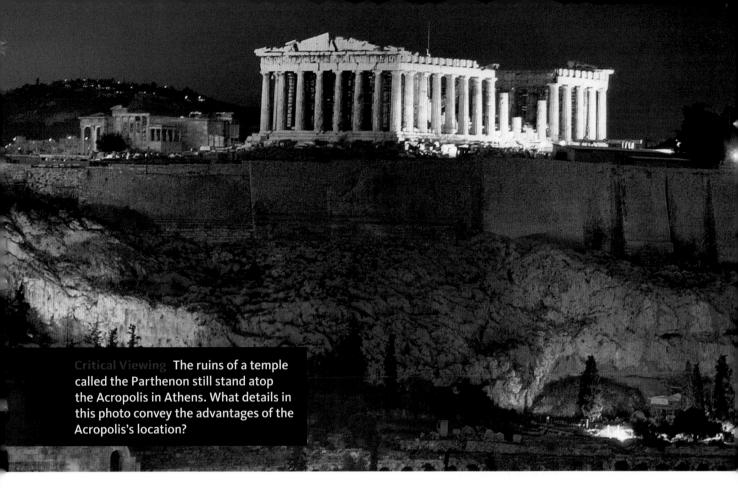

The ruins of a temple called the Parthenon still stand atop the Acropolis in Athens. What details in this photo convey the advantages of the Acropolis's location?

EARLY GOVERNMENT

Greek city-states were as different as they were independent. Each city-state established its own way of governing its citizens. One form of governing was a **monarchy**, a government ruled by a single person, such as a king. Another form was an **aristocracy**, a government ruled by a small group of elite, landowning families.

Aristocratic rule was soon challenged by a growing merchant class. As trade expanded, the merchants became more powerful. The 600s saw increasing tensions involving aristocratic landowners and an uneven distribution of wealth. These tensions led to fighting and civil strife. Sometimes powerful men took advantage of the situation and seized power as **tyrants**. Some tyrants were ruthless, but others made positive changes, including giving farms to the landless and work to the unemployed. Not everyone favored their rule, though. In order to take power from tyrants, merchants formed an **oligarchy**, or a government ruled by a few powerful citizens.

Eventually, some city-states, such as Athens, wanted to give citizens a greater voice and began to experiment with a new type of government. You will read more about this government later in the chapter.

REVIEW & ASSESS

1. **READING CHECK** How were ancient Greek city-states alike and different?

2. **DETERMINE WORD MEANING** Based on what you have read, from what ancient Greek word do you think the word *politics* originates?

3. **ANALYZE CAUSE AND EFFECT** How did the geography of Greece influence the development of city-states?

1.5 Colonization and Trade

The ancient Greeks were always on the look out for fertile land and materials such as timber, metals, and luxury goods. Together these prompted the Greeks to trade and settle around parts of the Mediterranean where they could control the land.

MAIN IDEA

Ancient Greeks spread their culture around the Mediterranean and Black seas.

NEW SETTLEMENTS

Growing city-states meant growing populations and new problems. The hot, dry, and mountainous Greek countryside did not have enough usable farmland to feed everyone. As hunger fueled unrest, the leaders of city-states had two choices. They could fight other city-states for space or they could reduce their own populations.

Most did both. Between 750 and 550 B.C., the city-states waged wars with one another for control over limited natural resources. They also sent people overseas to establish new colonies in places with better farmland and valuable raw materials. Remember, a colony is an area controlled by a distant ruler. City-states selected their colonists by lottery and often prevented them from returning to Greece. The rulers wanted to make sure the new colonies would stay populated.

Greek city-states established hundreds of colonies in the Mediterranean region. Most colonies were situated on or near the coastlines of the Black and Mediterranean seas. They were located in present-day Spain, France, and Italy, in North Africa, and on the islands of Sardinia, Corsica, and Cyprus.

The new colonies were self-governing, but they maintained close political and economic links with their parent city-states. Although colonists adopted some local ways, they remained proudly Greek in their culture and outlook. They shared a common language, worshipped the same gods, and took part in Greek festivals such as the Olympic Games.

WATER HIGHWAYS

Colonies served many purposes for the ancient Greeks. Overall, they allowed access to land and resources not available in Greece. Some colonies were specifically set up to secure and control trade routes.

The Mediterranean and Black seas were relatively easy to navigate. Because most colonies were positioned near good harbors, sea trade flourished throughout the region. Expert sailors on well-built merchant ships carried raw materials such as silver and tin from present-day Spain and France back to Greece.

The flow of new resources to and from these colonies stimulated the production of goods. These goods were then traded at home and abroad. Trade boosted Greece's growing economy, as did the introduction of coins after 600 B.C.

Wide-ranging sea trade also encouraged cultural diffusion, or the spread of ideas from one culture to another. This dual exchange of goods and ideas was important in shaping civilizations in the ancient world. For example, the ancient Egyptians welcomed learning about Greek military skills. Ancient Greece had a strong cultural influence on early Rome and carried Mediterranean culture as far away as

ATLANTIC OCEAN

EUROPE

Olbia
Panticapaeum
Black Sea
Phasis
Trapezus
Danube

Spina
Massilia
ITALY

Hemeroscopium

Byzantium
Abydos
Phocaea
ANATOLIA
ASIA

Ionian Sea
GREECE
Athens
Corinth
Sparta
Miletus
Al Mina

Sicily
Gela
Syracuse
Crete
Cyprus

Mediterranean Sea

Cyrene
EGYPT

AFRICA

Region of Greek influence
Major trade route
Greek trade goods found

0   200   400 Miles
0   200   400 Kilometers

N W E S

present-day France. The ancient Greeks also incorporated ideas from other cultures. Elements of Egyptian culture influenced Greek art and architecture. Some historians think that ancient Greeks may have gotten their ideas of city-states, colonization, and sea trade from the Phoenicians.

One of the major effects of cultural diffusion in the ancient Mediterranean was the Greek adoption of the Phoenician alphabet. The Greeks made changes to the Phoenician alphabet, which then became the foundation of the modern alphabet we use today.

GREEK POTTERY IN ITALY

Tuna fish decorate this pottery cup found in the Apulia region, in the heel of Italy's boot. The cup may have been produced there by Greek colonists, or it may have been a trade good. Archaeologists believe the cup dates to about 500 B.C. In what ways does this cup represent Greek colonization and trade?

REVIEW & ASSESS

1. **READING CHECK** Why did the ancient Greeks establish colonies in the Mediterranean region?

2. **ANALYZE CAUSE AND EFFECT** In what ways did trade and cultural diffusion shape the ancient Greek world?

3. **INTERPRET MAPS** How far north did Greek influence reach as a result of trade?

Sparta's
Military Society

One of the greatest rivalries in the ancient world was between the city-states of Athens and Sparta. The Athenians, whom you'll learn about in the next lesson, emphasized culture and learning. The Spartans, though, were the fierce warriors of ancient Greece. They fought hard and could handle more pain than anyone. They were almost unbeatable, thanks to tough military training.

MAIN IDEA

Sparta was a powerful ancient Greek city-state devoted to war.

STRONG WOMEN

This bronze sculpture from Sparta reflects the expectation that Spartan girls and women be tough. Girls' education focused on physical strength and athletic skills, and Spartan girls learned how to defend themselves.

SPARTAN SOCIETY

The Spartans lived in one of the most fertile areas of southern Greece. The city-state of **Sparta** was located in the Eurotas river valley, protected by mountains that made attacking this city-state difficult. This physical separation may have led to an outlook and values in sharp contrast with those of other ancient Greek city-states.

Spartan government was an unusual blend of rule by kings, elected officials, and the ruling class. Two kings who shared power ruled Sparta. Together, they led Sparta's armies into battle. Real power rested with the five officials who were elected each year by an assembly of Spartan citizens. In addition, the two kings and a council of elders, made up of 28 men over 60 years of age, proposed laws. The Spartans' unique government helped maintain a balance of power and prevent revolts.

Spartan society was a rigid hierarchy. Groups of citizens were ranked by importance based on wealth and power. Elite, landowning families of Sparta formed the upper class. A second class included free noncitizens from the villages around Sparta. They were farmers and traders and sometimes served in the army.

The lowest social class was made up of the **helots**, or state-owned slaves captured from conquered lands. Helots farmed the Spartans' land and were only allowed to keep a tiny portion of their harvest. The helots outnumbered the Spartans, and fear of helot uprisings was a main reason for Sparta's military society. The army was at the center of everything in Sparta—and everything in Sparta was centered on the army.

DAILY LIFE

Spartan soldiers considered it an honor to die in battle for Sparta, but they did not die easily. At seven years of age, all boys were taken from their families and raised by the state to be soldiers. Their training was brutal. They wore thin tunics and no shoes, even in winter. Their meals were purposely small and nasty so that they had to steal food to survive but were punished if caught.

Such intense physical training and endless military drills created strong and obedient

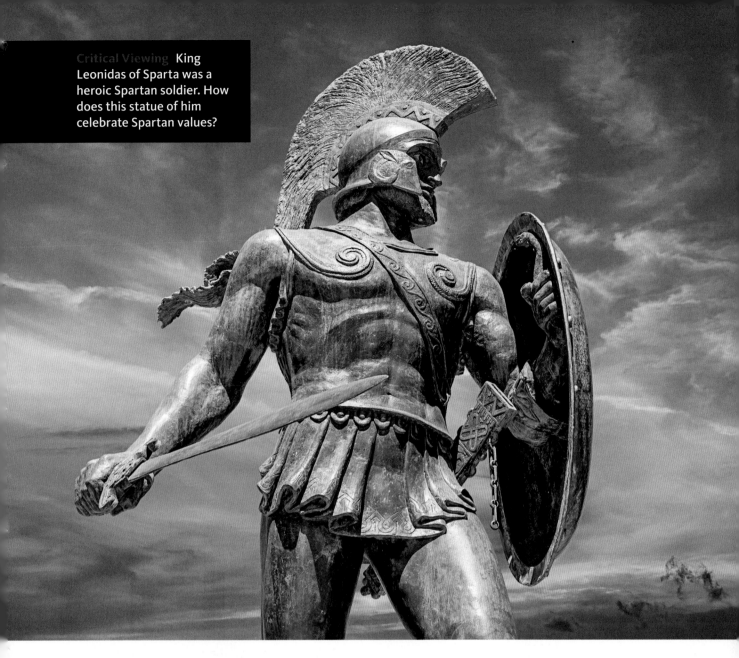

Critical Viewing King Leonidas of Sparta was a heroic Spartan soldier. How does this statue of him celebrate Spartan values?

soldiers. At age 20, they joined a military mess, or regiment, a commitment that dominated the rest of their lives.

Family life supported Sparta's military values. Women's primary role was to produce future soldiers for the state, and husbands and wives spent much time apart. One result of this separation was that Spartan women lived their daily lives independent of men. Spartan women could also own property.

Sparta's extraordinary commitment to war transformed this city-state into an ancient power, but this success came at a price. Although Sparta boasted the best soldiers, it claimed few artists, philosophers, or scientists, unlike its rival Athens.

REVIEW & ASSESS

1. **READING CHECK** What was one reason Sparta developed a military society?

2. **SUMMARIZE** In what ways was Sparta's government unique?

3. **ANALYZE CAUSE AND EFFECT** What effect did Sparta's commitment to the military have on other aspects of its society and culture?

DAILY LIFE IN ATHENIAN ART

The art on ancient Greek pots allows a glimpse into daily life in ancient Greece. Study each pot. Then decide what you think the art portrays. Compare your ideas with the descriptions of the art below.

1. Athletes throw a ball to a trainer.
2. A servant attends to a woman tying a shoe.
3. A merchant watches over his goods.
4. A priest and an acolyte [assistant] light a fire.
5. A young woman combs her hair.
6. An athlete learns how to throw a discus.

Athens's Democratic Society

The city-state of Athens was named for its devotion to Athena, the Greek goddess of wisdom. Ancient Athenians developed one of the world's great forms of government.

MAIN IDEA

The culturally rich city-state of Athens developed democracy.

DAILY LIFE

The daily lives of people in ancient **Athens** helped shape their approach to governing. Citizenship was open to adult men who had been born in Athens. Foreign-born residents could live in Athens. However, they did not generally become citizens, vote, or own property—even though they paid taxes and fought in the army. Slaves were at the bottom of society.

Athenian women were firmly controlled by their husbands. Wealthy women ran the household and raised children, but they could not go out alone. Poorer women had more freedom but had to work for wages.

Children were raised much differently in Athens than in Sparta. Athenians valued education, and boys attended school if their families could afford it. After a well-rounded education, Athenian boys went through two years of military training in preparation for citizenship. Athenian girls did not attend school, but they learned household skills at home. Poor children worked from an early age.

BEGINNINGS OF DEMOCRACY

Even as the city-state of Athens thrived, many Athenians felt they had little voice in their government. Unlike Sparta, Athens replaced its monarchy with an aristocracy. Trouble arose when aristocratic families began to fight with each other and farmers started to protest decreasing wealth and land. A time of increasing strife and, on occasion, violence in Athens followed. A harsh code of laws made things worse.

In 594 B.C., the aristocrats responded to the crisis by granting special powers to a trusted man named **Solon**. He improved conditions for the poor by limiting the power of the aristocracy and allowing an assembly of free citizens to pass laws. In 508 B.C., Athens established **democracy**, a form of government in which citizens have a direct role in governing.

Athenians were less devoted to war than were Spartans. Although their citizen-soldiers were capable, they did not form a professional army. To defend itself, Athens joined forces with other city-states, including Sparta. In 490 B.C., the Persians attacked Greece from the east. The resulting war would test Spartans and Athenians alike.

REVIEW & ASSESS

1. **READING CHECK** What role do citizens play in a democracy?

2. **COMPARE AND CONTRAST** How was daily life for Spartan women and children different from daily life for Athenian women and children?

3. **INTEGRATE VISUALS** How do the depictions of ancient Greek women on the pots fit with the text's description of them?

2.3 Uniting Against the Persians

When the Persians attacked Greece, they triggered the Persian Wars. We know much about these wars from the ancient Greek historian Herodotus. Modern historians consider him to be reliable even though it's likely that he exaggerated the size of the Persian threat. Whatever the numbers, these wars changed the course of Greek history.

MAIN IDEA

City-states in ancient Greece united to drive back invasions by the Persian Empire.

26.2

The modern marathon has its roots in the Persian Wars. According to one legend, upon defeating the Persians at Marathon, Miltiades sent his best runner to Athens to announce the victory. After he reported the news, the runner collapsed and died.

The distance from Marathon to Athens was just over 24 miles. Today's race measures 26.2 miles.

IONIAN REVOLT

In 546 B.C., the Persian Empire conquered Ionia, an area of Greek colonies on the west coast of present-day Turkey. Life under Persian rule was not especially harsh, but the Ionians wanted to regain their independence. They rebelled in 499 B.C. with the support of Athens. Despite Athenian help, Persia crushed the Ionian revolt in 494 B.C. The Persian emperor **Darius I** vowed to punish Athens as revenge for helping Ionia.

In 490 B.C., the Persian army landed at Marathon, just over 24 miles east of Athens. Knowing they were outnumbered by at least two to one, the Athenians knew their strategy would have to be clever—and bold. As the Persian foot soldiers stood in formation, the Greek general Miltiades (mihl-TY-uh-deez) ordered his troops to lock shields and advance at a full run. The Greeks charged into the surprised Persians, forced them back to their ships, and claimed victory over them.

DEFEAT OF THE PERSIAN EMPIRE

Ten years after the Battle at Marathon, **Xerxes** (ZURK-seez), Darius's successor, invaded Athens. In 480 B.C., hundreds of Persian ships and more than 150,000 soldiers went on the attack. Athens was ready this time—and it did not have to face the Persians alone. Athens had forged strong **alliances**, or partnerships, with other Greek city-states, including Sparta. Because the Athenians needed more time to prepare for battle, King Leonidas of Sparta occupied the important mountain pass of **Thermopylae** (thur-MAHP-uh-lee). Leonidas's small army fought off the Persians, giving the Greeks time to assemble further south.

The Athenians fought on. At the Battle of Salamis (SAL-uh-mihs) a small fleet of Greek warships called **triremes** (try-REEMZ) faced the Persian navy. The Greeks lured the Persians into a trap in the strait at Salamis and destroyed nearly a third of the Persian fleet. In 479 B.C., a large and united Greek army finally defeated the Persians at the Battle of Plataea. After this, the Persians left Greece and never invaded again. Although the war flared on and off for a few more decades, Greece was safe. Athens and Sparta emerged triumphant as the most powerful city-states in Greece.

POWER ROWERS
Rowing was exhausting work, and rowers endured sweltering heat and cramped conditions.

LONG AND LEAN
These warships were 120 feet long and 18 feet wide and could reach speeds of up to 10 miles an hour.

ROWING MASTER
The rowing master shouted commands to the rowers.

WATER'S EDGE
Rowers on the lowest level of the trireme were only inches away from the water.

EXTRA DEFENSE
Spearmen accompanied the rowers on Greek triremes to defend against enemies trying to board the ship.

SECRET WEAPON
A bronze-covered ram at the front of the trireme could pierce the hulls of enemy ships.

GREEK TRIREMES

The word *trireme*, which means "three-oared," accurately describes these Greek warships, which had three levels of oars on each side. Greek triremes were smaller, faster, and more maneuverable than larger ships. Built specifically for battle, these lightweight, wooden ships were powered by up to 170 rowers, 85 rowers per side.

REVIEW & ASSESS

1. **READING CHECK** How were the Greeks able to defeat the Persians at the Battle of Salamis?

2. **COMPARE AND CONTRAST** How did the size and strategy of the Greek army contrast with that of the Persians?

3. **ANALYZE VISUALS** Why do you think triremes were effective warships?

480 B.C.

Heroic events inspire exciting movies. Here, outnumbered Spartan soldiers force Persians over a cliff in a scene from the 2007 film *300*. At the Battle of Thermopylae in 480 B.C., 6,000 Greek soldiers led by Spartans fought off more than 100,000 Persian soldiers. Exhausted, the soldiers battled bravely, but their strength was running out. King Leonidas of Sparta realized the battle was lost and ordered most of the soldiers to withdraw. He and his 300 elite Spartans stayed behind to protect the retreating army and delay the Persians. It meant certain death. The ensuing battle was fierce. When swords broke, the Spartans fought with bare hands. None escaped alive. Thanks to the sacrifice of the 300, the Greeks were able to regroup and eventually defeat the Persians. How do the actions of Leonidas and the 300 reflect the culture of Sparta?

VOCABULARY

Complete each of the following sentences using one of the vocabulary words from the chapter.

1. According to an ancient myth, King Minos of Crete built a large maze, or _____, beneath his palace.

2. The *Odyssey* is a(n) _____ that was written by Homer and tells the many adventures of Odysseus.

3. _____ is the Greek word for city-state.

4. In ancient Greek city-states, the _____ was the city's marketplace and social center.

5. Typically built on a hilltop, the _____ was a city's last line of defense.

6. During the Persian Wars, Athens formed _____ with other Greek city-states.

7. In Spartan society, _____ were slaves from conquered regions.

8. Gold and tin are examples of _____.

READING STRATEGY

9. **ORGANIZE IDEAS: COMPARE AND CONTRAST** If you haven't already, complete your graphic organizer to compare and contrast life in Sparta and Athens. Then answer the question.

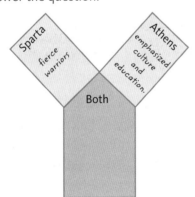

How was life in Sparta and Athens similar? How was it different?

MAIN IDEAS

Answer the following questions. Support your answers with evidence from the chapter.

10. Where did the Minoan civilization settle and flourish? **LESSON 1.1**

11. How did the Mycenaeans gain wealth and power in the Mediterranean? **LESSON 1.2**

12. What are epic poems and what kinds of stories do they tell? **LESSON 1.3**

13. What was the function of the polis as it developed in Greek civilization? **LESSON 1.4**

14. How did sea trade affect ancient Greek civilization? **LESSON 1.5**

15. What were the advantages and disadvantages of Sparta's military society? **LESSON 2.1**

16. How did the roles of Athenian men and women differ? **LESSON 2.2**

17. What caused the Persian Wars? **LESSON 2.3**

CRITICAL THINKING

Answer the following questions. Support your answers with evidence from the chapter.

18. **SYNTHESIZE** What were some of the developments that led to the establishment of a cultured and influential civilization in ancient Greece?

19. **COMPARE AND CONTRAST** How were the Minoan and Mycenaean civilizations alike? How were they different?

20. **DRAW CONCLUSIONS** Why were epic poems and their heroes important to the ancient Greeks?

21. **EVALUATE** Why was the Greek adoption of the Phoenician alphabet an important development?

22. **YOU DECIDE** Which city-state—Athens or Sparta—had the most effective system of government? Support your opinion with evidence from the chapter.

INTERPRET MAPS

Study the map of the Persian Wars. Then answer the questions that follow.

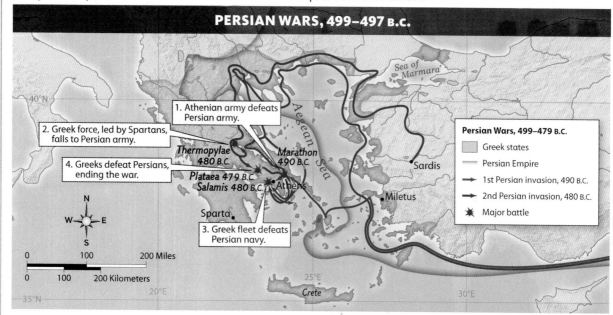

PERSIAN WARS, 499–497 B.C.

1. Athenian army defeats Persian army.
2. Greek force, led by Spartans, falls to Persian army.
4. Greeks defeat Persians, ending the war.
3. Greek fleet defeats Persian navy.

Thermopylae 480 B.C.
Marathon 490 B.C.
Plataea 479 B.C.
Salamis 480 B.C.
Athens
Sparta
Sardis
Miletus
Sea of Marmara
Aegean Sea
Crete

Persian Wars, 499–479 B.C.
- Greek states
- Persian Empire
- 1st Persian invasion, 490 B.C.
- 2nd Persian invasion, 480 B.C.
- Major battle

0   100   200 Miles
0   100   200 Kilometers

23. How did the routes of the first and second Persian invasions differ?

24. Which of the major battles shown was a naval battle?

ANALYZE SOURCES

Read the following description of Darius I, the emperor of Persia, written by Herodotus after the Ionian revolt.

> Darius did, however, ask who the Athenians were, and after receiving the answer, he called for his bow. This he took and, placing an arrow on it, shot it into the sky, praying as he sent it aloft, "O Zeus, grant me vengeance on the Athenians."
>
> Then he ordered one of his servants to say to him three times whenever dinner was set before him, "Master, remember the Athenians."

25. What does this description of Darius I reveal about him?

WRITE ABOUT HISTORY

26. INFORMATIVE Suppose you have been asked to participate in a radio program that examines important topics from history. Write a paragraph to inform your audience about the beginnings of democracy in ancient Greece between 600 and 500 B.C.

TIPS

- Take notes from the lesson about Athens's democratic society.
- Introduce the topic clearly.
- Develop the topic with relevant, well-chosen facts, concrete details, and examples.
- Use vocabulary from the chapter to explain democratic ideas.
- Provide a concluding statement that summarizes the information presented.

SECTION 1 THE GOLDEN AGE OF GREECE

SS.6.C.1.1; SS.6.C.2.1; SS.6.G.2.5; SS.6.W.3.2; SS.6.W.3.4; SS.6.W.3.5; SS.6.W.3.6;
LAFS.68.RH.2.5; LAFS.68.RH.3.7

KEY VOCABULARY

direct   immortal
democracy   mythology
golden age

NAMES & PLACES

Cleisthenes   Parthenon
Delian   Pericles
  League

SECTION 2 THE PELOPONNESIAN WAR

SS.6.G.1.4; SS.6.W.1.3; SS.6.W.3.3; SS.6.W.3.4; SS.6.W.3.6; LAFS.68.RH.1.1;
LAFS.68.RH.1.2; LAFS.68.RH.2.4; LAFS.68.RH.2.5; LAFS.68.RH.3.7; LAFS.68.WHST.1.1;
LAFS.68.WHST.3.9

KEY VOCABULARY

plague   truce
siege

NAMES & PLACES

Peloponnesian War
Thucydides

SECTION 3 ALEXANDER THE GREAT

SS.6.G.1.4; SS.6.G.1.5; SS.6.G.1.7; SS.6.G.2.1; SS.6.G.2.5; SS.6.G.2.6; SS.6.W.3.7;
LAFS.68.RH.1.2; LAFS.68.RH.2.5; LAFS.68.RH.3.7

KEY VOCABULARY

catapult   Hellenistic
cosmopolitan   phalanx

NAMES & PLACES

Alexander the Great
Philip II

SECTION 4 THE LEGACY OF ANCIENT GREECE

SS.6.C.1.1; SS.6.C.2.1; SS.6.W.3.2; SS.6.W.3.5; SS.6.W.3.6; LAFS.68.RH.1.2;
LAFS.68.RH.2.5; LAFS.68.RH.3.7

KEY VOCABULARY

comedy   representative
jury   democracy
philosophy   tragedy

NAMES & PLACES

Aesop   Plato
Aristotle   Socrates
Homer

READING STRATEGY

DETERMINE WORD MEANINGS
Many English words are based on
Greek words. This chart shows some
common Greek roots and their
meanings. As you read the chapter,
write down examples of words you
find that include these roots.

Root	Meaning
cosm-	universe
-cracy	government
dem-	people
-logy	speech
myth-	story
phil-	love
poli-	city
soph-	wise

Cape Tainaron, located at the southernmost point of Greece, was known in ancient times as the "Gate to Hades," or what the Greeks thought of as hell.

Pericles and Democracy

When you go out with your friends after school, how does your group decide what to do? Does one friend make this decision? Do two or three take charge? Or do you all have a say? If you all weigh in, that's democracy, a concept that began in Athens more than 2,500 years ago.

MAIN IDEA

Athens established the world's first democracy.

ELECTED BY LOTTERY

Athenians used this machine, known as a *kleroterion*, to elect officials. Each eligible male placed a token with his name on it in one of the slots. A series of balls were then released from a tube to determine whose tokens would be chosen.

SEEDS OF DEMOCRACY

As you may recall from the previous chapter, the leader Solon made life better for the poor. He canceled their debts, freed enslaved farmers, and abolished unfair payments to greedy landowners.

Solon also reduced the power of the aristocracy. He organized citizens into four classes based on wealth. Rich men still had more power, but all male citizens, rich and poor, were allowed to join the assembly and help elect leaders. Solon also created a council chosen by lottery, or chance, from the assembly. Solon made Athenian government fairer, but it was not yet a true democracy.

Around 500 B.C., a leader named **Cleisthenes** (KLYS-thuh-neez) took things further. Under his rule, the assembly members debated openly and heard court cases. Citizens were organized into groups based on where they lived. Each group sent 50 representatives a year to the Council of 500. The council proposed laws and debated policies, and the assembly voted on them. The citizens were now fully engaged in government. This was democracy—but a limited one. Only male property owners born in Athens could participate. Women, foreigners, and slaves had no political rights.

ATHENS'S GREATEST LEADER

Pericles (PEHR-uh-kleez), one of Athens's greatest leaders, expanded this limited democracy into one that would allow all male citizens to participate in government. He transferred the remaining powers of the aristocrats to the assembly. He paid jurors, which allowed poor citizens to take time off to serve the state. This idea was later extended to all public officials, who previously were unpaid. Pericles also opened up powerful political positions to the middle classes. Neither social class nor poverty was a barrier to political power anymore. Athens now had a **direct democracy**, in which citizens gathered together to vote on laws and policies. Athenian democracy formed the basis of the constitutional democracy in the United States, hundreds of years later.

Pericles also transformed Athens from a city ravaged by war to a center of learning, creativity, and beauty. By encouraging the work of great thinkers and artists, Pericles guided Athens through a **golden age**—a period of great cultural achievement.

PERICLES

Job: Athenian statesman and leader
Education: Taught by Anaxagoras, who was known for his clear thinking and oratorical skills
Home: Athens

TO-DO LIST

He had three goals for Athens: to strengthen democracy, to increase Athens's power in the wider world, and to beautify the city.

FINEST HOUR

He introduced reforms that made Athens a fairer and more democratic society.

DEATH

He was among the many victims of a brutal plague that fell upon Athens in the year after the Peloponnesian War. He died in 429 B.C.

TRIVIA

Sculptures and illustrations from this period always portray him wearing a helmet. It is said that he wore the helmet to hide his oddly shaped head.

REVIEW & ASSESS

1. **READING CHECK** What is one way that Pericles expanded democracy in Athens?

2. **COMPARE AND CONTRAST** What are the similarities and differences between the accomplishments of Solon and Cleisthenes?

3. **MAKE INFERENCES** How did Pericles' decision to pay public officials help strengthen democracy?

Sanctuary of Zeus
This structure was dedicated to Zeus, the king of the gods.

Parthenon
This important temple was dedicated to Athena. It contained a gold and ivory statue of the goddess as well as the city's treasury.

Sanctuary of Artemis
This shrine was dedicated to the goddess Artemis, who was the protector of pregnant women.

Statue of Athena
This statue stood 33 feet tall and was visible from as far away as three miles.

Erechtheion (ee-REHK-thee-on)
This temple was named after an early king of Athens.

Propylaea (prop-uh-LEE-uh)
This was the gateway to the Acropolis.

Temple of Athena Nike
Athena's role as goddess of victory in war was celebrated through this temple.

THE ACROPOLIS, C. 400 B.C.

Under the rule of Pericles and with the guidance of sculptors and artists, the Acropolis of Athens was constructed on a rocky hill in the center of the city. The fortress loomed high over the rest of Athens, and the most important buildings and temples were situated there. The Acropolis was easier to defend from invading armies than was the rest of the city.

1.2

The Athenian Empire

The war with Persia made the Greeks realize that there really is strength in numbers. So Athens and numerous other city-states joined forces to protect themselves against enemies. But Athens was always the strongest of the city-states, and it soon became apparent that Athenians had their own interests in mind.

MAIN IDEA

Athens grew into a powerful empire and was rebuilt to reflect its important status.

THE DELIAN LEAGUE

To defend themselves from Persia, which still posed a possible threat, Athens and the other city-states formed an anti-Persian alliance. The **Delian** (DEE-lee-uhn) **League**, formed in 478 B.C., was based on the island of Delos, where funds were kept to fight future wars with Persia.

Each city-state contributed cash, ships, or soldiers and had equal votes in the league's council. However, Athens was always the league's leader and took control over the other city-states in the alliance.

Pericles used the league's money to build Athens's powerful navy. This naval force allowed Athens to rule the Mediterranean region and the Delian League. In 454 B.C., the league's treasury was moved from the island of Delos to Athens. The other city-states in the alliance were now powerless against Athens.

The Spartans were not happy that the Athenians were gaining so much power. Although distracted by regular slave revolts, Sparta remained a major power. It established its own network of alliances called the Peloponnesian League. Resentment built between the two leagues, causing tension to run dangerously high.

REBUILDING THE CITY

Meanwhile, Athens was still in ruins from the Persian Wars. The Delian League began funding the rebuilding of Athens, which would be grander than ever.

The city walls were rebuilt. Then Pericles rebuilt the Acropolis with richly decorated temples and monuments. One structure on the Acropolis was the **Parthenon** (PAHR-thuh-nahn), the awe-inspiring temple that was dedicated to Athens's goddess, Athena. The city's leaders poured money into beautifying the city with the finest architecture, art, and sculpture. Pericles transformed Athens into one of the most magnificent cities in the ancient world. It was a fitting capital for a powerful empire.

REVIEW & ASSESS

1. **READING CHECK** How did the Delian League make Athens more powerful?

2. **ANALYZE CAUSE AND EFFECT** How did the Spartans respond to the creation of the Delian League?

3. **INTEGRATE VISUALS** Why do you think the Parthenon was located on the Acropolis?

1.3 Religion and the Gods

 Greek gods and goddesses may seem more like cartoon superheroes than divine deities. According to Greek belief, the gods looked and acted like humans: They married, had children, got jealous, and started wars. But they did it all with fantastic superpowers! Ordinary people had to either keep them happy or face their wrath.

MAIN IDEA

The Greeks believed that the many gods they worshipped could strongly influence daily life.

BELIEFS

Greek gods played an important role in ancient Greece. The gods were considered **immortal**, or able to live forever. Like the Mesopotamians and Egyptians, the Greeks believed that unhappy gods showed their displeasure by causing problems in people's lives. Greeks obtained the gods' help by leaving offerings outside temples—the gods' earthly homes. Temples were usually impressive stone buildings housing a statue of the god. A city's biggest temple was dedicated to its patron god, who protected it.

There were hundreds of Greek gods. According to Greek belief, the top 12 gods were the Olympians, or the ones who lived in luxury on Mount Olympus, the highest mountain in Greece. A holy day, celebrated with colorful and noisy public festivals, was dedicated to each god and goddess. These special days involved great processions, offerings, poetry recitals, and competitive sports, including the original Olympic Games. For private worship, most Greek homes had small altars where people would pray to the gods.

MYTHS

The Greeks had a close relationship with their gods, who often got involved in human affairs. This is how Greek religion blended with **mythology**—a collection of stories that explained events, beliefs, or actions. In Greek myths, the gods, kings, heroes, and ordinary people had amazing adventures together. The gods often rewarded or punished humans for their deeds. These stories were written down to form a group of exciting tales that are still popular today. One of these myths appears on the next page.

The 12 Olympians

Zeus King of the gods

Hera Queen of the gods

Aphrodite Goddess of love and beauty

Apollo God of the sun and music

Ares God of war

Artemis Goddess of the moon and hunting

Athena Goddess of wisdom and war

Demeter Goddess of the harvest

Dionysus God of wine

Hephaestus God of fire and metalworking

Hermes Messenger of the gods

Poseidon God of the sea

THE MYTH OF DAEDALUS AND ICARUS

On the island of Crete, there lived a skilled craftsman named Daedalus. Daedalus wanted to leave the island with his son, Icarus, but the king would not let him go. So he came up with a plan to escape. He took feathers and wax and constructed two pairs of wings that would allow him and Icarus to fly like the birds.

As Daedalus attached the wings to his son's arms, he told Icarus to follow him closely. "If you fly too low, the sea will soak the wings. If you fly too high, the sun will burn them," he warned.

The father and son were soon flying through the air. Icarus grew excited and began to fly higher and higher in spite of his father's warning. Apollo, the god of the sun, decided to teach the boy a lesson, and soon the wax holding Icarus's wings together was melting away. Icarus tumbled down to the water below. Daedalus could only watch helplessly as his beloved son was claimed by the sea.

When he safely reached land, Daedalus built a shrine to Apollo and hung his wings on it. He never tried to fly again.

REVIEW & ASSESS

1. **READING CHECK** What role did gods and goddesses play in the lives of the ancient Greeks?

2. **MAKE INFERENCES** What lesson do you think Apollo was trying to teach Icarus?

3. **DRAW CONCLUSIONS** Why were myths important to ancient Greek culture?

War Breaks Out

 As Athens became wealthier and more powerful, other city-states, especially Sparta, became suspicious and fearful of Athens's future plans. Athens and Sparta had created very different societies. Athens championed a democratic government, while Sparta focused on military strength. These differences contributed to a growing distrust that exploded into war.

MAIN IDEA

Rivalry between Sparta and Athens plunged Greece into war.

TENSIONS RISE

In addition to societal differences, Sparta resented Athens's use of money from the Delian League. Remember, Athens had used this money, intended to protect all of the city-states, for its own benefit. When the city-states protested this inequality and attempted to free themselves from Athenian rule, Pericles punished them. By 431 B.C., Sparta had had enough of Athenian aggression and declared war on Athens. The **Peloponnesian War** had begun.

Sparta had a strong army and Athens had a strong navy. This contrast in military strength forced the two sides to develop very different plans for winning the war. Athens, under Pericles, avoided fighting Sparta and its allies on land and planned to attack from the sea. Athens withdrew behind its strong city walls. Its ships kept the city stocked with supplies and were also used to raid its enemies' land.

Meanwhile, Sparta marched its army into Athenian lands expecting a big battle, but the Athenian army stayed protected behind the city walls. The frustrated Spartans attempted to weaken the Athenian economy by burning its crops. Though the walls protected Athenians from the Spartans, they could not prevent a devastating attack from an unexpected enemy.

A PLAGUE STRIKES ATHENS

In 430 B.C., Athenians began suffering from rashes, headaches, vomiting, and fever. This was probably an outbreak of typhoid fever, a highly infectious disease. In the narrow streets of Athens, overcrowded with refugees from the countryside, the fever quickly became a deadly **plague**, or a disease that causes many deaths. In four years the plague killed one in three Athenians—about 60,000 people— including Pericles. Disease was doing more damage than Sparta's soldiers.

Elsewhere the war raged on with brutal acts committed by both sides. It was typical for a captured city to have all its male citizens executed and its women and children enslaved. Despite all the deaths, the war seemed unwinnable. Athens was dominant at sea and Sparta ruled on land, but neither was able to overpower the other. In 421 B.C., Athens signed a **truce**, or an agreement to stop fighting. Sparta and Athens entered a period of peace, but it would not last for long.

THE PELOPONNESIAN WAR, 431–404 B.C.

Black Sea

THRACE

MACEDONIA

422 B.C.

429 B.C.

Sea of Marmara

410 B.C.

405 B.C.

411 B.C.

Aegean Sea

406 B.C.

PERSIAN EMPIRE

•Sardis

424 B.C.

•Thebes

Ionian Sea

Corinth•

•Athens

407 B.C.

418 B.C.

•Miletus

Delos

425 B.C.

•Sparta

N
W   E
S

Mediterranean Sea

Crete

0   50   100 Miles
0   50   100 Kilometers

	Sparta and allies
	Athens and allies
	Neutral states
✶	Spartan victory
✳	Athenian victory

MYRTIS, A VICTIM OF PLAGUE

Myrtis is the name given to the remains of an 11-year-old Athenian girl who died of the plague around 430 B.C. Her body was found in a mass grave in a subway tunnel in the 1990s. Myrtis's skull was in good enough condition to be reconstructed. Scientists built up layers of artificial skin and muscle tissue and gave her brown eyes and hair and an appropriate hairstyle for the age. Myrtis's reconstruction is probably very close to what she actually looked like. It is rare and exciting to be able to look into the eyes of someone who lived some 2,500 years ago.

REVIEW & ASSESS

1. **READING CHECK** What caused tensions between Athens and Sparta? What did these tensions lead to?

2. **COMPARE AND CONTRAST** How did Sparta's and Athens's war strategies differ?

3. **INTERPRET MAPS** How did geography give Sparta an advantage during the war?

The **Defeat** of **Athens**

Both Sparta and Athens wanted to control all of Greece. Sparta thought its soldiers, with their strict military training, would crush any opponent. Athens attempted to dominate the region by building a powerful navy. But Sparta and Athens failed to notice that their constant warring was causing Greece to slowly fall apart.

MAIN IDEA

After many years of fighting, Greece found itself in a weakened and vulnerable state.

THE WAR DRAGS ON

The truce was supposed to last 50 years. Instead it ended in only two. Sparta and Athens were drawn back into war over the rich lands of Sicily, a fertile island near Italy that the Greeks had colonized. A dispute between a pro-Athenian colony and a pro-Spartan colony prompted Athens to invade.

In 414 B.C., Athens laid **siege** to Syracuse, Sicily's strongest and richest city. In a siege, soldiers surround a city in an attempt to take control of it. The invasion of Syracuse was disorganized, and Athens made many mistakes. Spartan reinforcements arrived and attacked the Athenians on land and sea. The Spartans sank all 200 of Athens's ships, and killed or enslaved 40,000 soldiers.

Meanwhile, Sparta seized control of the land around Athens, cutting off the Athenians' agricultural and economic resources. With Athens weakened, its allies revolted. Athens's situation just kept getting worse. The city-state had no good leaders left, and its naval fleet had been completely destroyed by Sparta.

In 412 B.C., Sparta strengthened its forces by allying with its old enemy Persia. The Spartan army steadily advanced on Athens, deliberately causing refugees to flee to the already overcrowded city. Blocked by Spartans on land and sea, a desperate Athens had only two choices: surrender or starve. In 404 B.C., Athens surrendered and the Peloponnesian War was finally over.

SPARTA IS VICTORIOUS

Sparta's fellow members in the Peloponnesian League wanted Athens to be completely destroyed and its people enslaved, but Sparta rejected these calls for revenge. Still, surrendering to Sparta was humiliating to the proud Athenians. The long walls linking Athens to the sea were torn down, and the Athenian navy was reduced to just 12 ships. As a final insult, Sparta replaced Athenian democracy with an oligarchy, a government made up of a small group of people. It was run by tyrants who ruled in a ruthless and controlling way. This form of leadership caused further conflicts within democracy-loving Athens.

The once powerful city of Athens was reduced to a second-rate state. However, Athens was not alone in its suffering. The long war had been costly in men, money, and resources to all the city-states involved. Greece as a whole was left weakened and vulnerable. To repair the damage, the city-states needed to cooperate with one another. Unfortunately, the end of the war did not stop conflicts from erupting. The city-states were soon warring among themselves again. In its weakened condition, Greece was a prime target for attack.

Critical Viewing Spartan soldiers raise their weapons for battle. What does the illustration suggest about how Spartan soldiers fought?

Spartan Warriors, Howard David Johnson, 2013

REVIEW & ASSESS

1. **READING CHECK** What finally caused Athens to surrender to Sparta, ending the Peloponnesian War?

2. **DETERMINE WORD MEANINGS** How does knowing that *olig-* means "few" and *arch-* means "ruler" clarify the meaning of *oligarchy*?

3. **ANALYZE CAUSE AND EFFECT** What were the effects of the Peloponnesian War on the Greek city-states?

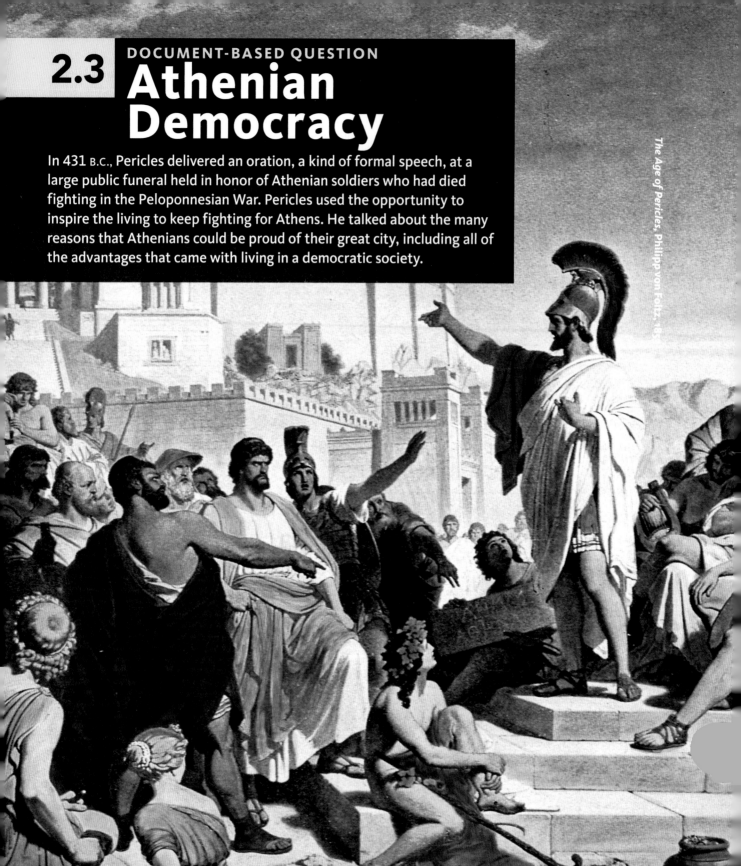

Athenian Democracy

In 431 B.C., Pericles delivered an oration, a kind of formal speech, at a large public funeral held in honor of Athenian soldiers who had died fighting in the Peloponnesian War. Pericles used the opportunity to inspire the living to keep fighting for Athens. He talked about the many reasons that Athenians could be proud of their great city, including all of the advantages that came with living in a democratic society.

The Age of Pericles, Philipp von Foltz, 1852

Critical Viewing An artist imagines what the scene might have looked like as Pericles delivered his oration. How do the Athenians appear to react to Pericles' words?

Primary Source: Speech

from *History of the Peloponnesian War*
by Thucydides (translated by Rex Warner)

Thucydides (thoo-SIH-duh-deez) was a Greek historian and general best known for his historical account of the events of the Peloponnesian War. As an Athenian military commander, he failed to prevent the capture of an important city from Sparta and was exiled for 20 years. During this time, he was able to witness events firsthand and interview participants much as a modern journalist would. His account provides a detailed record of Pericles' funeral oration. In this excerpt, Pericles reminds Athenians of the power they have as members of a democratic society.

CONSTRUCTED RESPONSE According to Pericles, what was special about the Athenian system of government?

> Our constitution is called a democracy because power is in the hands not of a minority but of the whole people. When it is a question of settling private disputes, everyone is equal before the law; when it is a question of putting one person before another in positions of public responsibility, what counts is not membership of a particular class, but the actual ability that the man possesses. No one, so long as he has it in him to be of service to the state, is kept in political obscurity because of poverty.

DOCUMENT TWO

Primary Source: Artifact

Ostracon, Greece, c. 400s B.C.

Ostracism was an enforced banishment. Athenians used it to prevent an individual from gaining too much power. Each citizen carved the name of someone he believed to be dangerous on a piece of pottery called an ostracon, seen at right. If the same name appeared often enough, the named person had to leave Athens. He did not lose citizenship, property, or wealth, but he was forbidden to return for ten years.

CONSTRUCTED RESPONSE What does the practice of ostracism tell you about Athenian values?

SYNTHESIZE & WRITE

1. **REVIEW** Review what you have learned about democracy in Athens from the text and the sources above.

2. **RECALL** On your own paper, write down the main idea expressed in the speech and artifact.

3. **CONSTRUCT** Write a topic sentence that answers this question: What was most important in Athenian democracy—the individual or the community?

4. **WRITE** Using evidence from the speech and artifact, write an argument to support your answer to the question in Step 3.

Philip of Macedonia

Your king wants to conquer Greece, located just south of your homeland. Weakened from internal fighting, Greece has become a prime target for attack. You and your fellow soldiers grip your 18-foot-long spears tighter as Greek soldiers approach. You are terrified, but you trust King Philip II. His military skills are extensive. In his capable hands, the act of war is turned into an art.

MAIN IDEA

Greece became unified under the military influence of Philip II.

CONQUEROR OF GREECE

The Greeks didn't think much of the kingdom of Macedonia (ma-suh-DOH-nee-uh), located just north of Greece. They dismissed its residents as uncultured foreigners. However, in 359 B.C., **Philip II** seized the Macedonian throne. He was an intelligent general and a clever politician—skills he combined with ambition, determination, and ruthlessness. An inspiring king, Philip completely controlled all political, military, legal, and religious matters.

Philip admired many things about Greece, including its ideas and art. He set his sights on uniting the Greek city-states with his own kingdom to create a combined kingdom strong enough to conquer the Persian Empire—his ultimate goal.

Philip built a powerful professional army and used new warfare methods. For example, he placed large groups of soldiers close together, forming an almost unstoppable battle formation called a **phalanx** (FAY-langks). Each soldier carried a spear that was much longer than the enemy's. The soldiers stood close to one another so that their shields overlapped, making it difficult for the enemy to attack them. Another new method of waging war was the use of war machines like the **catapult**, which hurled huge stones to shatter city walls.

Philip conquered the lands around Macedonia and seized Greek colonies that were rich in natural resources like gold mines, increasing his wealth. Greek city-states were still weak from the Peloponnesian War and were constantly quarrelling among themselves.

They were no match for Philip's strong army, great wealth, and political skill. By 348 B.C., Philip had won control of much of Greece. Any remaining Greek resistance crumbled when Athens and the strong city-state of Thebes fell to Philip at the Battle of Chaeronea (kair-uh-NEE-uh) in 338 B.C. Philip had united Greece for the first time ever. However, his son, **Alexander the Great**, would soon surpass his achievements.

YOUNG ALEXANDER

Born in 356 B.C., Alexander demonstrated his courage at a young age. One story tells how 12-year-old Alexander bravely stepped up to a nervous wild horse named Bucephalus (byoo-SEHF-uh-luhs), spoke gently to calm him down, and then rode him. Philip proudly announced that Macedonia would never be big enough for such a brave boy—and he was right.

Alexander trained for war with "the companions," a group of aristocratic sons

The Battle of Issus, House of the Faun, Pompeii, c. 80 B.C.

who became his loyal lifelong friends. His most important training came from his father, who took Alexander into battle with him. This gave his son firsthand experience in planning and carrying out a war.

The Greek scientist and great thinker Aristotle (A-ruh-stah-tuhl) was Alexander's tutor. He taught him geography, science, and literature. Alexander was greatly influenced by Homer's *Iliad* and kept a copy of it under his pillow. He wanted to be like the *Iliad*'s courageous hero, Achilles (uh-KIH-leez). According to myth, Achilles was one of the greatest warriors Greece had ever known.

Alexander soon became a warrior himself. At the age of 16, he was fighting off invasions and founding cities. In 336 B.C., Philip was assassinated, and 20-year-old Alexander became king.

The people of Thebes rebelled after Philip's death. They thought Macedonia would become weak without him. They could not have been more mistaken. Alexander marched into Greece to assert his leadership. He destroyed Thebes, terrifying all of Greece into submission. Alexander was well on his way to becoming "the Great."

REVIEW & ASSESS

1. **READING CHECK** What was Philip II's key achievement in Greece?

2. **ANALYZE CAUSE AND EFFECT** Why were the Greek city-states unprepared for an attack by Philip II?

3. **IDENTIFY MAIN IDEAS AND DETAILS** What evidence from the text demonstrates that Philip II was an intelligent general?

ALEXANDER
THE GREAT 356 B.C. – 323 B.C.

According to legend, the city of Gordium in Asia Minor contained a knot so complex that it was impossible to untie. Whoever could unravel the Gordian knot would conquer Asia. When Alexander saw the knot, he drew his sword and asked, "What does it matter how I untie it?" He then sliced the knot in two.

- 💼 **Job:** King of Macedonia and general of the army
- ✒️ **Education:** Taught by Aristotle, the great Greek thinker and scientist
- 🌐 **Home:** Born in Pella, Macedonia

FINEST HOUR
He led his unbeaten army to conquer lands as far east as India.

WORST MOMENT
In a drunken rage, he murdered his friend Cleitus.

FRIENDS
- Ptolemy (boyhood friend and general in the army)
- Hephaestion (lifelong friend and second-in-command)
- His soldiers

ENEMIES
- Thebans (Greek warriors)
- Darius (Persian king)
- Porus (Indian king)

TRIVIA
To honor his beloved horse, Alexander named a city in present-day India after him: Bucephala.

ALEXANDER'S TRIUMPHS

In 334 B.C., Alexander set out to fulfill his father's plans to conquer Persia. Philip was a skilled politician and general, but Alexander was even more gifted. He was a military genius who never once lost a battle. Alexander invaded and freed Persian-controlled Anatolia (present-day Turkey). Then he marched his army south toward Egypt, taking control of Persia's Mediterranean naval bases along the way. Persia responded with an attack from its huge army. However, Alexander cleverly forced the battle to occur on a narrow coastline, which destroyed Persia's advantage of having more soldiers.

When Alexander arrived in Egypt, the people, who had been living under Persian rule, greeted him as a liberator and crowned him pharaoh. Here, as elsewhere, Alexander won the support of conquered people by honoring local traditions. While in Egypt, he founded Alexandria, the first of many cities to bear his name. As a center of education,

Danube R.

Black Sea

CAUCASUS MOUNTAINS

Aral Sea

Syr Darya

Caspian Sea

Amu Darya

Chaeronea 338 B.C.

Granicus 334 B.C.

ANATOLIA

40°N

Alexandria Eschate

Thebes
Athens
Sparta
Miletus

Issus 333 B.C.

Euphrates R.

Tigris R.

Gaugamela 331 B.C.

Ecbatana

Bactra

Alexandria Areion

Mediterranean Sea

Tyre

Babylon

Susa

Alexandria Arachoton

Bucephala

Indus R.

Alexandria

Memphis

Persepolis

30°N

EGYPT

Nile R.

Persian Gulf

N
W E
S

Red Sea

0   200   400 Miles

0   200   400 Kilometers

Alexander's empire

Route of Alexander and his armies

Major battle site

Arabian Sea

20°N

20°E   30°E   40°E   50°E   60°E   70°E

culture, and trade, Alexandria was one of the most important cities in the ancient world.

In 331 B.C., Alexander defeated the Persians near Babylon and soon controlled the rest of the Persian Empire. Instead of returning home to celebrate, Alexander and his soldiers continued east. They conquered present-day Afghanistan and Uzbekistan before turning toward what is now India, which was then thought to be the edge of the world. In 326 B.C., Alexander crossed the Indus River and won a number of bloody battles, but his soldiers had had enough. Deeply homesick after 11 years away, they wanted to return home. Alexander reluctantly agreed. Over the course of 13

years, Alexander had carved out an empire stretching 3,000 miles from Europe to India. Legend says that he wept because he had no more worlds to conquer.

ALEXANDER'S DEATH

Thousands of soldiers died during the long trip home. Alexander himself did not survive the return journey. In 323 B.C., he became sick with a fever while in Babylon and died a few days later at the age of 32. His generals fought each other for control of the empire, which eventually fell apart. Alexander's empire was replaced with four kingdoms: the Egyptian, Macedonian, Pergamum (PUR-guh-muhm), and Seleucid (suh-LOO-suhd) kingdoms.

REVIEW & ASSESS

1. **READING CHECK** How did Alexander the Great win the support of the people he conquered?

2. **COMPARE AND CONTRAST** How were Philip II and Alexander similar and different as leaders?

3. **INTERPRET MAPS** What physical feature marks the eastern extent of Alexander's empire?

This statue, known as *Winged Victory of Samothrace*, is an example of Hellenistic sculpture from the second century B.C. It depicts Nike, the Greek goddess of victory. The head and arms of the statue have been lost.

The Spread of Hellenistic Culture

People enjoy going to museums to check out new exhibits. The library is the perfect quiet spot for research and reading. Sports fans gather in stadiums to be entertained by sporting events. Theaters showcase the latest dramatic play for an eager audience. Thousands of years ago, ancient Greeks enjoyed these very same activities.

MAIN IDEA

Alexander's conquests spread Greek culture across Asia.

CULTURAL BLEND

Hellas is Greek for "Greece," and the three centuries after Alexander's death are called the **Hellenistic** era because the known world was dominated by Greek culture. Alexander founded Greek colonies wherever he went, and Greek culture spread from these centers through cultural diffusion. Thousands of Greek colonists carried Greek practices and ideas to the plains of Persia, deserts of Egypt, mountains of Afghanistan, and river valleys of northern India. Each area adopted and adapted Greek culture differently, blending it with its own culture.

Alexander founded more than 70 cities, each with Greek designs and features such as temples, gymnasiums, and theaters. These cities flourished, cementing Greek influence in faraway places for centuries. The ultimate Hellenistic city was Alexandria, Egypt's new capital.

WORLDLY ALEXANDRIA

Alexandria became one of the largest, wealthiest, and most cultured cities in the ancient world. Many parks and open spaces created a pleasant environment, and the main streets were lined with colonnades, a series of columns that support a roof to provide shade. Alexandria's multiethnic mix of Greeks, Egyptians, Jews, and others created a **cosmopolitan**, or worldly, atmosphere.

In addition to housing Alexander's tomb and countless temples, Alexandria also had many magnificent buildings, including a museum used as a research center and a library known as the Great Library. It boasted a copy of every book written in Greek—some 500,000 scrolls. The library drew scholars and scientists from around the world. Meanwhile, Alexandria's wealth attracted the best artists, sculptors, writers, and musicians. The city was the cultural and trade center of the Hellenistic world.

REVIEW & ASSESS

1. **READING CHECK** How did Alexander spread Greek culture across Asia?

2. **DRAW CONCLUSIONS** What made Hellenistic culture unique?

3. **IDENTIFY MAIN IDEAS AND DETAILS** In what ways was Alexandria the cultural center of the Hellenistic world?

4.1 Philosophy and Literature

What is right? What is wrong? What is good? What is bad? We all think we know the answers, but do we really? These are some of the questions posed by Greek thinkers over 2,000 years ago. Today we are still searching for the answers.

MAIN IDEA

Greek ideas and writings remain influential today. They are the foundation of Western thought.

SOCRATES, PLATO, AND ARISTOTLE

Philosophy comes from a Greek word meaning "love of wisdom." Philosophers try to understand the universe and our place in it. Instead of explaining the world through gods and myths, they use logic and reason. Greek city-states provided an open environment where philosophers excelled. They also studied and taught other subjects, such as science, math, and biology.

Socrates (SAH-kruh-teez) was an Athenian philosopher interested in ethics, or the study of right and wrong. He challenged people to think more deeply, asking probing questions like, "What is justice?" His question-and-answer teaching style became known as the Socratic method. Socrates' methods made him unpopular among the leaders of Athens. He was accused of not believing in the official gods and of encouraging young

Athenians to rebel. He was put on trial, found guilty, and sentenced to death.

Socrates taught **Plato** (PLAY-toh), one of the most influential philosophers in history. Plato believed that this world was a shadow of a superior world. He disliked democracy, believing instead that philosopher-kings should rule. Plato founded an elite academy, where he taught **Aristotle**, the tutor of Alexander the Great.

Aristotle searched for understanding by examining the world closely. He categorized everything, laying the foundations for the study of biology, law, physics, and politics. Aristotle opened an academy, the Lyceum, where anyone could study a wide range of subjects. Together these three Greek philosophers formed the basis of modern Western philosophy, mathematics, and science and continue to influence our thinking.

EPICS AND HISTORIES

Homer was the most famous writer of epic poetry, a form of poetry that combines elements of drama and narrative. With their mythical beasts, interfering gods, and adventurous heroes, Homer's epics about the Trojan War—the *Iliad* and the *Odyssey*—continue to entertain modern readers. Another Greek writer still popular today was a slave called **Aesop** (EE-sahp). He wrote a series of fables, or short stories with animals as the central characters. Each fable taught a moral lesson.

The Greeks were among the first people to research their past and write it down accurately. When the Greek historian Herodotus (hih-RAH-duh-tuhs) wrote a history of the Persian Wars, he made sure to check his sources and to understand the significance of the events he described. He is considered the father of history. Similarly, Thucydides wrote an accurate account of the Peloponnesian War, while Xenophon (ZEH-nuh-fuhn) described life in Greece. They provided useful insights into ancient Greece and created a model for the future study of history.

THE SCHOOL OF ATHENS (Detail)

The Renaissance artist Raphael worked on this fresco over a three-year period. It was painted on a wall in the pope's palace in Rome. The painting shows the greatest thinkers of classical Greek society. There are mathematicians, natural philosophers, artists, and scientists. They all lived at different times, but Raphael painted them under one roof. The two central figures are Plato and Aristotle, who have had a lasting effect on Western thought.

Detail from *The School of Athens*, Raphael, A.D. 1511

Aristotle
Aristotle believed in studying the world as it is, including politics and biology.

Socrates
Socrates taught his pupils to question everything and to think for themselves.

Plato
Plato believed that all things on Earth were lesser versions of their ideals in heaven.

REVIEW & ASSESS

1. **READING CHECK** What are some of the subjects that ancient Greek thinkers studied and taught?

2. **DRAW CONCLUSIONS** What was unique about Aristotle's philosophy?

3. **ANALYZE CAUSE AND EFFECT** How did Herodotus and Thucydides influence the writing of history?

4.2

Arts and Architecture

A well-known ancient Greek tyrant cruelly enjoyed burying his enemies alive. Surprisingly, actors performing a Greek play were able to make him cry during sad scenes. The tyrant would weep for the suffering the actors mimicked onstage. Greek drama was powerful.

MAIN IDEA

The Greeks developed forms of art and architecture that are still appreciated today.

GREEK MASKS

Greek actors hid their faces with masks that represented the faces of a play's characters. Since three actors played multiple roles, the masks helped the audience recognize character changes.

DRAMA AND SCULPTURE

The Greeks loved the theater. Plays sometimes lasting entire days were performed in huge semicircular theaters, or amphitheaters. Greek drama evolved from plays honoring the god Dionysus (dy-uh-NY-suhs) into two main forms. **Comedy** was humorous and often mocked famous people. **Tragedy** was serious, with characters suffering before an unhappy ending.

Only three male actors performed each play, which required each actor to play many parts. The chorus, a group of actors who spoke, sang, and danced together, narrated the story. Costumes, props, and music brought the action to life.

The greatest Greek playwrights were Sophocles (SAH-fuh-kleez), Aeschylus (EHS-kuh-luhs), and Euripides (yu-RIH-puh-deez), who all wrote tragedies, and Aristophanes (a-ruh-STAH-fuh-neez), who wrote comedy.

Greek sculptors were dedicated to capturing the human form in their art. They carved sculptures from marble, wood, and bronze. The sculptures were painted to look amazingly alive. The Colossus of Rhodes was a 100-foot-tall bronze statue of the sun god Helios, similar in style to the Statue of Liberty. It was once considered one of the Seven Wonders of the Ancient World, but the original no longer stands. In fact, many of the best examples of Greek sculpture are actually newer Roman copies of Greek originals.

This theater in Taormina, Sicily, is one of the best-preserved examples of a Greek amphitheater. What modern structure does this theater resemble?

COLUMNS AND TEMPLES

Ancient Greek architecture was a democratic art. It expressed beauty and harmony for everyone to enjoy. Temples were designed to be admired from outside, and all followed a similar plan. The temple usually faced east, toward the sunrise. The main room was rectangular and contained a statue of the temple god. Columns supported the roof. The features of Greek architecture continue to influence the style of buildings today. The Supreme Court Building in Washington, D.C., is a good example of this influence.

THREE COLUMN TYPES

Doric
Mainland, western colonies

Corinthian
More rarely found

Ionic
Eastern Greece and the islands

REVIEW & ASSESS

1. **READING CHECK** What art forms did the Greeks develop that we still appreciate today?

2. **COMPARE AND CONTRAST** What is the difference between the two main forms of Greek drama—comedy and tragedy?

3. **IDENTIFY MAIN IDEAS AND DETAILS** The text states that Greek architecture was a democratic art form. What evidence supports this claim?

432 B.C.

The Parthenon, one of the world's most recognizable buildings, was completed in 432 B.C. It took workers almost 15 years to build this magnificent marble temple, which honored Athena, goddess and protector of Athens. Like much Greek architecture, the Parthenon was made to be looked at from the outside. Its elegant proportions communicated a sense of harmony and balance. Inside, towering from floor to ceiling, was a 33-foot gold and ivory statue of Athena. The Parthenon was both an expression of Athens's wealth and a symbol of its cultural, political, and military superiority. What details in the Parthenon's design help convey these ideas?

4.4 Democracy and Law

Sometimes we might take our system of government for granted. However, our democracy is a legacy that has been passed down to us from thousands of years ago. Our modern ideas of democracy, justice, and citizenship all have their roots in ancient Greece.

MAIN IDEA

The Constitution of the United States was influenced by ancient Greek ideas.

GOVERNMENT OF THE PEOPLE

Ancient Greece was the birthplace of democracy and citizenship. Thousands of Greek citizens met regularly to vote on policies and laws. Greek colonies in Italy spread democracy to the ancient Romans, who carried it around the ancient world. They firmly established Greek political ideas in Europe. From these ideas evolved our modern ideas about government and civic life.

Ancient Greece also laid the foundations of American constitutional democracy. The cornerstone of Greek democratic ideas was that political power should rest with the people. The Greeks established the concept of citizenship with its rights and responsibilities toward the state and a duty to participate in politics and civic life.

The Greeks also embraced the principle of political equality, in which one citizen has one vote and where officials are paid, allowing the poor to serve as well as the rich. The Greeks put checks and balances into place. They limited terms of office and separated the three key branches of government—lawmaking, executive, and judicial—to prevent any one branch from becoming too powerful.

The **representative democracy** of the United States is based on the Greek system. Because the U.S. population is so large, its millions of citizens cannot vote directly on policies. Instead, citizens exercise their political power by electing representatives to vote on their behalf.

RULE OF LAW

Greek democracy was built on the rule of law. Greek citizens proposed and voted on laws that were enforced in courts. These courts established innocence or guilt through trials by **jury**. A jury is a group of people chosen to decide guilt or innocence in a trial. Greek jurors were selected randomly so that the results would be impartial. They also were paid so that even poor citizens could take part.

In Greek trials, the accuser and the accused represented themselves. There were no lawyers. Both parties had the same amount of time to speak, and both relied on witnesses. Under oath, witnesses sometimes testified to events but usually provided character statements.

Both sides presented their case, but they did not sum up the evidence, as lawyers do in court cases today. Nor was the jury allowed to discuss the case. Instead, jurors voted immediately by placing metal discs called ballots into a pot. The jury also passed sentence. Some penalties were automatic, such as death for murder, but more involved fines. Few people were actually imprisoned. There were no appeals, and the entire process was completed in a day.

Supporters of immigration rights march through downtown Los Angeles. How are these people demonstrating citizenship?

REVIEW & ASSESS

1. **READING CHECK** Why were jury members chosen randomly and why were they paid?

2. **ANALYZE CAUSE AND EFFECT** What ancient Greek ideas laid the foundation for the U.S. system of government?

3. **COMPARE AND CONTRAST** What are the differences between ancient Greek trials and modern trials in the United States?

VOCABULARY

Use each of the following vocabulary words in a sentence that shows an understanding of the meaning of the word.

1. **direct democracy**
   Athens's government was a direct democracy, in which citizens voted for or against laws.

2. **immortal**

3. **plague**

4. **siege**

5. **philosophy**

6. **comedy**

7. **tragedy**

8. **jury**

READING STRATEGY

9. **DETERMINE WORD MEANINGS** Copy the chart below and add your examples of words that include each Greek root. Then write a paragraph about Greek culture that includes each word.

Root	Meaning	Example(s)
cosm-	universe	
-cracy	government	*democracy*
dem-	people	*democracy*
-logy	speech	
myth-	story	
phil-	love	
poli-	city	
soph-	wise	

MAIN IDEAS

Answer the following questions. Support your answers with evidence from the chapter.

10. How did Athens become a powerful empire after the Persian Wars? LESSON 1.2

11. Why did the Greeks make offerings to the gods and goddesses they worshipped? LESSON 1.3

12. What caused the outbreak of the Peloponnesian War between Athens and Sparta? LESSON 2.1

13. How did Sparta defeat Athens and end the Peloponnesian War? LESSON 2.2

14. What was Phillip II's most important achievement in Greece? LESSON 3.1

15. Why did Alexander's conquests end? LESSON 3.2

16. How is Hellenistic culture an example of cultural diffusion? LESSON 3.3

17. What evidence is there that the ideas of the Greek philosophers and writers are still important today? LESSON 4.1

CRITICAL THINKING

Answer the following questions. Support your answers with evidence from the chapter.

18. **DRAW CONCLUSIONS** What are three ways in which Greek influences are felt today?

19. **ANALYZE CAUSE AND EFFECT** How did the plague contribute to the failure of Pericles' war strategy against the Spartans?

20. **EVALUATE** What factors contributed to Philip II's success in conquering and unifying Greece?

21. **YOU DECIDE** Where would you rather have lived—Athens or Sparta? Why? Support your opinion with details from the chapter.

Study the map of the Hellenistic world after Alexander's death, when his empire broke apart. Then answer the questions that follow.

THE HELLENISTIC WORLD, 241 B.C.

Legend:
- Egyptian Kingdom
- Macedonian Kingdom
- Pergamum Kingdom
- Seleucid Kingdom

22. Into what four kingdoms did Alexander's empire separate?

23. Which kingdom appears to have the least territory?

ANALYZE SOURCES

Read the following excerpt from the American Declaration of Independence. Then answer the question.

> We hold these truths to be self-evident, that all men are created equal, that they are endowed by their Creator with certain unalienable Rights, that among these are Life, Liberty, and the pursuit of Happiness.

24. How are the thoughts on democracy expressed by the authors of the Declaration of Independence similar to those of the Athenians?

WRITE ABOUT HISTORY

25. INFORMATIVE Write a three-paragraph speech for new American citizens explaining how democratic concepts developed in Greece laid the foundation for democracy in the United States.

TIPS

- Take notes from the lessons about Pericles and democracy and the legacy of ancient Greece.
- Introduce the topic clearly.
- Develop the topic with relevant, well-chosen facts, concrete details, and examples.
- Use vocabulary from the chapter as appropriate.
- Use appropriate transitions to clarify the relationships among concepts.
- Provide a concluding statement that summarizes the information presented.
- Use an audio recording device to record your speech. Be sure to speak loudly and clearly.

NATIONAL GEOGRAPHIC

ON **LOCATION**
WITH

William
PARKINSON

NATIONAL GEOGRAPHIC GRANTEE

▶ Check out more on myNGconnect

In the field, Parkinson uses hi-tech equipment like this Real-Time-Kinetic GPS. It makes accurate maps by communicating with multiple satellites at one time.

FROM VILLAGE TO CITY

Like many kids who grew up in the Midwest, I loved searching for arrowheads in the fields and woods. Finding them made me want to learn more about people who lived long ago. Lucky for me, I had excellent college professors who encouraged me to study archaeology, and now I'm living my dream!

Today, I study how small farming villages turned into big cities. From an archaeological perspective, cities are weird. Until about 8,000 years ago humans lived in small groups and moved around as hunter-gatherers. Today, more than half of all humans live in cities. This has dramatic implications for our future. Archaeologists have done a good job explaining human development from hunter-gatherers to settled farmers. However, we still don't really understand how those early villages turned into massive cities.

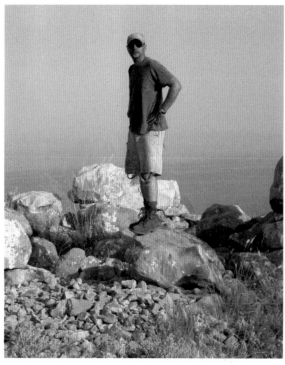

Bill Parkinson explores a coastline while conducting an archaeological survey in Diros Bay, Greece.

A TEAM SPORT

In Europe and the Near East, the turning point came during the Neolithic and the Bronze Ages. My team has been excavating an ancient farming village in Greece, just outside a big cave called Fox Hole Cave. This cave was used for rituals and habitation during the Neolithic period, when the first farmers emerged in southeastern Europe. Greek archaeologists have explored this cave for 40 years, and we wanted to build on their great work. Archaeology is a team sport that relies on the collaboration of many different specialists, so we brought together an international crew to study the cave.

Our excavations show that people built an agricultural settlement at the site about 6,000 years ago. This settlement gives us greater insight into how early agricultural villages developed. I'm studying a similar site from the same time period in Hungary, so we're able to compare and contrast how societies changed over time in different parts of the world. Now we are publishing the results of our research, another crucial part of archaeology. Soon we'll be back in the field, hunting for the next clues about how ancient villages transformed into cities.

WHY STUDY HISTORY ❓

❝ Nothing can describe how exciting it is to put your trowel in the ground and uncover something nobody has seen for several thousand years. *It never gets old.* ❞ —William Parkinson

NATIONAL GEOGRAPHIC

Greek Statues Sparkle Once Again

BY A. R. WILLIAMS

Adapted from "2,500-Year-Old Greek Statues
Sparkle After Facelift," by A. R. Williams,
news.nationalgeographic.com, June 19, 2014

IESL-FORTH

Four marble maidens from ancient Greece have gotten a makeover. Using a specially designed laser, conservators have stripped away the black grime that covered the statues. Sculpted in the late fifth century B.C., the figures served as columns for the Erechtheion, one of the temples that stood on the Acropolis. The maidens, known as the Caryatids, stand more than seven and a half feet tall and hold the roof of the Erechtheion's south porch on their heads.

As Athens rapidly industrialized over the past century, the Caryatids suffered from the effects of air pollution. Their golden hue turned dark, and their features began to dissolve under the constant assault of acid rain. In 1979 the figures were moved to protect them from further damage. Cement replicas were installed in their place on the Erechtheion's porch.

The Caryatids got their makeover in the public gallery of the Acropolis Museum. Conservators focused on one figure at a time in a makeshift room whose walls were sheets of heavy fabric hung from a frame. A video

monitor outside allowed visitors to see the statues slowly changing color. The curtain walls protected museumgoers' eyes from the laser system that conservators, wearing protective goggles, used to clean the statues. This system uses two pulsed beams of radiation—one infrared and the other ultraviolet—to zap away dust, soot, minerals, and metals.

Conservators and technicians considered several different kinds of cleaning, including chemicals and micro-sandblasting. The dual-wavelength laser system was the best option. It allows for safe, controlled cleaning that leaves the marble's ancient patina intact.

A future project may reveal even more of the maidens' original beauty. Their clothing was once brightly painted. However, centuries of winter rain have washed away all visible traces of pigment. Modern imaging techniques can peer into the invisible parts of the light spectrum and find long-faded hues. The result may be even more dazzling than the maidens' current makeover.

For more from National Geographic
Check out "Behind the Tomb" on myNGconnect

UNIT INQUIRY: DEFINE GOOD CITIZENSHIP

In this unit, you learned about ancient Greek civilization and its influence on our modern world. Based on your understanding of the text, what new form of government was central to Greek civilization? What role did citizenship play in Greek civilization and government?

ASSIGNMENT Create your own definition for good citizenship. Your definition should include a clear statement of what constitutes good citizenship and why it is important today. Be prepared to present your definition to the class and explain your reasoning.

Plan As you write your definition, think about the active role citizens played in ancient Greek civilization and government. Also think about the rights and responsibilities ancient Greek citizens had and how those ideas have influenced our ideas about citizenship today. You might want to use a graphic organizer to help organize your thoughts. ▶

Produce Use your notes to produce descriptions of the elements that make up your definition of good citizenship.

Present Choose a creative way to present your definition to the class. Consider one of these options:

- Create a video presentation using examples from everyday life showing good citizens "in action" in their community.

- Design a good citizenship medal to present to someone who exemplifies what it means to be a good citizen.

- Design a good citizenship brochure that outlines citizens' rights and responsibilities.

Good Citizenship

1. The Minoans and the Mycenaeans were the first advanced Greek civilizations.

2. Ancient Greek city-states established colonies and trade networks throughout the Mediterranean.

3. The city-state of Athens developed the world's first democracy.

4. Alexander the Great conquered Persia, Egypt, Afghanistan, and India, building a vast empire that spread Greek culture.

5. The ancient Greeks influenced Western art, architecture, literature, philosophy, science, medicine, government, and law.

6-10. **NOW IT'S YOUR TURN** Complete the list with five more things to remember about Greek civilization.

THE WORLD OF THE ROMANS

NATIONAL GEOGRAPHIC

ON **LOCATION** WITH

Steven Ellis
Archaeologist

Have you ever heard the expression "All roads lead to Rome?" Well, 2,000 years ago, all roads actually did lead to Rome. Though it began as a small town on the Tiber River in Italy, in only a few centuries Rome came to dominate the Mediterranean and build a civilization that stretched from northern Europe to Syria. I'm Steven Ellis, and I work with National Geographic. Welcome to the world of the Romans!

< **CRITICAL VIEWING** The ruins of Pompeii, seen here in the shadow of Mount Vesuvius, continue to reveal much about the lives of the ancient Romans. What details do you notice in the photo that resemble features you might see in a town or city today?

Ancient Rome

44 B.C.
Julius Caesar is assassinated by a group of Roman senators.

753 B.C.
According to legend, Romulus founds the city of Rome. *(illustration of Romulus on a coin)*

509 B.C.
Rome becomes a republic.

100 B.C.

800 B.C.

The World

750 B.C.
EUROPE
Greek city-states flourish with shared Greek identity but individual loyalties, customs, and governments.

334 B.C.
EUROPE
Alexander the Great begins to build his massive empire.
(detail from statue of Alexander)

264

COMPARE TIME LINES

What other world event happened around the time Rome became an empire?

A.D. 26–29
Jesus preaches religious ideas that will form the basis of Christianity.

A.D. 476
Invasions bring about the fall of the Western Roman Empire.
(painting of the sack of Rome)

A.D. 177
The Roman Empire reaches its greatest extent, stretching over parts of Europe, Asia, and Africa.

A.D. 395
The Roman Empire is divided into the Eastern and Western empires.

27 B.C.
Rome becomes an empire, and Augustus becomes its first emperor.

A.D. 300

A.D. 500

A.D. 100

**A.D. 250
AMERICAS**
The Maya build great cities and make significant advances in learning.
(Maya pyramid)

**A.D. 300s
AFRICA**
The kingdom of Aksum in East Africa reaches its height under Ezana.

**10 B.C.
ASIA**
The Silk Roads connect China to the Mediterranean.

FROM REPUBLIC TO
EMPIRE
146 B.C.–A.D. 117

Find Rome on the map. That's how it began: as a small dot in a land once known as Italia. Actually, Rome was even smaller, since it began as a village of farmers. But the Romans developed a civilization that grew to become one of the greatest empires the world has ever seen.

At its full extent, the Roman Empire stretched over three continents. It was held together by taxes, the powerful Roman army, and an amazing network of roads. Through periods of peace and war, Rome remained the center of the Western world for hundreds of years.

What body of water probably helped link the Roman Empire?

Hadrian's Wall

North Sea

Caledonia
Hadrian's Wall
Hibernia

BRITANNIA
Londinium

Germania

MAGNA GERMANIA
12 B.C.–A.D. 9

Rhine
Vistula
Elbe

GERMANIA INFERIOR
GERMANIA SUPERIOR

PANNONIA INFERIOR

Seine
LUGDUNENSIS
BELGICA
Rhine
Danube
RAETIA
NORICUM
PANNONIA SUPERIOR

Loire
Gallia
Lake Geneva
Alps
AQUITANIA
ALPES GRAIAE ET POENINAE
Lake Garda
Po
DALMATIA
Rhône
ALPES COTTIAE
Adriatic Sea

NARBONENSIS
ALPES MARITIMAE
ITALIA

CORSICA
Rome ★

Ebro
TARRACONENSIS
LUSITANIA
Tagus
Hispania
Emerita Augusta

SARDINIA
Tyrrhenian Sea

Balearic Islands

BAETICA
Mediterranean
SICILIA
Carthage

MAURETANIA TINGITANA
Volubilis
MAURETANIA CAESARIENSIS
AFRICA

Atlantic Ocean

A F R I[CA]

Time Line of Good and Bad Emperors

 "Bad" emperor
Historians traditionally call the first three emperors below "bad" because they abused their power.

 "Good" emperor
The other five emperors are considered "good" because, like Augustus, they presided over a period of peace and ruled wisely.

 Caligula
A.D. 37–41
- Reigned as a cruel tyrant
- Insisted on being treated as a god

 Nero
A.D. 54–68
- Committed many murders
- Did nothing while much of Rome burned

 Domitian
A.D. 81–96
- Ruled as a dictator
- Murdered many of his enemies

 Nerva
A.D. 96–98
- First emperor chosen for the job
- Tried to end tryannical rule

0 50 100 150 200 250 kilometers
0 50 100 150 200 250 miles
Places on the map are labeled with their early Latin names.

The Arch of Constantine, Rome

Detail of Trajan's column, A.D. 113, Trajan's Forum, Rome

As a vassal of Rome, this kingdom managed much of its internal affairs, but Rome controlled its foreign affairs.

E

Sarmatia

Dniester

Dnieper

BOSPORAN KINGDOM

Caucasus Mts.

Volga

Caspian Sea

Black Sea

DACIA

Danube

MOESIA INFERIOR

MOESIA SUPERIOR

THRACIA

Byzantium (Constantinople)

BYTHINIA ET PONTUS

CAPPADOCIA

ARMENIA A.D. 114–117

Lake Sevan

Lake Van

Parthia

ASSYRIA A.D. 116–117

MESOPOTAMIA A.D. 115–117

Tigris

Euphrates

A S I A

Asia Minor

MACEDONIA

Aegean Sea

ASIA

GALATIA

EPIRUS

LYCIA

CILICIA

SYRIA

Persian Gulf

Athens

ACHAEA

Sparta

Ionian Sea

CRETA

Tripolis

CYPRUS

JUDAEA

Jerusalem
Dead Sea

ARABIA

The curled fingers were part of a statue that stood in Arabia around A.D. 160.

Sea

Ptolemais

CYRENE

Alexandria

Nile

AEGYPTUS

I

C

A

■ Roman Territory, 201 B.C.	▨ Area ruled by the time of Caesar Augustus' death, A.D.14	▨ Region temporarily held by Rome, with dates
■ Gains by 100 B.C.	▨ Gains by Emperor Trajan, A.D. 117 (Roman Empire at its greatest extent)	▨ Vassal of Rome
■ Area ruled by the time of Julius Caesar's death, 44 B.C.		∿∿ Fortified frontier

Trajan
A.D. 98–117

• Brought Empire to greatest extent
• Created aid program for the poor

Hadrian
A.D. 117–138

• Fortified the Empire's borders
• Enforced peace

Antoninus Pius
A.D. 138–161

• Reigned over period of peace and prosperity
• Specified that Marcus Aurelius succeed him

Marcus Aurelius
A.D. 161–180

• Fought off invaders
• Reigned as a just and lawful man

10

THE ROMAN REPUBLIC

509 B.C. – 44 B.C.

SECTION 1 EARLY ROME

 SS.6.C.1.2; SS.6.C.2.1; SS.6.E.1.1; SS.6.G.1.4; SS.6.G.1.6; SS.6.G.1.7; SS.6.G.2.1; SS.6.G.2.4; SS.6.G.2.5; SS.6.G.2.6; SS.6.W.3.8; SS.6.W.3.10; SS.6.W.3.16; LAFS.68.RH.1.2; LAFS.68.RH.2.5; LAFS.68.RH.3.7

KEY VOCABULARY		NAMES & PLACES	
consul	peninsula	Aeneas	Romulus
dictator	plebeian	Cicero	and Remus
legend	republic	Cincinnatus	Senate
patrician	tribune	Etruscans	Tiber River
	veto	Forum	Twelve Tables

SECTION 2 SOCIETY AND CULTURE

 SS.6.E.1.1; SS.6.G.2.5; SS.6.G.2.6; SS.6.G.4.1; SS.6.W.3.12; SS.6.W.3.16; LAFS.68.RH.1.2; LAFS.68.RH.2.4; LAFS.68.RH.2.5; LAFS.68.RH.3.7

KEY VOCABULARY		NAMES & PLACES
aristocracy	patriarchy	Council of Plebs
pantheon		

SECTION 3 THE ARMY AND EXPANSION

 SS.6.E.1.1; SS.6.G.1.4; SS.6.G.1.7; SS.6.G.2.2; SS.6.G.2.5; SS.6.W.1.4; SS.6.W.3.8; SS.6.W.3.9; SS.6.W.3.12; SS.6.W.3.14; LAFS.68.RH.1.3; LAFS.68.RH.2.5; LAFS.68.RH.3.7

KEY VOCABULARY		NAMES & PLACES	
legionary	province	Carthage	Punic Wars
		Hannibal	

SECTION 4 THE END OF THE REPUBLIC

 SS.6.W.1.3; SS.6.W.3.8; SS.6.W.3.11; LAFS.68.RH.1.1; LAFS.68.RH.1.2; LAFS.68.RH.2.5; LAFS.68.RH.3.7; LAFS.68.RH.3.8; LAFS.68.RH.3.9; LAFS.68.WHST.1.2; LAFS.68.WHST.3.9

KEY VOCABULARY		NAMES & PLACES
civil war	reform	First Triumvirate
		Julius Caesar

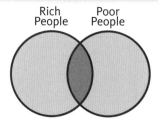

Temple of Venus and Rome

READING STRATEGY

ORGANIZE IDEAS: COMPARE AND CONTRAST When you read, you often compare and contrast one thing with another to help you understand new information. As you read the chapter, use a Venn diagram like this one to compare and contrast the lives of rich people and poor people in the Roman Republic.

Rich People   Poor People

Painting of gladiators in the Colosseum

Claudian Aqueduct

This model of Rome shows the city as it might have looked in A.D. 312.

The Geography of
Ancient Rome

If you wanted to build a Mediterranean empire, you'd probably start from Rome. The city lies near the heart of the sea. Geographically, it's the best place to begin a conquest of the Mediterranean.

MAIN IDEA

Rome's location had many geographic advantages that helped it grow and become powerful.

THE ITALIAN PENINSULA

Italy lies on a **peninsula**, or land surrounded by water on three sides, in the Mediterranean Sea. It is shaped like a boot and looks as though it is kicking a football—the island of Sicily—toward North Africa. Italy is attached to the rest of Europe by a massive range of snow-covered mountains called the Alps.

Another mountain range, the Apennines (A-puh-nynz), runs down the center of Italy. These mountains slope through wooded hills to sunny coastal plains and the blue waters of the Mediterranean. In time, the Romans would come to call the Mediterranean *Mare Nostrum* (MAHR-ay NOHS-truhm), or "Our Sea."

Rome was founded on seven hills on the volcanic west coast of Italy. The Romans embraced the advanced cultures of their neighbors to the north and south. Ideas adopted from these cultures helped Rome flourish and grow strong.

THE CITY OF ROME

Rome's geography helped it survive and thrive. What first made Rome important was its strategic position. It was located at a key crossing point of the **Tiber** (TY-bur) **River**.

The location was also a natural stopping point on the valuable trade routes running north to south and inland from the sea. The city was far enough from the coast to escape deadly attacks by pirates and enemies but close enough to benefit from the Mediterranean's busy sea trade. Olive oil and wine were among Rome's most commonly traded items.

The circle of seven hills on which Rome was built rose above the river and also provided protection against attack. These seven hills became Rome's center. Romans built important government buildings there. The hills were also home to religious temples and entertainment facilities. Roads branched off from this area to the outside world.

The land around the city had fertile soil, a good water supply, and a mild climate. These qualities helped Rome's agriculture flourish and support the large population needed to wage and win wars in the ancient world. As the Roman historian Livy boasted, "With good reason did gods and men choose this site for founding a city."

Rome's central location helped it take over much of Italy. Then Italy's central location helped Rome become a powerful force in the Mediterranean. Around the sea, the riches of Europe, Southwest Asia, and North Africa were temptingly close. Control of the Mediterranean seemed within the grasp of a strong, ambitious, and determined civilization like Rome.

Alta Semita

Quirinal Hill

Viminal Hill

Clivus Patricus

Esquiline Hill

Temple of Jupiter

Capitoline Hill

Senate House

Forum

Regia

Palatine Hill

Caelian Hill

Via Appia

Circus Maximus

Tiber River

Aventine Hill

ALPS

100 Miles

100 Kilometers

Apennines

Corsica

Rome ITALY

Sardinia

40°N

Mediterranean Sea

Sicily

10°E

REVIEW & ASSESS

1. **READING CHECK** How did Rome's geographic advantages help the city grow and gain power?

2. **FIND MAIN IDEAS AND DETAILS** What physical features helped protect Rome from invasion?

3. **INTERPRET MAPS** Where did the Romans build most of their buildings? What might be a good reason for this location?

1.2 The Founding of Rome

Three thousand years ago, a few small huts stood scattered across the hills that overlooked the Tiber River's swampy floodplain. Within just 250 years, this humble landscape was transformed into the heart of a mighty empire.

MAIN IDEA

Rome grew from a tiny village to a city between 753 and 509 B.C.

MYTHICAL BEGINNINGS

The Romans loved stories, especially bloody ones with great heroes. One of the most popular **legends**, or stories about famous people and events in the past, was about the founding of Rome. Not only did the story contain a hero and plenty of blood, but it also linked Rome to the great civilization of ancient Greece.

According to the legend, a Trojan hero named **Aeneas** (ih-NEE-uhs) was the ancestor of Rome's founders—the twin brothers **Romulus** (RAHM-yuh-luhs) and **Remus** (REE-muhs). As babies, the brothers were abandoned. They were rescued by a wolf and raised by a shepherd. When they grew up, the brothers founded their own city. In 753 B.C., Romulus became the first king of the city, which he named Rome, after himself.

Research actually supports a part of the story of Romulus and Remus. Archaeologists have uncovered ruins suggesting that the hills around Rome contained many small villages in 1000 B.C. Some of these villages merged with villages in the valleys to create a larger settlement around 750 B.C. This was early Rome.

EARLY ROMANS

At this time, Italy was a patchwork of different peoples with their own rulers, customs, and languages. Most of Rome's original residents were Latins, who came from an area around the Tiber River called Latium. The Latins were not united, and their many cities were often at war with one another as well as with neighboring peoples. In its early days, Rome was a small village in a violently competitive world.

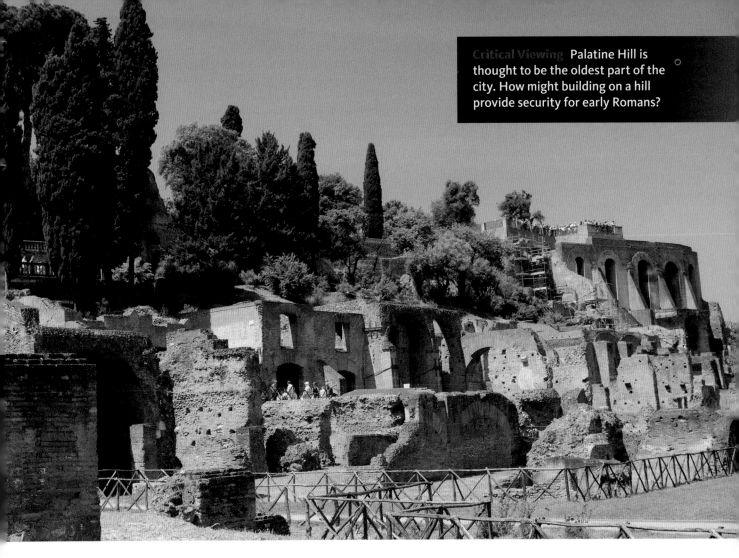

What helped make Rome strong was that it welcomed people from many different lands. Foreigners of different classes and professions settled in the city and helped it grow in size and strength. The people who most influenced early Rome were the Greeks to the south and the **Etruscans** (ih-TRUHS-kuhnz) to the north.

The Greeks dominated the Mediterranean and had many colonies in southern Italy. Through travel and trade, they introduced the Romans to important advances in agriculture, architecture, and learning.

The Romans learned to grow olives and modified the Greek alphabet for writing. Roman poets copied the Greek style of the long epic poem.

The Etruscans were expert traders, metalworkers, and engineers. Three Etruscan kings who came to rule Rome brought these professional skills with them. They laid out the city's streets in a grid plan around a central square. The Etruscans replaced mud huts with stone houses and built Rome's first temples and public buildings. By 509 B.C., Rome was becoming the city we still see traces of today.

REVIEW & ASSESS

1. **READING CHECK** How did people from different cultures help Rome develop into a city?

2. **IDENTIFY MAIN IDEAS AND DETAILS** According to legend, how was Rome founded?

3. **MAKE INFERENCES** What does the willingness to adopt other peoples' ideas suggest about Roman values?

Republican Government

You wouldn't have wanted to meet the Etruscan king Tarquin the Proud in a dark alley. He ruled as a tyrant—a cruel ruler—and had many of his opponents killed. In 509 B.C., the people of Rome overthrew Tarquin and established a new form of government.

MAIN IDEA

Rome developed a republican form of government that protected the rights of ordinary citizens.

THE YOUNG REPUBLIC

In a **republic**, citizens vote for their leaders. Only free adult men were citizens in Rome, but not all citizens were equal. Roman society was divided into two groups: the patricians and the plebeians. The **patricians** (puh-TRIH-shuhnz) were wealthy landowners. The **plebeians** (plih-BEE-uhnz), who included poorer farmers and craftsmen, made up the majority of Rome's citizens but were under-represented in the government.

The plebeians wanted a say in how Rome was run. As a result, in 494 B.C., they went on strike. The plebeians left the city, shutting down Roman shops and businesses, and set up their own government. Economic activity came to a halt. Once the patricians started losing money, they became frightened and agreed to share their power. In time, the plebeians were allowed to elect their own representatives, called **tribunes**, who fought to protect the rights of ordinary citizens.

The plebeians had one more demand. Because Rome's laws were not written down, the patricians often interpreted them to favor their rich friends. The plebeians fought back. They insisted that the laws be not only written down but carved into bronze tablets and displayed for all to see. These laws became known as the **Twelve Tables**. They protected all Roman citizens from injustice. Some of these laws are the basis of our own laws today.

ROMAN GOVERNMENT

Rome's new, more representative government furthered the development of democratic principles first introduced in the Greek city-state of Athens. The government contained three branches. An executive branch led the government and the army, a legislative branch made the laws, and a judicial branch applied the laws.

The Romans put in place a system of checks and balances, similar to that used in the United States, to prevent any one branch from becoming too powerful. They also replaced the position of king with two leaders called **consuls**. The consuls shared power so equally that they had the right to **veto**, or reject, each other's decisions.

The legislative branch was made up of the **Senate**, elected judicial officers, and two assemblies. The Senate advised the consuls. The assemblies represented the plebeians. In the beginning, most of the 300 members of the Senate were patricians. Over time, however, plebeians were also allowed to participate.

Senators often spoke out about issues in the Senate House and in public squares. One of Rome's most brilliant speakers was **Cicero** (SIH-suh-roh), who often used his speeches to attack those who he believed were a threat to the republic.

Cicero Denounces Catiline, Cesare Maccari, 1888

In times of crisis, the Romans appointed **dictators** who had complete control but were expected to give up power after danger had passed. One such Roman dictator was **Cincinnatus** (sihn-suh-NA-tuhs). In 458 B.C., Rome's army was facing defeat by a fierce enemy, and the Senate wanted Cincinnatus to take charge. He accepted the dictatorship, defeated the enemy, and then surrendered his power and returned to his farm. The example set by Cincinnatus was celebrated by the Romans, who valued the idea of civic duty—putting service to the community ahead of personal interest.

REVIEW & ASSESS

1. **READING CHECK** How did the Roman government come to protect the rights of the citizens?

2. **COMPARE AND CONTRAST** In what ways are the governments of the Roman Republic and the United States similar?

3. **DRAW CONCLUSIONS** Why was it important to the plebeians to have Roman laws written down?

The ruins of the Roman Forum represent different periods of Rome's ancient history. Here older ruins of buildings surround the Arch of Titus. The Colosseum stands in the background.

The Roman Forum

The Roman Forum was the place to be. It was the place to meet, shop, do business, worship, celebrate, and be entertained. This public square was one of the liveliest and most important places in all of Rome.

MAIN IDEA

The Roman Forum was the political, religious, economic, and social center of the Roman Republic.

BURIAL GROUND TO PUBLIC SQUARE

The **Forum** developed over several centuries in a valley between the Palatine and Capitoline hills. In heavy rain, the banks of the Tiber River would burst, flooding the marshy valley. Long before Rome was founded, this scrap of swamp had been used as a burial ground. However, once Rome began to grow and its population spilled down the hills, the swamp became a piece of desirable real estate. Around 600 B.C., an Etruscan king built a sewer to drain the area and created an open public square paved with pebbles. The Roman Forum was born.

Everyone came to the Forum. It was the city's open-air market, where Romans could buy everything from local fruit and vegetables to imported Greek pottery. Rome's oldest road, the Via Sacra, looped through the Forum. Along the road, the early kings of Rome built a royal residence, shops, houses, and temples dedicated to their many gods and goddesses. At first these buildings were little more than mud huts or raised-earth platforms. Over time, these were replaced with permanent structures, and the Forum became the center of Rome's religious, economic, and social activity.

THE CENTER OF ROME

After the republic was founded, the Forum also became the center of Roman politics. Although the Forum's open space remained small, huge public and government buildings sprang up around it. The Temple of Saturn, dedicated to one of Rome's most important gods, became the treasury, holding the growing riches of the republic. The Curia was the meeting place of the Roman Senate. Political activity, ranging from public speeches to rioting mobs, took place at the Forum. Because it was where ordinary Romans gathered, the Forum was the perfect place to display the Twelve Tables.

The Forum also provided a setting for public spectacles. Crowds came to watch theatrical performances and athletic games. Even the funerals of important men were held at the Forum.

In later centuries, the Forum's buildings were transformed from brick to marble, and great bronze statues were added. Later rulers built other public places, but none ever rivaled the importance of the great Roman Forum.

REVIEW & ASSESS

1. **READING CHECK** Why did the ancient Romans gather in the Forum?

2. **IDENTIFY MAIN IDEAS AND DETAILS** How did the Forum change over time?

3. **MAKE INFERENCES** How did the Roman Forum reflect the democratic values of the Roman Republic?

2.1 Men and Women

Growing up in Rome wasn't easy. There were no laws to protect children. Boys were expected to head their own families one day, but most girls never had any real control over their futures.

MAIN IDEA

Men and women had different roles in Roman society.

MEN IN ANCIENT ROME

If you were born a boy in Rome, you already had a head start in life. Rome was a **patriarchy** (PAY-tree-ahr-kee), or a society in which men have all the power. Only men could vote or hold public office, fight in wars, and perform important ceremonies. In Rome's patriarchy, men were in charge of everything—especially the family.

The family was at the core of Roman society. At the head of every family was the senior male, the *paterfamilias* (pa-tur-fuh-MIH-lee-uhs). He made all decisions. He could put family members on trial and punish them—even execute them. The Twelve Tables eventually limited the power of the paterfamilias, but he still had a lot of control over his family.

Boys from poorer families received little education and often could not read or write. Instead they went out to work beginning at an early age. Wealthier families sent their sons to school. Classes started at dawn, and teachers, who were often Greek slaves, taught reading, writing, and arithmetic. Public speaking was another important lesson. Long poems had to be memorized, and mistakes were often punished with a beating.

After the age of 14, boys destined for government jobs continued their education with private tutors at home. At the age of 17, boys were considered to be men and registered as Roman citizens in the Forum.

WOMEN IN ANCIENT ROME

Roman women had more rights than women in ancient Greece, but those still didn't amount to much by modern standards. Roman women were subject to the authority of men—their husbands, fathers, or brothers. They could not vote or hold public office, though they could eventually own property and manage their own businesses and finances. A wife could also manage her husband's business, and women with powerful husbands had some political influence.

In Rome, a woman's main role was to be a good wife and mother. For many, this meant doing the daily domestic chores of spinning yarn, making clothes, cooking, cleaning, and looking after the children. Sometimes women would have paying jobs as well. In wealthier families, the wife managed the household and its finances, but slaves did all the physical labor.

If they were lucky, some girls from wealthy families learned basic reading, writing, and arithmetic at home. However, they mostly learned household skills to prepare them for married life, which could begin when girls were as young as 12. Most marriages had little to do with love but were arranged to benefit the family. However, divorce was easy and acceptable, and ambitious politicians might remarry many times to gain support from increasingly important families.

Critical Viewing This fresco, a style of painting on fresh plaster, shows a Roman woman and man holding writing tools. Based on the details you can see in the fresco, what conclusions can you draw about these people?

Portrait of Terentius Neo and His Wife, artist unknown, A.D. 1st century

REVIEW & ASSESS

1. **READING CHECK** What was a woman's role in Roman society?

2. **DETERMINE WORD MEANINGS** How does knowing that *pater* is Latin for "father" help clarify what *patriarchy* and *paterfamilias* mean?

3. **COMPARE AND CONTRAST** How did roles differ for boys and girls in Rome?

2.2 Rich and Poor

If you were rich in Rome, life was good, but if you were poor, life was miserable. The huge gap between rich and poor was reinforced by a rigid class structure that kept all Romans firmly in their places.

MAIN IDEA

Roman society was divided among different classes of people.

CLASS DIVISIONS

At the top of society was the **aristocracy**, the small group of wealthy patricians who owned most of the land and dominated the government. The majority of citizens were plebeians. Some were well-off and owned farms or businesses, but many were very poor. At the bottom was Rome's huge population of slaves.

The wealthiest families lived in luxurious country estates. These were built around elegant courtyards and decorated with works of fine art. Slaves did the hard work, leaving the homeowners free to conduct business, take part in politics, or spend time on their hobbies.

Most poor Romans lived and worked on small farms. Often, the wealthy used their money to buy up land and create huge farms worked entirely by slaves. This practice forced many farmers off their farms and into the city to look for work. There they lived in overcrowded buildings and worked at manual labor for very low wages.

Romans' diets also differed greatly. The poor used cheap pottery bowls to eat porridge or bread with vegetables. Meat was a luxury. Only the largest houses had kitchens, so even wealthier plebeians relied on restaurants for hot food. There they could eat fish, cooked meat, and vegetables and perhaps a dessert of sweet pastries. The very rich enjoyed lavish banquets with dozens of courses, including exotic foods.

Around 287 B.C., the plebeians finally achieved political equality when their representative assembly, the **Council of Plebs**, was allowed to make laws for all citizens. However, the patricians continued to dominate society.

SLAVES IN THE REPUBLIC

Slaves were the largest class in Rome, but they had the fewest rights. They were considered property to be bought and sold. Some slaves were prisoners from Rome's conquests. However, most were bought from foreign traders.

Slaves were very useful in Rome's economy. Most worked at manual labor, from household chores to construction work or agriculture. Skilled slaves might be craftspeople, while educated slaves might be teachers, doctors, or managers of their master's business. The worst slave jobs were in the mines or factories, where the work was tough, the conditions were harsh, and the life expectancy was short.

Some slaves were treated well, but others suffered very badly. Excessive punishments could spark rebellion. A slave named Spartacus led the most famous rebellion in 73 B.C. For about two years, his slave army fought the Roman soldiers and controlled large areas of the countryside. When Spartacus was finally defeated, 6,000 of his followers were executed as a warning to other slaves.

A WEALTHY ROMAN FAMILY'S HOME

The diagram below shows four key areas in a house belonging to a wealthy family. While the house contained rooms for the family's private use, much of the space was designed for business and social gatherings.

1 ENTRANCE HALL
The front door opened up on a large entrance hall. Most mornings clients seeking favors waited here for the chance to pay their respects to their patron, or financial supporter.

3 OFFICE
This room was located behind the reception area and functioned as the patron's office. The room could also be used for family gatherings.

2 RECEPTION ROOM
In this large, airy space, the patron showed off his wealth and received visitors. The rectangular space beneath the opening in the roof served to collect rainwater.

4 COURTYARD
A roofed porch enclosed the courtyard garden. The space often included fountains, benches, and sculptures. In the richest homes, the porch's inner walls were often decorated with frescoes.

REVIEW & ASSESS

1. **READING CHECK** How did the lives of the Roman classes differ?

2. **INTEGRATE VISUALS** In what ways might plebeian or slave homes have differed from the home illustrated above?

3. **MAKE INFERENCES** How do you think the patricians reacted at first to the plebeians' political equality?

2.3 Gods and Beliefs

To Romans, the wrath of their gods was always present. They felt that honoring the gods—or at least not upsetting them—was a matter of life and death.

MAIN IDEA

Religious worship was an important part of Roman life.

Ten Gods of Ancient Rome

Jupiter King of the gods

Saturn God of agriculture

Mercury Messenger of the gods

Apollo God of poetry and music

Mars God of war

Neptune God of the sea and earthquakes

Ceres Goddess of the harvest

Juno Goddess of women; wife of Jupiter

Diana Goddess of the moon and the hunt

Venus Goddess of love and beauty

ROMAN WORSHIP

Roman religion was based on a **pantheon** (PAN-thee-ahn), or group of many gods, most adopted from the ancient Greeks. These gods had Roman names and were believed to have human traits and to control areas of Roman life. For example, Jupiter was the king of the gods. Juno was the goddess of women, marriage, childbirth, and children. Mars was the god of war, and Venus was the beautiful goddess of love.

The pantheon constantly grew to include the gods of people Rome conquered. Later, the Romans worshipped their rulers as gods after their death. Some rulers claimed to be living gods, but this claim made them very unpopular.

Romans worshipped their gods almost anywhere. Nearly every home had a shrine where the paterfamilias would make daily offerings to the gods that protected his family and his house. Priests managed temples for the most important gods. The priests conducted the rituals that Romans believed would secure the gods' favor.

The Roman calendar had many religious festivals that attracted huge audiences. The government funded many of them to ensure that the gods granted Rome good harvests or victories in war. These festivals included colorful processions, feasts, music, dance, theater, and sports.

THE ROMAN WAY

Roman gods had human traits that often highlighted the qualities most prized by the Romans. The Romans were a very practical and ambitious people, so they valued qualities that would help them achieve success. They considered the Greek virtues of beauty, grace, and elegance as nice but not essential. Instead, they preferred qualities like discipline, strength, and loyalty. Discipline and strength helped Romans endure hardship and overcome problems. Loyalty bound strong individuals together into even more powerful groups.

These valued qualities emphasize an important aspect of the Roman personality—*gravitas* (GRA-vuh-tahs). Having gravitas means being solemn and serious. Romans respected people who acted with great consideration, determination, and energy. These characteristics helped the people of the Roman Republic accomplish remarkable achievements in war, politics, law, commerce, and engineering. These qualities came to be known as "the Roman Way."

Critical Viewing A statue of Neptune, god of the sea, stands above the flowing water of Rome's Trevi Fountain. What details in the statue convey the qualities that the ancient Romans admired?

Trevi Fountain, Nicola Salvi and Giuseppe Pannini, 1762

REVIEW & ASSESS

1. **READING CHECK** Why was the worship of gods an important part of Roman life?

2. **SUMMARIZE** In what ways did the Romans expect the gods to affect daily life?

3. **DRAW CONCLUSIONS** What qualities did the Romans value? Why did they value these qualities more than others?

3.1 The Roman Army

War in the ancient world was extremely physical, and the Romans were good at it. The republic developed a formidable fighting force of well-trained professional soldiers called the legion. It was the ultimate weapon of ancient warfare.

MAIN IDEA

Organization and training brought Rome's army military success.

THE ROMAN LEGION

It was a privilege to serve in Rome's legions. At first only property-owning citizens could join, and they had to supply their own weapons. A legion contained around 4,200 men, and each consul led an army of two legions. When the battle season finished in October, everybody went home.

Yet as the republic fought longer wars farther from Rome, citizens who owned property became reluctant to serve. In 107 B.C., the consul Marius (MAIR-ee-uhs) found himself short of recruits, so he allowed poor, landless citizens to volunteer. The government supplied their equipment, which included a bronze helmet, mail armor, a short sword, a javelin, and an oval shield. These men became professional soldiers known as **legionaries**.

Marius also reorganized the legions for maximum strength and flexibility. He often grouped squads of men into 100-man centuries, or units. These units, in turn, were grouped into 600-man cohorts, or divisions. Ten cohorts made up a legion, now 6,000 strong. This command structure gave Roman generals control over large numbers of men, and it continues to be a model for modern military organization.

The legions became an efficient military machine that Rome used to conquer its enemies and expand its territory. Rome recruited additional soldiers from the regions it defeated, which led to more military might and manpower. If a Roman army was defeated, Rome would send an even bigger army the next time. This stubborn determination made Rome unstoppable.

Roman soldiers kept fit by running, marching, and practice fighting. They could march 20 miles a day wearing armor, swim or cross rivers in boats, and build bridges.

This photo shows a reenactment of a Roman army battle formation. As you can see, Roman legionaries usually fought in tight lines with their shields held before the attacking enemy. Why might this battle tactic, or strategy, have been effective?

< A Roman legionary stands guard in a reenactment of ancient warfare.

LIFE OF A LEGIONARY

Legionaries joined young and served for a maximum of 16 years. A recruit had to pass a physical inspection. Then in front of the legion's revered flag, the eagle, he swore an oath to serve the republic. This oath inspired a powerful sense of duty to comrades, to commanders, and to Rome itself.

Daily life revolved around a squad that trained, marched, and fought together. Soldiers built strong bonds of friendship and loyalty through sharing a tent, duties, and meals. When off duty, a legionary might play games or visit the public baths. However, duty always came first. While bravery led to rewards, failure led to severe punishment.

Training was key to the legions' success. Legionaries learned to carry out complicated instructions in the chaos of battle. At the end of each day, they built a fortified camp with deep ditches and high walls called palisades. Over time, they also built the straight roads and strong bridges that connected the republic and carried its men into battle.

REVIEW & ASSESS

1. **READING CHECK** How did the Roman army's organization and training lead to success?

2. **IDENTIFY MAIN IDEAS AND DETAILS** What were the duties of a legionary?

3. **SUMMARIZE** What changes did Marius make to the Roman army?

3.2 ROMAN ARMOR

"The infantry soldier carries so much equipment that he differs little from a mule," said an observer from the first century A.D. Along with his armor, shield, and weapons, which combined weighed some 50 pounds, a soldier had to carry food, tools, and personal belongings that could double the weight. Based on what you see here, what might have been some challenges that Roman soldiers encountered on and off the battlefield?

The ridge protected against vertical sword strikes.

Wide cheek flaps protected the face but eft ears exposed to hear orders.

Galea, or Helmet
The iron helmet followed a design used by warriors from Gaul.

Breastplate
Made of steel plates bound by leather straps, it weighed about 20 pounds and was lined with padding for comfort.

A wide projection shielded the neck and deflected blows from behind.

Javelin
The heavy javelin was thrown at close range and was designed to bend on impact.

Sword
Legionaries wore it on the right; officers wore it on the left.

Hooded Cloak
Wool kept soldiers warm.

Stake
Each soldier carried two to build a palisade.

Iron Pick
Picks were used in camp construction.

Canteen
Canteens held *posca*, a mixture of vinegar and water.

The shield's iron boss and rim were used as weapons to punch the enemy.

Sheath
Made of wood, it was covered in decorative leather.

Tunic
Soldiers wore red wool tunics under armor.

Shield
The leather-covered wooden shield weighed over 20 pounds. A legion's unique emblem was painted on the front.

Rucksack
The carryall contained tools and rations.

Around two feet long, the javelin's iron spear had a pyramidal, or arrow-shaped, tip.

Made of ash, the javelin's shaft measured between four and five feet.

Scabbard
Made of iron and often engraved, the scabbard had rings to attach it to the belt.

Sandals
Sandals were made from a single piece of leather. They had thick soles and were studded with iron tacks.

Ladle
Soldiers carried cooking and eating utensils.

Dagger
The short dagger had a stone handle and was worn on the hip.

3.3 Hannibal
and the Punic Wars

To win in the big leagues, you've got to take on the champion. In 264 B.C., Rome turned its might against the Mediterranean superpower of Carthage. The two enemies fought a series of wars, called the **Punic** (PYOO-nihk) **Wars**, that lasted, off and on, for about 100 years.

MAIN IDEA

Rome and Carthage fought the Punic Wars for control of the Mediterranean Sea.

War Elephants

Hannibal's war elephants were the "battle tanks" of the ancient world. Their size and power made them a terrifying and innovative battle weapon. Normally gentle creatures, however, the elephants had to be provoked and prodded to attack.

THE FIRST PUNIC WAR

The North African city of **Carthage** was immensely rich. It had grown from a Phoenician colony (*Punic* is Latin for "Phoenician") into a trading empire. Carthage had established colonies and trading ports around the western Mediterranean, and the city controlled valuable mineral resources in North Africa and present-day Spain. In time, Rome began to compete with Carthage for control of the sea.

The First Punic War broke out in 264 B.C. over the strategic island of Sicily (see the map in Section 3.5). The war was fought mainly at sea, but Carthage's navy was vastly superior to

Rome's. After suffering a key defeat, Rome quickly built a fleet of 120 powerful warships that beat the Carthaginian navy in almost every battle. These victories allowed Rome to occupy the important islands of Sicily, Sardinia, and Corsica. In 241 B.C., Carthage surrendered to Rome. Its defeated general was Hamilcar Barca, the father of a young boy named **Hannibal**.

THE SECOND PUNIC WAR

When Hannibal was a child, he promised his father that he would always hate Rome. When he became a Carthaginian general, he made good on that promise. After Hannibal attacked one of Rome's allies in southern Spain, the Second Punic War began in 218 B.C. While the Romans planned a counterattack,

The Battle of Zama, Giulio Romano, 1570–80

In the early battles, many of the Roman soldiers, who had never seen an elephant before, fled in terror.

Hannibal outsmarted them. He led about 60,000 soldiers and a herd of war elephants out of Spain and across the Alps to invade the Italian Peninsula by land. This astonishing action caught the Romans by surprise. Hannibal swiftly defeated the Roman army in battle after battle as he swept south toward Rome itself.

By 216 B.C., Hannibal was in southeast Italy, facing a huge Roman army at Cannae (KA-nee). Although outnumbered, Hannibal defeated the legions. His brilliant tactics are still studied at military academies today.

Rome fought on, however, and steadily wore down Hannibal's army. In 205 B.C., the Roman general Scipio (SIHP-ee-oh) was elected consul. He invaded North Africa in a plan devised to draw Hannibal out of Italy. It worked. Hannibal left Italy to defend his homeland. At the Battle of Zama (ZAY-muh) in 202 B.C., Hannibal and Scipio faced each other in a desperate fight. They were both brilliant generals, but after a long, bloody battle, Hannibal was defeated and later fled abroad to Asia Minor in present-day Turkey. In 201 B.C., the Second Punic War ended, and Rome once again ruled the western Mediterranean.

REVIEW & ASSESS

1. **READING CHECK** What events led Rome to fight two wars with Carthage?

2. **COMPARE AND CONTRAST** How were the two Punic Wars alike and how were they different?

3. **DRAW CONCLUSIONS** Why was Hannibal's trek through the Alps such an astonishing accomplishment?

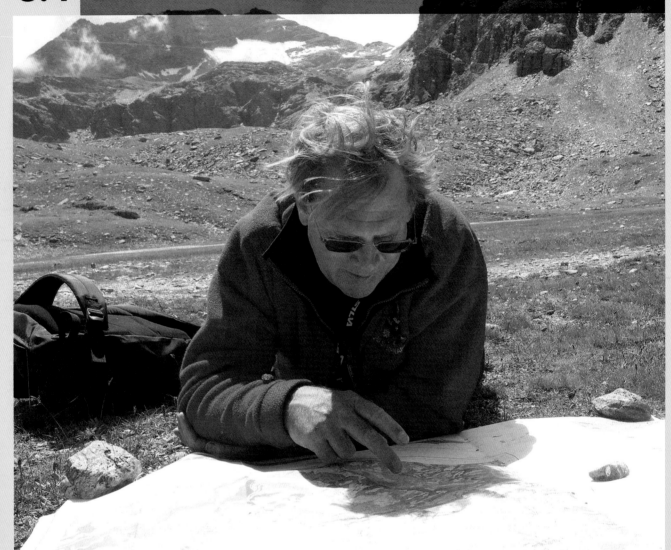

Searching for
Hannibal's Route

Patrick Hunt is a man on a mission to solve one of history's mysteries: Where did Hannibal cross the Alps? One of the most daring military maneuvers of all time, Hannibal's invasion of Italy in 218 B.C. required marching about 40,000 men and 37 elephants across these rugged mountains in winter. Hannibal didn't leave a map behind though. "For the last decade plus, we've been trying to pinpoint Hannibal's route," says Hunt. Because of his research, now he's close to an answer.

^ Patrick Hunt theorizes that Hannibal used the Col du Clapier-Savine Coche mountain pass, shown above, to cross the Alps into Italy.

Geo-archaeologist Patrick Hunt is rediscovering the route of Hannibal's army.

HANNIBAL'S FOOTSTEPS

Patrick Hunt is a National Geographic grantee and the director of the Hannibal Expedition. Since 1994, he has used everything from ancient literature to satellite imaging to find the mountain pass Hannibal traveled. "It's like looking for a needle in a haystack," Hunt says, "but it's not just for the sake of mystery." The Alps were considered impassable in winter. Historians know Hannibal crossed them, but they don't know how because they don't know where. If someone were to find the route, historians might begin to understand how Hannibal achieved this amazing military feat.

The Roman historians Polybius (puh-LIH-bee-uhs) and Livy (LIH-vee) wrote accounts of Hannibal's campaign. Although they use few place-names, they describe the geographic features Hannibal saw and the distances he traveled each day. Hunt uses these clues to work out probable routes. "It's a bit like sleuthing," he admits. "We've been over close to 30 Alpine passes, mostly on foot, constantly comparing how they fit the descriptions."

A SCIENTIFIC APPROACH

Geo-archaeology applies earth sciences such as geography and geology to archaeology. These sciences are vital to Hunt's search because he has to factor in 2,000 years of change. Mountains may look different because of erosion; climate changes may have moved the snow line. "The first thing we do on-site is to examine the basic rock types to check how stable the geology is," he says. "The more stable it is, the less likely it is to have changed much." It's a scientific approach and a physically challenging one, too. Several team members have suffered broken bones because of the treacherous working conditions.

HANNIBAL'S ROUTE

Through a process of elimination, Hunt is now confident he knows most of Hannibal's route. The view from the summit of the Col du Clapier-Savine Coche fits perfectly with the descriptions in the ancient texts. "Now we're looking for physical evidence, and we are focused on the campsites," he explains. "Ash has a chemical signature that lasts over 2,000 years. We think we've found the ash of Hannibal's camps and have pinpointed a major summit campground. Now we're looking at stone deposits that may mark graves. An elephant burial would be fantastic!"

"Hannibal is very close to my heart," asserts Hunt. "He lost close to 40 percent of his men crossing the Alps. That would be unacceptable today, but Hannibal went on to defeat the Romans multiple times. This is a man who wins battle after battle but ultimately doesn't win the war."

REVIEW & ASSESS

1. **READING CHECK** What tools is Patrick Hunt using to determine Hannibal's route through the Alps?

2. **INTERPRET MAPS** In what ways did the Alps both protect Rome and help Hannibal attempt a sneak attack?

3. **MAKE INFERENCES** What knowledge of geography and maps might Hannibal have had in order to believe his campaign over the Alps could be successful?

3.5 | Rome Expands

The geographic location of Rome made it the perfect place to begin building a Mediterranean empire. By 146 B.C., Rome had proved this point at the expense of its conquered neighbors. Its navy ruled the seas, its army dominated the land, and many once-great countries were now run by a Roman governor.

MAIN IDEA

Between 264 and 146 B.C., Rome's armies conquered a vast amount of land stretching from the Iberian Peninsula to Greece.

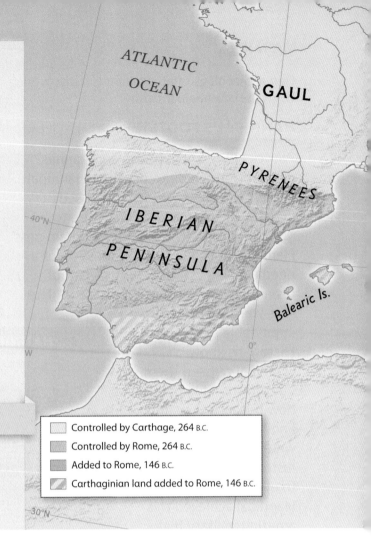

Controlled by Carthage, 264 B.C.
Controlled by Rome, 264 B.C.
Added to Rome, 146 B.C.
Carthaginian land added to Rome, 146 B.C.

The Catapult

The catapult was one of the Roman army's most effective weapons. It was capable of launching 60-pound rocks, long wooden beams, and even vats of fire. This powerful war machine relied on a system of tension and release to hurl missiles 500 to 1,000 feet across battlefields.

THE THIRD PUNIC WAR

After the Second Punic War, Carthage focused on trade and began to grow very rich. This worried the Romans, who were still suspicious of their old enemy. The famous Roman statesman Cato the Elder visited Carthage and was alarmed by its wealth, which he believed would be used to fight Rome. Cato shared his fears with the Senate in a unique way. Whenever he spoke, whatever the subject, he always ended with the dramatic exclamation *"Carthago delenda est"* ("Carthage must be destroyed").

Roman leaders eventually ordered the city of Carthage to be abandoned. Bullied into a corner, Carthage declared war. After decades of conflict, Rome decided that only the total destruction of its old enemy would do.

In 149 B.C., Rome laid siege to Carthage, surrounding it and stopping its food supply. Roman soldiers battered the city with huge rocks hurled from catapults and then stormed its shattered walls. The starving defenders fought bravely, but the Romans' victory was inevitable—and their revenge was merciless. The Romans sold Carthaginian survivors as slaves and destroyed every building. Carthage ceased to exist. Carthage and its adjoining lands were renamed the Roman **province** of Africa. The Iberian Peninsula, which Carthage had controlled, eventually became the Roman province of Hispania.

THE MACEDONIAN WARS

While Hannibal was rampaging through Italy in the Second Punic War, Philip V of Macedonia launched the First Macedonian War against Rome. Because Rome's army was focused on Hannibal, Rome could not fight against Macedonia and was forced to make peace. However, after Hannibal's defeat, two legions of battle-hardened Roman warriors invaded Macedonia, starting the Second Macedonian War.

The legions were pitched against the Macedonian phalanx, a solid body of troops bristling with long spears. The phalanx was strong, but it lacked the flexibility of the legion—and this flaw proved decisive. Once past the spears, fresh Roman reserves would fight ferociously until they destroyed the enemy army. These tactics defeated Philip's army in 197 B.C., ending the war. Macedonia later became a Roman province. Rome also destroyed the city of Corinth and conquered Greece, turning it into a Roman province in 146 B.C.

Roman power now extended from the Iberian Peninsula to the islands of Greece. Control of this vast area made Rome the new superpower of the ancient world and gave it control over vast economic resources.

REVIEW & ASSESS

1. **READING CHECK** In what order did the events of the Punic and Macedonian wars occur?

2. **INTERPRET MAPS** How did the defeat of Philip of Macedonia help Rome dominate the Mediterranean?

3. **ANALYZE LANGUAGE USE** How does Cato's exclamation about Carthage convey the Romans' fear of their enemy?

The Republic in Crisis

Politics in Rome had often been crooked, selfish, and occasionally even violent. But after 133 B.C., the corruption and greed spiraled out of control and threatened the survival of the republic.

MAIN IDEA

The Roman Republic collapsed into civil war following a series of major events.

ATTEMPTS AT REFORM

Expansion following the Punic Wars brought great wealth to the Roman Republic, but this wealth was not evenly distributed among the people. Roman generals returned with great riches from the conquered territories. They used their new wealth to buy large areas of farmland, which drove many small farmers out of business. Unemployment and poverty became common in the republic, but the rich ignored the problems of the poor.

In 133 B.C., the tribune Tiberius Gracchus (ty-BIHR-ee-uhs GRA-kuhs) proposed a bill to take land from the rich and give it to the poor for farming. He knew the senators would reject his bill, so he had it approved by the plebeian assembly instead.

The Senate was furious at being bypassed. In response, members of the Senate arranged to assassinate, or murder, Tiberius. Ten years later his brother, Gaius (GAY-uhs) Gracchus, tried to introduce **reforms**, or changes to make things better, in the Senate. He, too, was assassinated.

In 107 B.C., the people elected the army general Marius as consul. As you have learned, he allowed landless citizens to join the army. When these soldiers retired, they relied on the generosity of their generals to support them, which made them more loyal to their commanders than to the state.

BATTLES FOR CONTROL

Marius's reforms did not help him when a general named Sulla rose up against him. Sulla was a brilliant general with political ambitions of his own. He marched his army into Rome, starting a **civil war**, or war between groups in the same country, and took control of the Senate. Marius fled, and Sulla set himself up as dictator of Rome. He created a list of his enemies and had many of them killed.

When Sulla left Rome to fight in the east, Marius led his army into Rome and attacked Sulla's supporters. Sulla invaded Rome a second time and regained control. By 81 B.C., he was declared dictator once again.

In the following decades, crises arose that forced the Senate to give extraordinary powers to two generals named Pompey (PAHM-pee) and Crassus. You have read about the slave rebellion that spread throughout the republic in 73 B.C. Pompey and Crassus combined their two large armies to put down the rebellion.

By 63 B.C., the republic was in chaos, and the consul Cicero argued strongly for reducing the powers of the army and restoring the government's system of checks and balances. However, his words failed to persuade Rome's leaders.

FACTORS THAT WEAKENED THE REPUBLIC

- Greed of the rich
- Inequality between rich and poor
- Failed reforms
- Ambitious generals and powerful armies
- Soldiers' shifting loyalty to their generals
- Civil war

Critical Viewing Sulla, shown here on horseback, never lost a battle. What qualities of a successful general are conveyed in this painting?

Sulla at Orchomenos, R. Weibezahl, 1832

REVIEW & ASSESS

1. **READING CHECK** What happened when Marius and Sulla fought over Rome?

2. **IDENTIFY MAIN IDEAS AND DETAILS** What problems led to civil war in Rome?

3. **FORM OPINIONS** Could Roman leaders have helped the republic survive? Why or why not?

4.2

GAIUS JULIUS
CAESAR 100 B.C. – 44 B.C.

Julius Caesar is by far the most famous Roman. He overcame obstacles to success with his military brilliance, political cunning, and amazing speeches. When his power-sharing triumvirate collapsed, he led his army into Rome and was voted dictator for life by the frightened Senate. Caesar's rule marked the end of the republic.

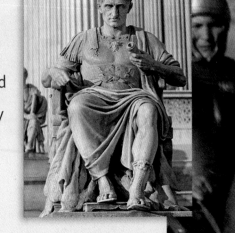

💼 **Job:** Dictator for life
📝 **Education:** Taught by Greek tutors
🌐 **Home:** Rome

FINEST HOUR

His conquest of Gaul was his most impressive military achievement.

WORST MOMENT

His enemies finally won when dozens of them joined in stabbing him to death.

FRIENDS

‹ Cleopatra VII, Queen of Egypt
- Commoners of Rome
- Veteran soldiers

TRIVIA

His most noted connection was with Egypt's last queen, Cleopatra VII. Both a love affair and a political alliance, their relationship was short lived. It began in 48 B.C. and ended with Caesar's assassination in 44 B.C.

THE FIRST TRIUMVIRATE

Generals Crassus and Pompey were elected consuls in 70 B.C. However, they soon made themselves unpopular with the Senate by seizing much of its power for themselves. As a result, the Senate turned to a rising political star, **Julius Caesar**.

Caesar had already proved himself as a politician and general. Pompey and Crassus used their influence to have him elected consul. In return, Caesar persuaded the Senate to pass Pompey and Crassus' legislation. This political alliance became known as the **First Triumvirate** (try-UHM-vuh-ruht)—a sharing of power between three people. The triumvirate lasted for about seven years but was always an uneasy alliance full of suspicions and jealousies.

The triumvirate granted Caesar a huge army, which he used to conquer Gaul (present-day France). This conquest extended Roman territory north and made Caesar very popular with the people. He also

Many movies and television series have focused on the life of Julius Caesar. Here, actor Ciarán Hinds portrays Caesar in the 2005 television series *Rome*.

won immense wealth and the fierce loyalty of his soldiers.

END OF THE REPUBLIC

In 53 B.C., Crassus died, and the triumvirate collapsed. Law and order in Rome broke down. To end the chaos, the Senate appointed Pompey sole consul. This, however, resulted in a power struggle between Caesar in Gaul and Pompey in Rome. To regain control, Caesar led his army into Rome, sparking a bloody civil war. In August 48 B.C., Caesar defeated Pompey and declared victory.

Many Romans expected Caesar to restore the republic, but he had other ideas. Backed by his army, he ruled alone. Caesar declared himself dictator for life and introduced reforms that were popular with the people, such as creating jobs for the poor. But the Senate hated his reforms. On March 15, 44 B.C., a group of senators assassinated Caesar.

Another civil war followed Caesar's death. Fourteen years later, the Roman Republic transformed into a monarchy and, ultimately, an empire.

Et tu, and tu, and tu, and tu, and tu?

Julius Caesar was assassinated by about 60 senators under a statue of his old enemy Pompey. According to legend, as Caesar died, he cried out to a man who he had thought was his friend, *"Et tu, Brute?"* ("And you, Brutus?")

REVIEW & ASSESS

1. **READING CHECK** What were Caesar's major successes and failures?

2. **SUMMARIZE** Why was Caesar assassinated, and what happened after he was killed?

3. **COMPARE AND CONTRAST** How does Caesar's career as a general compare with his role as a leader?

The Assassination of Julius Caesar

Caesar's assassination commanded much attention right after his death—and for many centuries after that. The ancient Romans commemorated, or remembered, the date with special coins. Historians who lived in later years tried to describe Caesar's death, and playwrights dramatized the event. We may never know all the details of his death, but the story and fate of a leader who became too hungry for power still fascinates us.

Critical Viewing The woman fainting in the painting is a soothsayer, or a fortune-teller, warning Caesar not to go to the Senate. What elements of this painting forewarn of a terrible event?

Julius Caesar on His Way to the Senate on the Ides of March, Abel de Pujol, c. 1850

Silver Denarius of Marcus Junius Brutus, Macedonia, 43–42 B.C.

This commemorative coin, called a denarius, shows the profile of Marcus Brutus, Caesar's former friend and assassin. The reverse features two daggers and a "cap of liberty." Underneath are the words EID MAR, or Ides of March. In the Roman calendar, the ides referred to the day that fell in the middle of the month.

CONSTRUCTED RESPONSE What did Roman leaders want people to remember about Caesar when they saw the commemorative coin?

DOCUMENT TWO

Secondary Source: Biography

from *The Lives of the Twelve Caesars*, by Gaius Suetonius Tranquillus, translated by J.C. Rolfe
In Volume 1 of his biography, written in the second century A.D., Suetonius describes Caesar's assassination by a group of senators who called themselves "the liberators."

CONSTRUCTED RESPONSE What does the violence of Caesar's death tell about the liberators' view of Caesar?

> When he saw that he was beset [surrounded] on every side by drawn daggers, he muffled his head in his robe . . . with the lower part of his body also covered . . . [H]e was stabbed with three and twenty wounds, uttering not a word . . . All the conspirators made off, and he lay there lifeless.

DOCUMENT THREE

Secondary Source: Drama

from William Shakespeare's *Julius Caesar*
In this excerpt from Act 3, Scene 2 of Shakespeare's play *Julius Caesar*, written in 1599, Mark Antony, a Roman politician and general, speaks at Caesar's funeral.

CONSTRUCTED RESPONSE According to Mark Antony, why was Caesar assassinated?

> Friends, Romans, countrymen, lend me your ears;
> I come to bury Caesar, not to praise him.
> The evil that men do lives after them;
> The good is oft interred [buried] with their bones;
> So let it be with Caesar. The noble Brutus
> Hath told you Caesar was ambitious:
> If it were so, it was a grievous [serious] fault,
> And grievously hath Caesar answer'd it.

SYNTHESIZE & WRITE

1. **REVIEW** Review what you have learned about the Roman Republic, Julius Caesar, and Caesar's assassination.

2. **RECALL** On your own paper, write down the main idea expressed in each document and in the photograph of the coin.

3. **CONSTRUCT** Construct a topic sentence that answers this question: What do the Roman leaders' actions and words tell about their view of Caesar?

4. **WRITE** Using evidence from the documents, write a paragraph that supports your answer to the question in Step 3.

The Assassination of Julius Caesar, Vincenzo Camuccini, 1798

MARCH 15, 44 B.C.

Julius Caesar met a violent end on this date, known as the Ides of March. After Caesar's assassination, the Ides of March came to represent an unlucky or ill-fated day, which is why today we hear, "Beware the Ides of March!" every March 15. In this dramatic painting, Caesar reaches out for help. He appears unable to believe that his own countrymen, most of whom he had handpicked to be senators, would assassinate him. What other details in the painting does the artist include to illustrate the intensity of the moment?

VOCABULARY

For each pair of vocabulary words, write one sentence that explains the connection between the two words.

1. **patrician; plebeian**
    At first wealthy patricians held much of the power, but over time the plebeians, who made up most of Rome's citizens, could also hold office.

2. **consul; veto**

3. **republic; tribune**

4. **aristocracy; patrician**

5. **plebeian; tribune**

6. **consul; dictator**

7. **legionary; province**

8. **civil war; reform**

READING STRATEGY

9. **ORGANIZE IDEAS: COMPARE AND CONTRAST** If you haven't already, complete your Venn diagram to compare and contrast the lives of rich people and poor people in the Roman Republic. Then answer the question.

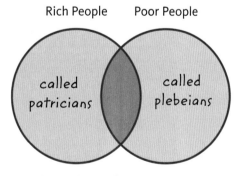

Rich People   Poor People

called patricians   *called plebeians*

How did the lives of the rich and poor differ in the Roman Republic? Did they share any similarities?

MAIN IDEAS

Answer the following questions. Support your answers with evidence from the chapter.

10. What geographic advantages helped Rome grow into a city? **LESSON 1.1**

11. How did different cultures help transform Rome from a small village into a city? **LESSON 1.2**

12. What was the purpose of the Twelve Tables? **LESSON 1.3**

13. What was the role of men in Rome's patriarchal society? **LESSON 2.1**

14. Why were slaves important to the Roman economy? **LESSON 2.2**

15. What factors made the Roman army successful? **LESSON 3.1**

16. What did Rome gain from its battles with Carthage during the Punic Wars? **LESSON 3.3**

17. What was the First Triumvirate? **LESSON 4.2**

CRITICAL THINKING

Answer the following questions. Support your answers with evidence from the chapter.

18. **MAKE INFERENCES** Based on what you've learned about ancient Rome, what factors helped the republic develop into a mighty power?

19. **DRAW CONCLUSIONS** Why did the Romans replace the position of king with two consuls and give each the right to veto?

20. **COMPARE AND CONTRAST** How did the lives of the rich and poor differ in the Roman Republic?

21. **IDENTIFY MAIN IDEAS AND DETAILS** What details in the chapter support the idea that the Roman Senate had a great deal of power?

22. **YOU DECIDE** Was Julius Caesar a great leader? Was he a dictator who abused his power? Did he fall somewhere in between? Support your opinion with evidence from the chapter.

Study the chart comparing the governments of the Roman Republic and the United States. Then answer the questions that follow.

GOVERNMENT	ROMAN REPUBLIC	UNITED STATES
Executive Branch	Led by two consuls elected for a one-year term; led government and army	Led by a president elected for a four-year term; heads government and military
Legislative Branch	• Senate of 300 members • Senate advised consuls and set policies • Two assemblies made laws and selected officials	• Senate of 100 members • House of Representatives of 435 members • Laws approved by both groups
Judicial Branch	• Eight judges oversaw courts and governed provinces	• Supreme Court of nine justices • Supreme Court interprets the Constitution and federal law
Legal Code	• Twelve Tables basis of Roman law • Twelve Tables established laws protecting citizens' rights	• U.S. Constitution basis of U.S. law • Constitution established individual rights of citizens and powers of government

23. In what ways are the branches of each government similar?

24. What do the legal codes of each government protect?

Read the following translation from one of the Twelve Tables. Then answer the question.

TABLE VII: Rights Concerning Land

The width of a road extends to 8 feet where it runs straight ahead, 16 round a bend . . .

Persons shall mend roadways. If they do not keep them laid with stone, a person may drive his beasts where he wishes . . .

Should a tree on a neighbor's farm be bent crooked by a wind and lean over your farm, action may be taken for removal of that tree.

It is permitted to gather up fruit falling down on another man's farm.

25. Why do you think the Romans included so much detail in the laws of the Twelve Tables?

26. ARGUMENT What arguments might a senator favoring Julius Caesar's assassination make? What arguments might a senator opposing his assassination make? Create an outline that lists points supporting each side.

TIPS

• Take notes from the chapter about Caesar's actions as a ruler and the manner of his death.

• Consider who benefited from Caesar's reforms and who benefited from his death.

• Consider how the Romans might have felt when Caesar declared himself dictator for life.

• Use vocabulary from the chapter in your outline.

• List the points that support assassination in the first part of your outline. List the points that support opposition to the assassination in the second part.

11

THE ROMAN EMPIRE AND CHRISTIANITY

44 B.C. – A.D. 476

SECTION 1 LIFE DURING THE EMPIRE

SS.6.E.1.1; SS.6.E.3.1; SS.6.E.3.2; SS.6.E.3.3; SS.6.G.1.4; SS.6.G.5.1; SS.6.G.5.2;
SS.6.G.5.3; SS.6.W.3.8; SS.6.W.3.11; SS.6.W.3.12; SS.6.W.3.14; LAFS.68.RH.1.2;
LAFS.68.RH.2.5; LAFS.68.RH.3.7

KEY VOCABULARY		NAMES & PLACES
aqueduct	gladiator	Augustus
arch	mosaic	Colosseum
emperor		Pax Romana
fresco		Pompeii

SECTION 2 CHRISTIANITY

SS.6.G.1.4; SS.6.G.1.5; SS.6.G.4.4; SS.6.W.1.3; SS.6.W.3.13; SS.6.W.3.18; LAFS.68.RH.1.1;
LAFS.68.RH.2.5; LAFS.68.RH.3.7; LAFS.68.WHST.1.2; LAFS.68.WHST.3.9

KEY VOCABULARY		NAMES & PLACES	
catacomb	parable	Christianity	Paul
epistle	pope	Constantine	Roman
missionary		Gospels	Catholic
		Jesus	Church
		New	Twelve
		Testament	Apostles

SECTION 3 DECLINE AND FALL OF THE EMPIRE

SS.6.G.1.4; SS.6.G.1.7; SS.6.W.3.8; SS.6.W.3.15; LAFS.68.RH.2.5; LAFS.68.RH.3.7

KEY VOCABULARY	NAMES & PLACES
barbarian	Attila
tetrarchy	Diocletian

SECTION 4 THE LEGACY OF ROME

SS.6.C.1.2; SS.6.C.2.1; SS.6.W.3.8; SS.6.W.3.10; SS.6.W.3.14; SS.6.W.3.17; LAFS.68.RH.2.5

KEY VOCABULARY	NAMES & PLACES
bas-relief	Latin
oratory	Virgil

READING STRATEGY

ORGANIZE IDEAS: SEQUENCE EVENTS

When you sequence events, you place them in the order in which they occurred. As you read the chapter, use a time line like this one to keep track of key people and events in the Roman Empire.

People and Events of the Roman Empire

The Colosseum is made of stone and concrete. Early Roman theaters were built into hillsides for extra support, but the Colosseum is a freestanding structure.

Spectators entered and exited through 76 gates that sat just inside the 80 arches surrounding the ground floor.

The Roman Colosseum was opened in A.D. 80 and is still standing today.

Augustus
and the Pax Romana

When Julius Caesar was assassinated, Romans rolled their eyes and thought, "Here we go again." After decades of dictatorships and civil wars, they hoped for stability in the empire. They got it, but the republic was dead. A new type of leader was about to rule Rome for the next 500 years.

MAIN IDEA

Augustus transformed Rome from a violent republic into a peaceful empire.

A NEW EMPIRE

After Caesar's death, his heir, Octavian, found himself at the center of a deadly power struggle. At 18 years old, he had to kill or be killed. He survived and thrived. Octavian defeated his rivals, killed Caesar's assassins, and crushed revolts. He emerged victorious, immensely rich, and all-powerful. In 31 B.C., he became Rome's sole ruler. Four years later, the Senate gave him the name **Augustus**, or "exalted one."

Augustus was smarter than Caesar had been. He used his wealth and political skill to take control of the army and secure the people's support. He also won over the Senate, which awarded him dictator-like powers. He did all this while working within the law and appearing to uphold republican ideals. The Senate, among other institutions, continued, but Augustus controlled its decisions. He was the supreme ruler in Rome, or its **emperor**. His powers were granted for life and could be passed to a successor, which was something that made the Romans uneasy. They didn't want to return to the harsh rule of kings. However, the people accepted Augustus because he moved slowly, carefully, and legally. Above all, he finally brought peace to Rome.

PEACE UNDER AUGUSTUS

Augustus' reign began the **Pax Romana**, or "Roman Peace"—200 years of peace and prosperity enjoyed across the empire. The Pax Romana was possible because Augustus tackled some long-standing problems. The poor thanked Augustus for guaranteeing free handouts of grain. Most of the people might not have noticed that Augustus' newly paid officials were improving government. However, everyone took immense pride in his transformation of Rome into an impressive capital with magnificent marble monuments. Meanwhile, Augustus' new laws were restoring order, and he actively encouraged art, literature, and education.

Augustus also cleverly prevented any threat that might have been posed by the army. He cut its size in half but kept out-of-work veterans happy with grants of land. Soldiers still serving were kept constantly busy defending and expanding the empire's frontiers. The army also now had standardized pay and conditions and a new oath of loyalty to the emperor himself.

The elite Praetorian (pree-TAWR-ee-uhn) Guard were the only soldiers stationed in Rome, and they were committed to upholding the emperor's authority. In addition, to protect the empire's coasts and shipping trade, Augustus created Rome's first permanent navy. All of these changes helped ensure long-term stability for the empire and for many Roman emperors to come.

GAIUS OCTAVIAN
AUGUSTUS

💼 **Job:** First emperor of Rome

FINEST HOUR

Augustus was able to peacefully pass on all his imperial powers. He left a secure, stable, and prosperous empire to his adopted son Tiberius.

WORST MOMENT

A major military embarrassment occurred in A.D. 9 when Germanic barbarians destroyed three Roman legions.

TRIVIA

Although often ill, Augustus lived to be 77. Shortly before he died, the month of August was named after him.

Augustus of Pirmaporta, c. 20–17 B.C.

REVIEW & ASSESS

1. **READING CHECK** What is the Pax Romana?

2. **IDENTIFY MAIN IDEAS AND DETAILS** What are three things Augustus did to secure people's support?

3. **MAKE INFERENCES** Why do you think Augustus was careful to reward soldiers and reduce the size of the army?

307

1.2 Growth and Trade

During the Pax Romana, you could travel easily and safely across the entire Roman Empire. By A.D. 117, that meant you could cross most of the known western world. It was a merchant's dream, and the economy boomed as Romans enjoyed goods imported from almost everywhere.

MAIN IDEA

As the Roman Empire expanded, trade became easier and the economy boomed.

IMPERIAL EXPANSION

Under Augustus, the Roman army became the mightiest in the world. Its relentless march expanded the empire's frontiers and cultural influence farther than ever before. Soldiers in forts on three continents—Europe, Asia, and Africa—protected the empire's frontiers from attacks by numerous enemies. The soldiers could be soaking in the rains of northern Britain, sweltering in the deserts of southern Egypt, battered by Atlantic winds in western Spain, or swimming in the waters of the Red Sea.

Some of the frontier military camps became permanent settlements. Soldiers stationed at these settlements often stayed in the community when they retired. This practice helped expand Roman culture and influence in the region.

The Roman Empire did not always rely on military conquest to expand its borders. If an area looked like it would be difficult or costly to conquer outright, Augustus would support a local ruler. In return, the territory would be required to provide the empire with military aid if needed. In this way, Augustus was able to expand the empire while saving the expense of an all-out war. This arrangement also made it easier for Augustus to invade the territory in the future if he felt that it was necessary.

A network of roads, bridges, and tunnels built by soldiers connected these far-flung frontiers. It allowed the army to march swiftly across great distances and quickly crush trouble wherever it arose. The roads helped the army keep order, but they also benefited everyone in the empire. The official mail service used the roads to keep information flowing across the empire. Rest areas and inns for overnight stays were built at regular intervals. Everyone in the empire could travel farther, faster, more easily, and more safely than ever before.

A BOOMING ECONOMY

These excellent roads also stimulated the economy by making it easy to transport and sell goods throughout the empire—basic goods as well as luxuries. Even citizens with limited incomes could afford African olive oil and Spanish salted fish. This flow of goods around the empire created a thriving economy as well as a sense of community. Roman merchants gained great benefits from all of this trade.

Rome's craftspeople produced beautiful objects that archaeologists have found as far away as Vietnam, but what flowed out of the empire most was money. The city of Rome itself was the main consumer of imports, or goods brought from other places. Rome especially needed food to feed its huge population. Agriculture, though still Rome's largest industry, was focused on luxuries such as fruit.

EUROPE

BRITAIN

ATLANTIC
OCEAN

GAUL

SPAIN

Black Sea

Rome

Mediterranean Sea

To China

AFRICA

EGYPT

Red Sea

Tropic of Cancer

To India

Roman Empire at its height, c. A.D. 117
Trade routes
Slave trade
Goods traded

Gems		Spices	
Grain		Textiles	
Marble		Timber	
Metals		Wild animals	
Olive oil		Wine	

0   300   600 Miles
0   300   600 Kilometers

The most important Roman goods in terms of the quantity traded were wine, olive oil, and grain. Traders moved these bulky goods by ship before transferring them to slower ox-drawn carts. Adventurous traders looked far beyond the empire's borders. These merchants would sail east to India or travel the Silk Roads to China. There they sought to trade wool, gold, and silver for luxuries such as silks, spices, and gems.

The introduction of a standard currency, or money, throughout the empire made it easier to conduct trade as well as collect taxes and pay soldiers. The empire made coins called *denarii* (dih-NAIR-ee) out of silver and *sesterces* (SEHS-tuhrs) out of brass. Roman coins were accepted not only in the empire but also beyond. The expanded empire and the Pax Romana were certainly good for business.

REVIEW & ASSESS

1. **READING CHECK** What factors encouraged trade in the Roman Empire?

2. **INTERPRET MAPS** From which locations in the empire did Rome import grain to feed its citizens?

3. **ANALYZE CAUSE AND EFFECT** What were two positive effects of the flow of goods throughout the empire?

Roman Engineering

Step outside your door and you'll see a road. Follow the road and you'll reach a city. In the city, you'll find large concrete buildings. Two thousand years ago, Roman engineers were perfecting the techniques that enabled the building of these "modern" constructions.

MAIN IDEA

The Romans were skilled engineers who helped transform how things were built.

ROMAN INVENTIONS

Arch
A curved structure over an opening

Vault
An extended series of arches

Dome
A rotated series of arches

ROADS

Before the Romans began building their network of roads, travel generally meant following dirt tracks. Rome's first great road was the Appian Way built in 312 B.C. It connected Rome with southern Italy. As the empire expanded, its armies built new roads back to the capital—which is where the saying "All roads lead to Rome" comes from.

The army used specialized tools and lots of human power to build roads. Soldiers marked the route, dug foundations, and built up the road with several layers of material. The center of the road was slightly higher than the edges, which helped rain run into drainage ditches.

Where possible, the soldiers built the road wide and straight, making marches shorter and easier. Engineers developed special techniques to overcome obstacles. Roads sometimes included bridges over rivers or tunnels through hills. Every mile a milestone marked the distance to major cities. By A.D. 300, the Romans had built about 53,000 miles of roads.

ARCHES AND AQUEDUCTS

Concrete is not usually very interesting, but at the time of Augustus it transformed construction. The Romans developed a new, stronger type of concrete and used it to build huge freestanding structures, like the Pantheon in Rome. This building, shown on the next page, was built in 27 B.C. as a temple to all the gods of ancient Rome.

Roman architecture was modeled on Greek architecture, but the use of arches, vaults, and domes created a distinctive Roman style. An **arch**, or curved structure over an opening, is strong and inexpensive to build. Lengthening an arch creates a vault, and joining a circle of arches at their highest point creates a dome.

Long stone channels called **aqueducts** (AK-wih-duhkts) carried clean water from hilltops into cities and towns. The engineers' precise calculations over long distances ensured a steady flow of water. Rome received 35 million cubic feet of water every day. While most of an aqueduct ran underground, sometimes huge arched bridges were built to carry the water across valleys. Many of these magnificent structures still stand as reminders of Roman engineering ability: building big and building to last.

Critical Viewing This interior photo of the Pantheon shows the oculus—the opening in the center of the dome. What mood did Roman architects create using a tall dome with an opening at the top?

REVIEW & ASSESS

1. **READING CHECK** What techniques and constructions did Roman engineers develop?

2. **SUMMARIZE** What was the process Roman soldiers used to build roads?

3. **MAKE INFERENCES** How did aqueducts help unify the empire?

1.4 The Colosseum

Just as you might go to a stadium to watch a ball game, the Romans went to an amphitheater for entertainment—but the "games" they watched were far more dangerous than the toughest sports we see today.

MAIN IDEA

The Colosseum was the stage for brutal games to entertain the Roman people.

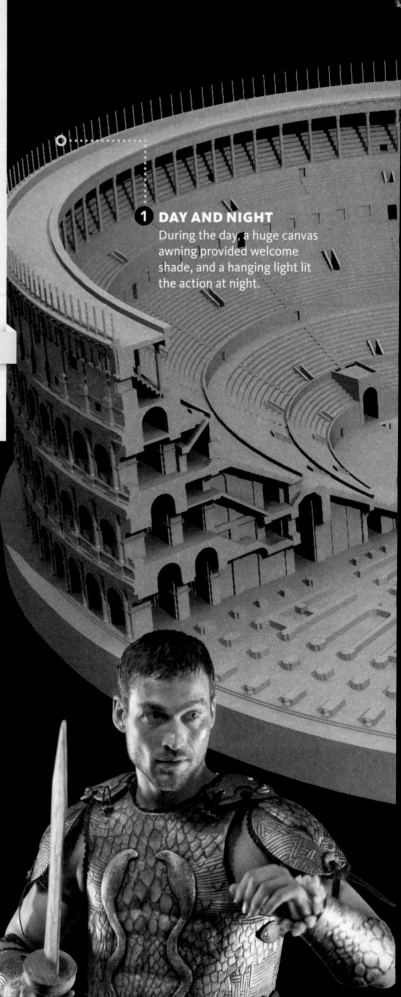

1 DAY AND NIGHT
During the day, a huge canvas awning provided welcome shade, and a hanging light lit the action at night.

A COLOSSAL STADIUM

The **Colosseum** in Rome was the world's largest amphitheater. The emperor Titus (TY-tuhs) opened it in A.D. 80. The building was designed to seat 50,000 spectators. An expertly engineered network of arches carried the structure's huge weight of stone.

Violent death was what Romans came to see at the Colosseum. In the morning, exotic animals hunted down defenseless criminals. After a break to clear the bodies, the main event began—the gladiators.

The **gladiators**, usually slaves or criminals, fought each other to the death. A successful gladiator might win fame, fortune, and his freedom.

The games, which could last 100 days, were usually paid for by the emperor. He hoped they would distract the poor from their problems.

Modern sports stadiums copied the Colosseum's design of tiered seating encircling a central stage.

2 GOING UP
Underground elevators lifted the gladiators and animals into the arena.

3 BEHIND THE SCENES
Cages beneath the stage held the wild animals that would be featured in the games.

REVIEW & ASSESS

1. **READING CHECK** What were some of the games that took place at the Colosseum?

2. **MAKE CONNECTIONS** How did the Colosseum influence the design of modern sports stadiums?

3. **MAKE INFERENCES** Why do you think the emperor might have wanted to distract the poor from their problems?

1.5 Villas and Frescoes

Whether you rented rooms in a block of apartments or were rich enough to own a house, summer in the city of Rome was seriously hot for everyone. Summer also brought the risk of deadly diseases. There was no air conditioning to keep you cool and no antibiotics if you got sick. If you were really rich, you'd head for the fresh, clean air of your country home.

MAIN IDEA

Wealthy Romans lived in luxurious country houses called villas.

LIFE IN A ROMAN VILLA

Villas were large country houses designed to impress. Visitors entered through huge doors into a bright central courtyard. This was the main living room, where Romans would relax and entertain. They knew their guests would admire expensive features such as fountains, magnificent marble statues, and portraits of important ancestors. Many other rooms for working, eating, and sleeping stood beyond the courtyard.

Roman interior designers favored large rooms with high ceilings. Usually there were only a few pieces of very fine furniture, which were often beautifully carved or decorated. A very expensive design feature in Roman villas was mosaic (moh-ZAY-ihk) floors. A **mosaic** contains tiny colored stone cubes set in mortar to create a picture or design. A mosaic floor was a work of art, and keeping it clean was essential. Villas had many slaves who did all the work, from tending the fields to cleaning, cooking, and serving meals.

The Villa Adriana at Tivoli (TIH-vuh-lee) near Rome is a luxurious example of a country house that is still visible today. Built by the emperor Hadrian, it formed a vast group of 30 buildings, many copied and named after places Hadrian had admired on his travels. Covering an area equal to about 270 football fields, the villa included a theater, a stadium, baths, a library, and a palace.

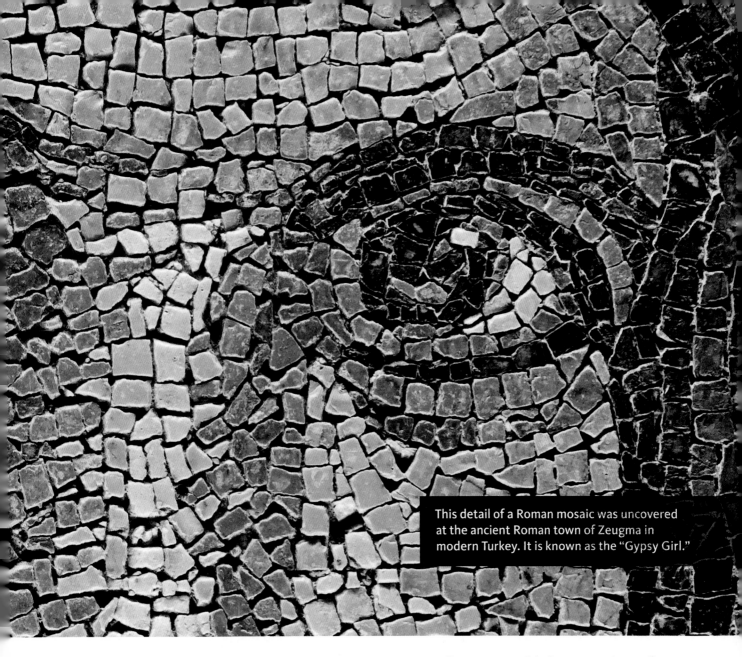

This detail of a Roman mosaic was uncovered at the ancient Roman town of Zeugma in modern Turkey. It is known as the "Gypsy Girl."

FRESCOES

The Romans learned the art of painting frescoes from the ancient Greeks. A **fresco** is a picture painted directly onto the wall while the plaster is still wet. Rich Romans covered their walls with these paintings. Talented Greek artists were often employed to paint these frescoes.

Roman frescoes could show a variety of scenes such as landscapes, famous battles, and views of everyday life. Some pictures even included family members, posed to show off wealth and status. The Romans were great lovers of art, which they used to emphasize their position in society. To rich Romans, appearance was everything.

REVIEW & ASSESS

1. **READING CHECK** What kinds of luxurious features did the villas of wealthy Romans often have?

2. **MONITOR COMPREHENSION** For what purpose did wealthy Romans employ talented Greek artists?

3. **SYNTHESIZE** What was the relationship between art and status in Roman culture?

1.6 Pompeii

As dawn broke on August 24, A.D. 79, the citizens of **Pompeii** (pahm-PAY) rolled out of bed and dressed for another day. Around noon, a dog was chained to a post, a crate of new pottery waited to be unpacked, and a kettle was filled with water. Then disaster struck. Within days, the whole city became a "living" history—entombed in ash for 1,900 years.

MAIN IDEA

The ruins and remains of Pompeii provide insight into everyday Roman life.

MODERN VESUVIUS

Mount Vesuvius is still an active volcano, and about 2.4 million people live in nearby Naples and its suburbs.

Vesuvius has erupted several times since the destruction of Pompeii. The last eruption was in 1944. Experts believe it is not a question of *if* the volcano will erupt again, but *when*.

DISASTER STRIKES

Pompeii was an average city resting in the shadow of Mount Vesuvius (vuh-SOO-vee-uhs), a volcano on Italy's western coast. The paved streets of the city followed an orderly pattern, and citizens there had all the civic comforts expected. Some 20,000 people worked, played, ate, slept, and lived within Pompeii's city walls until the afternoon of August 24, A.D. 79.

The Roman writer Pliny the Younger was near Pompeii that day. He had once described the city as "one of the loveliest places on Earth." After the events that occurred in Pompeii, he described a nightmare.

A violent explosion brought the city to a standstill. Pliny watched in horror as Mount Vesuvius erupted, shooting gas mixed with rock and ash high into the sky and creating an immense black cloud that blocked out the sun. Panic-stricken citizens fled as ash rained down.

As lava crept toward the city, fires raged and buildings collapsed. A vast volcanic ash cloud swept in to suffocate the city, burying its people and their possessions nearly 25 feet deep. A cloud of poisonous gas overtook and killed anyone who had not yet escaped. Over the next few days, lightning, earthquakes, and tidal waves followed. Finally after three days, Vesuvius went quiet—as silent as the deserted city of Pompeii.

This man died fleeing the eruption of Mount Vesuvius, which rises in the background. Pompeians' final moments were preserved by the ash from the volcano and then revealed using plaster casts.

A CITY PRESERVED

The volcanic ash that buried Pompeii also helped preserve its contents. The city's ruins were first discovered in the late 1500s. By 1861, archaeologists began carefully uncovering and working to protect their extraordinary find. Removing the ash, the scientists found houses, shops, and public buildings that contained mosaics, frescoes, and even graffiti. Many of the items had obviously been abandoned suddenly, in the first moments of the eruption. These artifacts offer a revealing glimpse into everyday Roman life. The ash preserved items such as leather shoes, wooden furniture, food, and a library of scrolls.

The ash also preserved some of its victims. It hardened around the bodies. Over time the bodies decayed and left behind an empty space. By pouring plaster into these spaces, archaeologists created exact casts of people, animals, and plants at their moment of death. All the discoveries are moving reminders of how suddenly death came to the city of Pompeii and froze it in time under a blanket of ash.

REVIEW & ASSESS

1. **READING CHECK** What items in Pompeii were preserved after the eruption?

2. **SEQUENCE EVENTS** What was the order of events that occurred in Pompeii on August 24, A.D. 79?

3. **ANALYZE CAUSE AND EFFECT** How were the ruins of Pompeii preserved?

The Origins of Christianity

A man named Jesus who lived in Nazareth was a Jew whose beliefs became a threat to Jewish and Roman leaders. His teachings formed the foundation of a religion that has powerfully shaped the world for over 2,000 years.

MAIN IDEA

Christianity developed in Jewish communities and was based on the teachings of Jesus.

JEWISH ROOTS

As the empire expanded, the Romans were usually tolerant of the many different religions practiced throughout the empire. As long as people worshipped their emperor as a god, they could follow whatever faith they liked. This was not a problem for most religions. The exception was Judaism, the religion of the Jewish people.

As you've already learned, the Romans captured the Jewish city of Jerusalem in 63 B.C. This brought the Jewish people under Roman control. At first the Romans allowed the Jews to worship one God. Over time, tensions grew. Rome began to enforce emperor worship, and the tensions exploded into conflict. In A.D. 70, Rome defeated the Jews, who then scattered throughout the empire. This helped spread a new religion that was developing in the Jewish community: Christianity.

JESUS OF NAZARETH

Christianity is based on the teachings of **Jesus**, a man born into a poor family in Judea around 6 B.C. Most of what we know about Jesus' teachings comes from the four **Gospels**. These books were written after Jesus' death by four of his followers—Matthew, Mark, Luke, and John. The Gospels are part of the **New Testament**, which presents the history, teachings, and beliefs of Christianity. According to historical record, Jesus was a practicing Jew and worked as a carpenter. When he was about 30 years old, he began to teach ideas that differed from Jewish practices. Biblical accounts claim that Jesus could perform miracles, such as healing the sick.

In time, Jesus traveled around Judea preaching and gathering disciples, or followers. He chose his closest followers, known as the **Twelve Apostles**, to help spread his teachings. He often used **parables** (short stories about everyday life) to make his religious or moral points. In his Sermon on the Mount, Jesus declared that love for God and charity toward all people were more important than following Jewish law. He also promised that those who sought God's forgiveness for their sins would go to heaven after death. To his followers, Jesus became Christ, "the anointed one." They believed he was the promised Messiah—the one who would free them.

According to Christian writings, Jesus criticized Jewish practices while visiting Jerusalem during the Jewish observance of Passover. Jesus was arrested and turned over to Roman authorities. Pontius Pilate, the Roman governor of Judea, sentenced Jesus to death by crucifixion—being nailed to a cross and left to die. Jesus' body was buried, and then, according to the Gospel accounts, he was resurrected, or rose from the dead, and ascended into heaven. For Christians, the resurrection signals victory over sin and death. The man called Jesus was gone, but Christianity was just beginning.

The Last Supper, Leonardo da Vinci, 1498

1 2 3 4 5 6 7 8 9 10 11 12 13

THE LAST SUPPER

Leonardo da Vinci completed this painting in 1498. It was painted directly on the wall of a church in Milan, Italy.

Jesus and his Twelve Apostles have gathered for a final Passover supper. The painting depicts the moment when Jesus tells his Apostles that one of them will betray him. Da Vinci captures a range of emotions among the Apostles and a sense of calm in Jesus. According to Christian belief, the Apostle Judas would betray Jesus after the meal. The next day Jesus was put to death.

LEGEND

1 Bartholomew

2 James Minor

3 Andrew

4 Judas

5 Peter

6 John

7 Jesus

8 Thomas

9 James Major

10 Philip

11 Matthew

12 Thaddeus

13 Simon

REVIEW & ASSESS

1. **READING CHECK** What were some of Jesus' teachings?

2. **SEQUENCE EVENTS** What were the key events in the life of Jesus?

3. **MAKE INFERENCES** What do you think makes parables an effective way to teach Christian ideas?

2.2 Christianity Spreads

Faith is very personal. We follow a particular religion (or no religion) for different reasons. Early Christians were the same way. Christianity had broad appeal and attracted a wide mix of people. They all believed that Jesus was the Messiah.

MAIN IDEA

Christianity attracted many followers and spread throughout the Roman Empire.

APPEAL OF CHRISTIANITY

At first all Christians were practicing Jews who still met in synagogues, places for Jewish worship. However, soon Christianity placed less emphasis on the laws of Judaism and welcomed Gentiles (GEHN-tylz), or non-Jews. As a result of the split from Judaism, Christianity grew and developed its own identity.

Christianity appealed to a lot of people. The religion's main appeal was the promise of salvation made possible by the sacrifice of Jesus. Many followers were also attracted by Christianity's rejection of the Roman focus on wealth and image. They preferred Jesus' focus on living simply and peacefully, sharing property, and providing charity to help the less fortunate. The poor liked the way Christian communities shared their wealth and established hospitals, schools, and other public services to improve their lives. Women and slaves liked Christianity because it treated them more like equals than other religions and Roman society did. Finally, many people embraced the idea of a personal relationship with God.

SPREADING THE WORD

In spite of Christianity's broad appeal, the religion's survival was far from certain, and it could easily have faded away. Instead it thrived because Jesus' followers spread his teachings fast and far. Through the Roman road network, Christianity spread rapidly in Jewish communities across the empire. Another big break was that the Romans confused Christianity with Judaism, and so they ignored the new religion, which allowed it to grow.

Even so, life as a Christian wasn't easy. The Romans often persecuted, or

THE SPREAD OF CHRISTIANITY, c. A.D. 500

— Boundary of Roman Empire, c. A.D. 395
▢ Christian areas, c. A.D. 325
▢ Christian expansion, c. A.D. 500

Black Sea

Danube R.

ITALY
Rome

SYRIA

Tigris R.

Euphrates R.

Persian Gulf

50°E

30°N

Damascus
Nazareth
JUDEA
Jerusalem

Mediterranean Sea

EGYPT

Nile R.

Red Sea

Tropic of Cancer

20°N

‹ Christianity spread to scattered places throughout the Mediterranean during Roman rule, including to places such as present-day Ethiopia, Egypt, Syria, and even Spain. In the years after the fall of the empire, it spread further and far beyond the Roman Empire's former borders.

punished, Christians for their beliefs. However, one of Christianity's fiercest persecutors, a man named **Paul**, eventually became its biggest champion.

Paul was most responsible for spreading early Christianity. He was a well-educated Jew and a Roman citizen. He converted to Christianity while traveling on the road to Damascus. According to Paul's own account, he had a vision in which Jesus was revealed to him as the Son of God. As a result, Paul became a **missionary**, a person who travels to another country to do religious work.

He began spreading Jesus' teachings. Paul was often arrested, but he always escaped to preach again. He wrote many letters, or **epistles** (ih-PIH-suhls), explaining Jesus' teachings by answering specific questions. According to tradition, Paul was killed in a Roman massacre of Christians in A.D. 64. By then, Roman leaders realized that Christianity was a separate religion from Judaism and a popular religion—too popular. Fearful that Christianity might threaten the stability of the empire, Roman rulers made the religion's practice illegal.

REVIEW & ASSESS

1. **READING CHECK** How did Christianity spread throughout the Roman Empire?

2. **INTERPRET MAPS** What natural features served as the northern border for Christian expansion by A.D. 500?

3. **MAKE INFERENCES** Why was Paul an effective spokesperson for spreading the teachings of Christianity?

New Testament Literature

The Christian Bible is made up of two parts: the Old Testament (or Hebrew Bible) and the New Testament. The New Testament includes the Gospel of Luke and Paul's Epistles. At the core of the New Testament teaching is the death and resurrection of Jesus, giving the world a "new covenant" (new testament) that would enable all who repented of their sins to enter the kingdom of heaven.

This painting shows a moment from Jesus' parable of the Prodigal Son.

The Prodigal Son, Lucio Massari, c. 1614

The Parable of the Good Samaritan

This parable was recorded in the Gospel of Luke in the first century A.D. The Samaritans (suh-MEHR-uh-tuhns) were a community of people who were generally distrusted by the Jews, the audience of the parable. According to the Gospel of Luke, Jesus tells this parable to answer the question "Who is my neighbor?"

CONSTRUCTED RESPONSE How does the Samaritan's response to the beaten man differ from the responses of the priest and Levite?

Good Samaritan, Julius Schnorr von Carolsfeld, 1860

A man was going down from Jerusalem to Jericho, when he fell into the hands of robbers. They stripped him of his clothes, beat him, and went away, leaving him half dead. A priest happened to be going down the same road, and when he saw the man, he passed by on the other side. So too, a Levite [a Jew], when he came to the place and saw him, passed by on the other side. But a Samaritan, as he traveled, came where the man was; and when he saw him, he took pity on him. He went to him and bandaged his wounds, pouring on oil and wine. Then he put the man on his own donkey, took him to an inn, and took care of him. The next day he took out two silver coins and gave them to the innkeeper. "Look after him," he said, "and when I return, I will reimburse you for any extra expense you may have."

Luke 10:30—35

from Paul's Epistle to the Galatians

Paul wrote his letter to the Galatians (guh-LAY-shuhnz) in the first century A.D. The Roman province of Galatia contained a number of early Christian communities. In his letter, Paul stresses some important ideas of the Christian faith.

CONSTRUCTED RESPONSE What important Christian ideas is Paul stating in this epistle?

You all are sons of God through faith in Christ Jesus, for all of you who were baptized . . . have clothed yourselves with Christ. There is neither Jew nor Greek, slave nor free, male nor female, for you are all one in Christ Jesus.

Galatians 3:26—28

SYNTHESIZE & WRITE

1. **REVIEW** Review the ideas expressed in the parable of the Good Samaritan and Paul's Epistle to the Galatians.

2. **RECALL** On your own paper, write down the main idea expressed in each document.

3. **CONSTRUCT** Write a topic sentence that answers this question: What are some fundamental Christian ideas about how people should treat one another?

4. **WRITE** Using evidence from the documents and from the chapter, write a paragraph that supports your answer to the question in Step 3.

2.4

The **Early** **Christian** Church

Being different can make you a target for attacks. Early Christians were violently attacked, but their courage and determination ensured Christianity's survival.

MAIN IDEA

In time, Christianity became the official religion of the Roman Empire.

CONSTANTINE

Constantine was very generous to his supporters. Historians have suggested that he could afford to be so generous only because he robbed temples and used tax money for his own purposes. It is also clear that some of his supporters gained favor by faking conversions to Christianity.

THE CONVERSION OF CONSTANTINE

As you have learned, Christians were often persecuted by their Roman rulers. In A.D. 35, a Christian named Stephen became the first of thousands of Christian victims. He was killed for his religious beliefs. Roman leaders punished Christians for refusing to worship the emperors.

This persecution only got worse. In A.D. 64, the emperor Nero blamed Christians for a great fire that swept through Rome. He had thousands of Christians put to death. Just being a Christian became punishable by death. As a result, worshippers were forced to meet in secret. They buried their dead in hidden underground chambers called **catacombs** (KA-tuh-kohms).

In A.D. 312, Christian persecution had reached its highest point when an amazing change began. On the eve of a battle for control of the empire, a young Roman leader named **Constantine** prayed for help. He believed his prayers were answered with a vision of the Christian cross. The vision led him to paint a symbol on his soldiers' shields. Constantine went on to win the battle. As a result, he immediately put an end to Christian persecution.

Constantine made many other changes after he became emperor. He built churches in Roman lands and declared Sunday the Christian day of rest. He even had Christian symbols placed on coins. Constantine ruled for a long time. However, it was only after Constantine's rule that the emperor Theodosius officially closed all the temples to the Roman gods and made Christianity the official religion of Rome.

Catacombs

Catacombs are underground burial chambers. They often have tunnels with spaces cut into the walls for the bodies. Some catacombs also have large chambers where funeral feasts were held. There are about 40 early Christian catacombs around Rome, and they are the most extensive of any known catacomb system in the world. Shown below is the Catacomb of Priscilla in Rome, Italy.

< Saint Peter's Basilica, in present-day Vatican City

FORMATION OF THE EARLY CHURCH

With the legalization of Christianity, Christian communities could openly share their beliefs. Church leaders from across the empire held councils, or meetings, to discuss Christianity and the writings of religious scholars. Their discussions helped them define Christian beliefs and practices.

Christian practices were then communicated to Christian churches throughout the empire and beyond. Each church was led by a priest, and groups of churches were overseen by a bishop. The first bishop of Rome, according to Christian tradition, was the apostle Peter, who died for his beliefs in A.D. 64. Constantine had a church, St. Peter's Basilica, built over the

apostle's tomb. The photo above shows the basilica, which was rebuilt in the 1600s. In time the bishop of Rome became the most important bishop, or **pope**. He was seen as the leader of the unified church, known as the **Roman Catholic Church**.

Church leaders standardized Christian beliefs into a common creed, or statement of beliefs. One such statement was the definition of God as a Holy Trinity: the union of Father, Son (Jesus), and Holy Spirit. Worship in the Christian church focused on some common sacraments, or religious ceremonies, such as baptism, an individual's acceptance by the church. As Christianity grew more structured and became more organized, it became a powerful religion.

REVIEW & ASSESS

1. **READING CHECK** How did Christianity become the official religion of the Roman Empire?

2. **DESCRIBE** How was the leadership of the early church organized?

3. **DRAW CONCLUSIONS** In what way did their persecution help unite the Christians?

The Third Century Crisis

Despite the occasional unbalanced emperor, the Roman Empire ran smoothly for 200 years. Then things began to fall apart. Disputes over who should be emperor caused the return of political violence and civil war. In some years, four or even six emperors were on the throne. By A.D. 235, the Roman world had plunged into a crisis.

MAIN IDEA

Military problems led to a crisis in the Roman Empire.

MILITARY PROBLEMS

So what went wrong? Arguably the empire had physically outgrown the emperor's ability to govern it. At its height, the Roman Empire stretched from Scotland to the Sahara, an area about half the size of the United States. This vast expanse, with huge geographic and cultural differences, was very difficult to govern effectively.

Defending such a large area also proved difficult. Rome faced attacks on two fronts at the same time, which drained money and resources all across the empire. In the east, Rome fought the powerful Parthian Empire from Persia, while Germanic tribes raided Rome's northern borders.

Meanwhile, warring groups within the empire once again fought to decide who would be emperor. Civil wars bled the empire of desperately needed food, money, and soldiers. As emperors fought expensive wars they could not win, enemies from outside the empire attacked. With so many Roman soldiers engaged in warfare, the invaders plundered, or stole riches from, the unguarded interior. It was a sure sign of trouble when cities, including Rome, rebuilt their long-neglected defensive walls. These military problems provoked further political and social problems.

POLITICAL, ECONOMIC, AND SOCIAL PROBLEMS

War was not only dangerous for soldiers; it was disruptive for everyone. Emperors were blamed for not protecting the empire, and they were regularly replaced or murdered. Fifty different emperors ruled between A.D. 235 and 285. People living in what would become Spain, France, and Britain preferred to trust local rulers. They broke from Rome to form a separate Gallic Empire. These events weakened imperial authority and prevented the strong, decisive, and long-term action needed to restore order.

This constant warfare also ruined the economy. Trade was interrupted, and the empire had to rely on its inadequate agricultural resources. The people suffered food shortages and higher taxes. Wars are expensive, and the emperors expected the people to pay for them. Even heavier taxes were enforced when the imperial currency lost value. This affected rich and poor but mostly the poor.

Ordinary people grew angry, criminal organizations grew, and outbursts of mob anger increased. It even became difficult to recruit local officials. Nobody wanted these jobs because people risked a beating for doing them. In these unstable times, good citizenship took second place to looking after oneself.

DECLINE OF THE ROMAN EMPIRE

Illustration of a parade honoring victories of Emperor Augustus

Stone relief showing a government bureaucrat at work

Military Reasons

- Fighting the Parthian Empire in the east
- Fighting Germanic tribes in the west
- Fighting civil wars at home

Political Reasons

- Difficult to govern huge empire
- Frequently changing emperors
- Power gained by local leaders

Relief depicting a tax payment

Illustration of a Roman party with the poor waiting on the rich

Economic Reasons

- Trade interrupted
- People heavily taxed
- Lower value of currency

Social Reasons

- Unrest from gap between rich and poor
- More criminal organizations
- Civic responsibility no longer important

REVIEW & ASSESS

1. **READING CHECK** Why did the size of the Roman Empire cause military problems?

2. **ANALYZE CAUSE AND EFFECT** What was the result of the emperors' expensive wars?

3. **DRAW CONCLUSIONS** How did Rome's military problems lead to political, social, and economic problems?

3.2 | Eastern and Western Roman Empires

The Roman Empire was too big for one person to manage. Unfortunately that didn't stop ambitious men from trying and failing. Then Rome's luck changed. In A.D. 284, the throne was seized by an emperor who had the sense and strength to make the big changes that could keep the empire alive.

MAIN IDEA

In A.D. 285, the Roman Empire was divided into the Western Roman Empire and the Eastern Roman Empire.

DIOCLETIAN DIVIDES THE EMPIRE

The new emperor was named **Diocletian** (dy-uh-KLEE-shuhn), and he had a lot on his plate. He faced endangered frontiers, overstretched armies, economic collapse, weak imperial authority, and widespread unrest. However, Diocletian had a radical plan: In A.D. 285, he divided the empire in two. Diocletian ruled the Eastern Roman Empire, and his trusted friend Maximian ruled the Western Roman Empire. Each man appointed a junior emperor to rule with him. This rule by four emperors, called a **tetrarchy** (TEH-trahr-kee), worked really well at first.

Each emperor focused on his specific region while cooperating to introduce reforms.

Together they increased the army to 400,000 men and reorganized and strengthened the frontier forces. They also created a mobile field army ready to tackle trouble wherever it broke out. On the political front, Diocletian and Maximian reformed government administration and divided the provinces into more manageable units. To promote unity, they enforced emperor worship and the Latin language everywhere. They encouraged economic recovery by reforming tax laws, controlling inflation, and stabilizing the currency. The empire was on the road to recovery, and after 20 years, Diocletian and Maximian retired, letting the junior emperors take over. However, this was as good as the tetrarchy got.

CONSTANTINE MOVES THE CAPITAL

You've learned that the emperor Constantine made the practice of Christianity legal in the empire. Before he did that, he had to fight to become emperor. Constantine's father was emperor of the Western Roman Empire. When Constantine's father died in A.D. 306, however, the tetrarchy refused his claim to be western emperor, sparking a civil war. Constantine won the war and became emperor of east and west. However, Constantine was more interested in the eastern half of his empire.

ATLANTIC OCEAN

Western Roman Empire
Eastern Roman Empire

Rome's importance had long been decreasing. Emperors no longer lived in Rome, and Italy had lost its privileged status.

The differences between east and west were increasing. The east produced more people, more food, more taxes, and more soldiers, while the west just grew weaker. So Constantine moved the capital from Rome to the ancient Greek city of Byzantium, which he renamed Constantinople. (Today the city is called Istanbul.) He built his new capital on the strategically important Bosporus, a narrow stretch of water separating Europe and Asia.

Constantine also continued the reforms begun by earlier emperors, earning the title "the Great." However, his sons plunged the empire into another civil war. The emperor Theodosius later reunited the empire, but the division of east and west became permanent after his death in A.D. 395. From then on, the fortunes and futures of the two empires were very different.

ROMAN EMPIRE: EAST AND WEST, c. A.D. 395

NATURAL BORDERS The Rhine and Danube rivers on the northern border of the Roman Empire were difficult to cross, which made it easier for the Roman army to defend the empire.

CONSTANTINOPLE Constantine's new capital on the Bosporus provided easy access to many resources and allowed the empire to control trade.

ROME Diocletian's decision to rule the Eastern Roman Empire made it clear that Rome was no longer the center of political power.

EUROPE

Rhine R.

Danube R.

Black Sea

Bosporus

Constantinople

Rome

ASIA

AFRICA

Mediterranean Sea

REVIEW & ASSESS

1. **READING CHECK** Why did Diocletian divide the Roman Empire in two?

2. **INTERPRET MAPS** In what ways was Rome's location similar to that of Constantinople?

3. **IDENTIFY PROBLEMS AND SOLUTIONS** What was Diocletian's plan for ruling the vast empire more efficiently?

Critical Viewing This painting shows Attila the Hun attacking a Roman city. In what ways has the artist made Attila seem very fierce?

End of the Western Roman Empire

If you lived in the Western Roman Empire in A.D. 375, you'd be unhappy with the way things were going. While the west struggled to rule itself, feed itself, pay its bills, and defend its borders, you would enviously watch the Eastern Roman Empire grow richer, stronger, and more stable. However bad things got, you could never imagine a world without the Roman Empire—but that reality was just 101 years away.

MAIN IDEA

Invaders attacked the Western Roman Empire and caused its downfall.

FOREIGN INVADERS

Diocletian and Constantine only delayed the end of the Western Roman Empire. The end came in the form of **barbarians**, a Greek word Romans used to describe all people outside of the empire. Three main tribes of barbarians would finally tear the Western Roman Empire apart. The Visigoths (VIH-zuh-gahths) and Vandals were Germanic tribes from northern Europe. Looking for better farmland, both groups migrated south toward the Roman frontier.

The Huns formed the third tribe of barbarians. Migrating from Asia, they were nomads, or wandering cattle herders. Their skill with horses and bows made them a ferocious fighting force. Beginning in A.D. 445, a man named **Attila** was their sole ruler.

THE WESTERN ROMAN EMPIRE FALLS

Attila and his army swept into Europe. Forced into the Western Roman Empire by the Huns, the Visigoths soon invaded Italy. Around the same time, the Vandals invaded Gaul and then Spain. By now the emperor, who had few Roman soldiers to call on, had to enlist barbarian fighters to defend the empire.

On August 24, 410, the Visigoths shocked the world by sacking, or destroying, Rome. They then conquered Gaul and Spain, driving the Vandals into North Africa. Then came Attila. The Huns attacked Gaul in A.D. 451, and the emperor relied on barbarian armies to fight them. Rome had lost control. In A.D. 476, the last emperor quietly left the throne.

The Western Roman Empire was broken up into many Germanic kingdoms, and the Eastern Roman Empire became known as the Byzantine Empire. The Roman Empire was over. Historians argue about why the Western Roman Empire fell. Did it end naturally because of internal failings? Was it brought down by external forces? Or was it simply transformed into something new?

REVIEW & ASSESS

1. **READING CHECK** What three barbarian tribes invaded Roman territory, leading to Rome's downfall?

2. **SEQUENCE EVENTS** What events led to the fall of the Western Roman Empire?

3. **DRAW CONCLUSIONS** Why were so many tribes able to invade the Western Roman Empire?

Latin and Literature

Students learning Latin have a rhyme: "Latin is a language as dead as dead can be. First it killed the Romans, and now it's killing me." But Latin is not dead. Latin is still used—especially by scientists and doctors. In fact, you use Latin words every day. It's part of Rome's legacy, or heritage.

MAIN IDEA

The Latin language spread across the empire and influences the way we speak and write today.

AN INFLUENTIAL LANGUAGE

As you've learned, the Roman Empire had dozens of languages, but the language spoken in Rome was **Latin**. Although Greek was also commonly used, Latin was established as the official language for international communication, government, law, and trade. It was used for official business from Britain to Egypt.

The Romans brought writing to northern Europe, and we still use the Latin alphabet today. However, back then the alphabet had only 22 letters. The letters *i* and *j* were interchangeable, as were *u* and *v*. The letters *w* and *y* did not exist at all.

After the Roman Empire fell, the Latin language lived on. Over time, new languages, called Romance languages, developed from Latin. These languages include French, Italian, Spanish, and Portuguese. Each language is distinctive but shares a common root in Latin, the "Roman" in *Romance*. The English language was greatly influenced by the Romance languages and uses many Latin words, including *campus, census, curriculum, index, item, sponsor,* and *stadium*.

ORATORY, POETRY, AND PHILOSOPHY

In addition to language, Rome left behind a legacy in literature, featuring speeches, poetry, and philosophical works. **Oratory**, or public speaking, was especially prized, and promising young men were trained in the art of argument and persuasion. As you learned previously, Cicero was one of Rome's greatest orators, and his speeches are still studied by serious students of public speaking.

The Romans also loved poetry, which was based on Greek traditions. The ultimate poem was the epic, a long story describing a hero's adventures. The most celebrated Roman epic was **Virgil's** *Aeneid* (uh-NEE-uhd), which fills 12 volumes. Written between 30 and 19 B.C., it tells the story of Aeneas, the legendary founder of Rome.

Roman philosophy was another extension of Greek ideas. Philosophy is the study of reality, knowledge, and beliefs. Ethical and religious arguments interested Romans more than theory and speculation. The Greek Stoic (STOH-ihk) philosophy was especially influential in Roman life. It stressed a practical approach to life in which people performed their civic duty and accepted their circumstances—good or bad.

The Roman Catholic Church became the keeper of Roman literature for centuries after the empire fell. It preserved works that could be used to educate young men in morality, government, and law. A 15th-century fascination with the ancient world revived the popularity of Roman literature and has ensured its widespread circulation ever since.

LATIN AND ENGLISH

Many English words have Latin roots, or origins. Examine the prefixes and suffixes listed. What words can you add?

-ty, -ity

FORMS NOUNS FROM ADJECTIVES

Similarity
Technicality

Sub-

UNDER

Submarine >
Subway

Re-

AGAIN

Rebuild
Remake

-ation

FORMS NOUNS FROM VERBS

Celebration
Formation

Pre-

BEFORE

Preview
Prepay

Dis-

NOT ANY

Disbelief
Disrespect

-ment

FORMS NOUNS FROM VERBS

Entertainment
Statement

-ible, -able

FORMS ADJECTIVES FROM VERBS

∧ *Flexible*
Likable

Post-

AFTER

Postgame
Postwar

-fy, -ify

FORMS VERBS AND MEANS "TO MAKE"

< *Purify*
Humidify

LEGEND

 Prefix   Prefix Definition Suffix   Suffix Explanation Example Words

---

REVIEW & ASSESS

1. **READING CHECK** How has the English language been influenced by Latin?

2. **SEQUENCE EVENTS** What sequence of events helped keep Latin alive?

3. **MAKE INFERENCES** How did Roman ideas about philosophy support the ancient Roman approach to life?

4.2 Art, Architecture, and Law

The Romans shaped the ancient world for a thousand years. But what have they ever done for us? Well, quite a lot actually. If you know what to look for, you can spot Rome's legacy in modern-day art, architecture, and law.

MAIN IDEA

The Romans developed many ideas that continue to influence our lives today.

ART AND ARCHITECTURE

As with their philosophy, Romans preferred a realistic approach to art. The paintings and statues that decorated their homes showed people and things as they really looked. Like the Romans, people today often display realistic family portraits, although photos have generally replaced statues.

The Romans also made mosaics and frescoes popular on floors and walls around the world. Roman frescoes can be compared to modern murals and even some street art. The Roman **bas-relief** (bah-ruh-LEEF) is a realistic sculpture with figures raised against a flat background. These sculptures appear on monuments such as the National World War II Memorial in Washington, D.C. The photo on these pages is an example of a Roman bas-relief carved into the side of a sarcophagus, or stone coffin.

Rome's architectural influence is everywhere. Starting from the ground up, the Romans showed the world the benefit of an extensive, well-built, and well-maintained all-weather road network. European roads still follow Roman routes and sometimes cross original Roman bridges.

When a new Roman town was created, city planners took into account the city's climate and geography. The Romans always tried to establish a grid pattern for the streets. That means that the streets formed a network of intersecting horizontal and vertical lines. Many towns and cities use this pattern today.

Like the Romans, modern builders rely on concrete to build strong, tall, and unusual buildings. Roman architectural styles such as columns, arches, and domes can be seen in the U.S. Capitol and other buildings. Many modern stadiums follow the design perfected in the Colosseum.

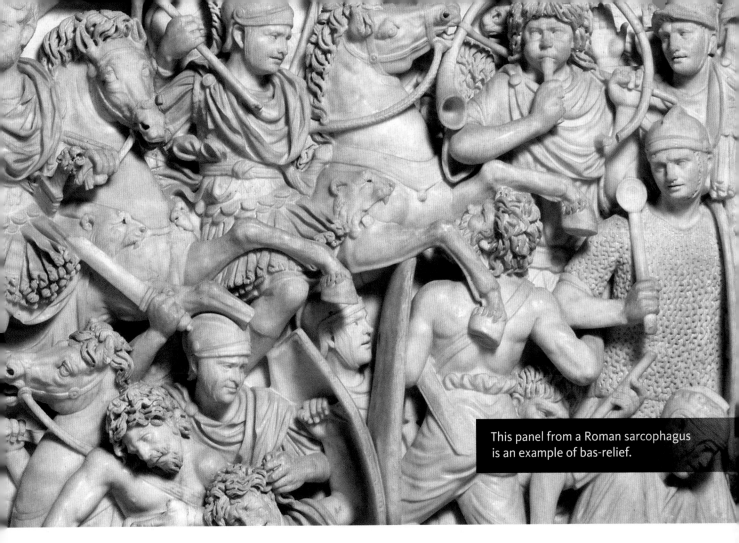

This panel from a Roman sarcophagus is an example of bas-relief.

LAW AND GOVERNMENT

Rome even influences the way people today live. Roman ideas of civic duty are encouraged in the United States and elsewhere. The structure of the U.S. government reflects elements of the Roman Republic, including representative assemblies and the system of checks and balances. Roman laws are the basis of law codes around the world, including that of the United States. The ideas of a fair judge, presumption of innocence, and equality under the law also come from the Romans.

The Latin language is still very much a part of modern law and other fields and professions. Legal documents, science papers, and memorial inscriptions are rich with Latin text. As you learned earlier, many everyday English words have their roots in Latin. Studying Latin can also make it easier to learn other modern languages that have Latin roots.

So don't just think about the legacy of Rome, search it out. It's in our language, laws, government, art, and architecture. The Romans are everywhere.

REVIEW & ASSESS

1. **READING CHECK** What Roman achievements in art and architecture influence our lives today?

2. **MAKE CONNECTIONS** How has the government of the Roman Republic influenced the structure of the U.S. government?

3. **COMPARE AND CONTRAST** How are the layouts of many towns and cities today similar to those in ancient Rome?

A.D. 52

The system of aqueducts that supplied water to Rome and its empire was a major feat of engineering. In the capital city itself, 11 aqueducts carried fresh water from the area's surrounding rivers and lakes, some as far as 57 miles away. Not all of these structures were architectural masterpieces like the Claudian Aqueduct (shown here), which was completed in A.D. 52. Many consisted of simple underground pipes through which water flowed to various tanks throughout the city. The Roman aqueduct system fell apart after the breakdown of the empire, but the basic engineering principles behind its construction are still in use today.

VOCABULARY

Match each word in the first column with its definition in the second column.

WORD	DEFINITION
1. aqueduct	a. the practice and skill of public speaking
2. fresco	b. thousands of tiny colored stone cubes set in plaster to create a picture or design
3. parable	c. a painting done on plaster walls
4. barbarian	d. a system of government in which there are four rulers
5. oratory	e. a member of a tribe outside the empire
6. bas-relief	f. a simple story told to make a moral point
7. tetrarchy	g. a stone channel that carries water
8. mosaic	h. a sculpture with figures raised against a flat background

READING SKILL

9. **ORGANIZE IDEAS: SEQUENCE EVENTS** If you haven't already, complete your time line of key people and events in the Roman Empire. Then answer the question.

People and Events in the Roman Empire

31 B.C.
Augustus
became
emperor

Which person or event do you think had the greatest impact on the Roman Empire? Why?

MAIN IDEAS

Answer the following questions. Support your answers with evidence from the chapter.

10. What was accomplished during the Pax Romana? **LESSON 1.1**

11. What effect did safe seas and a network of excellent roads have on the Roman Empire's economy? **LESSON 1.2**

12. What role did Constantine play in the growth of Christianity? **LESSON 2.4**

13. Why did Diocletian divide the Roman Empire into the Eastern and Western Roman Empires? **LESSON 3.2**

14. How did Roman ideas about government and law influence the government of the United States? **LESSON 4.2**

CRITICAL THINKING

Answer the following questions. Support your answers with evidence from the chapter.

15. **FORM AND SUPPORT OPINIONS** What was the main reason the Roman Empire became so powerful and long lasting?

16. **SYNTHESIZE** What steps did Augustus take to secure the support of the Roman people and bring peace to the Roman Empire?

17. **EVALUATE** What role did technology play in Roman architecture?

18. **ANALYZE CAUSE AND EFFECT** How did the Roman Empire's vast geographic expanse become a serious disadvantage in the third century? What was the effect of this disadvantage?

19. **MAKE CONNECTIONS** How did the Latin language influence the Romance languages and English?

20. **YOU DECIDE** Do you think Augustus was a great emperor or a clever politician? Support your opinion with evidence from the chapter.

ROAD NETWORK OF THE ROMAN EMPIRE, c. A.D. 117

Roman Empire, c. A.D. 117
Roman roads

21. Where is Rome located in relation to the rest of the Roman Empire?

22. In A.D. 117 how far north and how far south did the Roman Empire extend?

ANALYZE SOURCES

Read the following selection from Jesus' Sermon on the Mount. Then answer the question.

> Blessed are the poor in spirit, for theirs is the kingdom of heaven.
>
> Blessed are the meek, for they will inherit the Earth.
>
> Blessed are the merciful, for they will be shown mercy.
>
> Blessed are the pure in heart, for they will see God.
>
> —Matthew 5:3–8

23. SYNTHESIZE How might these teachings from Jesus have helped guide people to lead their lives during the Roman Empire?

WRITE ABOUT HISTORY

24. EXPLANATORY Many social, political, and economic problems contributed to the decline and fall of the Roman Empire. Put yourself in the position of a senator at that time. Write a speech explaining three of these problems.

TIPS

- Take notes as you review the portion of the chapter about the decline and fall of the Roman Empire.
- State your main idea and supporting details in a clear, well-organized way.
- Present evidence to support your explanation.
- Use vocabulary from the chapter.
- Make a concluding statement based on your explanation of and evidence about the decline and fall of the Roman Empire.
- Use an audio recording device to record your speech. Be sure to speak loudly and clearly.

ON **LOCATION**
WITH Steven
ELLIS

NATIONAL GEOGRAPHIC GRANTEE

▶ **Check out more on myNGconnect**

Archaeologist Steven Ellis surveys the ruins of Pompeii. His project focuses on the city's common people, which is a new approach to archaeological excavation.

NOT JUST DIGGERS

That's the misconception that annoys us the most! I dig up cities, yes, but it's what I learn from those cities that is important. Discovering artifacts is pretty cool, but piecing them together to tell a 2,000-year-old human story—that's what I find really exciting.

Pompeii is better preserved than any other Roman site, and because it's a city, you can relate to it more easily than, say, the pyramids. It's also got the drama of its sudden death, but we want to uncover its life. Pompeians lived in houses and went to shops and schools. I love that familiar urban element. They also had very different rules and did things differently. I think it's fascinating to try and recognize those similarities and differences.

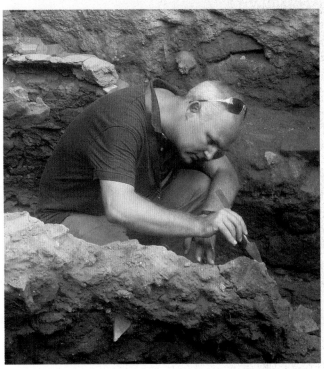

Archaeologists like Steven Ellis spend long hours in the field, carefully uncovering signs of past civilizations.

TELLING THE HUMAN STORY

For 200 years we've mostly looked at what the rich were doing by unearthing the grandest buildings. I'm using archaeology to tell the story of ordinary people, the other 98 percent of the population. It's a fairly new approach. I was the youngest archaeological director at Pompeii, and I was also the new guy with new questions. I said, "I want to work in areas that you've ignored." So I'm looking at shops, bars, restaurants, and houses. They don't have fine art, but they do have bones, seeds, and pieces of pottery that tell us a story. Some of our discoveries are pretty obvious, like the fact that poor people lived in smaller houses and ate cheaper foods off cheaper plates. But they're expanding our understanding of Roman society beyond just the rich and revealing the complex layers of life in the middle and working classes.

Excavating in poorer communities is incredibly gratifying because you've got to work harder at it. The rich lived in the best houses, with the best decorations and the most stuff. This all survived better, so it's easier to uncover and study. I'm proud that we are excavating the stories of families whose histories would otherwise never be told.

WHY STUDY HISTORY ?

❝ I study history because it's fascinating and *because I can.* In some countries, people are forbidden to study their own history, and that's a tragedy. I love finding out how similar or different people were from us. ❞ —Steven Ellis

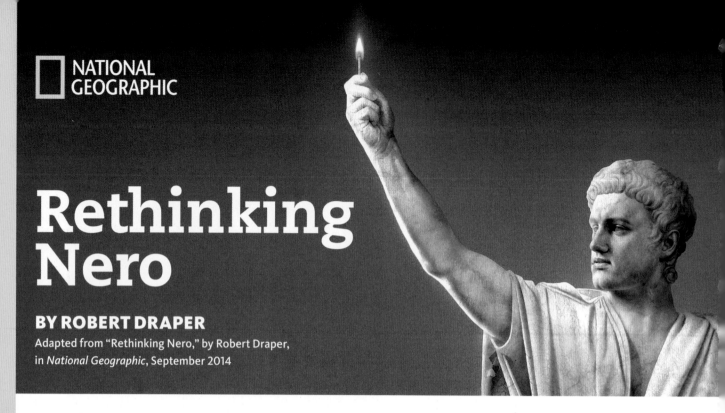

NATIONAL GEOGRAPHIC

Rethinking Nero

BY ROBERT DRAPER

Adapted from "Rethinking Nero," by Robert Draper,
in *National Geographic*, September 2014

As the city of Rome burned in A.D. 64, the infamous emperor Nero allegedly sat around playing his violin. He also may have killed two of his wives, his mother, and his stepbrother. In the accounts of many historians, he is described as a murderer and a lunatic. But now some scholars are rethinking Nero's reputation.

In 2007, archaeologist Fedora Filippi discovered the base of a column while digging under a busy street in Rome. Burrowing further, she encountered a portico and the edge of a pool. After a year of analysis, she concluded that she had discovered the enormous public gymnasium built by Nero a few years before the Great Fire. At first her discovery garnered little attention. But it was an important find. "The gymnasium was part of a big change Nero brought about in Rome," Filippi says. "Before, such baths were only for the aristocrats. This changed social relations because it put everyone on the same level, from senators to the horsemen."

Nero's gymnasium and events early in his reign suggest that he was a reformer who desired the admiration of his people. He ended the secret trials of the previous emperor, issued pardons, and was reluctant to sign death warrants. He praised Greek culture, encouraging Greek-style contests of athletics and poetry. Instead of looting other countries to gain wealth, Nero taxed wealthy Romans to raise funds, a practice that made him unpopular with the most powerful members of society. These early accomplishments likely alienated him from the Roman senators. But his own outrageous behavior later in his reign is the reason why he went down in history as a madman.

"Nero was a fool obsessed with his own power, but a fool can also be charming and interesting," says Roman archaeologist Andrea Carandini. He became powerful by appealing to the popular desires and prejudices of his people. In turn, he cherished the masses who adored him.

Romans themselves were conflicted about their ruler. "He was a monster," says Roberto Gervaso, author of the biographical novel *Nerone*. "But that's not all he was."

For more from National Geographic
Check out "Roman Frontiers" on myNGconnect

UNIT INQUIRY: BUILD AN EMPIRE

In this unit, you learned about ancient Rome and its legacy. Based on your reading, what factors can help make an empire great? What factors can lead to its decline?

ASSIGNMENT Design an empire that you think would be successful today. The empire should have a geographic location, a government, an economy, a social structure, and its own culture. Be prepared to present your empire and explain it to the class.

Plan As you build your empire, think about ancient Rome—what made it successful and what made it grow weak. Make a list of these factors and try to incorporate or avoid them in your own empire. Use a graphic organizer like this one to help organize your thoughts. ▶

Produce Use your notes to produce detailed descriptions of the elements of your empire. Write them in outline or paragraph form.

Present Choose a creative way to present your empire to the class. Consider one of these options:

- Create a multimedia presentation using photos to represent different elements of your empire.

- Write an introduction to a travel guide that describes your empire.

- Draw a map of your empire to accompany the description of its overall structure.

Geography | Government | Economy

My Empire

Social Structure | Culture

RAPID REVIEW
UNIT 4

THE **WORLD** OF THE **ROMANS** TOP TEN

1. In the Roman Republic, power was shared between elected consuls and assemblies to prevent individuals from becoming too powerful.
2. After many civil wars, Rome became an empire ruled with absolute authority by a single emperor.
3. The wise rule of the emperor Augustus ushered in the Pax Romana, 200 years of peace and prosperity.
4. The Colosseum hosted spectacular and bloody games where gladiators fought to the death.
5. Romans spoke Latin, and we still use many Latin words today.

6-10. **NOW IT'S YOUR TURN** Complete the list with five more things to remember about the world of the Romans.

AMERICAN AND ASIAN CIVILIZATIONS

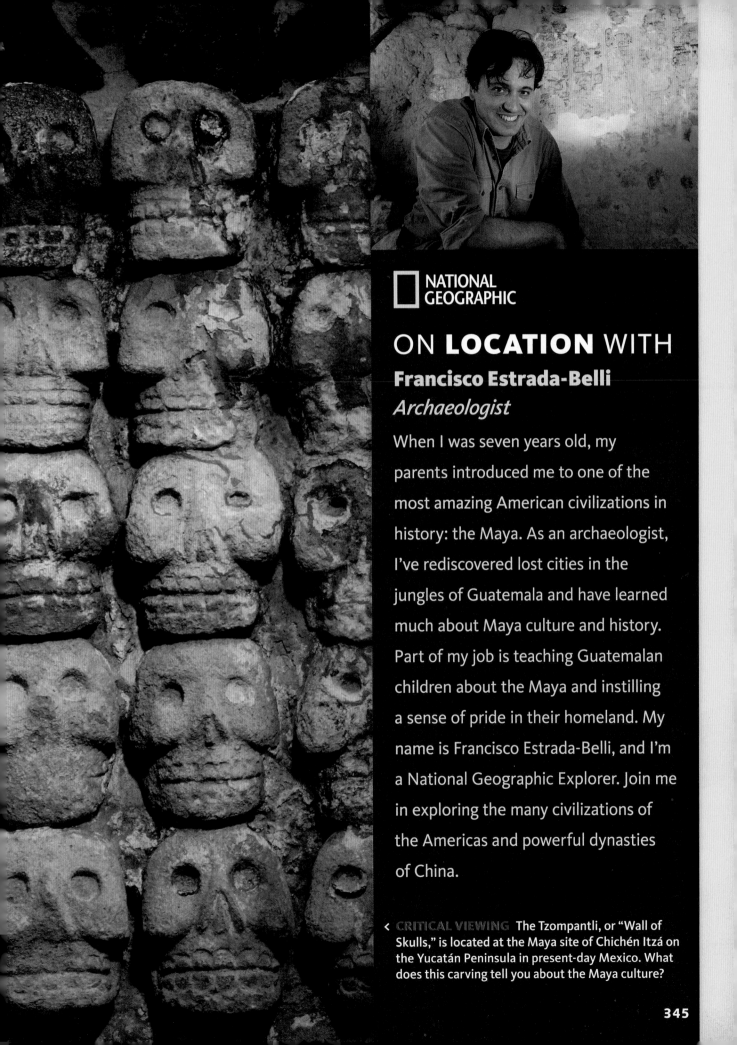

ON **LOCATION** WITH

Francisco Estrada-Belli
Archaeologist

When I was seven years old, my parents introduced me to one of the most amazing American civilizations in history: the Maya. As an archaeologist, I've rediscovered lost cities in the jungles of Guatemala and have learned much about Maya culture and history. Part of my job is teaching Guatemalan children about the Maya and instilling a sense of pride in their homeland. My name is Francisco Estrada-Belli, and I'm a National Geographic Explorer. Join me in exploring the many civilizations of the Americas and powerful dynasties of China.

< CRITICAL VIEWING The Tzompantli, or "Wall of Skulls," is located at the Maya site of Chichén Itzá on the Yucatán Peninsula in present-day Mexico. What does this carving tell you about the Maya culture?

American
Civilizations

A.D. 250
The Maya Classic
Period begins.
*(carving on a
Maya stele)*

500 B.C.
The Zapotec build
Monte Albán.

900
The ancient
Pueblo build
Pueblo Bonito.

1200 B.C.
The Olmec
civilization begins
in Mesoamerica.

A.D. 500

1200 B.C.

581
Wendi reunifies
China under
the Sui dynasty.

1045 B.C.
Zhou dynasty begins
800-year rule in China.

c. A.D. 220
Buddhism begins to
grow in popularity
after the collapse of
the Han dynasty.

Asian
Civilizations

How long after the Olmec arose did the Zhou dynasty begin in China?

1325
The Aztec found Tenochtitlán and build a great civilization.
(clay vessel of Aztec maize goddess)

1450
The Inca build Machu Picchu in the Andes Mountains.

1200
More than 20,000 people live in the Mississippian city of Cahokia.

1519
Spanish conquistadors arrive in the Aztec Empire.

1300

1600

1000

1209
The Mongols, led by Genghis Khan, invade northern China.

1405
Zheng He begins the first of seven voyages from China, exploring Asia and Africa.

c. 1041
The Chinese use movable type to print books cheaply and easily.

1644
The Manchus overthrow the Ming and found the Qing dynasty.

Early North American Civilizations, c. 1400

- Arctic & Subarctic
- California
- Eastern Woodlands
- Great Basin
- Great Plains
- Northwest Coast
- Plateau area
- Southwest
- Southeast

Early Mesoamerican Civilizations

- Olmec, c. 900 B.C.
- Zapotec, c. 500 B.C.
- Maya, c. A.D. 900
- Aztec, c. A.D. 1519

Early South American Civilizations

- Moche, c. A.D. 700
- Nazca, c. A.D. 600
- Wari, c. A.D. 1000
- Sican, c. A.D. 1400
- Inca, c. A.D. 1532

AMERICAN and ASIAN CIVILIZATIONS
900 B.C.–A.D. 1532

The first civilizations in the Americas arose in Mesoamerica. From the Olmec to the Aztec, these civilizations spanned thousands of years and left their imprint on the region and the world. Early South American civilizations developed in the Andes Mountains around the time of the Maya. They adapted to the challenges of their rugged, dry environment and built great centers of power. Hundreds of different civilizations populated North America. Their civilizations did not develop in the same way as those in other parts of the Americas, but they were just as sophisticated.

Between 960 and 1200, the Song dynasty, with its many inventions and booming economy, made China the world's most advanced society of the time. In the 1200s, China was conquered by the Mongols, who would establish the largest land empire in history.

What Mesoamerican civilization thrived during the time of the Song dynasty?

Asian Civilizations

Mongol homeland, 1200

Song Dynasty (China), 1100

Grand Canal

Great Wall

Karakorum

MONGOL HOMELAND

G O B I

Sea of Japan

Huang He (Yellow R.)

Huang He (Yellow R.)

Yangtze R.

Mekong R.

Kaifeng

Yellow Sea

Yangzhou

Chang Jiang (Yangtze R.)

Chang Jiang (Yangtze R.)

East China Sea

SONG DYNASTY (CHINA)

Hangzhou

Guangzhou

Hainan

PACIFIC

OCEAN

South China Sea

Philippines

800 miles

800 kilometers

600

600

400

400

200

200

0

0

Borneo

12

MESOAMERICA

1200 B.C. – A.D. 1521

SECTION 1   THE OLMEC AND THE ZAPOTEC

SS.6.G.1.4; SS.6.G.1.6; SS.6.G.1.7; SS.6.G.2.1; SS.6.G.2.3; SS.6.G.2.6; SS.6.G.3.1; SS.6.G.3.2;
SS.6.G.5.1; SS.6.W.2.10; LAFS.68.RH.1.3; LAFS.68.RH.2.4; LAFS.68.RH.2.5; LAFS.68.RH.3.7

KEY VOCABULARY		NAMES & PLACES
cacao	slash-and-burn	Mesoamerica
highland	agriculture	Monte Albán
lowland	terrace	Olmec
maize		Yucatán Peninsula
mother culture		Zapotec

SECTION 2   THE MAYA

SS.6.G.1.4; SS.6.G.1.7; SS.6.G.2.1; SS.6.W.1.3; SS.6.W.1.4; SS.6.W.1.5; SS.6.W.2.10;
LAFS.68.RH.1.1; LAFS.68.RH.1.2; LAFS.68.RH.1.3; LAFS.68.RH.2.4; LAFS.68.RH.2.5;
LAFS.68.RH.2.6; LAFS.68.RH.3.7; LAFS.68.WHST.1.2; LAFS.68.WHST.3.9

KEY VOCABULARY	NAMES & PLACES
codex	El Mirador
creation story	Maya
glyph	*Popol Vuh*

SECTION 3   THE AZTEC

SS.6.G.1.4; SS.6.G.1.5; SS.6.G.1.7; SS.6.G.2.4; SS.6.W.1.4; LAFS.68.RH.2.5; LAFS.68.RH.3.7

KEY VOCABULARY		NAMES & PLACES
chinampa	noble	Hernán Cortés
communal	serf	Moctezuma II
conquistador		Templo Mayor
		Tenochtitlán
		Teotihuacán

READING STRATEGY

IDENTIFY MAIN IDEAS AND DETAILS
When you identify key topics in a text, you need to support them with details from the text. As you read the chapter, use diagrams like this one to identify details about each Mesoamerican civilization.

Main-Idea Diagram

Main Idea: Olmec Civilization
Detail:
Detail:
Detail:
Detail:
Detail:

The Temple of the Great Jaguar at Tikal, Guatemala, served as a tomb for a Maya ruler. Its steep staircase is divided into nine levels and may represent the nine levels of the underworld in Maya religious belief.

The Geography of Mesoamerica

You walk among the ruins, gazing at the remains of temple complexes, carved stone sculptures, and towering pyramids. Are you visiting a city that thrived during the time of ancient Egypt? No. You're in the middle of a jungle in a region of North America known as Mesoamerica.

MAIN IDEA

Geographic factors greatly influenced the development of civilizations in Mesoamerica.

HIGHLANDS AND LOWLANDS

Thousands of years ago, advanced civilizations arose in **Mesoamerica**, which stretches from southern Mexico into part of Central America. Like the ancient civilizations of Mesopotamia, Egypt, India, and China, Mesoamerica's civilizations thrived largely as a result of climate and fertile river valleys.

Mesoamerica's landscape is divided into two main geographic areas: **highlands**, or land high above the sea, and **lowlands**, or land that is low and level. The highlands lie between the mountains of the Sierra Madre, a mountain system in Mexico, and consist of fairly flat and fertile land. This land was good for agriculture, but it also posed some challenges for its early residents. They were rocked from time to time by volcanic eruptions and powerful earthquakes. The lowlands are less active. They lie along the coast of the Gulf of Mexico. They are also found in the jungles of the **Yucatán** (you-kuh-TAN) **Peninsula**, which is located between the Gulf of Mexico and the Caribbean Sea.

If you hiked from the lowlands to the highlands, you would experience a wide variety of climates, from tropical rain forests to very cold, dry zones in the higher mountains. In general, the climate in the highlands is cooler and drier than that in the lowlands, where it can rain more than 100 inches a year. The lowlands are also crisscrossed by many rivers. Some of these rivers flood during heavy seasonal rains and wash fertile silt onto their floodplains.

AGRICULTURE

Early Mesoamerican farmers learned what crops would grow well in the different climates of the highlands and lowlands. In the drier highland areas, the main crops included **maize** (also known as corn), squash, and beans. Farmers in the lowlands grew these three crops as well as palm, avocado, and **cacao** (kuh-COW) trees. Cacao beans were used to make chocolate. Sometimes the beans were even used as money.

Mesoamerica's farmers developed different agricultural practices in the region's varied landscapes. In drier areas, farmers redirected the course of streams to irrigate their fields. In the dense lowland jungles, farmers cleared fields through a technique known as **slash-and-burn agriculture**, shown on the opposite page. Slash-and-burn agriculture can result in soil erosion and eventually harm an ecosystem. However, Maya farmers avoided this problem by allowing their fields time to regrow vegetation. These agricultural techniques helped ancient cultures produce food surpluses and allowed people to do jobs other than farming. As a result, civilizations began to arise in Mesoamerica more than 3,000 years ago—first the Olmec and later the Zapotec.

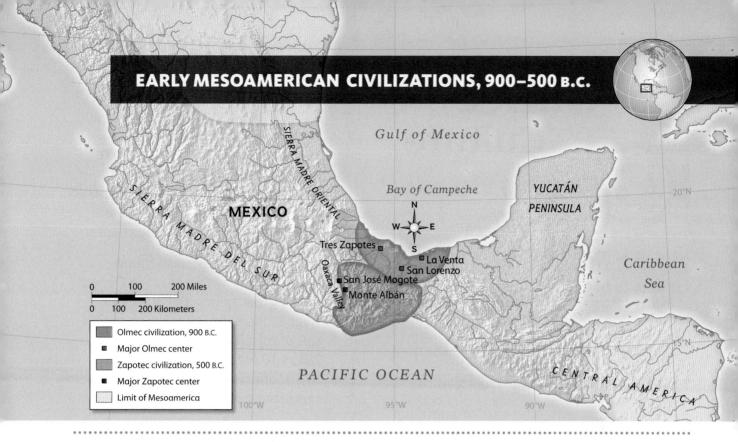

EARLY MESOAMERICAN CIVILIZATIONS, 900–500 B.C.

Gulf of Mexico

SIERRA MADRE ORIENTAL

MEXICO

SIERRA MADRE DEL SUR

Bay of Campeche

YUCATÁN PENINSULA

20°N

Tres Zapotes

La Venta
San Lorenzo

Oaxaca Valley
San José Mogote
Monte Albán

Caribbean Sea

PACIFIC OCEAN

CENTRAL AMERICA

15°N

100°W   95°W   90°W

0   100   200 Miles
0   100   200 Kilometers

- � Olmec civilization, 900 B.C.
- ■ Major Olmec center
- Zapotec civilization, 500 B.C.
- ■ Major Zapotec center
- Limit of Mesoamerica

SLASH-AND-BURN AGRICULTURE

1 Slash
Wooded areas and jungles are too thick to plant crops. Farmers slash, or cut down, trees.

2 Burn
Fallen trees and leaves are burned to clear the land. Ash produced by the fires is used as fertilizer.

3 Fertilize and Plant
Cleared land is fertilized with ash. Farmers plant crops such as maize and squash.

4 Migrate
Farmers move on to new locations after soil on cleared land becomes less productive.

REVIEW & ASSESS

1. **READING CHECK** What geographic factors influenced the development of civilizations in Mesoamerica?

2. **INTERPRET MAPS** Why do you think the Olmec and Zapotec civilizations developed along coastal areas?

3. **COMPARE AND CONTRAST** How did agricultural techniques differ in Mesoamerica's highlands and lowlands?

Olmec Culture

After a long search, the foreman has finally found the right rock. It's huge and heavy. He directs his men to begin their work. Their task: to haul the rock 50 miles through the jungle to the city where an artist will carve it into a sculpture. Their challenge: to move the rock without using a wheeled cart or animals. Welcome to the world of the Olmec.

MAIN IDEA

The Olmec civilization that arose in Mesoamerica was one of the region's earliest civilizations and influenced later cultures.

JAGUAR GOD

The Olmec worshipped many gods, but one of the most important was the jaguar god. When Olmec priests visited the spirit world, the priests believed they transformed into powerful jaguars.

OLMEC CITIES

The **Olmec** (AHL-mehk) culture began along Mexico's Gulf Coast around 1200 B.C. The development of this culture led to the birth of Mesoamerica's first civilization.

Like the ancient civilizations of Mesopotamia, Egypt, India, and China, the Olmec emerged on the floodplains of rivers. Heavy rains caused these rivers to flood and deposit fertile silt on their plains. The rich soil allowed farmers to grow abundant crops. In time, the culture's economy expanded and cities, including San Lorenzo, La Venta, and Tres Zapotes, began to develop. (See the map in Lesson 1.1.)

Olmec cities contained pyramids and temples built on earthen mounds. The Olmec also built courts where athletes played a game that was a sort of combination of modern soccer and basketball. You will learn more about this game later in the chapter.

Archaeologists have also found extraordinary works of art in Olmec cities. Chief among these are the huge stone heads the Olmec carved out of rock. The heads stand as tall as 10 feet and can weigh up to 20 tons. They are believed to represent different Olmec rulers.

DAILY LIFE AND LEGACY

Workers, including those who hauled the rocks for the stone sculptures, and farmers made up most of Olmec society. They were at the bottom of the civilization's class structure. Rulers were at the top, followed by priests, merchants, and artists. The farmers and workers lived in simple houses made of wood or mud. The upper classes lived in more elaborate stone structures and wore fine clothes and precious jewelry.

Archaeologists are not sure why, but around 400 B.C., the Olmec civilization disappeared. However, elements of the civilization's legacy can be seen in later civilizations. The Olmec had established an extensive trade network. In addition to the exchange of goods, the trade routes carried Olmec culture throughout Mesoamerica. As new civilizations arose, their people were influenced by Olmec art and religious practices. As a result, many archaeologists consider the Olmec to be the **mother culture** of Mesoamerica.

Critical Viewing The rock this head was carved out of may have been rolled onto a log raft and floated downriver. Why might Olmec laborers have chosen to use this method to move the head?

REVIEW & ASSESS

1. **READING CHECK** What geographic features played a key role in the development of Olmec civilization?

2. **INTERPRET VISUALS** What does the stone head suggest about the power and authority of Olmec rulers?

3. **DRAW CONCLUSIONS** What conclusions can you draw about daily life for most of the Olmec people?

Critical Viewing This mural by Mexican artist Diego Rivera shows Zapotec artists at work. What details in the mural convey class differences in the society?

1.3 The Zapotec and Monte Albán

 As the Olmec declined, the Zapotec people were developing an advanced society to the southwest. Although their culture reflected Olmec influence, the Zapotec developed their own distinct and powerful civilization. They became a leading player in Mesoamerica.

MAIN IDEA

The Zapotec established a civilization and controlled the Oaxaca Valley for more than 1,000 years.

PEOPLE OF THE VALLEY

The **Zapotec** people would build one of the first major cities in Mesoamerica, but their beginnings were humble. They developed their society in the Oaxaca (wuh-HAH-kah) Valley, a large, open area where three smaller valleys meet. (See the map in Lesson 1.1.) This fertile area, with its river, mild climate, and abundant rainfall, proved excellent for growing crops, especially maize.

For centuries, the Zapotec lived in farming villages located throughout the Oaxaca Valley. Then, around 1300 B.C., a settlement called San José Mogote (san ho-ZAY moh-GOH-tay) emerged as the Zapotec center of power. Leaders built temples there and had artists decorate them with huge sculptures. In time, nearly half of the Zapotec people lived in San José Mogote.

URBAN CENTER

Around 500 B.C., the center of power shifted when the Zapotec built a city known now as **Monte Albán** (MAHN-tay ahl-BAHN) high atop a mountain. The site overlooked the Oaxaca Valley. Its location helped the Zapotec defend themselves against their enemies. Monte Albán must have been a spectacular sight. The city's rulers flattened the top of the mountain and built great plazas on it filled with pyramids, palaces, and even an astronomical observatory.

Monte Albán became the center of the Zapotec civilization. There, the Zapotec built magnificent tombs in which they buried the bodies of wealthy people wearing their gold jewelry. The Zapotec believed the deceased would carry the jewelry into the afterlife. Artificial **terraces**, or stepped platforms built into the mountainside, provided additional area for building and agriculture.

Around A.D. 750, Monte Albán's power began to weaken. By 900, the city had disappeared. Economic difficulties may have caused the decline, but no one knows for sure. Like the fall of the Olmec, the decline of the Zapotec civilization remains a mystery.

REVIEW & ASSESS

1. **READING CHECK** What geographic features of the Oaxaca Valley encouraged the development of the Zapotec civilization?

2. **MAKE INFERENCES** How do you think the location of Monte Albán helped the Zapotec defend themselves from their enemies?

3. **DETERMINE WORD MEANINGS** What does *deceased* mean in the phrase, "the deceased would carry the jewelry into the afterlife"?

2.1

Maya
Social Structure

Can people be made of corn? According to Maya tradition, they can. But it took the Maya gods a while to figure out how to do it. At first, they made people out of things like mud and wood, but these creatures couldn't speak. Finally, the gods mixed their blood with maize flour. The result? Walking, talking human beings. No wonder the early Maya called themselves "the people of the maize."

MAIN IDEA

Maya society was structured according to a class system, and religion shaped daily life.

CLASS SYSTEM

The **Maya** emerged around the same time as the Zapotec. Their culture began to develop to the east of the Zapotec in areas of present-day southern Mexico and Central America around 1500 B.C. These areas included lowlands in the north, highlands in the south, the forests of the Yucatán Peninsula, and the tropical jungles of Mexico and Guatemala.

Like Olmec farmers, Maya farmers developed successful agricultural practices. They produced surpluses of crops, including beans, chili peppers, cacao beans, and, of course, maize, which the Maya considered sacred. These surpluses allowed some people to become priests, merchants, and craftspeople and some villages to gain great wealth. Wealthier villages with religious ceremonial centers arose around 500 B.C. In time, these villages grew into cities.

The development of Maya cities produced a class system with four main classes. At the top was the king, who performed religious ceremonies and was believed to have descended from the gods. Next came priests and warriors. The priests decided when farmers could plant and when people could marry. They also conducted important religious rituals and ceremonies. Warriors were well respected and well trained.

Merchants and craftspeople followed these upper classes. Craftspeople made articles out of pottery and designed buildings and temples. The merchants sold and traded goods—often with buyers in other Maya cities. Finally, farmers—who made up the majority of the population—and slaves were at the bottom of the heap. Most of the slaves were prisoners of war. They were given the worst jobs and were often killed when their masters died.

DAILY LIFE

Class determined where people lived and how they dressed. People who belonged to the upper classes lived in stone buildings and wore colorfully decorated clothes and jewelry. Farmers wore plain clothes and lived in mud huts.

While the wealthy enjoyed a comfortable lifestyle, farmers worked hard in the heat to grow their crops. On hillsides they carved out terraces on which to grow their maize, cacao beans, and chili peppers. In drier areas they dug channels that carried river water to their fields. In addition to doing their own work, sometimes farmers had to tend the king's fields and build monuments and temples in his cities.

MAYA MAIZE GOD

The maize god was one of the most important Maya gods. The god often appeared as a handsome young man with hair made of maize silk. The god represented the cycle of life (birth, death, rebirth) as well as the cycle of maize (planting, harvesting, replanting).

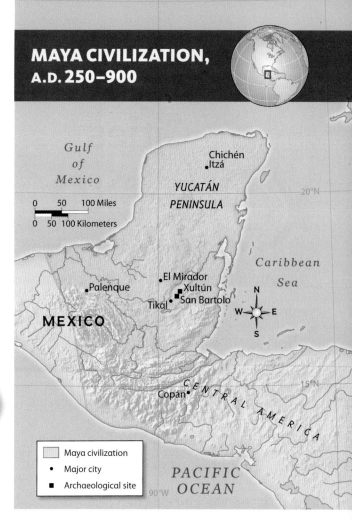

MAYA CIVILIZATION, A.D. 250–900

Gulf of Mexico

Chichén Itzá

YUCATÁN PENINSULA

20°N

0   50   100 Miles
0   50   100 Kilometers

Caribbean Sea

El Mirador
Palenque   Xultún
Tikal   San Bartolo

N W E S

MEXICO

15°N

Copán   CENTRAL AMERICA

☐ Maya civilization
• Major city
■ Archaeological site

PACIFIC OCEAN

90°W

Eventually the Maya learned how to track seasonal changes. This knowledge helped them predict the best time to plant and harvest their crops. You will learn more about how the Maya measured time later in the chapter.

Above all, however, the farmers looked to their gods to control the weather and increase their harvests. Religion was central to everyone's lives, and the Maya worshipped many gods, including the gods of fire, sun, war, rain, and maize. (You can learn more about the importance of the maize god in the feature above.) All of these gods were thought to influence every aspect of the people's lives—in both good and bad ways.

To please the gods, the Maya made frequent offerings of food, animals, plants, and precious objects. As you have already learned, the Maya believed that the gods had given their blood to create people. In return, the Maya sometimes offered their own blood or made human sacrifices to honor the gods. Just as maize nourished people, the Maya believed that blood nourished the gods. Rather than sacrifice one of their own, however, the Maya often sacrificed a member of the lowest class in their society: a slave.

REVIEW & ASSESS

1. **READING CHECK** What were the four main classes of early Maya society?

2. **INTERPRET MAPS** On what geographic landform were many of the major Maya cities located?

3. **COMPARE AND CONTRAST** How did the daily life of farmers differ from that of people belonging to the wealthier classes?

Maya Cities

In the 1800s, explorers battled mosquitoes, illness, and thick jungle growth in their search for the ruined remains of the Maya civilization. Their efforts paid off. When they came upon the half-buried monuments in the ancient Maya city of Copán, one of the explorers—John Lloyd Stephens—was so fascinated by what he saw that he purchased the site on the spot.

MAIN IDEA

The Maya built sophisticated cities that contained impressive structures and artwork.

CLASSIC PERIOD

Many of the great Maya cities lay hidden beneath the jungle growth for centuries. One of the earliest of these cities was **El Mirador**, which has been called the "cradle of the Maya civilization." (See the map in Lesson 2.1.) The city flourished from about 300 B.C. to A.D. 150 and was home to as many as 200,000 people. Most Maya cities, however, developed during the Classic Period, which lasted between A.D. 250 and 900. These cities included Copán (koh-PAHN), Tikal (tee-KAHL), Chichén Itzá (chee-CHEHN ee-TSAH), and Palenque (pah-LEHNG-keh). Although

each was an independent city-state ruled by a king, trade linked the city-states. Merchants from the cities exchanged goods such as salt and jade jewelry and often paid for them with cacao beans.

Most Maya cities followed a similar layout. A large plaza in the center of the city served as both a public gathering place and market. Each city also contained a palace for the king, administrative buildings, temples, and stepped pyramids. The pyramids rose hundreds of feet in the air and were lined with steep staircases. Many of the pyramids featured platforms at the top. Priests conducted ceremonies on the platforms so that the entire population could witness them.

The Maya built temples on the top of some of the pyramids. A huge ball court was constructed at the foot of at least one of these pyramids in each city to allow athletes to play the sacred Mesoamerican ball game. The Maya played this game, which began with the Olmec, to honor their gods. The illustration on the opposite page shows Maya athletes in action on the court.

CULTURE AND ART

Like the ball game, many other aspects of Maya culture and art were linked to religion. Artists made sculptures that honored and brought to life the various Maya gods. They also carved stone slabs called stelae to honor their kings. Artists carved a king's likeness on the slab and recorded his actions on it as well—actually setting his story in stone.

All of these stories were probably passed down orally from generation to generation. This oral tradition continued long after the great Maya civilization had come to an end. It may have been weakened by war, food shortages, or overcrowding. For whatever reason, by A.D. 900, the Maya had abandoned many of their cities. When Spanish conquerors arrived in the 1500s, only weakened city-states had been left behind—a shadow of their former glory.

MESOAMERICAN BALL GAME

The game the Maya and other Mesoamerican peoples played on a court like this one was much more than a game. It was often a matter of life and death. The captain of the losing Maya team probably climbed the temple steps to be sacrificed to the gods.

Players weren't allowed to touch the ball with their hands. They could only bounce the ball off their knees, hips, and elbows.

The solid ball was hard enough to break bones, so the players wore some heavy padding.

The goal of the game was to launch the ball through a stone ring. Since this wasn't easy, a game could go on for days.

REVIEW & ASSESS

1. **READING CHECK** What was the layout of most of the great Maya cities?

2. **INTEGRATE VISUALS** Based on the illustration and what you have learned about the Mesoamerican ball game, what qualities were probably necessary to play the game?

3. **MAKE INFERENCES** How do you think the Maya reacted as they witnessed a religious ceremony performed at the top of a towering pyramid?

Uncovering
Maya Murals

Sometimes you're just lucky. Ask **William Saturno**. He had spent three days—instead of the three hours he thought the trip would take—trudging through the jungles of Guatemala looking for carved Maya monuments. During the search, he and his team had been lost and near death. When a pyramid appeared in the midst of the dense undergrowth, Saturno ducked inside it to escape the terrible heat. He turned around to find a stunning Maya mural of the maize god looking right back at him. Now Saturno's lucky find is rewriting Maya history.

^
William Saturno is dedicated to preserving and interpreting the remains of the early Maya. In this photo, he removes debris from a mural he uncovered at the Maya site of Xultún.

MAIN IDEA

Archaeologist William Saturno's discoveries have challenged ideas about the early Maya and provided insight into their way of thinking.

A LUCKY FIND

National Geographic Explorer William Saturno has spent his life studying the Maya and searching out the civilization's secrets. His greatest discovery occurred in 2001, when he found the mural at a site he later named San Bartolo.

Portrait of a scholar in the San Bartolo mural

Saturno spent several years excavating the wall painting, which represented the Maya creation story in graceful and sophisticated detail. However, when Saturno dated the work of art, he found that it had been created around 100 B.C.—more than 300 years before the Maya Classic Period had even begun. As Saturno says, "Clearly Maya painting had achieved glory centuries before the great works of the Classic Maya."

The far end of the mural revealed another surprise—the portrait of a king. "Some scholars thought that at this early stage in Maya history, the Preclassic, city-states had not yet evolved into full-fledged monarchies, with all the trappings seen later," explains Saturno. "But here was a king, named and titled, receiving his crown. In short, this one chamber upended much of what we thought we knew about the early Maya."

ROOM OF WONDER

About ten years later and just five miles from San Bartolo, Saturno got lucky again. He was digging under a mound in the Maya site of Xultún (shool-tuhn) when a student assistant claimed he'd found traces of paint on a wall. "I was curious," Saturno says. "So I excavated to the back wall, and I saw a beautiful portrait of a king. There he was in Technicolor, with blue feathers."

After more painstaking work, Saturno uncovered an entire room with paintings of other figures and a wall covered with columns of numbers. He thinks that mathematicians had been using the walls like a whiteboard to see whether the movements of the moon and planets matched the dates they had calculated. The mural and numbers dated back to about A.D. 750, around the time Xultún was beginning to decline.

According to Saturno, the Maya knew the collapse of their city had begun. Still, as he says, "They wanted to tie events in their king's life to larger cosmic cycles. They wanted to show that the king would be okay and that nothing would change. We keep looking for endings. It's an entirely different mind-set. I would never have identified this nondescript [uninteresting] mound as special. But this discovery implies that special things are everywhere."

REVIEW & ASSESS

1. **READING CHECK** Why are William Saturno's discoveries so remarkable?

2. **DRAW CONCLUSIONS** Saturno emphasizes the luck he's had in his explorations, but what other qualities must he possess to carry out his work?

3. **ANALYZE LANGUAGE USE** Saturno says that the Maya had "an entirely different mind-set." What do you think he is suggesting about how the Maya viewed the world?

2.4

Legacy of the Maya

In 2012, the prediction went viral: On December 21, the world was going to end. The prediction was based on the Maya calendar, which some people claimed would end on that day. But the date simply marked the completion of a 5,125-year cycle. The Maya had calculated that a new cycle would begin on the 22nd.

MAIN IDEA

Important advances in mathematics, astronomy, and writing allowed the Maya to create their calendar.

MAYA NUMBERS

The Maya represented numbers using only three symbols: a shell for zero, a dot for one, and a bar for five. A few of the numbers are shown above. Try using the symbols to create some simple subtraction problems.

MATH AND ASTRONOMY

The Maya were superb mathematicians. Like the people of ancient India, they developed the concept of zero. They also developed a sophisticated number system using positions to show place value and to calculate sums up to the hundreds of millions.

Such calculations were used to record astronomical observations as well. Maya astronomers observed the sun, moon, planets, and stars and were able to predict their movements with great accuracy—all without the aid of any instruments. Instead,

they studied the sky from temples and observatories. Astronomers used their observations to calculate the best times for planting and harvesting crops and for religious celebrations.

These astronomical observations and calculations were used to develop an elaborate 365-day calendar that was nearly as accurate as our own. Remember the room that William Saturno uncovered in Xultún? The mathematical calculations on its walls were probably used to work out dates in the calendar.

WRITING SYSTEM AND BOOKS

Archaeologists gained a better understanding of the Maya people's scientific achievements and culture

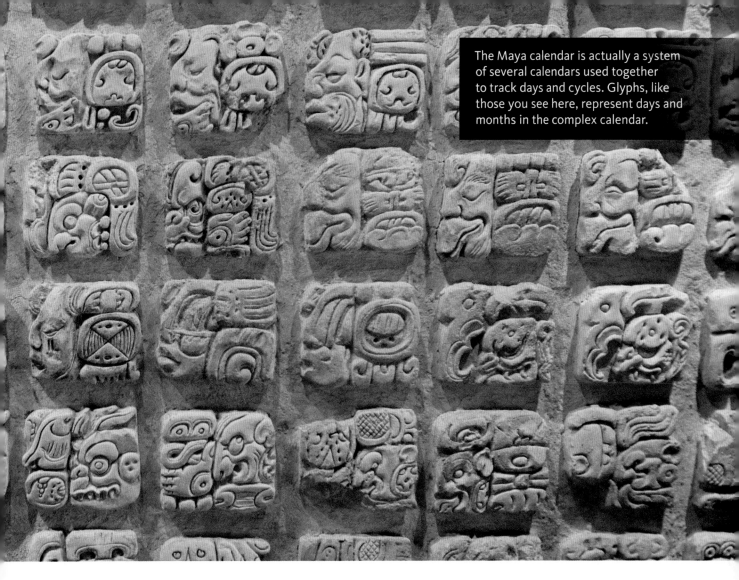

The Maya calendar is actually a system of several calendars used together to track days and cycles. Glyphs, like those you see here, represent days and months in the complex calendar.

once they began to crack the code of their writing system. The Maya used symbolic pictures called **glyphs** (glihfs) to represent words, syllables, and sounds that could be combined into complex sentences.

The Maya carved glyphs into their monuments, stelae, and tombs. Maya writers, called scribes, also used them to record their people's history in a folded book made of tree-bark paper called a **codex**. The Spanish conquerors destroyed most of the codices in the 1500s. However,

after the Spanish arrived, the Maya wrote other books in which they recorded Maya history and culture. The most famous of these books is called the *Popol Vuh*, which recounts the Maya creation story.

As you've already learned, the Maya civilization had greatly declined by A.D. 900. However, Maya people today still keep their culture alive. Many of them speak the Maya languages and tell their ancestors' stories. They are a living legacy of the Maya civilization.

REVIEW & ASSESS

1. **READING CHECK** What important mathematical ideas did the Maya develop?

2. **IDENTIFY MAIN IDEAS AND DETAILS** According to the text, why did Maya astronomers study the sun, moon, planets, and stars?

3. **ANALYZE CAUSE AND EFFECT** What breakthrough helped archaeologists gain a better understanding of Maya history and culture?

Every culture has a creation story: an account that explains how the world began and how people came to exist. Creation stories are often considered sacred and are usually passed down by oral tradition before they are written down. Like the excerpts you are about to read, creation stories often begin by describing how a god or gods brought order to the universe.

This page from a Maya codex contains painted figures, numbers, and astronomical tables.

from the *Popol Vuh*, translated by Dennis Tedlock

Spanish conquerors destroyed much of Maya culture in the 1500s. To preserve their sacred stories for future generations, Maya scribes wrote them down in the *Popol Vuh*. In this passage, two Maya gods form Earth from a world that contains only the sea.

CONSTRUCTED RESPONSE According to this passage, how did the Maya gods form Earth?

> "Let it be this way, think about it: this water should be removed, emptied out for the formation of the earth's own plate and platform . . ." they said. And then the earth arose because of them, it was simply their word that brought it forth. For the forming of the earth they said, "Earth." It arose suddenly, just like a cloud, like a mist, now forming, unfolding.

DOCUMENT TWO

Primary Source: Sacred Text

from the Book of Genesis

Genesis is the first book of the Hebrew Bible, a collection of sacred Jewish texts. It is also the first book of the Old Testament in the Christian Bible. Followers of both religions believe in a single God. In this passage from Genesis, which means "the origin, or beginning," God creates night and day.

CONSTRUCTED RESPONSE In this excerpt, what was the world like before God brought light to the earth?

> When God began to create heaven and earth—the earth being unformed and void [empty]. . .—God said, "Let there be light"; and there was light. God saw that the light was good, and God separated the light from the darkness. God called the light Day, and the darkness He called Night. And there was evening and there was morning, a first day.

DOCUMENT THREE

Primary Source: Myth

from *Pan Gu Creates Heaven and Earth*, translated by Jan and Yvonne Walls

Pan Gu is a god in an ancient Chinese creation story that has been told and passed down for more than 2,000 years. According to the story, Pan Gu created heaven and earth. In this passage, Pan Gu bursts from a disordered universe that is shaped like an egg.

CONSTRUCTED RESPONSE In this myth, what elements formed heaven and what elements formed the earth?

> Pan Gu, an enormous giant, was being nurtured [cared for] in the dark chaos of that egg. . . . Then one day he woke and stretched himself, shattering the egg-shaped chaos into pieces. The pure lighter elements gradually rose up to become heaven and the impure heavier parts slowly sank down to form the earth.

SYNTHESIZE & WRITE

1. **REVIEW** Review what you have learned about the creation stories and religious beliefs of early civilizations.

2. **RECALL** On your own paper, write down the main idea expressed in each document.

3. **CONSTRUCT** Write a topic sentence that answers this question: What are some common characteristics of creation stories?

4. **WRITE** Using evidence from the documents, write a paragraph to support your answer in Step 3.

Tenochtitlán:
An Aztec City

Thriving cities, massive temples, fierce warriors, strong armies. These are only a few characteristics of the Mesoamerican civilization called the Aztec. The Aztec were nomads from a mysterious land known as Aztlán—the origin of the name *Aztec*. Starting from only an island city in a swamp, the Aztec founded a powerful empire.

MAIN IDEA

The Aztec developed a mighty empire in central Mexico.

SETTLING IN CENTRAL MEXICO

Around A.D. 1300, Aztec nomads migrated into the Valley of Mexico, a thriving and populous region in the central part of Mexico. When the Aztec arrived, the valley was dominated by rival city-states. The Aztec settled there, adopted local ways, and served powerful kings as farmers and warriors. Then, in 1325, the Aztec founded their own city, **Tenochtitlán** (tay-nohch-teet-LAHN). Today Tenochtitlán is known as Mexico City.

The Aztec built Tenochtitlán on two islands in a swamp in the western part of Lake Texcoco. To feed their growing population, they constructed artificial fields called **chinampas** (chee-NAHM-pahz). Chinampa farmers piled layers of mud and vegetation to raise the soil level above the water. Then they planted trees alongside to mark off planting areas. Finally, they covered the areas with more soil, dug up from the bottom of the lake. Farmers planted maize, beans, and different kinds of squash on the chinampas. These remarkable fields produced many crops, and the Aztec population thrived.

One advantage of living in a lake was that canoes made transport easy, so trade flourished. In time, the Aztec established a twin city called Tlatelolco (tlaht-el-OHL-koh) in the northern part of Lake Texcoco. Tlatelolco had a huge marketplace. Every day, thousands of people crossed the lake in canoes and visited Tlatelolco's bustling market.

BUILDING AN EMPIRE

The Aztec developed into skilled warriors. At first they fought for other kings, but then they overthrew their masters and began fighting for themselves. They allied with two other cities, Texcoco and Tlacopan (tlaht-oh-PAHN), to form a powerful Triple Alliance that the Aztec would control by 1428. Well-trained Aztec armies marched steadily through Mesoamerica, forcing hundreds of small city-states to surrender to Aztec rule.

Aztec bureaucrats, or government officials, kept order and enforced the supply of tribute to Tenochtitlán. Tribute, or a payment for protection, was made in food, raw materials, goods, or labor. Over time, the Aztec grew rich and commanded a vast empire stretching from the Pacific Ocean to the Gulf of Mexico. Around six million people lived in the Aztec Empire at its height.

By 1519, about 200,000 people lived in Tenochtitlán, which had become the largest city in Mesoamerica. It was one of the most magnificent cities of its time. The pyramid of **Templo Mayor**, or the Great Temple, towered above the city. Dozens more temples and many beautiful palaces surrounded Templo Mayor. Four roads

THE AZTEC EMPIRE, 1503–1519

CHICHIMEC

HUASTEC

Oxitipán

METZTITLÁN

Zimapán

TARASCANS

El Tajín

Cazones R.

Tula *Valley of*

Lake
Cuitzeo

Lake
Texcoco

Mexico
TEXCOCO

Totlantzinco

Xocotla

Jalapa

Zempoala (Cempoala)

TLACOPÁN

Tlatelolco

TLAXCALA

Ixhuacán

Veracruz

TENOCHTITLÁN

Tlaxcala

Huexotzinco

Cholula

Orizaba

Gulf of Mexico

Balsas R.

Nexapa R.

Atoyac R.

Oztoma
Teloloapán

Mixtlán

Xicallanco

TEOTITLÁN

San Juan R.

Zacatula

Tetela

YOPITZINCO

Achiotla

Yanhuitlán
Zozollán

Grijalva R.

Usumacinta R.

Nochcoc

Acapulco
Ayutla

Grande R.

Monte
Albán

Milta

Grijalva R.

MIXTEC

Tehuantepec

Tototepec

Legend:
- Aztec Empire, 1503
- Moctezuma II's conquests
- **TEXCOCO** Triple Alliance
- Moctezuma II's offensives
- Route of Hernán Cortés, 1519

20°N

N W E S

PACIFIC OCEAN

XOCONOCHO
Huitztlán

Mazatlán

0   50   100 Miles
0 50 100 Kilometers

divided the city into quarters, each with distinct neighborhoods, leaders, farmland, markets, and temples. The island city was crisscrossed by canals and connected to the mainland by long causeways, or roads across the water. When Spanish explorers arrived in 1519, they marveled at Tenochtitlán's size and splendor.

PRECIOUS MASKS

This turquoise mask depicts the Aztec god Quetzalcoatl (kweht-sahl-koh-AHT-uhl), believed to be part bird, part snake. Aztec sculptors carved masks from volcanic rock and precious stones such as turquoise and jade.

REVIEW & ASSESS

1. **READING CHECK** What features made Tenochtitlán an awe-inspiring city?

2. **ANALYZE CAUSE AND EFFECT** How were the Aztec able to develop productive farm fields in the swampy lands around Tenochtitlán?

3. **INTERPRET MAPS** Use the map scale to determine how far the Aztec Empire extended from north to south in 1503.

Aztec Culture

In any big city, you will find people from all walks of life. The same was true for the great Aztec city of Tenochtitlán, where you might have met nobles, priests, soldiers, artisans, and slaves.

MAIN IDEA

Class structure and religious practices defined Aztec society.

CLASS STRUCTURE

The emperor was the most powerful person in Aztec society. He controlled all political and spiritual matters and served for life. Below him were the **nobles**. Nobles were the smallest but most powerful class. They inherited their status and held the top jobs as generals, priests, tax collectors, and judges. Some nobles even governed cities for the Aztec emperor.

Most Aztec belonged to the commoner class, which included merchants and artisans, farmers, and soldiers. Merchants and artisans were highly respected, and they lived in their own communities. Merchants traveled throughout the empire, trading goods. Artisans made and sold jewelry, ornaments, and clothes. Many Aztec were farmers who worked **communal**, or shared, land and had to give part of their harvest as a tax to the empire. Others were professional soldiers, some of whom gained wealth and privilege by distinguishing themselves on the battlefield.

Serfs and slaves occupied the lowest level of Aztec society. **Serfs** lived and worked on the private land of nobles. In addition to providing agricultural labor, serfs performed household tasks for landowners. Slaves were considered property and were usually prisoners of war. Slave status was not based on race, and children of slaves were born free.

AZTEC GODS

Religion was central to all classes of Aztec society. The Aztec were polytheistic. They worshipped as many as 1,000 gods and built hundreds of magnificent temples and religious structures in Tenochtitlán to honor those gods. Though people's individual homes were simply constructed, they almost always featured a shrine to the gods.

The Aztec followed many traditions that they shared with other Mesoamerican cultures. They believed they could please the gods with offerings and sacrifices. Some of these sacrifices were human.

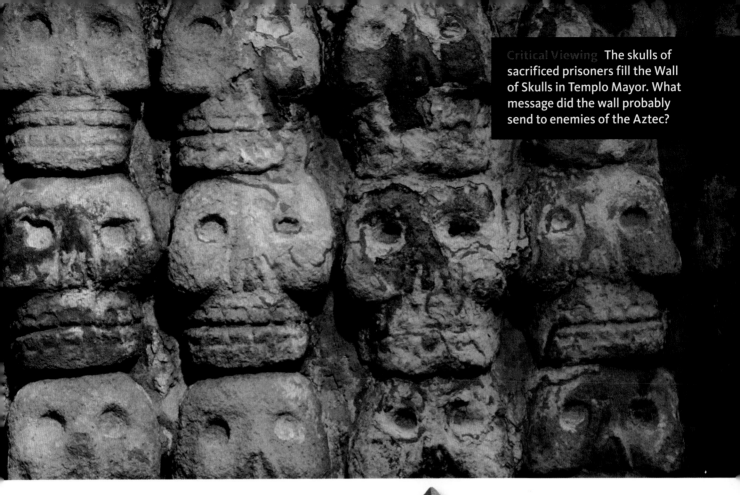

Critical Viewing The skulls of sacrificed prisoners fill the Wall of Skulls in Templo Mayor. What message did the wall probably send to enemies of the Aztec?

Most of the human sacrifices were prisoners of war. The Aztec considered themselves "the People of the Sun" and believed they nourished the sun with these sacrifices.

An important site for the Aztec was **Teotihuacán** (tay-oh-TEE-wah-khan), or "the place where the gods were born." Teotihuacán was located north of Tenochtitlán and built by an earlier people. This once-great city became sacred to the Aztec, who came later. The Aztec built onto the ruins they found there and revived worship at its many temples, including two vast pyramids dedicated to the sun and moon.

WARRIOR SCHOOLS

This Aztec sculpture depicts an Eagle Warrior. Much of the success of the Aztec Empire was due to its fierce warriors. All boys attended military training schools from a young age. At these schools, boys learned to fight in formation and use weapons.

REVIEW & ASSESS

1. **READING CHECK** Which social class in Aztec society had the most members?

2. **DRAW CONCLUSIONS** Why do you think merchants and artisans were highly respected members of the commoner class?

3. **COMPARE AND CONTRAST** In what ways were some Aztec religious practices similar to practices of other Mesoamerican cultures?

Aztec Defeat and Legacy

The Aztec founded thriving cities, developed rich cultures, and built a strong military. However, their empire lasted barely 200 years. It came to a sudden end when the Spanish arrived in the early 1500s.

MAIN IDEA

European invaders defeated the Aztec, who left behind a rich cultural legacy.

END OF THE EMPIRE

Aztec power depended on the empire's huge military, which conquered many people and then demanded tribute from defeated populations. Constant wars and regular rebellions, though, kept the Aztec Empire unstable. The unrest in the empire was made worse by the rule of **Moctezuma II** (mok-tih-ZOO-muh), who became emperor in 1502. He considered himself an equal to the gods. He also kept pressuring defeated peoples for more and more tribute to pay for his luxurious, wasteful lifestyle. Until 1519, he crushed one rebellion after another. Then the unthinkable happened.

That year **conquistadors** arrived from Europe. Conquistadors were Spanish conquerors who were greedy for gold and other riches from South and Central America. Although few in number, they were able to overpower the Aztec with superior weapons, such as guns and cannons, as well as horses. Aztec warriors armed with spear throwers and swords were no match for Spanish conquistadors. Spanish invaders also brought diseases such as smallpox that would eventually kill millions of native people throughout the Americas.

Believing the Spanish would liberate them from the tyranny of their rulers, some Aztec joined the conquistadors' leader, **Hernán Cortés**, in his battles. (See Cortés' route on the map in Lesson 3.1.) The conquest ended with a great siege of Tenochtitlán in 1521. The Spanish surrounded and systematically destroyed the great city. They rebuilt over the ruins, and that city became present-day Mexico City, Mexico.

AZTEC LEGACY

Because of their ruthless approach to conquest, the Spanish destroyed Aztec buildings, art, and literature. However, some Aztec ruins, artifacts, and writings survived the conquest. Archaeologists and historians study them to learn more about the Aztec.

The Aztec built huge monuments, especially temples for their gods. Aztec temples were positioned to line up with the sun and stars. The Aztec were skilled astronomers who could predict the movements of the sun, moon, planets, and stars. Like the Maya, the Aztec believed these movements directly affected their lives. They also used complex calendars to chart and record events, such as important religious rituals and the planting and harvesting of crops.

Aztec writing also gives archaeologists and historians a picture of their society. The Aztec recorded historical events, and they wrote inspiring speeches, poetry, legends, and prayers to their gods. Glyphs represented words that were painted into codices. Although few of the original codices survived, many were copied and translated by Spanish scholars. These colorful books offer a detailed and artistic picture of Aztec society.

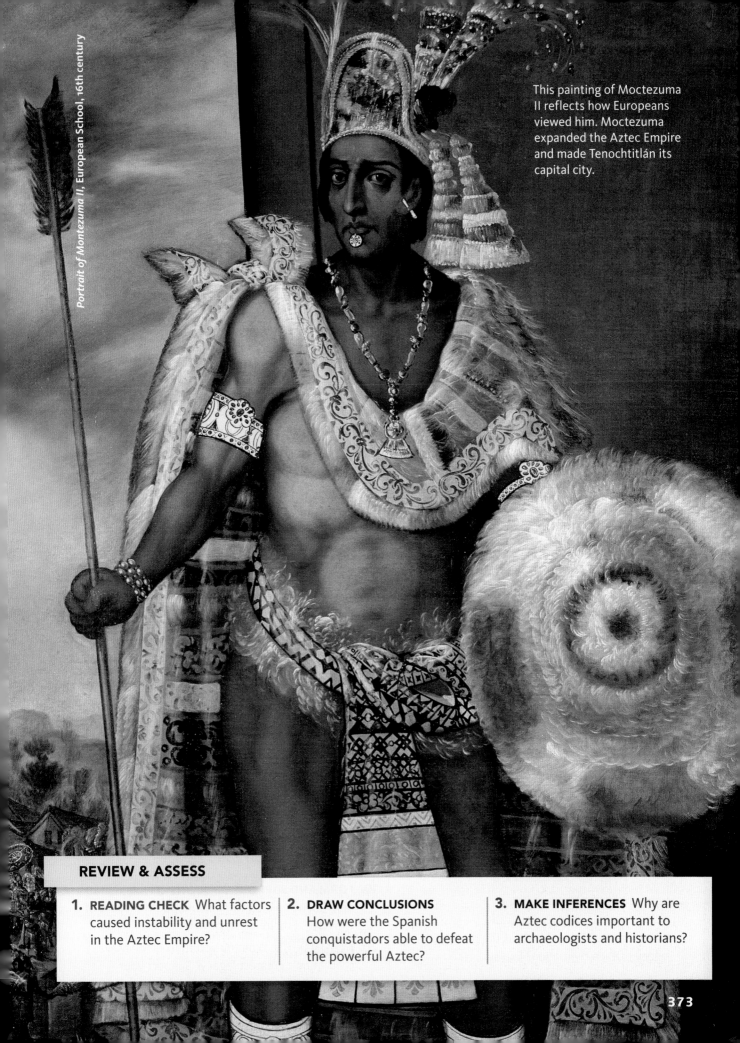

Portrait of Montezuma II, European School, 16th century

This painting of Moctezuma II reflects how Europeans viewed him. Moctezuma expanded the Aztec Empire and made Tenochtitlán its capital city.

REVIEW & ASSESS

1. **READING CHECK** What factors caused instability and unrest in the Aztec Empire?

2. **DRAW CONCLUSIONS** How were the Spanish conquistadors able to defeat the powerful Aztec?

3. **MAKE INFERENCES** Why are Aztec codices important to archaeologists and historians?

VOCABULARY

On your paper, match the vocabulary word in the first column with its definition in the second column.

WORD	DEFINITION
1. terrace	a. a civilization that greatly influences other civilizations
2. mother culture	b. a stepped platform built into a mountainside
3. codex	c. a symbolic picture used to represent a word, syllable, or sound
4. glyph	d. a Spanish conqueror who overpowered the Aztec
5. chinampa	e. a folded book made from tree-bark paper
6. conquistador	f. an artificial field

READING STRATEGY

7. **IDENTIFY MAIN IDEAS AND DETAILS** If you haven't already, complete your diagram for each Mesoamerican civilization. Then answer the question.

Main-Idea Diagram

Main Idea: Olmec Civilization

Detail: Developed along a floodplain

Detail:

Detail:

Detail:

Detail:

What feature do you think was the greatest legacy of each civilization? Explain.

MAIN IDEAS

Answer the following questions. Support your answers with evidence from the chapter.

8. Why is the Olmec civilization considered to be Mesoamerica's mother culture? **LESSON 1.2**

9. Why is Monte Albán considered one of the first major cities in Mesoamerica? **LESSON 1.3**

10. Which groups of people made up the largest social class in the Maya civilization? **LESSON 2.1**

11. During what time period did most of the great Maya cities develop? **LESSON 2.2**

12. What did the Maya use to develop their elaborate 365-day calendar? **LESSON 2.4**

13. Describe the class structure of society in the Aztec Empire. **LESSON 3.2**

14. How did instability contribute to the end of the Aztec Empire? **LESSON 3.3**

CRITICAL THINKING

Answer the following questions. Support your answers with evidence from the chapter.

15. **ANALYZE CAUSE AND EFFECT** What happened as a result of the Olmec's trade network?

16. **DRAW CONCLUSIONS** What conclusions can you draw about cacao beans based on the fact that the Maya often used them to pay for goods?

17. **COMPARE AND CONTRAST** What are some of the similarities surrounding the decline of the Zapotec and Maya civilizations?

18. **COMPARE AND CONTRAST** How is the development of Maya civilization similar to and different from that of the early river valley civilizations of Mesopotamia, Egypt, India, and China?

19. **FORM AND SUPPORT OPINIONS** In your opinion, was Moctezuma II an effective leader of the Aztec Empire? Why or why not?

20. **YOU DECIDE** What do you think is the Maya civilization's greatest legacy? Support your opinion with evidence from the chapter.

INTERPRET VISUALS

Study the images of a Maya pyramid and an ancient Egyptian pyramid. Then answer the questions that follow.

Maya pyramid

Egyptian pyramid

21. How are the pyramids alike, and how do they differ?

22. What challenges did both pyramid styles present to the people who built them?

ANALYZE SOURCES

This jade mask was placed over the face of King Pacal, a great ruler of Palenque, when he died. The mask shows the king's own features.

23. The Maya highly valued jade and often used it to represent the maize god. Study the mask. Why do you think the Maya associated jade with the maize god?

WRITE ABOUT HISTORY

24. EXPLANATORY How were the Olmec, Zapotec, Maya, and Aztec civilizations similar? How did they differ? Write a paragraph comparing and contrasting the civilizations for tourists who are planning to visit some of the civilizations' archaeological and historic sites. Consider such aspects of the civilizations as religion, art, architecture, daily life, social structure, and the sciences.

TIPS

- Take notes from the lessons about the Olmec, Zapotec, Maya, and Aztec civilizations. You might jot down your comparisons in a chart using the aspects listed above as headings in the chart.

- State your main idea clearly at the beginning of the paragraph. Support your main idea with relevant facts, details, and examples.

- Use vocabulary from the chapter in your paragraph.

- Provide a concluding statement about the similarities and differences among the Olmec, Zapotec, Maya, and Aztec civilizations.

SECTION 1 **PERUVIAN CULTURES**

SS.6.E.1.2; SS.6.E.2.1; SS.6.G.1.4; SS.6.G.1.5; SS.6.G.1.7; SS.6.G.2.1; SS.6.G.2.4; SS.6.G.5.1; SS.6.G.5.2; SS.6.W.2.10; LAFS.68.RH.1.2; LAFS.68.RH.2.5; LAFS.68.RH.3.7

KEY VOCABULARY

geoglyph   terrace
quarry   farming
quinoa

NAMES & PLACES

Atahualpa   Nasca
Francisco   Pachacuti
 Pizarro   Sicán
Machu   Wari
 Picchu
Moche

SECTION 2 **NORTH AMERICAN CULTURES**

SS.6.E.2.1; SS.6.G.2.1; SS.6.G.2.2; SS.6.G.2.4; SS.6.G.3.2; SS.6.G.4.1; SS.6.G.5.1; LAFS.68.RH.2.5; LAFS.68.RH.3.7

KEY VOCABULARY

adobe
confederation
kiva
mound builder
potlatch
shaman
totem pole
wigwam

NAMES & PLACES

Algonquin
Cahokia
Cherokee
Creek
Great Plains
Iroquois
Mesa Verde
Pueblo Bonito

READING STRATEGY

ORGANIZE IDEAS: SEQUENCE EVENTS In this chapter, the sequence of historical events is divided by geographic location. First you'll learn about events in South America, and then you'll learn about events in North America. Use a time line like this one to place all the events in the chapter in order so you can see what was happening in both locations at a specific time.

PERUVIAN CULTURES

NORTH AMERICAN CULTURES

The fine-line art that wraps around this Moche stirrup pot shows warriors running to the top of a mountain and back down again.

Pre-Inca Cultures

Humans have treasured gold for centuries. When people mold gold into necklaces and bracelets, the beautiful finish outshines all other metals. In the northern and western parts of South America, four cultures developed extraordinary skill in working with gold and other precious metals. These cultures lived in present-day Peru, which the Inca would dominate by A.D. 1400.

MAIN IDEA

Beginning around A.D. 100, four complex cultures thrived in Peru.

THE MOCHE AND THE NASCA

As in the four river valleys of Mesopotamia, Egypt, India, and China, unique and complex civilizations emerged in the Andes Mountains of South America. On the northwest coast of South America, the **Moche** (MOH-chay) culture flourished between A.D. 100 and 700. Their land was harsh—a desert that was squeezed between the Andes Mountains to the east and the Pacific Ocean to the west. Like other pre-Inca cultures and the Inca who came later, the Moche showed great creativity in adapting to this challenging environment. To irrigate the farm fields in their arid region, they built complex irrigation systems. They also developed a strong military and ruled nearly 400 miles of the Peruvian coast.

The Moche were also artists, as shown by the artifacts archaeologists have discovered. Moche artisans created beautiful ceramics, or bowls, statues, and other objects made from clay and then hardened under intense heat. The artisans decorated the vessels with detailed line drawings of animals and people, such as rulers and warriors. Just as impressive was Moche artists' work with gold, which they shaped into exquisite jewelry.

In south Peru, the **Nasca** culture thrived from about A.D. 200 to 600. It was one of the earliest complex cultures in South America. Nasca artisans were as highly skilled as those of the Moche culture, creating magnificent jewelry from gold, silver, and copper. They also formed ceramic pottery and decorated it with intricate designs from nature, such as birds and fish.

The Nasca left behind a mystery, though. They created enormous **geoglyphs**, or large geometric designs and shapes drawn on the ground. The shapes often took the form of animals or birds. The dry climate where the Nasca lived helped preserve the geoglyphs. However, archaeologists are still not absolutely certain what the purpose of the designs was.

THE WARI AND THE SICÁN

The greatest military power among pre-Inca cultures was the **Wari** culture, which dominated the high desert of central Peru from about A.D. 500 to 1000. With their strong military, the Wari overran the Nasca and other people and established the first empire in the region of the Andes Mountains. The Wari were also skilled farmers. To cultivate crops on the rugged terrain of the Andes, they created terraced fields, or flat fields dug out of the sides of hills.

In a recent find at El Castillo, a Wari city along the Peruvian coast, archaeologists

This giant spider geoglyph created by the Nasca still exists in the Nasca Desert of Peru. What clues in the photo reveal the geoglyph's size?

unearthed a royal tomb that revealed a great deal about Wari culture. The tomb contained the remains of four queens or princesses and other members of the nobility. Buried with the remains were golden earrings, copper axes, and silver bowls. The discovery indicates that not only did the Wari worship their ancestors but they were, like other pre-Inca cultures, gifted artisans with precious metals.

While the Wari ruled central Peru, the **Sicán** culture flourished in the mountains of northern Peru from about A.D. 800 to 1400. The Sicán created delicate jewelry from gold, silver, and copper. They perfected a technique of pounding gold into extremely thin sheets. Archaeologists found two strips of metal that were only 0.006 inches thick—almost as thin as a piece of paper.

The Sicán showed great respect for the creatures of the natural world. Artists created a mural that was decorated with waves, fish, the sun, and the moon. When the Sicán buried the dead, they prepared them for the next world by burying them with gold, copper, and shells to carry water. This practice revealed their belief in an afterlife.

REVIEW & ASSESS

1. **READING CHECK** Where did the pre-Inca cultures live?

2. **SUMMARIZE** What have discoveries of tombs revealed about pre-Inca cultures?

3. **COMPARE AND CONTRAST** In what ways were these four pre-Inca cultures similar?

1.2 PERUVIAN GOLD

Pre-Inca Peruvians were master artisans who created fine jewelry and adornments with precious metals such as gold, silver, and copper. They also made pottery that was both beautiful and functional. The artifacts shown here were part of a special exhibition by the National Geographic Museum in partnership with the government of Peru. What common themes do you notice in the artifacts featured below?

Nasca Bee
Pre-Inca artisans decorated clothing with gold appliqués like this bee, which mimics a Nasca geoglyph of the same shape.
(Banco Central de Reserva Del Perú, Lima, Perú)

El Tocado
The Sicán crafted this headdress with movable parts and radiating feathers. Note the enormous gold ear spools on each side.
(Y. Yoshii/PAS)

Diadem
This Moche headpiece, called a diadem, symbolizes power and authority. It is 12 inches wide, made from a single sheet of copper, and coated with gold.
(Museo Larco Lima-Perú)

Nose Ornament
Gold and silver are fused together in this bi-metal piece. Cats, which represented strength and fierceness, made frequent appearances in pre-Inca art.
(Banco Central de Reserva Del Perú, Lima, Perú)

Moche Mask
When copper is exposed to the elements, it changes in color from a shiny red-brown to a pale green, as it did on this funeral mask.
(Museo Larco Lima-Perú)

1.3

Inca Society and Government

The civilization known as the Inca began as a small mountain culture that lived high in the Andes Mountains. In only a few hundred years, the Inca had conquered large parts of South America and governed a huge empire.

MAIN IDEA

The Inca created and controlled a large empire in South America.

ORGANIZED EMPIRE

About the same time as the Aztec emerged in Mesoamerica, the Inca began their conquest of western South America. In A.D. 1200, the Inca were one of many small states occupying the Urubamba Valley, high in the Andes Mountains of present-day Peru. By 1440, the Inca ruled the region.

Under the leadership of the emperor **Pachacuti** (pah-chah-KOO-tee), the empire expanded rapidly. The name *Pachacuti* means "he who changed the world"—and this ambitious man certainly did that. Pachacuti conquered and ruled widespread areas through a powerful military and a strong central government. He also transformed the Inca capital, Cusco (KOO-skoh), into an impressive stone city of 100,000 people.

The Inca Empire stretched 2,600 miles from present-day Colombia to Argentina and included about 12 million people who spoke more than 20 languages. Despite its size, the Inca Empire was well organized. The hierarchy of Inca society helped rulers maintain tight control of the large empire.

At the top, the emperor had absolute power. Below him, four regional officers, or prefects, oversaw provincial governors, district officers, and local chiefs. The Inca economy was a command economy, which meant that the government determined what was produced and set prices and incomes. Inca subjects were considered a resource and whole populations were relocated if the state needed their labor elsewhere. Commoners worked on state-run farms and served in the army or on government building projects.

In order to manage the many details involved in running an empire, the Inca also had a large bureaucracy, or system of state officials. In fact, for every 10,000 Inca, there were 1,331 administrators. These administrators kept detailed records about all parts of the empire, from population to farm animals to trade.

MOUNTAIN LIFE

Like other early civilizations, the Inca Empire was built on agriculture. However, farming was difficult in the steep Andes. The Inca made up for the lack of flat farmland with a type of farming called **terrace farming**. They cut flat steps, or terraces, on the sides of mountains and then built stone walls to keep the terraces in place. Terrace farming produced potatoes, maize, and **quinoa** (KEEN-wah), a high-protein grain native to the Andes. In addition to farming, the Inca raised llamas and alpacas for meat and wool and for transporting goods and people across the mountains.

Inca religious rituals centered on the need to guarantee a good harvest. The Inca worshipped their emperor as the son of Inti, the Sun God, and believed the emperor helped humans communicate with the gods.

VENEZUELA

COLOMBIA

*Quito
ECUADOR

AMAZON

Amazon R.

BASIN

BRAZIL

•Cajamarca

PERU

SOUTH

10°S

Urubamba
Valley

AMERICA

Lima⊛

Ayacucho•

•Cusco

BOLIVIA

Maukallacta•

Lake
Titicaca

•La Paz

•Sucre

20°S

Tropic of Capricorn

CHILE

PACIFIC

OCEAN

ARGENTINA

30°S

Santiago⊛

ANDES

N
W · E
S

BUILDING AN EMPIRE

1400
The Inca lived in Urubamba Valley. They began their expansion around 1400.

1470
By 1470, the Inca had reached the coast and extended their power northward into present-day Ecuador.

1500
By 1500, the Inca had expanded as far south as present-day Chile. They united their vast empire using more than 14,000 miles of roads.

1532
The Inca reached the eastern slope of the Andes in the 1530s. By 1532, the Inca Empire included more than 300,000 square miles and 12 million people.

—— Inca roads
—— Present-day boundaries
⊛ Present-day capital city
• Other city

```
0        250        500 Miles
0    250    500 Kilometers
```

REVIEW & ASSESS

1. **READING CHECK** How did Pachacuti unify and control the Inca Empire?

2. **ANALYZE CAUSE AND EFFECT** What method did the Inca use to farm in the Andes Mountains?

3. **INTERPRET MAPS** What physical features limited eastward and westward expansion of the Inca Empire?

Inca Architecture

What do you do when you are faced with a problem? The Inca met the challenge of mountain living head-on by building some of the most remarkable structures you can imagine.

MAIN IDEA

The Inca used their building skills to adapt to their mountain surroundings.

MOUNTAIN BUILDERS

The Inca were gifted engineers and builders. They built an extensive network of roads that helped them transport people and goods. Bridges built of wood, stone, and even thick rope helped them cross rivers and deep canyons. Inca stone architecture was even more impressive. The Inca constructed walls, buildings, and entire cities out of enormous blocks of stone. They **quarried**, or extracted, the stone in the Andes without the use of iron or steel tools.

Machu Picchu (MAH-choo PEE-choo) sits high on a mountain in Peru. Built around 1450, this stone city survived Spanish conquest in the 1530s because the Spanish never found it. Machu Picchu included religious temples, royal residences, and homes for workers as well as waterworks and terraces for farming. Aqueducts made of stone carried water to the city—just as aqueducts carried water in ancient Rome.

Critical Viewing Machu Picchu sits 8,000 feet above sea level. Why might the Inca have built this city in such a remote place?

REVIEW & ASSESS

1. **READING CHECK** Why are the Inca known as highly skilled engineers and builders?

2. **MAKE INFERENCES** How did bridges and roads help the Inca manage their empire?

3. **DRAW CONCLUSIONS** Why did Machu Picchu survive the Spanish conquest?

1532

This 20th-century mural in Cajamarca, Peru, depicts the 1532 meeting of the Spanish conquistador **Francisco Pizarro** and **Atahualpa** (ah-tah-WAHL-pah), the Inca emperor. Pizarro had just 180 men with him, but they had the advantage of horses and superior metal weapons. Shortly after the meeting, Pizarro's men captured Atahualpa and killed his unarmed attendants. The Spanish ruled the Inca through Atahualpa for almost a year—and then executed him. By 1539, the Spanish had conquered the territory of the fallen empire. What details in the mural convey Atahualpa's power as emperor?

Madd

2.1 Northwest Coast Cultures

 North America is made up of vastly different landscapes, including rain forests, mountains, deserts, prairies, and woodlands. The hundreds of Native American cultures varied as much as North America's geography. In the Pacific Northwest, the forests and seacoast provided a hospitable environment for several cultures.

MAIN IDEA

Native American cultures of the Pacific Northwest thrived in a land of plentiful rainfall and dense forests.

NORTHWEST COAST TRIBES

Thirty distinct cultures lived in the Pacific Northwest region. This narrow strip of mountains and woodland followed the coast from present-day northern California to Alaska. It was one of the most densely populated parts of North America. The lakes, rivers, and ocean provided fish, shellfish, and whales. The forests offered plentiful plants and game. With such abundance, populations grew, and complex societies developed without any need to farm.

Along the southern coast of what is now the state of Alaska, the Tlingit (KLING–kit) people developed a thriving culture that was closely tied to the Pacific Ocean and the many rivers. In fact, the word *Tlingit* means "the People of the Tides." The Tlingit were superb sailors and fishers, and their most important food was salmon.

Because the Pacific Northwest receives ample rainfall, forests carpet the region. As a result, wood was central to Tlingit culture. Around A.D. 500, the Tlingit developed tools for splitting and carving wood. With those tools, they built permanent homes and crafted everyday necessities such as plates and utensils. They also used tools and fire to carve dugout canoes from logs. The canoes, some as long as 60 feet, were seaworthy and could sail for miles into the Pacific Ocean, allowing the Tlingit to hunt for whales.

Two other important Northwest Coast tribes—the Kwakiutl (kwahk-ee-YOU-tuhl) and the Haida (HIGH-dah)—lived south of the Tlingit. Both lived by hunting and gathering but settled in permanent villages. They used the forests' cedar trees to build large family houses. Like the Tlingit, they also built excellent seagoing canoes.

These tribes also traded extensively with neighboring cultures. Over time, trade allowed some families to become wealthy, and social classes developed. Social rank became hereditary and certain families had great influence based on their wealth and ancestry. These families demonstrated and shared wealth through gift-giving ceremonies called **potlatches**, in which they gave away gifts and food to their communities.

TOTEM POLES AND MASKS

The skillful wood carvings of Northwest Coast cultures reveal their relationship to the natural world and their belief in a spirit world. One example of their artistry is found in the intricate masks they carved and painted and then wore at ceremonies. A **shaman**, or a person who is believed to be able to help others communicate with the spirit world, guided the mask carving and led the ceremonies.

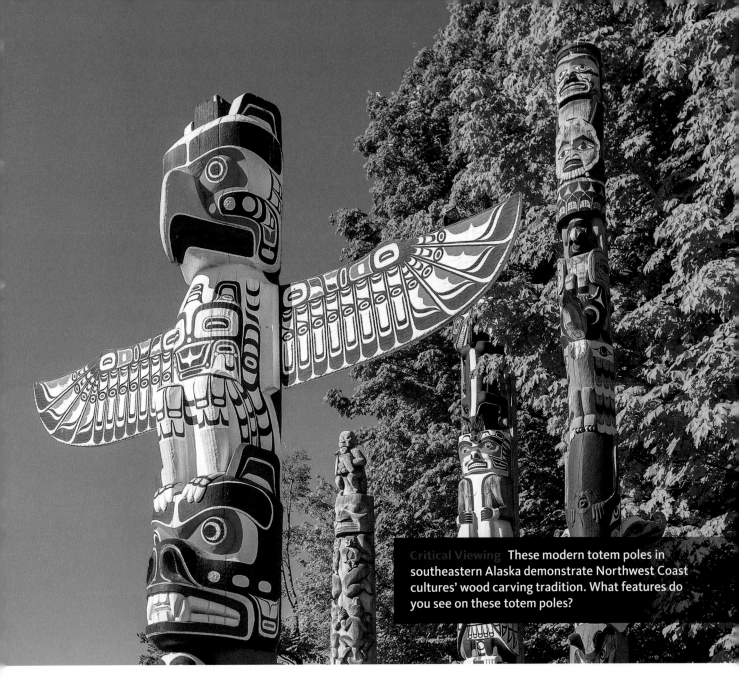

Critical Viewing These modern totem poles in southeastern Alaska demonstrate Northwest Coast cultures' wood carving tradition. What features do you see on these totem poles?

Totem poles are another example of Northwest Coast wood carving artistry. Totem poles are tall, elaborately carved and painted tree trunks that honor a revered being or guardian associated with a family. Totem pole carvings included colorful representations of animals of the region, such as bears, whales, and eagles. Other carvings included human figures, such as chiefs or ancestors and supernatural spirits. Totem poles told stories and legends as well as family and tribal histories. Wood rots easily in the region's damp climate, so few totem poles have survived more than 100 years. However, totem pole carving remains a Northwest Coast tradition today.

REVIEW & ASSESS

1. **READING CHECK** In what ways did the geography of the Pacific Northwest influence the culture of the Tlingit people?

2. **DRAW CONCLUSIONS** What was the function of the potlatch in the Kwakiutl and Haida societies?

3. **EVALUATE** What role did totem poles and masks play in the cultures of Pacific Northwest tribes?

The Ancient Pueblo

The American Southwest could not be more different from the Pacific Northwest. The Southwest is a harsh land of mountains and deserts, where temperatures can reach a scorching 120 degrees Fahrenheit. In this forbidding land, the ancient Pueblo developed a vibrant culture that was closely tied to the land.

MAIN IDEA

The ancient Pueblo adapted to their environment by farming the arid land and building complex structures.

DESERT DWELLERS

As early as 1000 B.C., the ancient Pueblo began to farm in various parts of the arid Southwest desert. They inhabited the Four Corners region, where present-day Arizona, Colorado, Utah, and New Mexico come together. Little by little, they began to build villages with permanent structures on high plateaus or in canyons. Some structures were dwellings made of stone and **adobe**, a clay used for building. Farm fields surrounded the villages. Using a technique called dry farming, the ancient Pueblo grew crops on the dry land, using very little water. The three staples of their diet were corn, beans, and squash.

The ancient Pueblo were skilled artisans who created baskets and pottery that were beautiful yet practical. They wove lightweight baskets and threaded together different materials to create brightly colored patterns. They used the baskets to carry objects and even to cook by placing hot stones in the baskets to heat the food. As they settled in permanent villages, the ancient Pueblo began to create extraordinary pottery, which was heavier but more permanent than baskets. They molded clay into jars, bowls, and pitchers.

PUEBLO BONITO AND MESA VERDE

One of the most impressive ancient Pueblo settlements was **Pueblo Bonito**, located in Chaco Canyon in northern New Mexico. It housed as many as 1,200 people and had more than 600 rooms and 30 kivas. **Kivas** were circular-shaped chambers in the ground used for ceremonies and social gatherings. Construction on Pueblo Bonito began around A.D. 850 and continued for another 200 years. The ancient Pueblo abandoned Pueblo Bonito sometime during the 1200s. Archaeologists are not sure why, but they believe that a severe drought may have forced people to migrate to other parts of the Southwest.

By 1200, the ancient Pueblo who lived in present-day southwestern Colorado built a series of dwellings into the sides of cliffs at **Mesa Verde**. They did this to defend themselves from invaders and provide protection from rain and the intense sun. Using advanced architectural skills, they built structures with several stories underneath cliff overhangs. The largest dwelling, Cliff Palace, featured more than 200 rooms and housed about 250 people. In all, the dwellings at Mesa Verde sheltered as many as 5,000 people.

The ancient Pueblo abandoned Mesa Verde by about 1300. In the late 1800s, two local ranchers discovered the ruins there, and in 1906, it became a U.S. National Park.

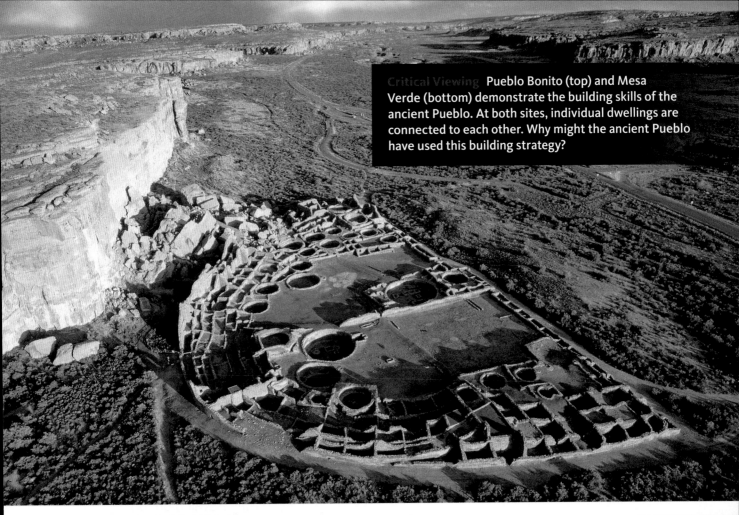

Pueblo Bonito (top) and Mesa Verde (bottom) demonstrate the building skills of the ancient Pueblo. At both sites, individual dwellings are connected to each other. Why might the ancient Pueblo have used this building strategy?

REVIEW & ASSESS

1. **READING CHECK** How did the ancient Pueblo survive on the harsh land?

2. **DRAW CONCLUSIONS** How did the ancient Pueblo show their skill as artisans?

3. **COMPARE AND CONTRAST** In what ways were Pueblo Bonito and Mesa Verde similar? How were they different?

2.3 Peoples of the Great Plains

Hunting might be a sport for some people in the 21st century, but for early Great Plains cultures, hunting was key to survival. Farming on dry grasslands did not always produce good harvests. So Great Plains tribes relied on other natural resources, such as the buffalo.

MAIN IDEA

Native Americans on the Great Plains depended on the land and especially on the buffalo for survival.

PLAINS DWELLERS

The **Great Plains** is a wide area of flat, windswept grasslands that stretches north from present-day Texas into Canada. Early tribes settled along the region's major rivers and established permanent villages.

To survive the bitter winters, some tribes built earth lodges out of soil and grasses to house whole families. They relied mostly on hunting, gathering, and fishing because farming was not easy on the dry grasslands of the plains.

The different tribes of the Great Plains each had their own spiritual beliefs and traditions. Many homes had altars for burning incense during prayers. Farming communities practiced religious ceremonies centered on a good harvest. Hunting tribes had ceremonies focused on visions and spirit beings that might enhance their hunting abilities. For example, young men participated in vision quests where they put their bodies through strenuous ordeals. The goal was to achieve a trancelike state and have a vision—often of an animal. Shamans would interpret their visions.

Another important spiritual practice for Great Plains people was the Sun Dance. The Sun Dance was an annual ceremony of drumming, dancing, singing, and praying for harmony among people and giving thanks for prosperity.

BUFFALO HUNTERS

One animal was central to the livelihood and the culture of the Great Plains people— the buffalo. Large herds grazed on the wide-open grasslands, and nomadic tribes followed their migrations. These tribes had no horses, so they traveled on foot.

Because buffalo are more aggressive than cattle, they will attack if provoked. Hunting buffalo was a risky business. Hunters agitated the herd into a thunderous stampede. Then they drove the buffalo over cliffs or into corrals where they killed the animals with arrows or spears.

Buffalo were a useful resource. Great Plains people ate buffalo meat raw, roasted, or as smoked jerky. They used buffalo skins for clothes and tents, bones for tools, sinew, or tendons, for bowstrings, boiled hooves for glue, and even buffalo dung for fuel.

In the 1500s, the Spanish introduced horses to North America, and some Great Plains people began to use them to hunt. Horses allowed the tribes to follow buffalo migrations across the plains. As hunting became more efficient, more tribes moved to the plains and became buffalo hunters. White settlers in the 1800s also hunted the buffalo, resulting in its near extinction.

Critical Viewing Before 1500, about 50 million buffalo roamed freely on the plains. By 1889, commercial hunting with horses and guns had reduced buffalo numbers to just 1,000. How might this overhunting have affected tribes on the Great Plains?

REVIEW & ASSESS

1. **READING CHECK** Why were buffalo important to the people of the Great Plains?

2. **ANALYZE CAUSE AND EFFECT** How did the introduction of the horse to North America affect life for tribes on the Great Plains?

3. **COMPARE AND CONTRAST** How were the religious practices of Great Plains tribes similar? How did they differ?

The Mound Builders and Cahokia

The Mississippi River Valley and prairies and woodlands further east supported many different Native American cultures. Some built mounds, others built cities—including one of the largest cities in North America.

MAIN IDEA

Native Americans from the Great Lakes to the Gulf of Mexico developed complex societies, large cities, and organized governments.

MOUND BUILDERS

East of the Mississippi River, woodlands and prairies covered the lands that stretch between the Great Lakes and the Gulf of Mexico. Between 1000 B.C. and A.D. 500, the Adena and then the Hopewell lived in this region. They are known as **mound builders** because they built huge mounds of earth. The mounds served religious and ceremonial purposes. Some mounds, such as the Great Serpent Mound built by the Adena in southern Ohio, formed the shape of animals.

The mound builders relied mostly on hunting and gathering, but they also tamed wild plants and farmed crops such as barley. Maize—called corn today—appeared around A.D. 100, probably brought there by traders. The Adena and Hopewell cultures developed highly organized and complex societies. Living in villages that dotted the region, they hunted, farmed, and traded. The Hopewell culture collapsed by A.D. 500 for reasons that remain unknown.

From 800 to 1700, a different mound building culture—the Mississippians—emerged in the Mississippi River Valley. The Mississippians eventually populated the region from present-day Ohio, Indiana, and Illinois, south to the Gulf of Mexico. Like the Adena and Hopewell, Mississippians built mounds that had sloping sides, steps, and flat tops. However, the Mississippians built their mounds around a central plaza, where they held feasts and ceremonies.

The fertile floodplains of the Mississippi River Valley supported farming. Because of the fertility of their lands, the Mississippians grew ample quantities of maize, beans, and squash. They also hunted, skillfully using bows and arrows. Because of their plentiful food, Mississippian settlements supported large populations. In fact, they were the most populous Native American settlements north of Mexico.

CAHOKIA

The largest and most complex city that the mound builders created was at **Cahokia**, in southwest Illinois. Cahokia contained more than 120 mounds covering 6 square miles and supported more than 30,000 people. A series of stockades surrounded much of the city and a grand plaza provided space for ceremonies and celebrations.

The centerpiece of Cahokia was Monks Mound, which rose 100 feet above the flat prairie and covered 16 acres. This mound contained 814,000 cubic yards of soil—enough to fill 45,000 dump trucks. The Cahokians moved all this earth without the use of dump trucks, though. They used baskets instead.

Building the mounds required a highly organized society. A powerful chief who lived in a palace on top of one of the mounds ruled the city. Archaeologists believe that

CAHOKIA

Cahokia was the largest of the many settlements that appeared along the Mississippi River beginning in A.D. 800. This model shows how Cahokia may have looked hundreds of years ago.

Cahokia Creek

Canteen Creek

Monks Mound

Borrow Pit, where earth was extracted to build the mounds

Grand Plaza

Stockades

when the chief died, the people destroyed the palace, added more earth to the mound, and built a new palace for the next ruler.

Cahokians engaged in widespread trade with other Mississippian cities and towns. Using the Mississippi River and other waterways, they exchanged freshwater pearls, silver, copper, beads, and pottery.

By 1400, Cahokia had been abandoned. Archaeologists are not sure why, but many think this once-mighty city may have been weakened by less abundant crop production, disease, overpopulation, or warfare.

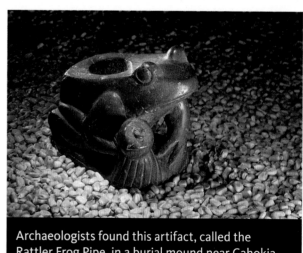

Archaeologists found this artifact, called the Rattler Frog Pipe, in a burial mound near Cahokia. They think it may represent a shaman in an amphibian disguise.

REVIEW & ASSESS

1. **READING CHECK** What purposes did mounds serve in the Adena, Hopewell, and Mississippian cultures?

2. **DRAW CONCLUSIONS** How was agriculture important to the way of life of Mississippian cultures?

3. **ANALYZE VISUALS** Based on the text and illustration of Cahokia, what purpose might the stockades have served?

2.5 Cultures in the East and Southeast

Like cultures in the Pacific Northwest, Native Americans who lived on the opposite side of North America relied on the plentiful wood and game from the forests and woodlands that surrounded them. Over time, they developed sophisticated ways of governing themselves.

MAIN IDEA

Native American cultures in the East and Southeast developed complex political organizations.

THE CHEROKEE AND THE CREEK

The **Cherokee** lived in the forests of the present-day states of Georgia, Tennessee, North Carolina, and South Carolina. They built permanent log cabins using the wood from the forests that surrounded them. The Cherokee hunted deer, elk, and bear, and they also farmed, growing crops such as corn, beans, and squash.

Individual Cherokee villages formed complex alliances with each other and with other cultures. During wartime, some villages were known as "red towns," where the people held war councils and ceremonies. Other villages were considered "white towns," or towns devoted to peace. Spanish explorers arrived in the mid-1500s, and

British colonists moved into the region in the 1700s. The Cherokee traded extensively with both groups, exchanging furs and animal hides for horses, fabrics, and firearms.

The **Creek** lived south and west of the Cherokee, in what are now the states of Alabama, Mississippi, Florida, Georgia, South Carolina, and Tennessee. Like the Cherokee, the Creek formed alliances with different tribes that spoke related languages.

The Creek had great respect for fire. Each settlement had a permanent fire, which the people believed was a symbol of the life-giving powers of the sun. The female head of each household lit a fire from the village's flame and then carried it to her family. With this custom, the Creek developed a strong sense of unity within the community.

An important custom that the Cherokee and the Creek shared was the Green Corn Ceremony. Corn was an important crop for both groups. The Cherokee and Creek held this ceremony when their corn first ripened, in early to mid-summer. Over a period lasting from four to eight days, they feasted, held dances, and repaired buildings. At the height of the ceremony, they relit the sacred fire at the center of the village's plaza.

THE ALGONQUIN AND THE IROQUOIS

The **Algonquin** and **Iroquois** dominated the woodlands of the Northeast, in present-day southern Canada, upper New York, and Pennsylvania. Each culture included different tribes with their own languages and customs. The woodlands provided wood, plants, and animals, but they could not support enough farming to sustain large cities.

Instead, farmers in temporary villages relied on slash-and-burn techniques. Algonquin and Iroquois farmers burnt fields out of the forests and grew crops such as corn, beans, and squash until the soil was exhausted, or depleted of nutrients. Entire villages would then move on and create new fields elsewhere.

This reproduction shows what an Iroquois longhouse may have looked like. Like wigwams, longhouses had domed roofs and were covered with tree bark for protection.

The Algonquin lived in **wigwams**, or domed huts built on a framework of poles and covered with skins or bark. Wigwams could be quickly moved and easily adapted to the changing weather. The Algonquin farmed for much of the year, but in winter moved around because they were hunting game. Chiefs led villages made up of related families. Villages traded and formed loose **confederations**, or groups of allies, to help each other through war or hardship.

In contrast to the Algonquin, the Iroquois developed a more formal political structure. They called themselves the "people of the longhouse." They lived in villages of longhouses, in which as many as 10 families lived. Iroquois tribes fought each other until the 1500s, when they formed the Iroquois League. This agreement formally bound together five tribes—Onondaga, Seneca, Mohawk, Oneida, and Cayuga—in a representative and democratic alliance.

REVIEW & ASSESS

1. **READING CHECK** What was the function of the Green Corn Ceremony in Cherokee and Creek culture?

2. **COMPARE AND CONTRAST** How did the political structures of the Algonquin and Iroquois differ?

3. **MAKE INFERENCES** How might the Iroquois League have helped end fighting among the Iroquois tribes?

VOCABULARY

Use each of the following vocabulary words in a sentence that shows an understanding of the term's meaning.

1. **quinoa**
   The Inca grew quinoa, a high-protein grain native to the Andes Mountains.

2. **wigwam**

3. **totem pole**

4. **terrace farming**

5. **adobe**

6. **confederation**

7. **potlatch**

8. **quarry**

9. **geoglyph**

READING STRATEGY

10. **ORGANIZE IDEAS: SEQUENCE EVENTS**
    If you haven't already, complete your time line to sequence events that occurred in civilizations in South and North America. Then answer the question.

A.D. 100
The Moche civilization began to flourish.

PERUVIAN CULTURES

NORTH AMERICAN CULTURES

A.D. 500
The Tlingit developed tools for splitting and carving wood.

What event affected civilizations in both South and North America in the 1500s?

MAIN IDEAS

Answer the following questions. Support your answers with evidence from the chapter.

11. What have archaeologists learned about pre-Inca cultures from various discoveries in Peru? **LESSON 1.1**

12. Why did the Inca Empire develop rapidly under the leadership of Pachacuti? **LESSON 1.3**

13. What factors helped Machu Picchu survive the Spanish conquest? **LESSON 1.4**

14. On what natural resources did Northwest Coast cultures rely? **LESSON 2.1**

15. How did the beginning of pottery making signal a shift in ancient Pueblo culture? **LESSON 2.2**

16. Why were buffalo important to the people of the Great Plains? **LESSON 2.3**

17. What made it possible for the Mississippi River Valley to support large cities? **LESSON 2.4**

CRITICAL THINKING

Answer the following questions. Support your answers with evidence from the chapter.

18. **EVALUATE** Were the cultures in South and North America successful in adapting to their environments? Explain your answer.

19. **COMPARE AND CONTRAST** In what ways does the development of pre-Inca civilizations compare to the development of different civilizations in the four river valleys of Mesopotamia, Egypt, India, and China?

20. **MAKE INFERENCES** Why was a network of roads important to the success of the Inca Empire?

21. **ANALYZE CAUSE AND EFFECT** How were complex societies in the Pacific Northwest able to develop and grow without farming?

22. **YOU DECIDE** Did the size of the Inca Empire contribute to its fall? Support your opinion with evidence from the chapter.

INTERPRET VISUALS

Study the photograph showing farming terraces built by the Inca. Then answer the questions that follow.

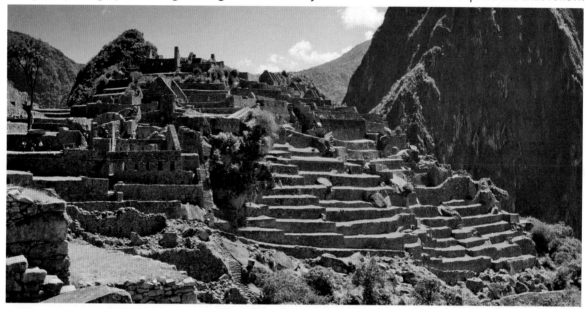

23. Use details in the photo to describe the method of terrace farming the Inca used.

24. Why might Inca farmers have preferred flat surfaces on which to grow crops?

ANALYZE SOURCES

While on an expedition in the Andes in 1911, American explorer Hiram Bingham and his guide discovered a city that had been hidden for nearly 400 years: Machu Picchu. Read the passage and then answer the question.

> We were confronted with an unexpected sight, a great flight of beautifully constructed stone-faced terraces, perhaps a hundred of them, each hundreds of feet long and ten feet high. . . . The flowing lines, the symmetrical arrangement of the [large stones], and the gradual gradation of the [layers], combined to produce a wonderful effect, softer and more pleasing than that of the marble temples of the Old World.
>
> from *Lost City of the Incas*, by Hiram Bingham, 1952

25. What were Bingham's impressions of the architecture at Machu Picchu?

WRITE ABOUT HISTORY

26. INFORMATIVE Suppose you are contributing to a booklet about Native American cultures. Write a paragraph that explores the impact of the Spanish use of guns and horses on either the Inca or the people of the Great Plains.

TIPS

- Take notes from the lessons about the Inca or the Great Plains peoples.
- Begin the paragraph with a clear topic sentence.
- Develop the paragraph with supporting details and examples of the impact of Spanish guns and horses on your chosen group.
- Use vocabulary from the chapter as appropriate.
- Conclude with a sentence about how changes resulting from the introduction of guns and horses affected the Inca or people of the Great Plains.

14 DYNASTIES OF CHINA

581 – 1500

SECTION 1 A GOLDEN AGE OF PROSPERITY

SS.6.E.1.1; SS.6.E.3.1; SS.6.G.1.4; SS.6.G.1.7; SS.6.G.4.4; SS.6.G.6.2; SS.6.W.4.4; SS.6.W.4.6; SS.6.W.4.8; SS.6.W.4.9; LAFS.68.RH.2.5; LAFS.68.RH.3.7

KEY VOCABULARY

commerce reincarnation
movable reunify
 type staple
nirvana
porcelain

NAMES & PLACES

Song Tang
Sui Wendi
Taizong Yangdi

SECTION 2 THE MONGOL EMPIRE

SS.6.E.3.2; SS.6.E.3.4; SS.6.G.1.4; SS.6.G.1.5; SS.6.G.1.7; SS.6.G.2.2; SS.6.W.1.3; SS.6.W.4.9; SS.6.W.4.10; SS.6.W.4.11; LAFS.68.RH.1.1; LAFS.68.RH.2.5; LAFS.68.RH.3.7; LAFS.68.RH.3.9; LAFS.68.WHST.1.2; LAFS.68.WHST.3.9

KEY VOCABULARY

khanate
steppe

NAMES & PLACES

Genghis Khan
Kublai Khan
Marco Polo
Yuan

SECTION 3 THE MING DYNASTY

SS.6.G.1.4; SS.6.W.1.1; SS.6.W.1.4; SS.6.W.1.5; SS.6.W.4.9; SS.6.W.4.10; SS.6.W.4.11; SS.6.W.4.12; LAFS.68.RH.1.2; LAFS.68.RH.1.3; LAFS.68.RH.2.5; LAFS.68.RH.3.7

KEY VOCABULARY

isolationism

NAMES & PLACES

Hongwu Qing
Manchus Yongle
Ming Zheng He

READING STRATEGY

DRAW CONCLUSIONS When you draw conclusions, you support them with evidence from the text. Use a graphic organizer like this one to draw conclusions about the impact of the Tang, Song, and Ming dynasties on Chinese civilization.

Tang, Song, or Ming Dynasty

Evidence	
Evidence	→ Conclusion
Evidence	

The north gate of Beijing's Forbidden City, known as the Gate of Divine Prowess, served as an entrance and exit for China's empresses.

故宫博物院

1.1 Reunification
Under the
Sui Dynasty

 A famous Chinese proverb says, "After a long split, a union will occur; after a long union, a split will occur." This saying reflects the belief that Chinese history has been a series of cycles alternating between strength and weakness. After a period of unrest, a strong leader establishes a powerful dynasty. It flourishes and then eventually declines until the people rebel and a new dynasty gains power. This dynastic cycle is a repeating theme in Chinese history.

MAIN IDEA

The short-lived Sui dynasty reunified China after centuries of civil war.

WENDI'S RULE

The Han dynasty, which began its rule of China in 206 B.C., ruled China for centuries, until weak rulers, rebellions, and powerful warlords caused its collapse in A.D. 220. China was plunged into nearly 400 years of civil war among many small kingdoms. The state belief system of Confucianism declined, though its ethical ideals and Chinese culture survived.

Then, in 581, the dynastic cycle turned again. A general named **Wendi** seized power and established a new dynasty called the **Sui** (sway). Wendi's conquests allowed him to **reunify**, or join together again, northern and southern China. He then faced the enormous challenge of restoring order across a vast and culturally diverse land.

To reunify China, Wendi strengthened the central government, limiting the power of local nobles and the bureaucracy. The government selected new officials by written examination and made sure they better reflected China's diverse ethnic groups. The military was organized and brought under Wendi's control.

Wendi also issued a new law code that combined northern and southern traditions. He gave farming land to former soldiers, established agriculture in the border regions of the empire, and extended the canal system. Wendi encouraged religious tolerance but also promoted the popular religion of Buddhism. When he died unexpectedly in 604, he left a strong empire for his son and successor, **Yangdi**.

THE GRAND CANAL

Yangdi loved luxury and built extravagant palaces in his new eastern capital at Luoyang (lu-WOH-YAHNG). Yangdi extended some of his father's useful public projects, such as restoring and expanding the Great Wall to help protect China's long and vulnerable northern border, and building state granaries to protect the food supply.

He also built the Grand Canal, connecting the southern Chang Jiang with the northern Huang He. This incredible 1,200-mile waterway had a road alongside it and became a vital communication link. It united China's economy, allowing southern China's plentiful resources to flow north where the government and armies were located. However, it came at a cost. Millions of peasants were forced to work on it, and many of them died.

Beijing

Luoyang
Xi'an
Huang He
(Yellow R.)
Grand Canal
Yangzhou

CHINA

Chian Jiang
(Yangtze R.)

Hangzhou

Yellow
Sea

East
China
Sea

PACIFIC
OCEAN

South
China
Sea

Sui dynasty, 581–618
Tang dynasty, 618–907
Grand Canal
Great Wall
Boundary of modern
China

INDIAN OCEAN

0   200   400 Miles
0   200   400 Kilometers

The people of China hated this forced labor and the high taxes imposed by both Wendi and Yangdi to pay for such projects. Yangdi also launched expensive and unsuccessful wars against Korea. The military campaign required more money and service from his unhappy subjects.

Yangdi grew increasingly unpopular until, in 611, a famine finally pushed the people to rebel. It was the dynastic cycle at work. Rich and poor rose up against Yangdi's harsh rule, and he was assassinated. The Sui dynasty proved to be short-lived. In 618, a new dynasty—the Tang—rose to power. These leaders would continue to unify China.

REVIEW & ASSESS

1. **READING CHECK** What is the Sui dynasty known for?

2. **MAKE INFERENCES** How did the Sui dynasty reflect the pattern of the dynastic cycle?

3. **INTERPRET MAPS** In what ways do the sizes and boundaries of the Sui and Tang dynasties compare to the size and boundary of present-day China?

The **Spread** of **Buddhism**

When bad things happen, it's common to question our beliefs and re-examine our understanding of the world. In trying to make sense of the suffering, we might find comfort in the spirituality of religion—the belief that a higher power can end the misery. The Chinese people found comfort in religion when they most needed it.

MAIN IDEA

In troubled times, many Chinese turned to Buddhism.

BUDDHISM IN CHINA

The collapse of the Han dynasty in A.D. 220 plunged China into chaos for a period that would last hundreds of years. In such troubled times, many Chinese turned from the practical belief system known as Confucianism to a new, more spiritual religion—Buddhism.

As you learned in Chapter 6, Buddhism was based on an understanding of life founded by Siddhartha Gautama in India around 500 B.C. He taught that the keys to a good life were revealed in the Four Noble Truths: Life is full of suffering; the cause of suffering is desire and ignorance; to end the cycle of desire is to end suffering; and one can be free of desires by following the Eightfold Path. The path promoted a balanced life in which the sum of a person's deeds, or karma, results in **reincarnation**, or rebirth, into another life. Through good karma over successive lifetimes, a person could reach the state of **nirvana**—an end of reincarnation and the suffering of life.

Foreign traders and missionaries brought Buddhism to China during the first century A.D. During the collapse of the Han dynasty and the civil war that followed, Buddhism's teachings provided comfort and offered a clear path beyond suffering. Buddhist texts were translated, and Buddhist practices were adapted into a distinctive Chinese form, which became very popular among all classes of people.

Over the following centuries, Buddhism's popularity rose and declined, but emperors often promoted it to gain the people's support, as Wendi had done. This promotion included building magnificent monuments and not taxing Buddhist religious lands. Meanwhile, Buddhism continued to spread rapidly across the east and southeast areas of Asia, especially Korea and Japan.

IMPACT ON CONFUCIANISM

After the chaotic period of civil war ended, Confucianism made a comeback during the 600s. The government reintroduced traditional Confucian-style tests for the civil service. Confucian principles of respect, responsibility, loyalty, and duty to family and the state became popular once again.

In contrast, Buddhism encouraged moral behavior but played down the importance of obedience to outside authority in favor of inner guidance. Daoism, which emphasized our essential unity with nature, also had a strong following. These three competing belief systems became interwoven. Confucianism's concern with earthly duty influenced the religious spirituality of Buddhism and Daoism. As a result, Confucianism once more emerged as an important part of Chinese society.

Critical Viewing This Buddhist cave painting from China shows a seated figure meditating. What do the details in this painting suggest about Buddhism?

REVIEW & ASSESS

1. **READING CHECK** After the collapse of the Han dynasty, why did many Chinese turned to Buddhism?

2. **SEQUENCE EVENTS** How was Buddhism first introduced in China?

3. **COMPARE AND CONTRAST** How do the main principles of Confucianism and Buddhism differ?

1.3 Tang and Song Dynasties

A picture is worth a thousand words—but it often does not last as long. Only words remain to capture the brilliance of Chinese painting from this era. For example, legend tells how the acclaimed Tang artist Wu Daozi (woo dow-dzuh) painted a mural that was so lifelike, he walked into it and disappeared forever.

MAIN IDEA

Under the Tang and Song dynasties, China grew and prospered.

THE TANG DYNASTY

Although unpopular, the Sui dynasty established solid foundations of government for future dynasties to build on. After the rulers of the **Tang** dynasty seized power in 618, they continued the Sui policy of tolerance toward China's many religions and cultures. They encouraged economic growth through agricultural reform and trade. The dynasty also strengthened the government by using civil service examinations to select government officials. These well-educated scholar-officials carried out government policy. They helped keep the government stable from one emperor to the next.

These reforms helped the Tang expand the empire into central and southern Asia.

(See the map in Lesson 1.1.) Meanwhile, literature and art flourished in a golden age. Few paintings survive, but beautiful sculptures reveal the talent of the artists of this period. Also, around 48,000 poems exist from this time. Tang officials were encouraged to write poetry.

Taizong (ty-johng) was the second Tang emperor and an admired figure in Chinese history. From 626 to 649, he used Confucian ideas to organize his government. Later, Wu Zhao (woo jow), the wife of Taizong's son and successor Gaozong, became China's only official female emperor by ruthlessly eliminating her rivals, including her own children. Despite the stormy succession, Wu Zhao had inherited a peaceful and well-run country. Her policies were sensible, improved the life of the people, and helped strengthen the empire. Later Tang emperors were less successful. Political instability sparked a long civil war in which millions died. Poor rulers, corruption, and rebellion weakened Tang authority until the dynasty lost power in 907. Once again, China plunged into chaos.

THE SONG DYNASTY

In 960, over 50 years later, the **Song** dynasty restored order. Though the Song rulers did not expand the territory of the empire, they introduced domestic improvements that made Song China the world's most advanced society of the time. Confucianism again became the state philosophy. Art and literature thrived while technology led to new inventions. Agriculture expanded with new techniques in drainage, irrigation, and terrace farming. Strains of rice from Southeast Asia doubled the harvest, and rice became China's **staple**, or main crop. In a short period, from 750 to 1100, China's population doubled to 100 million.

Meanwhile, this growth led to more rapid trade, and China's economy boomed. Farmers grew sugar cane, tea, bamboo, and hemp for trade, and the traditional crafts of

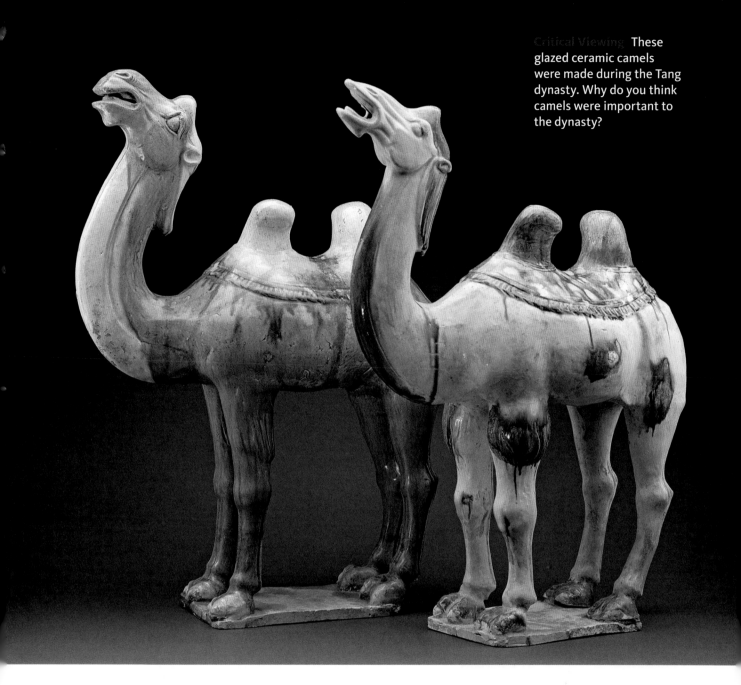

Critical Viewing These glazed ceramic camels were made during the Tang dynasty. Why do you think camels were important to the dynasty?

silk, paper, and ceramics grew in popularity. Improved roads and canals carried goods within China, while bigger ships carried exports overseas. For the first time, the state made more money from trade than from agriculture. Because of the strong economy,

China started banks and printed the world's first paper money. Economic prosperity led to the growth of cities, which became busy centers of culture and **commerce**, or the buying and selling of goods.

REVIEW & ASSESS

1. **READING CHECK**
   How did China change during the Song dynasty?

2. **MAKE INFERENCES** How did reforms introduced under the Tang dynasty contribute to China's golden age?

3. **ANALYZE CAUSE AND EFFECT**
   How did the growth of trade during the Song dynasty affect China?

The **Legacy** of **Chinese Inventions**

Imagine using dimes to buy a car. Maybe you'd start counting but soon give up. Dollar bills are far more convenient. Printed money was a Chinese invention, as were printed books, porcelain, navigational compasses, and gunpowder. All these new inventions were created during the Tang and Song dynasties. It's difficult to imagine our world without these items.

MAIN IDEA

Chinese inventions have helped shape the world we live in today.

PRINTING AND PAPER MONEY

The Chinese had invented paper around A.D. 100. About five hundred years later, they contributed another bookmaking breakthrough—block printing. This technique involved carving the text in reverse to stand out on a block of wood. The block was painted with ink and pressed onto paper to create a printed page. Carving the blocks for each page of each book was a long process.

Around 1041, the innovation of **movable type**, which used individually carved characters, made it easier and cheaper to print books. The new widespread distribution of books helped spread government regulations, literature, and the ideas of Confucianism and Buddhism.

Meanwhile, China's booming population and economy created a large demand for coins—by 1085 six billion coins were minted per year. The coins were too bulky for large transactions, so merchants began exchanging paper notes as IOUs. The money stayed in a bank but was owned by whoever held the note. Around 1100, the first government-backed currency was issued. Over time, the use of bank seals and increasingly complex designs helped discourage counterfeiting.

GUNPOWDER, THE MAGNETIC COMPASS, AND PORCELAIN

Gunpowder was an accidental discovery by Chinese alchemists attempting to turn worthless metals into gold. These early chemists found that sulfur, saltpeter, and charcoal made a powerful explosive when mixed together. The military found that gunpowder confined in an iron tube could shoot objects great distances. This discovery led to the development of cannons, guns, and fireworks. Later, Chinese armies used gunpowder in Central Asia, and the secret spread.

The Chinese had long used magnetic compasses for ceremonies, but in the 1100s they began using them for navigation. A sliver of magnetized iron hanging from a silk thread or floating in water would point north and south. This property allowed sailors to tell their direction without the sun or stars. Longer sea journeys also became possible, which increased China's maritime trade.

One especially prized trade item was **porcelain**—a strong, light, and nearly see-through ceramic. Porcelain's closely guarded secret was the blending of unique minerals and a glaze at very high temperatures. Because of these secret techniques, porcelain—or china, as it came to be called—was incredibly rare and precious.

Antique block characters for printing

Movable Type

The Chinese created block characters for use in movable type, a development that made printing easier. Artisans carved characters as individual clay tablets that could be arranged on a board to form text. After printing, the characters could be reused.

Song porcelain vase with celadon glaze

Porcelain

Techniques for creating porcelain were perfected during the Tang dynasty and reached the height of artistry under the Song. The formula used to create porcelain was a closely guarded secret.

Ancient Chinese nautical compass

Compass

The ancient Chinese had developed a compass that was used in rituals. During the Song dynasty, they discovered the secret to making a magnetic compass used for navigation.

Fireworks display

Gunpowder

After the invention of gunpowder, the military experimented with explosive arrows, grenades, rockets, and land mines, and finally developed firearms and fireworks.

REVIEW & ASSESS

1. **READING CHECK** What inventions occurred during the Tang and Song dynasties?

2. **DRAW CONCLUSIONS** Why did the invention of movable type help increase the spread of ideas?

3. **ANALYZE CAUSE AND EFFECT** How did the use of magnetic compasses for navigation affect China's trade?

2.1

GENGHIS
KHAN A.D. 1162 – 1227

Forget Rome or Britain. It was the Mongols who ruled the largest land empire in history. It stretched from present-day Korea to Hungary and included more than 100 million people of widely differing cultures. And the Mongols conquered all this territory in less than 100 years, thanks to the determination of one man—Genghis Khan.

Job: Universal ruler
Education: His harsh childhood
Home: Near the Onon River
Real Name: Temujin

FINEST HOUR

When he died, Genghis Khan had united the nomadic tribes, conquered China, and extended his rule over all of central Asia.

WORST MOMENT

The death of his father, a defeated Mongol chieftain, left young Temujin and his mother to eke out a living on the harsh steppe.

FRIENDS

Jamuka was a friend and rival whom Temujin later defeated to become universal ruler.

TRIVIA

It is said that Temujin was born grasping a clot of blood in his hand, which has been viewed throughout history as a mixed sign—an omen of his future fame (and notoriety).

THE MONGOL CONQUEST

The Mongols were a loose collection of independent nomadic tribes from the **steppes**—or vast, grassy plains—of northwest China. They spent their lives roaming, raiding, herding, and fighting across this landscape.

A child named Temujin (TEH-moo-juhn) was born on this landscape. He was the son of a defeated Mongol chieftain, and his childhood was harsh. However, Temujin was ambitious, clever, charismatic, and a great warrior. He became a tribal leader and, in 1206, the Mongol people gave him the title **Genghis Khan** (JEHNG-gihs KAHN), meaning "universal ruler."

Despite conflicts among the tribes, there was one thing they all needed—more grazing lands. Genghis Khan organized the diverse bands into a powerful military machine that would sweep mercilessly across Asia in one of history's most impressive conquests.

Legend:
— Silk Roads
— Route of Marco Polo
···· Great Wall
— Border of Mongol Empire

0   500   1000 Miles
0   500   1000 Kilometers

In 1212, Genghis Khan and the Mongols invaded northern China, destroying more than 90 cities and killing their inhabitants. Turning west, he destroyed an empire in what is now Iran. He then invaded southern Russia and, in 1215, destroyed China's capital.

When Genghis Khan died around 1226, he had conquered much of central Asia. Four of his sons shared his vast empire, dividing it into four **khanates**, or regions, and expanded their rule into Europe and southern China.

KUBLAI KHAN

China's next great leader was Genghis Khan's grandson, **Kublai Khan** (KOO-bluh KAHN). He rose to become leader of the Mongol Empire in 1264. Kublai Khan was determined to add to his empire by conquering all of southern China. By 1271, he had succeeded, giving the Mongols control over most of China. That year he declared himself emperor, adopting the dynastic name **Yuan** (yoo-ahn) and preparing to help his army meet new challenges.

REVIEW & ASSESS

1. **READING CHECK** How did the Mongols gain power?

2. **COMPARE AND CONTRAST** How were Genghis and Kublai Khan alike?

3. **INTERPRET MAPS** Which cities in the northwest were part of the Mongol Empire?

2.2

Life in Yuan China

You love your country but hate your rulers. The Mongols are in charge, and they discriminate against you. You pay higher taxes than foreigners, receive less justice, and are excluded from the best jobs—all because you're Chinese.

MAIN IDEA

The Mongols set up strict rules to control China.

YUAN GOVERNMENT

Kublai Khan adopted a less destructive approach to governing than that of his predecessors, trying to win over the Chinese people and preserve conquered towns instead of destroying them. Even so, any resistance was brutally punished. During the 1270s, Song loyalists continued to fight the Mongols in southern China. The Mongols defeated the Song uprising of 200,000 troops—and then killed the entire population of Hangzhou (hahng-joh) city. To avoid further suffering, remaining officials of the Song dynasty surrendered in 1279.

Kublai Khan was now ruler of all China—the first to unite all China since the end of the Tang dynasty, which ended in 907—and its first foreign ruler ever. He would rule for 15 years, until his death in 1294. His Yuan dynasty led China for a century, but it was not an easy time for the Chinese.

The Mongols were more used to fighting than governing, and controlling a country as large and sophisticated as China demanded a highly organized government. Under the Yuan dynasty, Chinese government continued much as before, with a strong central state built around a bureaucracy with Confucian rituals and ceremonies.

The big difference was that the Mongols excluded Chinese people from higher positions to stop them from having too much power. Instead, Mongols and foreigners, especially Muslims, received the top jobs. Foreigners migrated to China, including the famous Italian merchant **Marco Polo**, who served as a tax collector and special envoy to the emperor. However, Chinese scholars still had a strong unofficial influence, and Kublai Khan relied on Chinese advisors.

SOCIAL CLASSES

Most Chinese hated living under the Mongols, who treated them as second-class citizens in their own country. Society was divided into four classes. At the top were the Mongols, followed by non-Chinese foreigners. Then came the northern Chinese, who had lived longest under Yuan rule. At the very bottom of society were the southern Chinese, who made up 80 percent of the population.

Many peasant farmers in the bottom bracket of society were forced off their land when they could not pay their taxes. Unable to feed their families, many sold themselves into slavery far from home. The government forced peasants to work on extravagant imperial projects. The Yuan dynasty rebuilt Beijing as a wealthy city filled with magnificent palaces and pleasure gardens enjoyed by rich foreigners.

All this luxury came at a cost for the Chinese. The Mongols feared rebellion because of the pressures they placed on the Chinese. Looking for signs of revolt, agents working for the government kept a close eye on neighborhoods. They forced

People in China still use the Grand Canal, shown in this photograph, to move goods up and down the river.

every ten Chinese families to share a single knife. The government banned meetings and fairs and prevented the Chinese from going out at night or playing sports, thinking it was too much like military exercise.

The Yuan dynasty did make significant contributions, though. During its reign, trade and agriculture expanded. The Yuan built roads and extended the Grand Canal. The Mongol postal service provided efficient communication, and the government introduced an accurate calendar of 365.2

days. Also, with many Chinese scholars out of work, they had more time to write, and Chinese literature flourished.

Still, the Chinese remained hostile to Mongol rule and formed secret societies to plot rebellions. After Kublai Khan's death in 1294, the Yuan dynasty gradually declined. There were seven emperors in 40 years, none of them as gifted as Kublai Khan. Rebellions started to break out, and, by 1368, China was poised for yet another change in dynasties.

REVIEW & ASSESS

1. **READING CHECK** How did the Mongols treat the Chinese under their rule?

2. **MAKE INFERENCES** Why did Kublai Khan exclude the Chinese from important jobs in government?

3. **ANALYZE CAUSE AND EFFECT** Under the Yuan dynasty, how did the Mongols open China to foreigners?

Travels on the
Silk Roads

Under the Mongols, China continued to produce goods that were popular all around the world, especially silk and porcelain. The Mongols wanted to encourage commerce, and their control of China and all the lands that connected it to Europe helped trade flourish. The ancient trade routes, the Silk Roads, were revitalized, and new routes reached north to the Mongol capital of Karakorum. From here, great caravans could now travel in safety and ease across the lush plains that had previously been too dangerous because of tribal wars and banditry.

In this illustration from Marco Polo's book of his travels, traders bring spices from the western part of the Mongol empire to the east.

from *Book of the Wonders of the World* by **Marco Polo and Rustichello**, **15th century**

DOCUMENT ONE

from *Genghis Khan and the Making of the Modern World* by Jack Weatherford
Anthropologist Jack Weatherford presents a fairly positive view of the rule of the Mongols. Silk was one of China's most valued exports, and here Weatherford notes how Genghis Khan shaped its distribution.

CONSTRUCTED RESPONSE Why might the people living on the steppes benefit from Genghis Khan's rerouting of exports through their territory?

> A river of brightly colored silk flowed out of China. It was as though Genghis Khan had rerouted all the different twisting channels of the Silk Route, combined them into one large stream, and redirected it northward to spill out across the Mongol steppes.

DOCUMENT TWO

from *Travels* by Marco Polo
Marco Polo was a merchant from Venice whose adventures in Asia have become the most celebrated of the medieval world. His colorful descriptions of life in Mongol China paint a vivid picture of the court of Kublai Khan.

CONSTRUCTED RESPONSE Why would using experts to determine prices make trade fairer and easier?

> Several times a year, parties of traders arrive with pearls and precious stones and gold and silver and other valuables, such as cloth of gold and silk, and surrender them all to the Great [Kublai] Khan. The Khan then summons twelve experts . . . and bids them examine the wares that the traders have bought and pay for them what they judge to be their true value.

DOCUMENT THREE

Passport Medallion, c. 1300
Kublai Khan issued a medallion like the one at right to Marco Polo before he set off on his travels. It acted as a passport, helping Marco Polo access difficult areas and secure help and supplies from subjects of the Khan.

CONSTRUCTED RESPONSE How might Marco Polo have helped expand China's foreign contact and trade during the Mongol Empire?

SYNTHESIZE & WRITE

1. **REVIEW** Review what you have learned about the Mongol Empire.

2. **RECALL** On your own paper, write down the main idea expressed through each document and artifact.

3. **CONSTRUCT** Write a topic sentence that answers this question: During the Mongol Empire, how did Genghis Khan and Kublai Khan promote and increase trade?

4. **WRITE** Using evidence from the documents and artifact, write an informative paragraph to support the answer to the question in Step 3.

3.1 Return to Chinese Rule

After a challenging period of Mongol rule, the Chinese people found an unlikely rescuer in a peasant who led China's rebellion. China's next two emperors set out to restore the country to greatness. The Ming dynasty's capital was a spectacular new seat of power that would be used continuously for 500 years.

MAIN IDEA

The Ming dynasty restored China to greatness.

A NEW LEADERSHIP

By the 1360s, Mongol rule had weakened and rebellions broke out. The son of a peasant, Zhu Yuanzhang (joo yoo-ahn-jahng), emerged as a leader. In 1368, the rebels began driving the Mongols north of the Great Wall, eventually bringing an end to Mongol rule. Zhu declared himself **Hongwu** (hung-woo), or the first emperor of the **Ming** dynasty.

The Chinese again ruled China, and Hongwu set out to restore the country to greatness. He could be paranoid, controlling, and cruel, but he worked hard to improve the lives of peasants. Hongwu rebuilt China's agriculture system and supported the growth of manufacturing. He cut government spending and established efficient taxation. He based his rule on the principles of the Tang and Song dynasties, restoring Confucian values. Notices in villages outlined government policy and expectations of moral behavior.

Hongwu's son **Yongle** (yung-loh) was, like his father, a suspicious, ruthless, and tyrannical ruler. However, he also effectively continued his father's work rebuilding China. Yongle sponsored sea expeditions and encouraged local governments to build schools for commoners. He also sponsored great literary works and led armies to suppress China's neighbors.

IMPERIAL PALACE

Like many Chinese emperors, Yongle moved the imperial capital—this time north, to Beijing. This location placed Yongle near his supporters and closer to his armies guarding China's borders. Beijing was well organized. It was laid out in a grid aligned with the points of the compass and surrounded by 14 miles of 40-foot walls. To feed the vast numbers of people who flocked to the capital, Yongle extended the Grand Canal even farther, using advanced engineering to carry boats uphill.

At Beijing's heart was the Imperial Palace, or Forbidden City—so named because few were admitted and only with the emperor's permission. The Forbidden City would be the center of imperial power and government for the next 500 years. It took an estimated one million workers nearly 15 years to complete the palace, which was an architectural marvel. The huge complex boasted hundreds of buildings that towered over Beijing. It included luxurious private residences for the imperial family and more than 100,000 servants. The city's rectangular, symmetrical, and compass-aligned design was said to be in perfect harmony with the world. It remains the world's largest palace—the perfect place for the emperor to fulfill his role as a connection between the will of heaven and the practical rule of Earth.

FORBIDDEN CITY

Governments are often housed in imposing buildings that reflect the power of politics. But few are as impressive as the Imperial Palace in Beijing.

The **Imperial Garden** was filled with fragrant flowers, plants, and trees as well as sculptures and pavilions.

During the Ming dynasty, the **Palace of Heavenly Purity** served as the emperor's living quarters.

The **Palace of Earthly Tranquility** served as the living quarters of the empress.

The **Hall of Supreme Harmony** housed the emperor's golden Dragon Throne.

The **Meridian Gate** served as the main entrance and exit for the emperor.

REVIEW & ASSESS

1. **READING CHECK** How was the Ming dynasty established?

2. **ANALYZE CAUSE AND EFFECT** Why did Yongle move the imperial capital to Beijing?

3. **INTERPRET VISUALS** What did the impressive architecture of the Forbidden City symbolize?

Zheng He's Explorations

The sea beckoned to a young Chinese Muslim named **Zheng He** (jung huh), who rose through the ranks of the navy and, in 1405, began a series of seven voyages to Asia and Africa. His success was built on the accuracy of Chinese navigation—the best in the world.

MAIN IDEA

Chinese ships and navigational tools allowed China to spread its power and influence by sea.

THE VOYAGES OF ZHENG HE

Zheng He's expeditions included more than 300 ships and nearly 30,000 sailors. This show of force was about more than exploration and trade. It also communicated political power. Zheng He's main mission was to glorify Yongle by asserting Chinese control over trade routes and weaker countries. For three decades, Zheng He sailed 40,000 miles around Southeast Asia, East Africa, and the Middle East.

His ships returned to China laden with treasure and exotic luxuries such as gold, gems, rare spices, giraffes, and zebras. These expeditions established China's international reputation as goods and ideas were exchanged with more countries than ever before. However, not everyone was happy that China was reaching out to other lands.

5
1417–1419
Zheng He's treasure fleet visited the Arabian Peninsula and, for the first time, Africa. In Aden, the sultan presented exotic gifts such as zebras, lions, and ostriches.

6
1421–1422
Zheng He's fleet returned foreign ambassadors to their native countries after stays of several years in China.

7
1431–1433
The last voyage marked the end of China's age of exploration. Historians believe that Zheng He died on the return trip and was buried at sea.

SAUDI ARABIA
Jeddah · Mecca
Arabian Peninsula
Red Sea
YEMEN
Sanaa
Aden
Mukalla
SUDAN
SOMALIA
KENYA
Mogadishu
Baraawe
AFRICA
Nairobi
Malindi **5**
6
Pate I.
Lamu
7
Mombasa
Swahili coast
TANZANIA

1413–1415
As a result of the voyage, an estimated 18 countries sent tribute and foreign ambassadors to China.

1409–1411
During this voyage, Zheng He fought a land battle in Sri Lanka. The voyage was also marked by his offering of gifts to a Buddhist temple.

1407–1409
The fleet returned foreign ambassadors who had traveled to China on the first voyage from Sumatra, India, and elsewhere.

1405–1407
In July, the fleet, with 317 ships and 27,870 men, left Nanjing with silks, porcelain, and spices for trade.

ZHENG HE'S VOYAGES, 1405–1433

This map shows the main and subsidiary, or secondary, routes of Zheng He's seven expeditions. Note that the map labels include place names from the 1400s as well as present-day names.

—— Main route
- - - Subsidiary route
◦ Major trading center
4 Destination

Present-day boundaries shown
Scale varies in this perspective.

CHINA

Beijing

Great Wall

Grand Canal

Dalian

MING EMPIRE

JIANGSU

Origin of all 7 voyages — Nanjing

East China Sea

FUJIAN
Changle
Quanzhou
Xiamen

TAIWAN

ASIA

Yangtze

IRAN

4 Hormuz

Persian Gulf

OMAN

Dhofar

Arabian Sea

INDIA

BANGLADESH

Chittagong

YUNNAN
Kunyang

Bay of Bengal

1
2
3

Kozhikode (Calicut)

Malabar Coast
Cochin
Quilon
Jaffna

SRI LANKA
CEYLON

Colombo
Galle
Dondra Head

MALDIVES

Andaman Islands (India)

Nicobar Islands (India)

THAILAND
SIAM
Ayutthaya

CHAMPA

Hainan

South China Sea

Qui Nhon

CAMBODIA

VIETNAM

INDIAN OCEAN

EQUATOR

Banda Aceh
Semudera

Strait of

Kelantan

MALAYSIA

Pahang
Malacca

Sumatra

Palembang

INDONESIA

Java
Surabaya

Critical Viewing This illustration contrasts Zheng He's ship with that of a European explorer. What impression might the large Chinese ship have made when it arrived in a foreign port?

REVIEW & ASSESS

1. **READING CHECK** What was one of the purposes of Zheng He's voyages?

2. **MAKE GENERALIZATIONS** How did Zheng He's voyages demonstrate China's power?

3. **INTERPRET MAPS** How did Zheng He pay respect to Buddhism during his third voyage?

3.3 China Turns Inward

 An ostrich is believed to bury its head in the sand to avoid seeing its enemies. But that doesn't stop its enemies from seeing it—or attacking it. China could have learned a valuable lesson on what not to do from this bird.

MAIN IDEA

China isolated itself from the world, but foreign influences still brought the downfall of the dynastic system.

ISOLATION POLICY

China's great explorer, Zheng He, died during his seventh voyage and was buried at sea. His death marked the end of China's maritime expeditions. There were competing government factions for and against exploration, and when the emperor Zhengtong (jung-tung) took power in 1435, he stopped all future voyages, claiming that they were too expensive and they imported dangerous foreign ideas.

The Chinese considered themselves the most civilized people on Earth. They felt they were surrounded by barbarians and did not need the rest of the world. After a period of foreign rule and much instability in their history, it was understandable that the Chinese reacted this way. However, the effect of Zhengtong's decision was to surrender control of the region's seas and trade to ambitious European nations and Japanese pirates.

In the following centuries, China entered a long period of **isolationism**, during which it rejected foreign contact and influences. The government took up a defensive attitude and geared the economy toward self-sufficiency. Rulers banned foreign trade, kicked out foreigners, and tried to eliminate foreign influences from Chinese society.

Symbolic of this effort was the extension of the Great Wall, which the government rebuilt entirely in stone and completed with 25,000 watchtowers along its 5,500-mile length. The wall was a formidable physical sign of China's defensive isolation.

THE LAST DYNASTY

The world, however, would not leave China alone. Starting in the mid-1500s, the Ming dynasty faced more and more challenges. Pirate raids were common along the southeast coast. The Mongols invaded the north, and Japan conquered Chinese-protected Korea. The cost of these wars, on top of a lavish imperial lifestyle and corruption at court, spelled financial difficulties. The peasants paid taxes for all this while they were already coping with widespread crop failures, famine, and disease. The people rebelled, and Ming authority crumbled.

In 1644, rebels took over Beijing. In despair, the last of the Ming emperors hanged himself from a tree. Tribes north of the wall, the **Manchus**, united and took advantage of the confusion to seize power. They easily defeated the rebels and founded the **Qing** (chihng) dynasty.

China would remain under the Qing's foreign rule for nearly 300 years. The Qing kept native customs and the Ming government structure but also introduced some of their own traditions. They forced Chinese men to wear their hair as the Qing did, in a long braid. The Qing continued

Dynastic Time Line of China

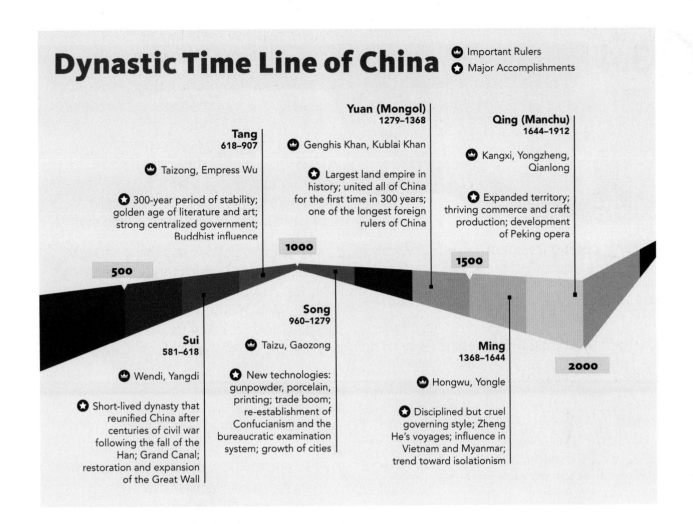

👑 Important Rulers
⭐ Major Accomplishments

Yuan (Mongol)
1279–1368
- 👑 Genghis Khan, Kublai Khan
- ⭐ Largest land empire in history; united all of China for the first time in 300 years; one of the longest foreign rulers of China

Tang
618–907
- 👑 Taizong, Empress Wu
- ⭐ 300-year period of stability; golden age of literature and art; strong centralized government; Buddhist influence

Qing (Manchu)
1644–1912
- 👑 Kangxi, Yongzheng, Qianlong
- ⭐ Expanded territory; thriving commerce and craft production; development of Peking opera

500 · **1000** · **1500** · **2000**

Sui
581–618
- 👑 Wendi, Yangdi
- ⭐ Short-lived dynasty that reunified China after centuries of civil war following the fall of the Han; Grand Canal; restoration and expansion of the Great Wall

Song
960–1279
- 👑 Taizu, Gaozong
- ⭐ New technologies: gunpowder, porcelain, printing; trade boom; re-establishment of Confucianism and the bureaucratic examination system; growth of cities

Ming
1368–1644
- 👑 Hongwu, Yongle
- ⭐ Disciplined but cruel governing style; Zheng He's voyages; influence in Vietnam and Myanmar; trend toward isolationism

China's isolationism, although they did embark on some successful wars that expanded the empire by the end of the 18th century. With peace and prosperity, the population started to increase again, reaching 300 million by 1800. At that time, many Chinese began to migrate to new lands that the Ming had conquered earlier.

Since 1514, European traders had been traveling to China. The Europeans were building strong trading colonies across Asia. The Qing tried to restrict European trade and refused to buy European goods. During the late 1700s, frustrated British merchants began smuggling the drug opium into China. They soon had a successful trade, but addiction ruined countless Chinese lives. The resulting Opium Wars weakened China internally and internationally. European powers seized Chinese territories and took control of the economy. After 1850, a string of rebellions weakened China, and, in February 1912, revolutionary forces overthrew the Qing dynasty. Two thousand years of imperial rule had come to a decisive end.

REVIEW & ASSESS

1. **READING CHECK** How did China try to isolate itself from foreign influences?

2. **COMPARE AND CONTRAST** How did China's policy toward the outside world at the beginning of the Ming dynasty differ from that at the end of the Ming Dynasty?

3. **INTEGRATE VISUALS** How does the time line illustrate the recurring theme of the "dynastic cycle" in Chinese history?

Exploring China's
Diverse Cultures

"When I was little I would identify the pieces of our Thanksgiving turkey and then reassemble the bones after the meal," laughs Christine Lee, a bioarchaeologist and a National Geographic Explorer. "My parents thought I was going to be a doctor!" Instead, she entered a relatively new science, bioarchaeology, which combines biology and archaeology, using the tools of both sciences to find out about the way ancient people lived.

^
This pit of human skulls was found during the excavation of Zhengzhou, a city from the Shang period about 3,750 years ago. Burial customs varied among several distinct cultures in early China.

MAIN IDEA

Bioarchaeology is providing insights into ancient China and Mongolia.

SKELETAL SECRETS

Christine Lee uses biological techniques to examine human skeletons found in archaeological sites. These new techniques allow researchers to piece together clues that tell the stories of long-dead individuals and groups. It is amazing what Dr. Lee can learn from even a single tooth.

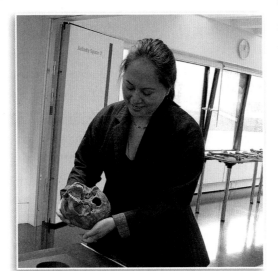
Dr. Christine Lee in the field

A skeleton reveals even more. "Bones can tell me a person's sex, age, and whether they worked hard or had an easy life," she says. "Were they right- or left-handed, did they walk long distances, ride horses, or spend lots of time kneeling? Did they have arthritis, leprosy, tuberculosis? Did they get kicked by a cow, fall off a horse, break their nose in a fight? Bones show me all this and more," says Dr. Lee. By comparing particular skeletal characteristics across populations, she can see how ancient peoples were connected. She can also find details that provide clues to ancient people's ancestral origins, movements, and marriages.

PUZZLES FROM THE PAST

Dr. Lee has worked all over the world but has a particular interest in Asia. In Mongolia, she was the lead bioarchaeologist on a team excavating a cemetery of the Xiongnu (shung-noo) people. These were the nomads whose raids drove China to build the 2,000-mile-long Great Wall to keep them out. The dig site was in the middle of the desert, a thousand miles from the Mongolian capital. "We stopped in a village and asked for directions and were told the site was cursed," she says. "When we got there it was eerily quiet . . . I always said if I ever felt the skeletons didn't want me there I would leave. I decided we could study the skeletons when they were brought to the museum—then we left."

Back at the museum, Dr. Lee's studies highlighted cultural differences between the ancient Xiongnu and their Chinese neighbors to the south. "The ancestors of today's Mongolians rode horses, ate meat, and had a certain cowboy wildness compared to the rigid society and structure on the other side of the Great Wall," she notes. This cultural contrast was reinforced by her excavations of another independent kingdom, the Dian (dee-ahn), a city society of farmers and fishers in southern China. Dr. Lee's findings suggest that the Xiongnu and the Chinese had very little interaction and almost never intermarried.

Dr. Lee feels a responsibility to uncover the stories of these cultures in China's history: "When I look at a 2,000-year-old skull it's like I'm saying, 'Don't worry. I will tell the world about you—I'll describe what your life was like and prove it had meaning.'"

REVIEW & ASSESS

1. **READING CHECK** How is bioarchaeology helping scientists gain insights into ancient China and Mongolia?

2. **IDENTIFY MAIN IDEAS AND DETAILS** What can Dr. Lee tell about ancient people's lives from their bones?

3. **COMPARE AND CONTRAST** According to Dr. Lee's studies, what important cultural differences existed between the Xiongnu people and their Chinese neighbors?

VOCABULARY

On your paper, write the vocabulary word that completes each of the following sentences.

1. General Wendi's conquests managed to _____ north and south China and establish a strong new dynasty called the Sui.

2. Chinese Buddhists believed that the state of _____ was an end to life's suffering.

3. During the Song dynasty, agricultural techniques improved and rice became China's _____.

4. A strong, nearly see-through ceramic called _____ was an especially valuable trade item.

5. The Mongols were a loose collection of nomadic tribes who roamed, raided, herded, and fought across the vast _____ of northwest China.

6. During Emperor Zhengtong's rule, China pursued a policy of _____, rejecting foreign contact and influences.

READING STRATEGY

7. **DRAW CONCLUSIONS** If you haven't already, complete your graphic organizer to draw conclusions about the impact of the Tang, Song, and Ming dynasties on Chinese civilization. Then answer the question.

Tang Dynasty

Evidence		Conclusion
Encouraged economic growth through agriculture and trade	→	
Evidence	→	
Evidence	→	

Which dynasty do you think had the greatest impact on Chinese civilization? Explain your reasoning.

MAIN IDEAS

Answer the following questions. Support your answers with evidence from the chapter.

8. What happened after the collapse of the Han dynasty in A.D. 220? **LESSON 1.1**

9. Why did many Chinese turn away from traditional Confucianism and embrace Buddhism? **LESSON 1.2**

10. What factors contributed to China's growth during the Tang and Song dynasties? **LESSON 1.3**

11. How did the Mongols gain power in China? **LESSON 2.1**

12. During the Yuan dynasty, how did the Mongols treat the Chinese under their rule? **LESSON 2.2**

13. How did the Ming dynasty restore Chinese rule to China? **LESSON 3.1**

14. What were the goals of Zheng He's voyages through Asia and Africa? **LESSON 3.2**

15. Why did China adopt a policy of isolationism during the Ming dynasty? **LESSON 3.3**

CRITICAL THINKING

Answer the following questions. Support your answers with evidence from the chapter.

16. **ANALYZE CAUSE AND EFFECT** Why was Wendi able to win the support of China's population?

17. **ANALYZE CAUSE AND EFFECT** How did Buddhism and Daoism influence Confucianism?

18. **EVALUATE** Which ancient Chinese invention benefitted people most: moveable type, porcelain, gunpowder, or the compass?

19. **SEQUENCE EVENTS** Describe the order of events in the Mongol creation of the world's largest empire.

20. **MAKE INFERENCES** How did Zheng He's maritime expeditions expand Chinese influence and demonstrate China's power and wealth?

21. **YOU DECIDE** Was Mongol rule good or bad for China? Support your opinion with evidence from the chapter.

INTERPRET VISUALS

Study the photograph of the seated Buddha statues in the Yungang Grottoes, a UNESCO World Heritage site in the Shanxi province of China. Then answer the questions that follow.

22. What spiritual qualities are conveyed through these statues of Buddha?

23. Why do you think these statues were carved in such a large scale?

ANALYZE SOURCES

Read the following poem, written by Li Po, one of the most popular Chinese poets of the Tang dynasty.

> **Zazen on Ching-t'ing Mountain**
>
> The birds have vanished down the sky.
> Now the last cloud drains away.
>
> We sit together, the mountain and me,
> Until only the mountain remains.

24. What is one Daoist or Buddhist ideal that is reflected in this poem?

WRITE ABOUT HISTORY

25. EXPOSITORY Suppose you are a historian being interviewed about China. The interviewer asks you, "How did the Great Wall become a symbol of China's policy of isolationism at the end of the Ming dynasty?" Write your answer in a brief paragraph.

TIPS

- Take notes from Lesson 3.3, "China Turns Inward."
- Begin the paragraph with a clear topic sentence.
- Develop the paragraph with supporting details and examples of the steps China took to pursue its policy of isolationism, particularly the expansion and fortification of the Great Wall.
- Use at least two vocabulary terms from the chapter.
- Conclude with an explanation of why the Great Wall became a symbol of China's policy of isolationism.

ON **LOCATION**
WITH **Francisco**
ESTRADA-BELLI

ARCHAEOLOGIST AND NATIONAL GEOGRAPHIC GRANTEE

▶ Check out more on myNGconnect

Francisco Estrada-Belli examines
the ancient stucco sculpture
he discovered in the buried
foundations of a rectangular
pyramid in Holmul, Guatemala.

HIDDEN CITIES

Exploring lost Mayan cities hidden deep in the jungles of Guatemala—that's my job! Every year we discover additional sites to explore to learn more about the Maya civilization, which thrived in Central America for nearly 1,500 years. It seems incredible, but in Guatemala you can still hack your way through the vegetation and come face-to-face with a long lost city.

As a child I visited the magnificent Mayan ruins of Tikal. I had so many questions! How did the Maya build such a great civilization in a jungle? Why did they leave their city? That's why I became an archaeologist: to try and answer some of those questions. I wanted to shed light on the beginnings of Maya civilization, so I chose to study the buried Maya city of Holmul, which had been partially excavated a hundred years ago and then forgotten. It was a good place to start. Exploring nearby, I found another lost Maya city called Cival. This turned out to be one of the earliest cities the Maya built, around 800 B.C. This was over 1,000 years before classic Maya civilization blossomed in cities like Tikal. By showing the complexity and innovation of early Maya settlements, including their architecture, our findings challenge the common belief that the early Maya were simple village farmers.

BURIED SCULPTURES

We've made many important discoveries, including a massive sculpture buried beneath a temple's rubble at Holmul. The site already had been ransacked by looters,

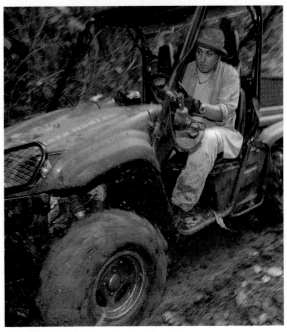

Archaeology can be messy. Here, Estrada-Belli uses a tractor to tow a car through the muddy Guatemalan jungle.

and if they had dug for another ten minutes, they might have found the sculpture. It's amazingly well-preserved—it even has a little color left on it—and it had almost been lost forever. That makes me feel as if we really rescued the past. I feel like I have made a really important contribution.

I love sharing all this new knowledge with others, not just academics but ordinary people and students. I want to help the modern Maya who live in the area, especially the children, reconnect with their glorious Maya past. Right now, they have little or no knowledge of their heritage, and I believe that people who know their past can live a better life.

WHY STUDY HISTORY ❓

❝ The past is irreplaceable, but the past is disappearing because of development, looting, and erosion. I study history because *the past is not a luxury, but instead a necessity* for cultures and for humanity as a whole to be able to live in peace. ❞ — Francisco Estrada-Belli

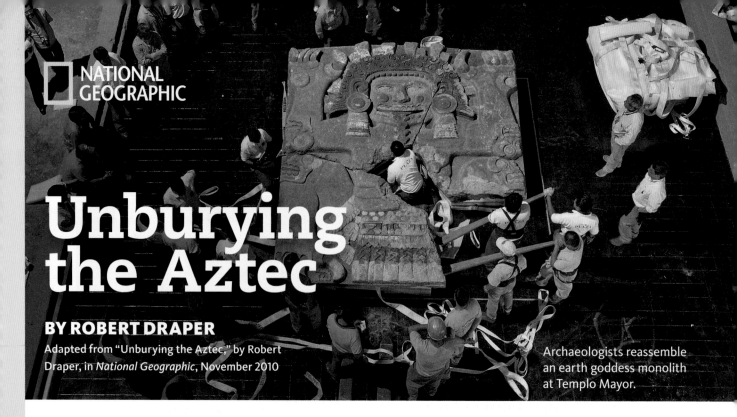

Unburying the Aztec

BY ROBERT DRAPER

Adapted from "Unburying the Aztec," by Robert Draper, in *National Geographic*, November 2010

Archaeologists reassemble an earth goddess monolith at Templo Mayor.

Archaeologist Leonardo López Luján might be on the verge of a major discovery. Since the Spanish conquest of Mexico in 1521, no Aztec emperor's remains have been discovered. Yet historical records say that three Aztec rulers were cremated and their ashes buried at the foot of Templo Mayor, in present-day Mexico City.

In 2008, López Luján unearthed a 12-ton monolith representing an earth goddess near Templo Mayor. Immediately, López Luján noticed that the monolith depicted a figure holding a rabbit, with ten dots above it. In the Aztec writing system, 10-Rabbit is 1502—the year that the empire's most feared ruler, Ahuitzotl (ah-WEE-tzoh-tuhl), died. López Luján is convinced that Ahuitzotl's tomb is somewhere near where the monolith was found.

Aztec power was fleeting. They ruled their empire for less than a century before the Spanish demolished it. The Aztec maintained what some scholars call "a cheap empire." The conquered were allowed to continue governing themselves as long as they paid tribute.

Ahuitzotl assumed the throne in 1486. As the eighth emperor, he stretched the empire to its breaking point. His armies made 45 conquests over 16 years, conquering areas along the Pacific coast, down into present-day Guatemala. He also sealed off trade from rivals to the west and increased control over subjugated territories. "He was more forceful, more brutal," says archaeologist Raúl Arana. "When people didn't want to pay tribute, he sent in the military. With Ahuitzotl, the Aztec went to the maximum expression of everything. And perhaps it was too much. All empires have a limit."

López Luján's work at the Templo Mayor site is slow, partly because of the challenges excavating in a modern city. Urban archaeologists have to dig around sewer and subway lines, avoid underground telephone, fiber optic, and electric cables, and maintain security for a dig in the middle of a city. "Sooner or later, we'll find Ahuitzotl's tomb," López Luján hopes. Whether or not he does, the Aztec mystique will continue to occupy modern Mexico's imagination.

For more from National Geographic
Check out "The Forgotten Road" on myNGconnect

UNIT INQUIRY: LEAVE A LEGACY OF INNOVATION

In this unit, you learned about American and Asian civilizations. Based on your understanding of the text, what new products, methods, and ideas did these civilizations invent or develop? Which of these innovations do you think has made a lasting legacy on the modern world?

ASSIGNMENT Choose an innovation that you think our modern civilization will leave as a legacy for a future civilization. The innovation you choose should come from the 20th or 21st century. Be prepared to present your legacy to the class and explain why you chose it.

Plan As you choose your innovation, think about how other innovations—such as the Chinese invention of paper—dramatically changed and influenced many civilizations past and present. Make a list of the ways in which the innovation you selected has affected or changed the modern world. You might want to use a graphic organizer to help organize your thoughts. ▶

Produce Use your notes to produce detailed descriptions of the impact your innovation has made on modern civilization and what impact you envision it having on a future civilization. You might want to write your descriptions in outline or paragraph form.

Present Choose a creative way to present your innovation to the class. Consider one of these options:

- Create a multimedia presentation using photos to illustrate different ways your innovation has affected or changed modern civilization.

- Design an advertisement for your innovation, providing a "before" and "after" view of our civilization with and without the innovation.

- Write a paragraph describing how you envision this innovation will impact a future civilization and why.

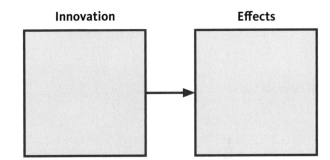

Innovation   Effects

1. The Olmec, Mesoamerica's mother culture, influenced later civilizations such as the Zapotec.
2. The Maya developed an advanced writing system, and they studied mathematics and astronomy.
3. Genghis Khan united the Mongol tribes and conquered Central Asia.
4. Traditionalist forces in China imposed centuries of isolationism to protect China's culture from foreign influence.
5. Chinese inventions spread worldwide, especially printing, paper money, magnetic compasses, gunpowder, and porcelain.

6-10. **NOW IT'S YOUR TURN** Complete the list with five more things to remember about American and Asian civilizations.

TO UNDERSTAND THE SIMILARITIES AND DIFFERENCES AMONG CIVILIZATIONS

You just plowed through five units introducing civilizations with similar but different languages, cultures, and religions. As global citizens, our call to action is to understand that each civilization has its own unique identity. Recognizing the inherent worth and equality of all civilizations and cultures—and, in fact, of all people—is at the heart of global citizenship.

On the Framework of World History chart at the beginning of this text, most of the civilizations in Units 3, 4, and 5 fall under "World Systems." The Greek, Roman, and Asian civilizations continued to build on the foundations that early civilizations had established. Some of the civilizations in the Americas fall under the second and third levels of that chart. Yet all these civilizations established sophisticated cultures. Understanding the similarities and differences among them is one reason we study history.

Fred Hiebert
▶ **Watch the Why Study History video**

These massive Roman aqueducts in Segovia, Spain, are evidence of ancient Roman technological advances in arch-building.

KEY TAKEAWAYS UNITS 3–5

PATTERNS IN HISTORY: SIMILAR DEVELOPMENTS ACROSS LOCATIONS

- Continued environmental adaptations in the Americas improve agricultural production.
- Trade takes off on a global scale, including a revitalization of the Silk Roads.

GOVERNMENT

- In Europe, emphasis shifts to protecting ordinary people, with the development of democracy in ancient Greece and Rome.
- New empires, including the Mongol in East Asia, rise to power.
- In the Americas, the Maya and Inca rise to power.

MOVEMENT OF PEOPLE AND IDEAS

- Hellenistic culture spreads through the empire-building of Alexander the Great.
- Roman culture spreads through colonization and trade.
- Buddhism spreads across China through trade and missionaries.

ARTISTIC EXPRESSION

- In Europe, new art forms include more realistic "selfies" in statues from ancient Greece and mosaics and frescoes of ancient Rome.
- Peruvian artisans in South America create fine jewelry out of gold, silver, and copper.

TECHNOLOGY & INNOVATION

Engineering and architectural developments include

- columns and temples from ancient Greece
- improved concrete and arches from ancient Rome
- the monumental structures of the Maya, Aztec, and Inca
- Chinese inventions, including movable type, the compass, and gunpowder

IT'S ABOUT BEING A GLOBAL CITIZEN.

As a global citizen, you are empowered to act responsibly in the 21st century by showing empathy and respect for others, making informed decisions and finding your own voice, and actively participating in a rich and diverse environment. Go for it!

STORIES MAKING
HISTORY

NATIONAL GEOGRAPHIC

History is a living thing, and you are part of it.

You've just read about centuries and centuries of events that may seem like they have little connection to your life—but you might be surprised. Those long-gone people and dramatic occurrences have brought us to where we are today, and the things happening all over the world while you sit in class each day will shape your life for years to come. If you don't keep an eye on the issues that will someday become the history of your generation, who will?

As this *World History* book went to the printer, important new National Geographic stories were just hitting the news. So we narrowed them down to the five stories that follow. Remember: These are just a few of the many intriguing stories surfacing around the world, and they're still developing. As a global citizen, it's up to you to ask yourself: What happened next? How did this turn out? **Go find out!**

Renewing Relationships: Cuba and the United States

Serving as The Geographer for National Geographic's Maps Division is an epic job. On any given day, Juan José Valdés and his team have the monumental task of creating and updating maps in a world where borders change frequently and sometimes without much notice. In 2011, Valdés stood expectantly outside a house in Havana, Cuba; but he wasn't in the country to make a map. He was visiting the place where he was born in 1953, and attempting to reconnect to a country he hadn't entered in 50 years.

^
The national flags of the United States and Cuba fly outside the Cuban hotel where the first U.S. congressional delegation to Cuba stayed in 2015.

Juan José Valdés

A year later, Juan visited Cuba again and reunited with his remaining family. A cousin approached him saying, "You are Cuban."

"Yes, I am Cuban," Juan answered, his voice trembling with emotion.

Like so many Cuban-Americans, Juan's life has been marked by enormous changes. When he was a child in Havana during the 1950s, a dictator named Fulgencio Batista ruled the country with an iron hand. A young law student and activist named Fidel Castro led rebels who waged a war to end Batista's rule. In 1959, Castro and his forces overthrew Batista.

Castro had promised free elections and other reforms. Yet once he took power, he quickly established a Communist government, in which the state owns or controls factories and other businesses. Castro refused to hold free elections, and he denied Cuban citizens freedom of speech and other rights most Americans take for granted. Castro also formed an alliance with the Soviet Union, in spite of the fact that the United States was in the middle of a Cold War with the Soviets. The U.S. response was swift and severe: diplomatic relations and trade with Cuba ended, and no one could travel between Cuba and the United States.

Hundreds of thousands of Cubans desperately wanted to leave Cuba for other countries like the United States. They didn't want to live in a Communist country. Juan's family could not leave right away, but they managed to get an airline ticket for Juan in 1961. At the age of seven, he traveled alone on an airplane to Miami, Florida. He lived with an elderly couple in Miami, until several months later, when his parents were able to leave Cuba and join him. Their family was reunited and built a life together in the United States.

Meanwhile, Cuba and the United States remained locked in tension. In April 1961, President John F. Kennedy authorized a group of American-trained Cuban exiles to attack Cuba at the Bay of Pigs and try to overthrow Castro. The invasion was a disaster for the United States. The Cuban exiles were outnumbered and many were captured. In October 1962, the Soviet Union tried to set up missiles with nuclear warheads in Cuba. This dangerous situation, known as the Cuban Missile Crisis, ended only when President Kennedy confronted the Soviets and forced them to remove the missiles.

But the world changes daily. On December 17, 2014, President Barack Obama announced that the United States would work to restore diplomatic and trade relations with Cuba and move to open an embassy in Havana, with Congressional approval. On April 11, 2015, President Obama met with Cuban President Raúl Castro in Panama in the first face-to-face discussion between the leaders of the two countries in more than 50 years. Both leaders expressed hope that the two countries will be able to interact without the tension and restrictions of the past.

This change is important for both nations, but it's also important for people like Juan Valdés who have roots in Cuba. As tensions between the countries continue to subside, Cuban-Americans will be able to travel more easily to Cuba and reconnect with relatives they left behind long ago. Yet change is never without complication. Cubans will have to adjust to the impact the lifted trade embargo has on the local economy they are used to. Others may find it unusual to welcome American tourists to their country after so many decades without them. It's likely that the Cuban people will find themselves and their country in a period of transition and adjustment for years to come.

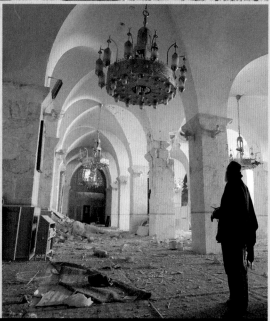

Saving Cultural Heritage

Home to some of the oldest cultures on earth and six UNESCO World Heritage sites, modern-day Syria lies along the eastern coast of the Mediterranean Sea with Iraq to the east, Turkey to the north, and Jordan to the south—at the heart of the region referred to as the Middle East. Syria's modern borders were drawn in the 20th century, and crossed diverse cultures. This diversity makes it a place where people from all faiths gather, where cultural heritage is a part of people's identity, and greatly influences their way of life.

^
Destruction and looting have drastically altered the Umayyad Mosque in Aleppo, Syria, as seen in these before and after shots of its exterior and interior.

Salam Al Kuntar
2015 Emerging Explorer

Dr. Salam Al Kuntar, an archaeologist who grew up in Syria, can tell you all about what it's like to live in a place so rich in cultural heritage.

As a young girl picking olives, pistachios, and almonds in her family's orchard in Syria, Al Kuntar also collected pottery shards left behind by ancient cultures. At the time, she dreamed of becoming an astronaut. Today, she laughs as she admits that instead of taking her up into the sky, her career sends her digging below the ground!

Named a National Geographic Emerging Explorer in 2015, Al Kuntar's work has taken on an unexpected urgency. She and a team of experts are working to save ancient evidence of Syria's diverse heritage from the ravages of war. Since civil war erupted in Syria in 2011, violence has sent millions of Syrians fleeing from their homes to live in refugee camps. Years into the conflict, millions of Syrian children are unable to go to school. Instead of focusing on homework assignments, they think about their family's safety and whether or not they'll have enough to eat.

Syria's ancient monuments and museums, too, have been the victims of careless government airstrikes as well as bombing and shelling by various opposition groups.

In the city of Aleppo in April 2013, for example, the minaret, or tower, on the Umayyad Mosque dating from 1090 A.D. was completely destroyed. Other fragile archaeological sites have been damaged, and thieves have been looting antiquities—objects or works of art from the ancient past—and selling them illegally outside of Syria.

Syria's Ma'arra Mosaic Museum, southwest of Aleppo, was once a *caravanserai*, or inn. It holds a collection of Roman and Byzantine mosaics more impressive than any other in the Middle East. The museum was near collapse from damages sustained because of the war until preservationists and volunteers stepped in. Their efforts saved the collection.

The physical destruction of something tangible like Syria's historical monuments actually is intended to rob people of something intangible—their cultural heritage and identity. The impact is deeply felt when people can no longer visit a place or a monument that they have memories of visiting with their grandparents. The stories they've carried with them since childhood become harder to remember and share. Al Kuntar warns that the war "is killing the hope for the future."

But there is still hope even under these difficult circumstances. Salam Al Kuntar's team works closely with local activists to document the destruction of monuments. They map and identify damage, apply a harmless glue to keep the tesserae, or small cubes that make up the mosaics, intact, and use sandbags and wrapping materials to protect them. People sometimes try to escape from the war and seek refuge inside some of the remote ruins. Al Kuntar's team does emergency repairs to shore up crumbling stone so it doesn't crush these frightened and exhausted guests.

As an archaeologist, Al Kuntar knows something very important that keeps her going under dangerous and discouraging conditions: this effort to destroy Syria's cultural heritage ultimately is not going to work. The fact is that their cultural heritage is embedded in the hearts and minds of the Syrian people—in their memories of family and country—and it cannot be destroyed. Salam Al Kuntar describes Syria's diversity as "precious," and is determined to protect it for future generations.

Our Shared History

Imagine if a symbol of the United States—for example, the Statue of Liberty—was stolen from New York Harbor and whisked away to another country. Most Americans would be angry that part of their history was lost to them. Across the world, this theft of the past happens regularly in areas that have been centers of civilization and are rich with archaeological sites and cultural artifacts. And it results in the same feeling of loss.

Top U.S. Customs agents at Dulles Airport in Washington, D.C., examine illegally shipped artifacts.

Bottom Left Head of a lamassu repatriated to Iraq

Bottom Right Paracas textile repatriated to Peru

Cultural artifacts are the little pieces of humanity left behind. They add to what we know of the human record, a non-renewable resource that we all share. When a cultural artifact is damaged or stolen, it is robbed of its identity and can never be replaced. The more conflict a region experiences, the less stable it becomes and the more vulnerable it is to looting, the illegal excavation and smuggling of cultural artifacts.

Some experts now work to help keep artifacts and identities where they belong. Dr. Fredrik Hiebert, National Geographic's Archaeology Fellow and an expert in documenting endangered collections around the world, calls these people "culture heroes" for their dedication to preserving the past. These historians, archaeologists, and anthropologists often support the goal of repatriation, the official returning of looted artifacts to their country of origin. National Geographic has helped bring about repatriations to Afghanistan, Egypt, and Peru.

Fred Hiebert

Afghanistan 2009 Afghanistan was a gathering place for cultures that traded along the Silk Roads. Invasion by the Soviet Union in 1979 began more than three decades of violence that continues today. As a result, Afghanistan's archaeological sites and museums suffered rocket attacks that destroyed cultural artifacts. Such unintended damage is called collateral damage. Other damage is caused intentionally. In 2001, for example, the Taliban used explosives to blow up giant sandstone Buddha statues dating from the 6th century A.D. For years, looting was widespread. More than 1,500 objects spanning thousands of years were confiscated at Heathrow Airport in London and repatriated to Afghanistan in 2009.

Peru 2015 Sometimes what happens to an artifact isn't necessarily the result of violence or war. The 2,300-year-old textile shown on the opposite page has had numerous adventures on its journey home—yet is still in perfect condition. It was discovered as part of a necropolis, or ancient cemetery, in the 1920s and excavated by the founder of Peruvian archaeology, Julio Tello. The textile was stolen from the National Museum in Lima, Peru, not once, but twice. The second time, it found its way to Texas, where U.S. Customs agents recognized the illegal shipment and returned it to the Peruvian embassy. National Geographic helped return the textile in good condition to the museum in 2015.

Egypt 2010 and 2015 In 2008, U.S. Customs agents in Miami, Florida, became suspicious about a shipment with inconsistencies in the paperwork accompanying it. Two years later, the sarcophagus of a man named Imesy who lived during the 21st dynasty of Egypt was repatriated to the Grand Egyptian Museum in Cairo.

In April 2015, National Geographic hosted a ceremony for dozens more illegally shipped artifacts being repatriated from the United States back to Egypt, including a rare nesting sarcophagus from the 26th dynasty and even some mummy parts. Attended by both the U.S. Customs officers and archaeologists involved in solving the case, the ceremony was a moving recognition of an international effort to stop the looting of cultural artifacts and preserve them for future generations.

Fred Hiebert believes that every country is entitled to its own history. He is part of an effort to develop an "antiquities protocol," a process that can be deployed when smuggled artifacts are discovered in the world's ports. Hiebert conducts emergency inventories of looted artifacts, creating a "passport" or permanent record for these objects. But he claims that education is just as important: training customs agents to safely handle artifacts and teaching local residents to become better stewards for the objects that represent their heritage. "Who owns the past?" Fred Hiebert asks, and he has a ready answer: "All of us."

Into the Okavango Delta: A Live-Data Expedition

Located on the continent of Africa in the northwestern part of Botswana, the Okavango Delta is one of the richest wildlife areas on Earth. Unlike most deltas, it doesn't flow into an ocean or sea—it's an inland delta made up of flat, grassy savannas that are flooded by the Okavango River during the winter. This miraculous ecosystem was declared the 1000th UNESCO World Heritage Site in 2015, in part because its unique, seasonal wetlands give many endangered large mammals salvation after their long migration across the Kalahari Desert.

^
National Geographic Emerging Explorers Steve Boyes and Shah Selbe and their team document and share their experiences with the species of the Okavango Delta.

Visible from space, the Okavango Delta is huge—the size of the state of Texas. It's one of Africa's last truly wild landscapes, like the Sahara, the Serengeti, and the Congo. 100,000 elephants roam free across the land. Lions, leopards, hyenas, rhino, cheetahs, crocodiles, and wild dogs also thrive here, as well as nearly 500 bird species and over 1,000 plants.

Since 2011, an expedition team made up of Ba Yei river bushmen and National Geographic Emerging Explorers Steve Boyes and Shah Selbe and their team has been making annual visits to the remote land of the delta in one of the first "live-data" expeditions. That means the team constantly uploads data from the field to their website—intotheokavango.org—via satellite. This data is also available through a public API, or application program interface, which allows anyone to analyze and examine the collected information. "We're connecting society with the wilderness," explains conservation biologist, and Into the Okavango expedition leader, Steve Boyes.

Every ten seconds, state-of-the-art sensors record personal data about expedition members, including heart rate, the amount of energy they are using, and GPS positional data. Cameras automatically take pictures of the team's current location and record sound clips every ten minutes. Team members also post water quality data, and document their animal and bird sightings. They tweet progress updates constantly for people who are tracking their movements online and analyzing the expedition's data.

This mobile computer station allows sensors to be programmed and data to be posted from the field.

Team members also respond to questions and suggestions from their followers.

The team has crossed the Okavango Delta five times so far in dug-out canoes, the traditional mode of transportation for Ba Yei river bushmen. Their goal is to continue conducting in-depth biodiversity surveys in this delicate ecosystem so that any major changes can be noted and addressed.

"We have unprecedented opportunities to improve the world. But only if we act in time." –Shah Selbe

In 2015, the team's two-month "Source to Sand" expedition includes plans to cover the entire Okavango River system. They'll start at the river's source in Angola and travel 1,000 miles down the river through Namibia's Caprivi Strip, into untouched wilderness in the heart of the Okavango Delta in Botswana.

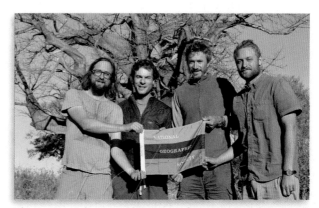

The team gathers in Okavango after a long trek in 2014.

This Okavango Delta exploration team has made an exciting step forward into expedition technology. For the first time, National Geographic explorers can share their movements, findings, and the sights and sounds of their surroundings, as well as their personal data, thoughts, and emotions in real-time while exploring one of the world's richest wilderness areas. This ground-breaking expedition gives people everywhere the chance to experience— and hopefully support—one of the world's most vibrant and important ecosystems.

Peacemaking Through Photography

The shifting nature of national boundaries is a theme throughout history as well as in current news stories. The world's newest nation is one of those stories. In July 2011, South Sudan became an independent country after citizens voted to break away from Sudan. Why did one country become two?

^
Photos taken by the students of National Geographic's South Sudan Photo Camp capture friends, family members, and daily life.

For the first half of the 20th century, Sudan was a British colony. During British rule, English-speaking Christians and members of many different tribes lived in the southern part of the country. Arabic-speaking Muslims lived in the northern part. When the British left in 1956, two civil wars took place: one in the 1960s and another in the 1980s. War finally ended, but old wounds and animosities did not disappear. A 2005 peace agreement included an option for independence. In January 2011, southern Sudanese people voted to split from Sudan. South Sudan became the world's newest country in July 2011, with the city of Juba as its capital.

Immediately, the new country faced a number of problems, including border disputes with Sudan. Then, in December 2013, widespread violence broke out between rival political groups. Since then, more than 10,000 South Sudanese have been killed, and 2 million have been internally displaced, or forced to leave their homes. Tens of thousands of South Sudanese have fled the country altogether, and many now live in neighboring Ethiopia as refugees. Both sides are responsible for violence committed against others based on their ethnic and tribal background. The fighting in South Sudan also disrupted farming, and now 11 million people face a serious food crisis.

In September 2014, National Geographic responded to the situation in South Sudan with an outreach program called Photo Camp. This program empowers young people to tell their own stories about their life and community through photography, guided by the mentorship of National Geographic photographers. Over a period of five days, 20 University of Juba students from different ethnic backgrounds learned photography from National Geographic photographers and photo editors. This lively group took nearly 32,000 images, including the ones you see on the left. They also engaged in cross-tribal peace-building activities.

Why photography? National Geographic photographers Ed Kashi, Matt Moyer, and Amy Toensing explain. According to Toensing, the students at Photo Camp are eager to learn about cameras and photography.

Moyer observes, "To see the students take the cameras and go into their communities, document positive things, and see their world with new eyes is just really inspiring."

National Geographic Photo Camp teaches photography skills, but it also encourages storytelling. Ed Kashi says, "I believe in the power of storytelling. And I believe in the importance of bridging these gaps of misunderstanding. Photo Camp represents that spirit, that desire to bring people together to share stories and to try to make the world a better place."

Participants in National Geographic's South Sudan Photo Camp examine the photos they took.

"We are the same—we are all South Sudanese."
–Mabil Dau Mabil, student

South Sudan participants responded to Photo Camp in a number of ways. For Catherine Koro, the benefits reached far beyond photography. She said, "It's about how you can look into something differently." Students saw their communities and each other with new eyes. Mabil Dau Mabil said they purposely avoided identifying themselves as belonging to the Dinka, Bari, Kuku, or Madi tribes.

These budding photographers understand that the story of South Sudan is just beginning. Even in the midst of the country's current turmoil, they remain hopeful. Akuot Chol Mayak predicts, "The world's eyes are on this nation, not because it's special, but because it is the newest. We are still on the move, but we shall reach there."

Think It Through

The articles in this section focus on history-making events and issues that have a profound effect on people and cultures across the globe. Consider and discuss the questions below to further your understanding of these important topics.

1 Choose one article that connects to your own life and experiences in some way and explain why. How does this article relate to your own personal history?

2 Which of the five articles would be most likely to motivate you to take action as a global citizen? How might you get involved?

3 Which topic are you most interested in finding out more about, and why? How might you seek additional information or updates?

Inquiry Project: Roundtable

Consider each of the newsworthy issues discussed in this section and select the one you feel is the most important or impactful within the world today. Why do you feel your chosen global issue is the most important one?

Assignment Become an expert on the issue you have chosen alongside others who have also chosen that issue. Participate in a roundtable discussion. Articulate why you feel your chosen issue is the most important one, and support your argument.

Plan Connect with other students in your class who share your opinion and discuss what you already know about this issue and what questions you still have. Develop a solid understanding of the topic by gathering information from multiple print and digital sources. Be sure to note your sources and summarize ideas in your own words.

Produce From your research, develop a list of reasons and arguments to support the notion that your chosen topic has the most impact on the world.

Present Participate in a classroom-wide roundtable discussion. Along with others who share your opinion about the topic you have chosen, work to explain why your topic has the most world impact. Use evidence from your research to support your argument. Listen respectfully as others present their viewpoints.

STUDENT
REFERENCES

AVAILABLE ONLINE

Skills Handbook
Primary Source Handbook
Geography Handbook
World Religions Handbook
Economics and Government Handbook

GLOSSARY

A

acropolis *n.* the highest point in an ancient Greek city

adobe *n.* a kind of clay that when dried is used as a building material

agora *n.* an open space in an ancient Greek city that served as a marketplace and social center

agriculture *n.* the practice of growing plants and rearing animals for food

alliance *n.* a partnership

anthropologist *n.* a scientist who studies the cultural development of humans

aqueduct *n.* a long stone channel that carries clean water

arch *n.* a curved structure over an opening

archaeologist *n.* a scientist who studies past human life by analyzing artifacts

aristocracy *n.* an upper class that is richer and more powerful than the rest of society

artifact *n.* an object made by humans from a past culture

artisan *n.* a person skilled at making things by hand

B

barbarian *n.* in this context, a person who lived outside the Roman Empire

barter *v.* to exchange goods

bas-relief *n.* a realistic sculpture with figures raised against a flat background

bureaucracy *n.* a system of government in which appointed officials in specialized departments run the various offices

C

cacao *n.* a bean used to make chocolate

caravan *n.* a group of people that travels together

caste system *n.* a rigid social hierarchy in India that divides people into hereditary classes

catacomb *n.* a hidden underground chamber where people are buried

catapult *n.* a weapon that hurls large stones

cataract *n.* a rock formation that creates churning rapids; also, a large waterfall

chinampa *n.* a floating field that supported agriculture

city *n.* a political, economic, and cultural center with a large population

city-state

city-state *n.* a self-governing unit made up of a city and its surrounding lands and settlements; a city that controls the surrounding villages and towns

civil war *n.* a war between groups in the same country

civilization *n.* a society with a highly developed culture and technology

clan *n.* a group of families that shares a common ancestor

codex *n.* a folded book made of tree bark paper

colony *n.* a group of people that settles in a new land but keeps ties to its native country

comedy *n.* a humorous form of Greek drama that often mocked famous people

commerce *n.* the buying and selling of goods

communal *adj.* shared

confederation *n.* a group of allies

conquistador *n.* a Spanish conqueror who sought gold and other riches in the Americas

consul *n.* one of two chief leaders elected yearly in ancient Rome

cosmopolitan *adj.* worldly

covenant *n.* a religious agreement

creation story *n.* an account that explains how the world began and how people came to exist

cultural diffusion *n.* the process by which cultures interact and ideas spread from one area to another

cultural hearth *n.* a place from which new ideas, practices, and technology spread

culture *n.* a group's way of life, including types of food, shelter, clothing, language, religion, behavior, and ideas

cuneiform *n.* the earliest form of writing, invented by the Sumerians

D

delta *n.* an area where a river fans out into various branches as it flows into a body of water

democracy *n.* a form of government in which citizens have a direct role in governing themselves or elect representatives to lead them

dharma *n.* the Buddha's teachings; divine law

dictator *n.* a person who rules with total authority

direct democracy *n.* a form of democracy in which citizens gather together to vote on laws and policies

domestication *n.* the raising of plants and animals to make them useful to humans

drought *n.* a long period of dry, hot weather

dynastic cycle *n.* the pattern of the rise and fall of dynasties in ancient and early China

dynasty *n.* a series of rulers from the same family

GLOSSARY

E

emperor *n.* the supreme ruler of an empire

empire *n.* a group of different lands and people governed by one ruler

epic poem *n.* a long story in the form of a narrative poem

epistle *n.* a letter

exile *n.* the forced removal from one's native country

F

famine *n.* an extreme lack of crops or food causing widespread hunger

fertile *adj.* encouraging the growth of crops and plants

filial piety *n.* the belief that children owe their parents and ancestors respect

fossil *n.* the remains of organisms that lived long ago

fresco *n.* a picture painted directly onto a wall

G

geoglyph *n.* a large, geometric design or shape drawn on the ground

gladiator *n.* a man in ancient Rome who fought others for entertainment

glyph *n.* a symbolic picture used to represent a word, syllable, or sound

golden age *n.* a period of great cultural achievement

government *n.* an organization set up to make and enforce rules in a society

H

Hellenistic *adj.* relating to Greek history or culture

helot *n.* a state-owned slave who was part of the lowest class of ancient Greek society

hero *n.* a character who faces a challenge that demands courage, strength, and intelligence

hierarchy *n.* a system in which people belong to social classes of different ranks

hieroglyph *n.* a picture representing an object, sound, or idea that was part of the ancient Egyptian writing system

highland *n.* a type of land that is high above the sea

hunter-gatherer *n.* a human who hunts animals and gathers wild plants to eat

I

immortal *adj.* able to live forever

inoculation *n.* a vaccine containing a mild form of a disease to prevent the development of that disease

irrigation *n.* the supply of water to fields using human-made systems

isolate *v.* to cut off from the rest of the world

isolationism *n.* a rejection of foreign contact and outside influences

J

jury *n.* a group of people chosen to make a decision based on evidence presented in a trial

K

karma *n.* in Hinduism, a state of being influenced by a person's actions and conduct; determines the kind of life into which a person will be reborn

khanate *n.* a region of the Mongol empire

kiva *n.* a circular-shaped chamber built in the ground by the ancient Pueblo

kosher *adj.* specially prepared according to Jewish dietary laws

L

labyrinth *n.* a maze

land bridge *n.* a strip of land connecting two landmasses

legacy *n.* the things, both cultural and technological, left to us from past cultures

legend *n.* a story from the past that is accepted as truth but cannot be proven

legionary *n.* a professional soldier in ancient Rome

lowland *n.* a type of land that is low and level

M

maize *n.* a type of corn first domesticated by early Mesoamericans

maritime *adj.* relating to the sea

matrilineal *adj.* relating to descendants traced through the mother

megafauna *n.* the large animals of a particular region, habitat, or geological period

GLOSSARY

metallurgy *n.* the science of obtaining metals in their natural form and preparing them for use

migration *n.* the movement from one place to another

missionary *n.* a person who goes to another country to do religious work; a person who tries to spread Christianity to others

monarchy *n.* a government ruled by a single person, such as a king

monotheism *n.* the worship of a single God

monsoon *n.* a strong seasonal wind in South and Southeast Asia

mosaic *n.* a grouping of tiny colored stone cubes set in mortar to create a picture or design

mother culture *n.* a civilization that greatly influences other civilizations

mound builder *n.* a Native American culture that built mounds and cities in the Mississippi River Valley region between 1000 B.C. and A.D. 500

movable type *n.* the individual clay tablets that could be arranged on a board to form text

mummy *n.* the preserved body of a pharaoh or other powerful person in ancient Egypt

myth *n.* an old story told to explain an event or justify a belief or action

mythology *n.* a collection of stories that explains events, beliefs, or actions

N

nirvana *n.* in Buddhism, a state of bliss or the end of suffering caused by the cycle of rebirth

noble *n.* a member of a high class in society who inherits his or her status

nomad *n.* a person who moves from place to place

O

oasis *n.* a fertile place with water in a desert

oligarchy *n.* a government ruled by a few powerful citizens

oracle bone *n.* an animal bone used to consult with the many gods worshipped by the Shang people

oral history *n.* an unwritten account of events, often passed down through the generations as stories or songs

oratory *n.* the art of public speaking

P

pantheon *n.* the gods of a group of people, a religion, or a civilization

papyrus *n.* a paperlike material made from reeds

parable *n.* in the Bible, a simple story to illustrate a moral or spiritual lesson

patriarchy *n.* a society in which men hold all the power

patrician *n.* a wealthy landowner in ancient Rome

peasant *n.* a poor farmer

peninsula *n.* a piece of land surrounded by water on three sides

phalanx *n.* in ancient Greece and Rome, a battle formation in which soldiers stood close together to protect themselves from enemy attack

pharaoh *n.* an ancient Egyptian ruler

philosophy *n.* the study of the universe and our place in it

plague *n.* a disease that causes many deaths

planned city *n.* a city built with a specific layout in mind

plebeian *n.* a common person in ancient Rome

polis *n.* a Greek city-state

polytheism *n.* a belief in many gods

pope *n.* the leader of the Roman Catholic Church

porcelain *n.* a strong, light, and translucent ceramic

potlach *n.* a gift-giving ceremony practiced by the Kwakiutl and Haida Native American tribes

primary source *n.* an artifact or piece of writing that was created by someone who witnessed or lived through a historical event

province *n.* an administrative district of a larger empire or country

pyramid *n.* a massive monumental tomb for a pharaoh

Q

quarry *v.* to extract stone from the earth

quinoa *n.* a high-protein grain native to the Andes Mountains in South America

R

rabbi *n.* a Jewish spiritual leader

raw material *n.* a substance from which other things are made

reason *n.* the power of the human mind to think and understand in a logical way

GLOSSARY

record keeping *n.* the practice of organizing and storing information

reform *n.* a change to make a situation better

reincarnation *n.* in Hinduism, the rebirth of a person's soul into another body after death

religion *n.* the belief in and worship of one or more gods and goddesses

representative democracy *n.* a form of democracy in which people are elected to vote on the citizens' behalf

republic *n.* a type of government in which citizens vote for their leaders

reunify *v.* to join together again

ritual *n.* a formal series of acts always performed in the same way; a religious ceremony

S

satrap *n.* a governor of a province in the Persian Empire

scribe *n.* a professional writer who recorded official information

secondary source *n.* an artifact or writing created after an event by someone who did not see it or live during the time when it occurred

serf *n.* a person who lived and worked on the private land of a noble or medieval lord

siege *n.* a military tactic in which troops surround a city with soldiers in an attempt to take control of it

silk *n.* a textile made from the cocoons of silkworms

silt *n.* an especially fine and fertile soil

slash-and-burn agriculture *n.* a method of clearing fields for planting

social class *n.* a category of people based on wealth or status in a society

specialized worker *n.* a person who performs a job other than farming, such as metalworking or toolmaking

staple *n.* a main crop produced in a specific place

steppe *n.* a vast, grassy plain

subcontinent *n.* a large, distinct landmass that is part of a continent

surplus *adj.* more than is required or necessary; extra

synagogue *n.* a Jewish place of worship

T

technology *n.* the application of knowledge, tools, and inventions to meet people's needs

temple *n.* a place of worship

terra cotta *n.* a fire-baked clay

terrace *n.* a stepped platform built into a mountainside

terrace farming *n.* a type of farming in which flat steps are cut into a mountain to provide farmland

tetrarchy *n.* a system of rule by four emperors

tolerance *n.* the sympathy for the beliefs and practices of others

totem pole *n.* a tall, elaborately carved and painted tree trunk common in Northwest Coast native cultures

trade *n.* the exchange of goods

tragedy *n.* a serious form of Greek drama in which characters endure suffering before an unhappy ending

tribe *n.* an extended family unit

tribune *n.* a representative who fought to protect the rights of ordinary citizens in ancient Rome

tribute *n.* a tax paid or goods and services rendered in return for protection

trireme *n.* an ancient Greek warship

truce *n.* an agreement to stop fighting

tyrant *n.* in ancient Greek city-states, a ruler who took power illegally

V

veto *v.* to reject a decision or proposal made by another government body

vizier *n.* a chief official in ancient Egypt who carried out much of the day-to-day work of governing

W

wigwam *n.* a domed tent used as housing by the Algonquin in North America

Y

yoga *n.* a series of postures and breathing exercises

Z

ziggurat *n.* a pyramid-shaped temple in Sumerian city-states

A

accurate *adj.* without mistakes or errors (page 364)

advance *v.* to move forward (page 238)

ambitious *adj.* having a desire for fame or success (page 410)

C

capacity *n.* the ability to do something (page 15)

collide *v.* to crash together (page 145)

commerce *n.* the buying and selling of goods and services (page 282)

commit *v.* to promise to do something (page 306)

communal *adj.* used or shared by a group of people (page 382)

concentrate *v.* to focus on (page 74)

D

determination *n.* the quality that makes someone continue to try doing a difficult task (page 284)

distinct *adj.* noticeably different or unique (page 388)

distinctive *adj.* different in a noticeable way (page 41)

dominate *v.* to have power over someone or something (page 112)

E

emerge *v.* to rise or appear (page 36)

eternal *adj.* existing at all times; lasting forever (page 150)

ethical *adj.* following accepted rules or behaviors (page 402)

F

flourish *v.* to be successful (page 270)

I

influence *v.* to affect or change someone or something indirectly (page 170)

interval *n.* the period of time between events (page 308)

P

policy *n.* a set of rules or ideas about how things should be done (page 127)

possession *n.* a personal article or possession (page 181)

predict *v.* to say that something will happen in the future (page 359)

privilege *n.* a right or benefit that only some people receive (page 114)

promote *v.* to encourage (page 154)

prosperous *adj.* successful, usually by making a lot of money (page 209)

R

reluctantly *adv.* with hesitation or doubt (page 245)

S

supervise *v.* to watch and oversee someone or something (page 69)

T

transform *v.* to dramatically change (page 26)

W

wage *n.* the amount of money a worker is paid (page 221)

SPANISH GLOSSARY

A

acrópolis *s.* punto más alto en una ciudad griega de la antigüedad

acueducto *s.* canal largo de piedra que transporta agua limpia

adobe *s.* tipo de arcilla que cuando se seca se usa como material de construcción

ágora *s.* espacio abierto en una ciudad griega de la antigüedad que servía como mercado y centro social

agricultura *s.* práctica de cultivar plantas y criar animales para obtener alimento

agricultura de tala y quema *s.* método de limpiar los campos para sembrar cultivos

aislacionismo *s.* rechazo al contacto extranjero y a las influencias externas

aislar *v.* apartar del resto del mundo

alianza *s.* acuerdo entre naciones para colaborar en la lucha contra los enemigos; asociación; pacto religioso

antropólogo *s.* científico que estudia el desarrollo cultural de los seres humanos

arco *s.* estructura curva colocada sobre una abertura

aristocracia *s.* clase alta que es más adinerada y más poderosa que el resto de la sociedad

arqueólogo *s.* científico que estudia el pasado de la vida humana mediante el análisis de fósiles y artefactos

artefacto *s.* objeto hecho por humanos pertenecientes a una cultura del pasado

artesano *s.* persona que se dedica a fabricar objetos de forma manual

B

bajorrelieve *s.* escultura realista que contiene figuras realzadas sobre un fondo plano

bancales *s.* tipo de agricultura en que se cortan escalones planos en una montaña para brindar terrenos de cultivo

bárbaro *s.* en este contexto, una persona que vivía fuera del Imperio Romano

burocracia *s.* sistema de gobierno en que funcionarios designados en departamentos especializados están a cargo de distintas oficinas

C

cacao *s.* grano que se usa para hacer chocolate

campesino *s.* granjero pobre

caravana *s.* grupo de personas que viajan juntas

catacumba *s.* cámara escondida bajo la superficie en donde se entierra a los muertos

catapulta *s.* arma que lanza piedras enormes

catarata *s.* formación rocosa que crea rápidos agitados; además, una cascada grande

cazador-recolector *s.* ser humano que caza animales y que cosecha plantas silvestres para alimentarse

chamán *s.* curandero de las culturas nativo-americanas

chinampa *s.* campo flotante que sustenta la agricultura

ciclo dinástico *s.* patrón del surgimiento y la caída de las dinastías de la China ancestral y antigua

cieno *s.* suelo especialmente fino y fértil

ciudad *s.* centro político, económico y cultural con una población grande

ciudad-estado *s.* unidad que se gobierna a sí misma, formada por una ciudad y sus territorios y asentamientos circundantes; ciudad que controla las aldeas y pueblos circundantes

ciudad planificada *s.* ciudad construida con un diseño específico en mente

civilización *s.* sociedad con una cultura y tecnología altamente desarrolladas

clan *s.* grupo de familias que comparten un ancestro en común

clase social *s.* categoría de personas basada en las riquezas o estatus en una sociedad

códice *s.* libro plegado hecho de papel de corteza de árbol

colonia *s.* grupo de personas que se asientan en un nuevo territorio, pero que mantienen sus lazos con su país nativo

comedia *s.* obra de teatro griega con un formato humorístico que solía burlarse de las personas famosas

comercio *s.* intercambio de productos; compra y venta de bienes

comunal *adj.* compartido

confederación *s.* grupo de aliados

conquistador *s.* explorador español que buscaba oro y otras riquezas en Centroamérica y América del Sur

constructores de montículos *s.* cultura nativo-americana que construyó montículos y ciudades en la región del valle del río Mississippi entre los años 1000 A.C. y 500 D.C.

cónsul *s.* uno de los dos jefes líderes elegidos cada año en la Antigua Roma

cosmopolita *adj.* internacional

crisol cultural *s.* lugar desde el cual se difunden nuevas ideas, prácticas y tecnología

cultivo básico *s.* cultivo principal producido en un lugar específico

cultura madre *s.* civilización que tiene una gran influencia sobre otras civilizaciones

cultura *s.* forma de vida de un grupo, que incluye tipos de alimento, vivienda, vestimenta, idioma, religión, comportamiento e ideas

cuneiforme *s.* primera forma de escritura conocida, inventada por los sumerios

D

delta *s.* área donde un río se divide en distintos brazos a medida que fluye hacia una masa de agua

democracia *s.* forma de gobierno en que los ciudadanos tienen un papel directo para gobernarse a sí mismos o para elegir a representantes que los gobiernen

democracia directa *s.* forma de democracia en que los ciudadanos se reúnen para votar sobre las leyes y las políticas

democracia representativa *s.* forma de democracia en que se eligen personas para que voten en representación de los ciudadanos

desertificación *s.* proceso mediante el cual las tierras fértiles se convierten en un desierto

dharma *s.* enseñanzas de Buda; ley divina

dictador *s.* persona que gobierna con total autoridad

difusión cultural *s.* proceso mediante el cual las culturas interaccionan y las ideas se propagan de un área a otra

dinastía *s.* serie de gobernantes de la misma familia

domesticación *s.* cultivo de plantas y animales de manera que fueran útiles para los humanos

E

edad de oro *s.* período de grandes logros culturales

emperador *s.* gobernante supremo de un imperio

epístola *s.* carta

escriba *s.* escritor profesional que anotaba información oficial

estepa *s.* planicie vasta y cubierta de hierbas

excedente *adj.* más de lo que se requiere o necesita; extra

exilio *s.* expulsión forzada del propio país de origen

extraer *v.* sacar piedras de la tierra

F

falange *s.* en la Antigua Grecia y Roma, formación de batalla en que los soldados se formaban juntos unos de otros para protegerse de los ataques de los enemigos

faraón *s.* gobernante egipcio de la antigüedad

fértil *adj.* que sustenta el crecimiento de cultivos y plantas

filosofía *s.* estudio del universo y de nuestro lugar en él

fósil *s.* restos de organismos que vivieron hace mucho tiempo atrás

fresco *s.* arte que se pinta directamente sobre una muralla

fuente primaria *s.* artefacto o texto escrito creado por alguien que presenció o vivió un acontecimiento histórico

fuente secundaria *s.* artefacto o texto escrito creado después de un acontecimiento por alguien que no lo vio o presenció durante el tiempo en que ocurrió

G

geoglifo *s.* diseño o forma geométrica grande dibujado sobre el suelo

gladiador *s.* hombre de la Antigua Roma que luchaba contra otros como espectáculo de entretención

glifo *s.* dibujo simbólico usado para representar una palabra, sílaba o sonido

gobierno *s.* organización establecida para hacer y reforzar las reglas de una sociedad

guerra civil *s.* guerra entre grupos de un mismo país

H

hambruna *s.* escasez extrema de cultivos o de alimentos que causa hambre generalizada

helenístico *adj.* relacionado con la historia o cultura griega

héroe *s.* personaje que enfrenta un desafío que requiere valentía, fuerza e inteligencia

historia de la creación *s.* narración que explica cómo comenzó el mundo y cómo nacieron las personas

historia oral *s.* registro no escrito de acontecimientos, que a menudo se transmite de una generación a otra a través de historias o canciones

hueso oracular *s.* hueso de animal usado para consultar a los muchos dioses adorados por el pueblo Shang

I

ilota *s.* esclavo que poseía el estado que era parte de la clase social más baja en la sociedad griega de la antigüedad

imprenta *s.* invento que usaba tipos móviles de metal para imprimir páginas

inmortal *adj.* que puede vivir para siempre

inoculación *s.* vacuna que contiene una forma leve de una enfermedad para prevenir el desarrollo de dicha enfermedad

irrigación *s.* suministro de agua para los campos mediante el uso de sistemas hechos por el hombre

J

jerarquía *s.* sistema en que las personas pertenecen a distintas clases sociales que tienen distintos rangos en la sociedad

jeroglífico *s.* imagen que representa un objeto, sonido o idea y que era parte del antiguo sistema de escritura egipcio

jurado *s.* grupo de personas escogidas para tomar una decisión con base en la evidencia presentada en un juicio

K

kanato *s.* región del Imperio Mongol

karma *s.* en el hinduismo, estado de estar influenciado por las acciones y el comportamiento; determina el tipo de vida en que una persona volverá a nacer

kiva *s.* cámara de forma circular construida en el suelo por los indígenas pueblo del pasado

kosher *adj.* preparado especialmente según las leyes dietéticas judías

L

laberinto *s.* lugar formado por encrucijadas, del cual es difícil salir

legado *s.* cosas, tanto culturales como tecnológicas, que nos quedan del pasado

legionario *s.* soldado profesional de la Antigua Roma

leyenda *s.* historia del pasado que se acepta como verdad, pero que no puede probarse

M

maíz *s.* tipo de elote que fue domesticado por los primeros mesoamericanos

marítimo *adj.* relacionado con el mar

materia prima *s.* sustancia a partir de la cual se fabrican otras cosas

matrilineal *adj.* relacionado con los descendientes que provienen de la madre

megafauna *s.* animales grandes de una región, hábitat o período geológico en particular

metalurgia *s.* ciencia que consiste en obtener materiales en su forma natural y prepararlos para el uso

migración *s.* mudarse de un lugar a otro

misionero *s.* persona que va a otro país para realizar labores religiosas; persona que trata de divulgar la cristiandad a otros

mito *s.* historia antigua contada para explicar un acontecimiento o justificar una creencia o acción

mitología *s.* colección de historias que explica acontecimientos, creencias o acciones

momia *s.* cuerpo preservado de un faraón u otra persona poderosa del Antiguo Egipto

monarquía *s.* gobierno liderado por una sola persona como, por ejemplo, un rey

monoteísmo *s.* alabanza a un solo Dios

monzón *s.* vientos estacionales fuertes en el Sudeste Asiático

mosaico *s.* agrupación de cubitos de piedra coloridos que se colocan sobre argamasa para crear un dibujo o diseño

N

nirvana *s.* en el budismo, un estado de dicha o del final del sufrimiento causado por el ciclo del renacer

noble *s.* miembro de la clase alta de la sociedad que hereda su estatus de sus antepasados

nómada *s.* persona que se muda de un lugar a otro

O

oasis *s.* lugar fértil con agua en un desierto

oligarquía *s.* gobierno liderado por unos pocos ciudadanos

oratoria *s.* arte del discurso público

P

panteón *s.* dioses de un grupo de personas, una religión o una civilización

papa *s.* líder de la Iglesia Católica Romana

papiro *s.* material parecido al papel que se hace a partir de juncos

parábola *s.* en la Biblia, un relato sencillo que ilustra una moraleja o una lección espiritual

patriarcal *adj.* dicho de una sociedad en que los hombres tienen todo el poder

patricio *s.* terrateniente rico de la Antigua Roma

península *s.* porción de tierra rodeada por agua en tres de sus costados

permutar *v.* intercambiar productos

piedad filial *s.* creencia de que los niños le deben respeto a sus padres y ancestros

pirámide *s.* tumba masiva y monumental construida para un faraón

plaga *s.* enfermedad que causa muchas muertes

plebeyo *s.* persona común de la Antigua Roma

poema épico *s.* historia larga escrita como un poema narrativo

polis *s.* ciudad-estado griega

politeísmo *s.* creencia en muchos dioses

porcelana *s.* cerámica resistente, liviana y translúcida

potlach *s.* ceremonia de entrega de obsequios practicada por las tribus nativo-americanas kwakiutl y haida

provincia *s.* distrito administrativo de un imperio grande o de un país

puente terrestre *s.* franja de territorio que conecta dos masas terrestres

Q

quínoa *s.* grano alto en proteínas originario de las montañas de los Andes en América del Sur

R

rabino *s.* líder espiritual judío

reencarnación *s.* en el hinduismo, el renacer del alma de una persona en otro cuerpo después de la muerte

reforma *s.* cambio hecho para mejorar una situación

registros *s.* práctica que consiste en organizar y almacenar la información

religión *s.* creencia en y alabanza de uno o más dioses y diosas

república *s.* tipo de gobierno en que los ciudadanos votan por sus líderes

reunificar *v.* volver a unir

ritual *s.* serie de actos formales que siempre se realizan de la misma manera; ceremonia religiosa

S

sátrapa *s.* gobernante de una provincia en el Imperio Persa

seda *s.* textil hecho de los capullos de los gusanos de la seda

sequía *s.* período largo de estado del tiempo seco y caluroso

siervo *s.* persona que vivía y trabajaba en los terrenos privados de un noble o de un señor medieval

sinagoga *s.* lugar de reunión religiosa para los judíos

sistema de castas *s.* jerarquía social rígida en India que divide a las personas en clases sociales hereditarias

sitio *s.* táctica militar en que las tropas rodean una ciudad con soldados en un intento por controlarla

subcontinente *s.* gran masa de tierra que es parte de un continente

T

tecnología *s.* aplicación de conocimiento, herramientas e inventos para satisfacer las necesidades de las personas

templo *s.* lugar de alabanza

terracota *s.* arcilla cocida al fuego

terrazas *s.* plataformas de estepa construidas en la ladera de una montaña

tetrarquía *s.* sistema de gobierno de cuatro emperadores

tierras altas *s.* terrenos que están sobre el mar

tierras bajas *s.* tipo de terrenos nivelados de poca altura

tipos móviles *s.* tablas de arcilla individuales que podían organizarse sobre un tablero para formar un texto

tirano *s.* en las ciudades-estado de la Antigua Grecia, gobernante que obtenía el poder de forma ilegal

tolerancia *s.* respeto por las creencias y las prácticas de otros

tótem *s.* tronco de árbol alto y elaboradamente tallado y pintado, común en las culturas nativas de la costa noroeste

trabajador especializado *s.* persona que realiza un trabajo que no está relacionado con la agricultura, como en la metalurgia o en la producción de herramientas

tragedia *s.* obra de teatro griega con un formato serio en que los personajes sufren antes de enfrentar un final triste

tregua *s.* acuerdo para detener un conflicto

tribu *s.* unidad familiar extendida

tribuno *s.* representante que luchó para proteger los derechos de los ciudadanos comunes en la Antigua Roma

tributo *s.* impuesto pagado o bienes y servicios proporcionados a cambio de protección

trirreme *s.* antigua nave de guerra griega

V

vetar *v.* rechazar una decisión o propuesta hecha por otro cuerpo gubernamental

visir *s.* oficial jefe en el Antiguo Egipto que realizaba la mayor parte del trabajo de gobernar cotidiano

W

wigwam *s.* tipo de choza con techo en forma de cúpula usada como vivienda por los indígenas algonquinos de América del Norte

Y

yoga *s.* serie de posturas y ejercicios de respiración

Z

zigurat *s.* templo con forma de pirámide en las ciudades-estado de Sumeria

A

ambicioso *adj.* que desea la fama o el éxito (pág. 410)

avanzar *v.* moverse hacia adelante (pág. 238)

C

capacidad *s.* habilidad de hacer algo (pág. 15)

colisionar *v.* chocar (pág. 145)

comercio *s.* compra y venta de bienes y servicios (pág. 282)

comprometerse *v.* prometer hacer algo (pág. 306)

comunal *adj.* usado o compartido por un grupo de personas (pág. 382)

concentrar *v.* enfocarse en algo (pág. 74)

D

determinación *s.* cualidad que hace que alguien continúe intentando realizar una labor difícil (pág. 285)

distintivo *adj.* notoriamente diferente o único (pág. 388)

dominar *v.* tener poder sobre alguien o algo (pág. 112)

E

eterno *adj.* que existe en todo momento; que dura para siempre (pág. 150)

ético *adj.* que sigue las reglas o comportamientos aceptados (pág. 402)

F

florecer *v.* tener éxito (pág. 270)

I

influenciar *v.* afectar o cambiar alguien o algo de manera indirecta (pág. 170)

intervalo *s.* período de tiempo entre los acontecimientos (pág. 308)

P

peculiar *adj.* diferente de una manera perceptible (pág. 41)

política *s.* conjunto de reglas o ideas sobre cómo deben hacerse las cosas (pág. 127)

posesión *s.* artículo o propiedad personal (pág. 181)

precisión *adj.* sin faltas ni errores (pág. 364)

predecir *v.* decir qué sucederá en el futuro (pág. 359)

privilegio *s.* derecho o beneficio que sólo reciben algunas personas (pág. 114)

promover *v.* animar (pág. 154)

próspero *adj.* exitoso, usualmente por ganar mucho dinero (pág. 209)

R

reaciamente *adv.* con incertidumbre o dudas (pág. 245)

S

salario *s.* cantidad de dinero que recibe un trabajador (pág. 221)

supervisar *v.* vigilar y monitorear algo o alguien (pág. 69)

surgir *v.* emerger o aparecer (pág. 36)

T

transformar *v.* cambiar dramáticamente (pág. 26)

INDEX

ACKNOWLEDGMENTS

Text Acknowledgments

425 Li Po, "Zazen on Ching-t'ing Mountain" from Crossing the Yellow River: Three Hundred Poems from the Chinese, translated by Sam Hamill. Copyright ©2000 by Sam Hamill. Reprinted with the permission of The Permissions Company, Inc., on behalf of Tiger Bark Press, www.tigerbarkpress.com.

NATIONAL GEOGRAPHIC LEARNING | **CENGAGE Learning**

National Geographic Learning gratefully acknowledges the contributions of the following National Geographic Explorers and affiliates to our program and to our planet:

Salam Al Kuntar, Archaeologist, National Geographic Emerging Explorer

Caroline Alexander, National Geographic Writer/Journalist

Nicole Boivin, Archaeologist, National Geographic Grantee

Steve Boyes, Conservation Biologist, National Geographic Emerging Explorer

Nina Burleigh, Journalist/Author

Michael Cosmopoulos, Archaeologist, National Geographic Grantee

Christopher DeCorse, Archaeologist, National Geographic Grantee

Steven Ellis, Archaeologist, National Geographic Grantee

Francisco Estrada-Belli, Archaeologist, National Geographic Grantee

Beverly Goodman, Geo-Archaeologist, National Geographic Emerging Explorer

Jeff Gusky, National Geographic Photographer

Fredrik Hiebert, Archaeologist, National Geographic Fellow

Patrick Hunt, Archaeologist, National Geographic Grantee

Louise Leakey, Paleontologist, National Geographic Explorer-in-Residence

Christine Lee, Bio-Archaeologist, National Geographic Emerging Explorer

Albert Lin, Research Scientist/Engineer, National Geographic Emerging Explorer

Jodi Magness, Archaeologist, National Geographic Grantee

Sarah Parcak, Archaeologist, National Geographic Fellow

Thomas Parker, Archaeologist, National Geographic Grantee

William Parkinson, Archaeologist, National Geographic Grantee

Matt Piscitelli, Archaeologist, National Geographic Grantee

Jeffrey Rose, Archaeologist, National Geographic Emerging Explorer

Max Salomon, National Geographic Producer

Aziz Abu Sarah, Cultural Educator, National Geographic Emerging Explorer

William Saturno, Archaeologist, National Geographic Grantee

Anna Secor, Political Geographer, National Geographic Grantee

Shah Selbe, Conservation Technologist, National Geographic Emerging Explorer

Maurizio Seracini, Cultural Heritage Engineer, National Geographic Fellow

Hayat Sindi, Science Entrepreneur, National Geographic Emerging Explorer

Christopher Thornton, Archaeologist, National Geographic Lead Program Officer of Research, Conservation, and Exploration

Soultana Maria Valamoti, Archaeologist, National Geographic Grantee

Juan José Valdés, National Geographic Geographer

Simon Worrall, National Geographic Writer

Xiaobai Angela Yao, Geographer, National Geographic Grantee

Dave Yoder, Photojournalist, National Geographic Grantee

Photographic Credits

COVER ©Neale Clark/Robert Harding World Imagery/Alamy iii (bl) ©Winn Brewer/National Geographic Learning. (bc) ©Winn Brewer/National Geographic Learning. (br) ©Chad Cohen/National Geographic Studio. iv (bl) ©Donnelly Photography/National Geographic Learning. (bc) ©Mary Lynne Ashley Photography/National Geographic Learning. (br) ©Andrew Faulds/National Geographic Learning. v (tl) ©Jeanine Childs/National Geographic Learning. vi (tl) ©Steven Ellis. (tc) ©Kenneth Garrett/National Geographic Creative. (tr) ©Rebecca Hale/National Geographic Creative. (bl) ©Sora Devore/National Geographic Creative. (bc) ©2011 The Field Museum, Photo by John Weinstein. (br) ©Christopher Thornton. vii (tl) ©Rebecca Hale/National Geographic Creative. (tcl) ©Rebecca Hale/National Geographic Creative. (tcr) ©Frank Wing. (tr) ©Mark Thiessen/National Geographic Creative. (bl) ©Mark Thiessen/National Geographic Creative. (bc) ©Mark Thiessen/National Geographic Creative. (br) ©Mark Thiessen/National Geographic Creative. viii (tl) ©Marcie Goodale/National Geographic Learning. (tc) ©Sora DeVore/National Geographic Creative. (tr) ©G. Vdokakis/Michael Cosmopoulos. (cl) ©Mark Thiessen/National Geographic Creative. (cc) ©Grace Parker. (cr) ©Matthew Piscitelli. (bl) ©Benjamin Grimes/National Geographic Creative. (bc) ©Georgios-Villy Kapetanakis. (br) ©Angelo Yao. ix (t) ©Nigel Pavitt/JWL/Aurora Photos. x (t) ©Kenneth Garrett/National Geographic Creative. xii (t) ©Herbert Esser/Panther Media/age footstock. xiii (t) ©Roger Ressmeyer/Corbis. xiv (t) ©Kenneth Garret/National Geographic Creative. xv (tl) ©Stringer/REUTERS. (tcl) ©Molhem Barakat/REUTERS. (cl) ©Frederik Hiebert. (bcl) ©Shah Selbe. (bl) ©2014 Holly Moses Edward/National Geographic Photo Camp South Sudan. GT1 ©ImageBroker/Alamy. GT3 (t) ©Ian Patrick/Alamy. (b) ©Raymond Gehman/National Geographic Creative. GT8 (b) ©Stephen Alvarez/National Geographic Creative. GT10 ©PictureLake/Alamy. GT12 (b) ©Brooks Kraft/Corbis News/Corbis. GT16 ©George H.H. Huey/Terra/Corbis. GT19 ©Panoramic Images/Getty Images. GT21 (t) ©Bill Hatcher/National Geographic Creative. GT22 (t) ©Daniel Dempster Photography / Alamy. (b) ©Michael Doolittle / Alamy. (c) ©Tom Bean/Alamy. GT23 (t) ©Frank Krahmer/Terra/Corbis. (c) ©Dmitiriy Bartosh/Geophoto/imagebroker/Alamy. GT24 (tl) ©Epa/Corbis Wire/Corbis. (tr) ©Denis Sinyakov/Reuters/Corbis. GT26 ©NASA Goddard Space Flight Center Image by Reto Stöckli (land surface, shallow water, clouds). Enhancements by Robert Simmon (ocean color, compositing, 3D globes, animation). Data and technical support: MODIS Land Group; MODIS Science Data Support Team; MODIS Atmosphere Group; MODIS Ocean Group Additional data: USGS EROS Data Center (topography); USGS Terrestrial Remote Sensing Flagstaff Field Center (Antarctica); Defense Meteorological Satellite Program (city lights)./NASA. GT27 (br) ©Michael Nichols/National Geographic Creative. (tr) ©U.S. Coast Guard photo. GT29 ©Tom Gilks/Alamy. 1 (tl) ©Winn Brewer/National Geogrpahic Learning. (bl) ©Fredrik Hiebert. 2 (bg) ©Sisse Brimberg/National Geographic Creative. (cl) ©Sora DeVore/National Geographic Creative. (c) ©William Saturno. (cr) ©G. Vdokakis/Michael Cosmopoulos. 3 (tr) ©Steven Ellis. (cl) ©Sarah Parcak. 4 (bg) ©Nigel Pavitt/JWL/Aurora Photos. 5 (tr) ©Kenneth Garrett/National Geographic Creative. 6 (tr) ©Raul Martin/National Geographic Creative. (tl) ©Keenpress/National Geographic Creative. (b) ©Berthold Steinhilber/laif/Redux. 7 (bc) ©Metta image/Alamy. (tl) ©Erich Lessing/Art Resource, NY. (tr) ©O. Lewis Mazzatenta/National Geographic Creative. 8 (tc) ©Wildnerdpix/iStock/Getty Images. (tr) ©LuismiX/MomentOpen/Getty Images. 9 (tr) ©Ronald Naar/ANP Photo/age footstock. (tc) ©Catalin Petolea/Alamy. (tl) ©Gertjan Hooijer/Shutterstock. 10 ©Paule Seux/Latitude/Corbis. 13

©Wil Matthews/500Prime. 14 ©Enguang Zhu/TAO Images Limited/Alamy. 16 ©Joel Sartore/National Geographic Creative. 16 (cll) ©Bridgeman-Giraudon/Art Resource, NY. (clr) ©Erich Lessing/Art Resource, NY. 20 ©National Geographic Studios. 23 ©Paul Franklin/World Illustrated/Photoshot . 25 ©Alexander Maleev/National Geographic. 26 ©Matthieu paley/National Geographic Creative. 28 ©Gianni Dagli Orti /The Art Archive at Art Resource, NY. 31 (bg) ©Album/Prisma/Newscom. (tr) ©The Trustees of the British Museum/Art Resource, NY. (cr) ©Album/Art Resource, NY. (br) ©Album/Art Resource, NY. 33 (bl) ©C M Dixon/AAA Collection/Ancient Art & Architecture Collection Ltd/Alamy. (t) ©Paule Seux/Latitude/Corbis. 34 ©Dmitry Ovcharov/500Prime. 41 (t) ©Aldo Pavan/Terra/Corbis. (br) ©De Agostini Picture Library/akg-images. 43 ©Nicolle Rager Fuller, National Science Foundation. 44 ©Guido Alberto Rossi/AGE Fotostock. 47 ©Vincent J. Musi/National Geographic Society/Corbis. 49 (cl) ©Kenneth Garrett/National Geographic Creative. (b) ©Balage Balogh /Art Resource, NY. (tr) ©DeA Picture Library/Art Resource, NY. (cr) ©Louvre, Paris, France/Bridgeman Images. (tl) ©Manuel Cohen/The Art Archive at Art Resource, NY. 50 (br) ©PjrStudio/Alamy. (tr) ©Vanni Archive/Art Resource, NY. (t) ©CDA/Guillemot/akg-images. (cr) ©Gianni Dagli Orti/The Art Archive at Art Resource, NY. (cr) ©Erich Lessing/Art Resource, NY. (b) ©Dagli Orti/De Agostini/Getty Images. 51 (c) ©Nathan Benn/Encyclopedia/Corbis. (bc) ©Phil Cawley/Alamy. (b) ©Erich Lessing/Art Resource, NY. (tl) ©Z. Radovan/Bible Land Pictures/akg-images. (tr) ©Kenneth Garrett/National Geographic Creative. (c) ©Nathan Benn/Ottochrome/Corbis. (bcr) ©The Metropolitan Museum of Art/ Art Resource, NY. (br) ©Alfredo Dagli Orti/The Art Archive at Art Resource, NY. 53 (bl) ©Nathan Benn/Ottochrome/Corbis. (t) ©Dmitry Ovcharov/500Prime. 54 (bg) ©Kenneth Garrett/National Geographic Creative. 55 (tr) ©Kenneth Garrett/National Geographic Creative. 56 (t) ©Jim Richardson/National Geographic Creative. 58 (bg) ©Kenneth Garrett/National Geographic Creative. 59 (tr) ©Christopher Thornton. 60 (bc) ©François Guenet/Art Resource, NY. (tl) ©The Trustees of the British Museum/Art Resource, NY. (tr) ©Bridgeman Images. 61 (tr) ©Dinodia Photo/age footstock. (br) Digital Image © 2014 Museum Associates/LACMA. Licensed by Art Resource, NY. (tl) ©Fitzwilliam Museum, Cambridge/Art Resource, NY. 62 (bl) ©Bilderbuch/Design Pics/Corbis. (br) ©Catherine Leblanc/Godong/Corbis. (tr) ©Ruggero Vanni/Corbis. 63 (bl) ©Lindsay Hebberd/Corbis. (tr) ©Aaron Geddes Photography/Moment/Getty Images. 64 ©Iain Masterton/Photographer's Choice RF/Getty Images. 70 ©Gianni Dagli Orti/Fine Art/Corbis. 71 ©François GuÃ/©net/akg-images. 72 ©Mary Evans Picture Library/The Image Works. 73 ©Bible Land Pictures/Zev Radovan/B/akg-images. 75 ©Scala/Art Resource, NY. 77 ©DeAgostini/Getty Images. 79 ©GraphicaArtis/Fine Art/Corbis. 83 ©James P. Blair/National Geographic Society. 85 (bc) ©Andy Crawford/Dorling Kindersley. (c) ©Tono Balaguer/easyFotostock/Age Fotostock. (tr) ©Photograph courtesy of Dr. Timothy Matney, Ziyaret Tepe Archaeological Expedition.. (tl) ©Alex Segre/Alamy. (cr) ©Imanhakim/Shutterstock.com. (tr) ©Gianni Dagli Orti /The Art Archive at Art Resource, NY. (bl) ©Dan Barnes/ Vetta/Getty Images. (tc) ©Blackbirds/Age Fotostock. 87 ©Iain Masterton/Photographer's Choice RF/Getty Images. 88 ©Dorothea Schmid/laif/Redux. 90 ©ImageBroker/Alamy. 95 ©Prisma/SuperStock. 96 Courtesy of Sarah Parcak. 97 ©AP Images/Space Imaging. 98 ©Sami Sarkis/Photolibrary/Getty Images. 101 ©De Agostini Picture Library/G. Dagli Orti/Bridgeman Images. 102 ©Scala/Art Resource, NY. 103 ©Gianni Dagli Orti/The Art Archive at Art Resource, NY. 105 ©Alfredo Dagli Orti/Fine Art/Corbis. 106 ©Kenneth Garrett/National Geographic Creative. 108 (tr) ©De Agostini Picture Library/A. Vergani/Bridgeman Images. (t) ©O. Louis Mazzatenta/National Geographic Creative. (bl) ©O. Loius Mazzatenta/National Geographic Creative. 110 (tl)©Kenneth Garrett/National Geographic Creative. (bl) ©CULTNAT, Dist. RMN-GP/Art Resource, NY. (cr) ©François Guenet/Art Resource, NY. (tr) ©Bpk, Berlin/Art Resource, NY. 111 (bl) ©François Guenet/Art Resource, NY. (cl) ©DeAgostini/

SuperStock. (tl) ©François Guenet/Art Resource, NY. (br) ©DeAgostini/SuperStock. (cr) ©François Guenet/Art Resource, NY. (tcr) ©CULTNAT, Dist. RMN-GP/Art Resource, NY. (tr) ©François Guenet/Art Resource, NY. 113 ©Kenneth Garrett/National Geographic Creative. 114 ©Gianni Dagli Orti/The Art Archive at Art Resource, NY. 116 ©The Trustees of the British Museum/Art Resource, NY. 117 ©O. Loius Mazzatenta/National Geographic Creative. 118 ©DEA/G Dagli Orti/De Agostini Editore/Age Fotostock. 121 ©Dorothea Schmid/laif/Redux. 122 ©Duby Tal/Albatross Aerial Perspective (Duby Tal)/AGE Fotostock. 125 ©De Agostini Picture Library/G. Nimatallah/Bridgeman Images. 126 (t) ©Hanan Isachar/Superstock. (cl) ©Colin Underhill/Alamy. 129 ©Grotesques, illustration from the Jewish Cervera Bible, 1299 (vellum), Asarfati, Joseph (fl.1299)/Instituto da Biblioteca Nacional, Lisbon, Portugal/Bridgeman Images. 130 ©cala/Ministero per i Beni e le AttivitÃ culturali/Art Resource, NY. 131 ©The Israel Museum, Jerusalem, Israel/Shrine of the Book/ Photo ©The Israel Museum, by Ardon Bar Hama/Bridgeman Images. 133 ©2008 by Crossway Bibles, a publishing ministry of Good News Publishers. Used by permission. All rights reserved. 134 ©Boris Diakovsky/Alamy. 137 ©BrAt82/Shutterstock. com. 138 ©Beverly Goodman. 139© Duby Tal/Albatross Aerial Perspective (Duby Tal)/AGE Fotostock. 141 (cr) ©Bettmann/Corbis. (t) ©Duby Tal/Albatross Aerial Perspective (Duby Tal)/AGE Fotostock. 142 ©Danish Siddiqui/Reuters. 147 ©Ursula Gahwiler/Robert Harding Picture Library Ltd/Alamy. 148 ©De Agostini Picture Library /A. Dagli Orti/Bridgeman Images. 149 (tl) ©Schoyen Collection. (t) ©Schoyen Collection. (tcl) ©Schoyen Collection. 151 (bl) © The Metropolitan Museum of Art. Image source: Art Resource, NY. (bc) ©V&A Images, London/Art Resource, NY. (br) © Smart-foto/Shutterstock.com. (t) ©Vivek Prakash/Reuters. 152 ©Helene Rogers/Art Directors & Trips Photo/Age Fotostock. 154 ©Sanjeev Gupta/epa/Corbis Wire/Corbis. 157 ©Dinodia/Dinodia Photo/Age Fotostock. 158 ©Moustafellou/IML/ Icarus/Age Fotostock. 161 (tl) ©Dinodia Photos/Hulton Archive/Getty Images. (cr) ©Leigh Prather/Shutterstock.com. (cl) ©Hero/Fancy/Age Fotostock. (tr) ©Rhimage/Shutterstock.com. 163 ©Danish Siddiqui/Reuters. 164 ©Xinhua/eyevine/Redux. 169 ©Roman Sigaev/ShutterStock.com. 170 ©Philip Lange/Panther Media/AGE Fotostock. 172 ©China Photos/Getty Images News/Getty Images. 174 (tr) ©The Art Archive/British Library. (tcr) ©Pure Rendereing Gmbh/National Geographic Creative. 176 ©Dave Porter Peterborough Uk/Photolibrary/Getty Images. 178 ©O. Louis Mazzatenta/National Geographic Image Creative. 179 ©O. Louis Mazzatenta/National Geographic Image Creative. 182 (c) ©Yi Lu/Viewstock/Collage/Corbis. (bl) ©Stockbyte/Getty Images. (bc) ©Smithsonian Institution, National Air and Space Museum. (br) ©Jeff Metzger/ShutterStock.com. 187 ©Adstock/UIG/age fotostock. 188 (b) ©bakelyt/age fotostock. (t) ©Private Collection/Art Resource, NY. (cr) ©Steshkin Yevgeniy11/ShutterStock.com. (br) ©Erich Lessing / Art Resource, NY. 189 (bl) ©photosindia/Getty Images. (cr) ©Hanyang University Museum, South Korea/Bridgeman Images. (tr) ©Senol Yaman/ShutterStock.com. 190 ©Danita Delimont/Alamy. 191 ©Leonid Bogdanov/Superstock. 193 (bl) ©DEA/E.Lessing/De Agostini Picture Library/Getty Images. (t) ©Xinhu/eyevine/Redux. 194 (bg) ©Christopher Thornton. 195 (tr) ©Christopher Thornton. 196 (t) ©Shreekant Jadhav/ephotocorp/Alamy. 198 (bg) ©Joe Scherschel/National Geographic Creative. (tr) ©Winn Brewer/National Geogrpahic Learning. (bl) ©Herbert Esser/Panther Media/age footstock. (br) ©Jim Haberman. (bc) ©Roger Ressmeyer/Corbis. 199 (bl) ©Scott Carr/500Prime. (bc) ©Kenneth Garret/National Geographic Creative. 200 (bg) ©Herbert Esser/Panther Media/age footstock. 201 (tr) ©William Parkinson. 202 (bc) ©Werner Forman/UIG/age footstock. (tr) ©Hercules Milas/Alamy. (tl) ©Werner Forman Archive/Bridgeman Images. 203 (tl) ©Ashmolean Museum, University of Oxford, UK/Bridgeman Images. (bl) ©Zhang Shui Cheng/Bridgeman Images. (tr) ©Hoberman/UIG/Bridgeman Images. 206 ©Vasilis Protopapas. 209 ©National Archaeological Museum, Athens, Greece/Bridgeman

Images. 211 ©De Agostini Picture Library/Bridgeman Images. 213 ©Bettmann/Corbis. 214 ©J.D. Dallet/Age Fotostock. 217 ©Akg-images/De Agostini Picture Lib./A. De Gregorio. 218 ©The Trustees of the British Museum/Art Resource, NY. 219 © Anastasios71/Shutterstock.com. 220 (tc) ©Erich Lessing/Art Resource, NY. (cl) ©Erich Lessing/Art Resource, NY. (tr) ©Alinari / Art Resource, NY. (br) ©Scala/Art Resource, NY. (bl) ©Ashmolean Museum/The Art Archive at Art Resource, NY. (tl) ©Leemage/Universal Images Group/Getty Images. 224 ©Warner Bros/Legendary Pictures/The Kobal Collection/Picture Desk. 227 ©Vasilis Protopapas. 228 ©Hercules Milas/Alamy. 230 ©John Hios/akg-images. 231 ©De Agostini Picture Library/G. Nimatallah/akg-images. 235 ©Mary Evans Picture Library / Alamy. 237 (bc) ©Orestis Panagiotou/EPA/Newscom. (bl) ©Yiorgos Karahalis/Reuters /Landov. 239 ©Howard David Johnson. 240 ©Phillipp von Foltz/akg-images. 241 ©Gianni Dagli Orti / The Art Archive at Art Resource, NY. 243 ©Erich Lessing/Art Resource, NY. 244 (tr) ©Dea/G. Dagli Orti/De Agostini Picture Library/Getty Images. 246 ©Dea/G. Dagli Orti/De Agostini/Getty Images. 249 ©Fine Art Images/Age Fotostock. 250 (t) ©Antonino Bartuccio/Grand Tour/Terra/Corbis. (cl) ©Dea/G. Dagli Orti/De Agostini Picture Library/Getty Images. 251 ©mart/Shutterstock.com. 252 ©Stelios Kritikakis/500px. 255 ©Lucas Jackson/Reuters. 257 ©Hercules Milas/Alamy. 258 (bg) ©William Parkinson. 259 (tr) ©William Parkinson. 260 (t) ©Thanassis Stavrakis/AP Images. 262 (bg) ©Roger Ressmeyer/Corbis. (t) ©James L. Stanfield/National Geographic Image Collection. 263 (tr) ©Steven Ellis. 264 (tr) ©Atlantide Phototravel/Corbis. (tl) ©Universal Images Group/Getty Images. (br) ©G. Dagli Orti/De Agostini Picture Library/Getty Images. 265 (tl) ©The Trustees of the British Museum/Art Resource, NY. (b) ©Jean-Pierre Lescourret/Corbis. (tr) ©Bridgeman Images. 266 (tr) ©Stephan Goerlich/imageBROKER/agefotostock. 267 (tr) ©DEA/G DAGLI ORTI/De Agostini Editore/agefotostock. (tl) ©Ivern Photo/agefotostock. (br) ©Robert Clark/National Geographic Creative. 268 (bg) ©Ruggero Vanni/Encyclopedia/Corbis. (cl) ©Cephas Picture Library/Alamy. 269 (cr) ©Glyn Thomas Photography/Alamy. (tr) ©Bettmann/Corbis. 270 ©Tantoon Studio/istock/Getty Images Plus/Getty Images. 272 (tl) ©Mystockicons/Digital Vision Vectors/Getty Images. (t) ©Gaertner/Alamy. 274 ©Tantoon Studio/istock/Getty Images Plus/Getty Images. 275 ©Ancient Art and Architecture Collection Ltd. / The Bridgeman Art Library. 276 ©Caroline Seidel/dpa/Corbis Wire/Corbis. 278 ©Tantoon Studio/istock/Getty Images Plus/Getty Images. 279 ©James L. Stanfield/National Geographic Image Creative. 280 ©Mystockicons/Digital Vision Vectors/Getty Images. 281 ©Peter Connolly/akg-images. 282 ©Mystockicons/Digital Vision Vectors/Getty Images. 283 ©James Hardy/PhotoAlto/Corbis. 284 ©Bogdan Cristel/X00337/Reuters/Corbis. 285 ©Taylor S. Kennedy/National Geographic Society/Corbis. 286 ©Gary Ombler/Dorling Kindersley. ©Gary Ombler/Dorling Kindersley. 287 (t) ©Gary Ombler/Dorling Kindersley. (tcl) ©Gary Ombler/Dorling Kindersley. (cl) ©Gary Ombler/Dorling Kindersley. ©Gary Ombler/Dorling Kindersley. (cr) ©Dorling Kindersley. (tl) ©Gary Ombler/DK Images. (tr) ©Gary Ombler/Dorling Kindersley. 288 (cl) ©Mystockicons/Digital Vision Vectors/Getty Images. (t) ©Bridgeman-Giraudon/Art Resource, NY. 290 ©Patrick Hunt. 292 (tl) ©Mystockicons/Digital Vision Vectors/Getty Images. (cl) ©Bettmann/Corbis. 295 ©akg-images. 296 (tr) ©Murat Taner/Comet/Corbis. (bg) ©Photos 12/Alamy. (cl) ©Louvre, Paris, France/Bridgeman Images. 298 ©Fine Art Premium/Corbis. 299 ©The Trustees of the British Museum / Art Resource, NY. 300 ©De Agostini Picture Library/L. Romano/Bridgeman Images. 303 ©Ruggero Vanni/Encyclopedia/Corbis. 304 ©Image Source/Aurora Photos. 307 ©Araldo de Luca/Fine Art/Corbis. 311 ©Hans Madej/Gruppe28/Aurora Photos. 312 (b) ©USA-TV/Kristy Griffen/The Kobal Collection/Picture Desk. (tl) ©Mystockicons/Digital Vision Vectors/Getty Images. 314 (tl) ©Tantoon Studio/istock/Getty Images Plus/Getty Images. (t) ©Marc Dozier/Latitude/Corbis. 316 ©Roger Ressmeyer/Eureka Premium/Corbis. 318 ©Tantoon Studio/istock/Getty Images Plus/Getty Images. 319 ©Scala/Ministero per i Beni e le Attività culturali/Art Resource, NY. 322 ©Alfredo Dagli Orti/The Art Archive at Art Resource, NY. 323 ©Album/Prisma/Album. 324 (tl) ©Tantoon Studio/istock/Getty Images Plus/Getty Images. (cl) ©Image Source/Corbis. (t) ©Michele Falzone/Alloy/Corbis. 325 ©Gallery with Loculus Tombs (fresco)./Catacombs of Priscilla, Rome, Italy/Bridgeman Images. 326 ©Tantoon Studio/istock/Getty Images Plus/Getty Images. 327 (bl) ©Dea/G. Dagli Orti/De Agostini/Getty Images. (br) ©akg-images. (tr) ©Dea/G. Dagli Orti/De Agostini Picture Library/Getty Images. (tl) ©Stefano Bianchetti/Fine Art/Corbis. 330 ©Private Collection/Look and Learn/Bridgeman Images. 331 ©Tantoon Studio/istock/Getty Images Plus/Getty Images. 332 ©Tantoon Studio/istock/Getty Images Plus/Getty Images. 333 (tr) © Ensuper/Shutterstock.com. (cl) © Ifong/Shutterstock.com. (br) ©Zoonar/A Maltsev/Age Fotostock. 334 (tl) ©Tantoon Studio/istock/Getty Images Plus/Getty Images. (t) ©Araldo de Luca/Corbis art/Corbis. 336 ©Guido Baviera/Terra/Corbis. 339 ©Image Source / Aurora Photos. 340 (bg) ©Steven Ellis. 341 (tr) ©Steven Ellis. 342 (t) ©Sam Weber/National Geographic Creative. 344 (bg) ©Kenneth Garret/National Geographic Creative. 345 (tr) ©Kenneth Garrett/National Geographic Creative. 350 ©Simon Norfolk/Institute. 354 ©Werner Forman/Universal Images Group/Getty Images. 355 ©Kenneth Garrett. 356 ©Gianni Dagli Orti/The Art Archive/Art Resource, NY. 359 ©The Trustees of the British Museum/Art Resource, NY. 362 ©Tyrone Turner/EPA/Alamy. 363 ©Kenneth Garrett/National Geographic Creative. 364 ©Egmont Strigl/imagebroker/Age Fotostock. 366 ©Ethnologisches Museum, Staatliche Museen, Berlin, Germany/Art Resource, NY. 369 ©Universal History Archive/UIG/The Bridgeman Art Library. 370 ©Kenneth Garret/National Geographic Creative. 371 ©Gianni Dagli Orti/The Art Archive/Art Resource, NY. 373 ©Palazzo Pitti, Florence, Italy / Bridgeman Images. 375 (tr) ©Rahmo/Shutterstock.com. (tl) ©f9photos/Shutterstock.com. (bl) ©Werner Forman/Universal Images Group/Getty Images. (t) ©Simon Norfolk/Institute. 376 ©Kenneth Garrett/National Geographic Society/Museos del Banco Central de Costa Rica. 379 ©Robert Clark/National Geographic. 380 (br) ©Museo Larco. Lima Peru. (tl) ©Kenneth Garrett/National Geographic Society/Museos del Banco Central de Costa Rica. 381 (br) ©Kenneth Garrett/National Geographic Society/Museos del Banco Central de Costa Rica. (t) ©Y. Yoshii/PAS. 384 ©Image Source/Getty Images. (bl) Kenneth Garrett/National Geographic Learning. 386 ©Mireille Vautier / Alamy. 389 ©Stuart Dee/Getty Images. 391 (b) ©Jason Langley/AGE Fotostock. (t) ©Richard A. Cooke/Encyclopedia/Corbis. 393 ©Joel Sartore/National Geographic Creative. 395 (br) ©Ira Block/National Geographic Creative. (t) ©Wood Ronsaville Harlin Inc/National Geographic Creative. 397 ©CharlineXia Ontario Canada Collection / Alamy. 399 (t) ©Kenneth Garrett/National Geographic Society/Museos del Banco Central de Costa Rica. (c) ©Mike Theiss/National Geographic. 400 ©Sean Pavone/Alamy. 405 ©Vidler Steve/Travelpix/Age Fotostock. 407 ©Private Collection/Paul Freeman/Bridgeman Images. 409 (bl) ©Science Source. (tr) ©RMN-Grand Palais/Art Resource, NY. (tl) ©Hjschneider/Shutterstock.com. (br) ©iBird/Shutterstock.com. 410 ©GL Archive/Alamy. 413 ©Robert Harding Picture Library/SuperStock. 414 ©Dea/J e Bulloz/AGE Fotostock. 415 ©Erik S. Lesser/epa/Corbis Wire/Corbis. 422 ©O. Louis Mazzatenta/National Geographic Creative. 423 ©Courtesy of Christine Lee. 425 (c) ©Ma Xiaoliang/TAO Images Limited/Alamy. (t) ©Sean Pavone/Alamy. 426 (bg) ©Bruce Smith. 427 (tr) ©Kenneth Garrett/National Geographic Creative. 428 (t) ©Kenneth Garrett/National Geographic Creative. 430 (tr) ©Winn Brewer/National Geogrpahic Learning. (bl) ©Hakbong Kwon/Alamy. (br) ©Terence Kong/500Prime. 431 (bg) ©David Santiago Garcia/Aurora Photos. 432 (tr) ©2014 Dotjang Agany Awer/National Geographic Photo Camp South Sudan. (cl) ©ed nazarko/500px. (c) ©2014 Emmanuela Henry Andrew Kenyi/National Geographic Photo Camp South Sudan. (cr) ©Bobby Haas/National Geographic Creative. (bl) ©David Doubilet/National Geographic Creative. (bcr) ©Jose Luis Gonzalez/REUTERS. (br)

©Mahmoud Hebbo/REUTERS. 433 (tl) ©Alexandre
Meneghini/REUTERS. (tcl) ©David Doubilet/National
Geographic Creative. (bcl) ©Richard Drew/AP Images. (bl)
©JD Dallet/arabianEye/Getty Images. (tr) ©2014 National
Geographic Photo Camp South Sudan. 434 (t) ©Stringer/
REUTERS. 435 (tl) ©Erin West Kephart/National Geographic
Learning. 436 (tl) ©Izzet Keribar/Lonely Planet Images/Getty
Images. (tr) ©Molhem Barakat/REUTERS. (cl) ©Izzet
Keribar/Lonely Planet Images/Getty Images. (cr) ©Molhem
Barakat/REUTERS. 437 (tl) ©Marcie Goodale/National
Geographic Learning. 438 (t) ©Frederik Hiebert. (cl) ©ICE/
Handout/REUTERS. (cr) ©Frederik Hiebert. 439 (c)
©Rebecca Hale/National Geographic Creative. 440 (t)
©Bobby Haas/National Geographic Creative. (tcl, bcl, cr)
©Shah Selbe. 441 (bl, cr) ©Shah Selbe. 442 (tl) ©2014 Simon
Odhol/National Geographic Photo Camp South Sudan. (tc)
©2014 Catherine Simon Arona Samuel/National Geographic
Photo Camp South Sudan. (tr) ©2014 Dotjang Agany Awer/
National Geographic Photo Camp South Sudan. (cl) ©2014
Holly Moses Edward/National Geographic Photo Camp
South Sudan. (c) ©2014 Simon Odhol/National Geographic
Photo Camp South Sudan. (cr) ©2014 Duku Stephen Savio/
National Geographic Photo Camp South Sudan. (bl) ©2014
Duku Stephen Savio/National Geographic Photo Camp
South Sudan. (bc) ©2014 Lisok James Moses/National
Geographic Photo Camp South Sudan. (br) ©2014 Samuel
Oyet Faustino/National Geographic Photo Camp South
Sudan. 443 (cr) ©2014 Lisok James Moses/National
Geographic Photo Camp South Sudan. 444 (tr) ©Beverly
Joubert/National Geographic Creative. R1 (bg) ©Kenneth
Garrett/National Geographic Creative.

Map Credits

Mapping Specialists, LTD., Madison, WI.
National Geographic Maps, National Geographic Society

Illustrator Credits

Unless otherwise indicated, all illustrations were created by
Precision Graphics.

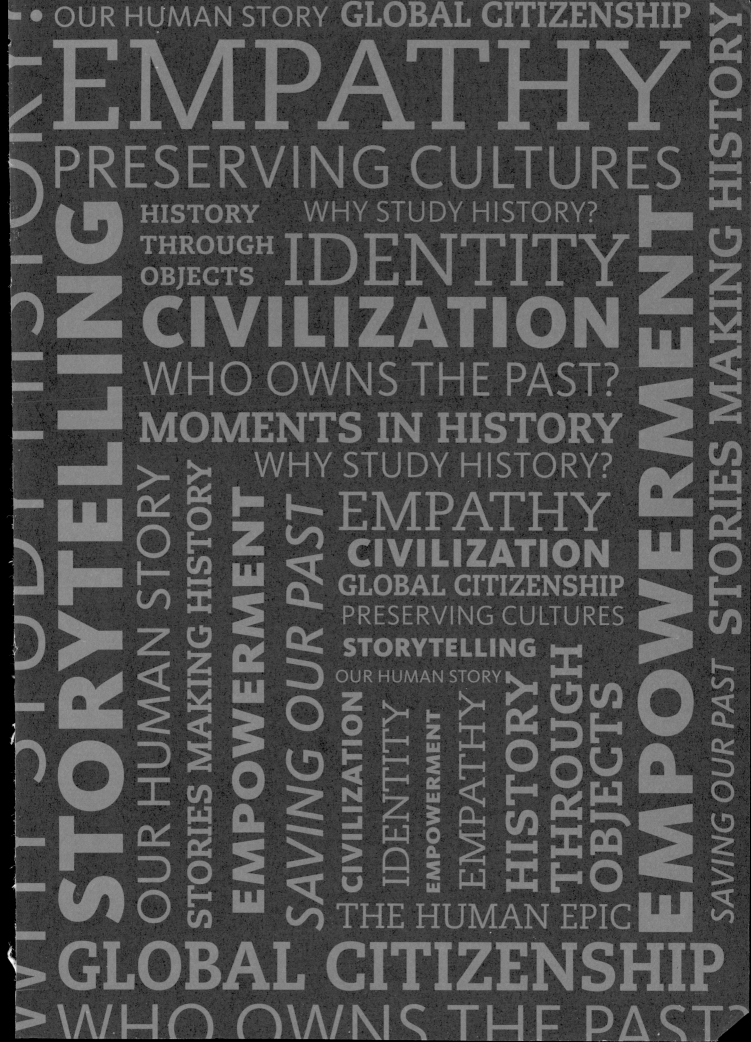

EMPOWERMENT

THE HUMAN EPIC GLOBAL CITIZENSHIP

STORYTELLING

WHY STUDY HISTORY? EMPATHY

IDENTITY CIVILIZATION

STORIES MAKING HISTORY

EMPOWERMENT

SAVING OUR PAST

EMPATHY

GLOBAL CITIZENSHIP

SAVING OUR PAST

HISTORY
THROUGH
OBJECTS

EMPOWERMENT
PRESERVING CULTURES
SAVING OUR PAST
WHY STUDY HISTORY?
GLOBAL CITIZENSHIP

IDENTITY

THE HUMAN EPIC
STORYTELLING
OUR HUMAN STORY

CIVILIZATION

PRESERVING CULTURES

GLOBAL CITIZENSHIP

PRESERVING CULTURES

EMPATHY

OUR HUMAN STORY

CIVILIZATION THE HUMAN EPIC

WHO OWNS THE PAST

STORIES MAKING HISTOR